I0819695

Daniel Johnston

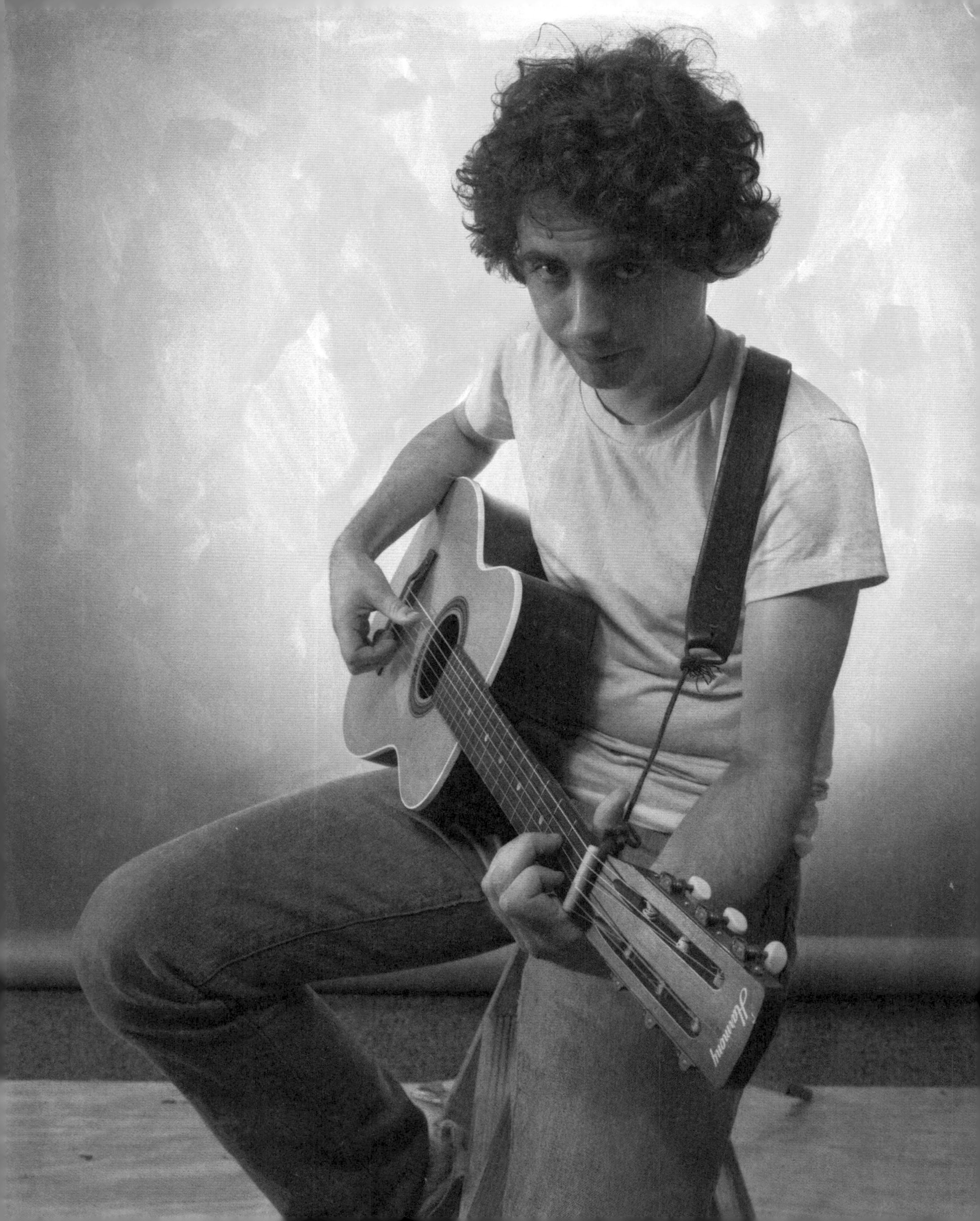
Harmony

Daniel Johnston

Lee Foster
Dick Johnston and Robin K. Williams

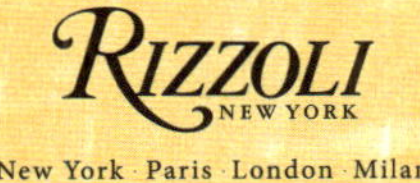

New York · Paris · London · Milan

All included works were drawn on 8½ x 11" typing paper, notebook paper, or card stock. Johnston used ballpoint pens, Sharpie markers, color markers, and highlighters. Artwork titles follow the artist's spellings.

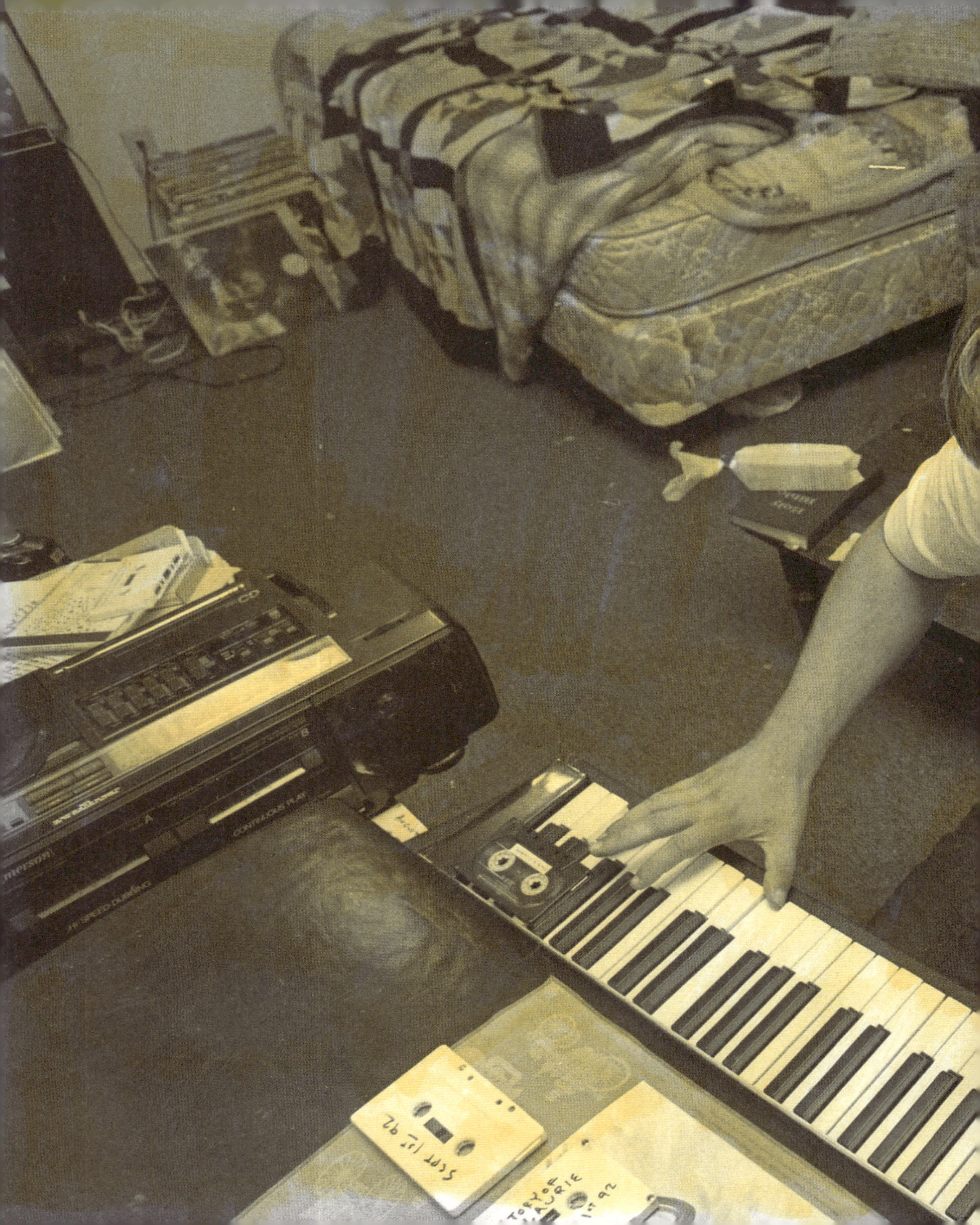
CD
CONTINUOUS PLAY
HI-SPEED DUBBING
SEPT 1st 92

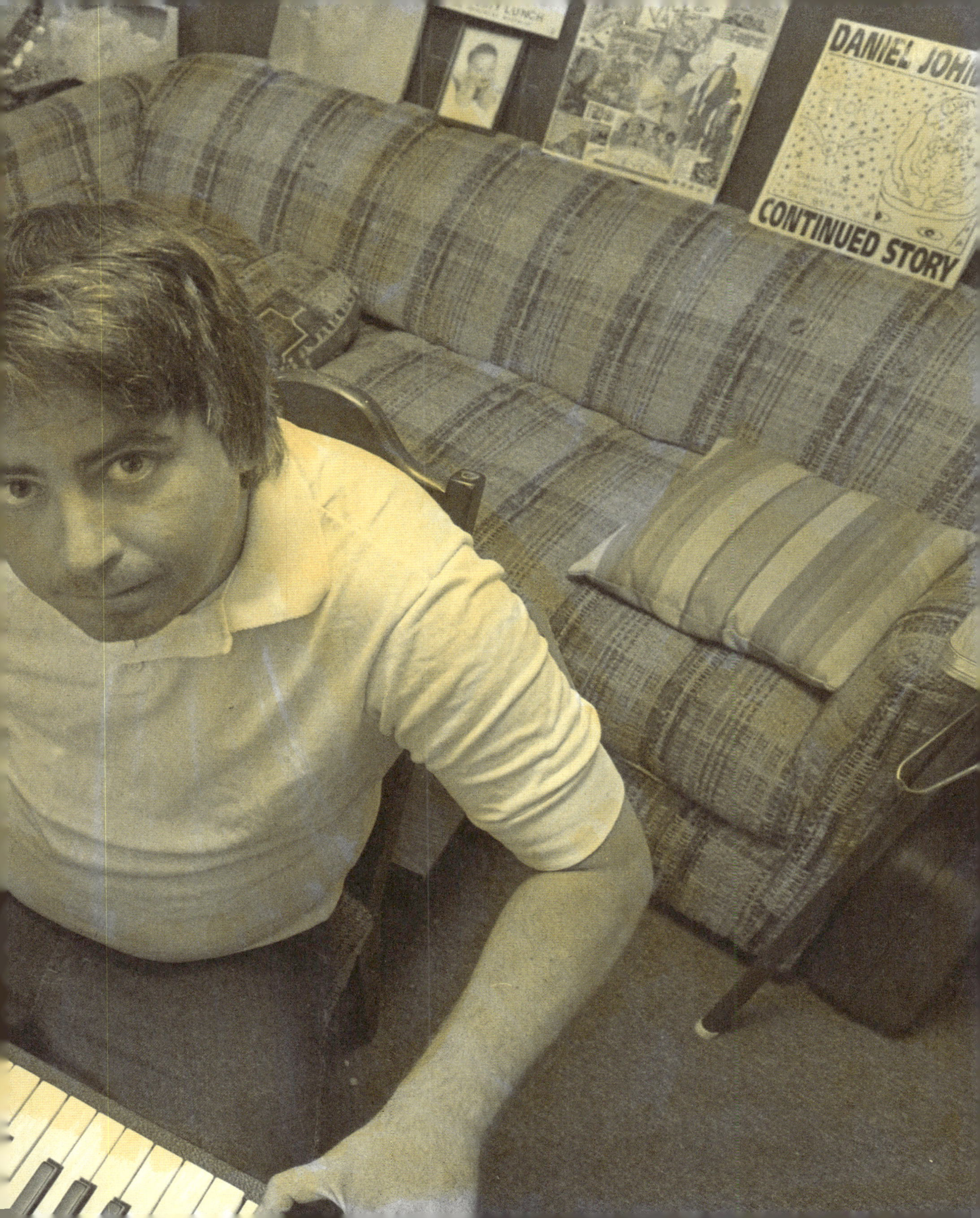
DANIEL JOHN
CONTINUED STORY

When I was very young, twenty-one, I had met and started dating a very handsome local rocker named Arthur. I'd never been taken anywhere on a trip for the weekend by a boyfriend, but his mother had a house in East Long Island and we were planning to go there. I was excited but I didn't know how it was going to go. We had the day there and before we fell asleep at his mom's house, he asked me if I had ever heard of Daniel Johnston. I hadn't—and he told me we should watch this documentary that came out called *The Devil and Daniel Johnston*. He put it on and fell asleep instantly—as usual.

But I was captivated by the movie.

I felt an instant kinship with him. He was fragile to say the least, on top of so many other things. But the only difference between him and me that I could see while I was watching was that he seemed more different—and he was—but in my heart I resonated more deeply to his demeanor and character and way of going about things than I had to anyone in a very long time. You can't make that feeling up when you see somebody and you shoot straight up out of bed because you just know that watching them in that moment is gonna change your whole life, and my life was truly never the same since then.

I had a new self-assuredness within me that just because I spoke or sang a little bit differently and felt a little different from most people I met, that I might just be able to make this whole thing work.

I couldn't even really tell Arthur about it because at the time I felt that what that documentary had given to me was so special that I wanted to hold it close to me, because I knew it might just be enough to keep me going.

Thinking about him and studying his music and his fears, on top of listening constantly to artists like Cat Power and Elliott Smith, gave me just enough juice at the time to keep me running until my battery almost burnt out weeks before meeting my manager Ben Mawson, and making my first record that people would soon talk about till this day—for better or for worse.

There have been about ten seminal moments in my thinking life when it came to my career and whether it could work and whether I would have the strength and stamina to keep going after six years of singing in bars, but getting familiar with Daniel was one of them.

I was lucky enough to meet him before he died. With someone like that, there really are no words you can tell them to explain to them how much they shaped your life. So I enjoyed the moment sharing a cigarette, and I'm thankful to this day that I got to share the same space with someone who didn't even know that their differences made me feel not so alone and were a big reason why I still do what I do today. Because making music ain't easy—but Daniel certainly made it look fun sometimes.

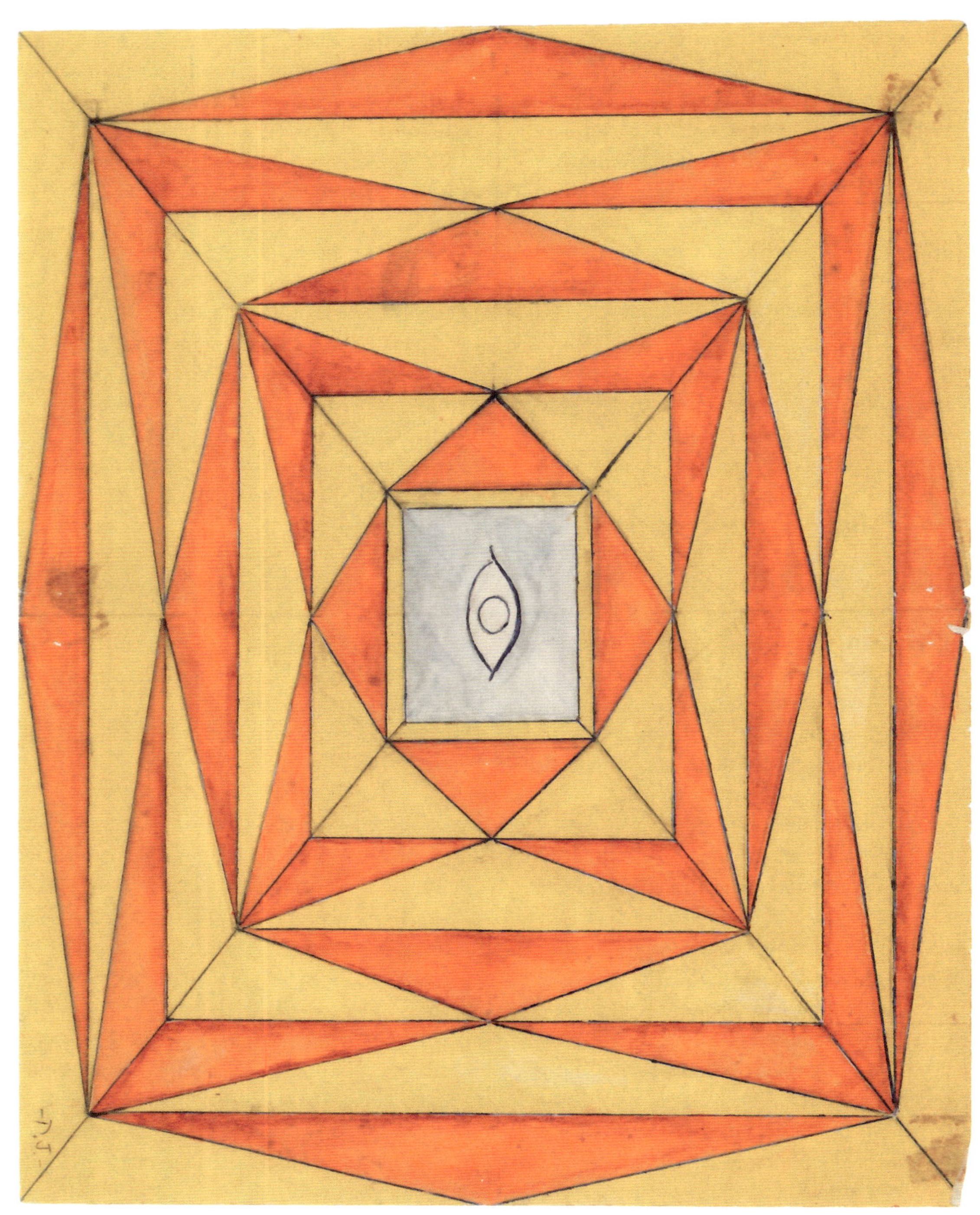

Untitled (Yellow, Orange)

I.
Symbolical Visions
1972–2000s

MY PLANET

THE EARTH
IS AN OLD CANVAS
PAINTED OVER
MANY TIMES

—— DAN JOHNSTON

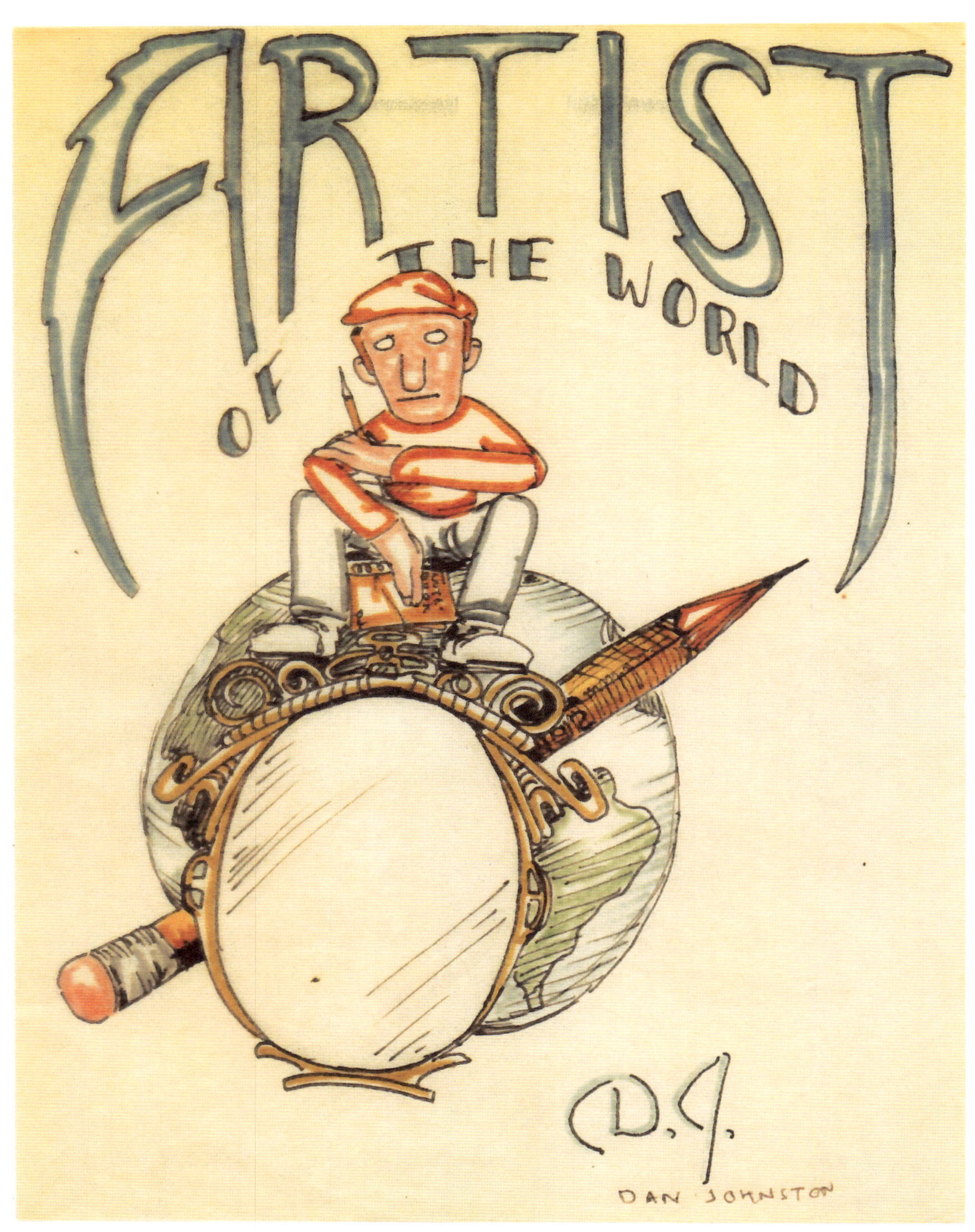

Artist of the World

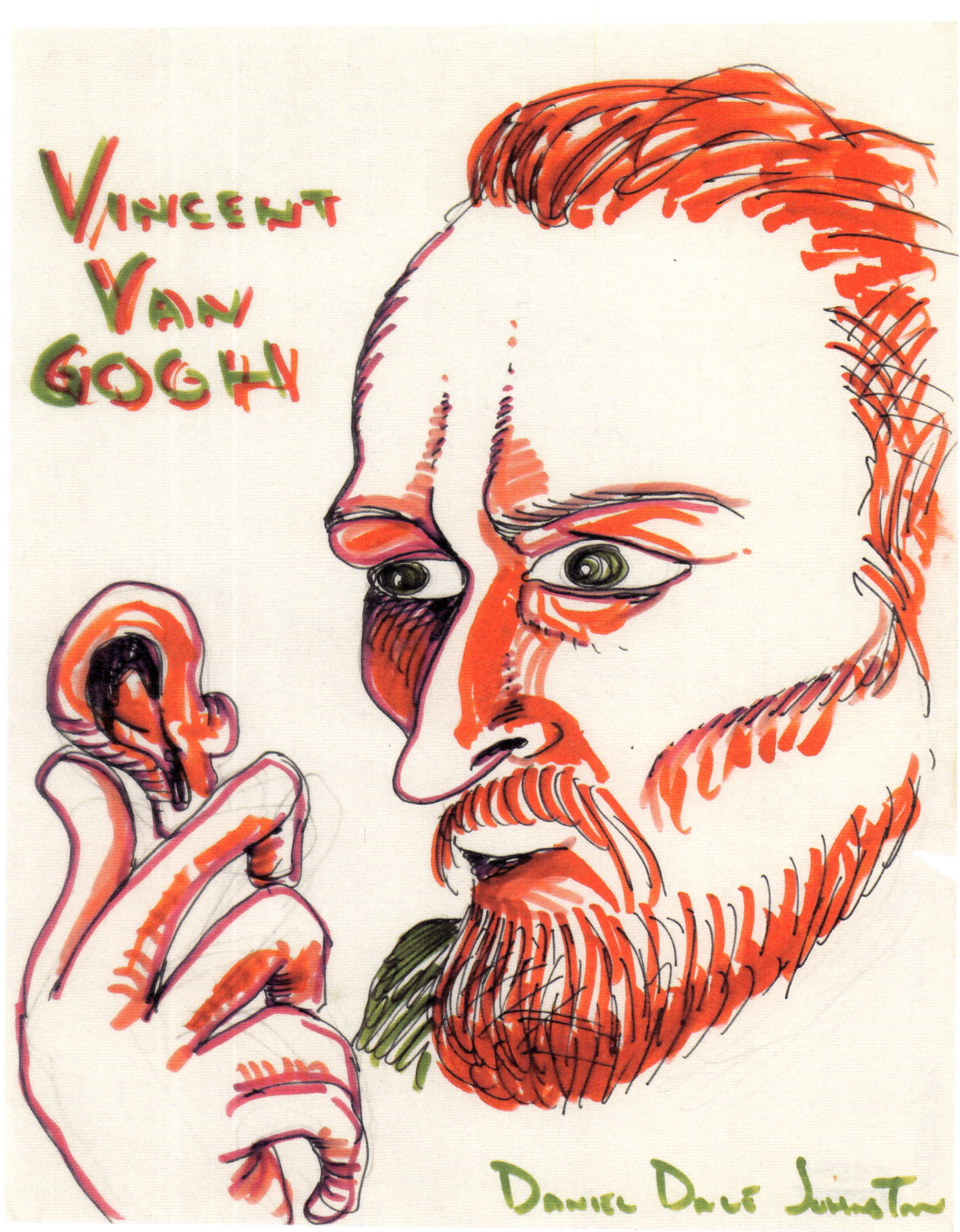

Vincent van Gogh

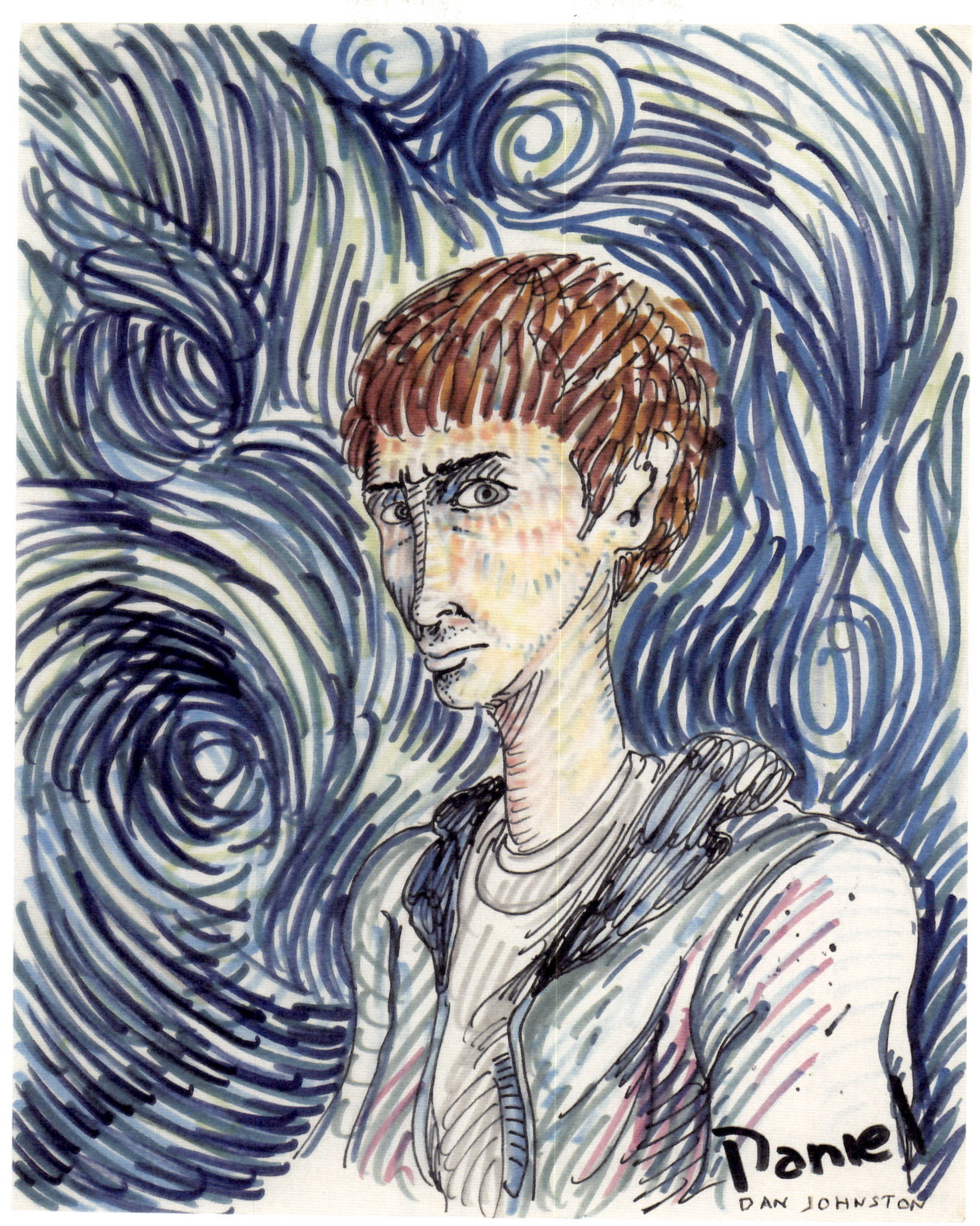

Self-Portrait (Starry Night)

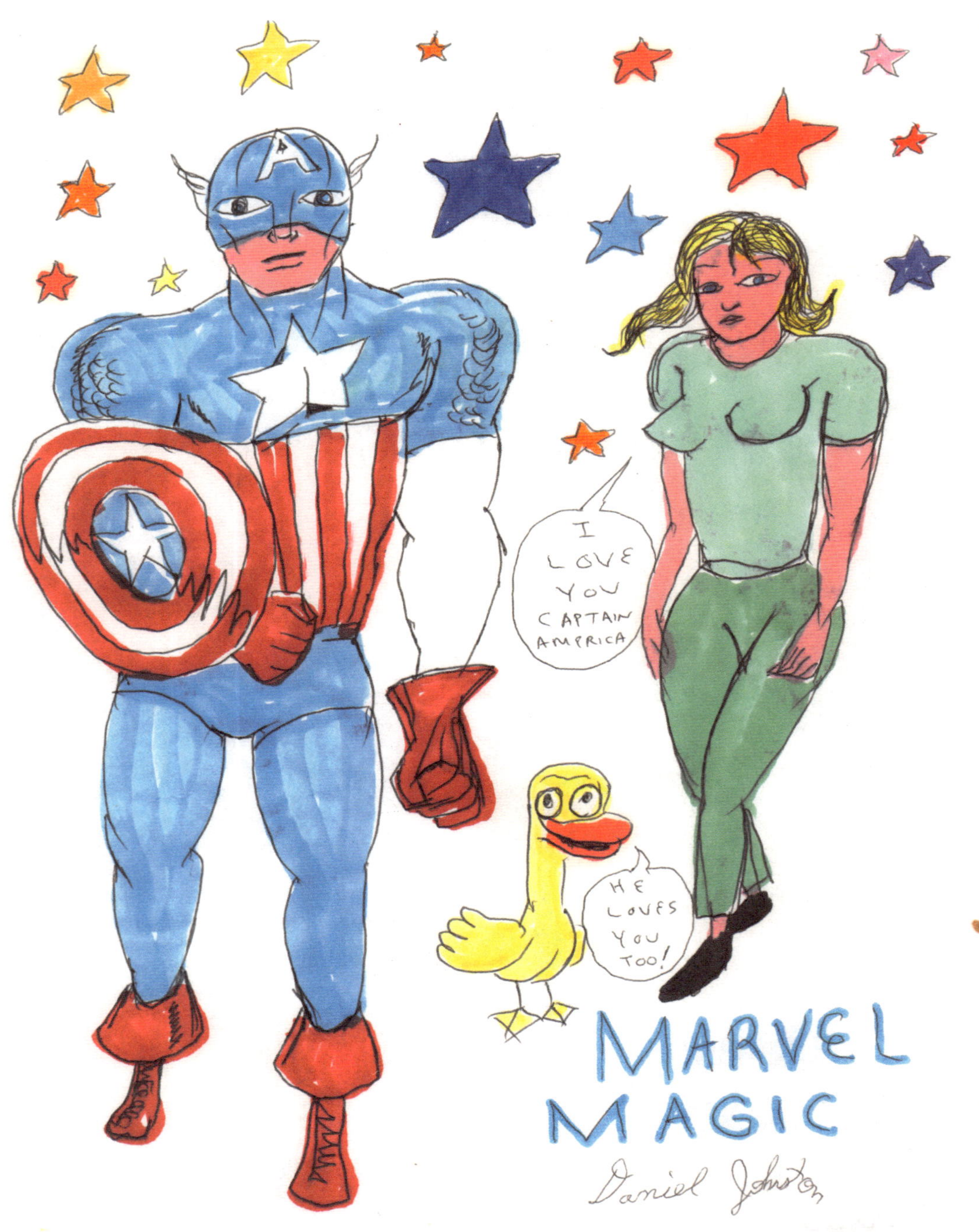

Marvel Magic

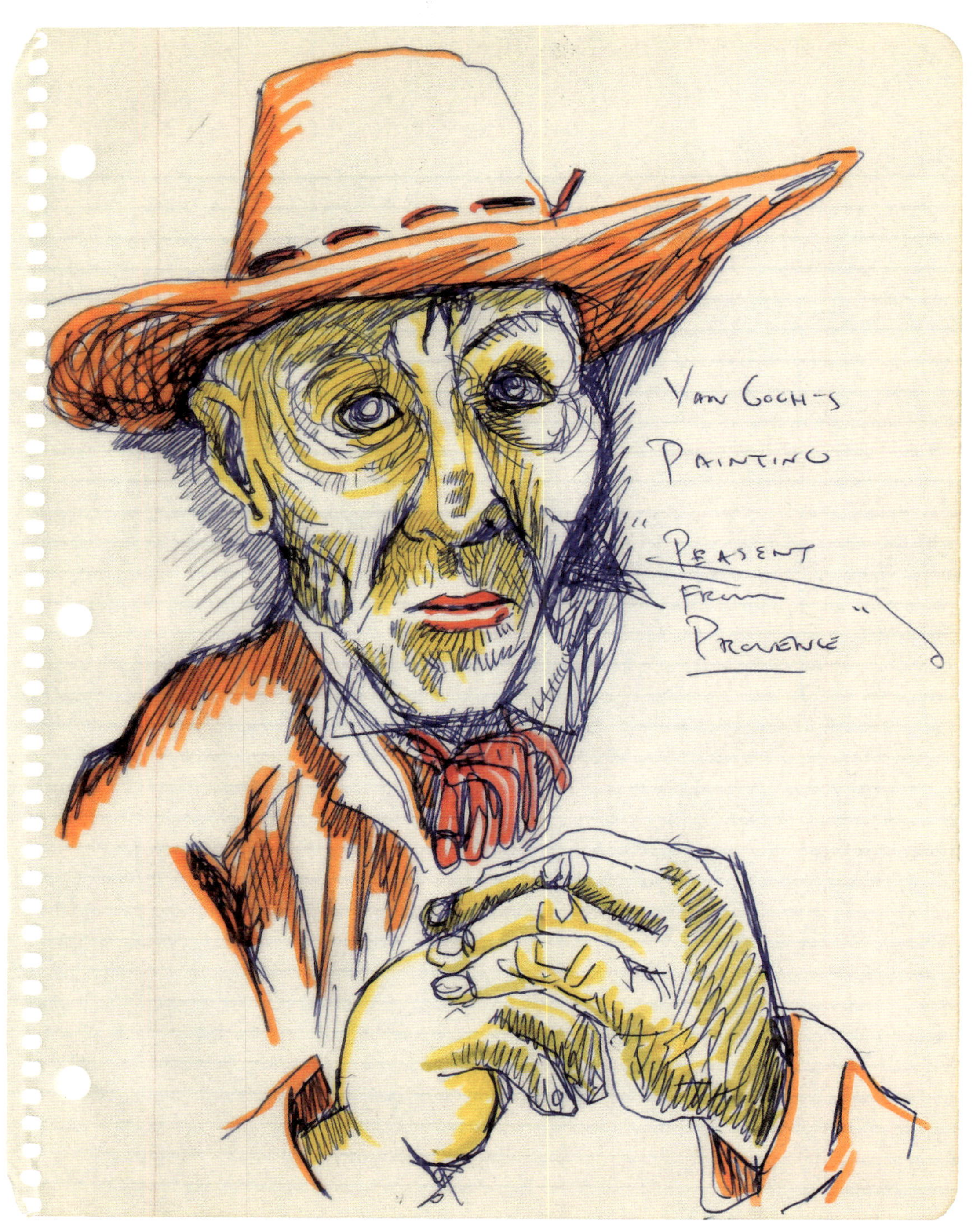

Peasent from Provence (Van Gogh)

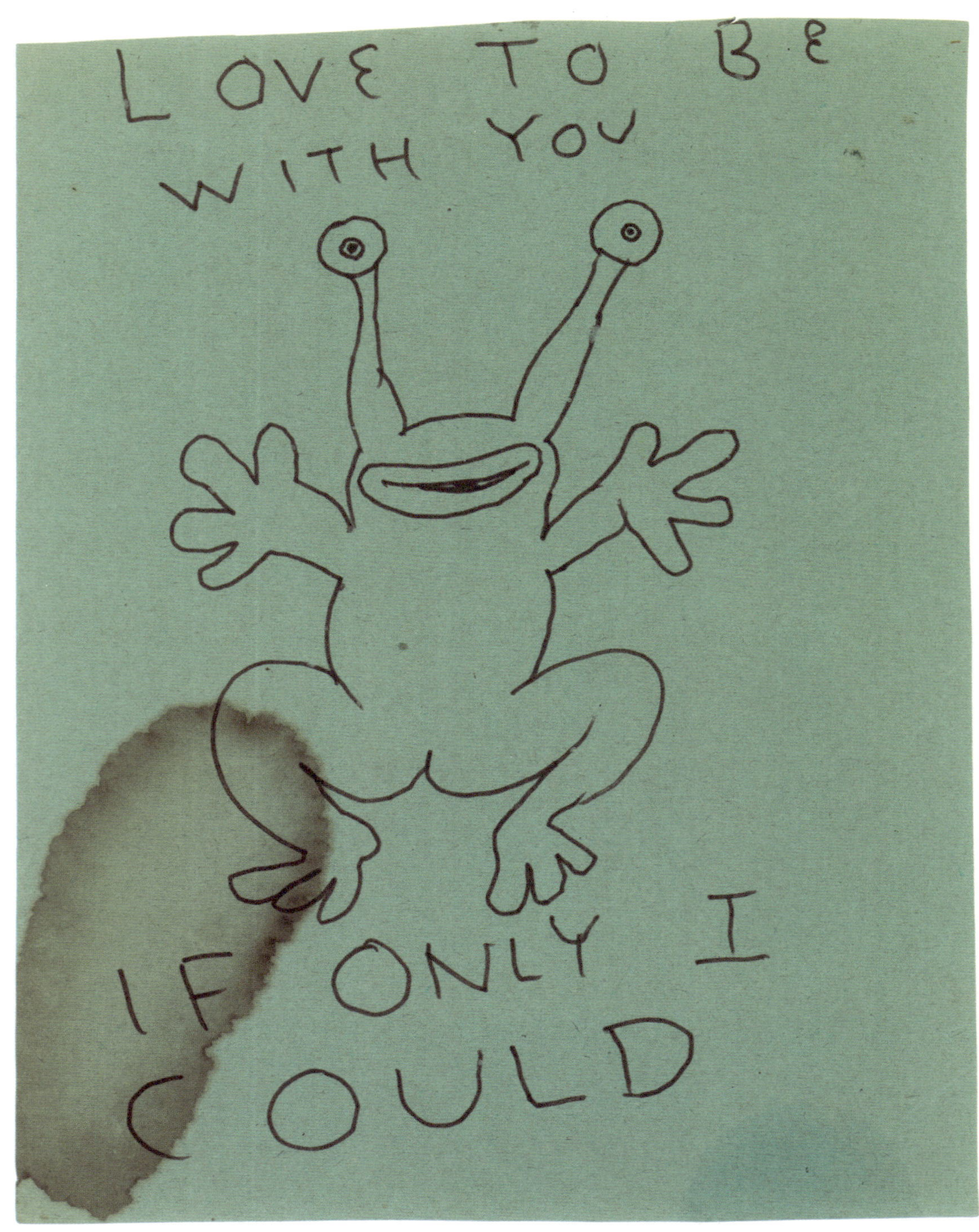

Love to Be with You If Only I Could

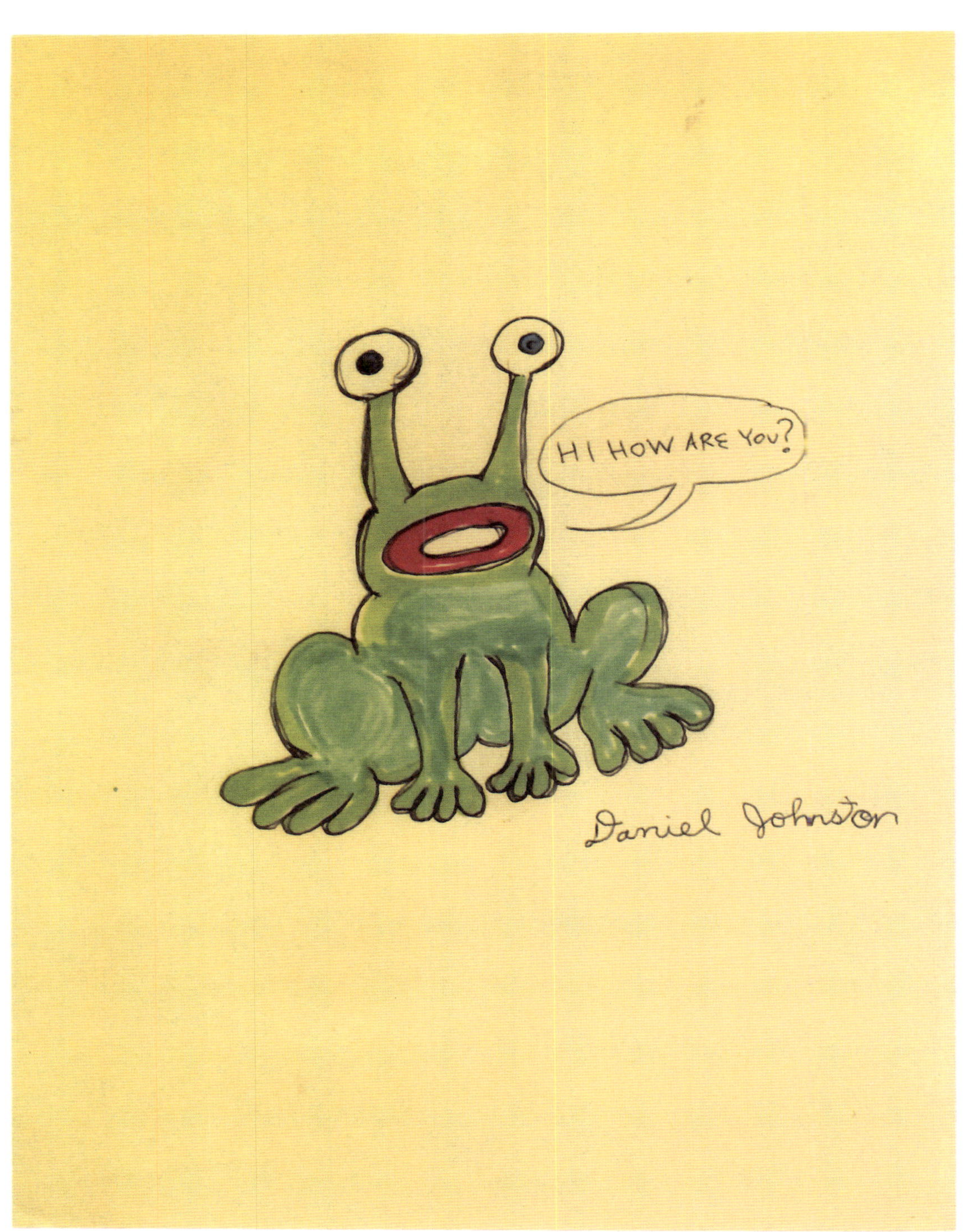

Hi How Are You?

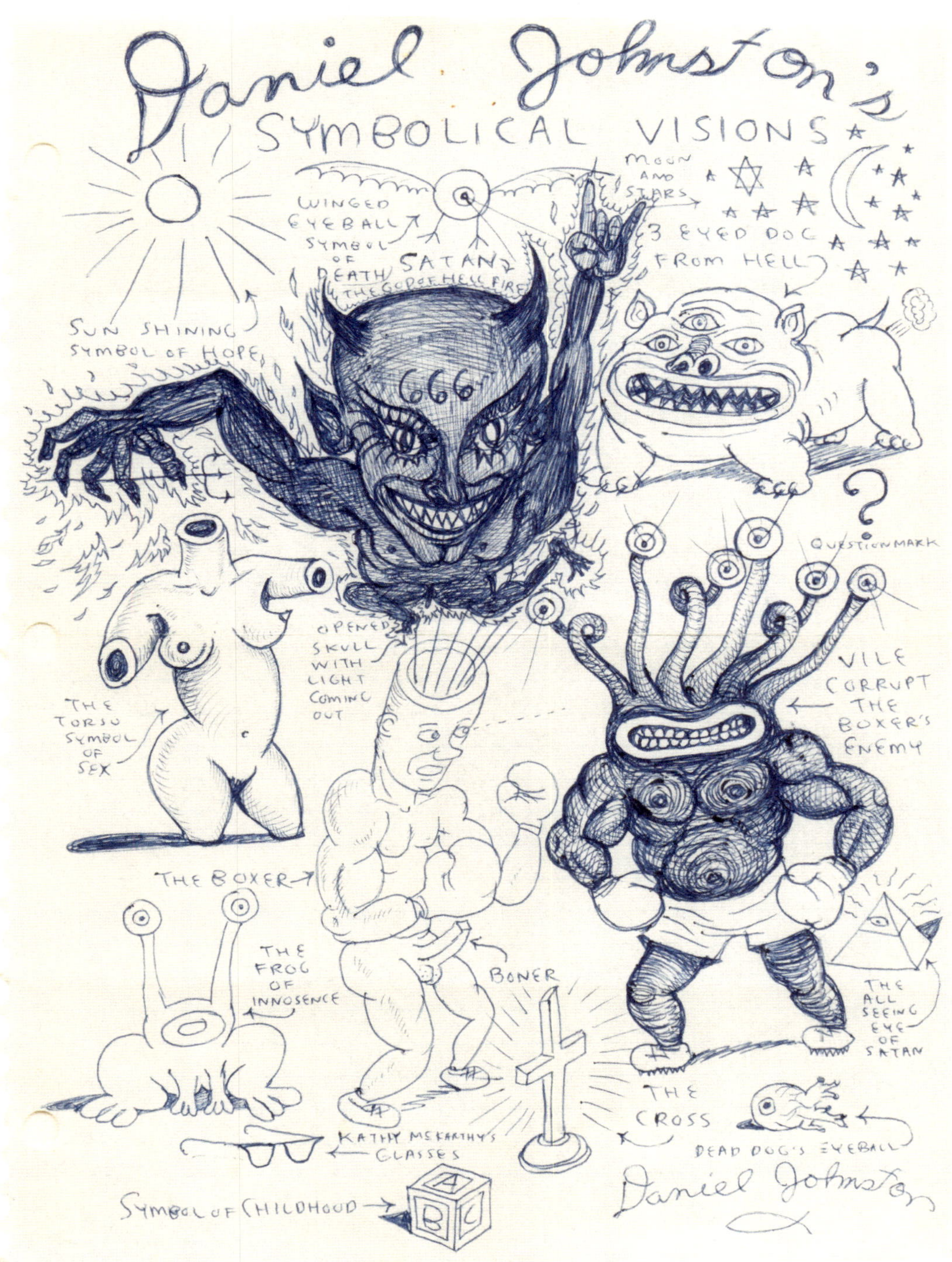

Symbolical Visions

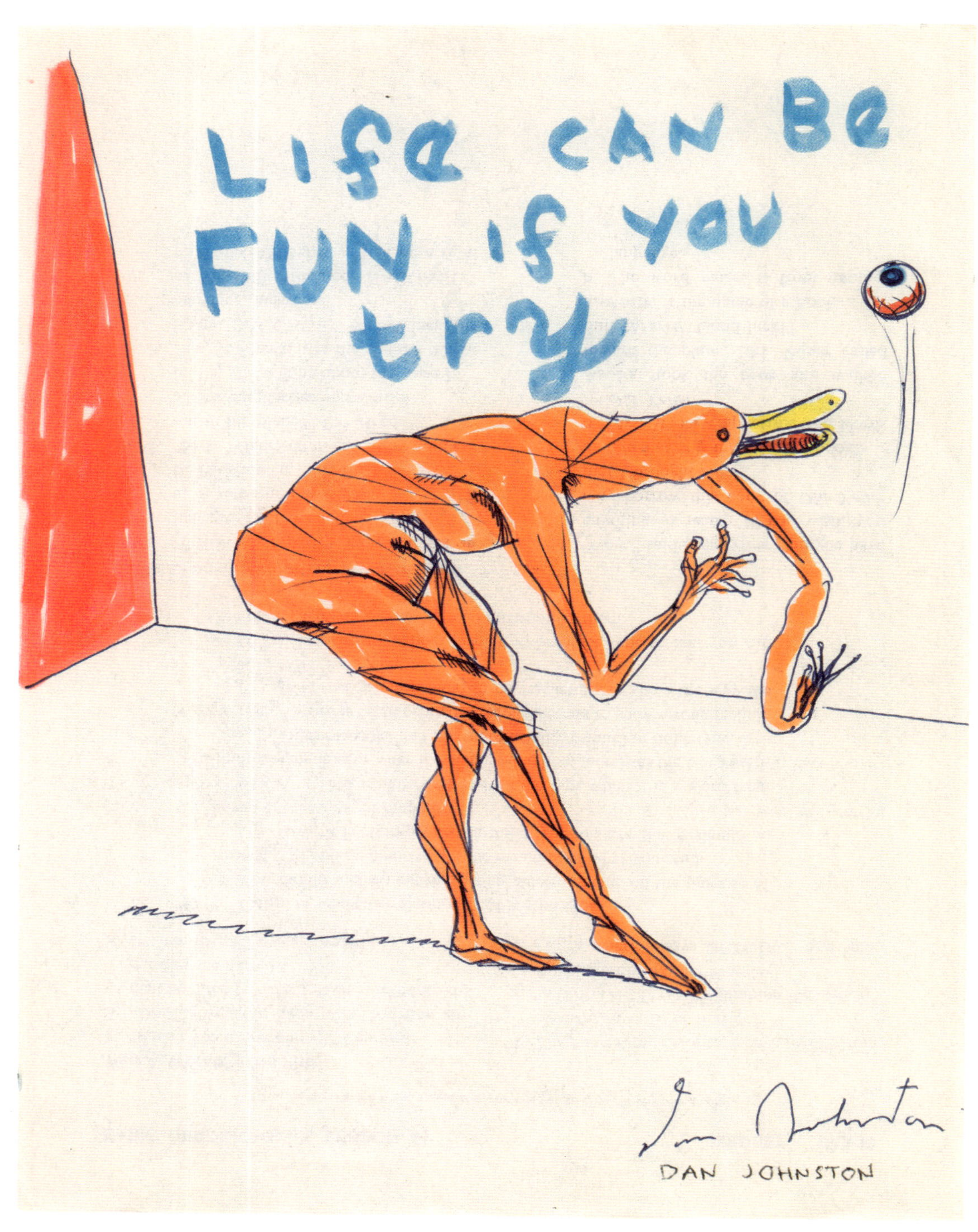

Life Can Be FUN If You Try

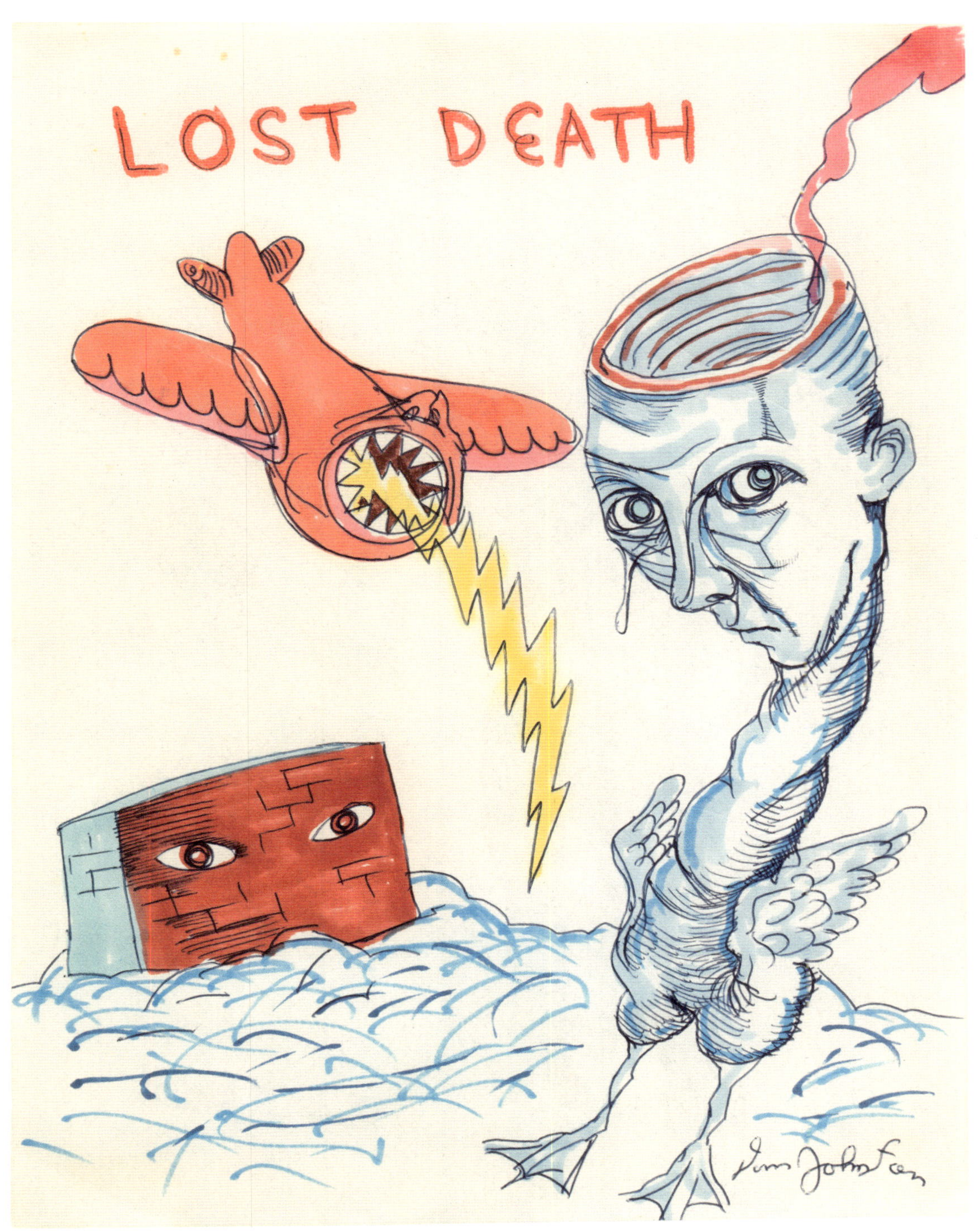

Lost Death

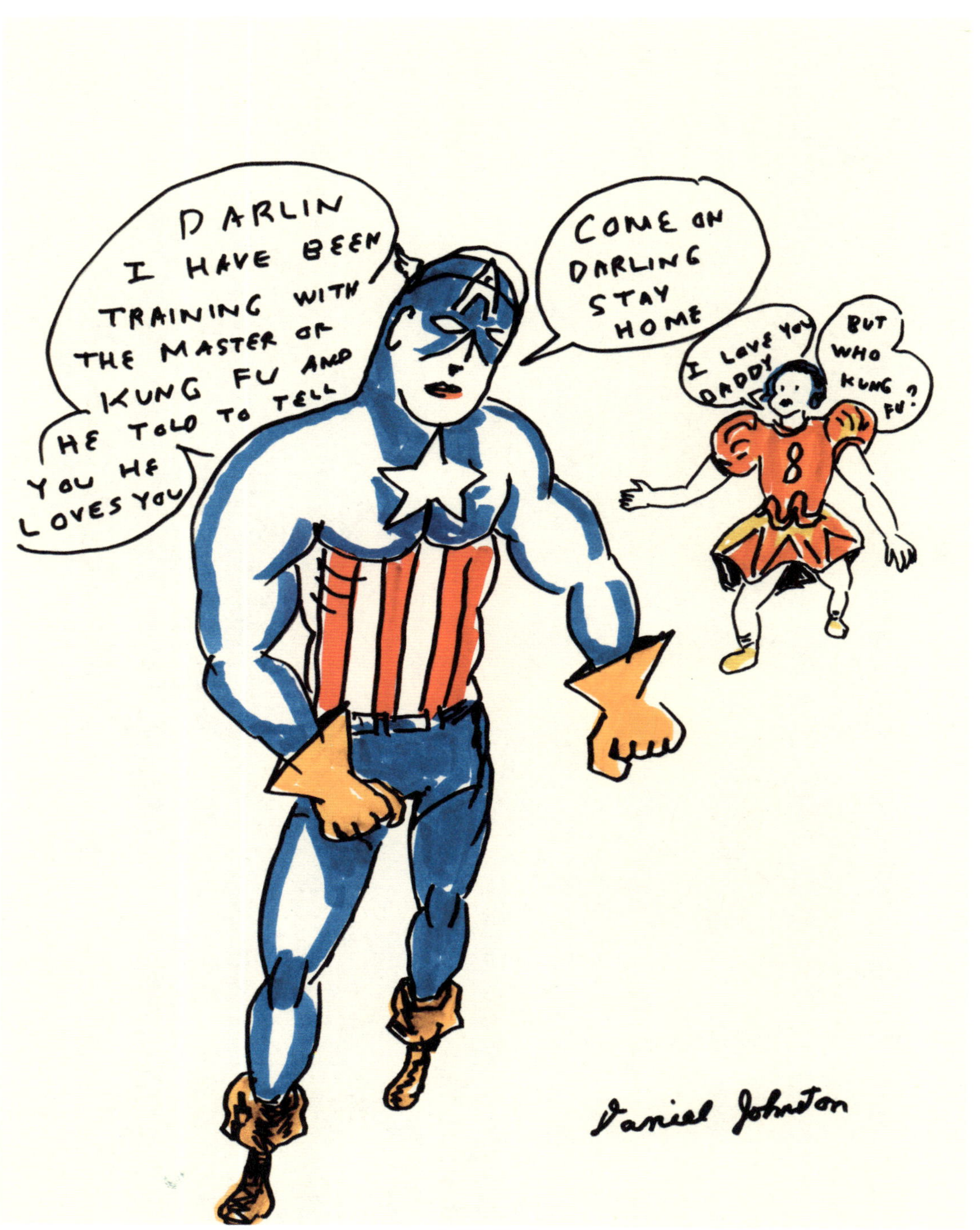

But Who Kung Fu?

THIS WORLD IS SO BIG AND I SO SMALL

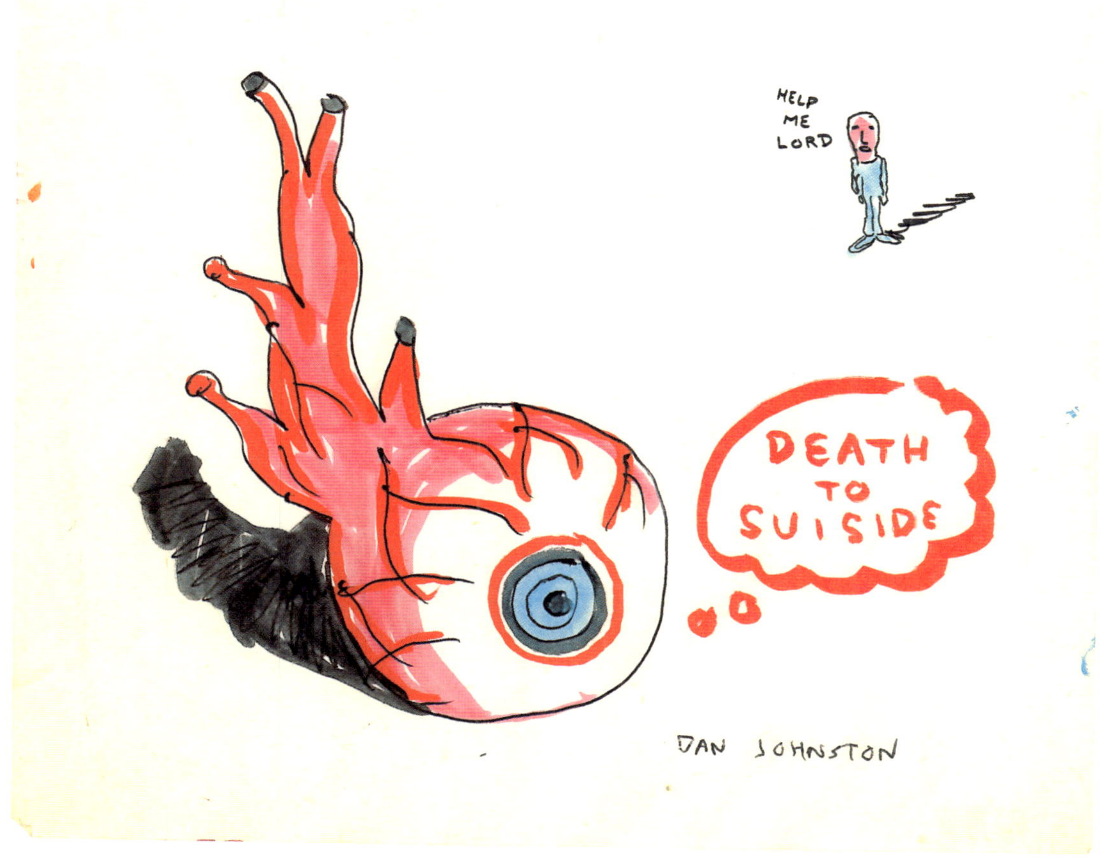

Death to Suiside

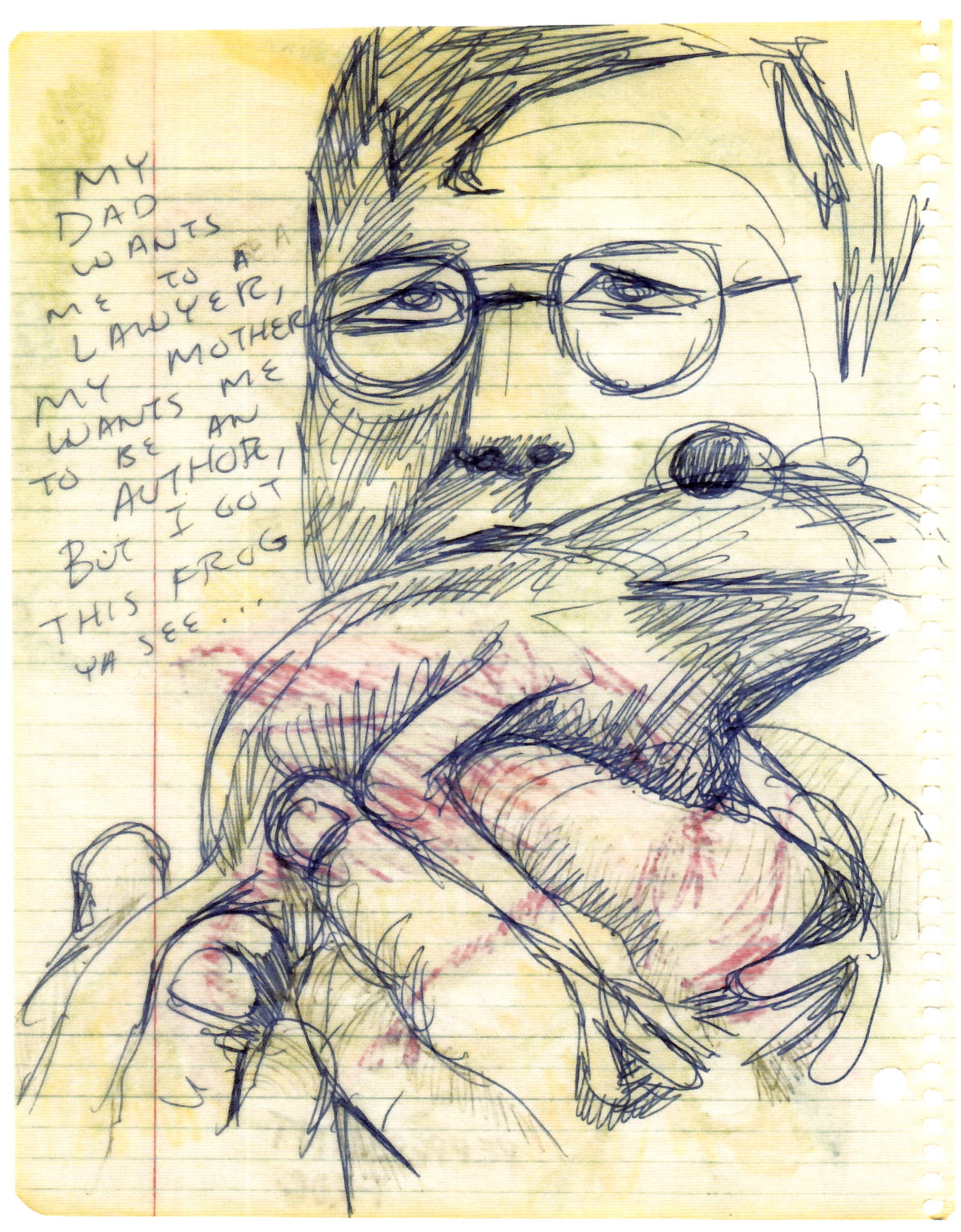

But I Got This Frog Ya See . . .

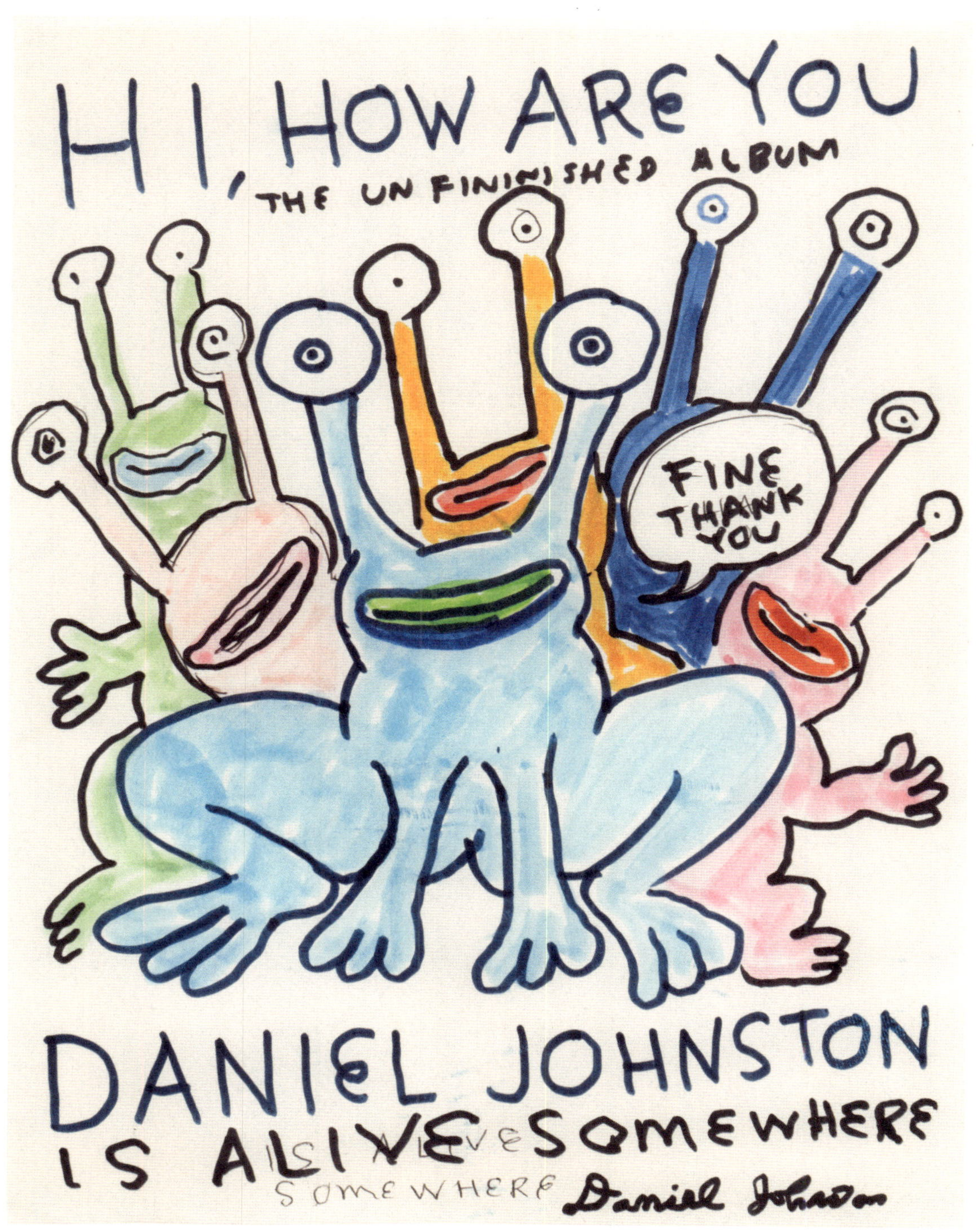

Daniel Johnston Is Alive Somewhere

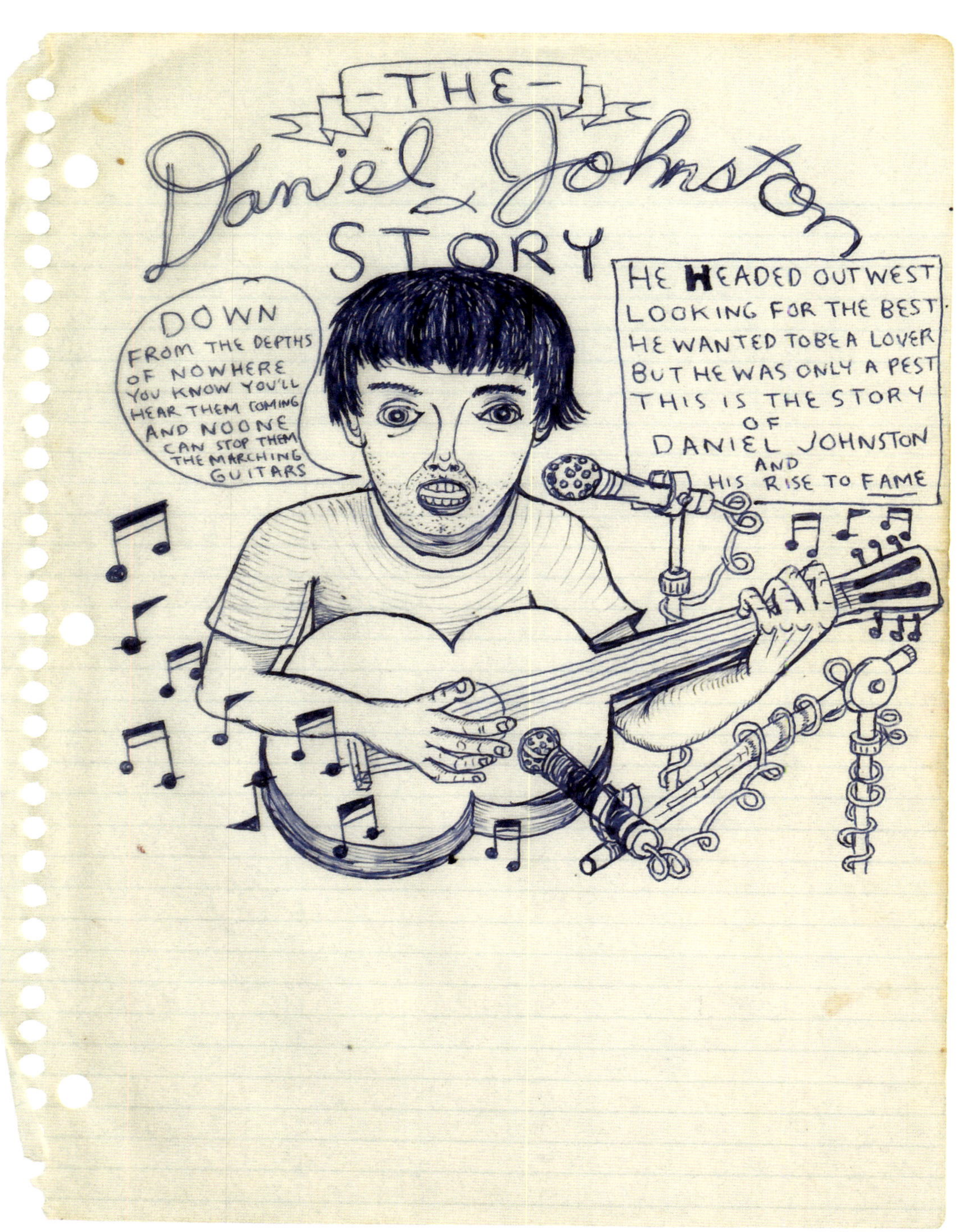

The Daniel Johnston Story

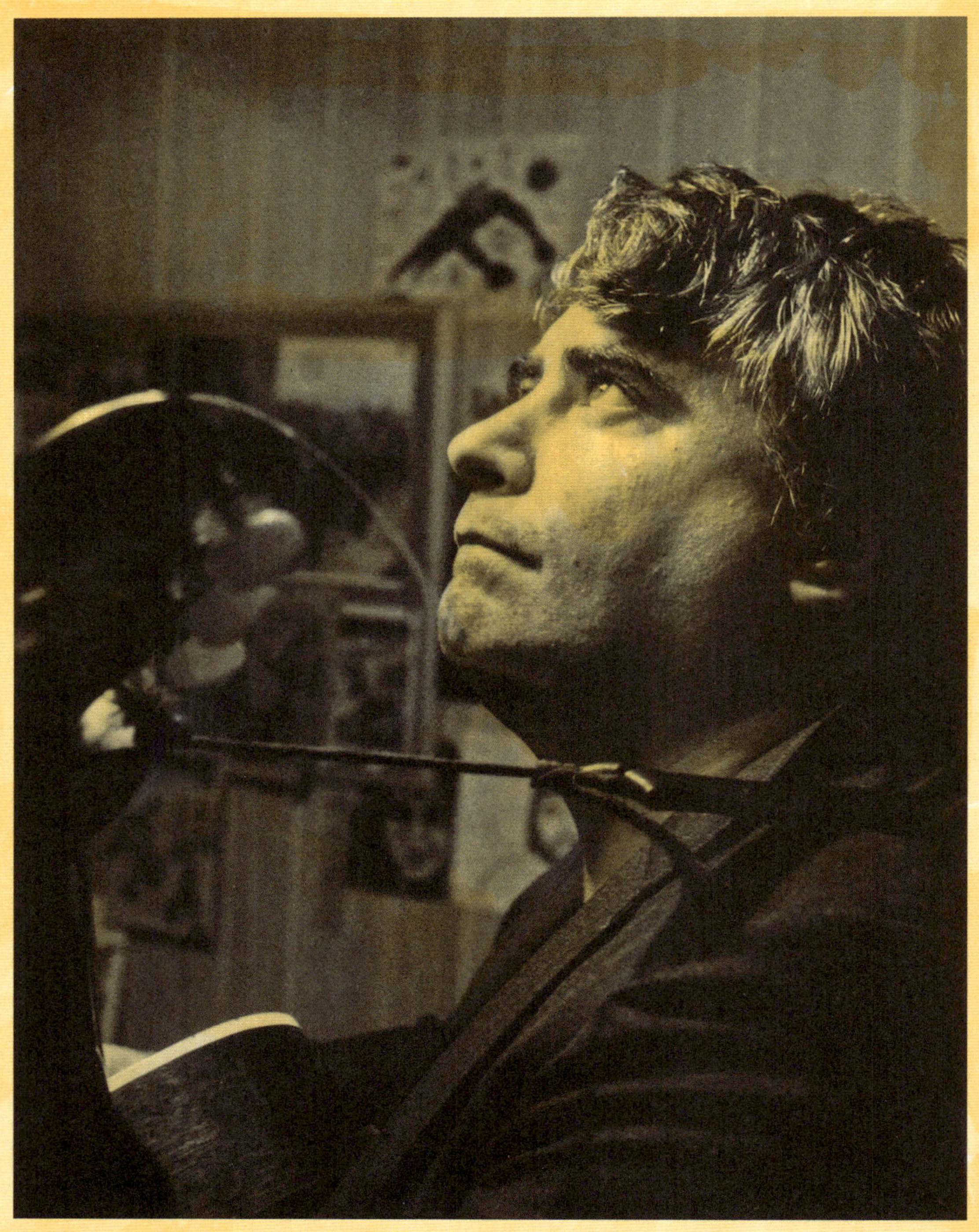

Lee Foster

Daniel Johnston Is Alive Somewhere

As a teenager I spent the early to mid-1990s paying close attention to all things Nirvana—and to the boom of great music that followed the band's rise. Full stop, I gave up my older sister's records and radio stations, grew my hair longer, and raided my dad's closet for flannel shirts. Pearl Jam and Soundgarden. The Smashing Pumpkins and R.E.M. PJ Harvey and Radiohead. I loved them all. So when Kurt Cobain first nodded in the direction of Daniel Johnston, I wanted to know more. Pre-Internet, though, we had to wait for information to reach us. Johnston was an obscure reference.

In the years that followed, I picked up what I could. Daniel was different. His voice and musical style were not palatable in a traditional way. He was an outsider. He was lo-fi. His mental health issues were obvious and out in front. To share his music with others, I felt I needed to serve up a preemptive explanation in the sort of "just-give-it-a-chance" kind of way—but then watched as new listeners were arrested by Daniel's words and earnestness. Songs like "True Love Will Find You in the End" and "Story of an Artist" are master classes in songwriting—simple, potent. Little by little, Daniel's message grew, made louder and more lasting by the praises of Jeff Tweedy, Tom Waits, Lana Del Rey, and others.

By 2019, I'd spent decades with Daniel's music and his lore. A favorite topic of musicians, I'd learned a lot about Johnston just being "in the room" at the recording studio where I worked. So when I discovered an original drawing on a friend's wall while visiting Los Angeles, I lost my composure. I'd never seen one of Daniel's drawings in the wild.

"How do you have that?" I interrupted, alarmed at how unhinged I sounded. The friend replied in some vague, brief way, as if protecting a treasure only he knew where to find. And it certainly was something precious.

Daniel had passed away only one month prior, so to be standing with something he'd made felt especially significant. It was also something my friend perhaps felt too sad to talk about. I let it go. When our visit was done, though, I ran red lights getting back to the hotel. A few hours later, I'd purchased my first Daniel drawing on eBay. One month later, I was on a plane to Texas to meet with Johnston's closest friends and relatives.

* * *

Once in Austin, I drove to the home of Daniel's longtime manager, Jeff Tartakov, who agreed to sell pieces from his collection—most notably *Symbolical Visions* (p. 21). It's the drawing Jeff calls "the Rosetta Stone" of Daniel's visual work in the documentary *The Devil and Daniel Johnston*. The piece first appeared as an illustration in the March 1989 issue of *SPIN* magazine. In the accompanying article, writer Louis Black summarizes a three-year period when Johnston achieved his dreams of becoming a successful musician and simultaneously experienced his first psychotic delusions.

The drawing identifies some of the internal and external forces that confounded Daniel, and points—perhaps without Johnston's knowledge—to Freud's ideas of id, ego, and the superego. This is the first floor of Daniel's psyche. And like much of his art, it is an examination of his primitive, impulsive thoughts pitted against his rational, moral ones. It acts as a snapshot of Daniel's mental state and manic internal battles.

After spending a few hours with Jeff, I packed up my newly acquired drawings and drove to Dick Johnston's home in Katy, Texas. Dick is Daniel's older brother and the sole supervisor of Daniel's estate. Almost immediately Dick began pointing to family photos, press clippings, notebooks, and drawings hanging on the walls and scattered about. Donny Veloz, who works with Dick, was there too.

I was a little wobbly with excitement as we finally sat at the dining room table to look at fifty or so drawings. Dick sat across from me, pointing to the different details of each piece. "Sometimes he signed a single drawing twice, or more times," he explained. "He'd come back to them months, or even years, later and make changes." Donny emphasized other features I shouldn't miss.

We spoke quietly together for an hour—and then an hour more. Donny excused himself around eight. Dick and I continued talking. At some point I realized that in all my excitement to see the artwork, I'd selfishly overlooked something: Daniel had been gone for less than three months.

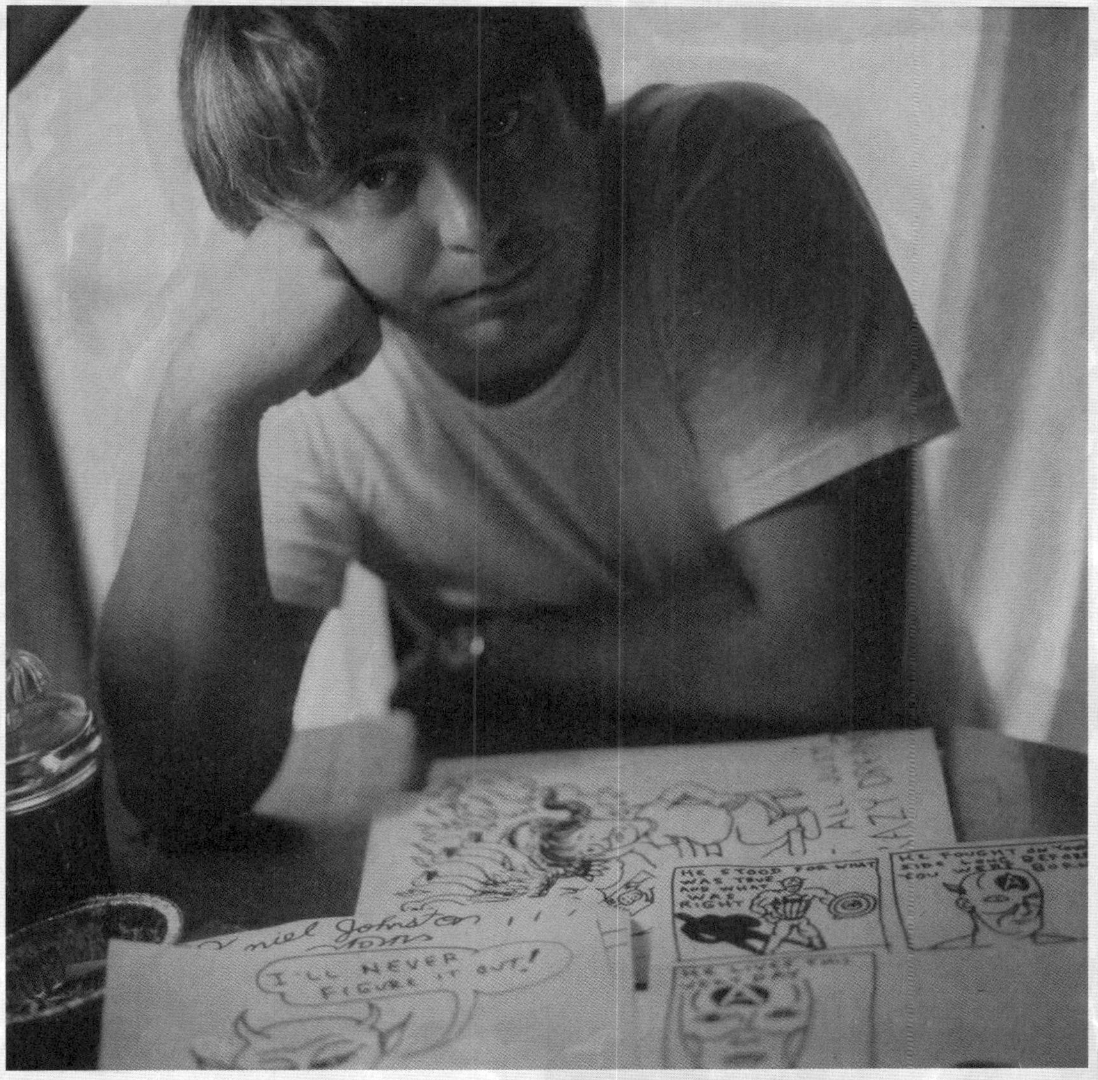

Dick was still mourning his brother; Donny, his friend. They were processing his absence with me in real time, and the experience seemed cathartic. Just as I was discovering Daniel, Dick and Donny were letting him go.

"When are you headed back to New York?" Dick asked.

"Tomorrow," I said. I looked at the time—it'd gotten late. I thought he'd probably like to go to bed, so I told him I should go.

"Or you could stay in the guest room," he offered. "I can show you more art. We could drive out to Daniel's house too."

"More art? This isn't all of it?" I couldn't believe it.

He looked at me silently over his glasses and grinned.

I canceled my return flight, and in the time it took me to grab my bag, Dick had already placed a box of binders on the bed, each one packed with drawings. "Here's enough for tonight," he said. He seemed tired, but happy.

I stayed up until four looking at each drawing, front and back. There were monsters. There were armies to fight the monsters. There were bigger monsters to fight the armies—angels and devils, innocence and evil. Negotiations between characters on almost every page quelled or processed whatever feelings Daniel felt in the moment he drew them. Alone in his brother's guest bedroom, I experienced Daniel's heartache, his tenderness, his curiosity, his humor. Most of all, I recognized his determination to overcome his difficulties, and that his expressions were so simple and exact. On a single sheet of standard-sized printer paper, Daniel could tell a formidable story.

The next day we drove to Daniel's home in Waller, Texas. Right away I noticed that the house appeared to have been untouched since his passing: a carton of milk still half full in the fridge, the dishes still dirty in the sink. When Daniel died, Dick and Donny simply shut the front door and locked it. I felt sad. It was all so deeply personal. Should I be here?

I scanned Daniel's massive collections of toys, Beatles memorabilia, DVDs, comic books, and PEZ dispensers. I sat in his TV chair. I played a few notes on his piano as I walked by it. It was all still here. A handwritten note on his desk read, "In my life of art and freedom there was a lot of shit thrown my way." Dick and I talked about what could be done with the contents of the home to preserve them but leave things untouched. On our drive back to Katy, we stopped at Daniel's grave to pay our respects, then again for Mexican food. Dick told more stories about his brother.

Back at Dick's house, he and Donny finally showed me the archive. There weren't dozens more drawings here. There were thousands. Rooms full. Surely one person couldn't have created so much art in a single lifetime. But Daniel did. Moreover, he made and released eighteen albums of recorded music and filled hundreds of notebooks, cassettes, and videotapes with his sketches, ideas, music, and imagination. Long before social media and smart devices were everywhere, Daniel explored all means possible to document his own existence. He wasn't just prolific; he was obsessed.

* * *

What I came to love about Daniel's art and music is the impulsiveness and imperfection of it all. He considered his audience, surely, but the work was never overcooked to accommodate anyone. These were his heartfelt feelings, and what is left on the page are Daniel's simple truths—mistakes and all. He could be precise in his message, but he was never precious in his expression. "Better done than perfect," as the saying goes.

His cheery drawings are the most endearing. In *Life Can Be FUN If You Try* (p. 22), a red duck on human legs pirouettes after a rogue eye that bounces around the room. Another piece, *I Feel Good in a Special Way* (p. 197), details a simply drawn figure surfing a wave—with red, blue, and yellow stars twinkling all around. In the background, a baby block represents Daniel's beloved childlike freedom and unbothered fun.

Other drawings are more troubled, dismayed, or ominous. *Lost Death* (p. 23) is the darker counterpart to *Life Can Be FUN If You Try*. The two drawings may well have been created on the same day with the same pens and markers, but with a stark difference in mood and message. In *Lost Death*, Daniel appears to have lost his mind. A tear runs down his cheek. Nearby, a wall represents the obstacles in his way, as he comes under fire from an attacking plane that barrels toward him. In another sorrowful piece, a blobby blue and pink baby sits in a corner staring at a lone painting, and asks, "oh, how come the channel won't change?" The baby block from *I Feel Good in a Special Way* is here too, blighted by another eyeball, perhaps a reference to the grown-ups that restrained Daniel's carefree behavior. "God Would Punish Even a Fantasy," the caption reads (p. 279).

Returning to *Symbolical Visions* (p. 21) to untangle more of Daniel's meanings, it seems the headless torso signifies sex; the winged eyeball, death; and the three-eyed dog from hell is an accomplice to Satan himself. The sun suggests hope, as do the cross, moon, and stars. Among these recurring symbols, however, a single figure emerges as Daniel's most celebrated and recognizable: Jeremiah the Frog. More commonly called the "Hi How Are You frog," the cartoon has long, ropey eyes that ascend high above its squat frog body.

The frog was first introduced to the public on the cover of Daniel's sixth self-released album, *Hi, How Are You*, recorded in 1983. Almost a decade later, the character was thrust into mainstream consciousness when Kurt Cobain wore a *Hi, How Are You* T-shirt to the 1992 MTV Video Music Awards. The now iconic character has since appeared in collaborations with Supreme and Vans for their skateboards, clothing, and shoes. A mural of Jeremiah has been a local Austin landmark since Daniel painted it in the mid-1990s.

But why a frog? Why the name Jeremiah? The allegorical meaning of the frog changes across cultures, but frogs are frequently seen as healing, or as representations of fertility, regeneration, and rebirth. In the book of Revelation, however, three frogs reflect the unholy trinity of the dragon, the beast, and the false prophet, all of which Daniel sometimes includes in his drawings.

Another explanation I've heard is that Daniel was quite fond of the singing, dancing frog from the 1955 animated musical short "One Froggy Evening." In the film, the frog demonstrates his talents only for the person who possesses the box wherein he resides. Or perhaps there is a much simpler reason. After all, "Jeremiah was a bullfrog."

Through my searches, three Jeremiah drawings struck me most, the first on the back of a notebook page (p. 26). In it, a man holds a frog and declares, "My dad wants me to be a lawyer, my mother wants me to be an author, but I got this frog ya see." It's one of the earliest mentions of the frog and appears to establish it as a symbol for Daniel's own innocence and commitment to protect it from outside pressures. The second drawing is a crude version of the frog on green construction paper (p. 18) that reads, "Love to Be with You If Only I Could." It's a sweet, simple sentiment marked by a stain from the artist's knocked-over soda. And the third drawing (p. 27)—an emotional discovery—is a family of happy, multicolored frogs gathered above the words "DANIEL JOHNSTON IS ALIVE SOMEWHERE."

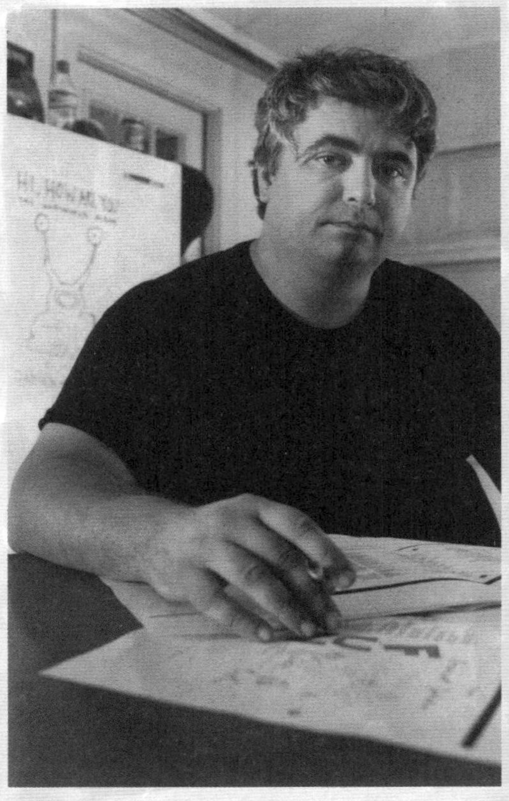

There are other notable constants in Daniel's art. Johnston often depicts himself as "Joe the Boxer," or as "Casper the Friendly Ghost." In many drawings, he is the "polka-dotted underwear guy"; in others the top of his head is lopped off and his brain is missing. Daniel also related to doomed film and literary characters like King Kong and Frankenstein's monster, and would sometimes recruit them for his drawings.

No matter which character Daniel inhabited, his own thoughts and feelings poured plainly onto the page. Like many artists, he processed his emotions by applying them to a persona and then allowing that character to bear the burden for him. He approached his relationships this way too and often grappled with family and romantic dynamics on the page. Most frequent of these are Johnston's mother and father. Mabel is often drawn quietly reading western novels in her chair or shown scolding Daniel for some chore he hasn't completed. Bill, though—a Second World War fighter pilot—was heroized in his son's drawings, and sometimes merged with Daniel's favorite comic-book superhero, Captain America. Bill takes a leading role in Daniel's drawings throughout his life and career.

Daniel's knowledge of comics and comic culture was encyclopedic—from the characters he loved most to the artists who created them. Jack Kirby (known as the William Blake of comics) was far and away Daniel's favorite comic-book artist. Johnston glorified him for decades with his own interpretations of the characters Kirby co-created. Legendary Marvel heroes and villains Iron Man, the Hulk, Doctor Doom, Red Skull, and Captain America, as well as the Avengers, were all inventions of Kirby and his partner Stan Lee.

Daniel emulated the storytelling style of Marvel and DC—it was how he learned to convey narratives through his drawings. He made the famous comic-book heroes his own, mixing them with original characters (e.g., pp. 16, 24). By the early 1990s, Johnston's versions of Captain America, Casper the Ghost, Joe the Boxer, Jeremiah the Frog, and Sassy Frass had all come together in the barren landscapes of Daniel's own universe. Johnston's technical abilities were now expertly practiced. If he could think it, he could draw it, and a new, more playful world emerged. As Daniel found his own visual style and voice, the cleverness, originality, and genius of his drawings began to soar.

At Dick's, I spent countless hours with Daniel's drawings. I found myself in tears with Johnston's most tender and sincere images, and then moments later laughing at his wit and frankness. Dick let me explore it alone, but he'd check in—usually to remind me to sleep, or eat. Some nights, though, he picked up the pages himself, and silently shuffled through them.

In those quiet hours sitting cross-legged on the floor, I discovered some of Daniel's most seminal drawings. On my last night at Dick's, I happened upon a letter from Daniel to his favorite songwriter, John Lennon, drafted as though the two were friends. Later, I found a drawing of John and Yoko, with the inscription, "We Miss You, John." I took the two pages to Dick the following morning. "I'd like to see if I can get these to John's family if you'll let me," I offered. "I'd like to try." He agreed but would only allow me to pay half price. "They'll be a gift from both of us this way. I like that." I liked it too. The drawing and the letter returned with me to Manhattan. On my flight home, I thought only of Daniel, his death, and the drawings inside my backpack.

A few months after my first visit, I returned to Katy to ask Dick if I could help share Daniel's work with the art community and his fans. First, we gathered music industry friends to pay tribute to Daniel on the one-year anniversary of his death. We called it *Honey, I Sure Miss You*—a lo-fi, pandemic-era compilation of bedroom and field performances interlaced with Daniel's illustrations. We launched a new website (storyofanartist.net) to make drawings available to collectors, then hosted Electric Lady Studios' first art exhibition in collaboration with the Outsider Art Fair and artist-curator Gary Panter. The Contemporary Austin then contacted us about organizing the retrospective *I Live My Broken Dreams*, Daniel's first solo museum show. To promote the exhibition, we were able to fulfill another of Daniel's lifelong dreams by putting his versions of Batman, Superman, and New Gods onto variant covers of the DC Comics series *Batman*—thanks in large part to curator Robin K. Williams and DC Comics editor-in-chief Marie Javins. And perhaps most important, we moved Daniel's archive of drawings, notebooks, and personal belongings to a secure storage facility in Houston, from which a selection of drawings and other items will be made available to admirers and collectors for years to come.

* * *

Back in New York from Katy, I adored the John and Yoko drawing and Daniel's letter to John. I drove them to a best-in-class conservator in Philadelphia to be framed. Having decided that the two pieces should be kept together, I asked the framer to fix the letter to the back of the drawing under plexiglass. It felt important: they should never be apart.

When it was done, I collected the frame and hung it in my office. In truth, I'd grown attached. These two pages had survived decades forgotten in a box, drafted from one amazing musician to another. And I'd found them. As much as I felt they belonged to someone else, I wanted to claim them as my own, at least for now. I reassured myself that I'd know when it was time to let go.

And then one night as I was making my late evening rounds at the studio, I happened upon an open door with Sean Lennon sitting inside. He was surrounded by musicians, instruments, microphones, and empty takeout containers—visiting someone he knew. I pulled Sean aside and told him the story. Later, I took the frame down from the wall and gave it to him. My task was complete.

Three days later I received a text from him—a photo of the framed drawing above his father's piano.

"Hung it up for Daniel," it read.

Lee Foster

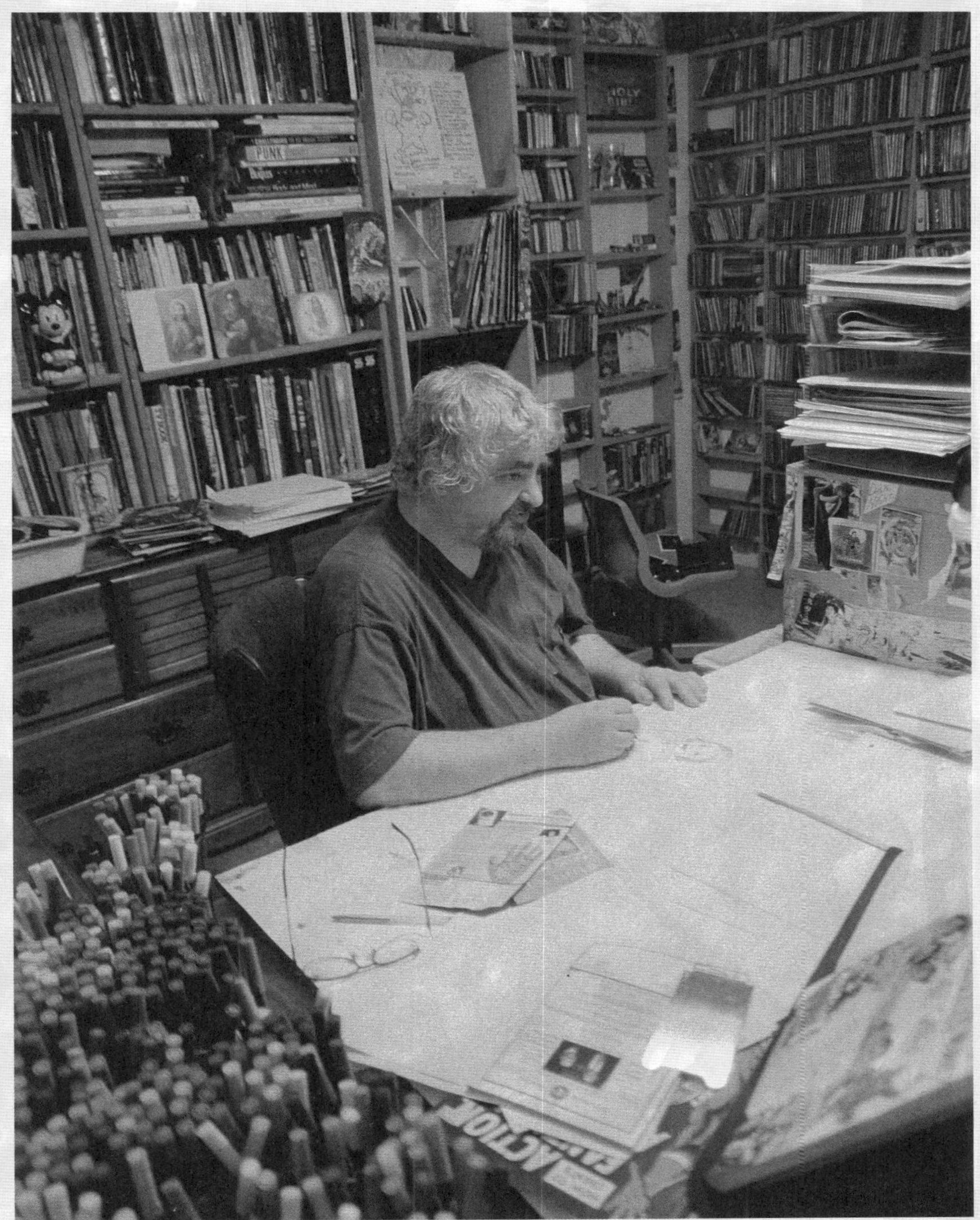

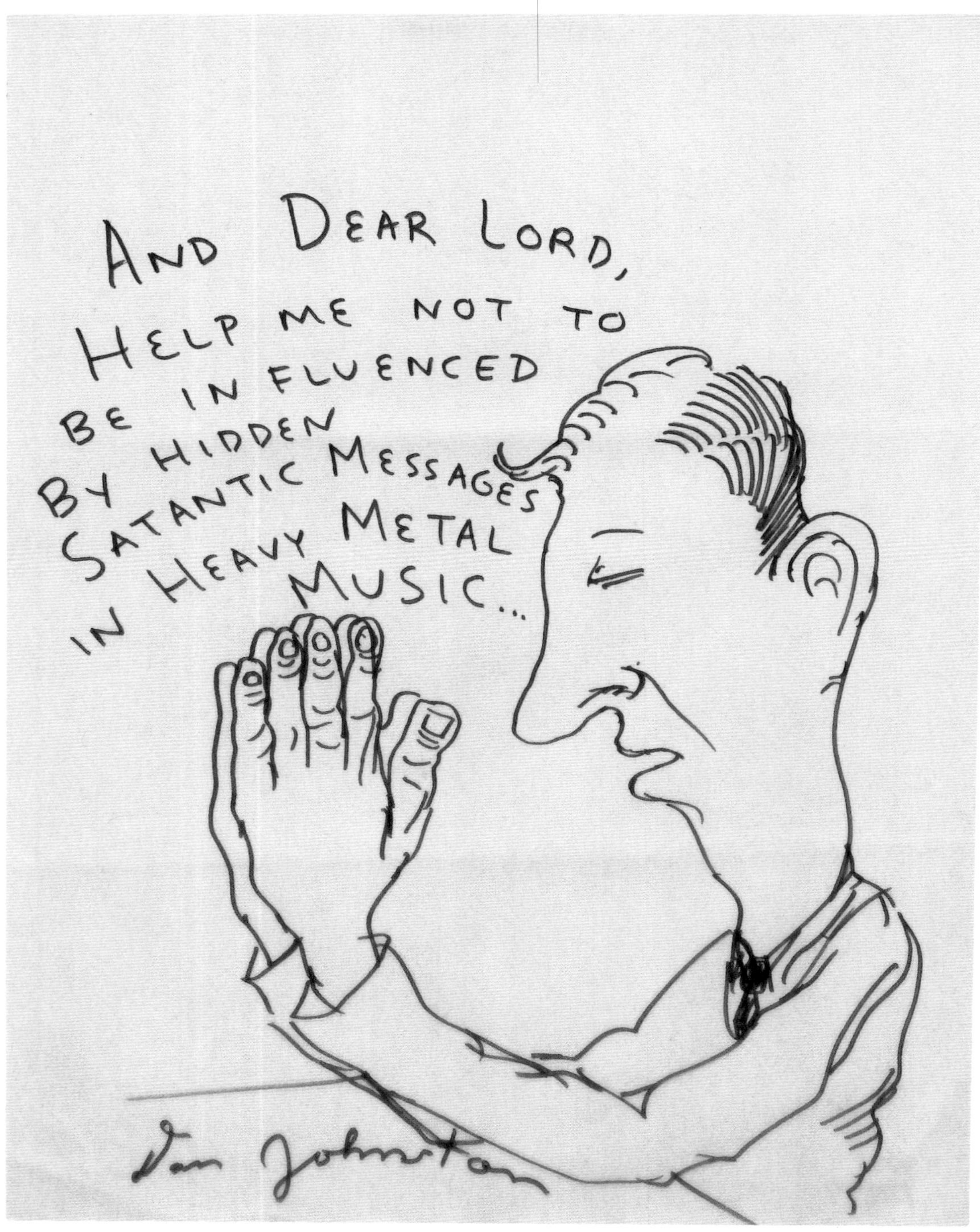

Heavy Metal Music

II.
Musicians
1975–1990s

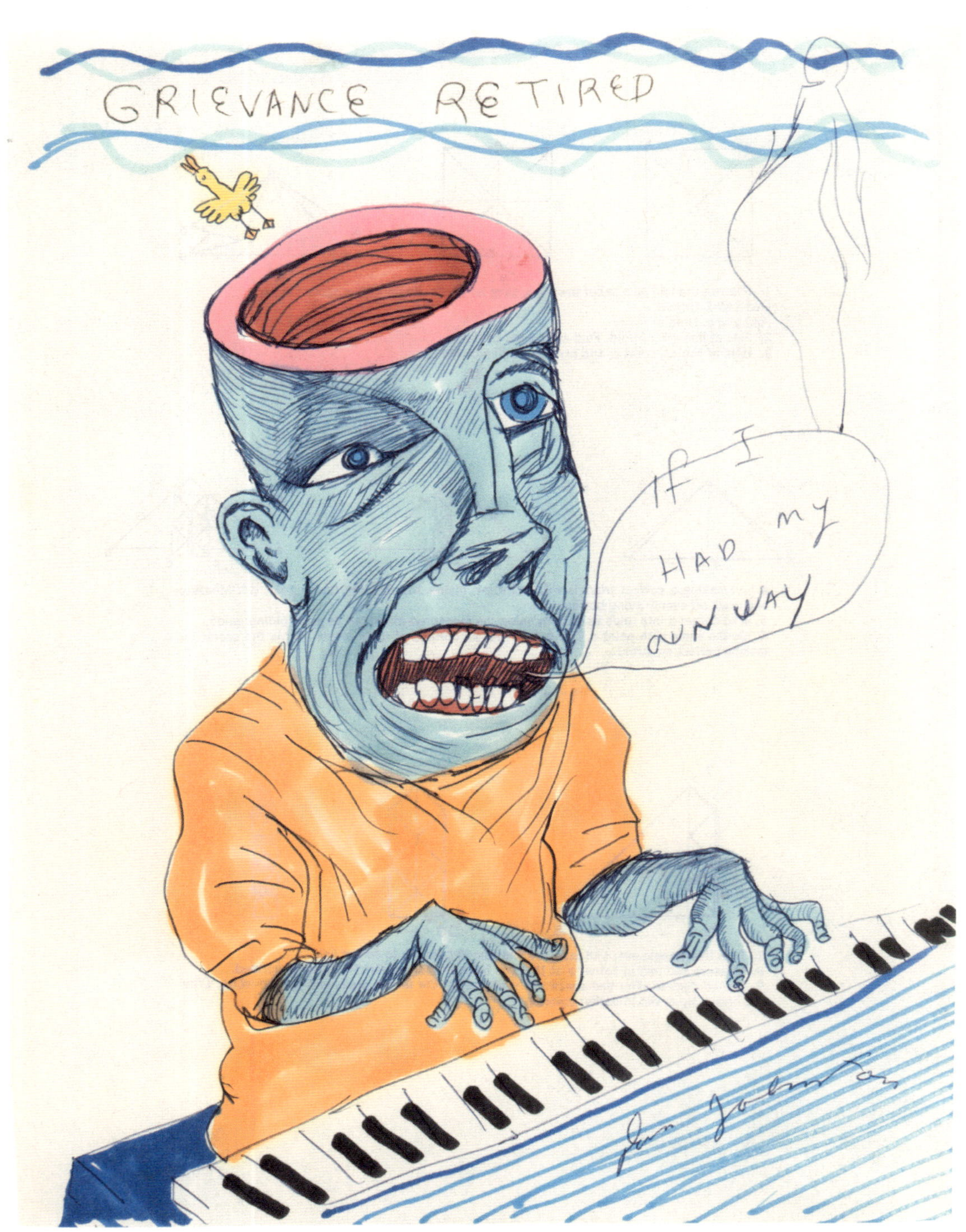

Grievance Retired

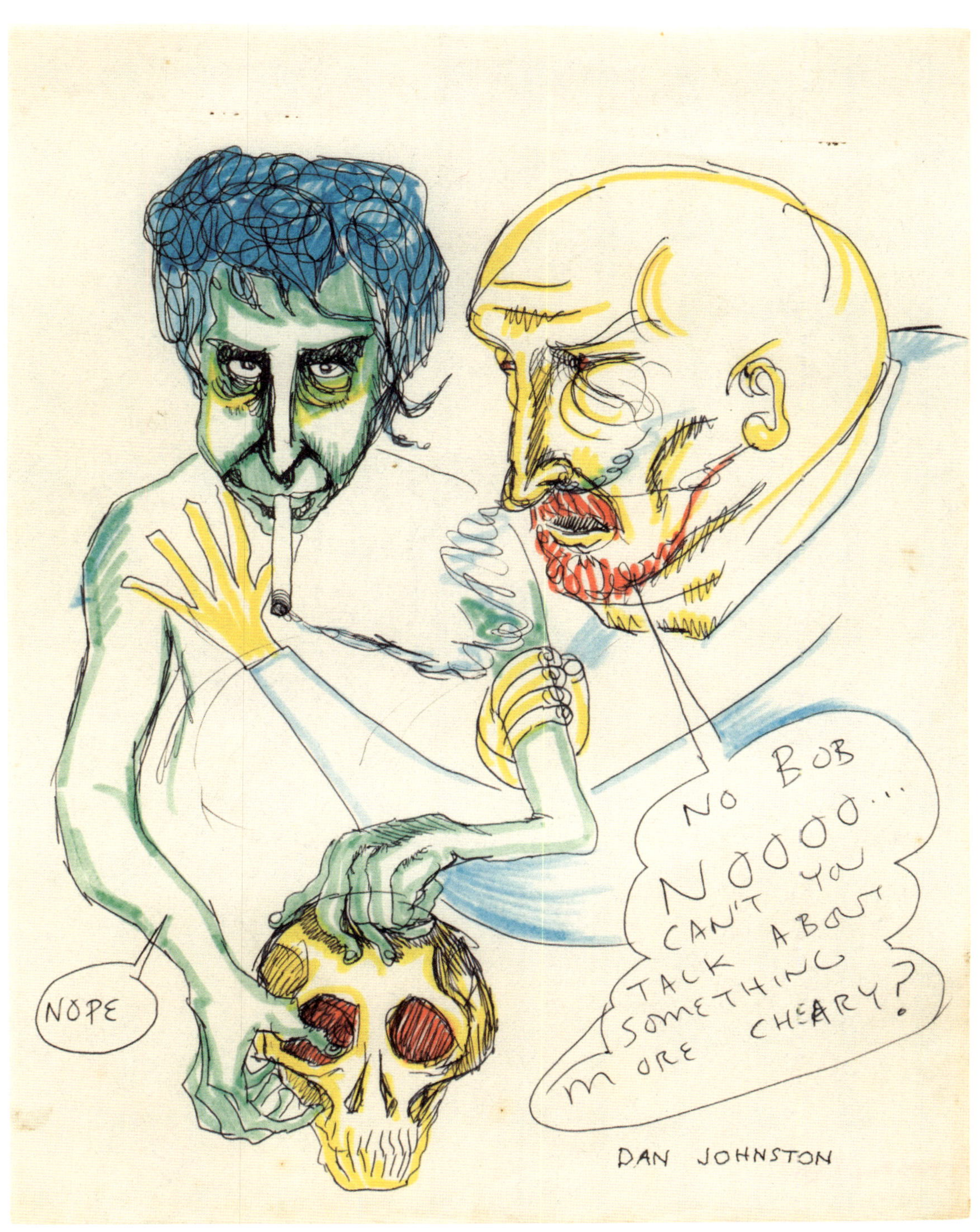

Talk about Something More Cheary? (Bob Dylan)

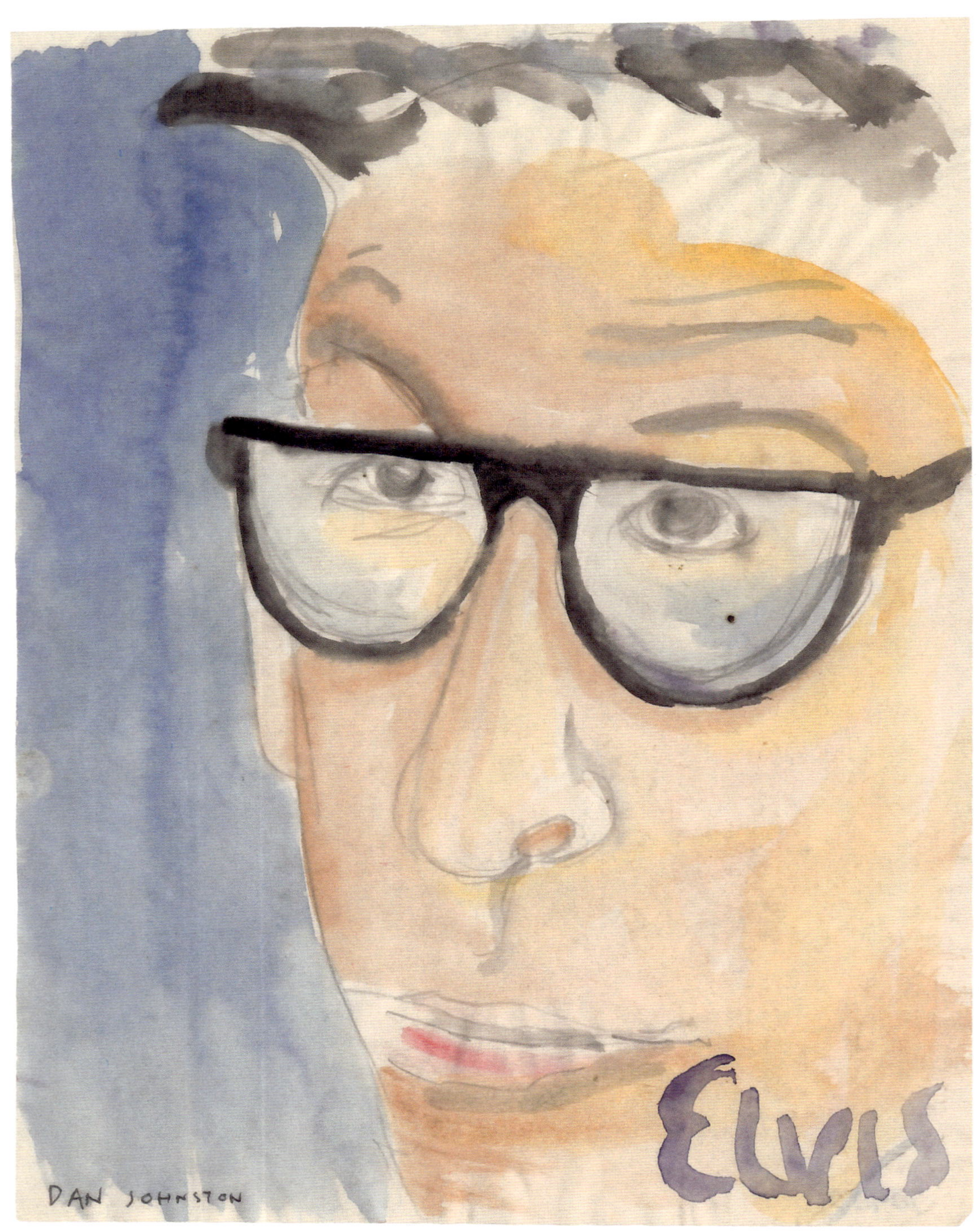

Elvis Costello

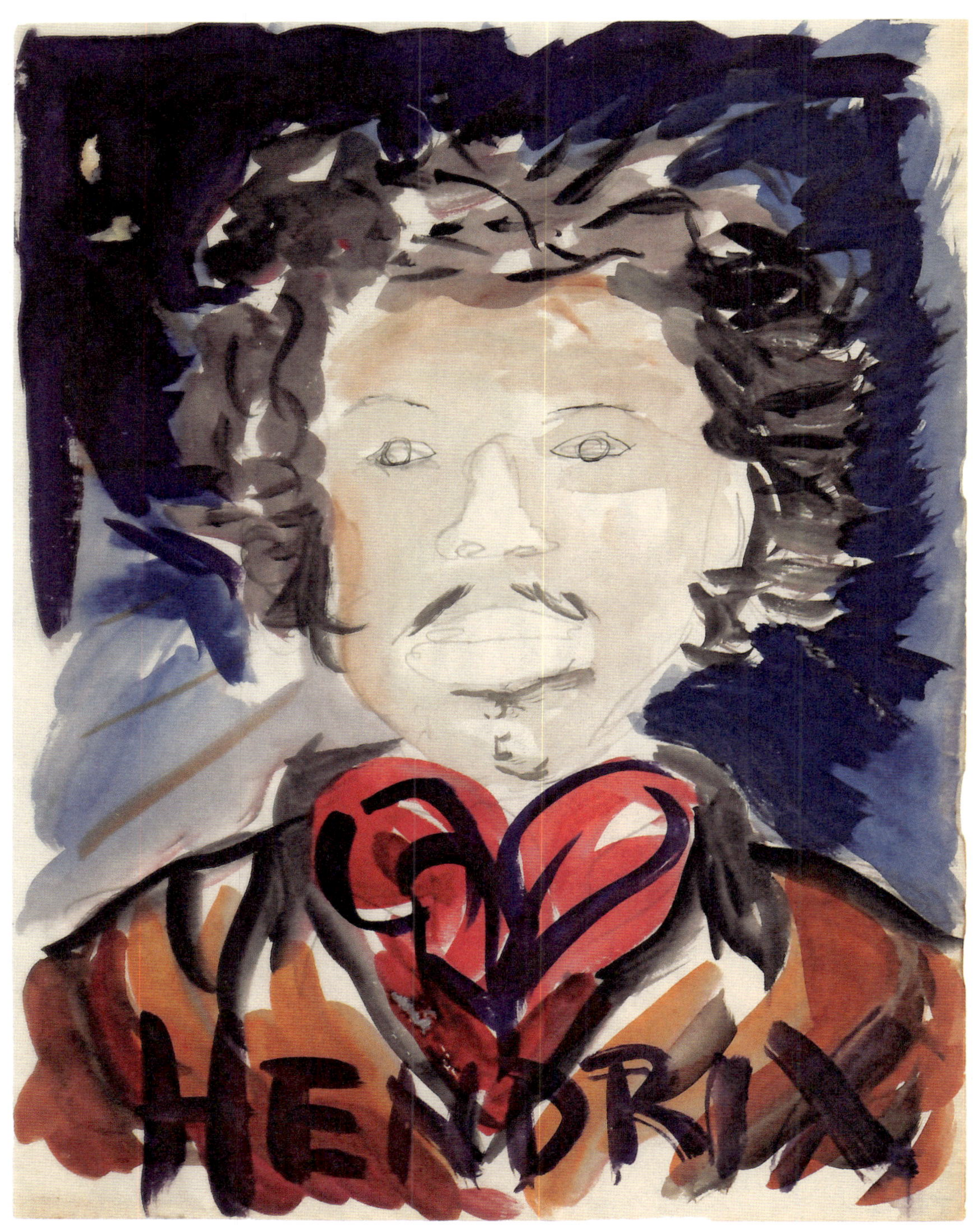

Jimi Hendrix

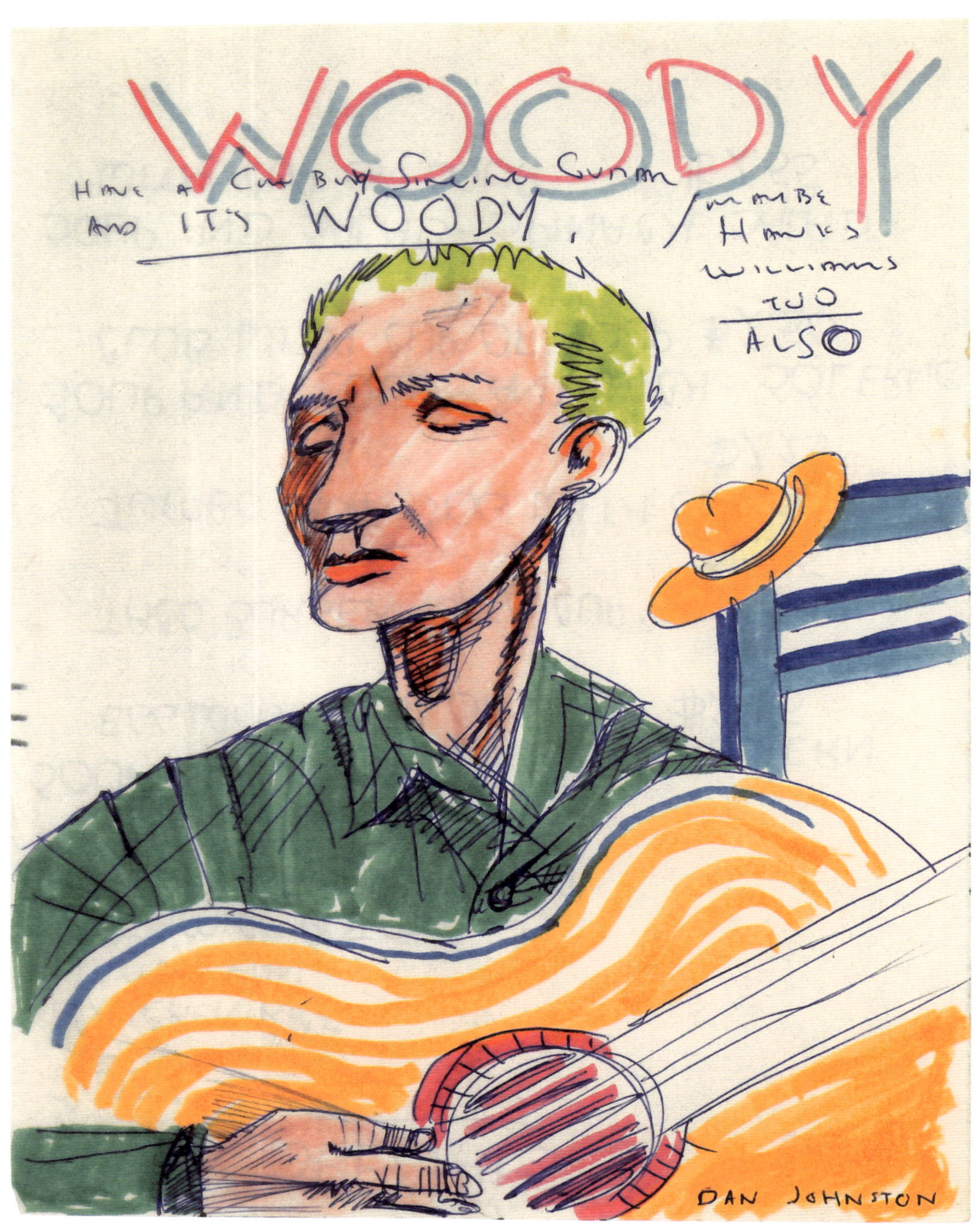

Woody Guthrie

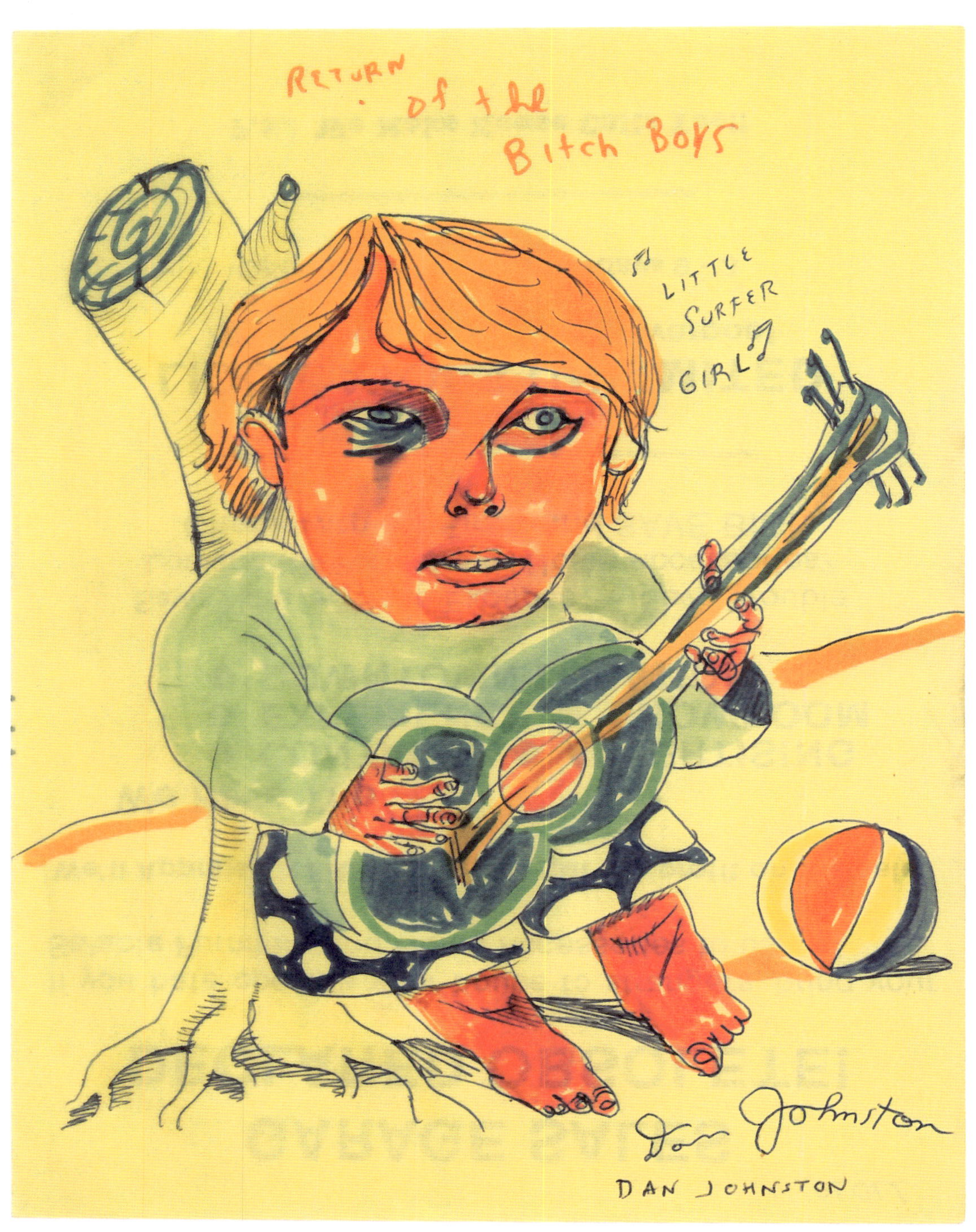

Return of the Bitch Boys

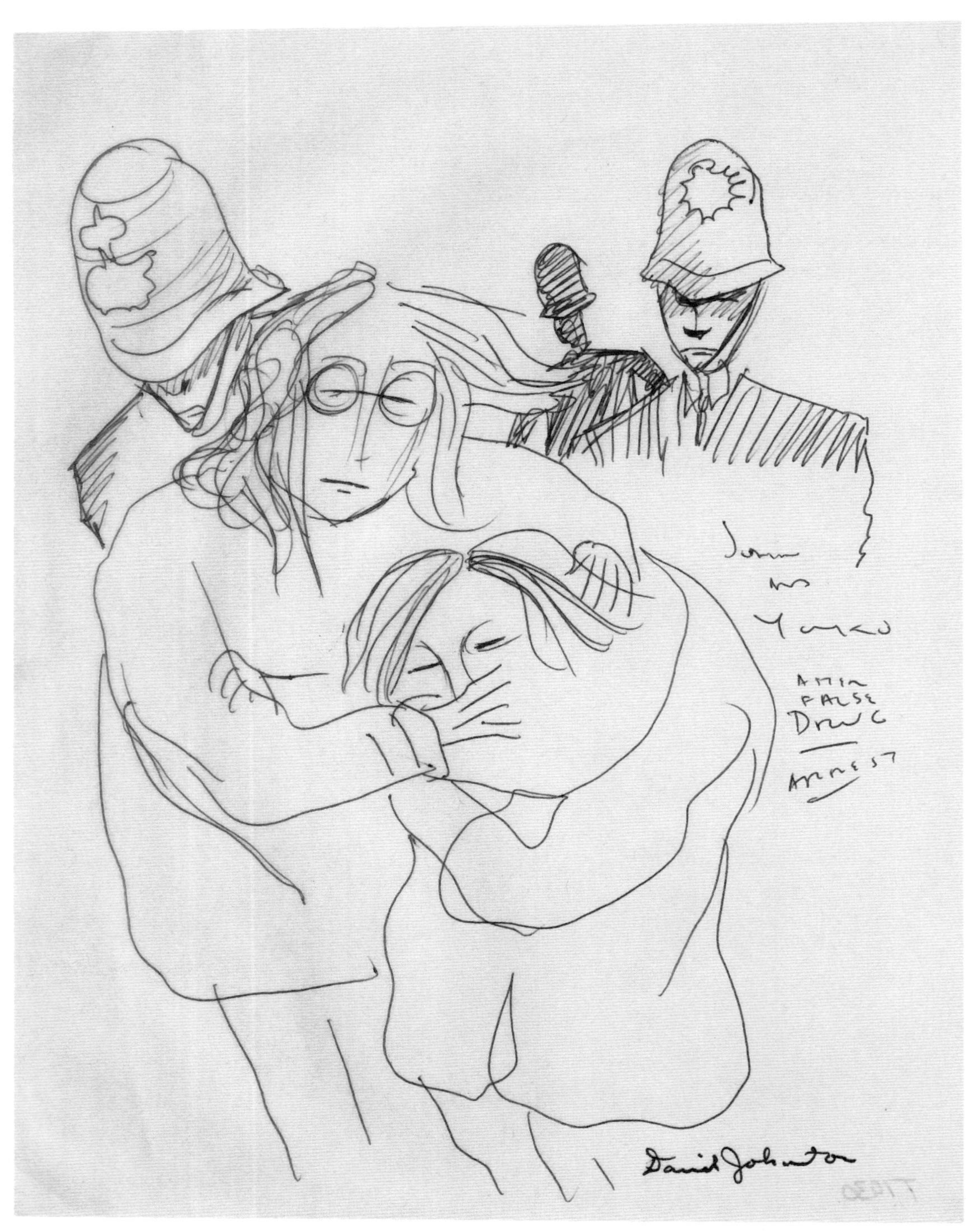

John and Yoko (After False Drug Arrest)

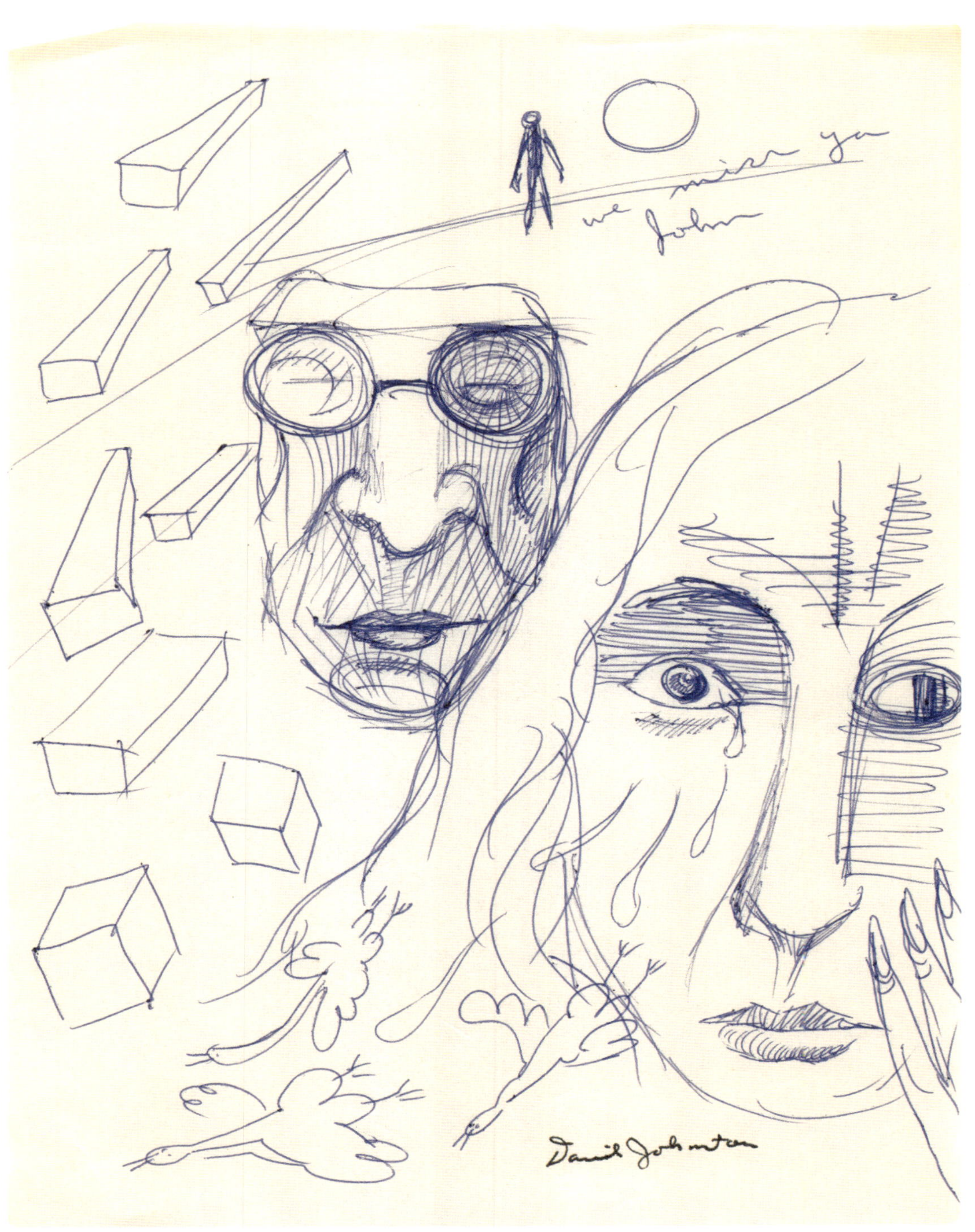

We Miss You John

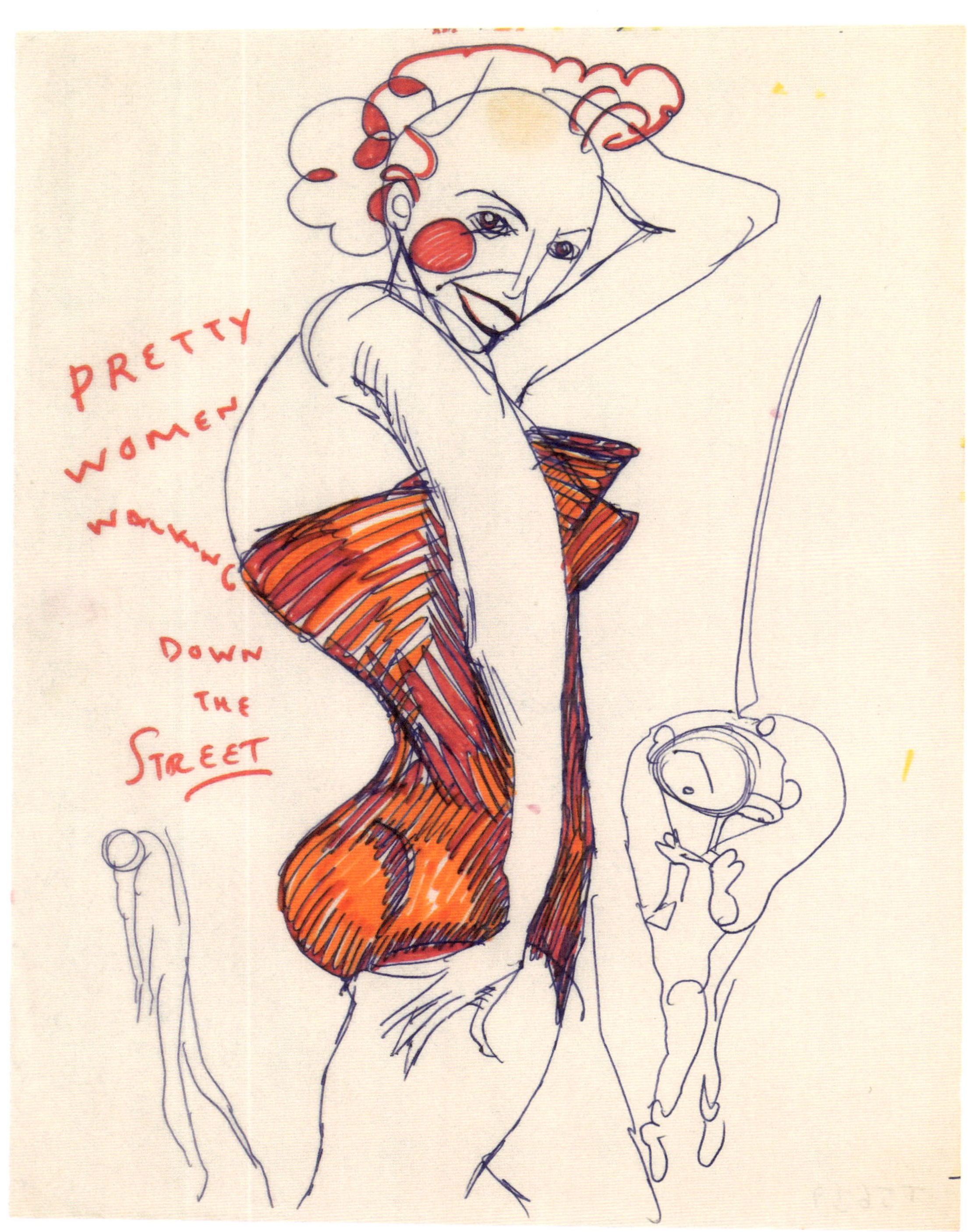

Pretty Women

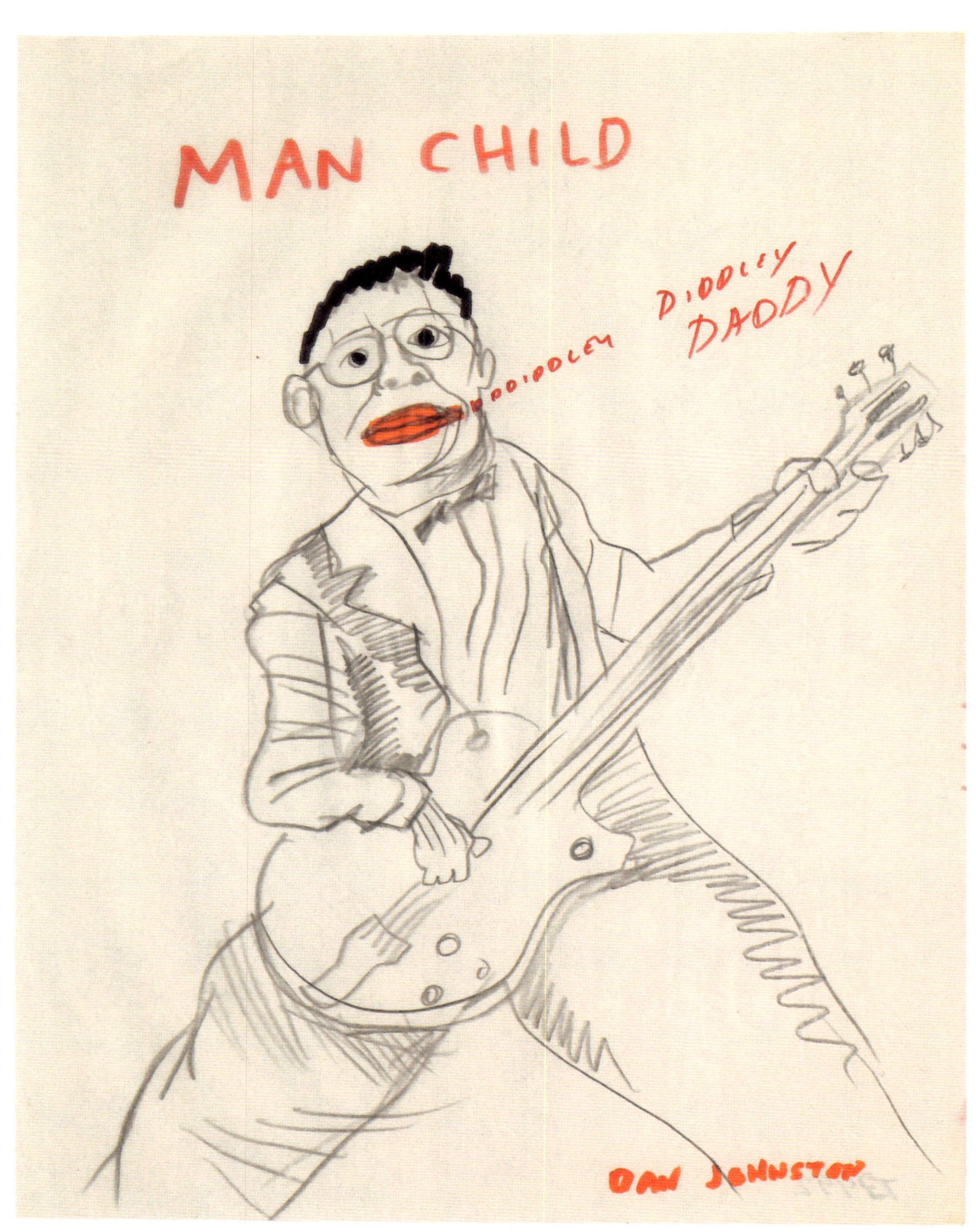

Man Child (Bo Diddley)

BUDDY
HOLY
IN LOVING MEMORY
SEPTEMBER 7, 1936
FEBRUARY 3, 1956

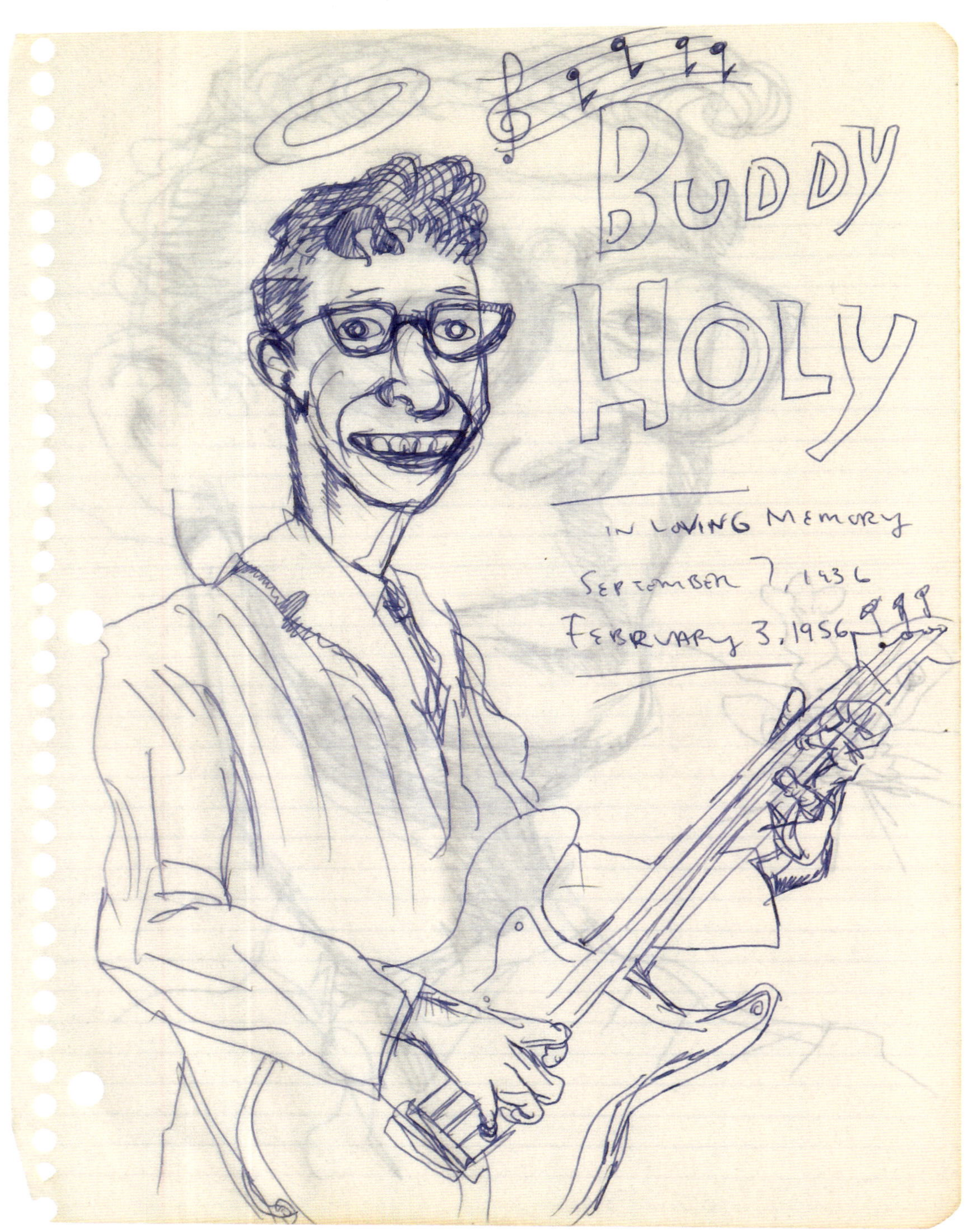

Buddy Holy

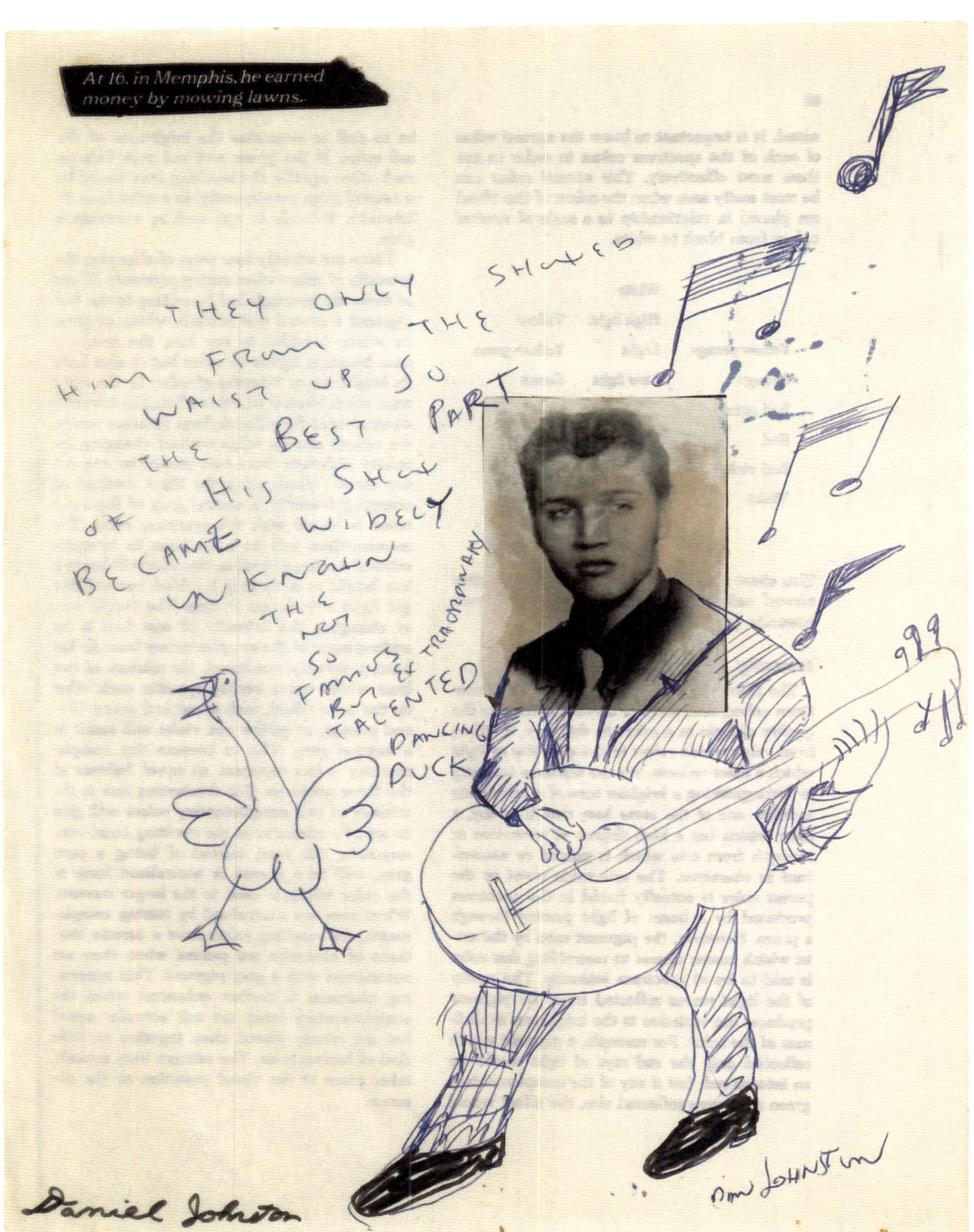

Elvis Presley

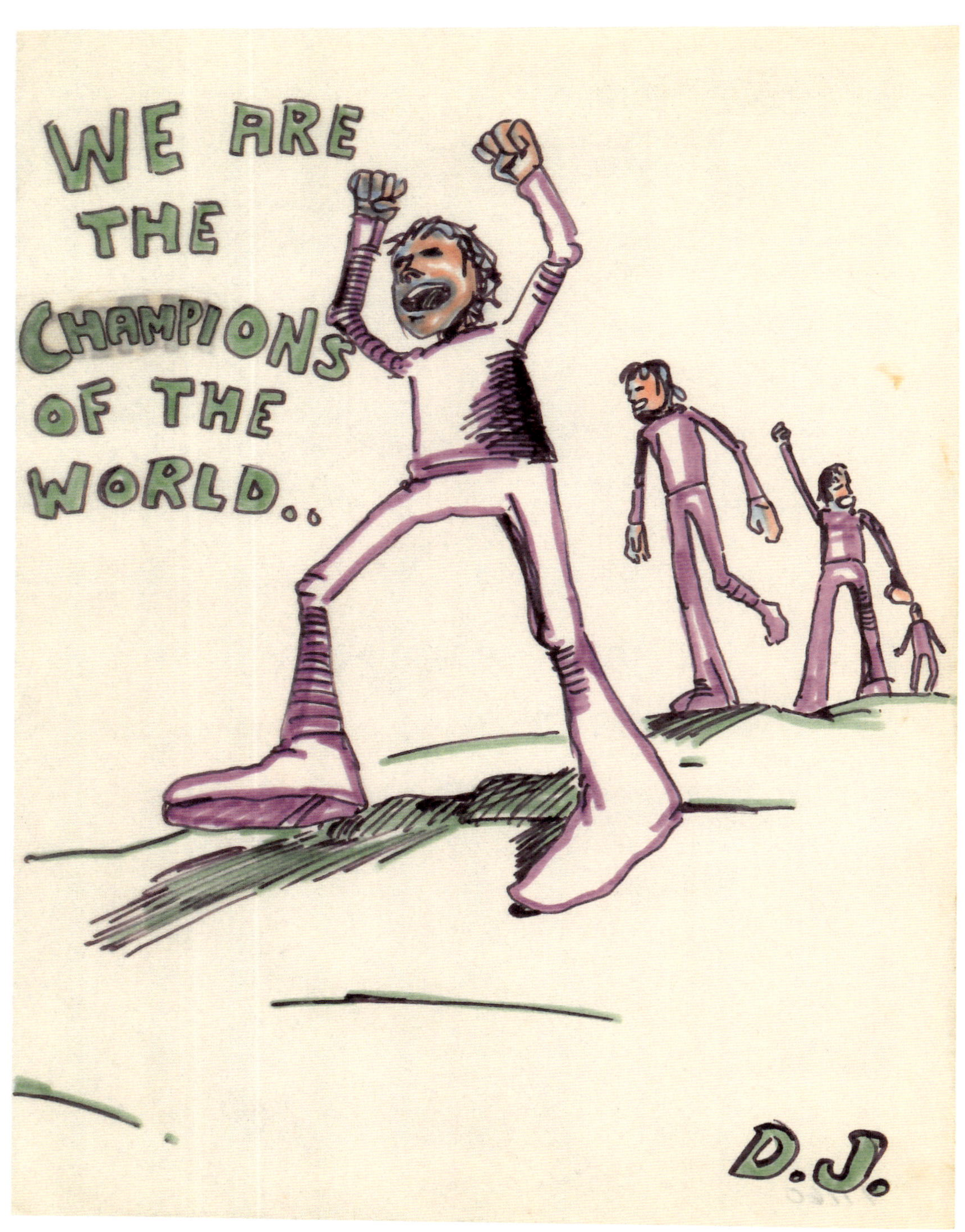

We Are the Champions (Queen)

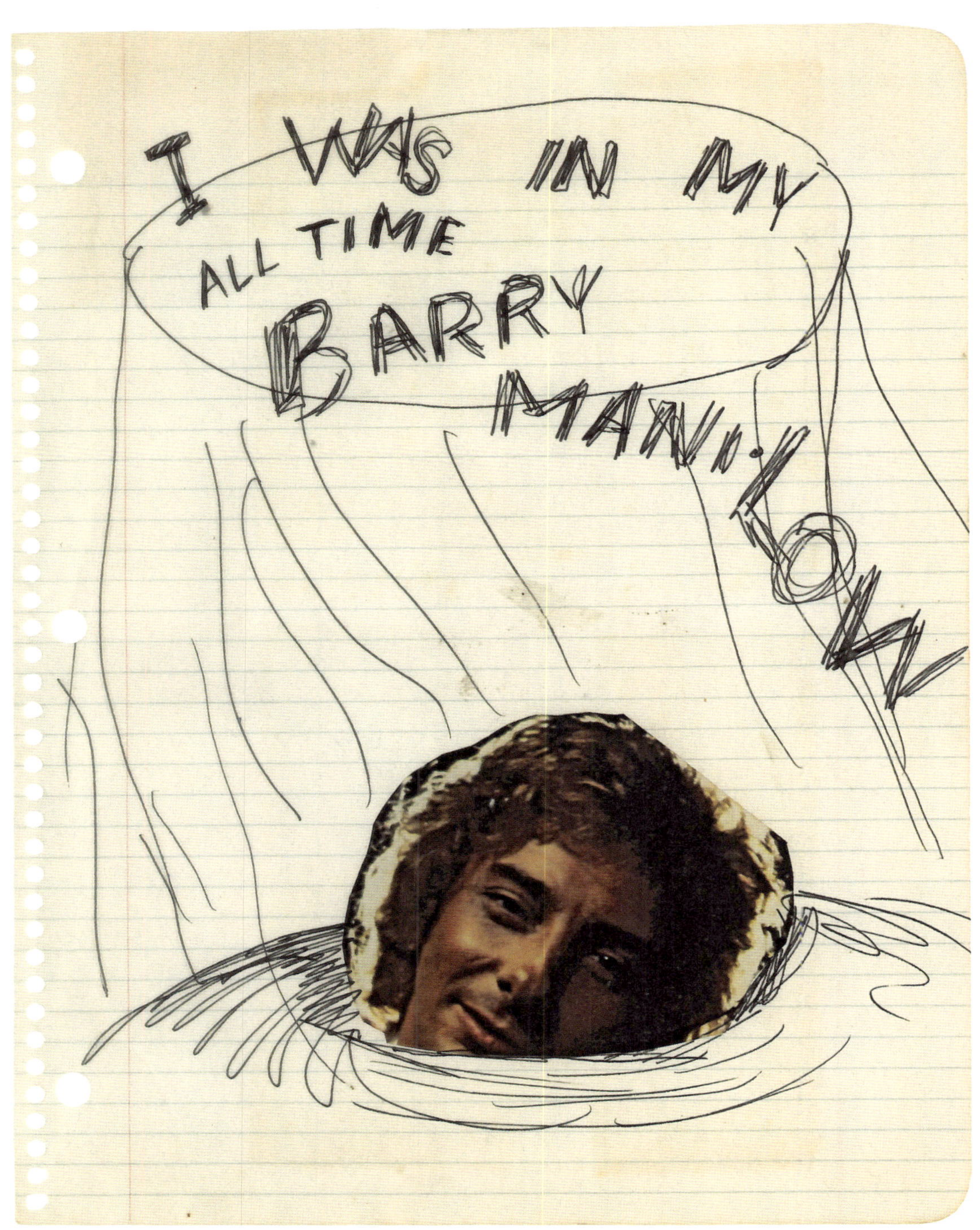

Barry Mani-Low

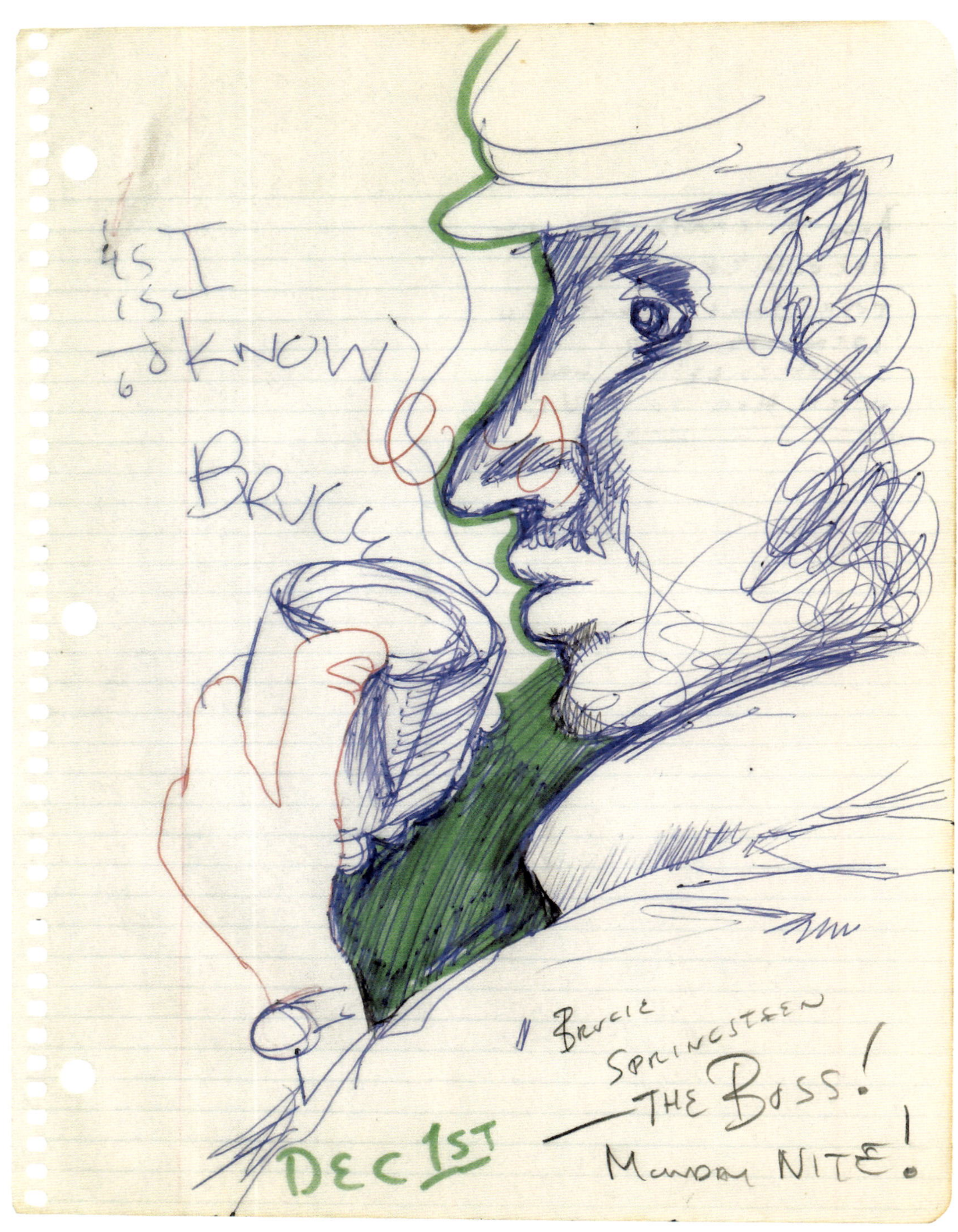

I Know Bruce

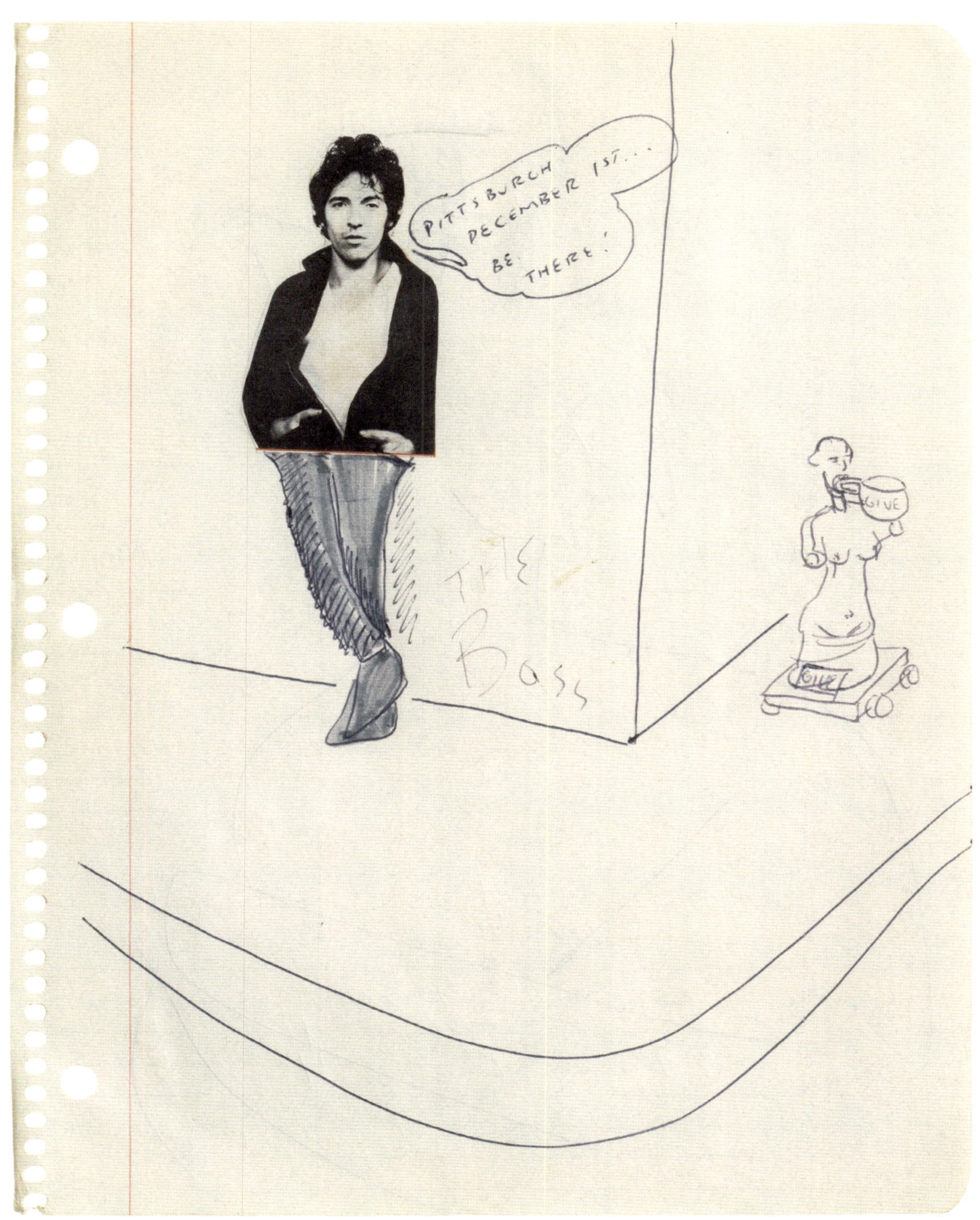

The Boss (Pittsburgh December 1st)

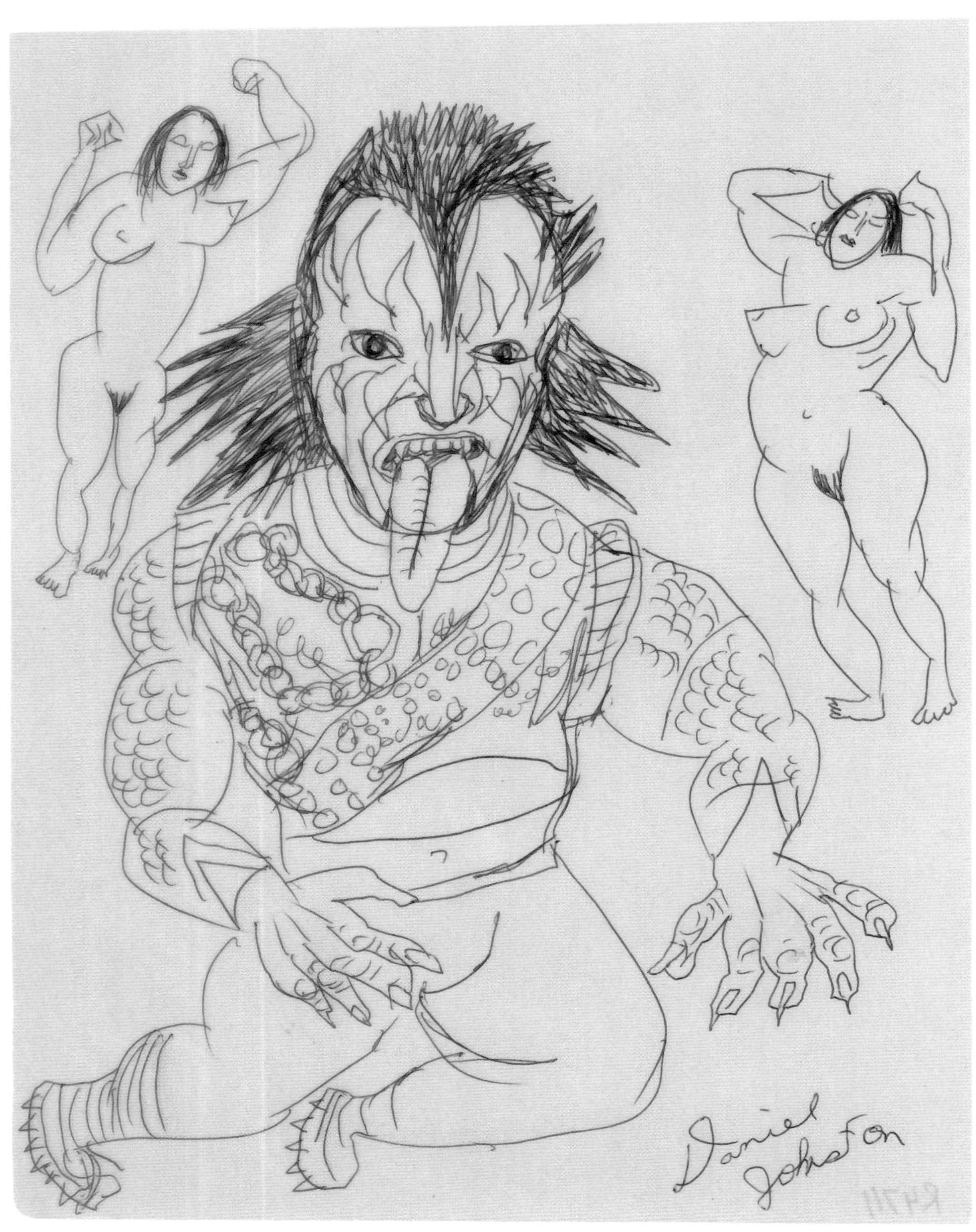

KISS

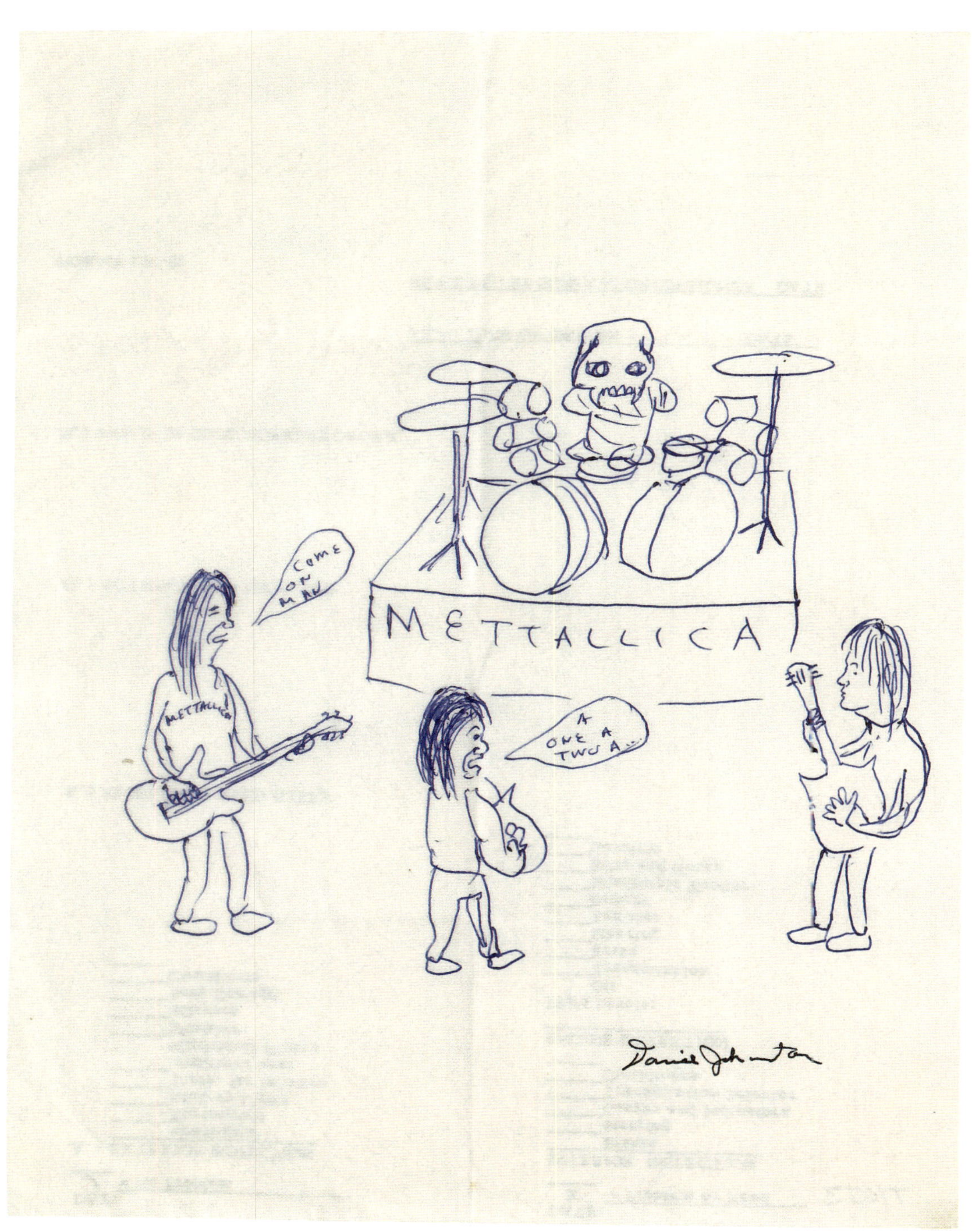
COME ON MAN
METTALLICA
METTALLICA
A ONE A TWO A...
Daniel Johnston

Metallica

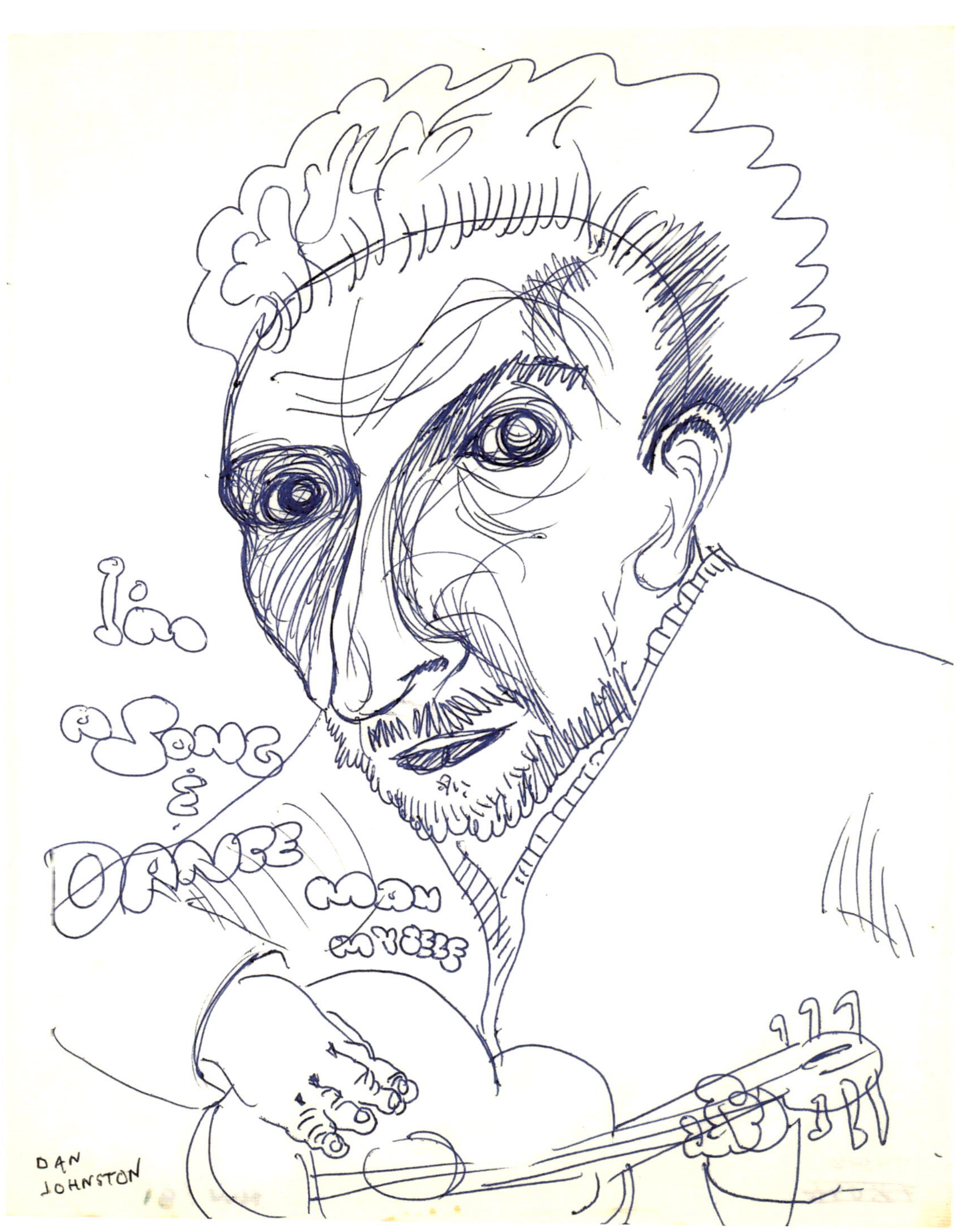

Song & Dance Man (Bob Dylan)

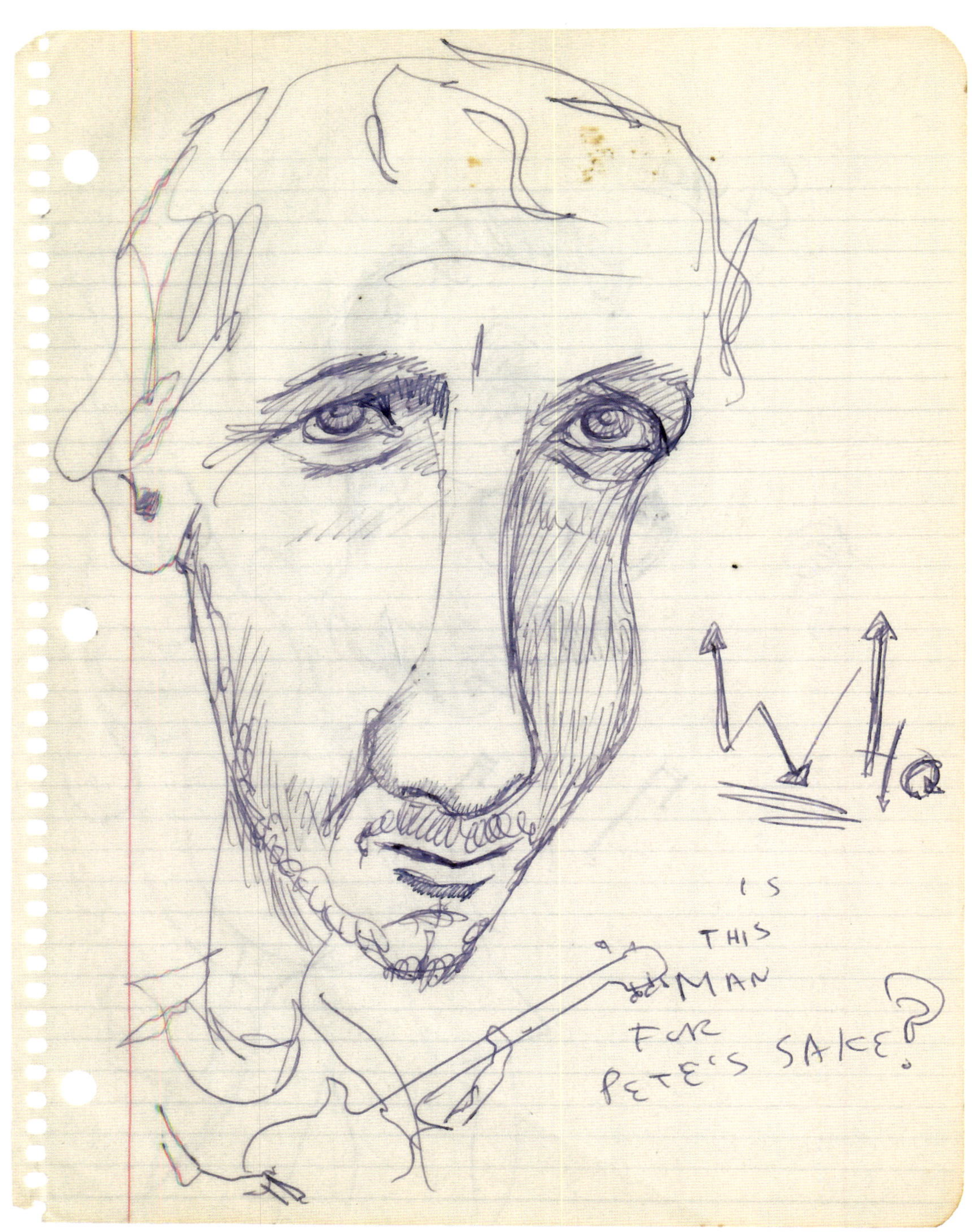

For Pete's Sake (The Who)

Like many before me, I came to the music of Daniel Johnston via *Hi, How Are You?* (1983). As I was an avid Nirvana fan thanks to my older sister, the alien image on Kurt's T-shirt at the 1992 MTV Video Music Awards (p. 303) rang familiar to me when I saw the cassette in a bargain bin at the Virgin Megastores on Tottenham Court Road.

The music was a shock at first, not necessarily because of its lo-fi nature compared to my other tapes. It was more relatable to me, as I would also record cassettes of music, taped in my bedroom, that I would hand out to friends. I didn't think it was possible to release music in this quality—a quality out of necessity—but also one that I have always felt, at its best, is integral to what the initial message could be.

Information wasn't completely easily available at the time, so when Jeff Feuerzeig's documentary *The Devil and Daniel Johnston* was released on DVD in 2006, I was quick to snap it up.

The DVD really struck me, watching this genius tortured and battling with the demons in his mind. It gave me yet another glimpse into the many different types of people who create, and use what they create as a form of escapism. And then seeing what happens when that art is reverberated and relatable to those all over, like myself in Essex, listening to the tape of this boy from West Virginia.

In the following years, I would go deeper into Daniel's world. The album *1990* would stay by my side while I traveled across England and through Europe, eventually to New York, which has now been my home for the last seventeen years.

It is surreal to be sitting here writing for this beautiful book. Daniel Johnston, who gave so much to his work, like so many artists before him, has become bigger than he could have possibly imagined and inspired many, many people. But then, as I get older and rewatch *The Devil and Daniel Johnston*, I'm struck by the person. He is a human with feelings, thoughts, bad days, many bad days, and some good days. When I used to listen to his music when I was younger, he seemed superhuman, incredible—how could someone make this? But now, as I listen, I feel the human, and I think to myself, how could he have made this?

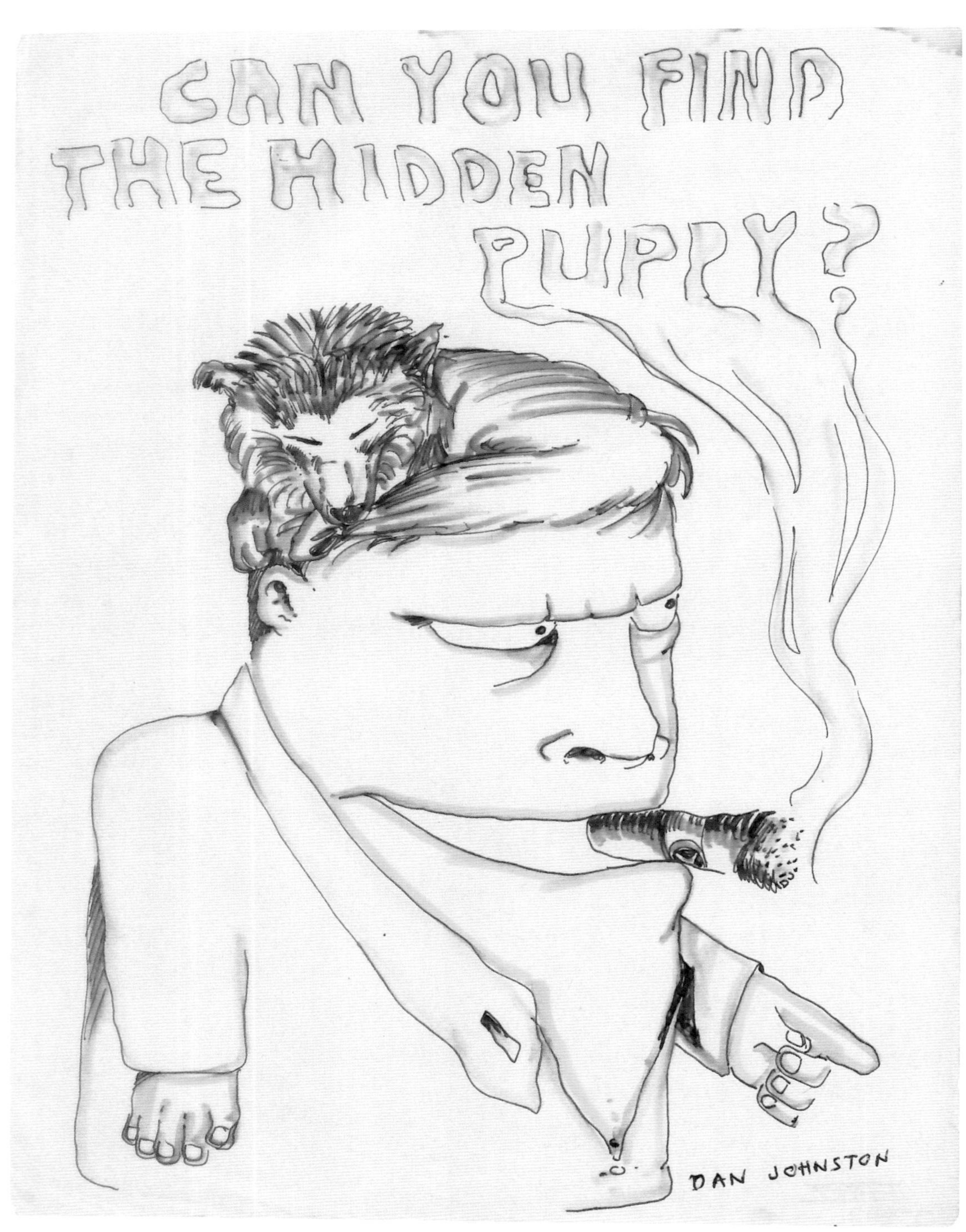

Can You Find the Hidden Puppy?

III.
High School
1975–1979

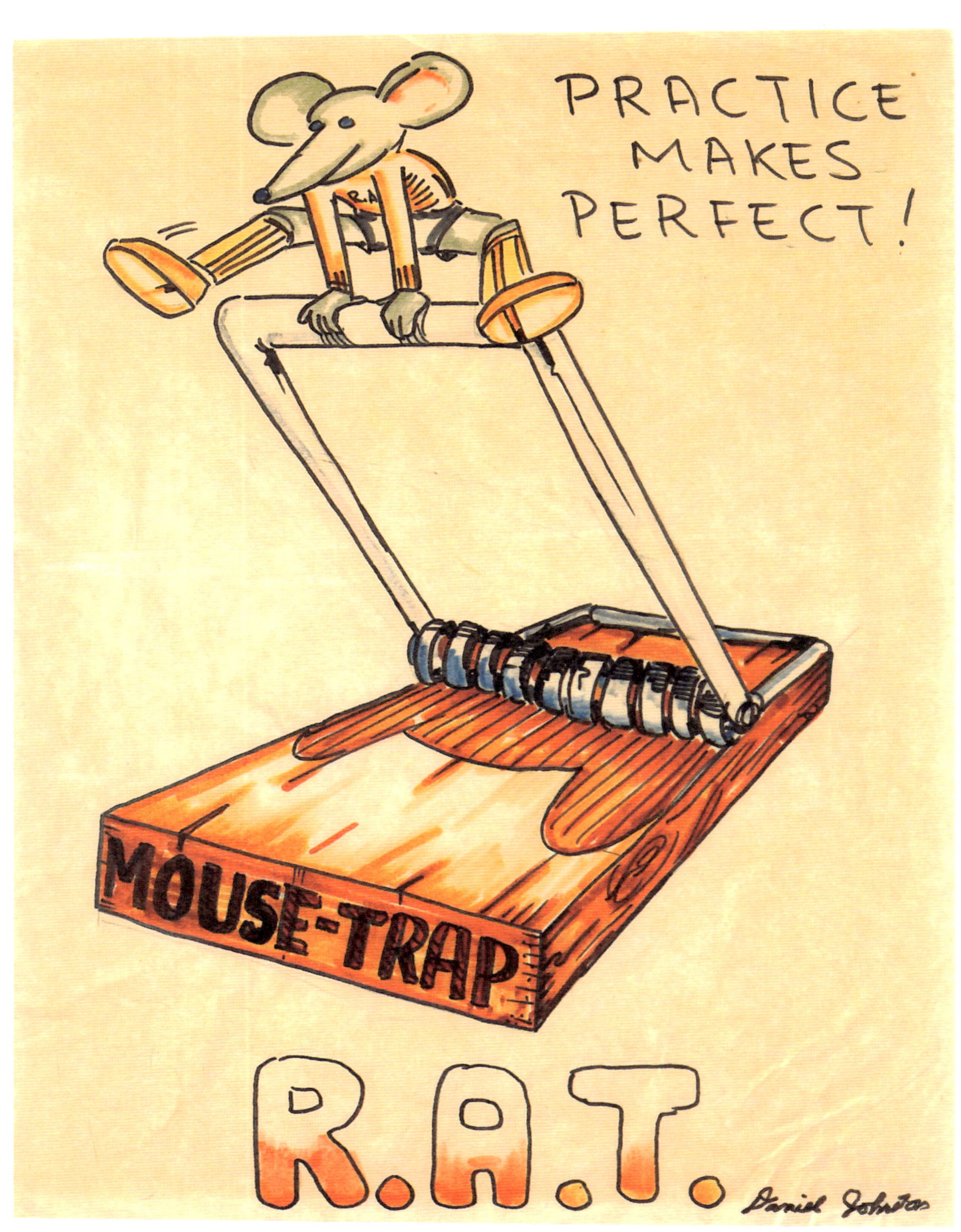

Mouse-Trap (Practice Makes Perfect)

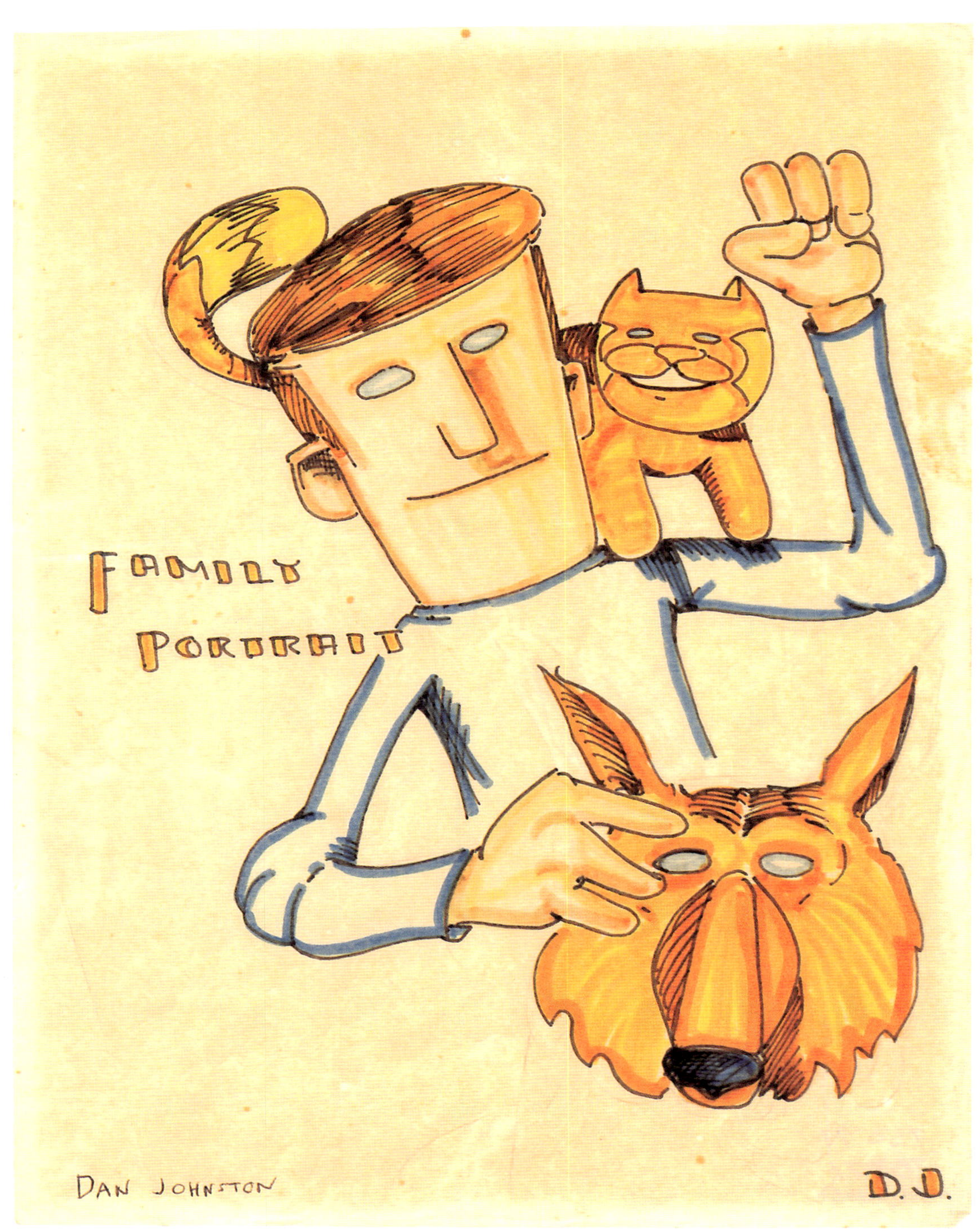

Family Portrait

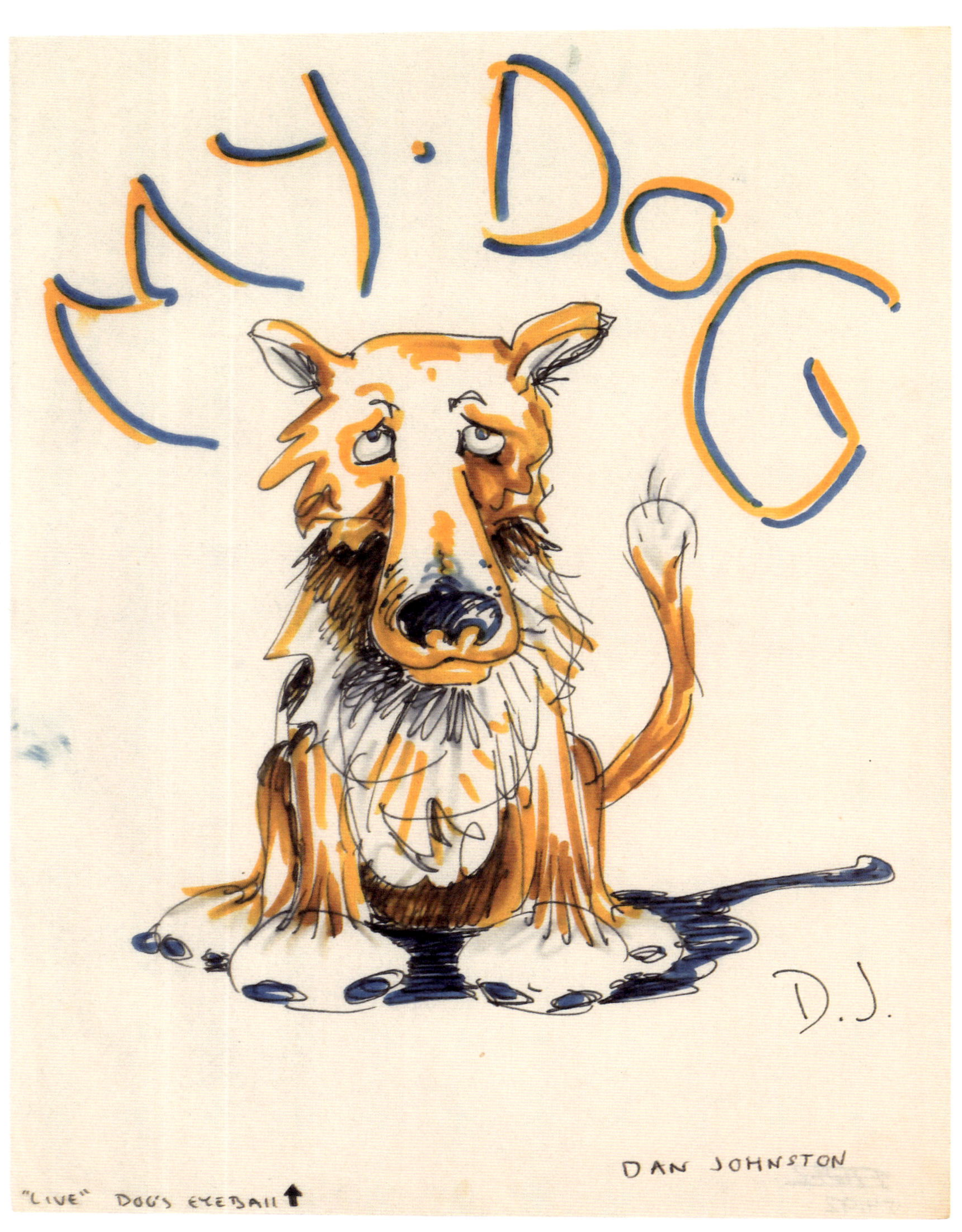

My Dog

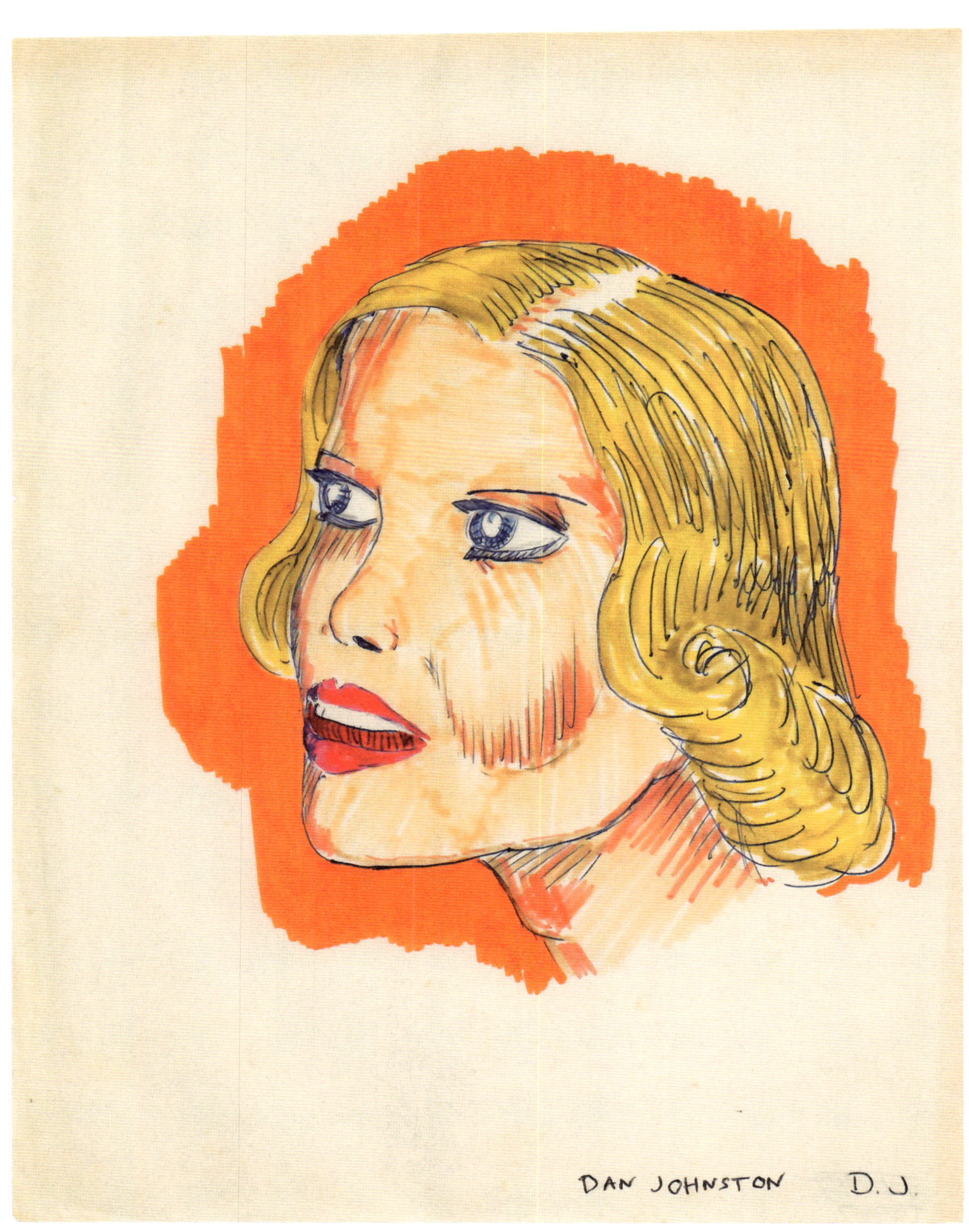

Untitled (Blonde)

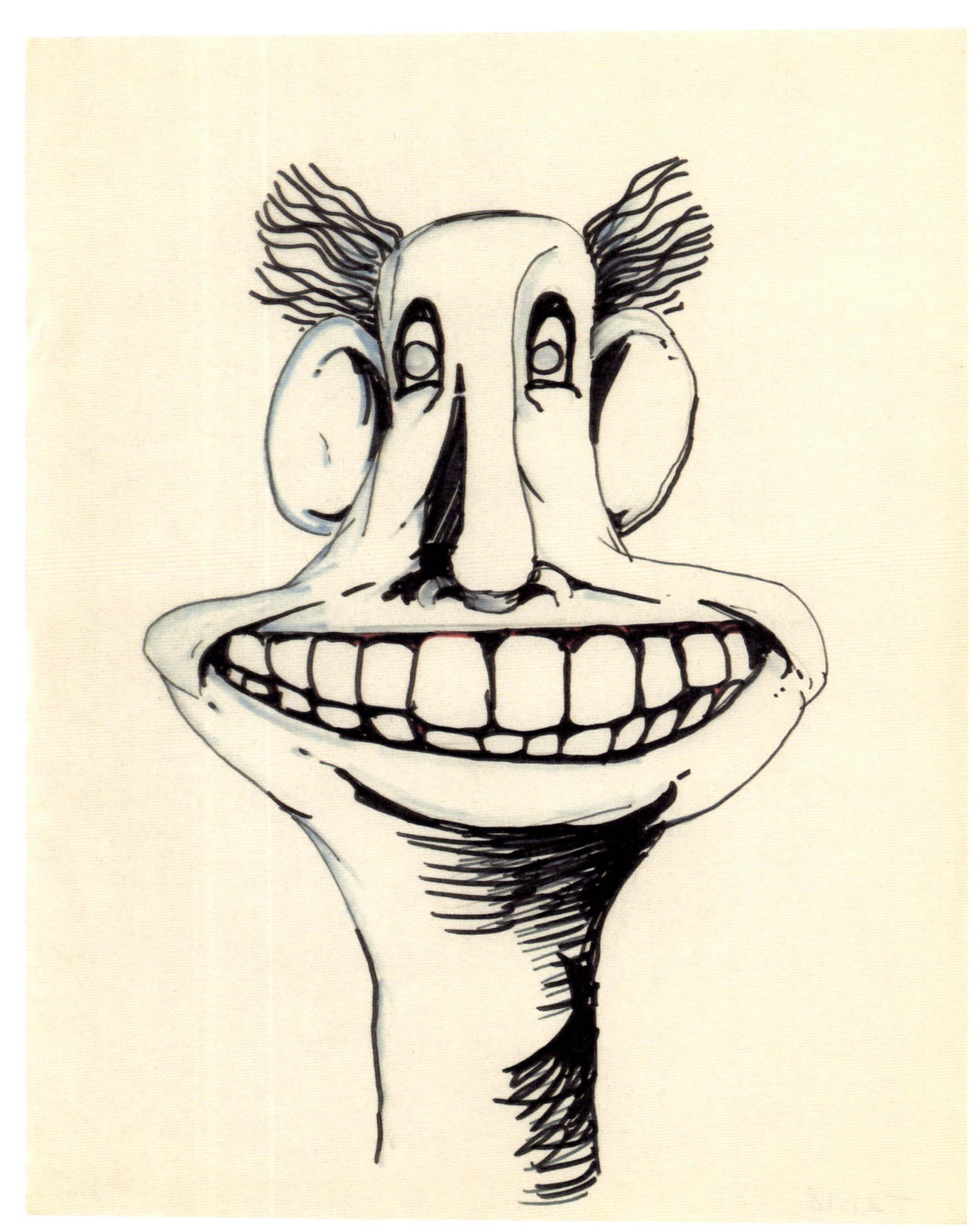

Untitled (Smile 1)

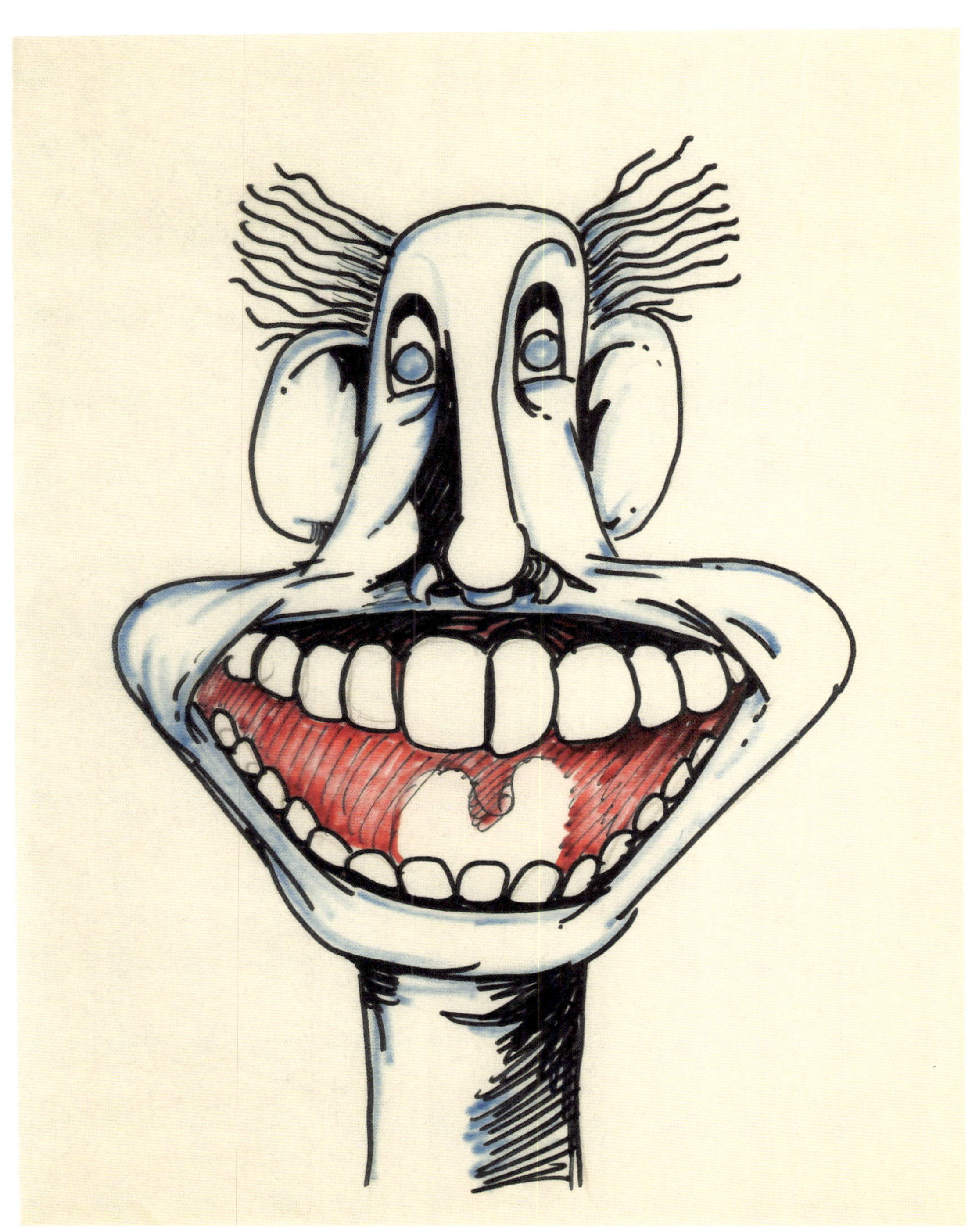

Untitled (Smile 2)

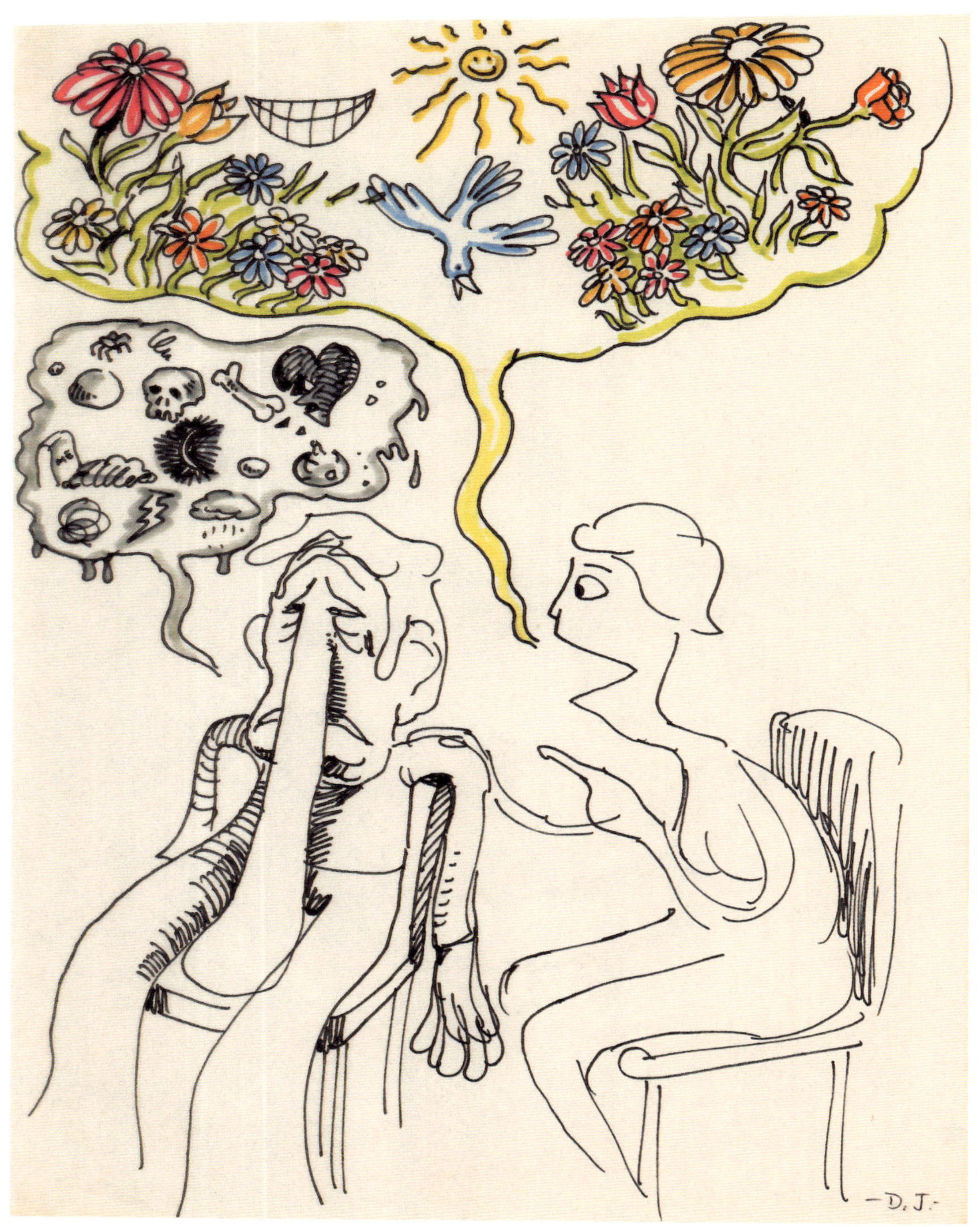

Blue Bird

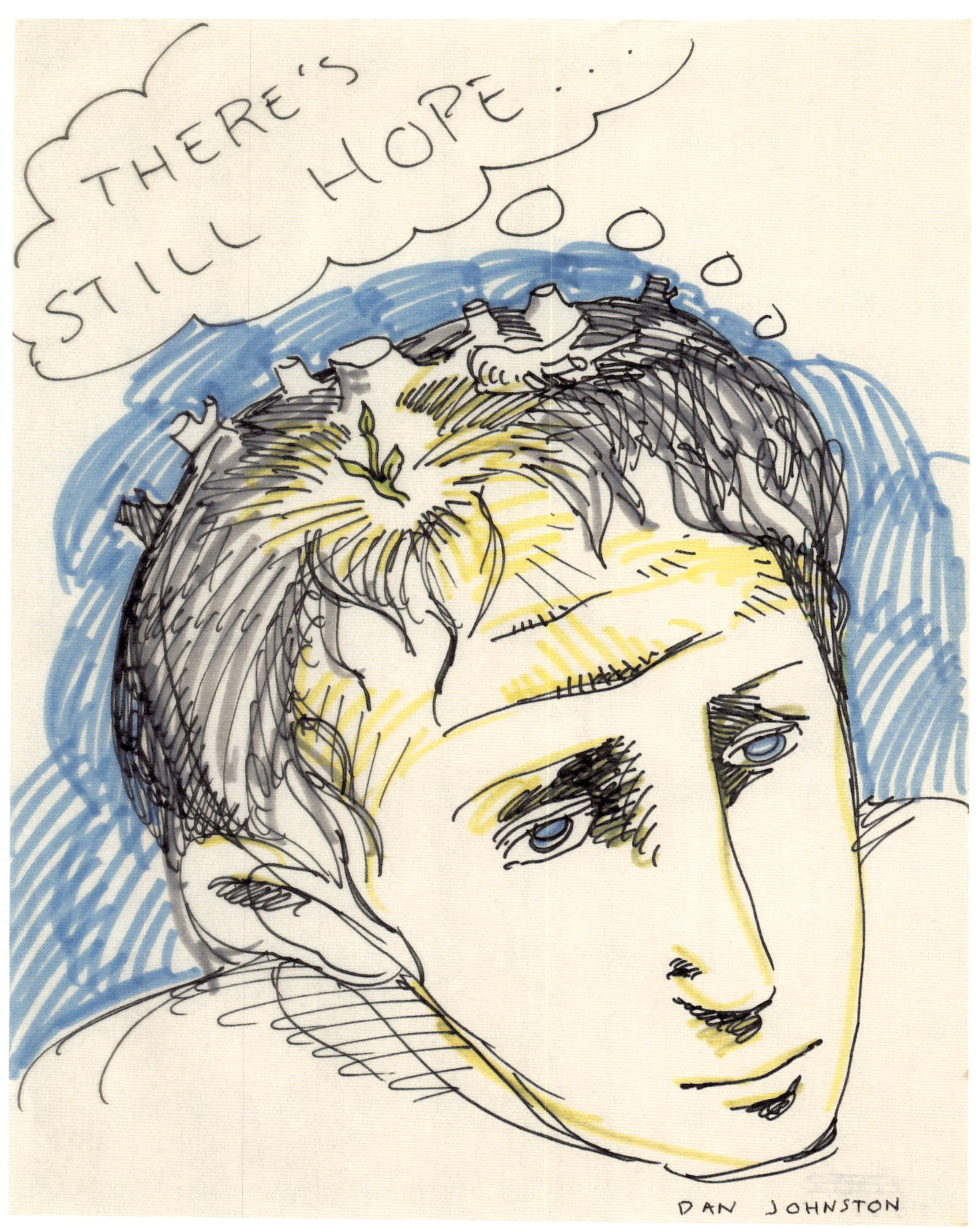

There's Still Hope

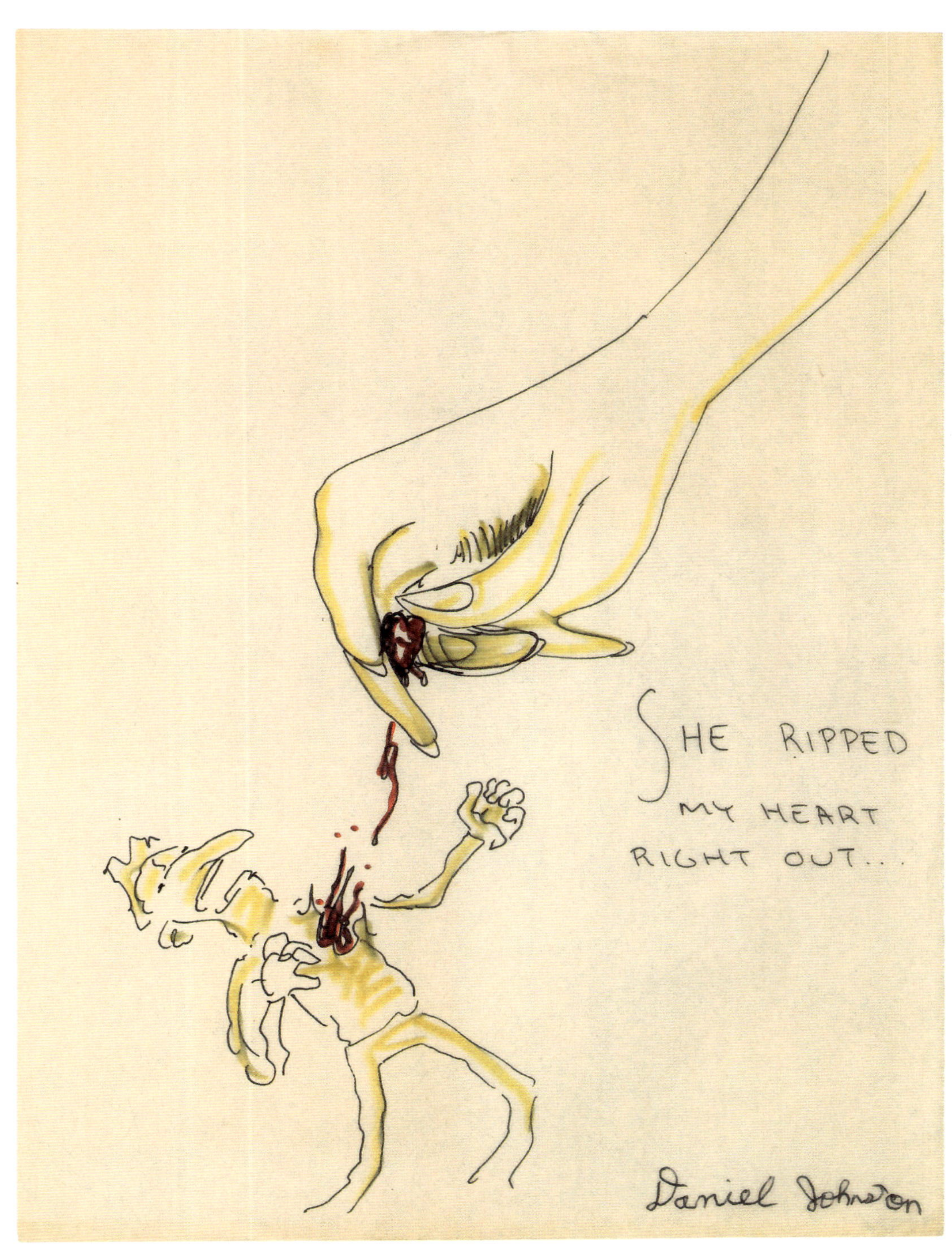

She Ripped My Heart Right Out

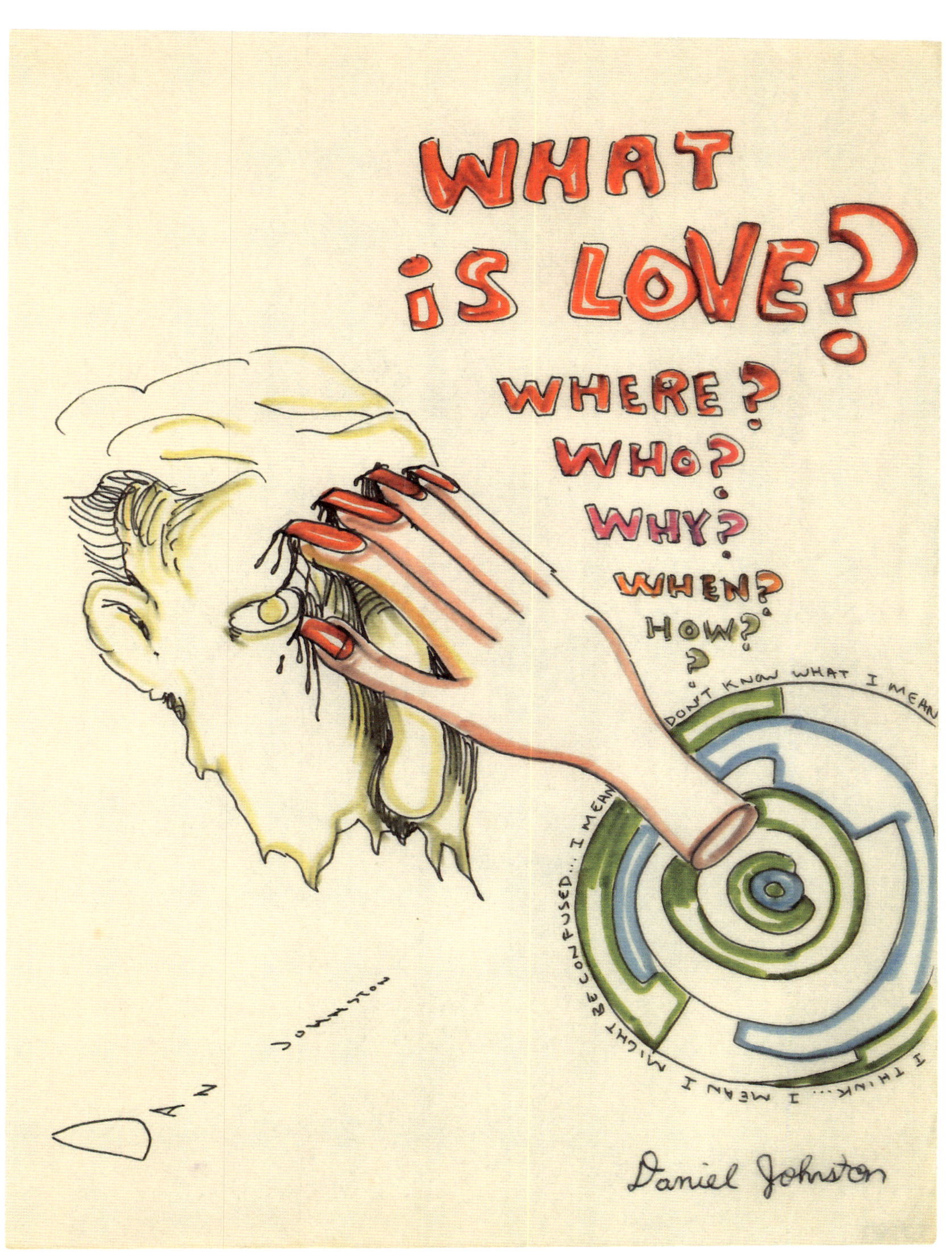
WHAT
IS LOVE?
WHERE?
WHO?
WHY?
WHEN?
HOW?
DON'T KNOW WHAT I MEAN
I THINK... I MEAN I MIGHT BE CONFUSED... I MEAN
DAN JOHNSTON
Daniel Johnston

What Is Love?

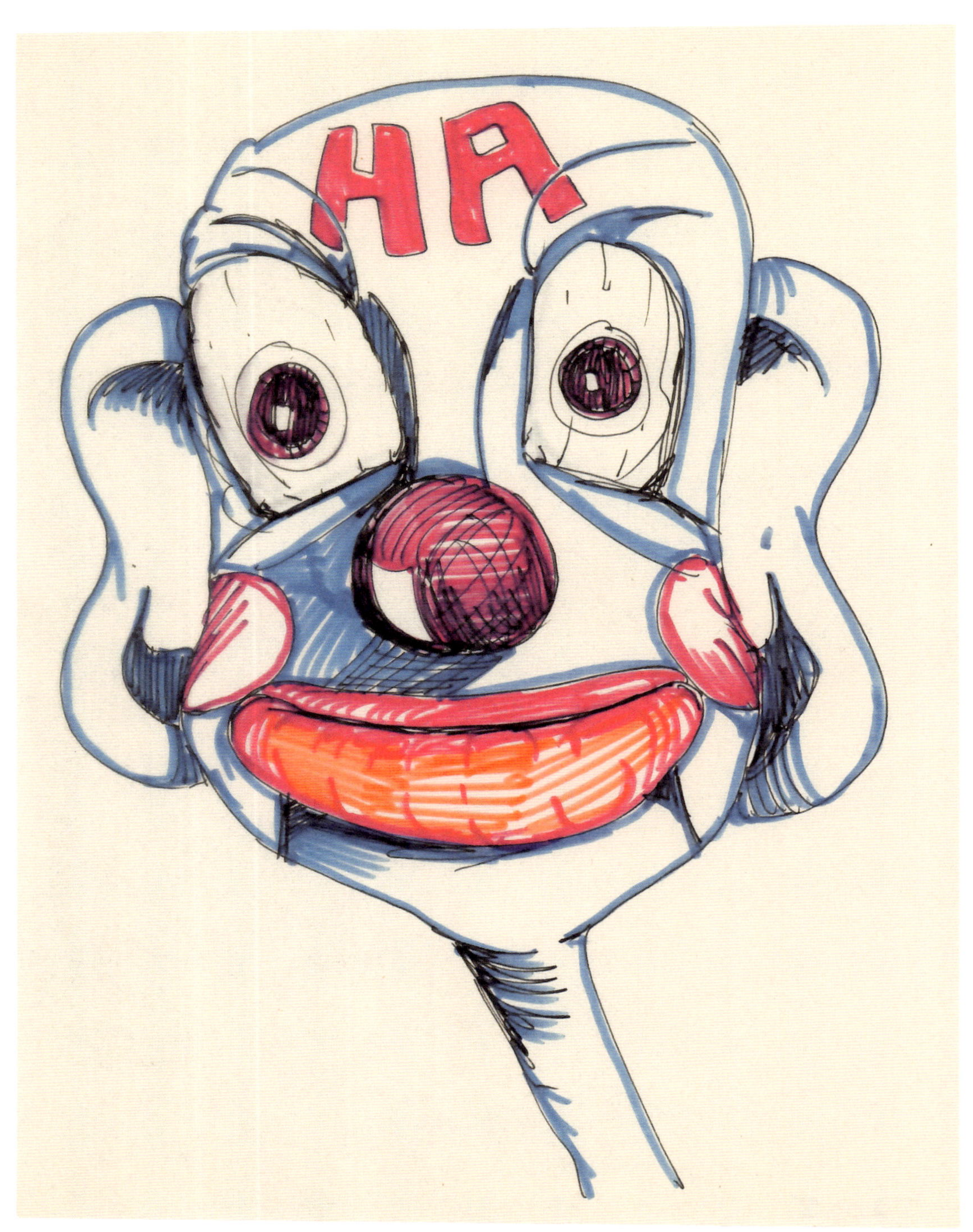

HA

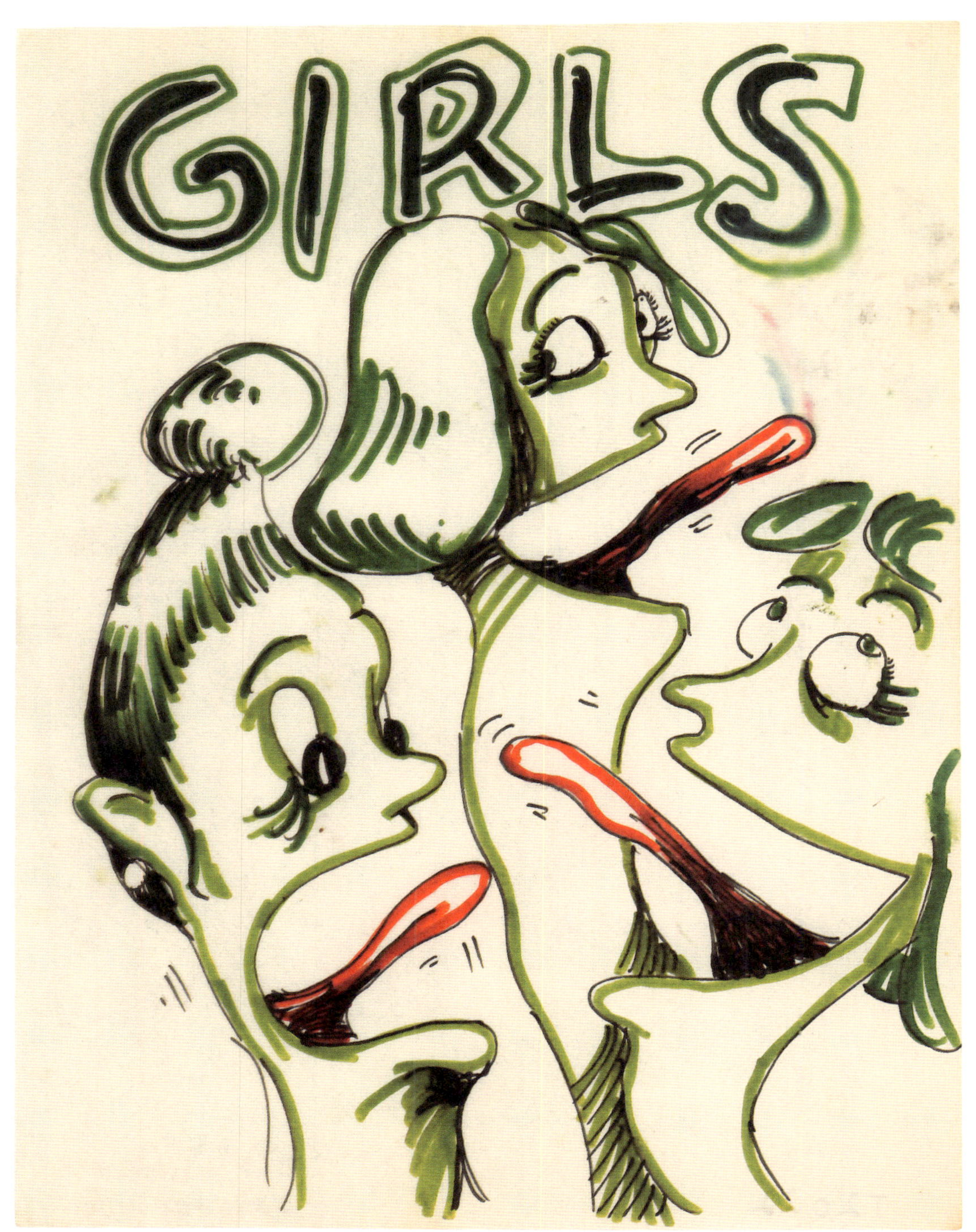

GIRLS

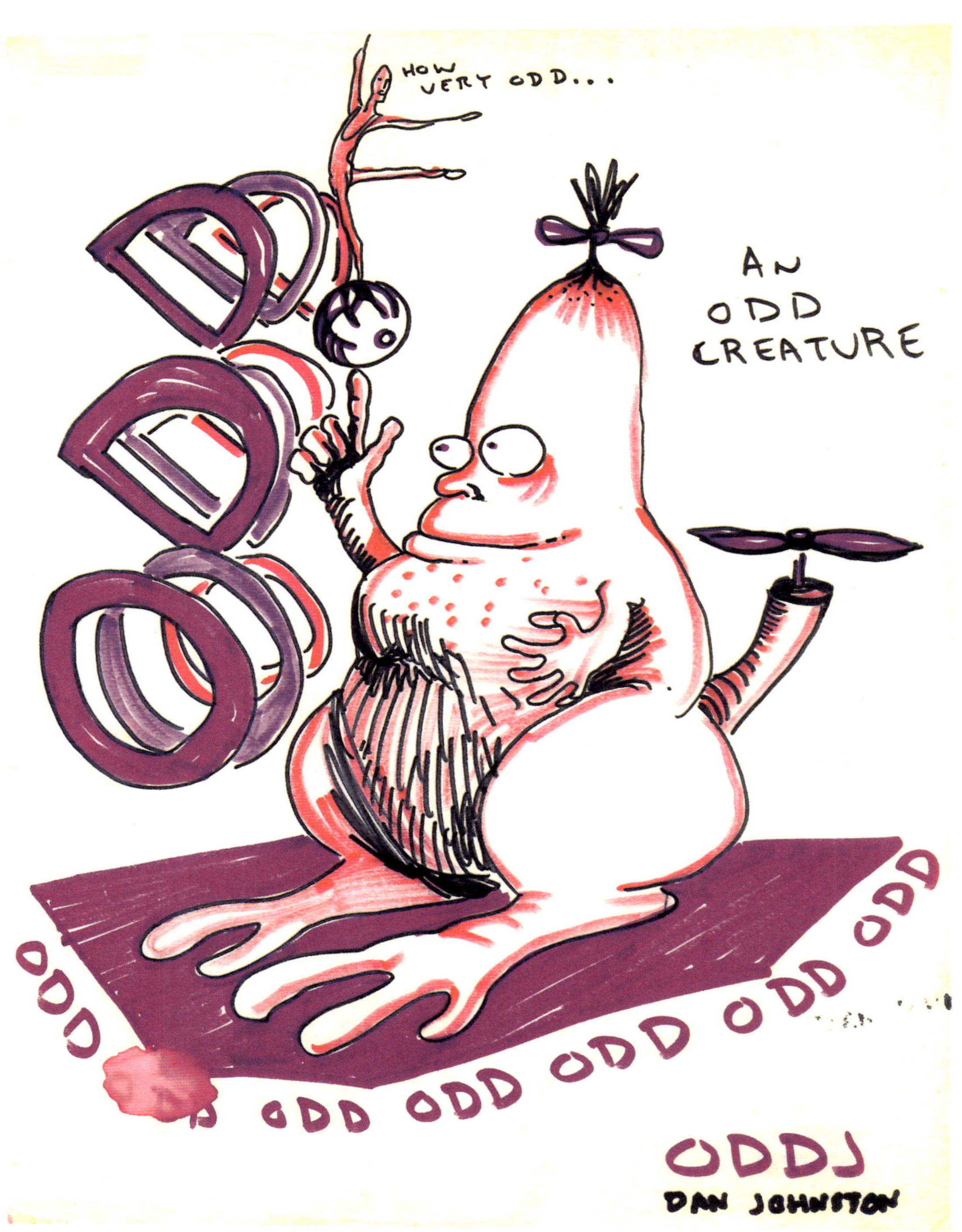

An Odd Creature

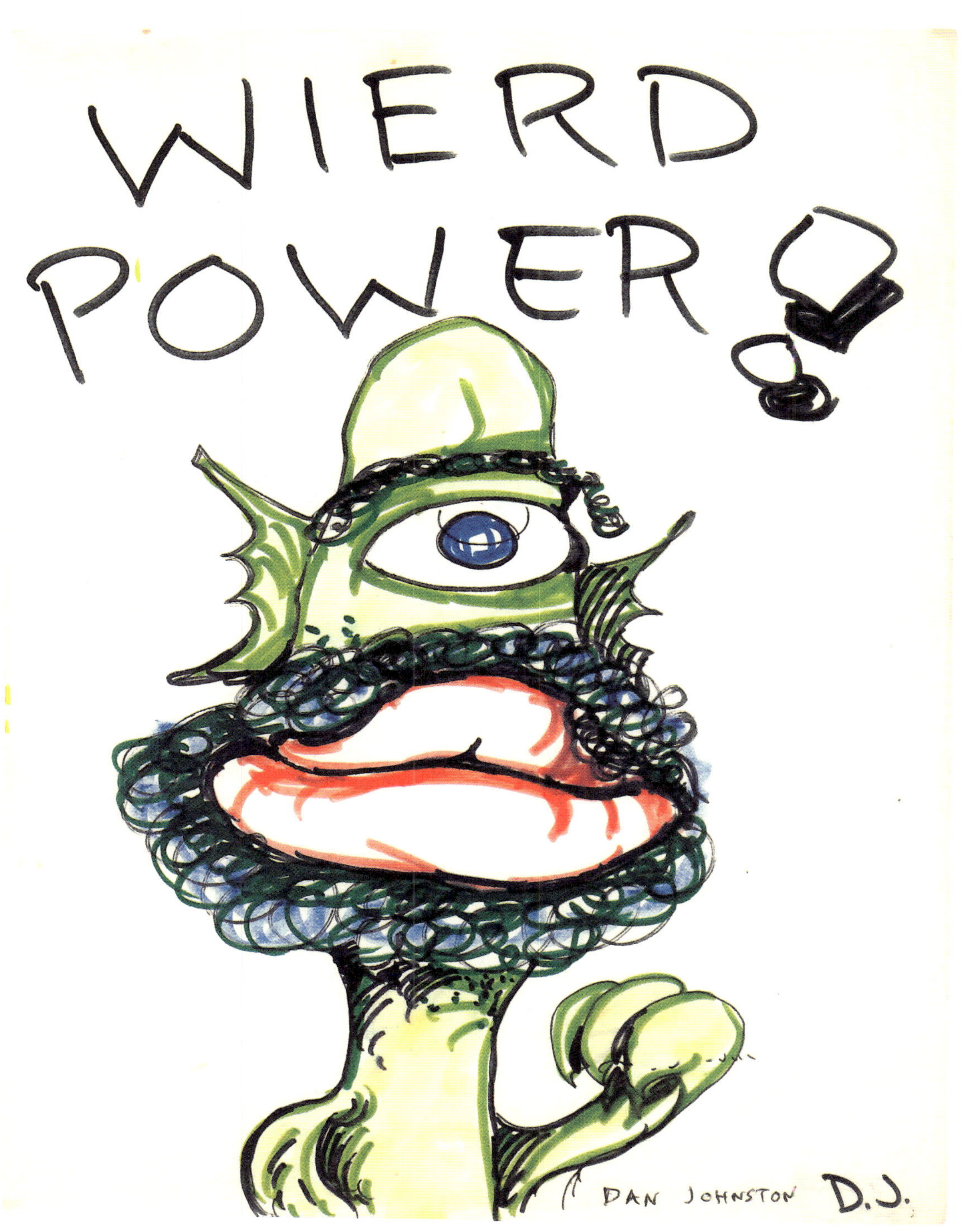

Wierd Power!

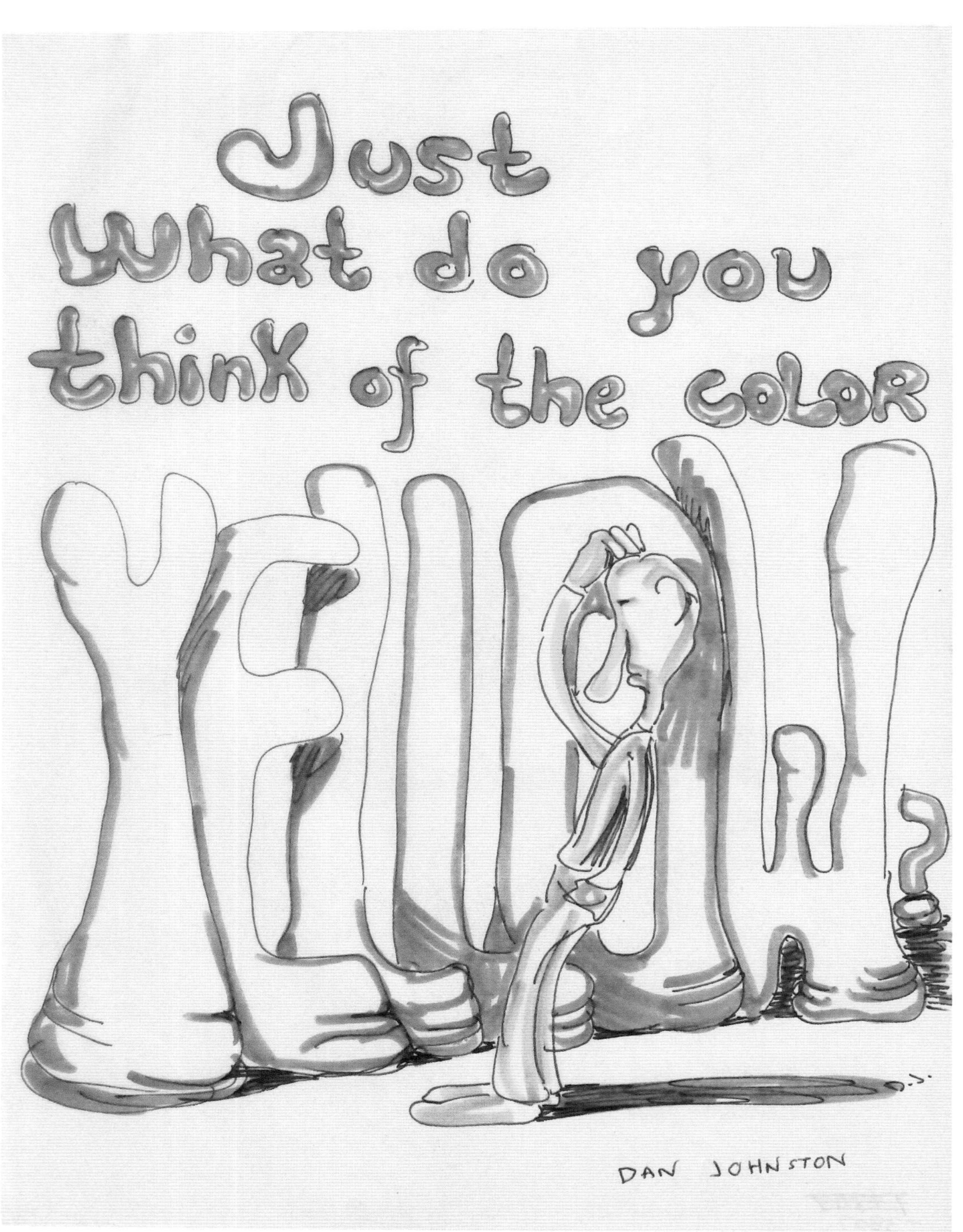

Yellow?

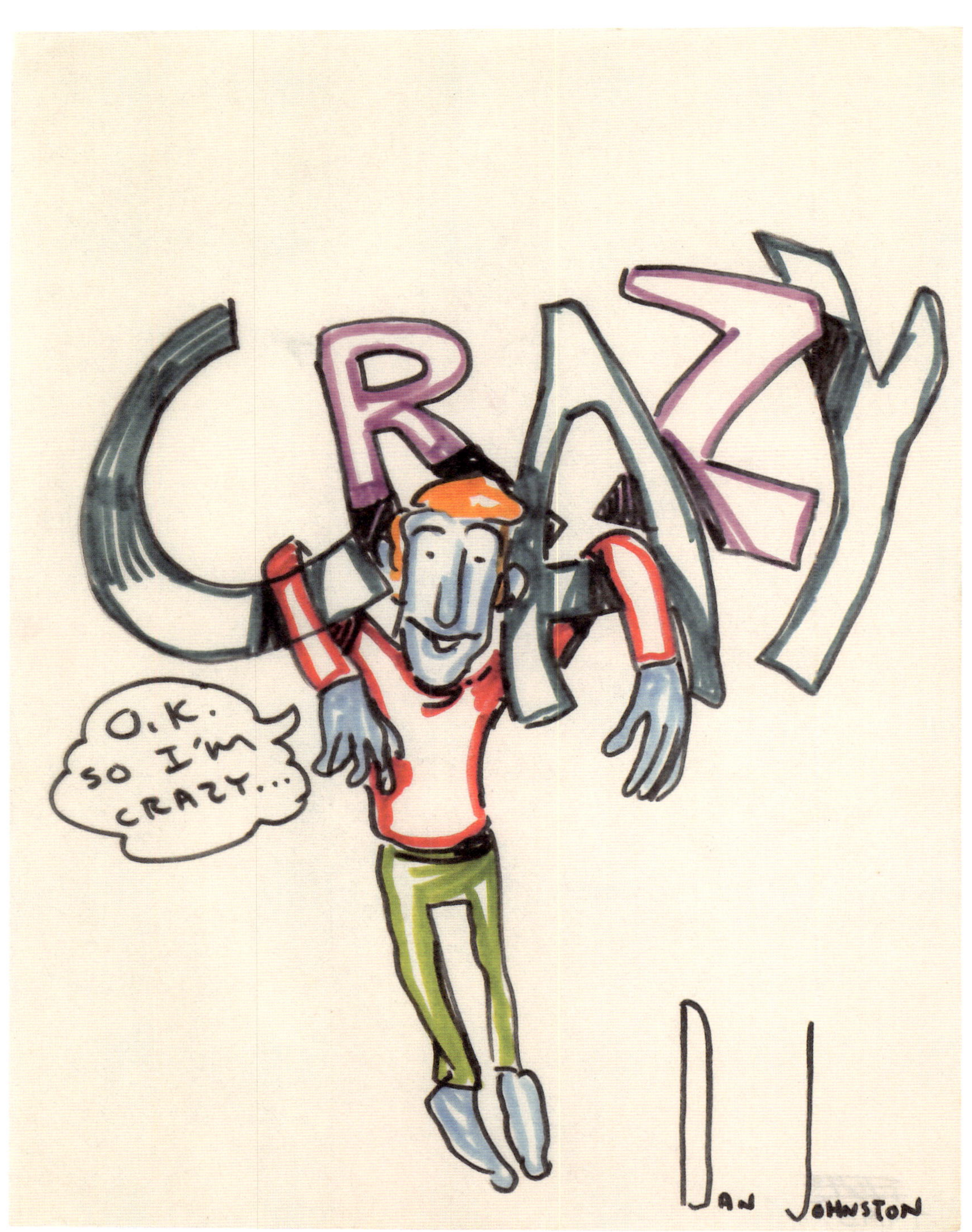

O.K. So I'm Crazy

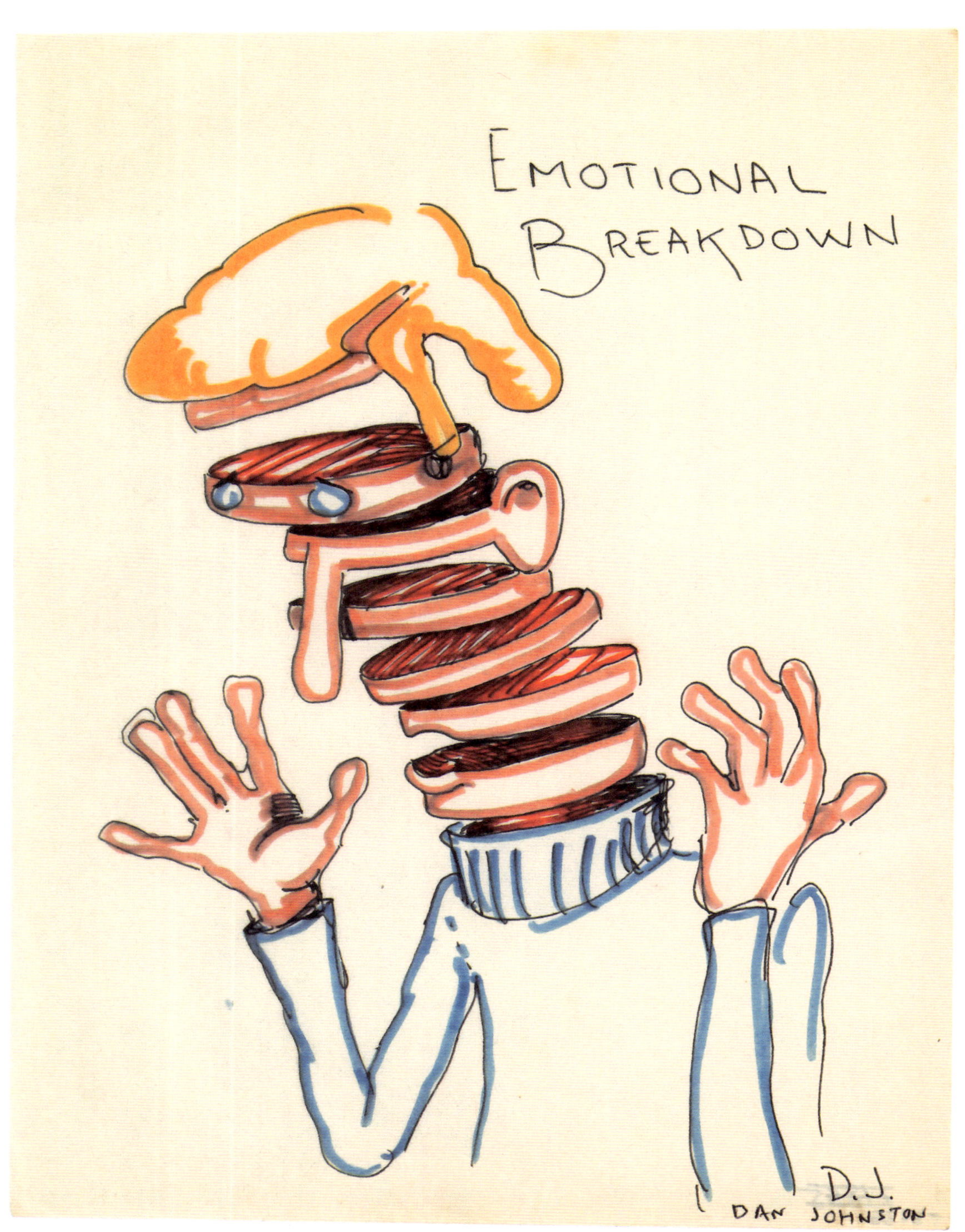

Emotional Breakdown

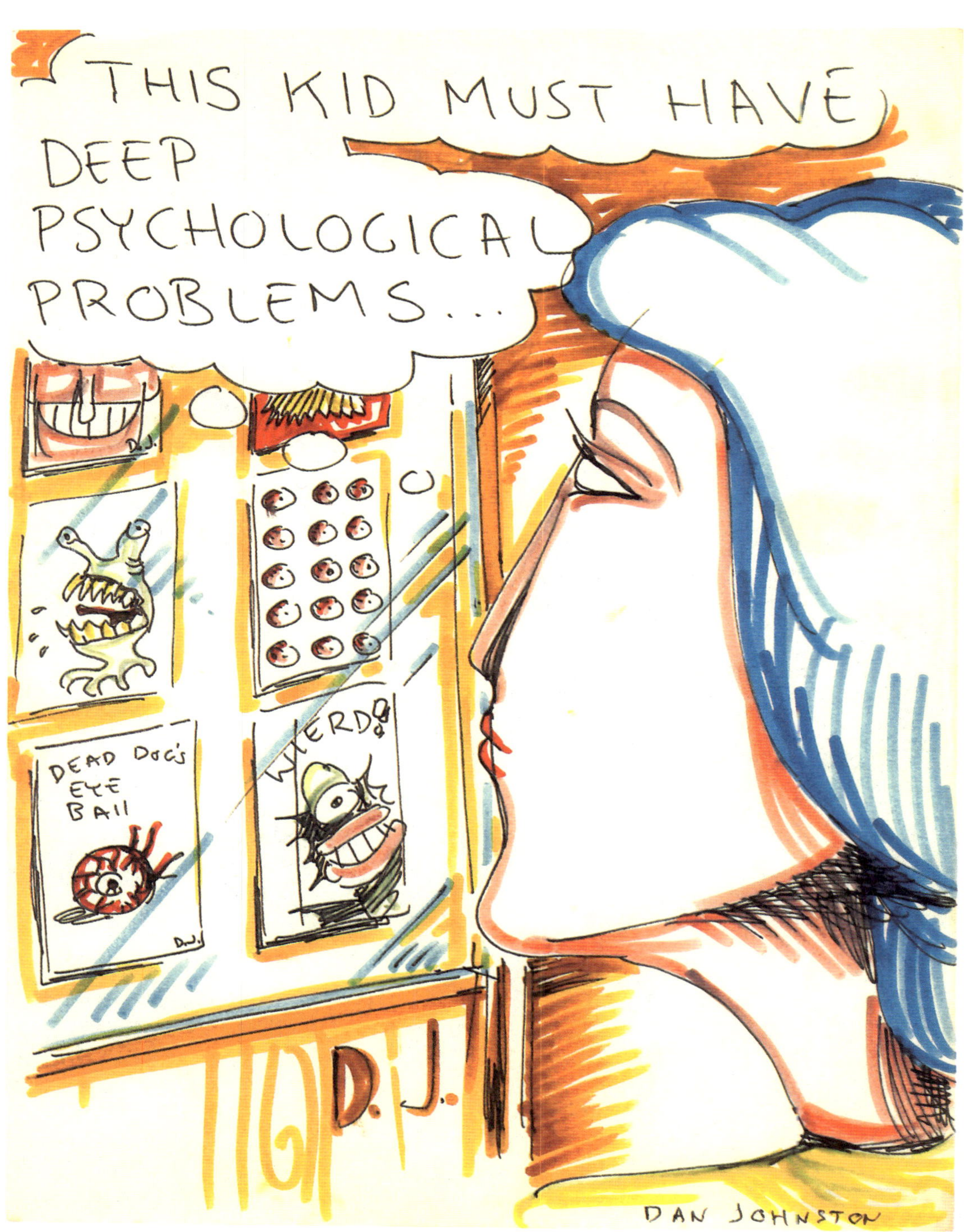

Deep Psychological Problems

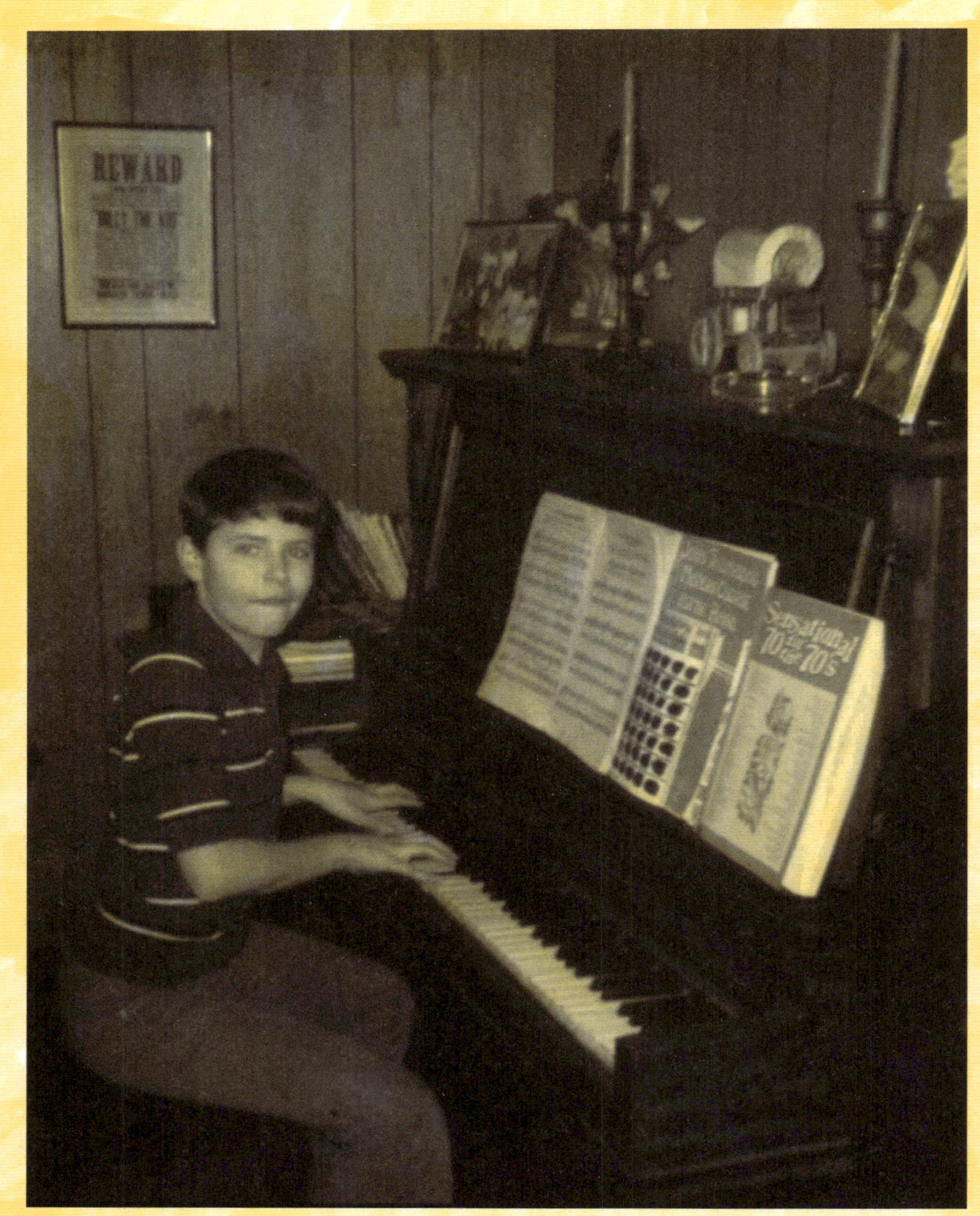
REWARD
Sensational

Dick Johnston

Singing My Songs and Whatnot

My brother, Daniel Johnston (Danny to us), aspired to be an artist from a very early age. When he was finishing sixth grade, the principal called him to his office. It wasn't the first time Mr. Stevens called Danny in. These talks were frequent enough to suggest they weren't effective. While Danny was a bright student, his academic performance was mixed. Danny was not a troublemaker, but he had an exuberance that gave him a reputation. Mr. Stevens always thought highly of him—he even took Danny home to meet his family for dinner. On this particular day, Mr. Stevens felt compelled to give Danny a speech, telling him to get his act together before he moved on to junior high.

"I won't be there to rescue you from your escapades," Mr. Stevens warned Danny. "You can't be cutting up, and certainly do not draw caricatures of your teachers on your homework!" He wasn't sure if he was getting through to Danny. So he asked, "Do you even know what you want to be? Do you have a plan for your life?"

"Yes!" Danny would tell the story decades later. He leaped out of his chair with his vision. "I'm going to be a great artist!"

At the time, Danny's vision was that he would draw comic books. Most kids enjoy comics, but Danny's interest went far deeper. He knew every artist's name and studied their methods and styles in great detail.

Let me back up and tell you a little about our family. Our dad, Bill, was born in Chester, West Virginia, in 1922. Chester was in the heartland of early industrial America—not far from Pittsburgh. In

World War II, Dad would serve in China as a fighter pilot in the famous Flying Tigers, a cause of great pride for Danny.

After the war, Dad enrolled in engineering classes in Bakersfield, California, where he met our mother, Mabel Voyles. Mom was one of ten children born on a farm in Delhi, California. When Dad was overseas, she was working for Lockheed, riveting airplanes in Bakersfield.

They married in 1947 and drove across the country to the hundred-acre farm in West Virginia that Dad's parents owned. In addition to the main house, the farm had a two-room cottage with a hand-pump water well, and a path (outhouse). The newlyweds moved in. Always the engineer, Dad elevated the cottage, dug out a basement beneath it, and expanded the house as their family grew with the arrivals of Sally (1948), Margy (1950), Cindy (1952), and then me (1954).

In 1958, we packed up and moved to California, where Dad worked as an engineer on the Minuteman missile system. Danny was born in Sacramento on January 22, 1961. We were uprooted again that same year when we moved to Brigham City, Utah, where Dad worked with another engineering company on the salt flats. We were there four years before returning to West Virginia, now with one more child.

Seven years younger than any of the rest of us, Daniel was the constant center of attention. Mom quickly learned to occupy his rambunctious side with a pencil and notepad when she needed him to be still. This got Danny started drawing very young, but it didn't keep him from absorbing everything going on. At church, his drawings would often be about the topics of his Bible class or the sermon.

The lines between real and make-believe were blurry for Danny, possibly enhanced by a special perk we enjoyed on some Friday nights: staying up late to watch a weekly program called *Nightmare*. It featured cheap sci-fi and horror flicks like *The Crawling Eye* and *Attack of the Killer Tomatoes!* This was the beginning of his lifelong interest in the genre.

He also had some strong reactions to make-believe. If someone put on a Halloween mask—not anything scary, but something like Disney's Snow White—he would scream nonstop until they took it off.

Mom related to Danny's creativity. She was a spontaneous singer at home, entertaining us with "Red River Valley" and other tunes from before our time. She liked to ascribe meaning to all kinds of sounds. She would say, "Listen, the birds are singing to us! What are they saying?" Danny always came up with an imaginative reply. When the teapot in the kitchen whistled, and my mother said, "My teapot is calling me!" Danny immediately interpreted: "He's telling you his seater is hot."

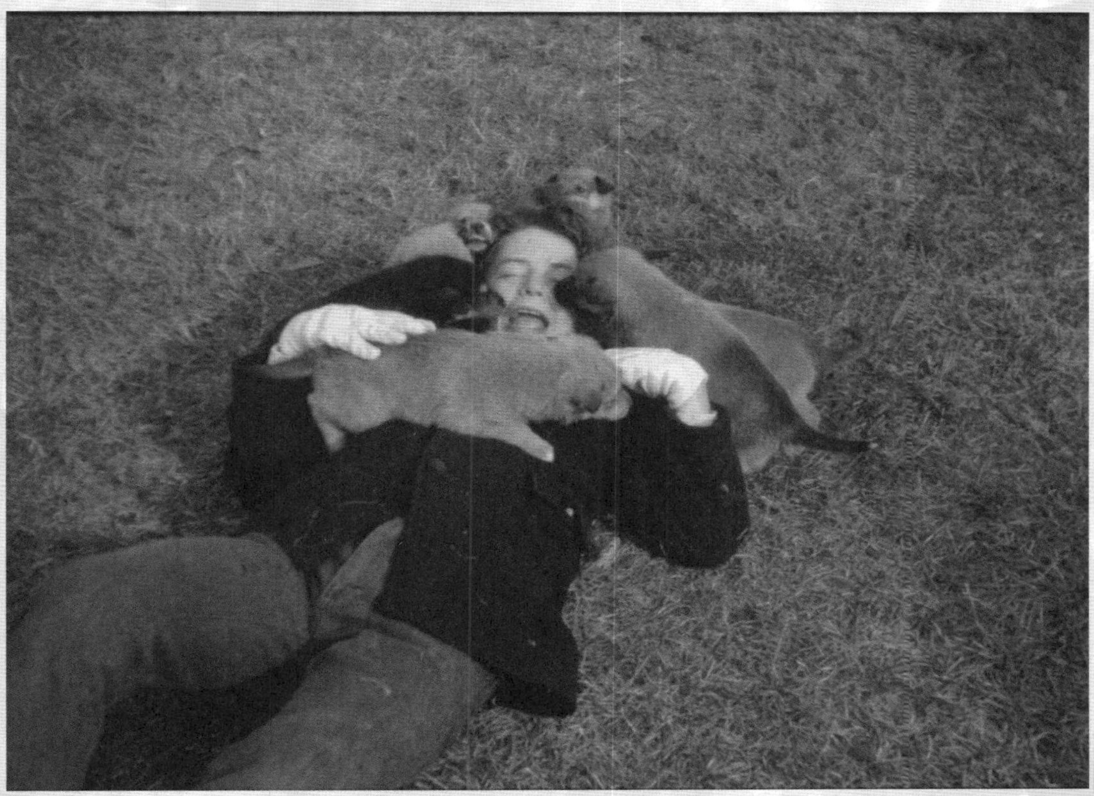

For Danny and me—four and eleven years old at the time—the move to West Virginia in 1965 was a dream, an adventure. The hills of the farm had expansive fields, a large orchard, springs and creeks, a pond, and three wooded valleys.

We occupied ourselves with playing pretend, hiking, exploring, hunting, camping ("sleeping out"), fishing, boating, swimming, sledding, building things in the snow, and shooting the new BB gun Dad gave me when it wasn't even my birthday or Christmas.

Mom and Dad hosted events, church fellowships, song nights, dinners, wiener roasts, and corn roasts, and we had sleepovers for the girls and campouts for the boys. We planted and harvested gardens, collected wild blackberries, pressed apple cider in the fall, and cut our own Christmas tree in the winter, hauling it home on a sled in the snow. Danny would capture this idyllic world in his song "Happy Time" (*Fun*, 1994):

"It must have been a happy time / The sun would shine / The candy bars / Kool-Aid

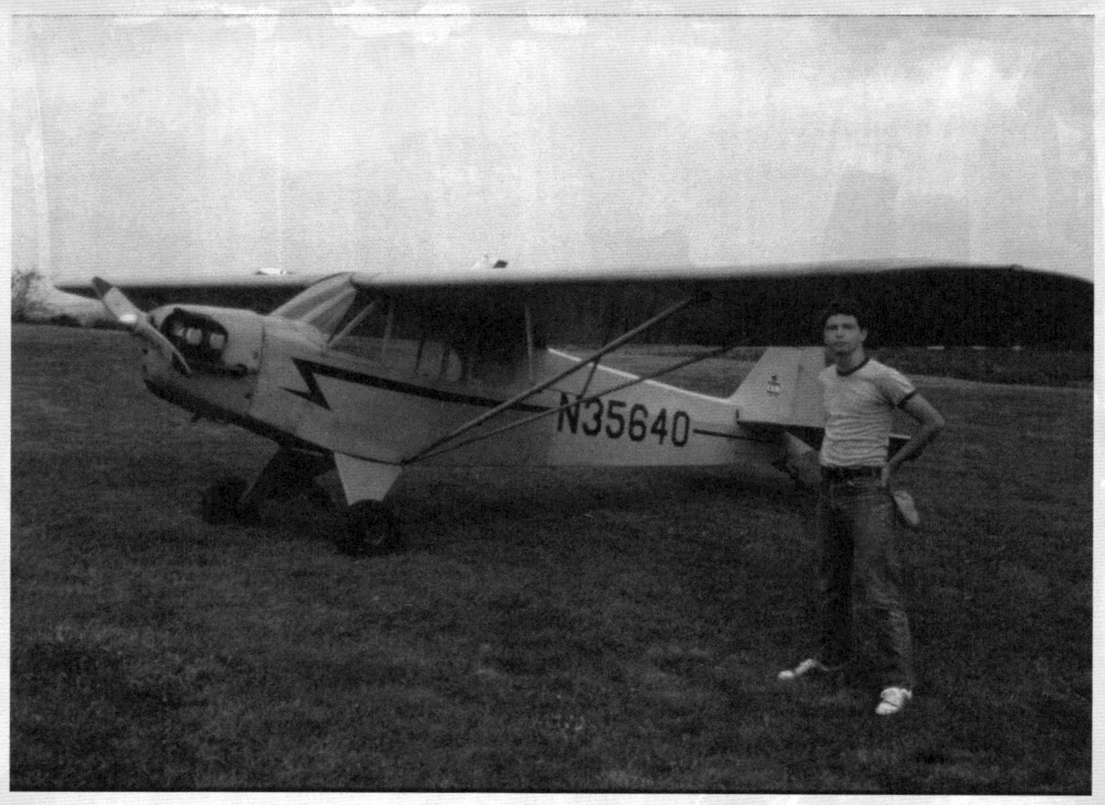

flowing like wine / The comic books / The TV shows / The bubble gum / The kitty cat / I was a time traveler / Listening to the heavenly laughter . . . The picture drawing /The pretend heroes / My favorite was Captain America / The little girl / The flowers in the yard / The dog and cat / The welcome mat / God told me to go out / Singing my songs and whatnot"

We spent Saturday nights at the table in the basement preparing for Bible class. The Bible was a treasure trove of interesting stories, and Danny and I were especially into the book of Proverbs. We were impressed with the weight of the stories, like the one in Genesis about Isaac's son Esau selling his inheritance to his brother Jacob for a bowl of stew.

Just as Danny and Mom liked to anthropomorphize animals and objects, the Bible transformed everyday life, giving it purpose and meaning and making it entertaining. Our own human experience is a message that offers advice and warnings. We needn't see the world as a string of disconnected surprises; we would view it as messages to guide (and challenge) us; to participate in the purpose of everything. Life (i.e., God) was shouting a message to us. We could reflect in awe and wonder on the indescribable marvel of human consciousness, and then crack a joke about it. This is what Danny shared in his art and his songs. These are the things that impressed him, frightened him, amazed him, defined him. Worthy things. Holy things.

For Danny, it was an appointed crusade: "God told me to go out / Singing my songs and whatnot." Everything in life was significant, intentional, and important. Overwhelmed by the prospect of "capturing it all," Daniel sometimes appeared to be without direction, jumping from one idea to another, spasmodically, making decisions intuitively, often overwhelming friends with his energy. His intensity and gregarious confidence would pull you into his vision.

But something else was happening over time—Danny's older siblings were gradually disappearing off to college. In 1972, I was the last to leave, and Danny was alone. That was also the year that Mr. Stevens warned Danny that life ahead would not be so kind.

Entering junior high school is tough, with new peer pressures and unwelcome emotional turmoil. Danny had bouts of depression and despair. These dark times he later recalled in the songs "Peek a Boo" and "Golly Gee." Mom took him to professionals for help. And he did get better, for a while. When I came back in the summer, Danny and I would always pick up where we had left off. But we inhabited a fragile world—the world of being a child—that eventually must end, and we both knew it.

Danny was well-liked everywhere. He would sit surrounded by a crowd of onlookers, drawing and entertaining with his caricatures and wittiness. For an elaborate 1976 Bicentennial celebration, he crafted large-as-life 3D displays that filled the school hallways.

The reputation Danny had as "the school artist" sustained his confidence into high school (p. 13), but when it came time for him to go to college, it was an emotional crisis. Still, he dutifully followed his siblings to Abilene Christian University in Texas, in the fall of 1979.

At first, he was the star of his art classes. He told me much later that since he had stubbornly refused the new techniques they were being taught, he began to fall behind. This letdown, along with a profound homesickness, crushed him, and he didn't make it through the semester.

Returning to West Virginia—looking to appease our parents—Danny enrolled at a branch of Kent State University in East Liverpool, Ohio. The school had a thriving art department, and there he flourished, making friends with many artists and musicians.

He experienced some of his greatest creativity in the years from high school through Kent State. He developed a whole line of characters like the one of himself with the top of his head cut open to expose ideas gushing out (p. 204), a scrawny duck with suppressed sexual desires (p. 22), and a man in underwear embarrassing himself in public (p. 146).

Danny wasn't planning or orchestrating anything; it was just flowing out of him. He carried notebooks with him everywhere and recorded everything—the mundane and the surprising, the beautiful and the frightening. Fear of death (p. 208), boy meets girl, the innocence of youth exploited and lost, and the search for purpose and meaning—it all poured out in a compulsive stream-of-consciousness comic strip of his life.

About this time, he gave me a tape of his songs and a canvas of our father sitting in his chair in the living room (much like the one on p. 105). Danny had captured the image and essence seen from our viewpoint when we were lying on the floor watching television in bold colors. The painting was genius, and I knew it.

When he played his songs for me on the piano in our basement, I thought they were very, very good, but I didn't think anyone would ever listen to them. I sensed that they lacked professional quality (recorded on a battery-powered cassette tape recorder), and while that didn't keep them from being amazing, I thought it might keep others from noticing them. Time would prove me wrong. Danny's music appealed to a broad audience, starting with musicians and artists themselves. People appreciated the raw honesty of his expression. But it would take time.

By 1983, he had struck a truce with our dad. They had reached an agreement that he could stay home and work on his music and art nonstop. I didn't know this when I invited Danny to come to Houston to work at AstroWorld amusement park for the summer. This untimely invitation launched him on an epic journey into the big wide wicked world, a world that fascinated and terrified Danny. The "grown-up" world.

Every bit of this was hard for Danny. I can't overstate this. He experienced his most dreaded fear (failure to make it on his own) and a new paranoia (he thought we would have him committed). Not true at all, but it was true to him.

Without warning, he disappeared with a traveling carnival. Five months later, he resurfaced in Austin, Texas. Comic artist P. Craig Russell had told Danny that Austin was where the underground comic scene was. There he appeared to flourish. He won over local musicians and audiences, and appeared on the MTV music showcase *The Cutting Edge* in 1985. Eventually Danny would be named best songwriter and best folk act at the Austin Music Awards. This newfound

Dick Johnston

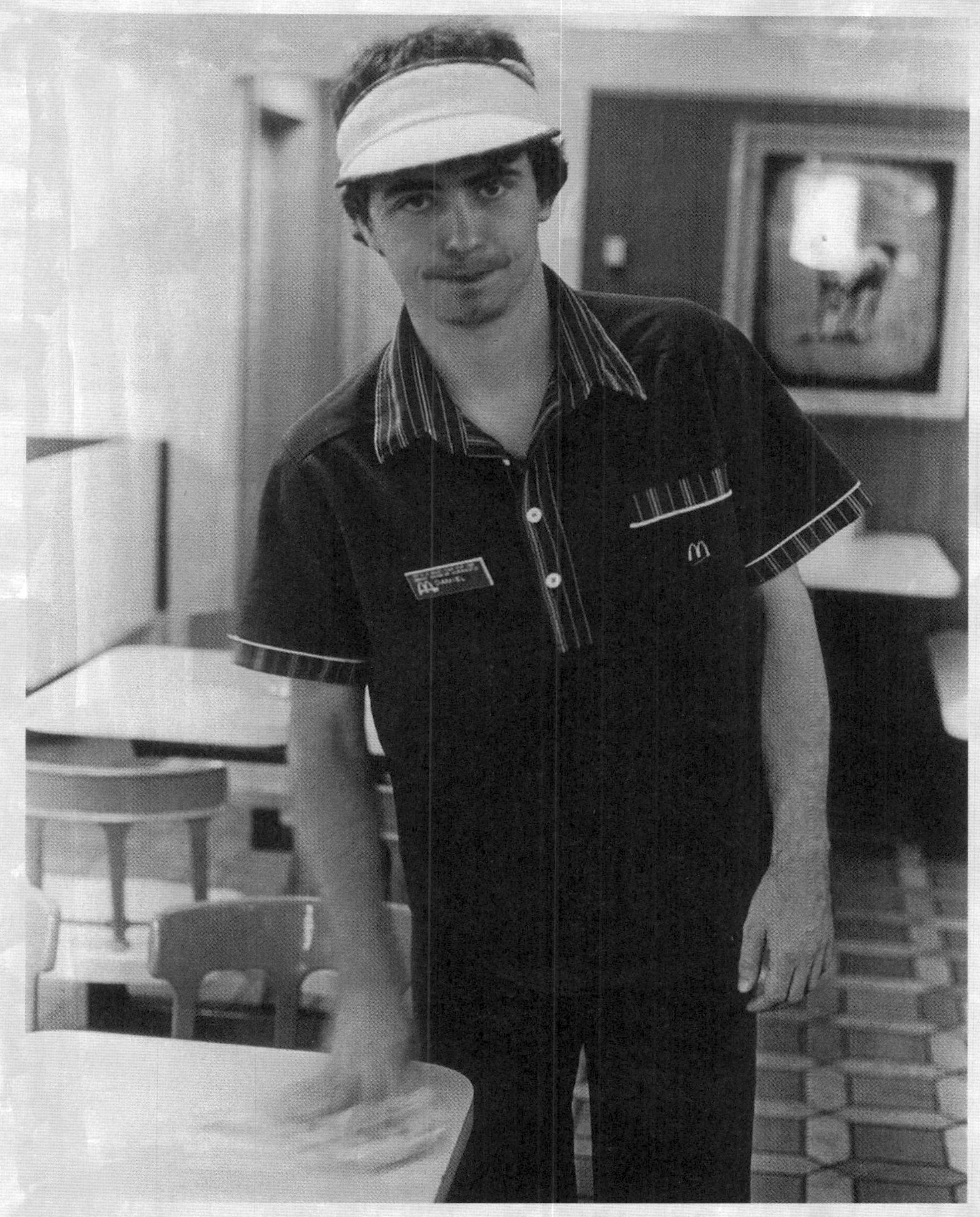

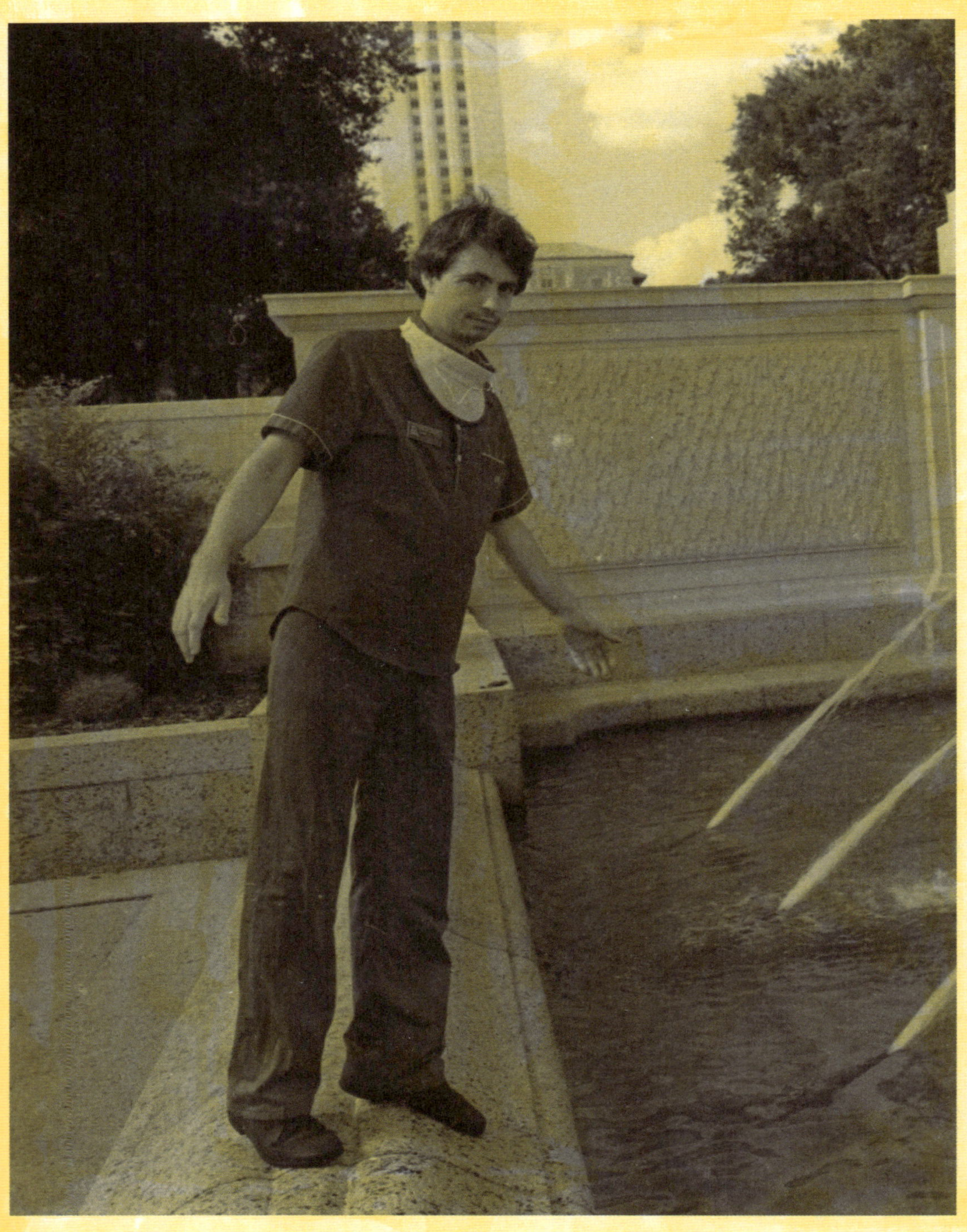

celebrity made demands on his employer, McDonald's: the press was calling all the time, and film crews were arriving to interview him in the restaurant.

Danny went through several managers, who worked furiously to have albums released. But he was barely surviving, living hand to mouth. If he wasn't eating expired entrees at McDonald's, he would leverage his notoriety to get free meals from local restaurants. Blowing all his paycheck at Half Price Books, he exchanged his art for comic books at Austin Books & Comics and for albums at the Sound Exchange.

Still, he told me he saw musical success only as a stepping stone to (and a distraction from) his becoming a great comic artist. Drawing constantly and gaining a following for it, if he squinted just right, he could imagine he was living the dream—the life of the starving artist.

Working frantically with troubles and depression mounting, he left Texas in 1987, abandoning many drawings. Friends salvaged them, and his art was shared, exchanged, and sold. It continued to circulate in Austin for years.

Back in West Virginia, he received professional help and put out two new albums, *1990* and *Artistic Vice*. On a manic excursion to New York City, he made studio recordings with Moe Tucker and Paleface and attended promotional events at the Knitting Factory and Pier Platters. Out of control, he was arrested for marking the inside of the Statue of Liberty. Friends tried to send him home, but he escaped to the streets, sleeping at the YMCA and singing with street musicians. After a trip to Maryland to record with Jad Fair, he went home, but his state of mind was fragile. His manic behavior frightened a woman so badly that she fled from him, breaking her ankles. After spending three days hiding in the woods around Chester, he was arrested and institutionalized. Our parents had some very difficult years then, navigating the legal and mental health systems, and Danny went through several sad years when he was overmedicated.

Once things improved, Dad flew Danny in his small plane to Texas for a SXSW show in 1990. Unbeknownst to Dad, manic Danny had decided he would be more creative if he chucked his meds. Danny did shows around Austin, and it was clear that he was a local celebrity. The experience peaked when Matt Groening met him backstage—Matt was a great fan of Danny's music and particularly his art.

On the return flight to West Virginia, Danny—now having gone a week without medication—went berserk. Imagining that he was Casper the Friendly Ghost, he physically wrested control of the plane from Dad and threw the keys out of the window. With the plane falling from the sky in a spin, Dad was able to put it into a controlled dive to gain air speed and then pulled up over some tall pine trees that lowered them to the ground. Bruised from head to foot, Danny would spend a year in an institution in Arkansas.

He finally returned home in time to move with our parents to Waller, Texas, where Dad was able to build Danny his own house next door. Dad would manage Danny's career, and then in 2001 I began accompanying Danny on tours and to art exhibitions. This was wonderful for me, because I witnessed firsthand the love people had for both his lo-fi music and his art. These tours seemed to work for Danny—as father or brother, we were able to keep him from getting into trouble and to spot manic behavior before it escalated.

With attention from art critics and collectors increasing, Danny's notoriety culminated in 2006, when he was included in the Whitney Biennial. We stepped out of a limousine and strode through a crowd of officials and reporters to enter the museum, where fourteen of his drawings hung on the wall. Daniel had arrived!

Returning home, away from the noise of the city, press, photo sessions, and autographs, I dropped Danny off at his house in Waller. I was talking about his fame when I noticed his countenance drop. He quietly said, "I just want to go to heaven."

That was Danny. As much as he wanted to be accomplished, as much as he had pursued fame and money, he also knew the pursuit could destroy a person. This perspective comes through in works like *The Eternal Battle* (p. 258), *Death Be Kind!* (p. 218), *Satan Will Die* (p. 284), and in his lyrics. After all, Danny once sang, "You'll never get to heaven if you've been there before."

In 2007, Danny experienced lithium poisoning from a slow buildup of his medications that left him unconscious for three weeks. His recovery was slow and difficult. For months, his drawings were jagged and unstable, yet it never occurred to him to stop. He said of his art, "It's the healthiest thing I do."

It may seem sad that someone with creative gifts encountered so many obstacles in pursuing his talent. I don't think his problems were the source of his creativity, but it might be accurate to say that they were fuel on the fire. Each piece of Danny's art is a frame in the movie of his fifty-eight-year life. It spans all genres—a cartoon, an adventure, a horror story, a romance, a tragedy, a sitcom. When *The Devil and Daniel Johnston* was made about Danny, he said, "The only thing missing was a laugh track!"

To date, most of my brother's artistic legacy hasn't seen the light of day. There is just so much material—hundreds of journals and many more drawings. But you can experience a wonderful selection of Daniel Johnston's work in these pages. If you can relate to the spirit of his art, and you can sense the beautiful and complex soul that produced it, you may come to love Daniel Johnston as much as I do.

Dick Johnston

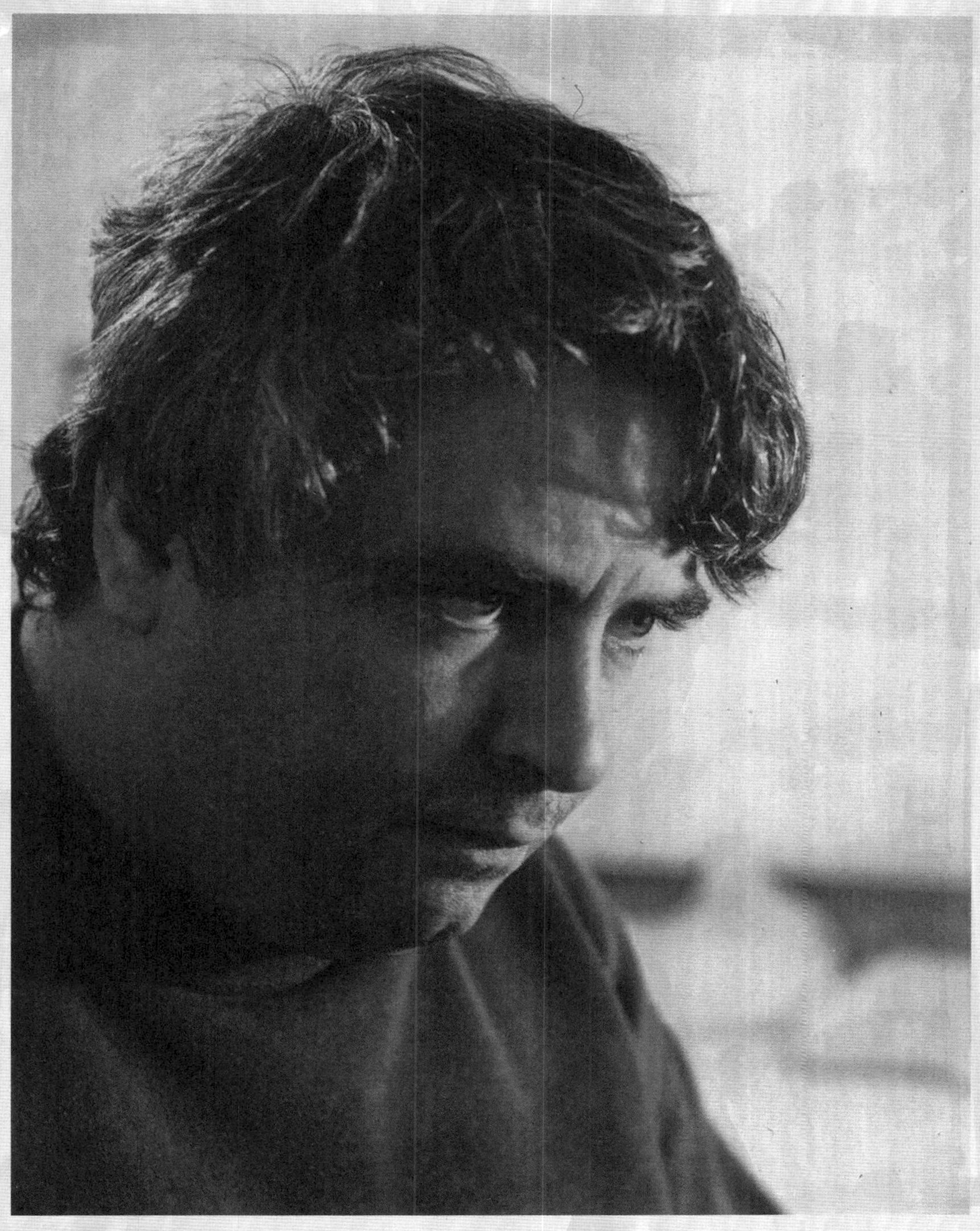

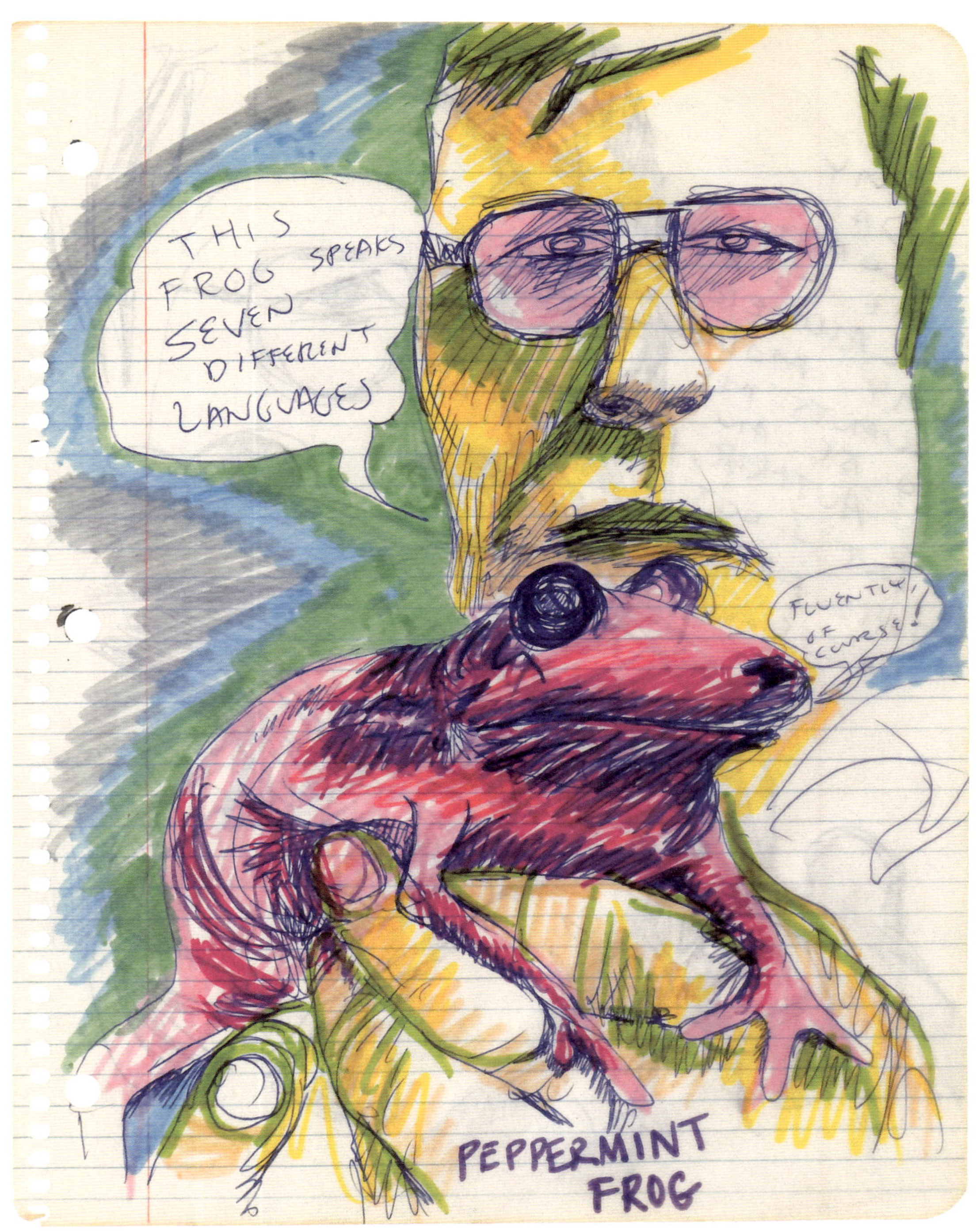

Peppermint Frog

IV.
Notebook Drawings
1980s–1990s

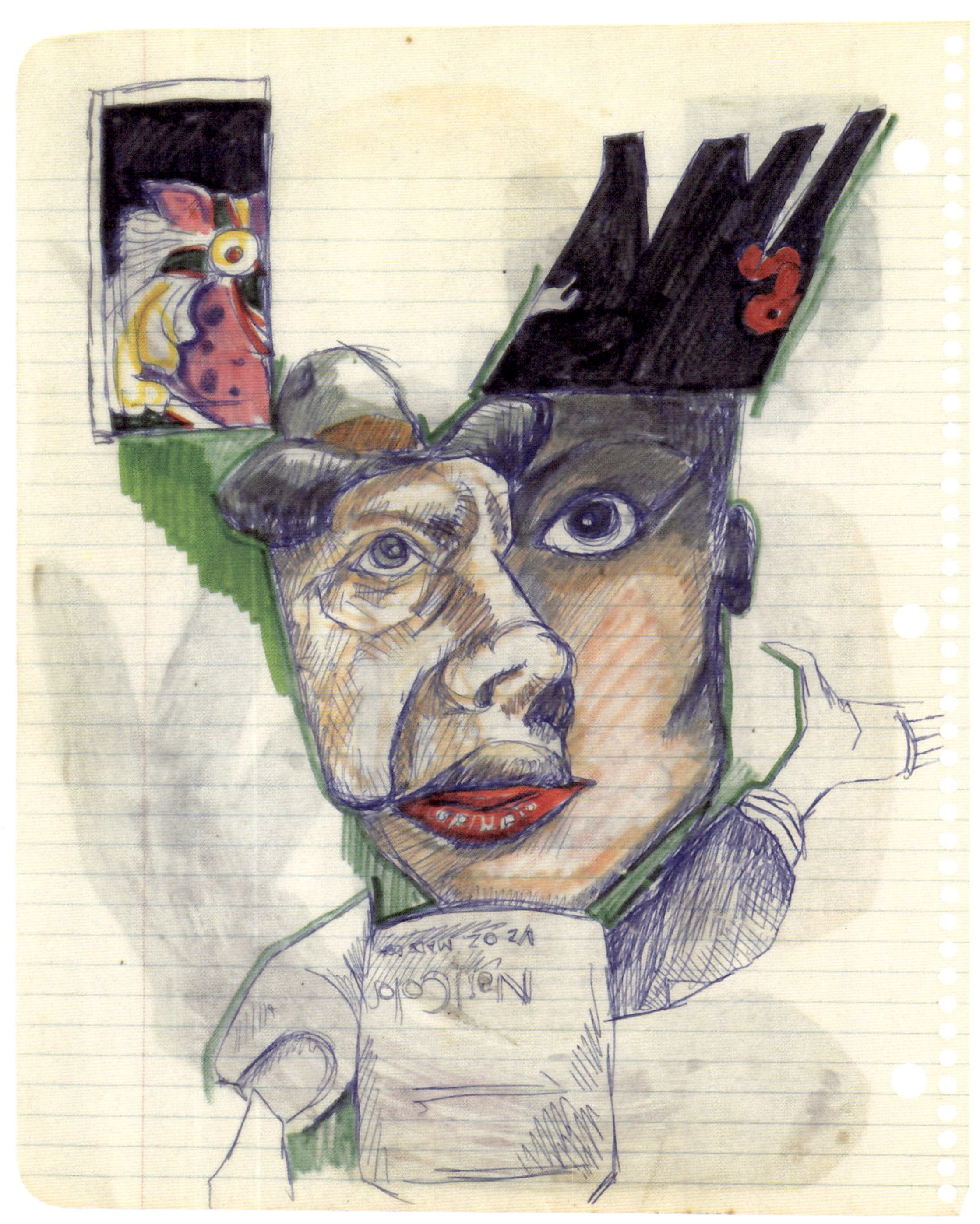

Nail Color

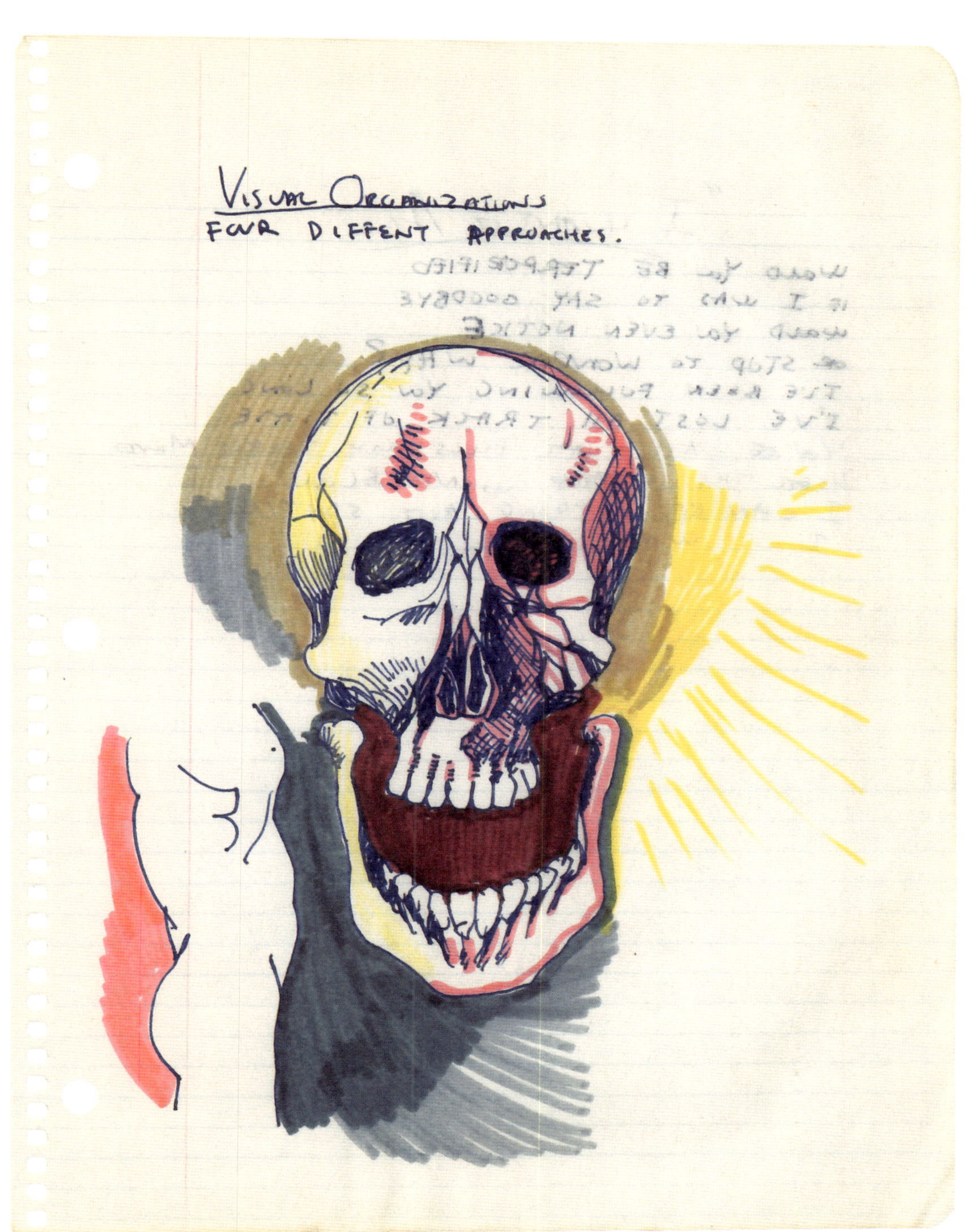
VISUAL ORGANIZATIONS
FOUR DIFFENT APPROACHES.

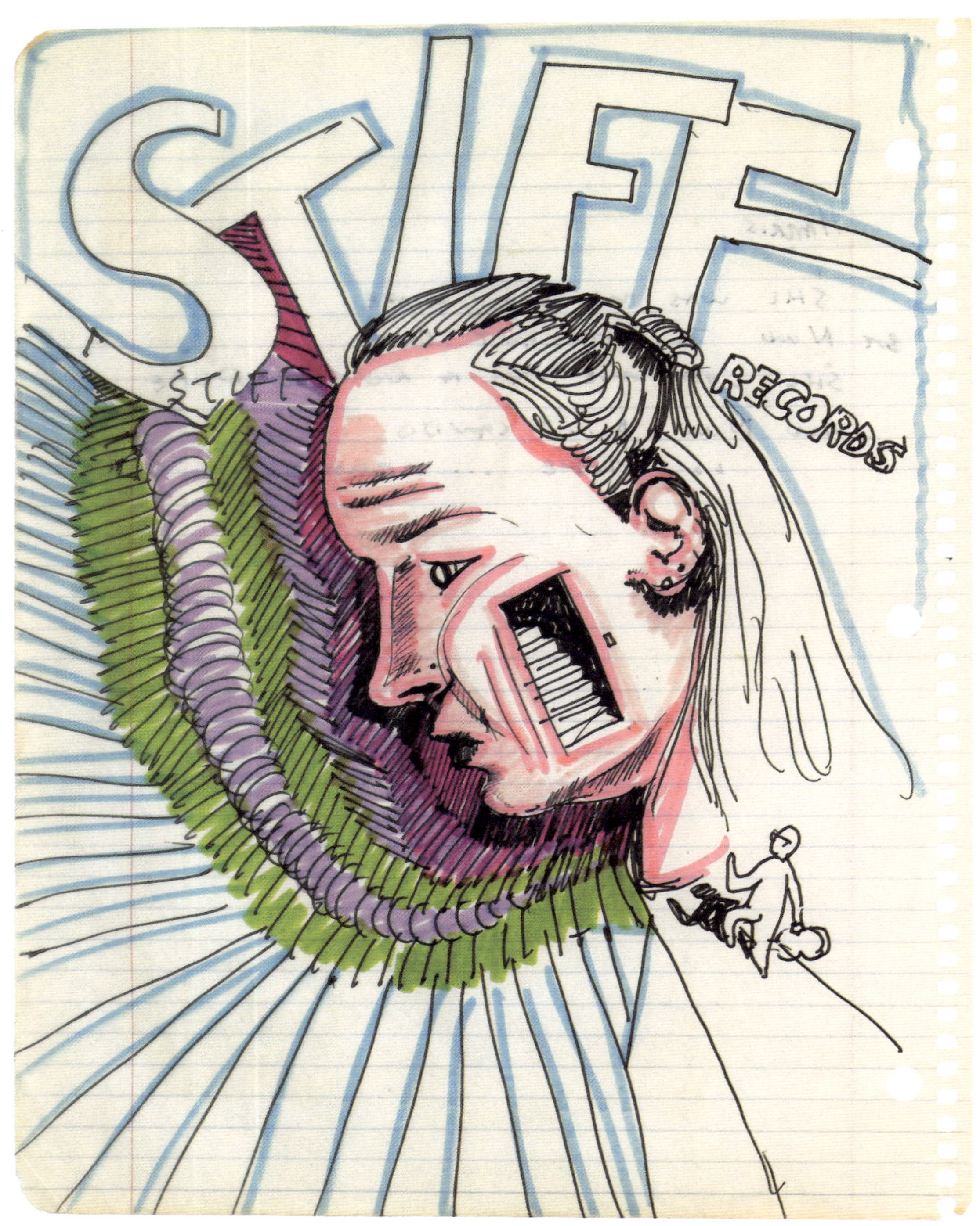

Stiff Records

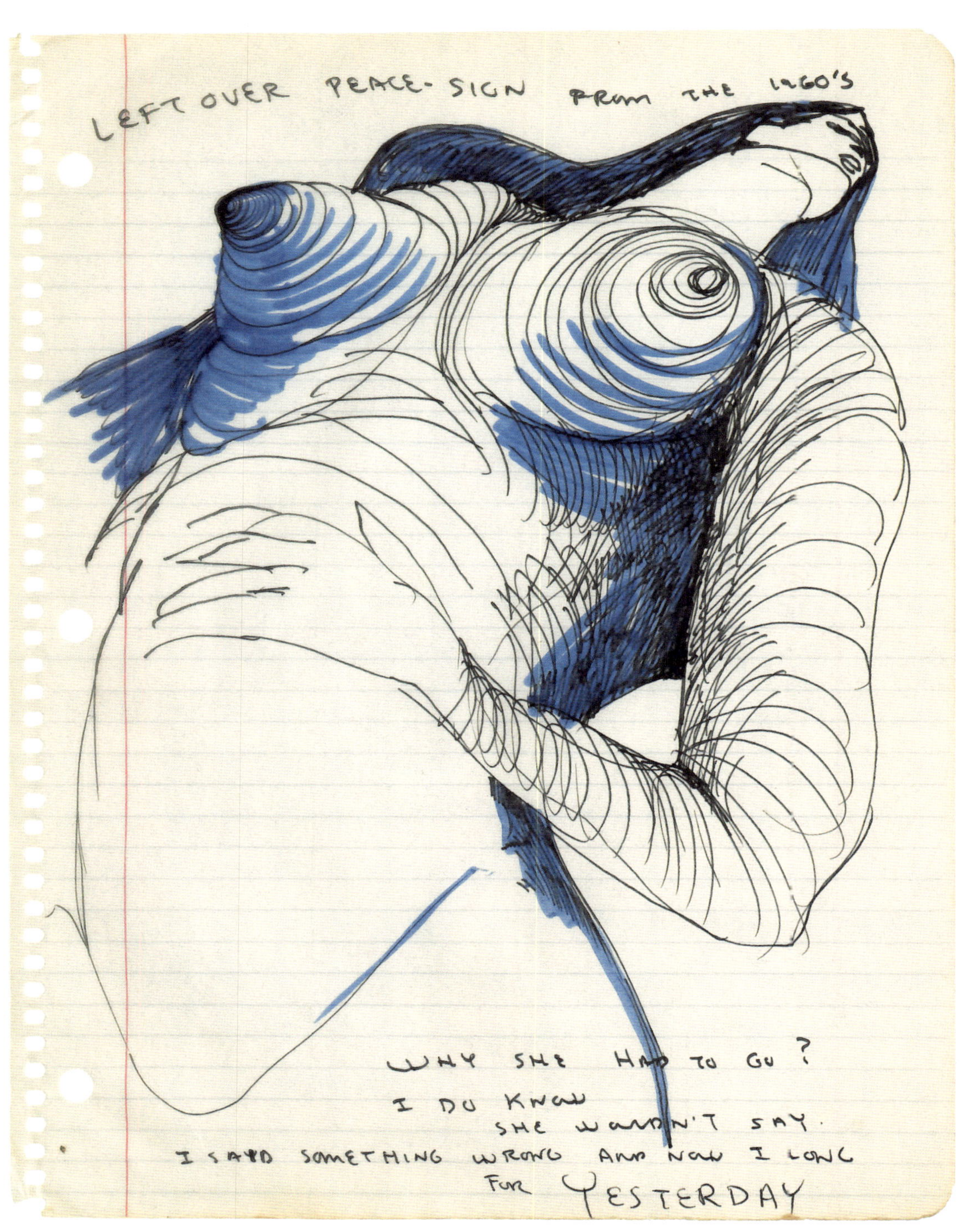

Why She Had to Go? (For Yesterday)

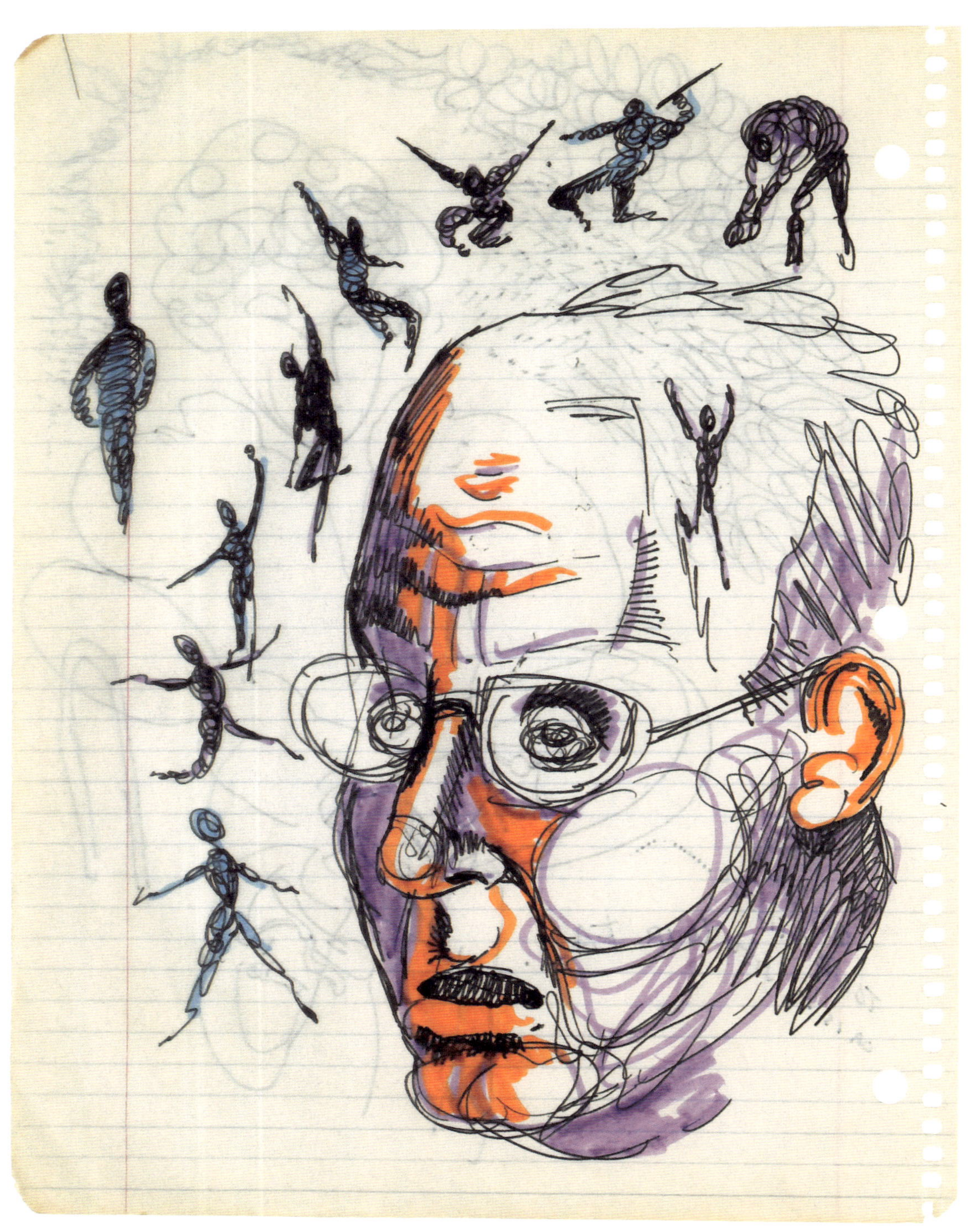

Untitled (Dancers and Glasses)

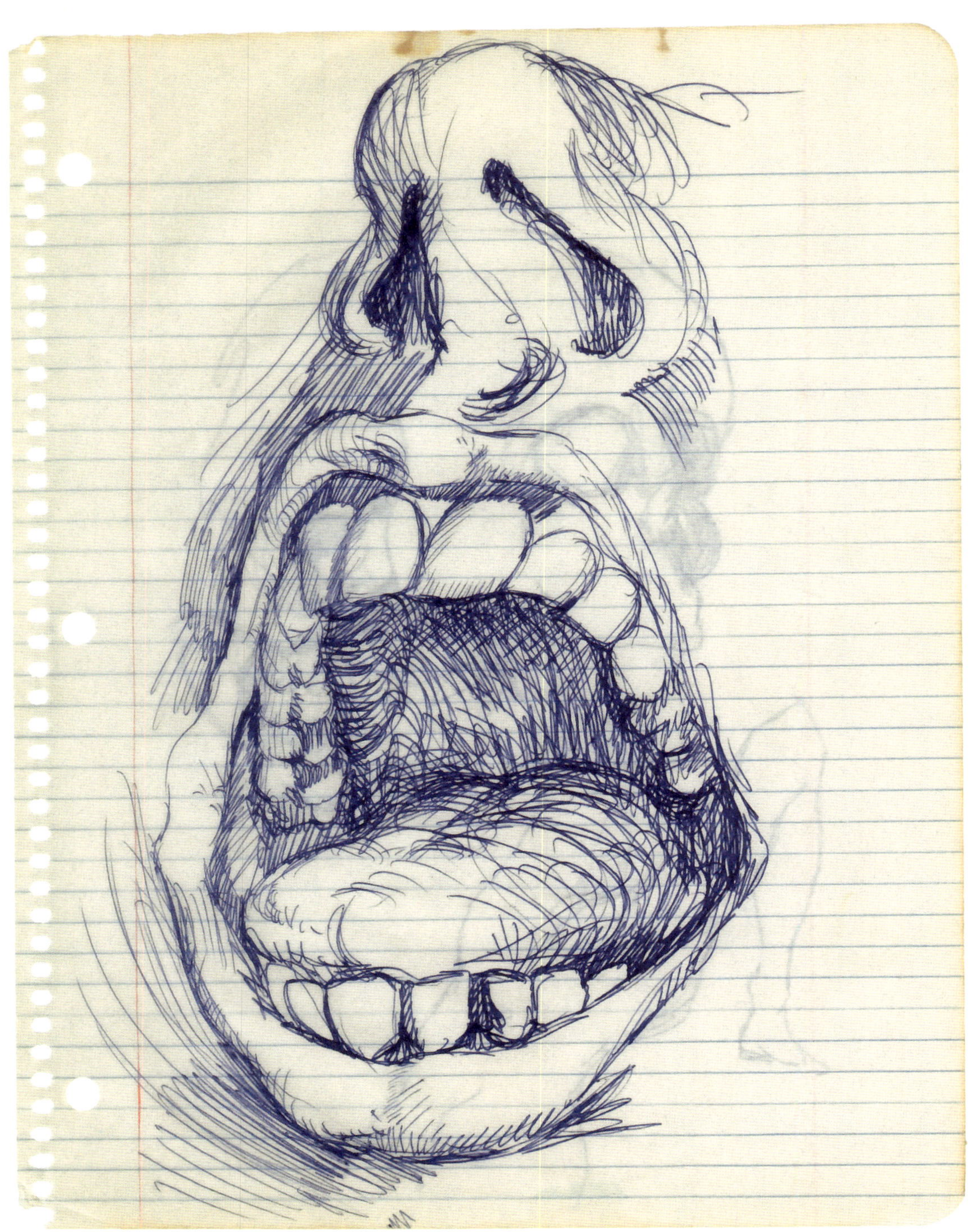

Untitled (Mouth Wide Open)

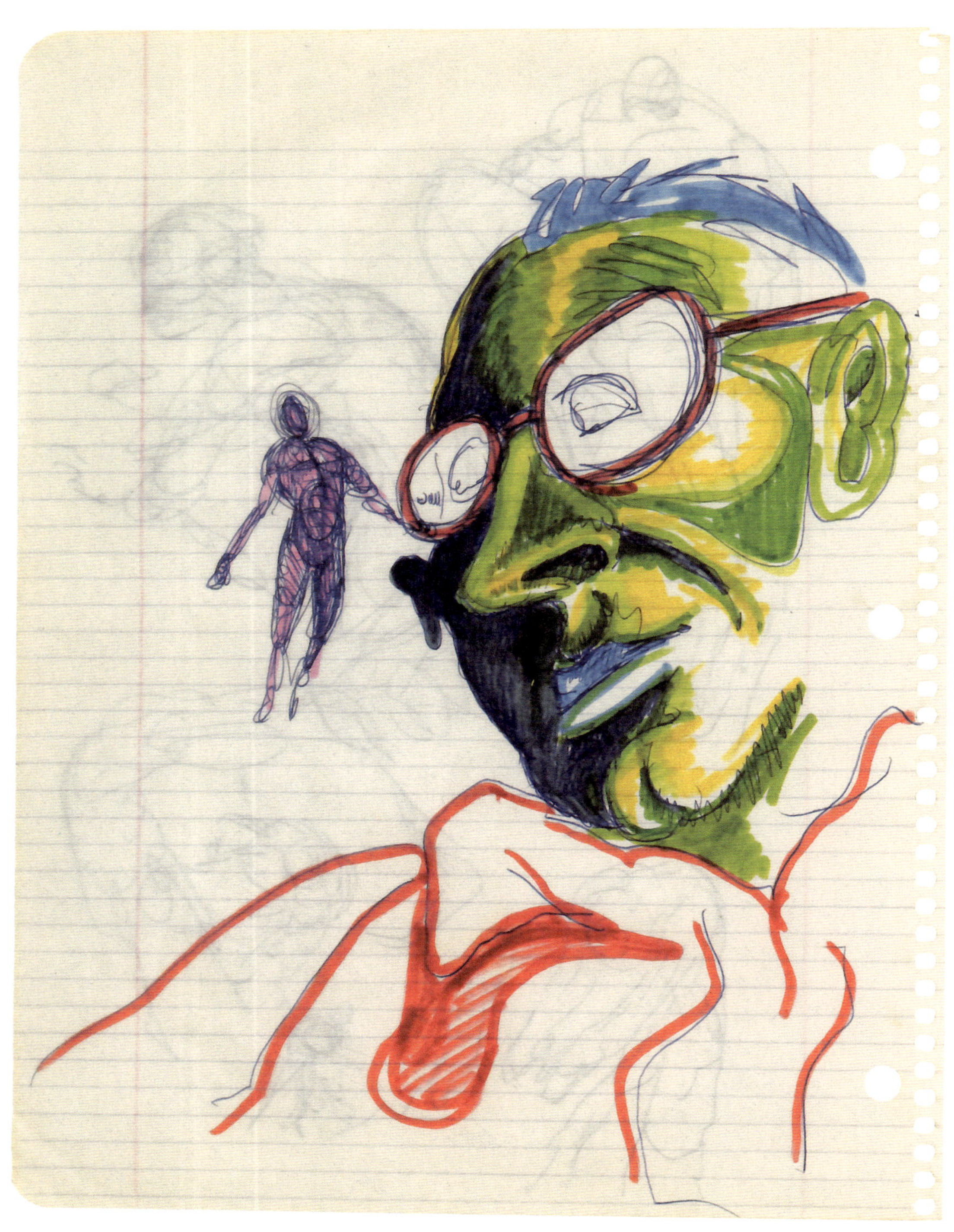

Untitled (Bill, Green Face)

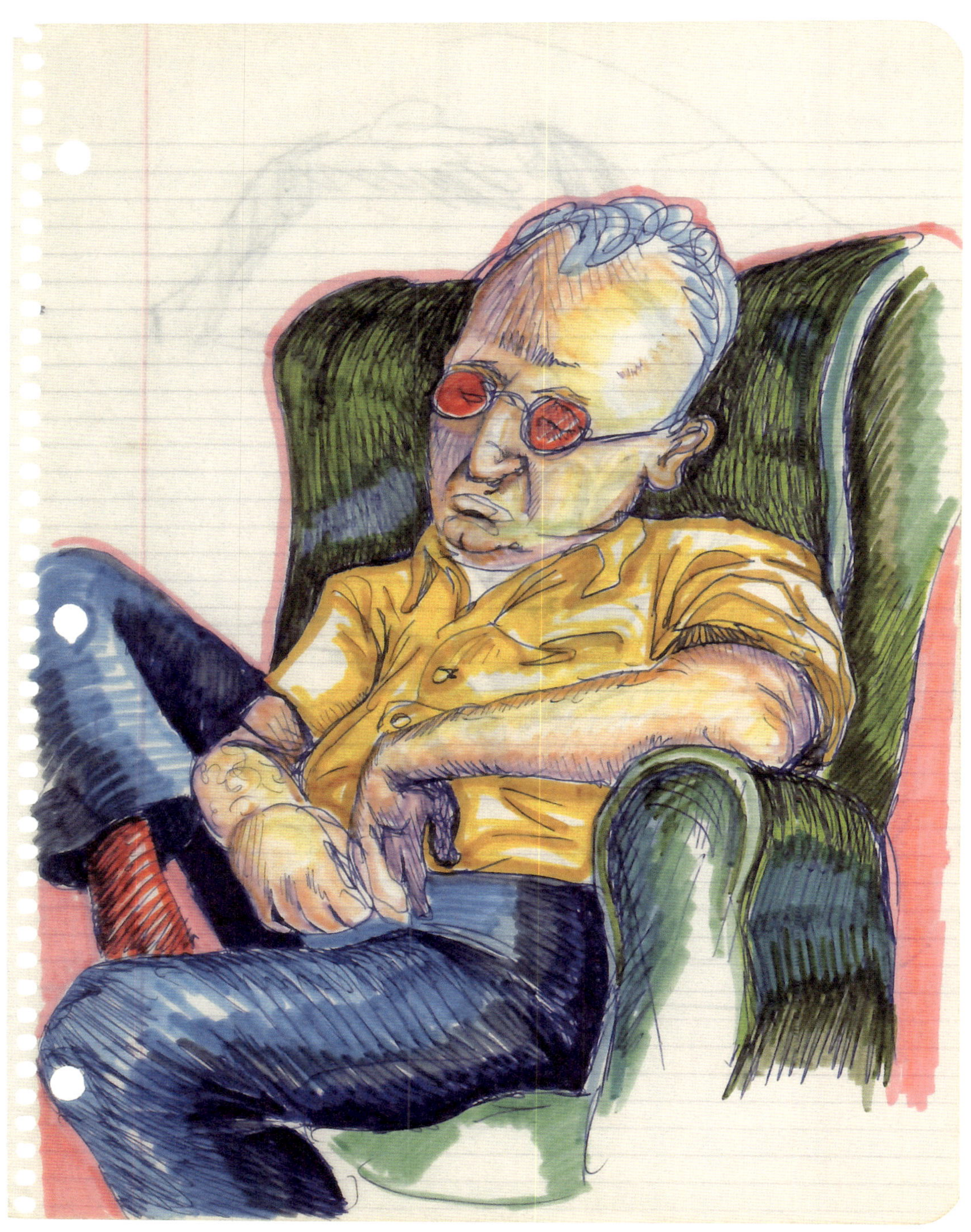

Untitled (Bill, Green Recliner)

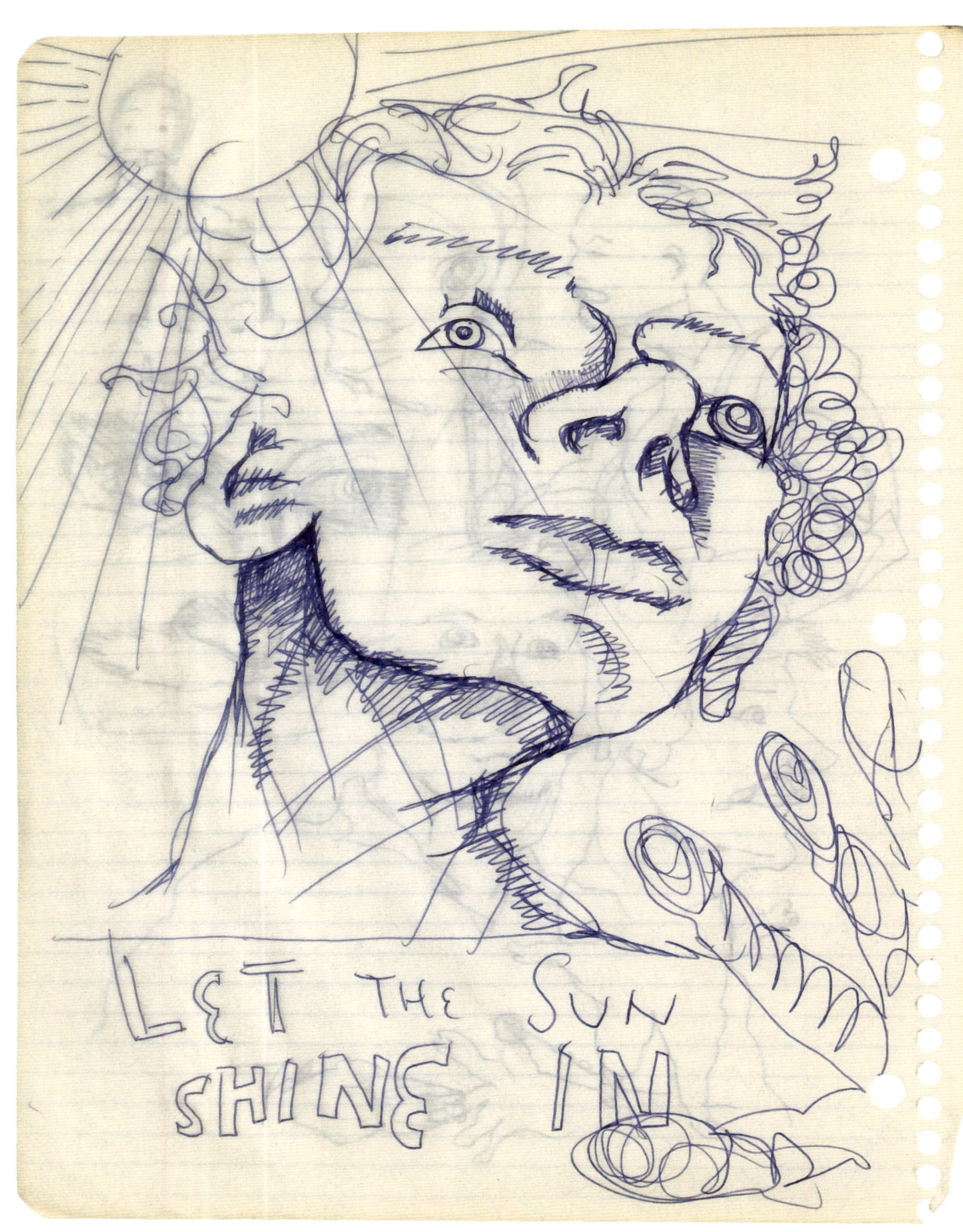

Let the Sun Shine In

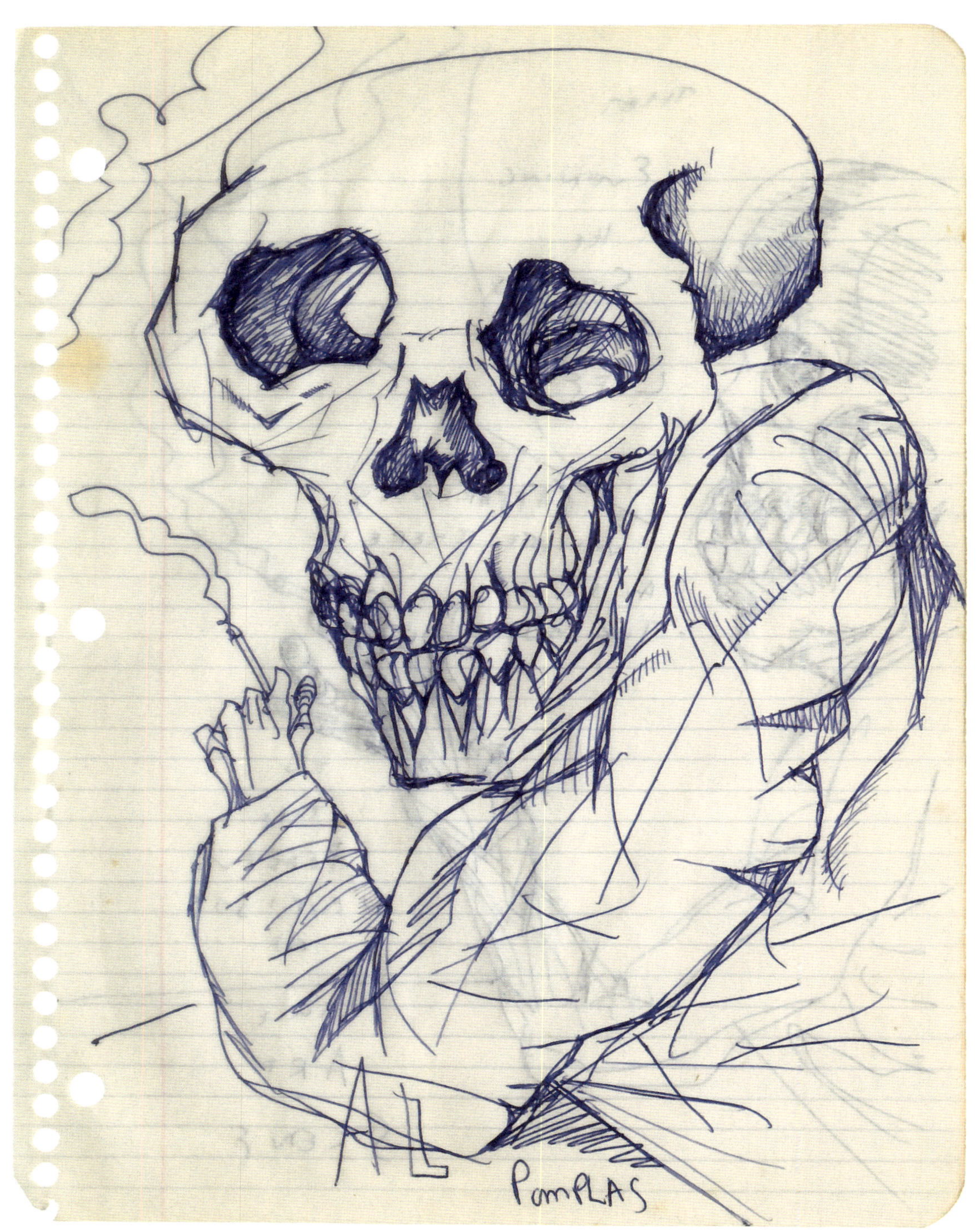

Al Pomplas

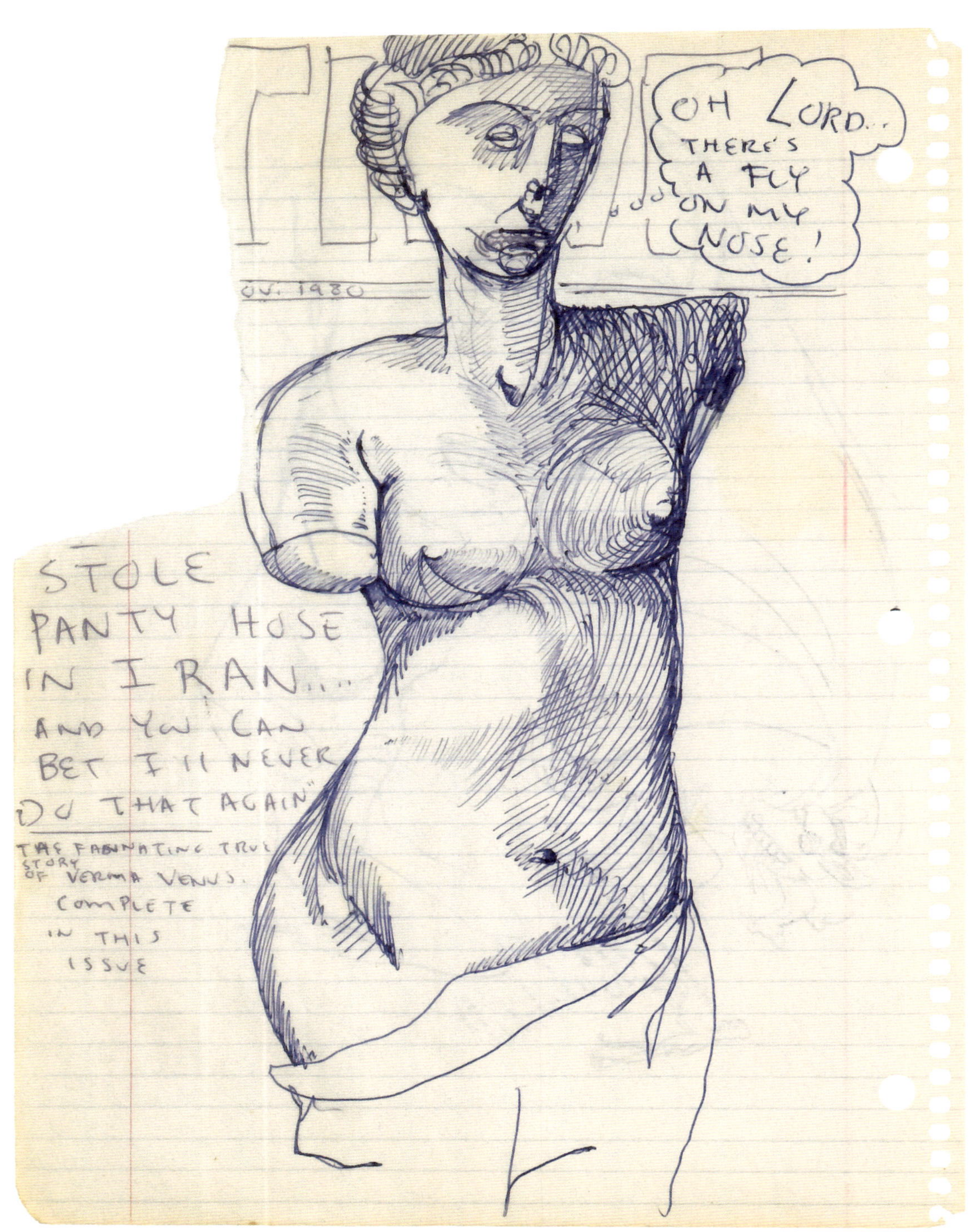

There's a Fly on My Nose

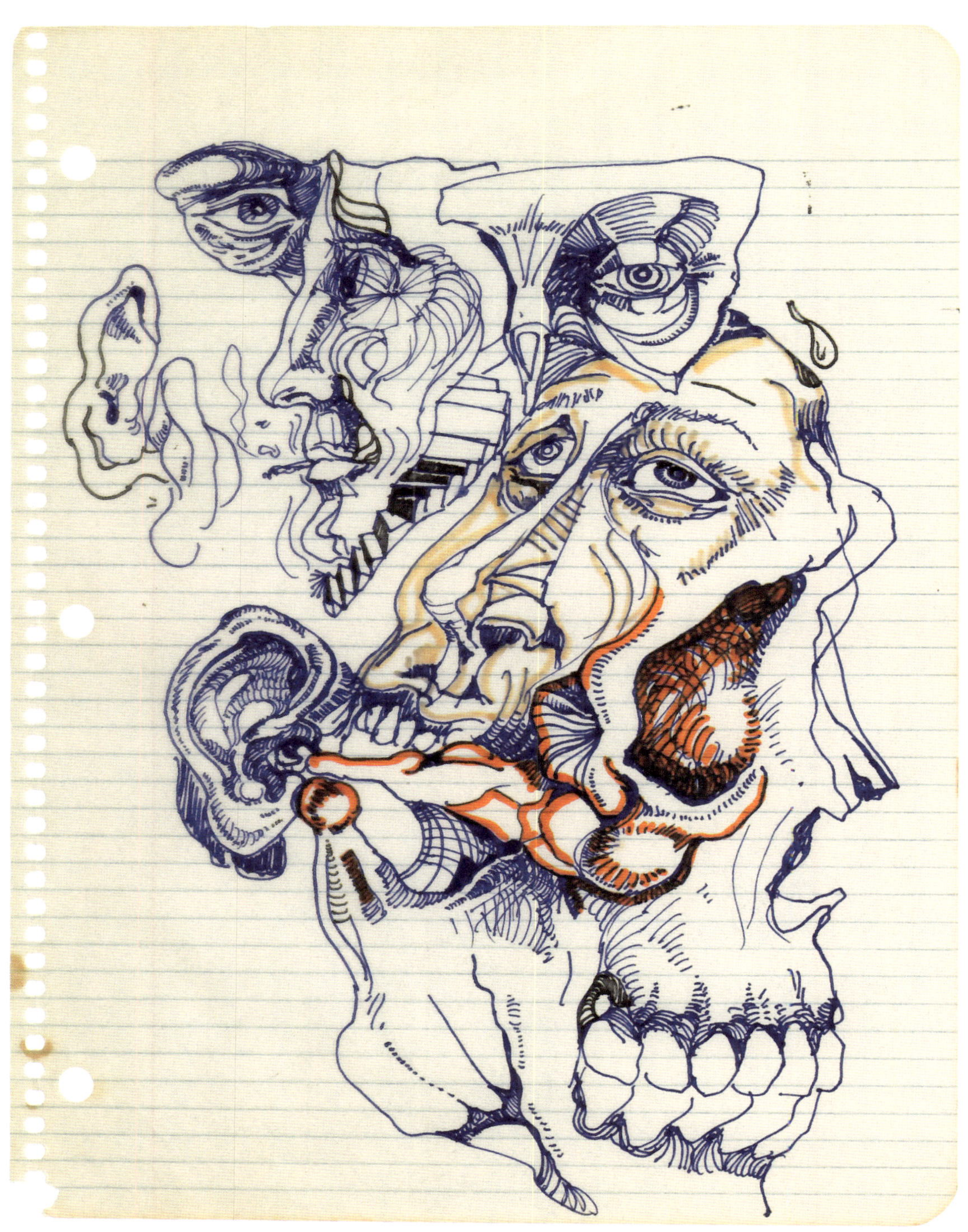

Untitled (A Mindful Skull)

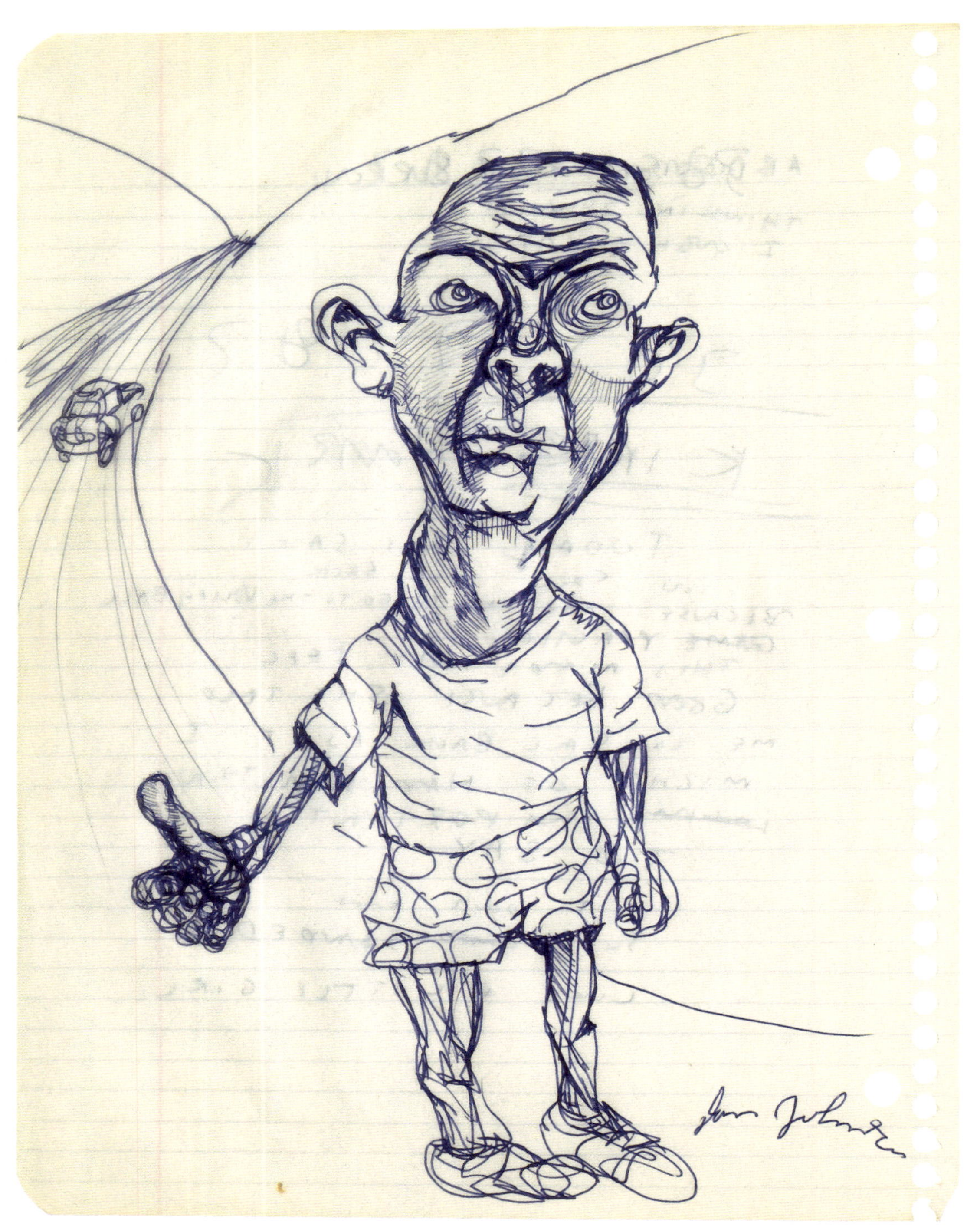

Little Hitchhiker

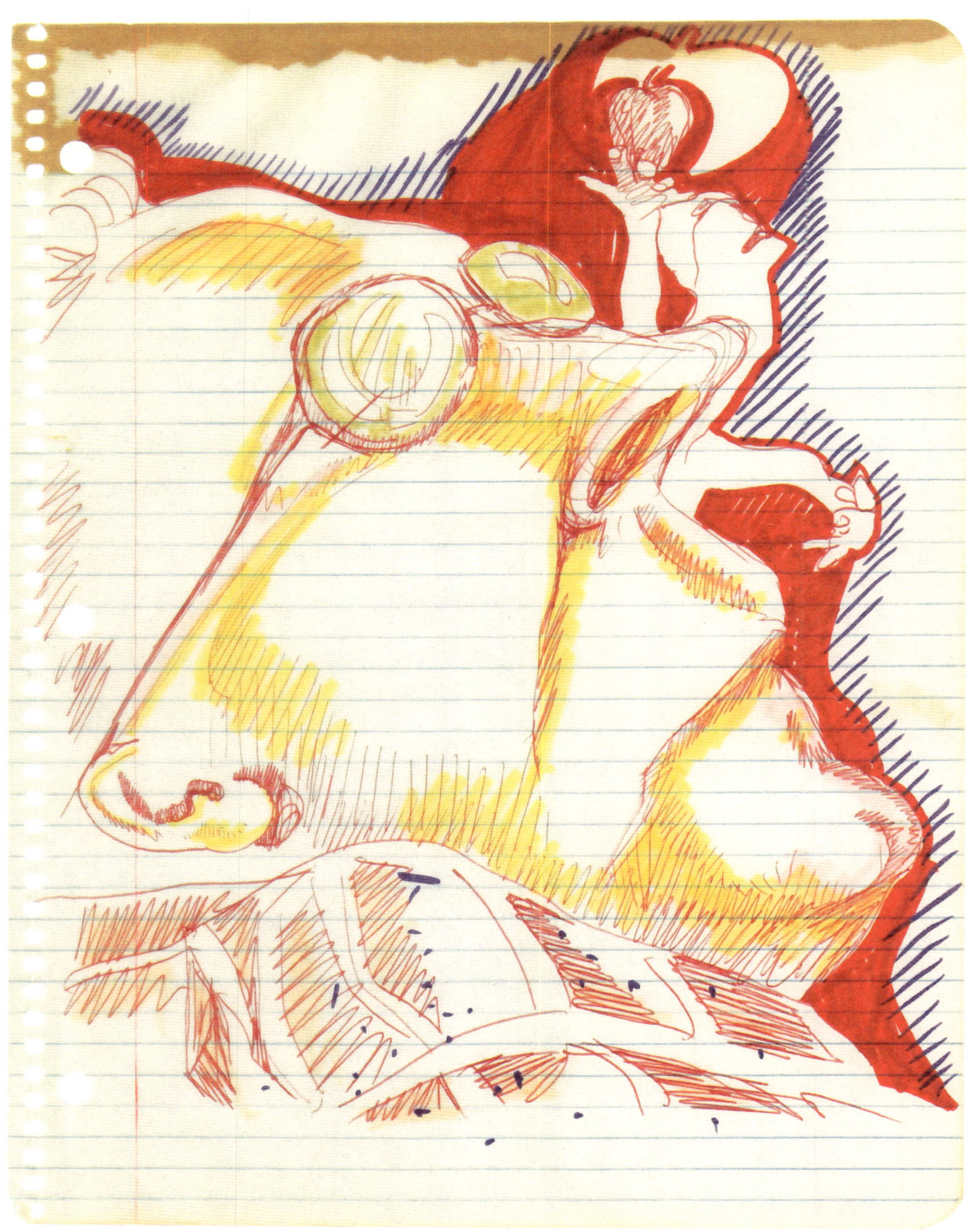

Untitled (Bill, Yellow Face)

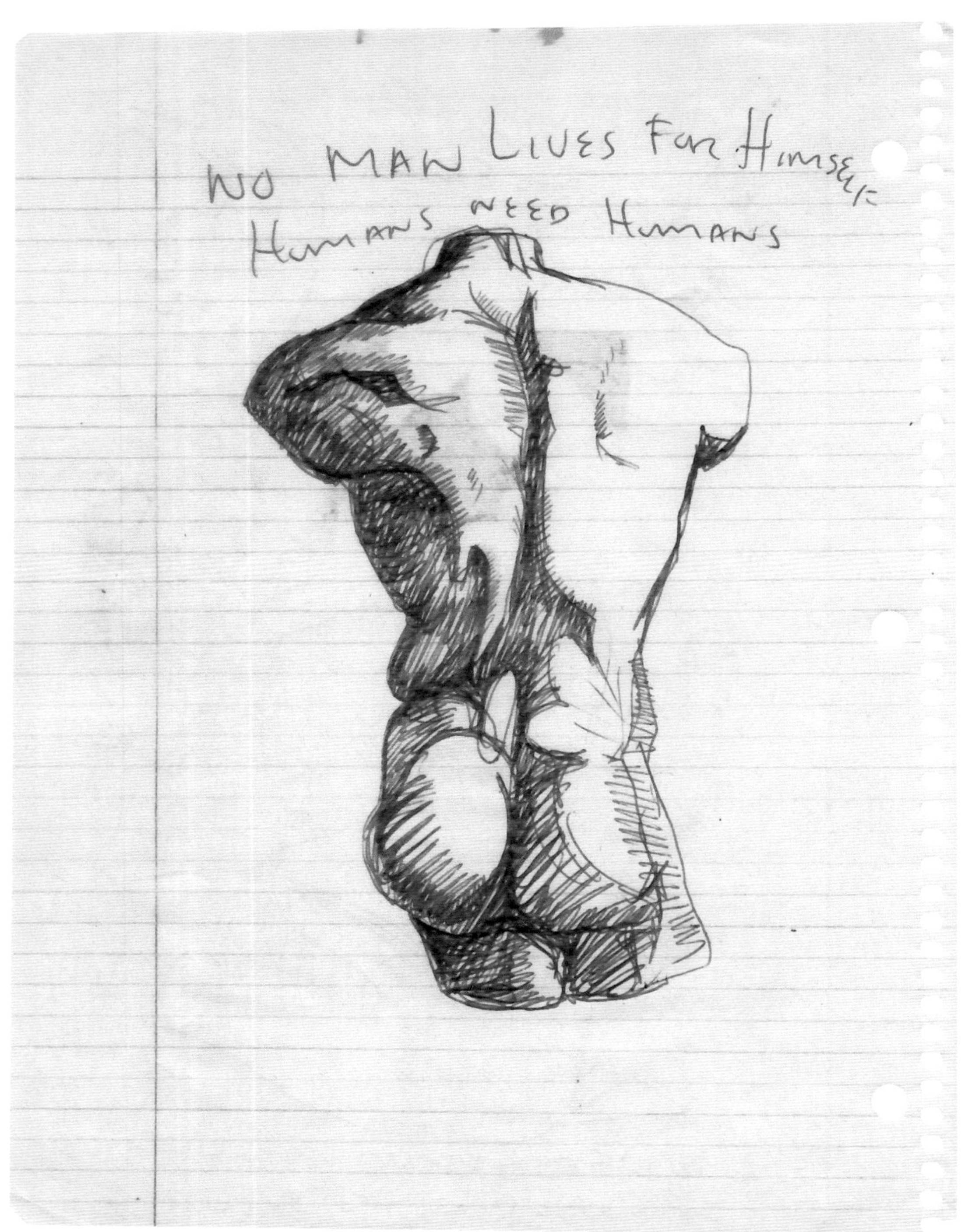

Humans Need Humans

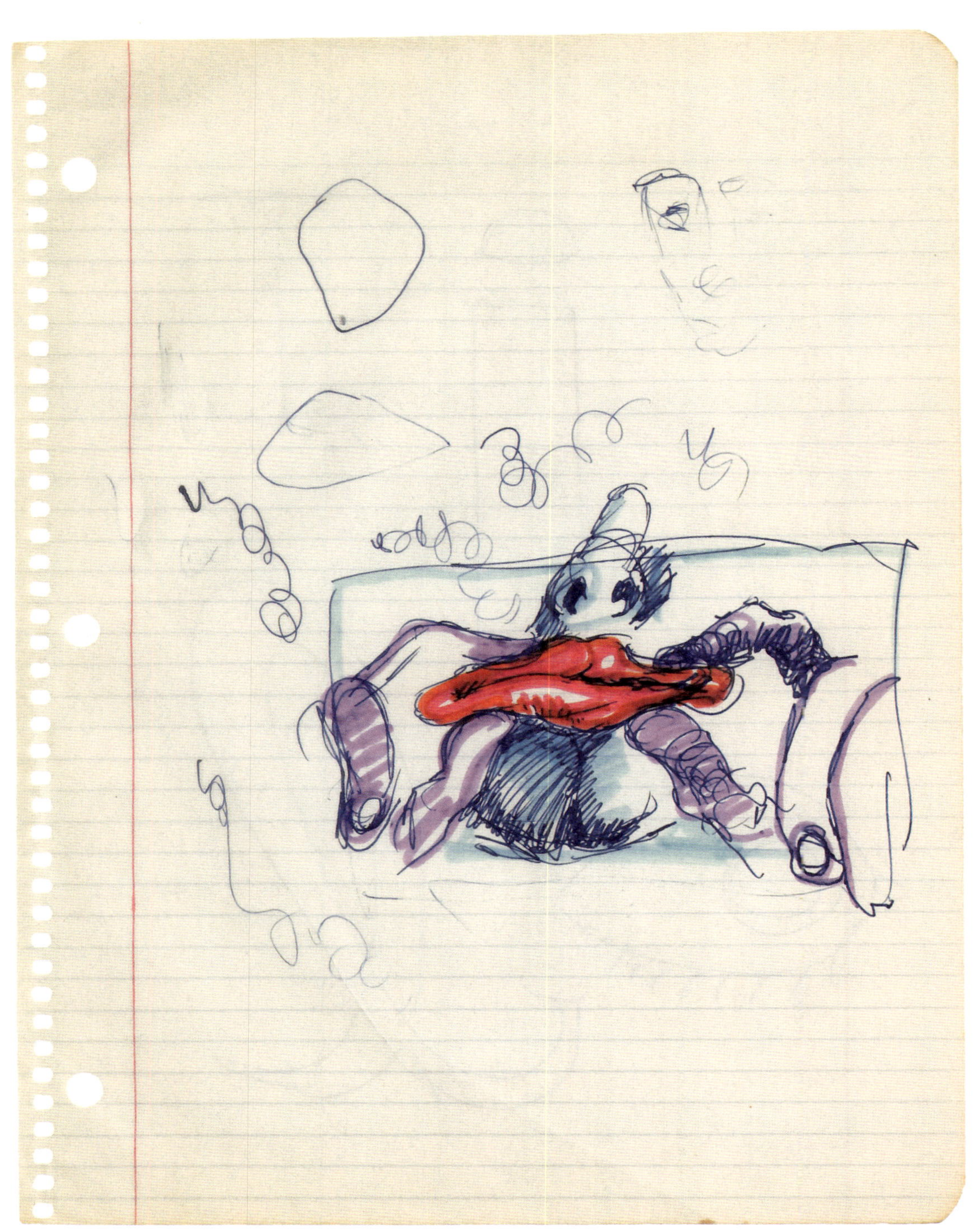

Untitled (Funny Face)

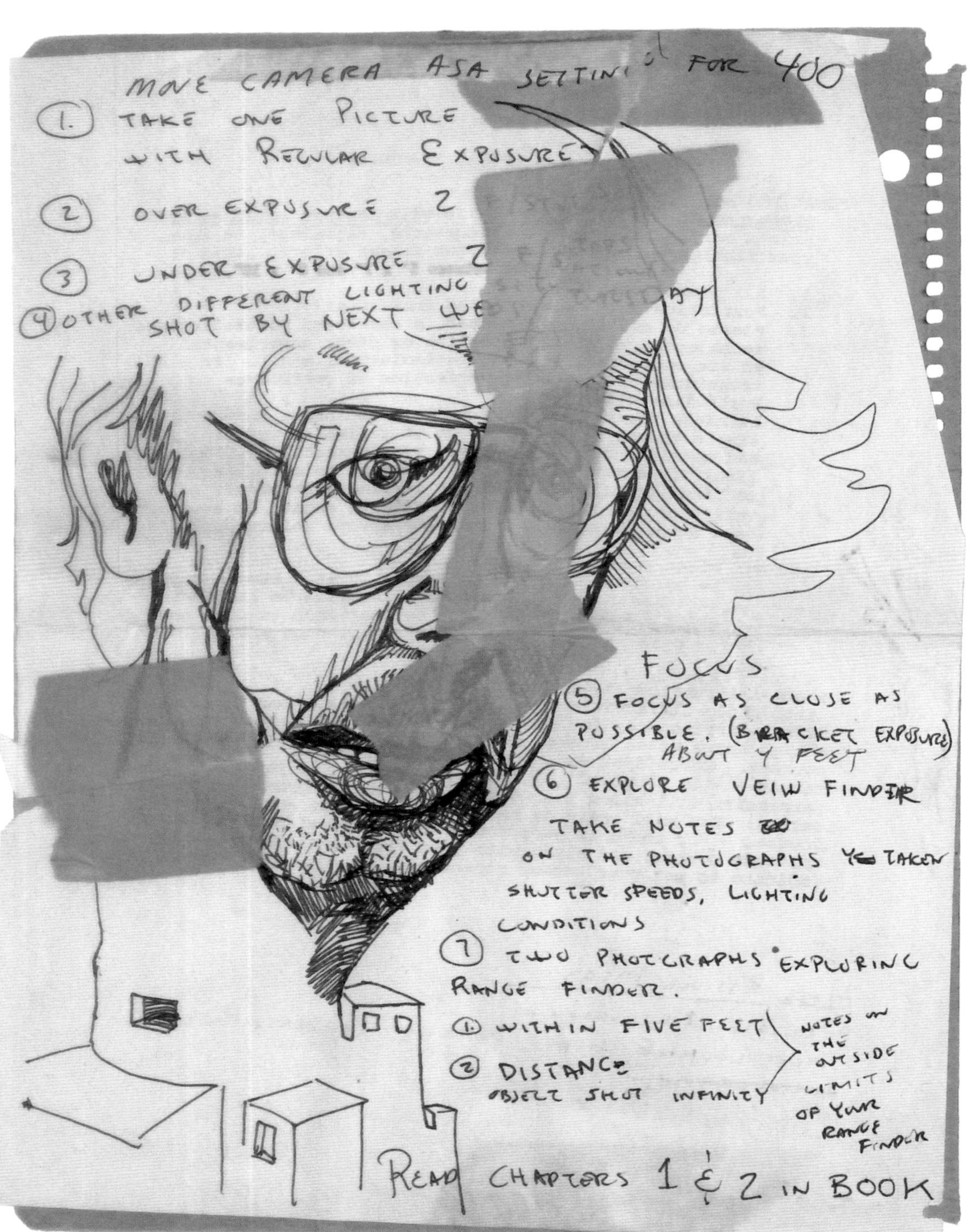

MOVE CAMERA ASA SETTIN FOR 400

(1.) TAKE ONE PICTURE
WITH REGULAR EXPOSURE

(2) OVER EXPOSURE 2

(3) UNDER EXPOSURE 2

(4) OTHER DIFFERENT LIGHTING
SHOT BY NEXT WE

FOCUS

(5) FOCUS AS CLOSE AS
POSSIBLE. (BRACKET EXPOSURE)
ABOUT 4 FEET

(6) EXPLORE VEIW FINDER

TAKE NOTES
ON THE PHOTOGRAPHS TAKEN
SHUTTER SPEEDS, LIGHTING
CONDITIONS

(7) TWO PHOTOGRAPHS EXPLORING
RANGE FINDER.

(1.) WITHIN FIVE FEET
(2) DISTANCE
OBJECT SHOT INFINITY

NOTES ON THE OUTSIDE LIMITS OF YOUR RANGE FINDER

READ CHAPTERS 1 & 2 IN BOOK

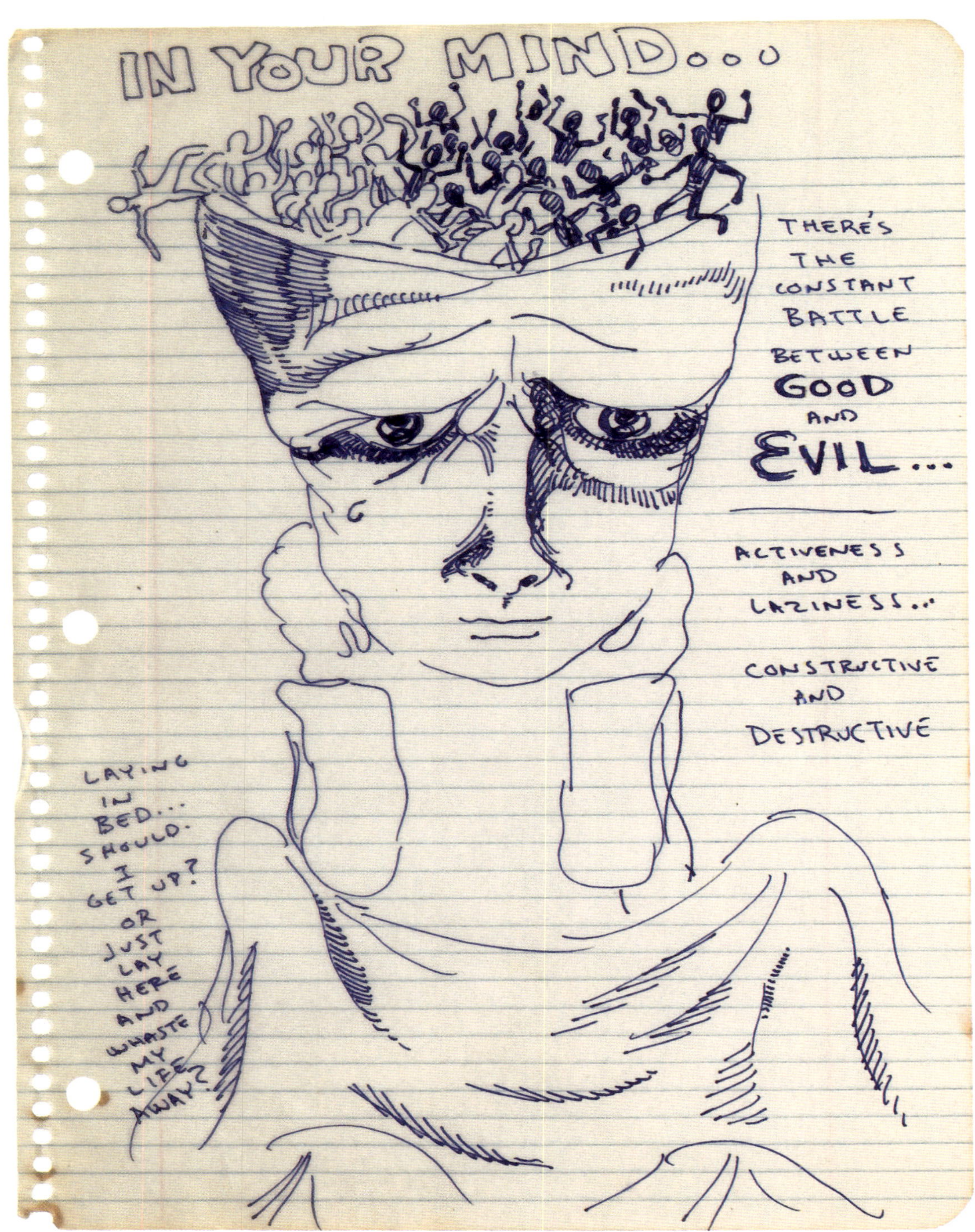

The Constant Battle

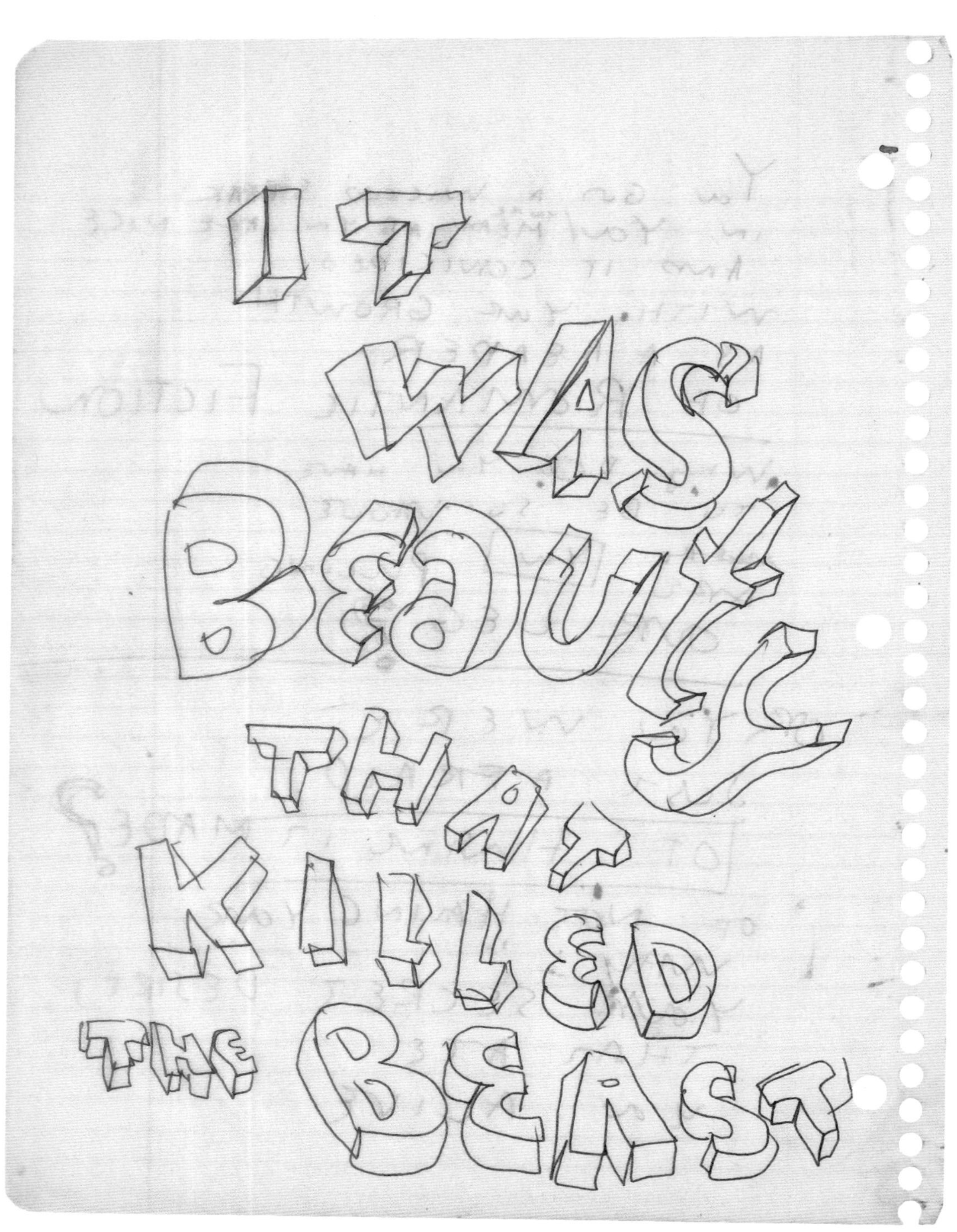

It Was Beauty That Killed the Beast

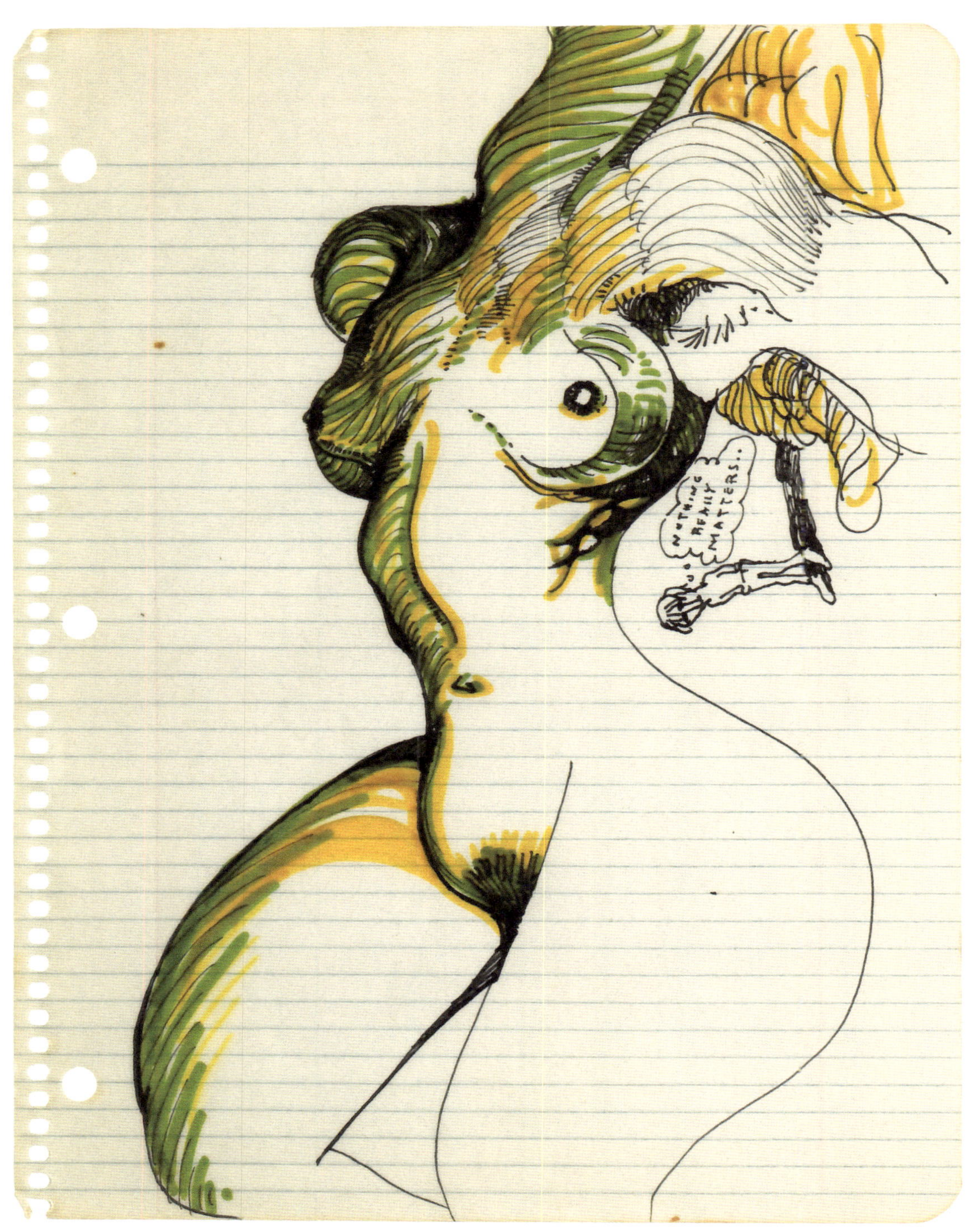

Nothing Really Matters

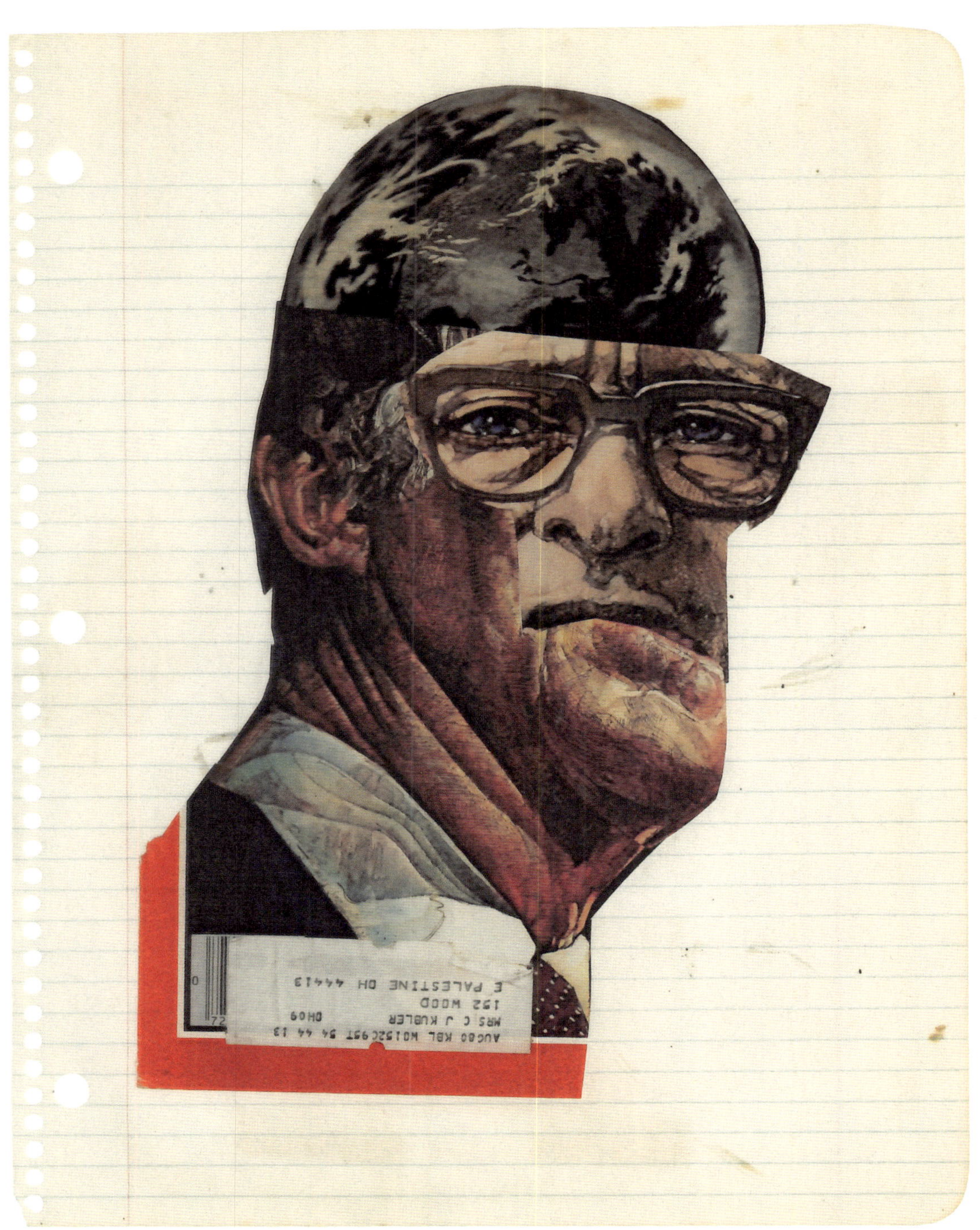

Palestine OH

I discovered Daniel the way I discover most of my favorite music: by pretending I knew who he was when someone I thought was cool asked me if I liked Daniel Johnston, and then listening at the earliest possible opportunity to make it not a lie.

In a way, I did already know him. His music had indirectly influenced me through the indie musicians I loved who had been influenced by him: from his confessional lyrics, to his punk rock acoustic guitar playing and his childlike voice. I was already a fan.

I immediately bought some of his drawings online. I got some of his early cassettes too, which he made by pressing record on a tape player, playing the songs in the order he liked, drawing some cover art, and then, when he wanted to make another one, just doing it all over again. Each one a completely unique recording and artifact.

I wolfed down all his music, connecting especially deeply with a song called "Peek a Boo." Every verse is a stream-of-consciousness chapter in his life.

Sometimes the words don't rhyme, as if the meaning of the words is so important that the whole thing stops being a song for a second. The last verse goes:

You can listen to these songs,
Have a good time and walk away.
But for me it's not that easy.
I have to live these songs forever.

I learned it on guitar and played it every time I had a show in Austin. When I got to the last verse, I'd almost completely stop playing guitar. I wanted to make sure people could hear the words. A confidence I didn't yet have singing my own songs. "Peek a Boo" made me want to write something myself one day I'd want to force people to hear.

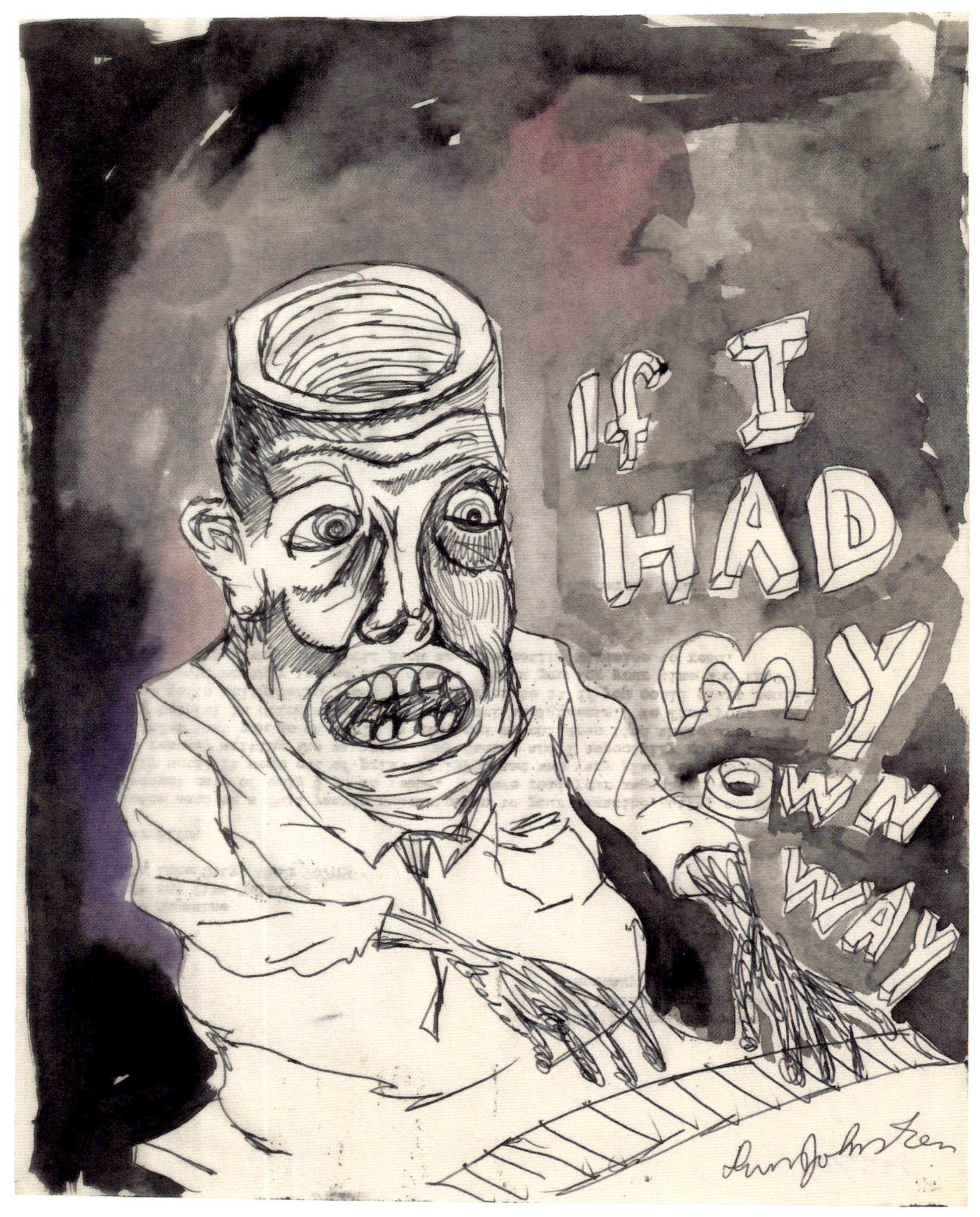

If I Had My Own Way

V.
My Pen Sits Lonely
1960s–1970s

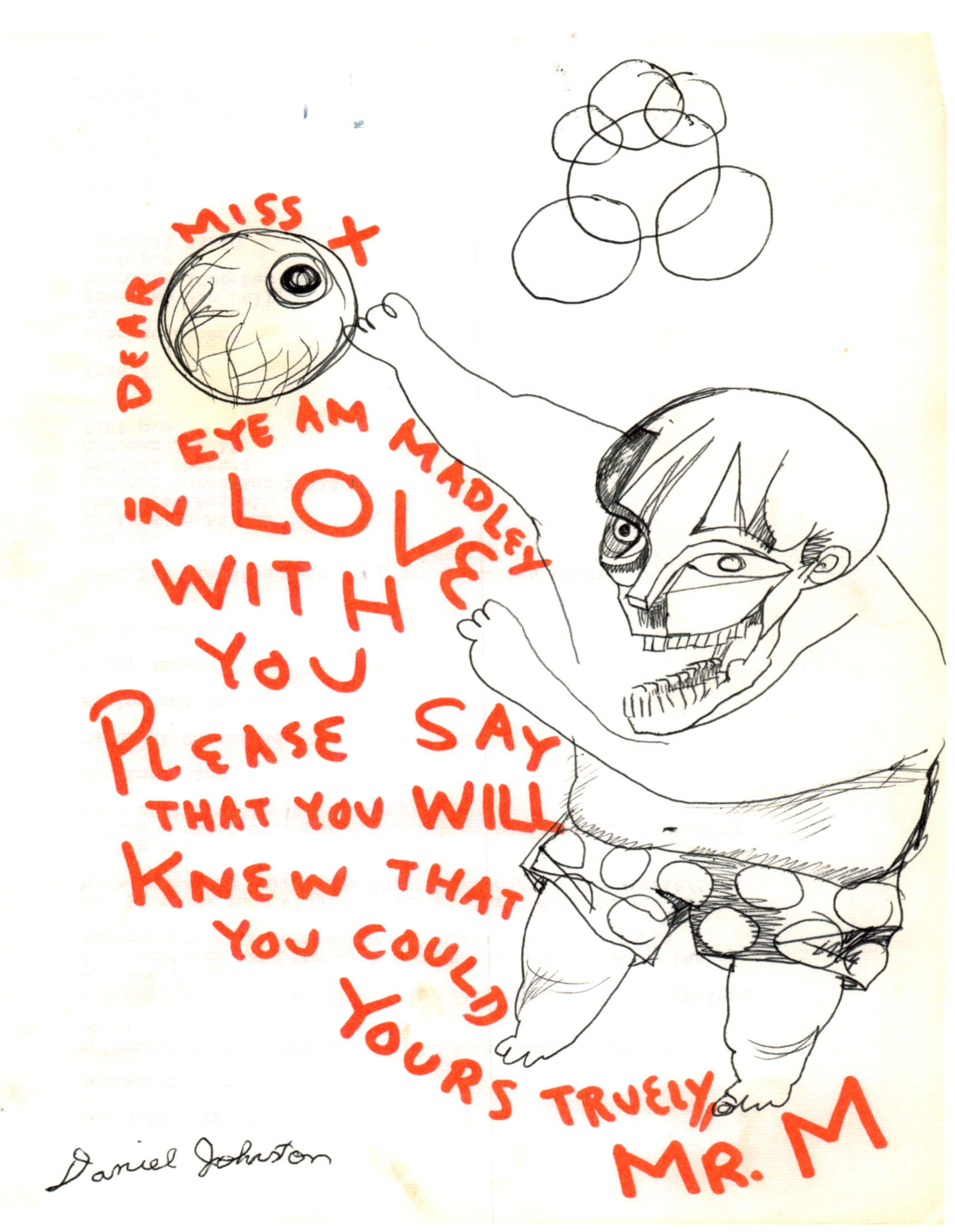
DEAR MISS X
EYE AM MADLEY
IN LOVE
WITH
YOU
PLEASE SAY
THAT YOU WILL
KNEW THAT
YOU COULD
YOURS TRUELY
MR. M
Daniel Johnston

Dear Miss X

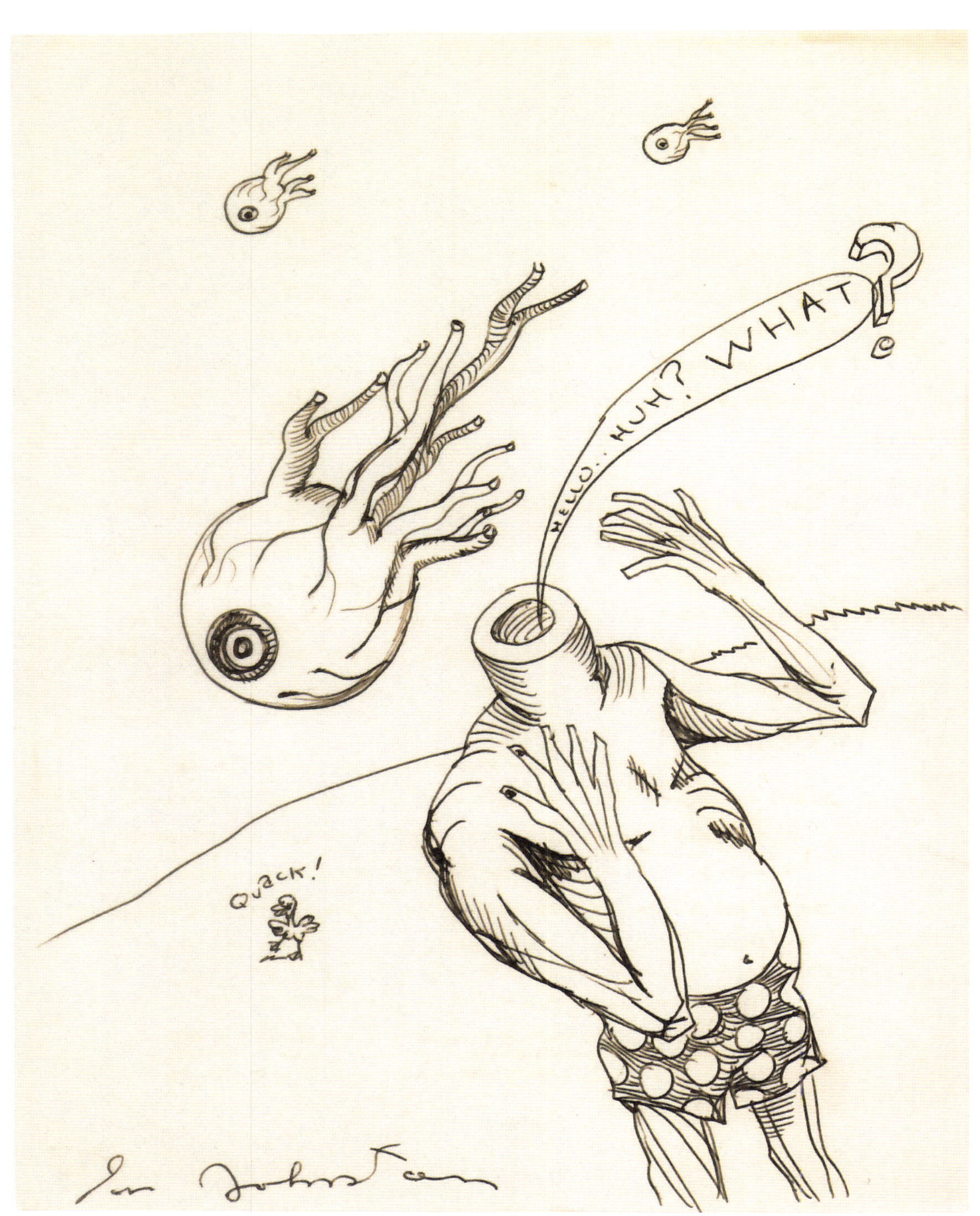

Hello . . . Huh? What?

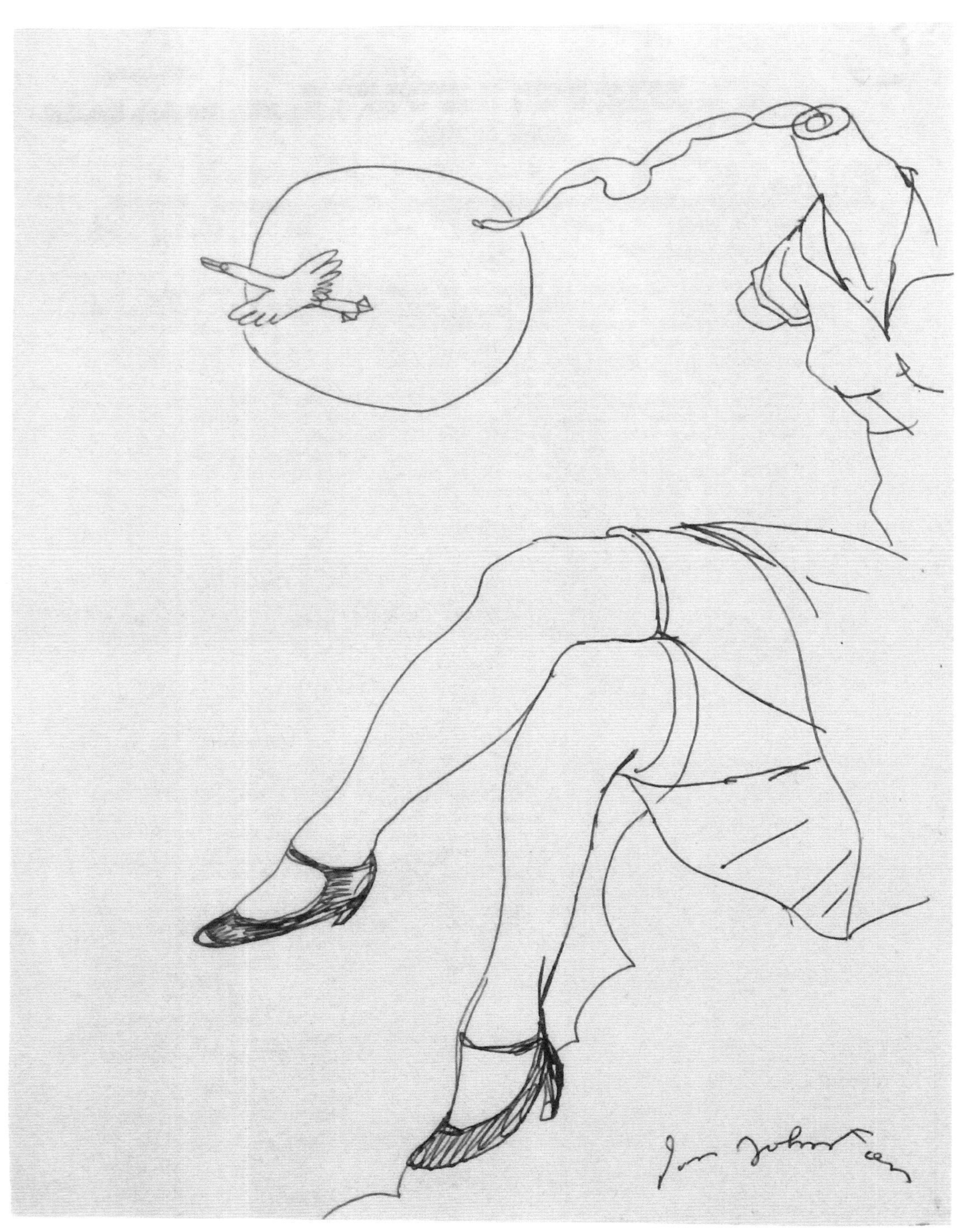

Untitled (Lady Bird)

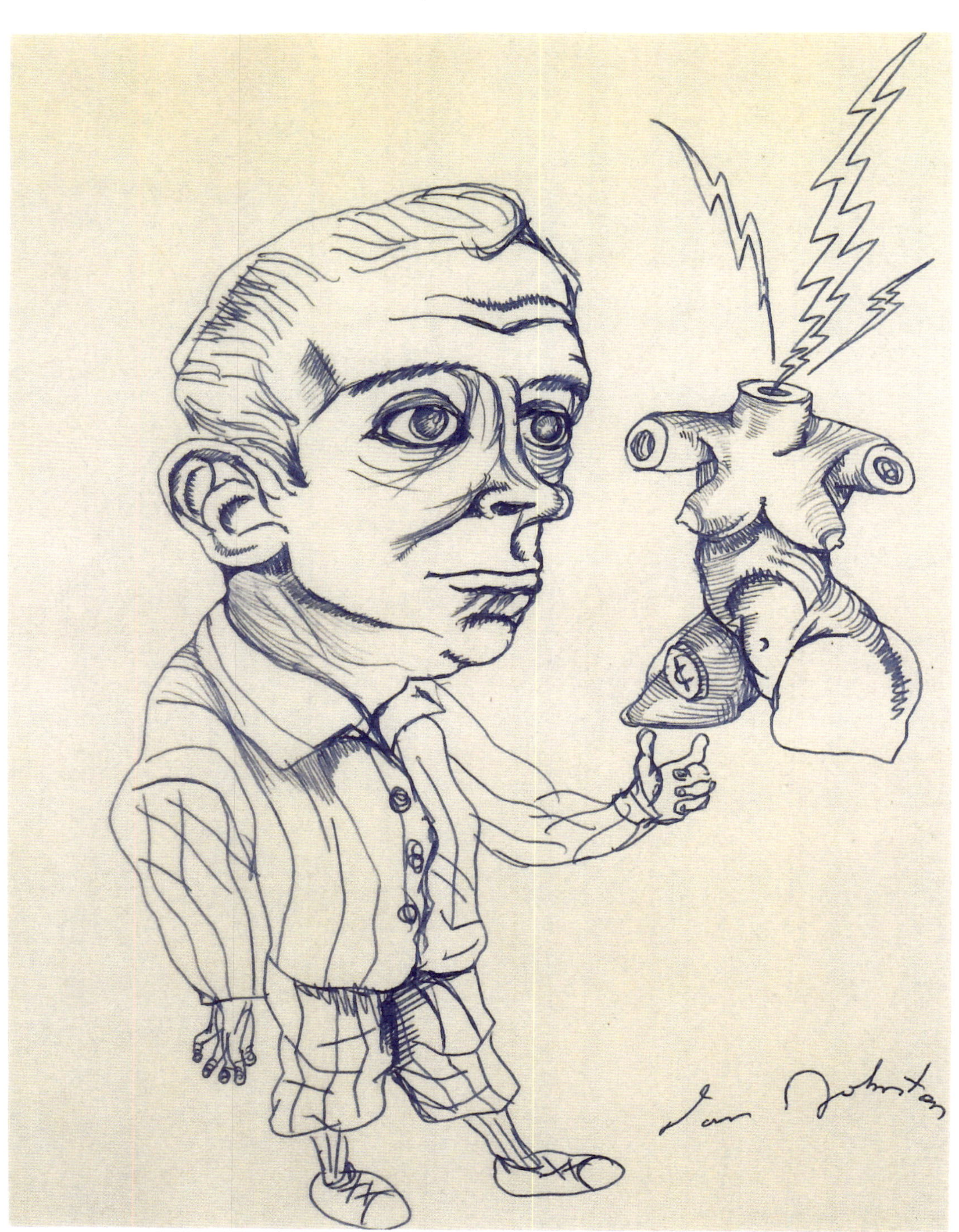

Untitled (Coin Toss)

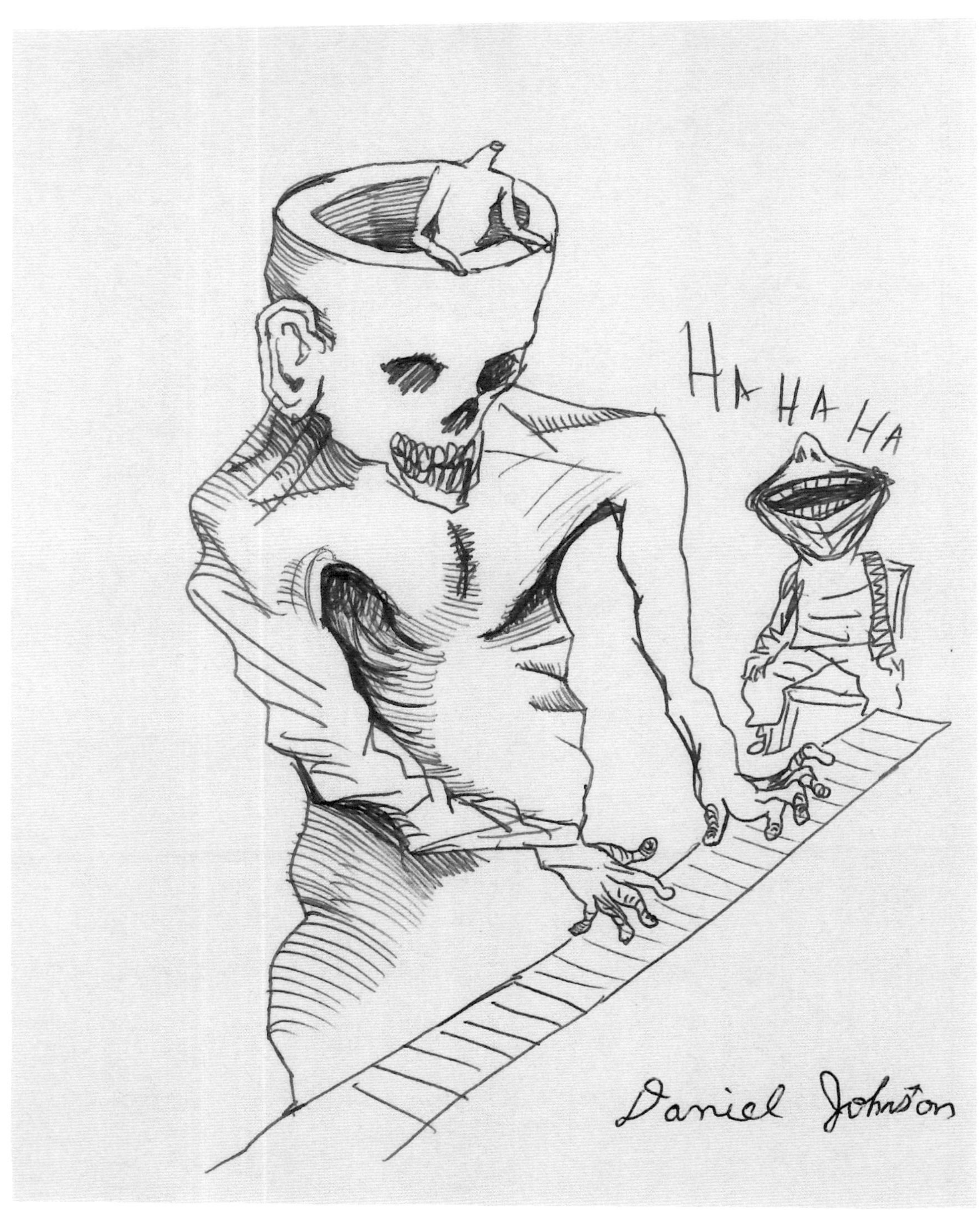

Ha Ha Ha

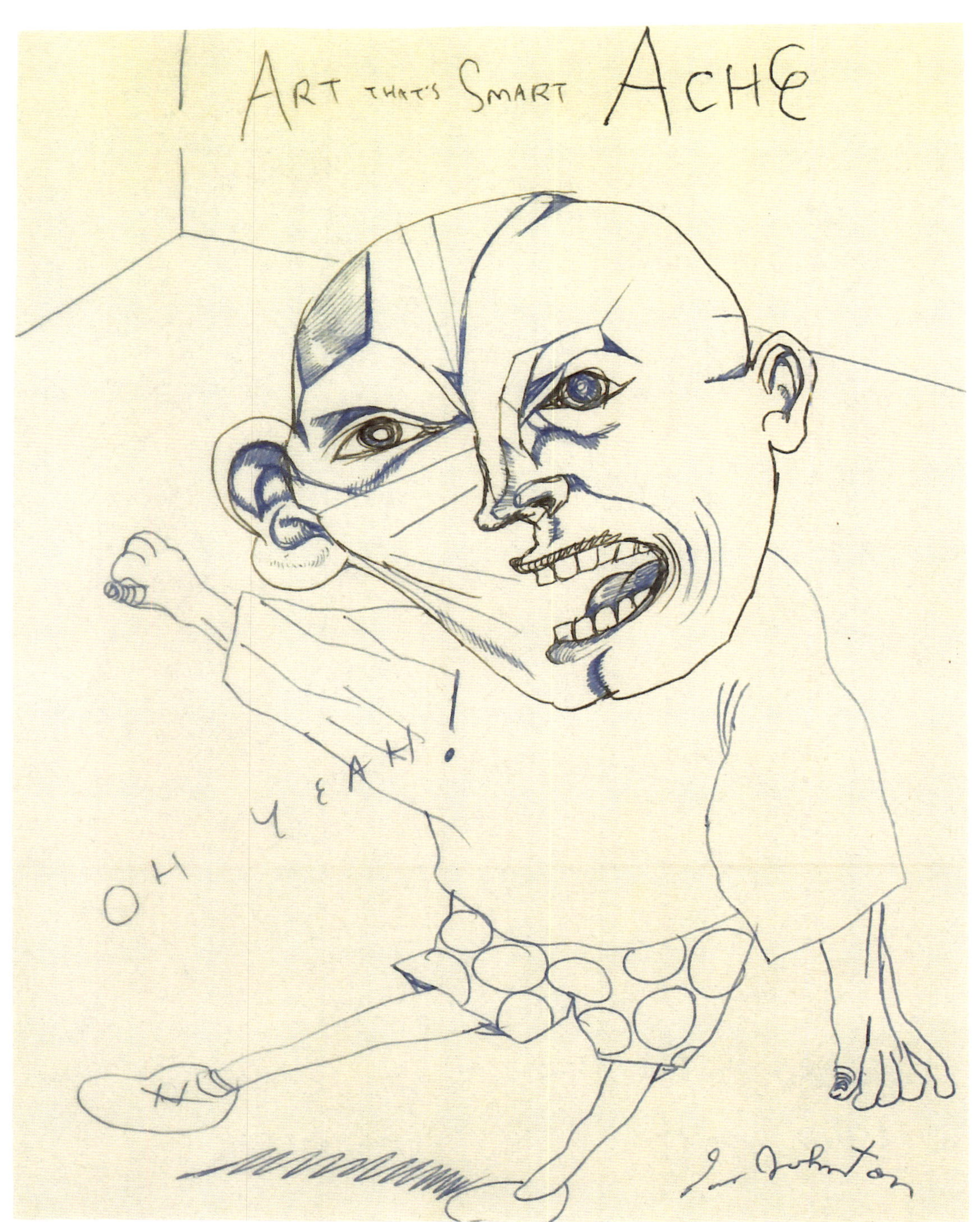

Art That's Smart

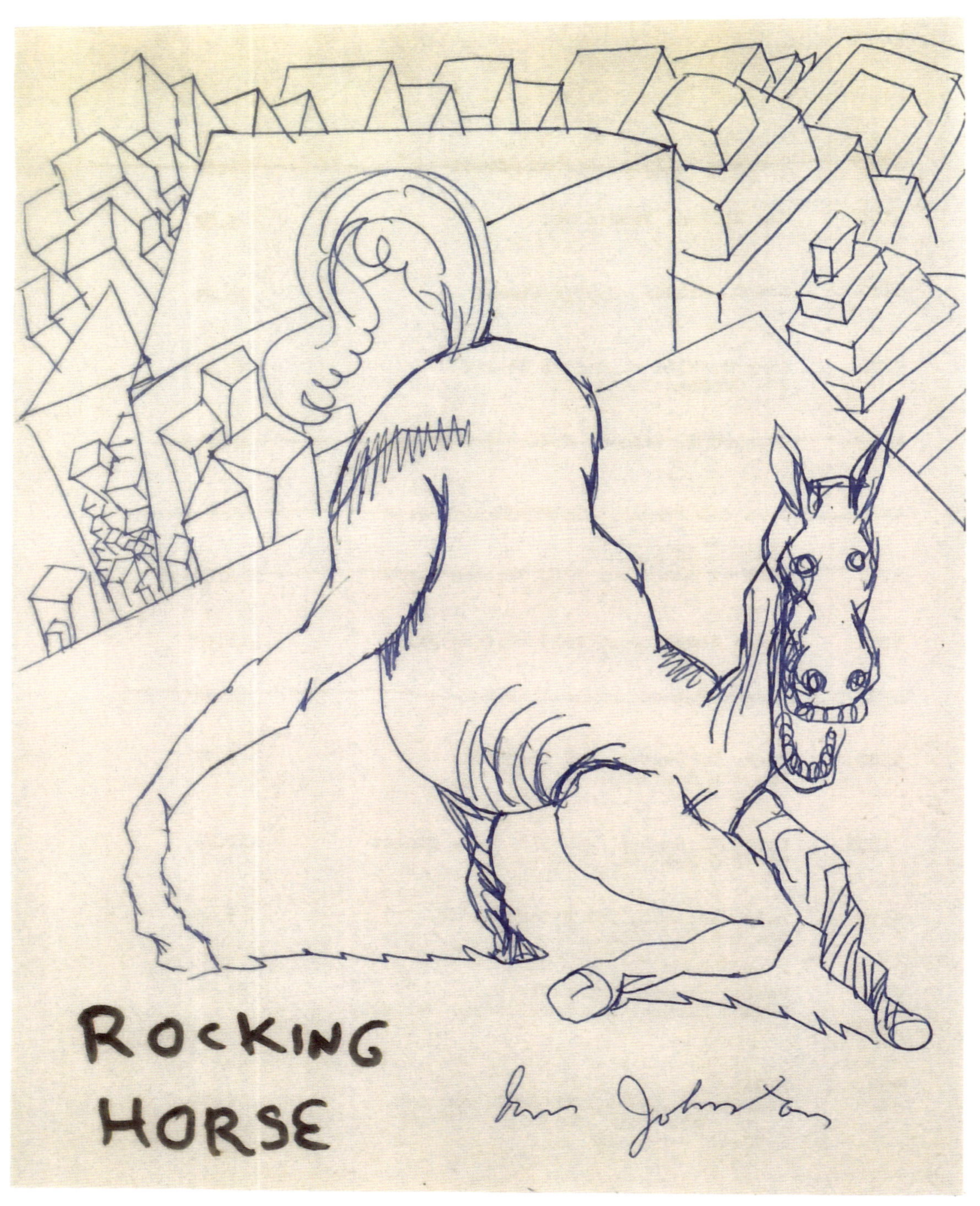

Rocking Horse

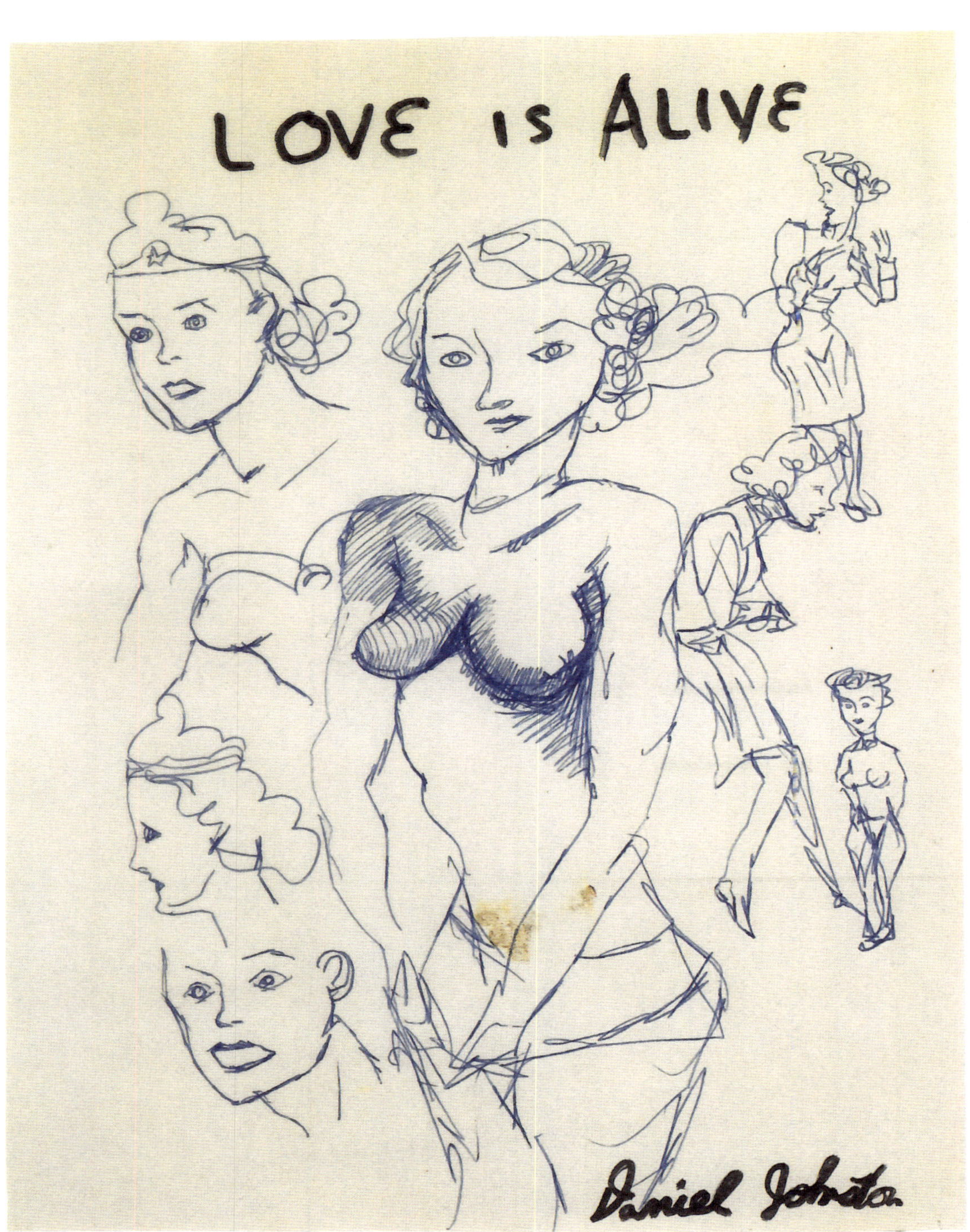

Love Is Alive

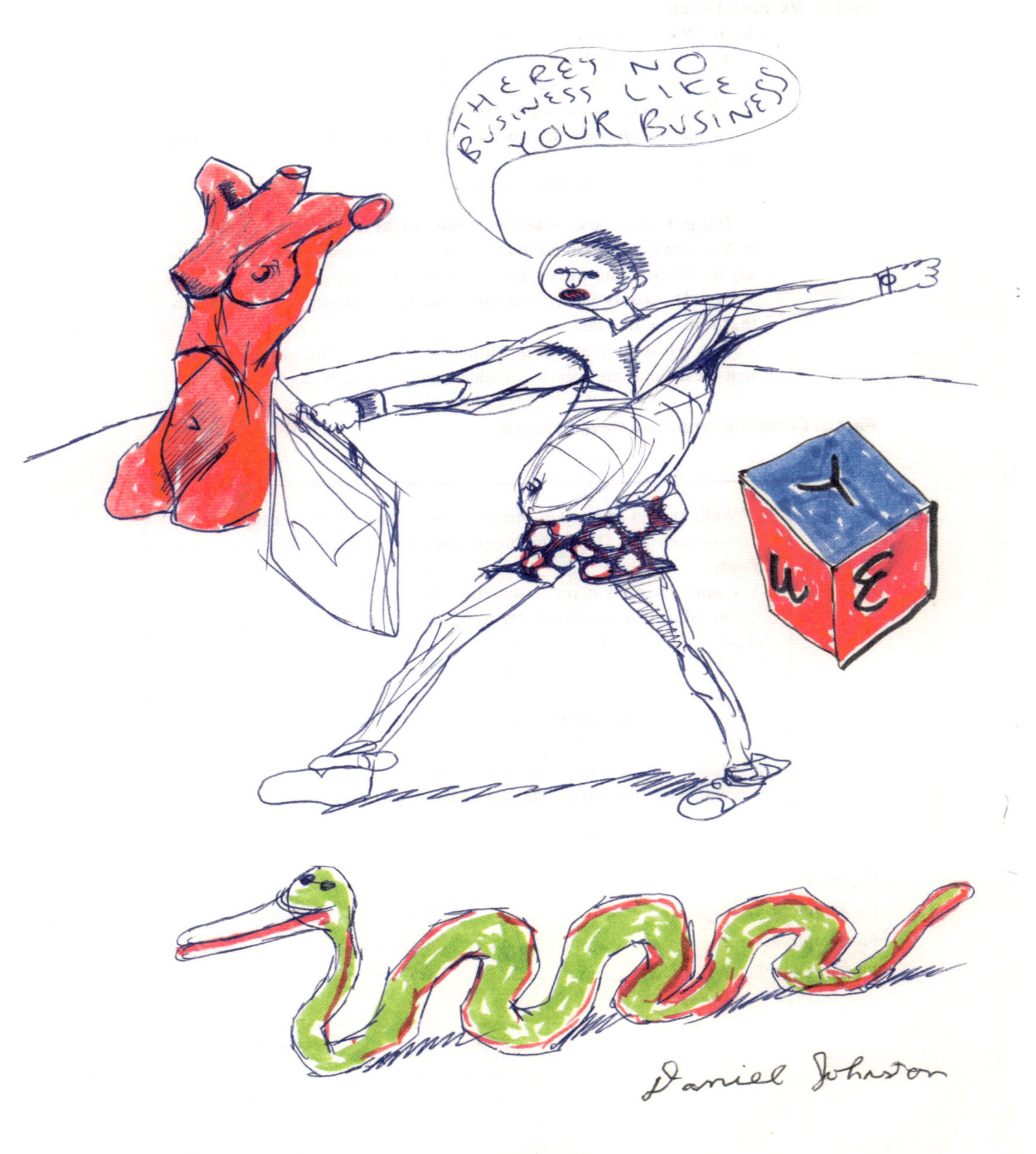

No Business Like Your Business

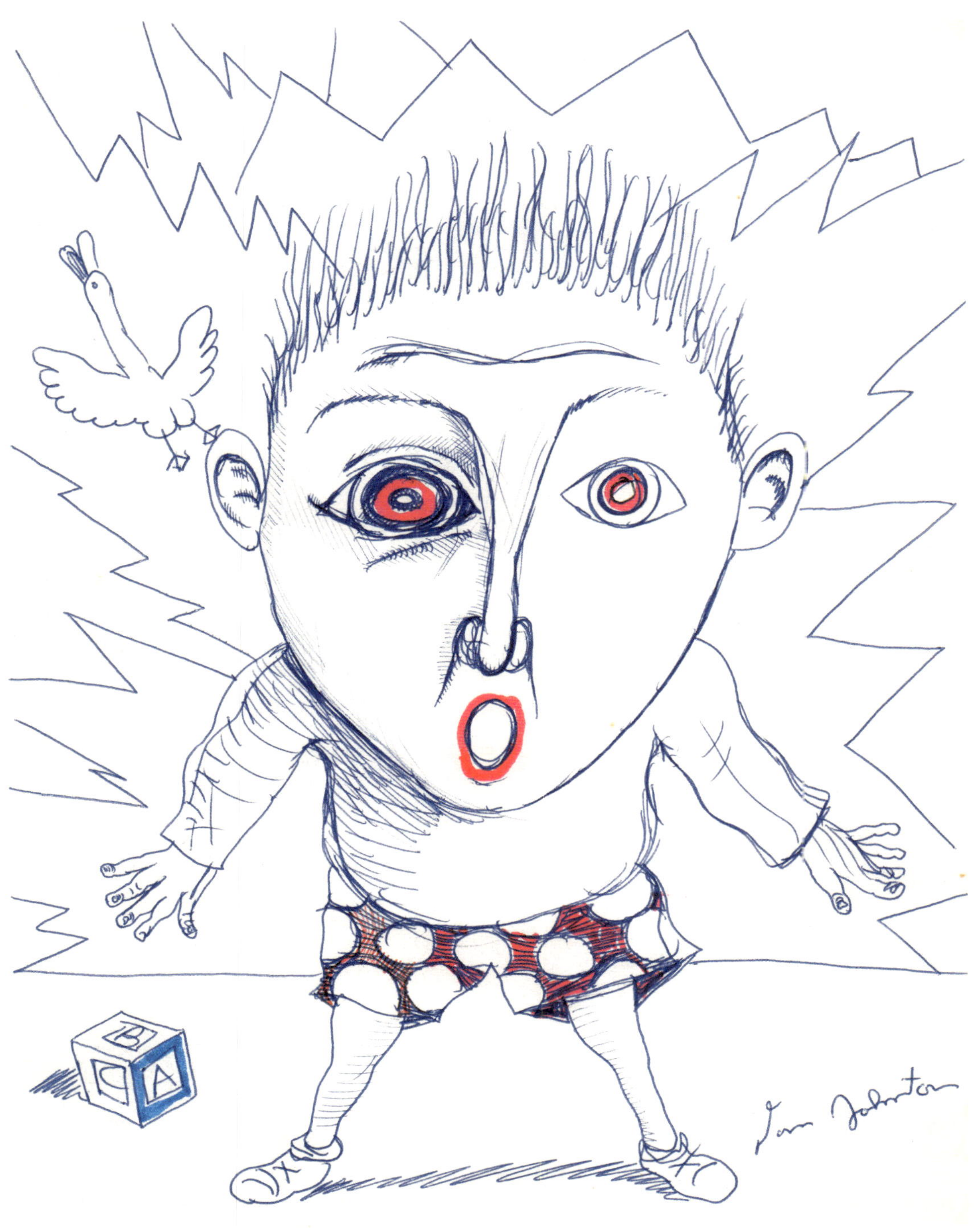

Untitled (Shocking)

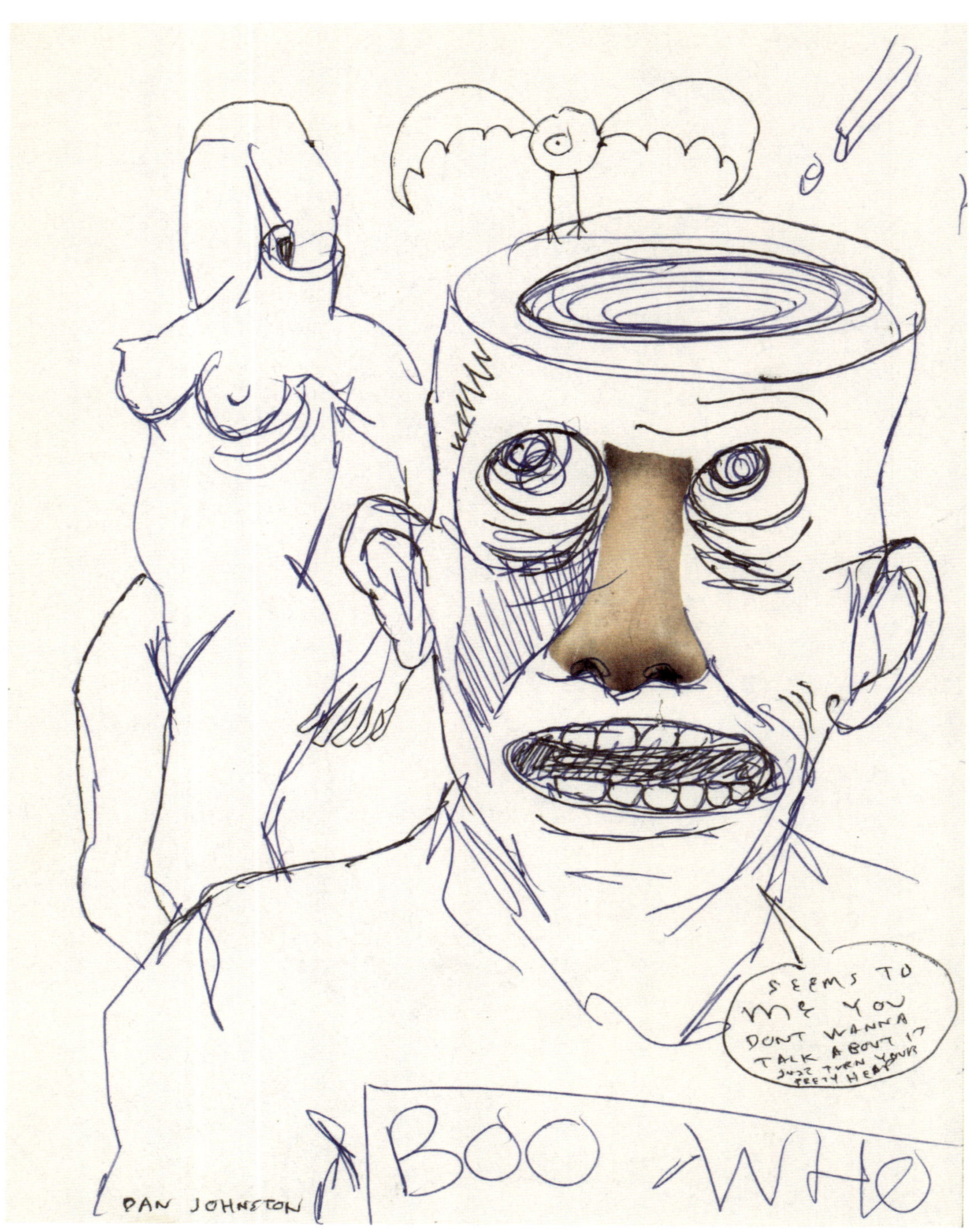
SEEMS TO
ME YOU
DONT WANNA
TALK ABOUT IT
JUST TURN YOUR
PRETTY HEAD
BOO WHO
DAN JOHNSTON

Boo Who

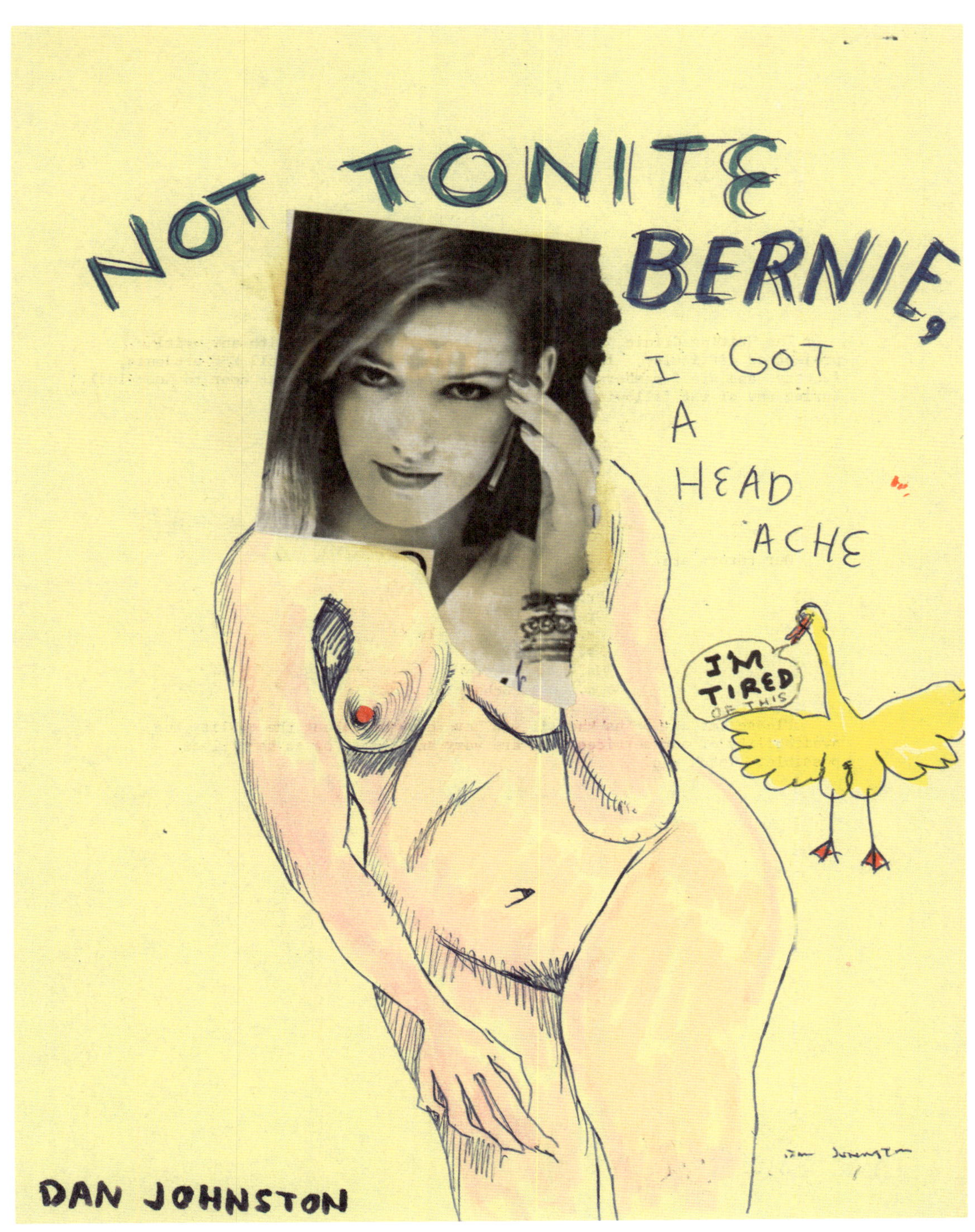

Not Tonite Bernie

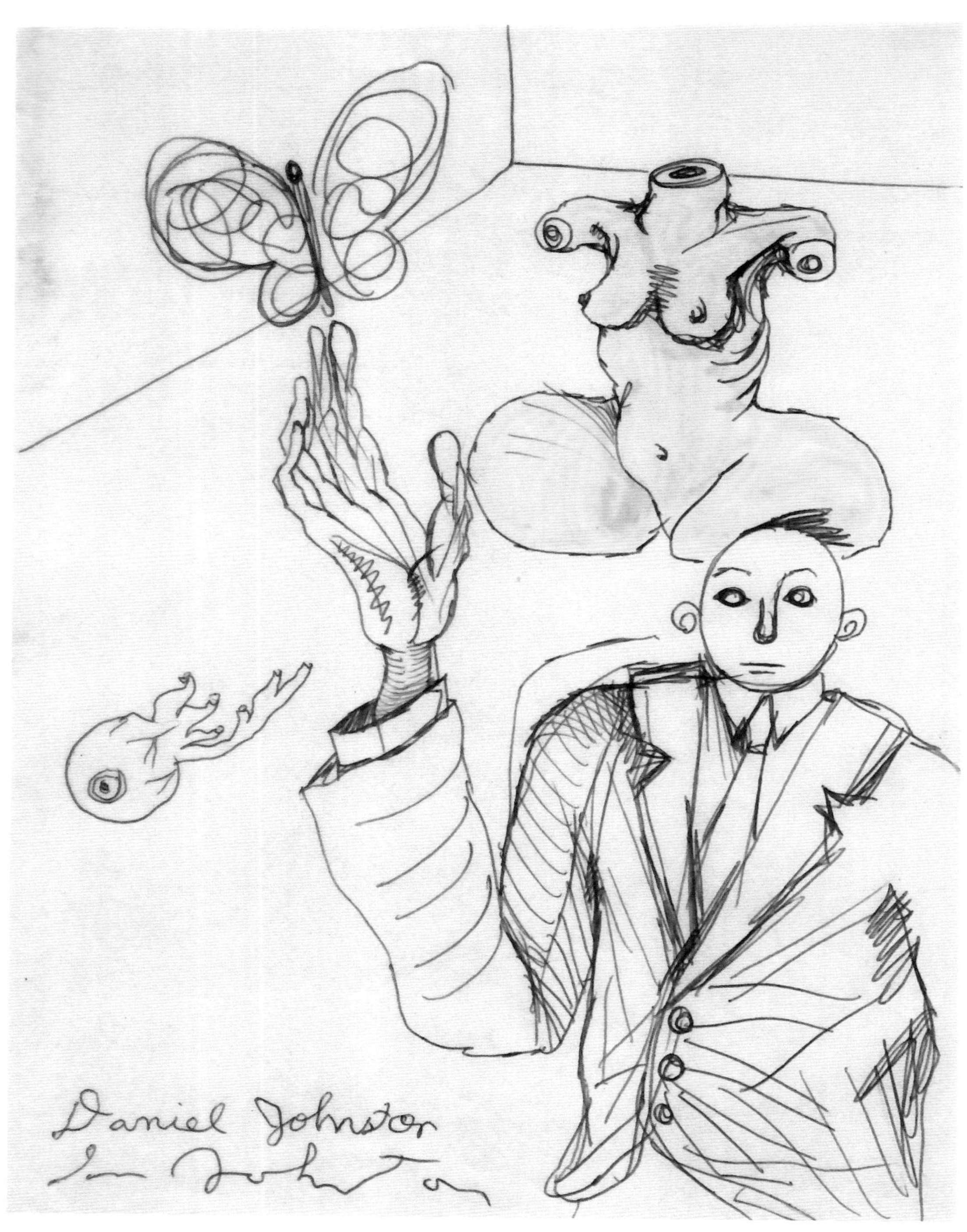

Untitled (Butterfly)

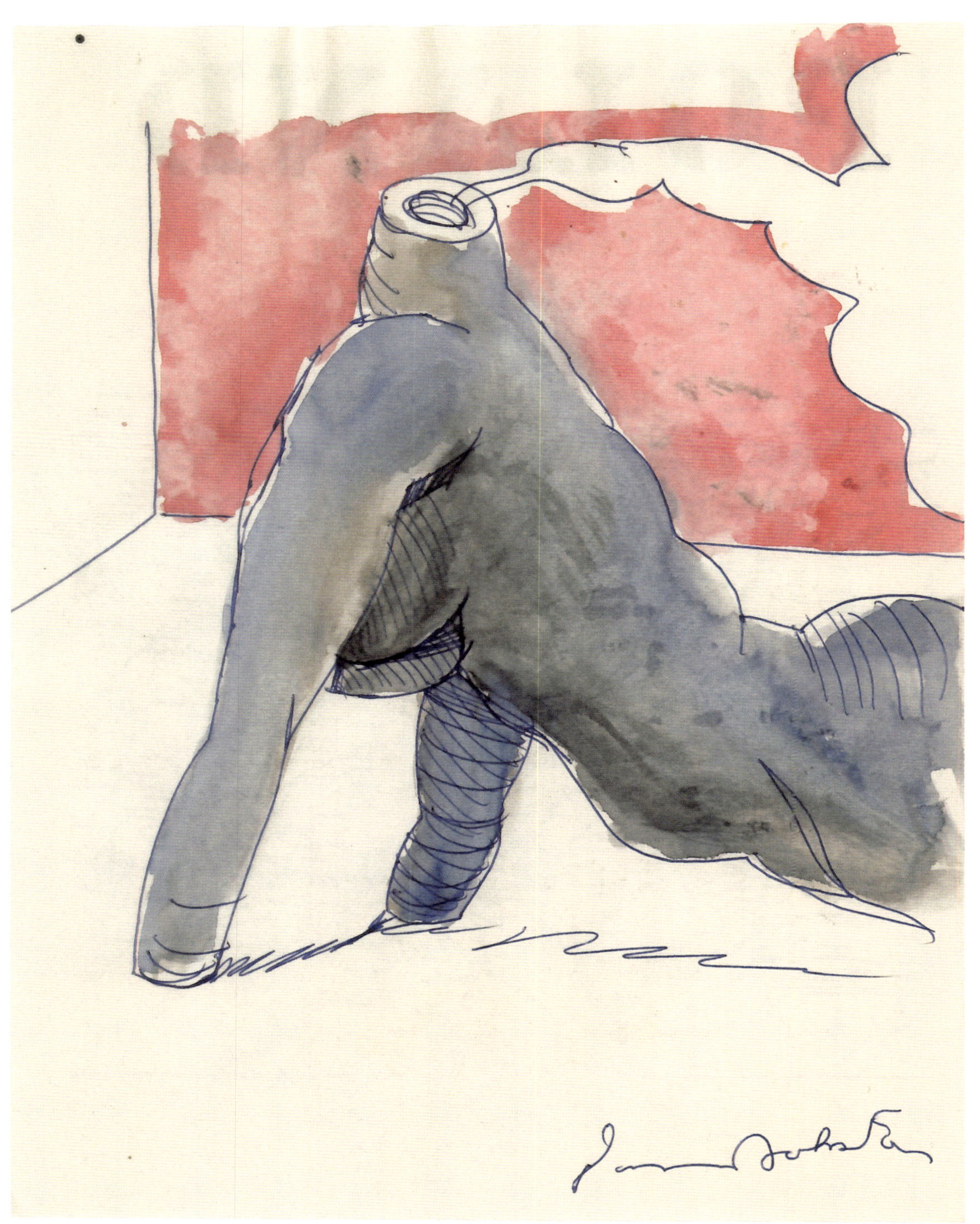

Untitled (Blue Torso)

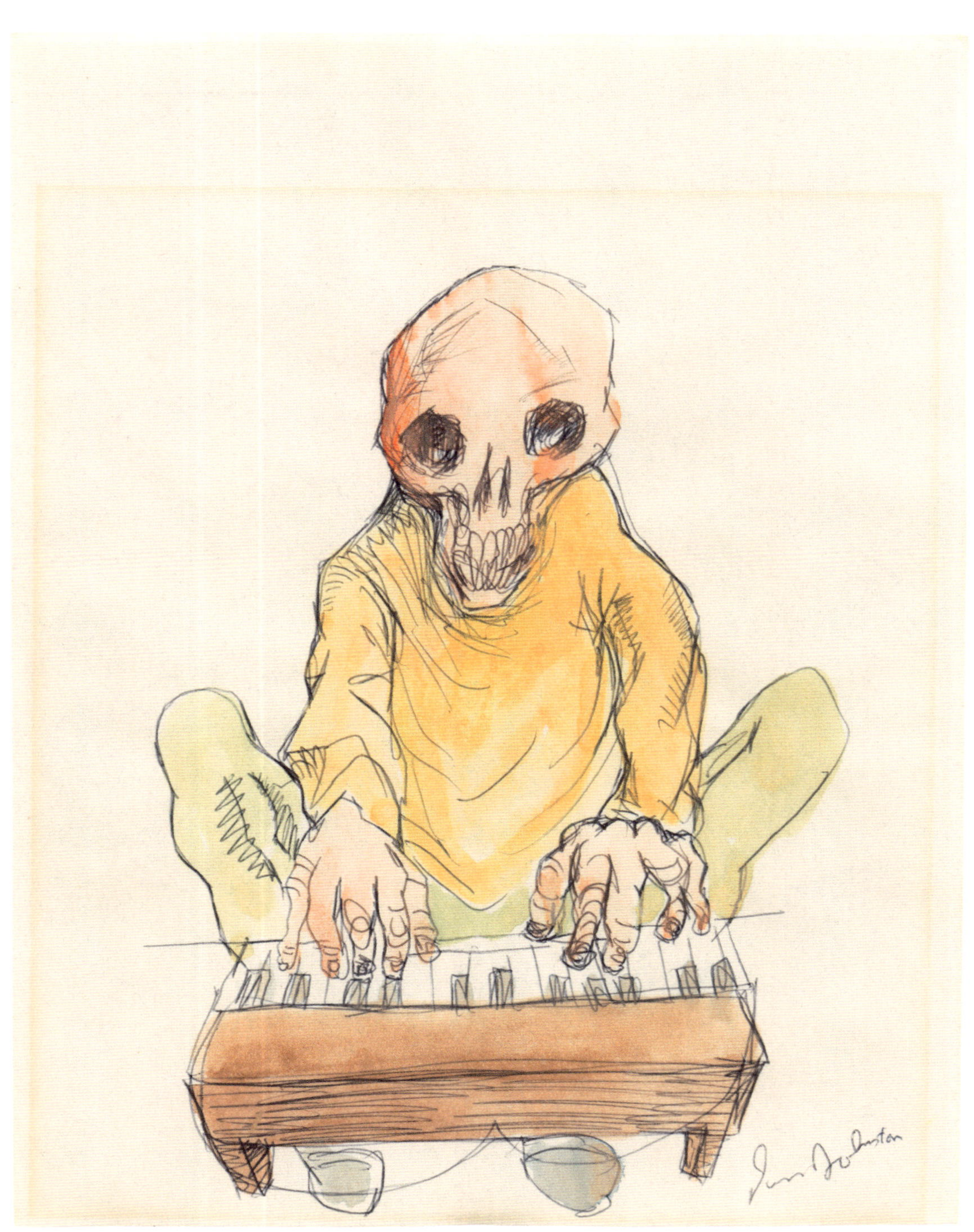

Untitled (Chord Organ)

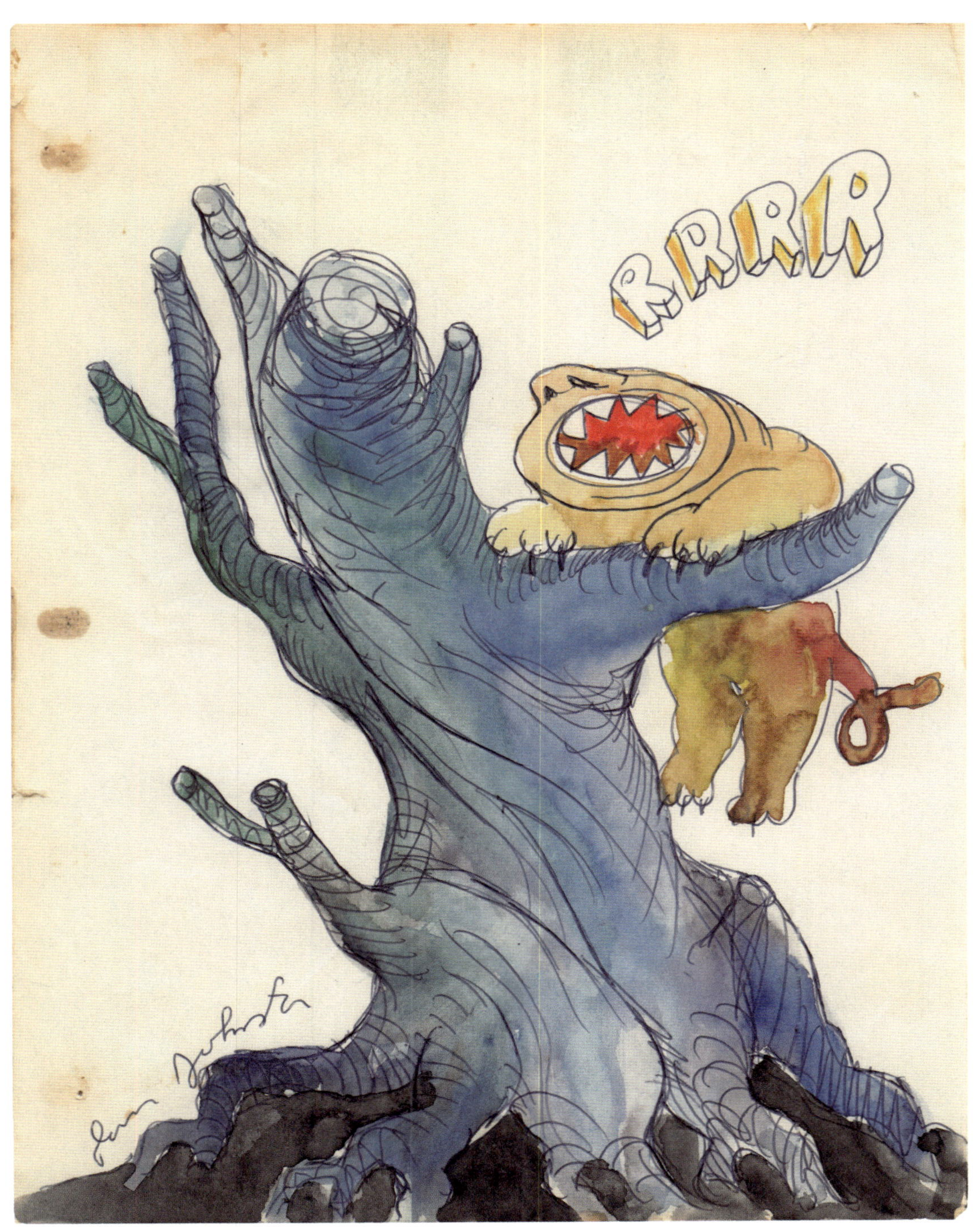

RRRR

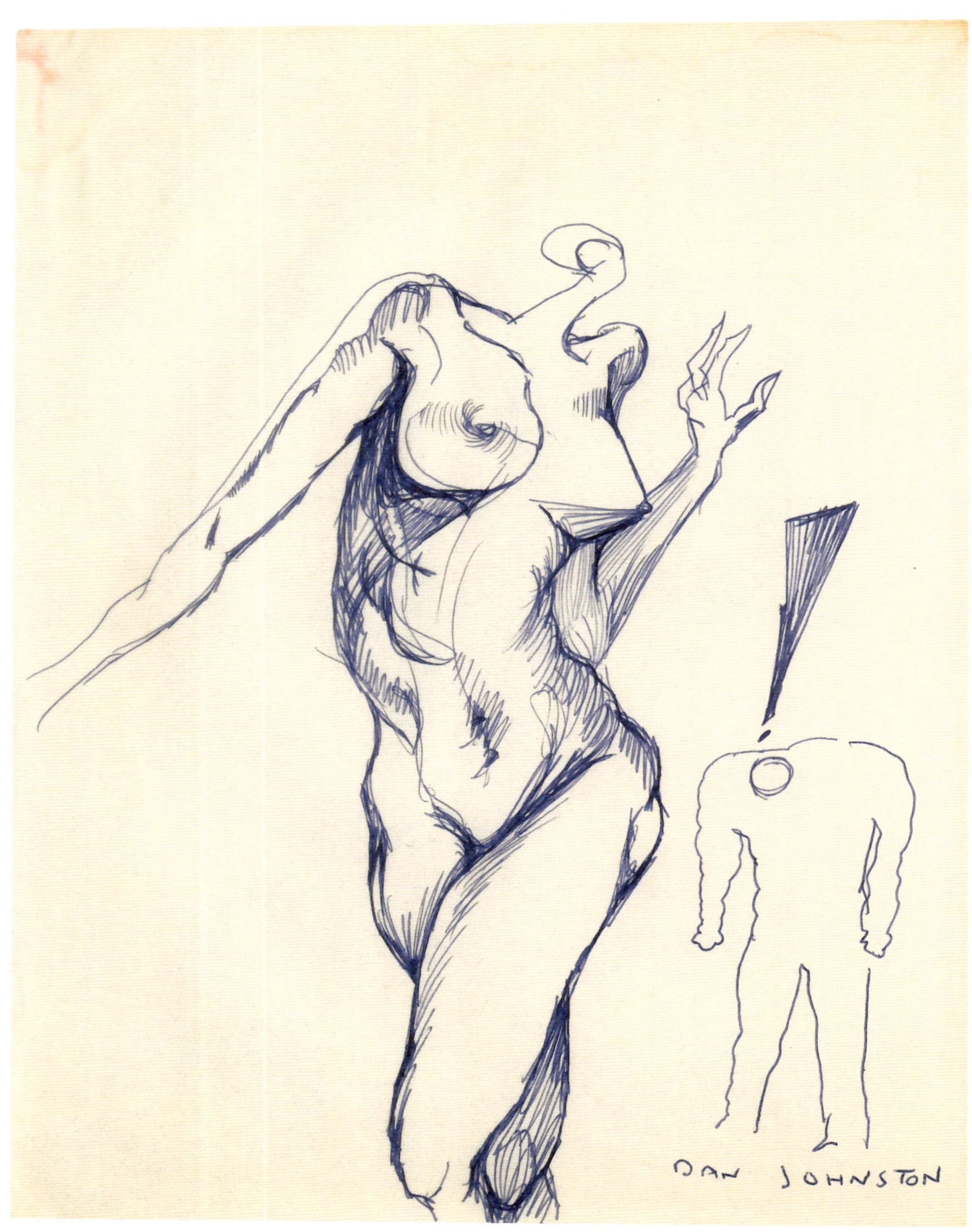

Untitled (Nude I)

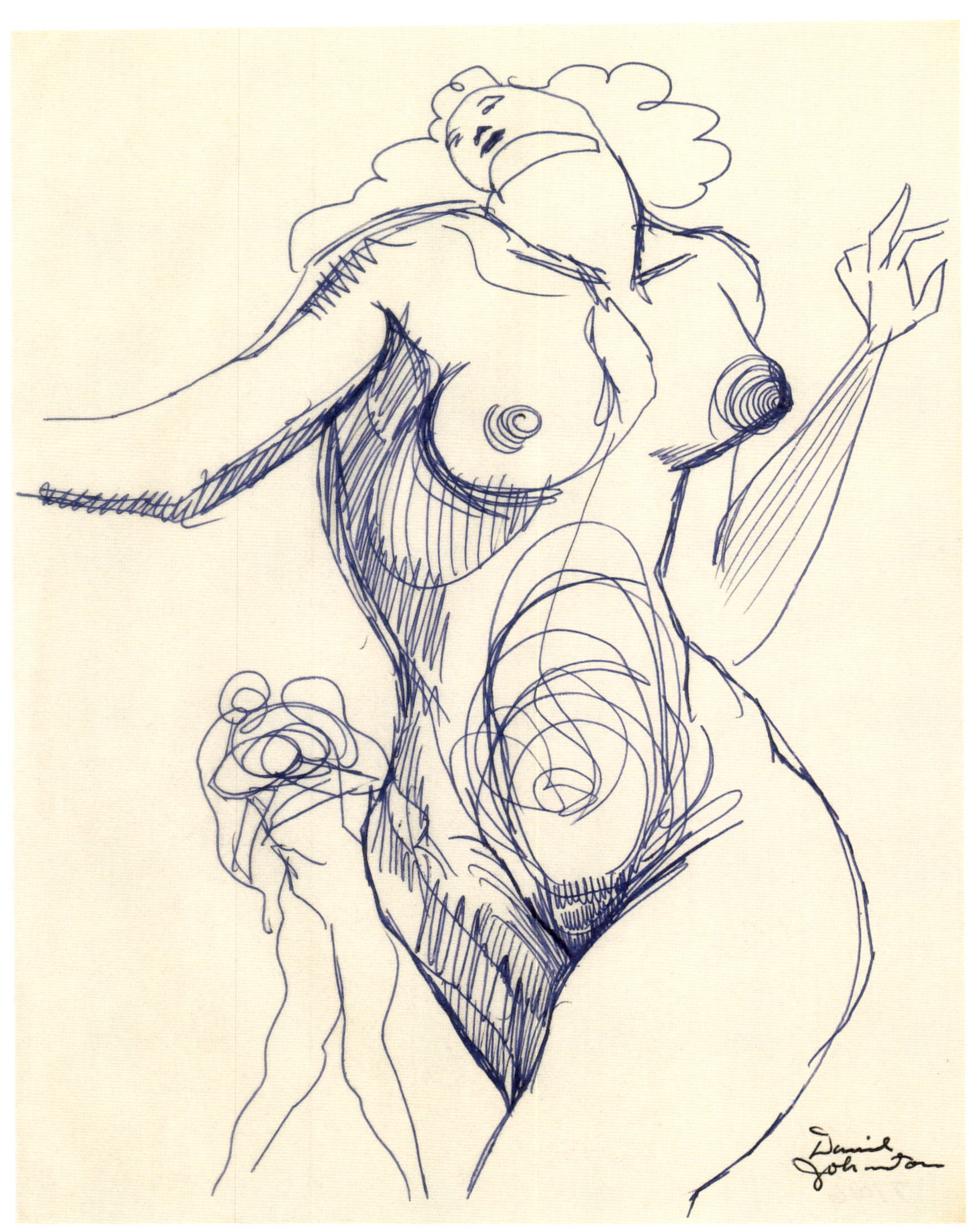

Untitled (Nude II)

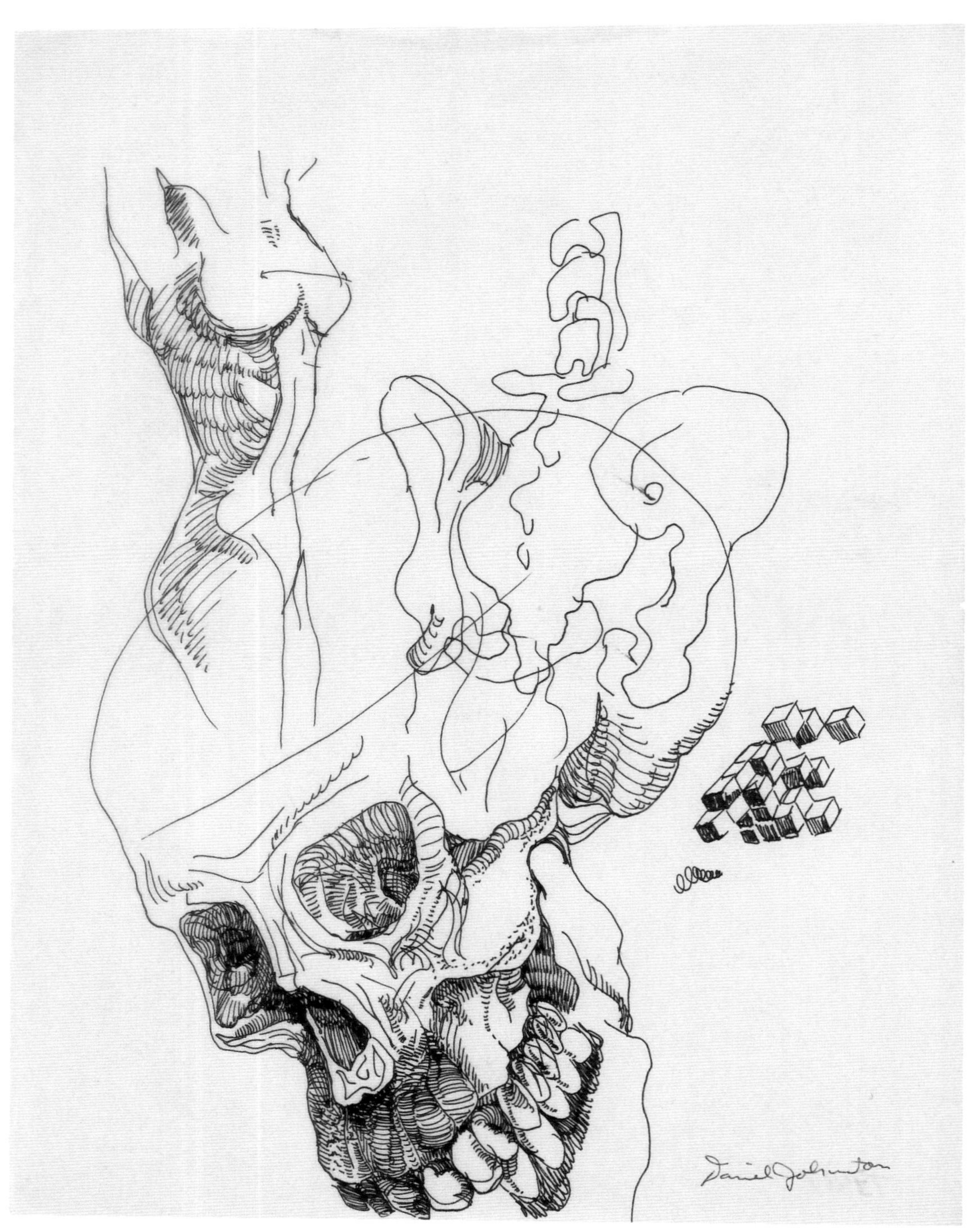

Untitled (Skull Study)

MY PEN SITS LONELY ON THE TABLE,
THERE'S NOTHING TO DRAW TODAY
SO MUCH HAPPENED
BUT I CAN'T REMEMBER A THING

Dan Johnston

Nothing to Draw Today

Every Daniel song feels like it just happened out of nowhere. Like there is zero processing that happens between what it sounds like inside of him and what we get. He has been a presence in my life since I wrote my first song and a touchstone—like Waits, Joni, Darnielle, or Springsteen—where I can always return free of all cynicism into the purest place of songwriting. The core of that, I've come to understand, is humor. I didn't get this when I was younger listening to Daniel. I felt all the pain. All the dissonance in the way it seemed the world interacted with him. All the sadness of wanting things to be a way that brings comfort and never getting it. But now, now he makes me laugh the same way life makes me laugh. His writing and delivery, a place I once thought too special and strange for the world that I know, are the clearest depiction of the actual world. Daniel writes about how we actually interact with each other. How we actually feel love and loss.

Took me a little bit of living to understand that Daniel wasn't my strange friend in my head showing me the edges of reality, but rather the true voice of how the world moves. For any area you could accuse him of being eccentric, he was actually just laying it down exactly as it was. The world is a Daniel Johnston song more than I ever knew. The vacillation from laughter to tears to silence to terror to the freedom of childhood in one verse of Daniel's writing is the honest experience of living. The gigantic questions of existence thrown away two seconds later by a joke are the actual conversations we have with those in our lives. He took care of us, his listeners, in that way. Never giving us a terrifying truth without an escape hatch right next to it. It's writing at its finest, and he's an artist who every artist I know will return to for guidance.

One time I got to be in a room with him and watch him perform. He played a few songs in a row, said nothing. Delivered that version of Daniel that was so tortured by the world. That version that was too rare to exist peacefully. The audience in Texas sat on the floor and met him with all of our personal versions of this place. He brought the room together almost like a mourners' circle of those who felt the world would run them over time and again. And after a few of the darkest, most connected songs I have experienced in a room, just at the moment that he held all of us at the edge of our existence, just at the moment that he brought god and truth into the space, before he had said one word not sung, just as the tension was at the greatest height, just as everyone wondered what soul-destroying song he would launch into next, Daniel leaned towards the mic . . . and delivered the most fucked-up World War II joke I have ever heard. The room erupts, the tension explodes away, and like his songs, he softens the harshness of life with a joke. And the great irony is that it's the joke that lets all the darkness ring so true. That's actually what it's like to be around, and Daniel, who some thought of as fringe, was telling that story better than anyone.

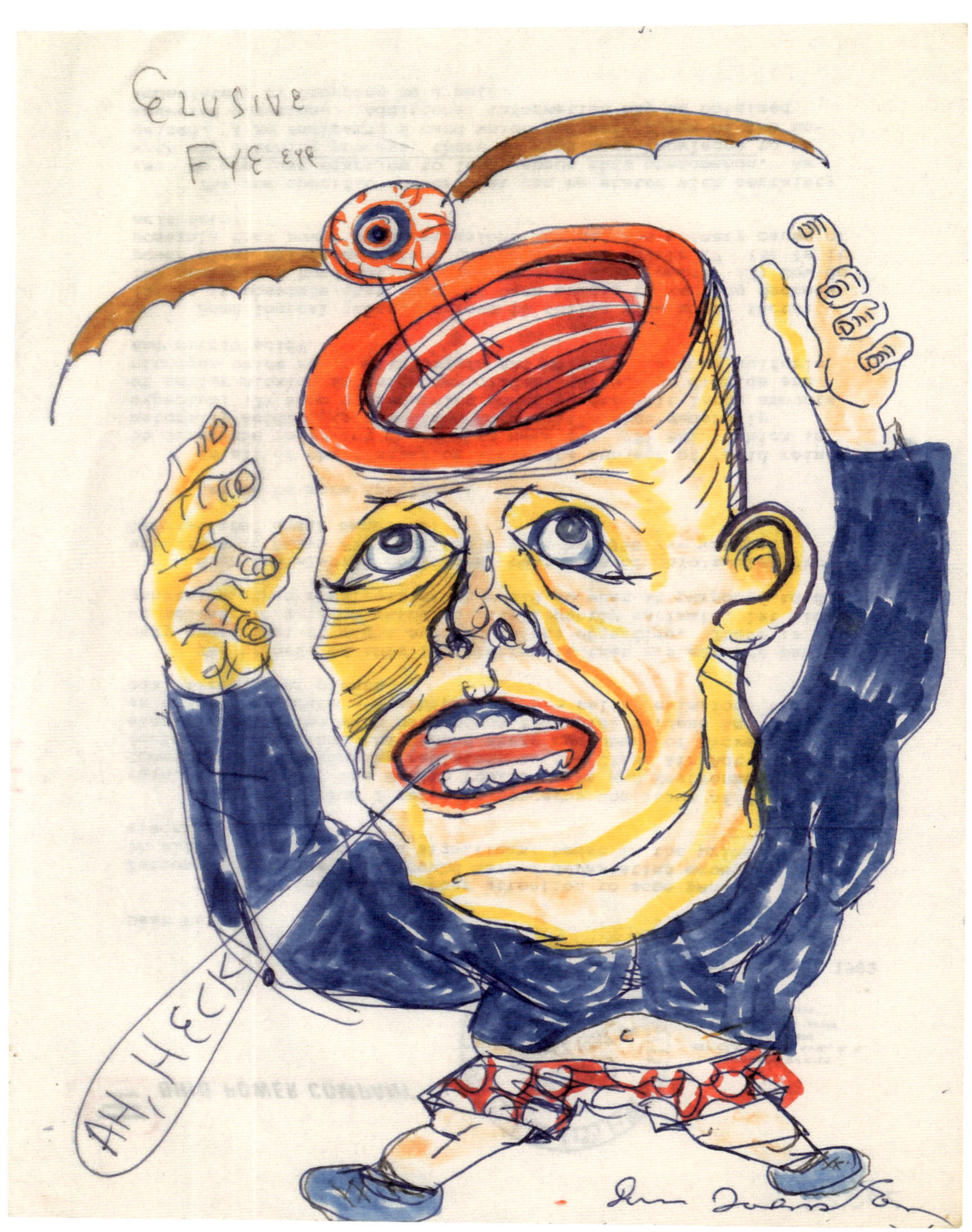

Elusive Eye

VI.
Pain
1979–1985

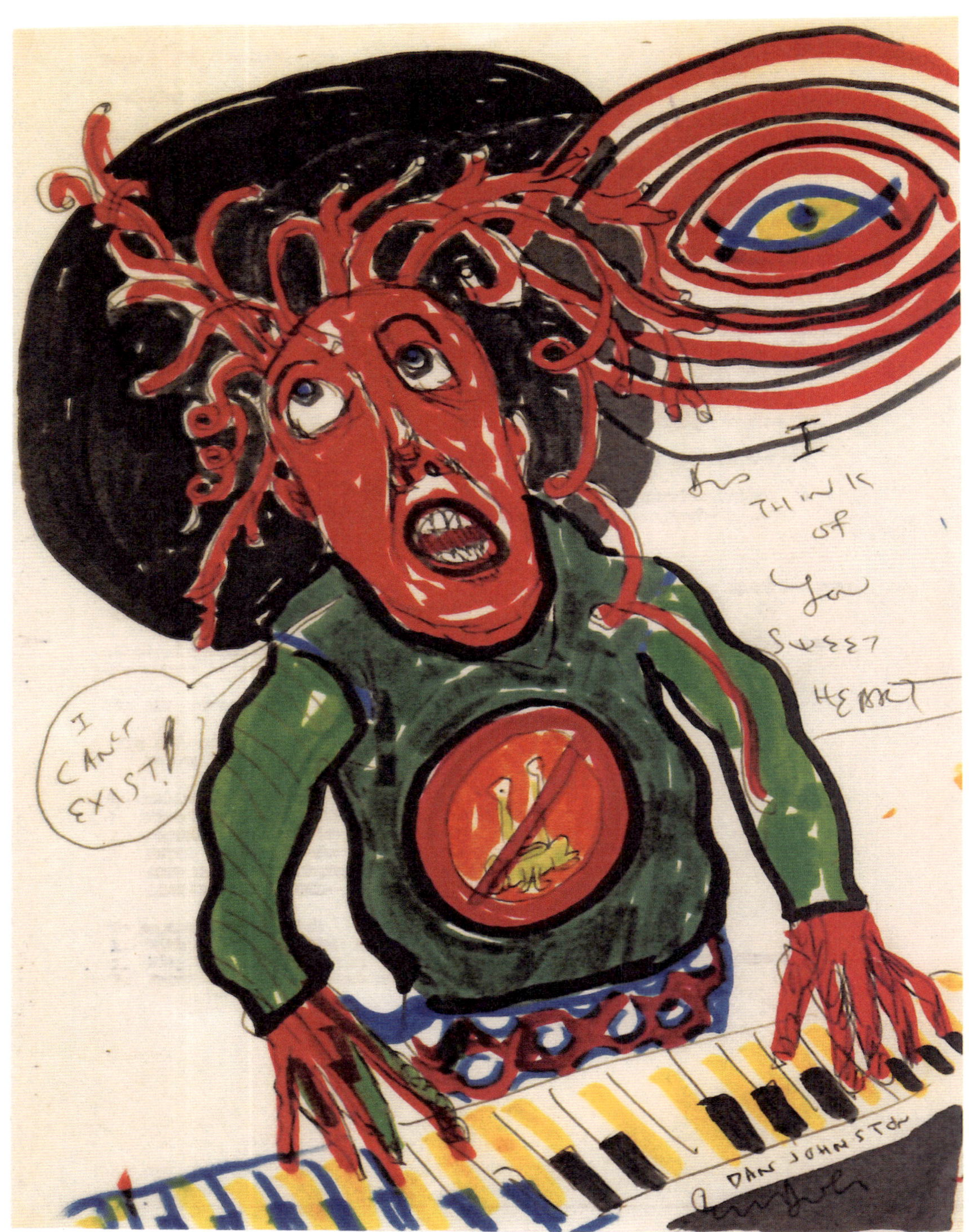

I Think of You Sweet Heart

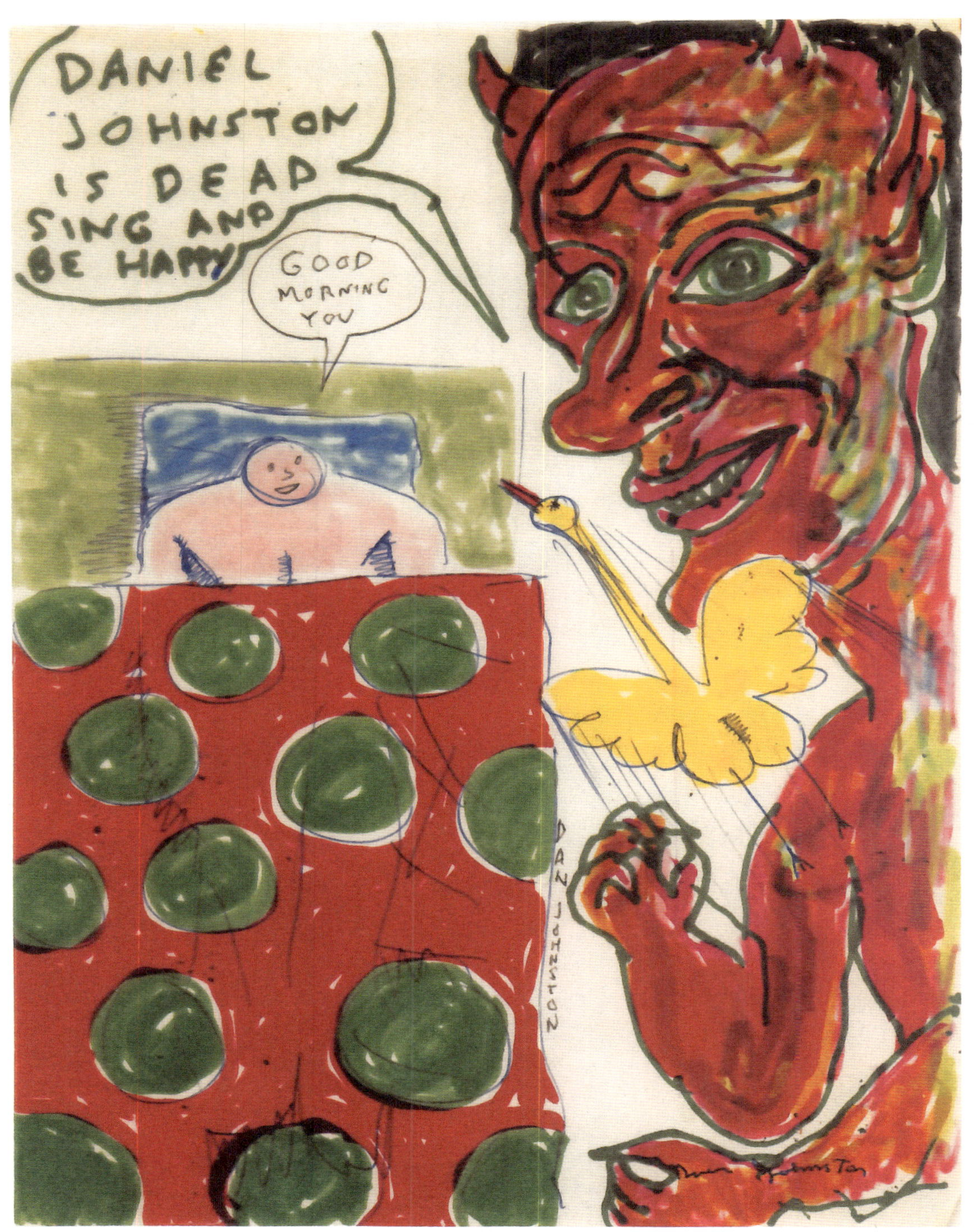

Daniel Johnston Is Dead

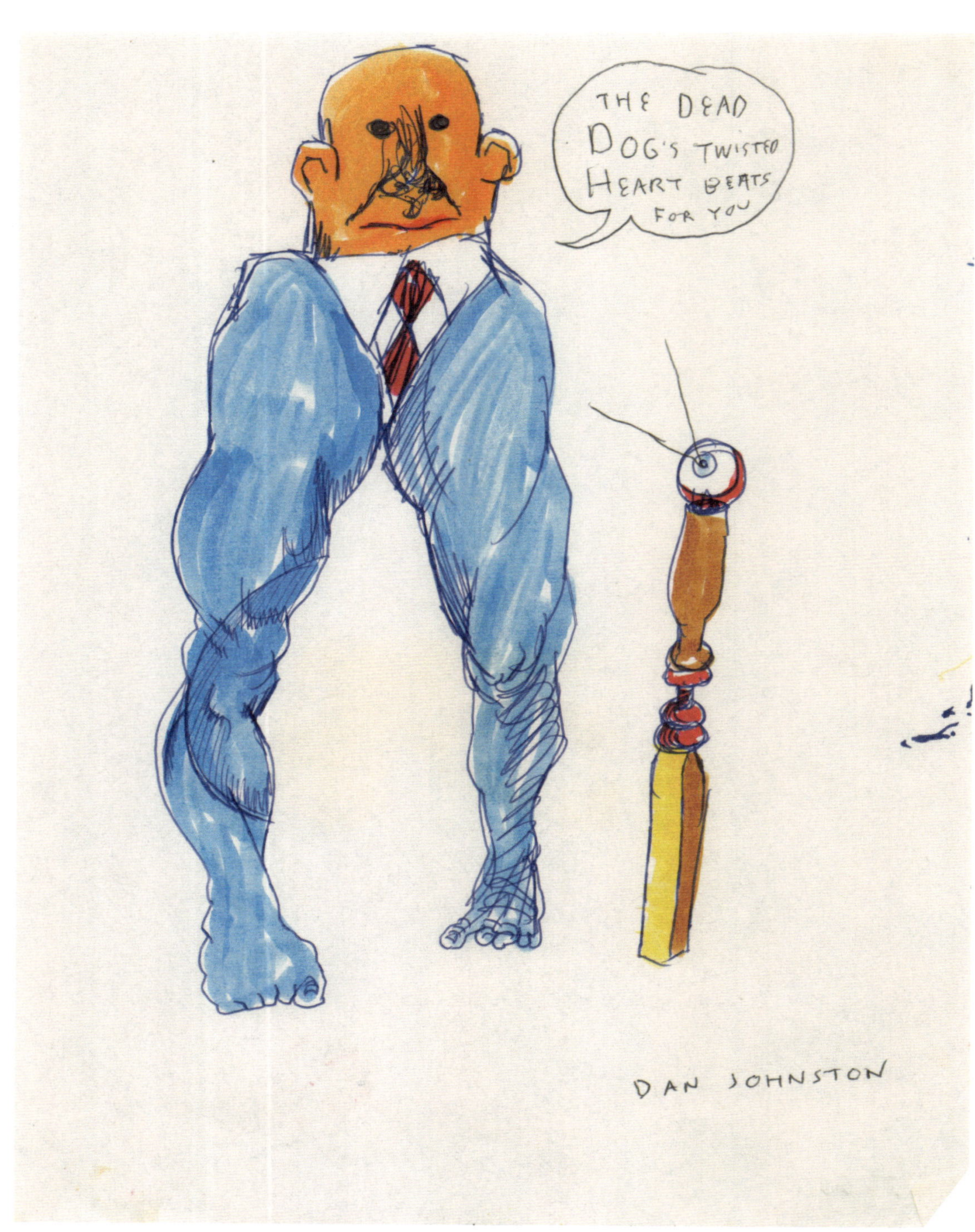

The Dead Dog's Twisted Heart

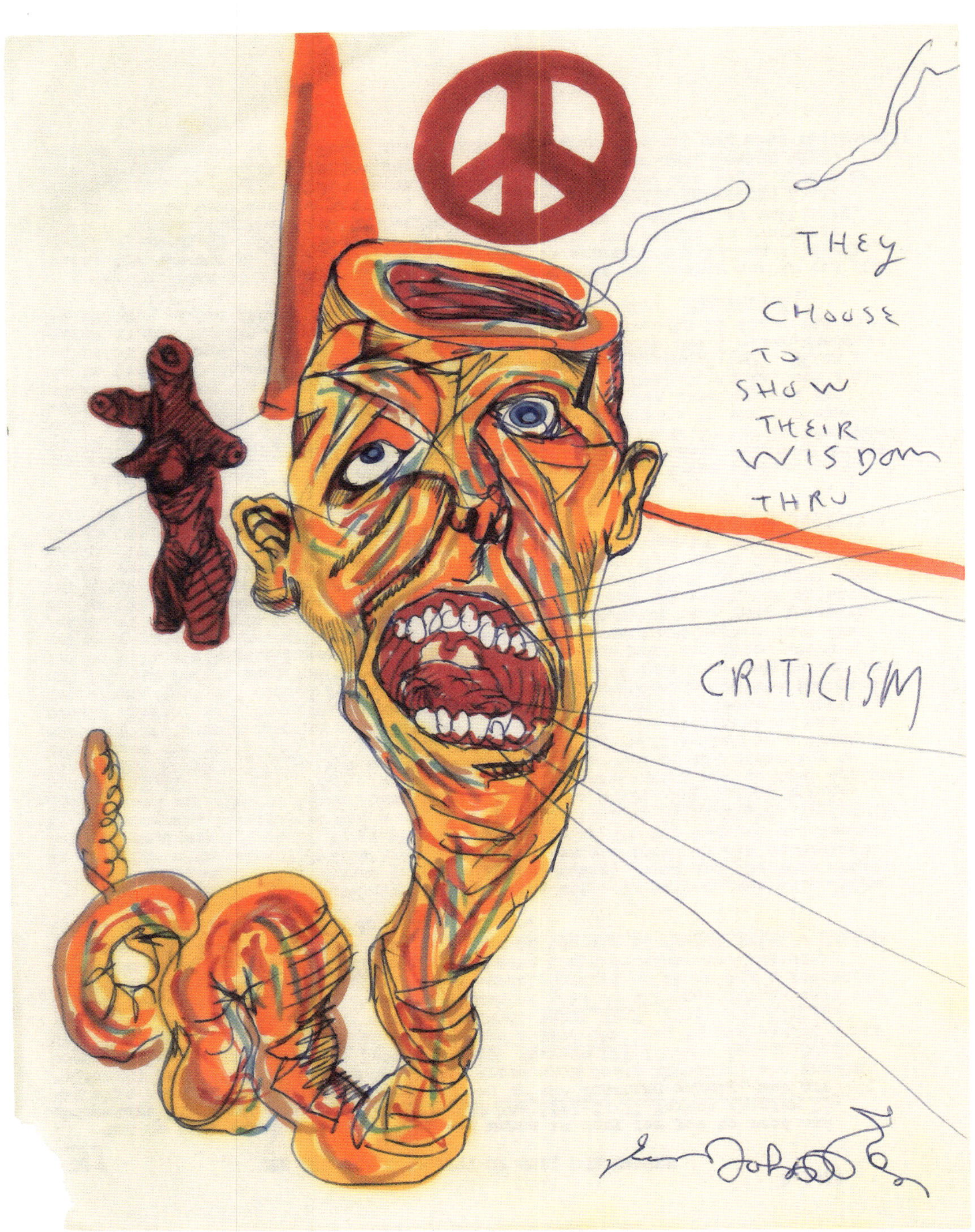

Wisdom Thru Criticism

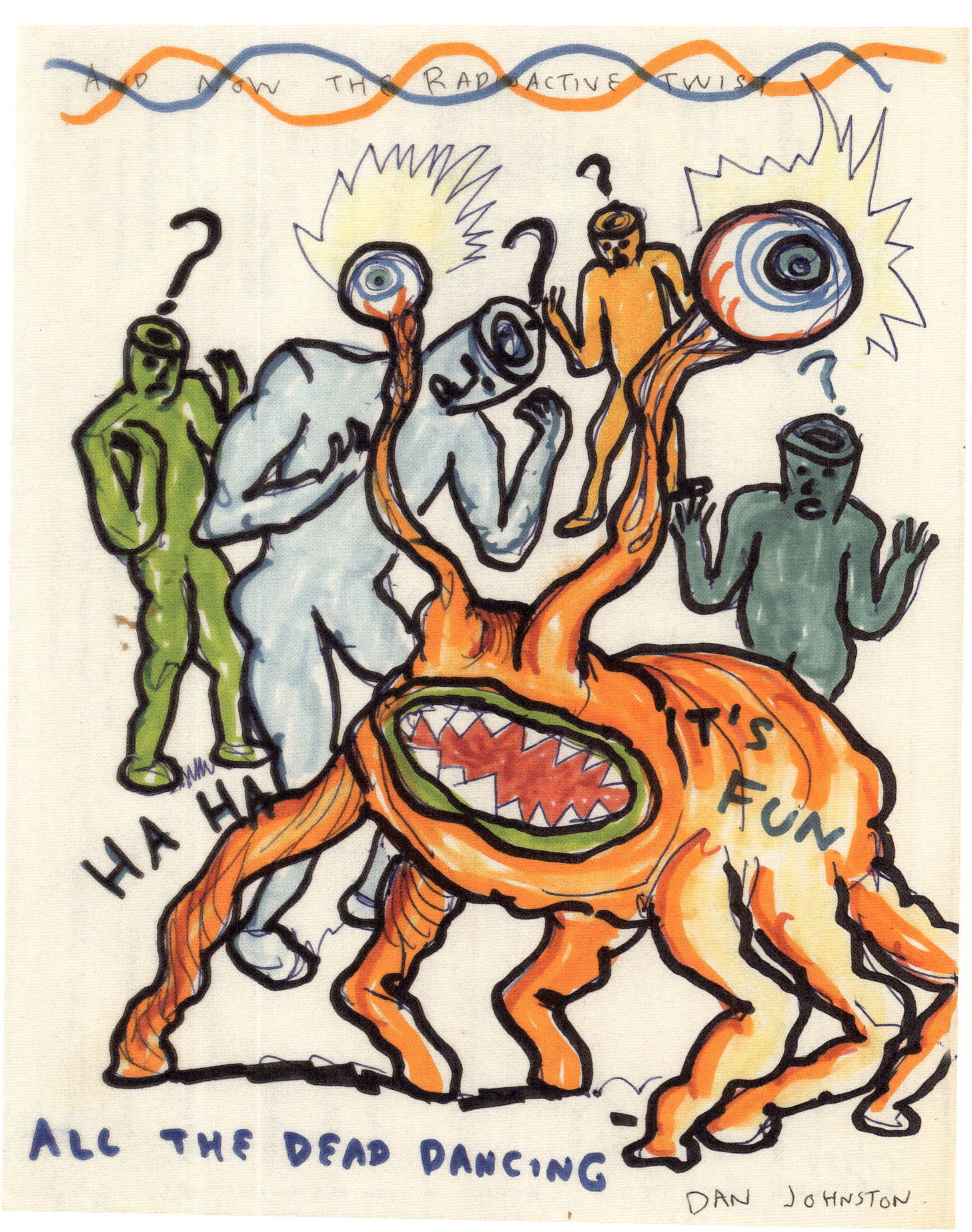

All the Dead Dancing

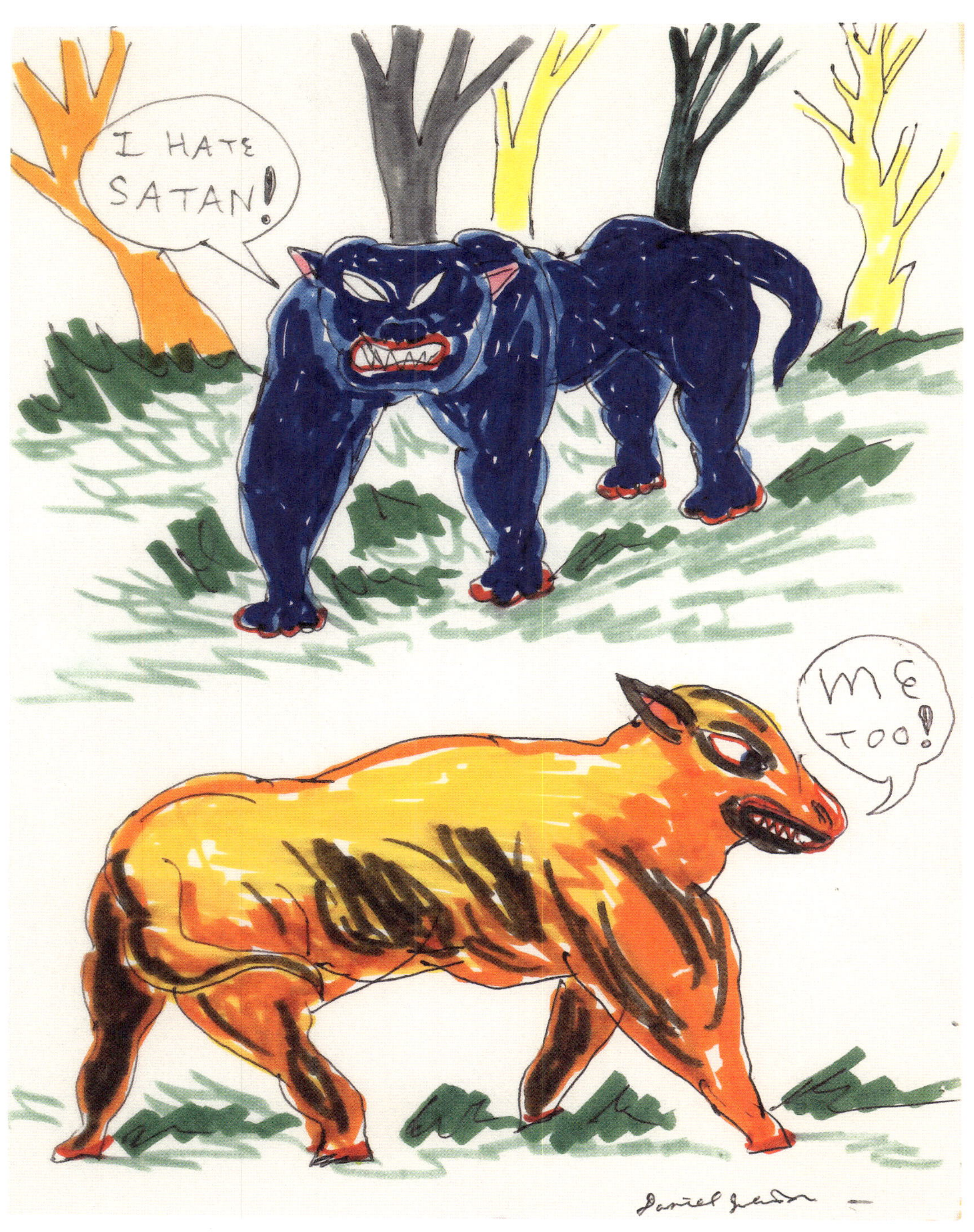

I Hate Satan!

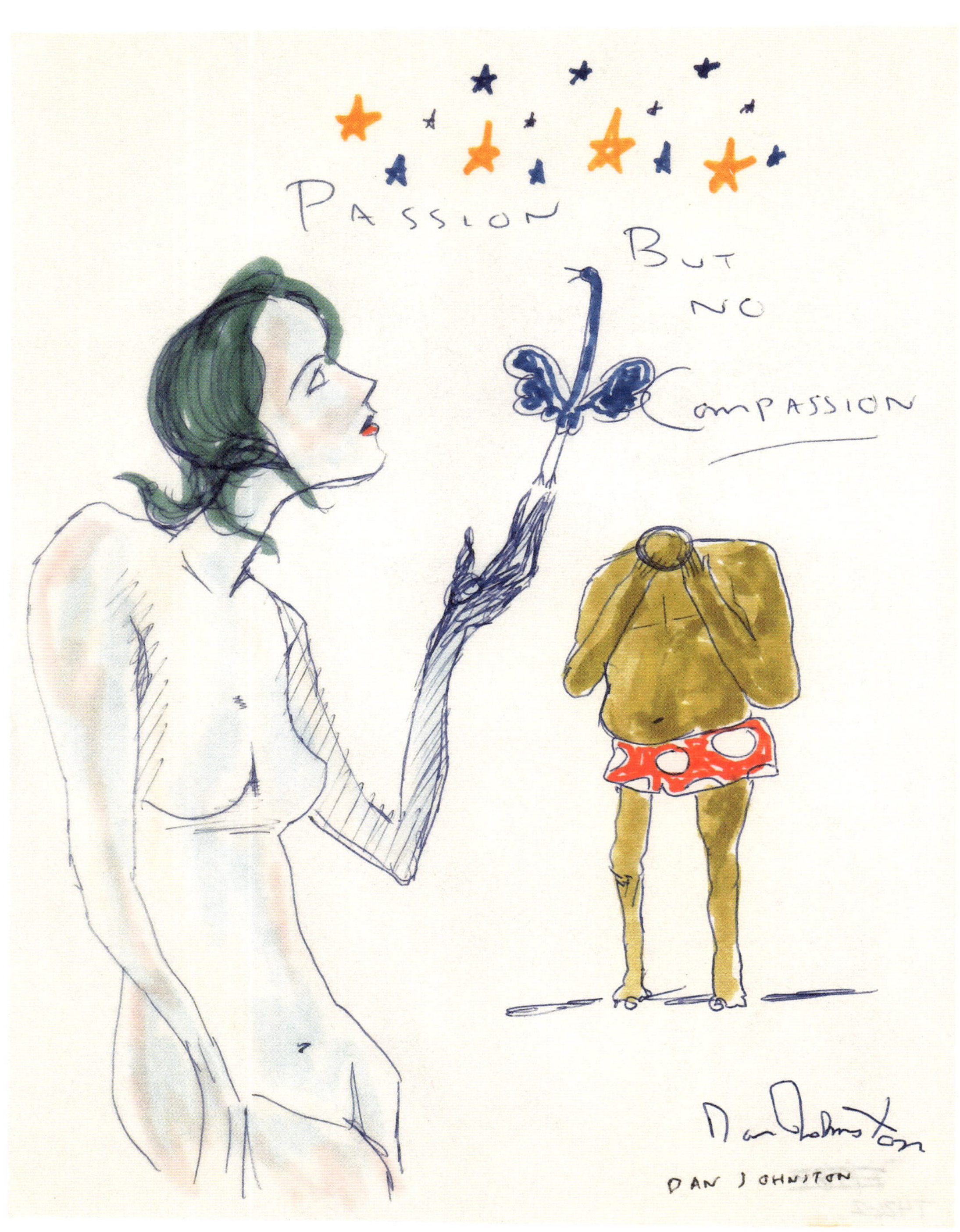

Passion but No Compassion

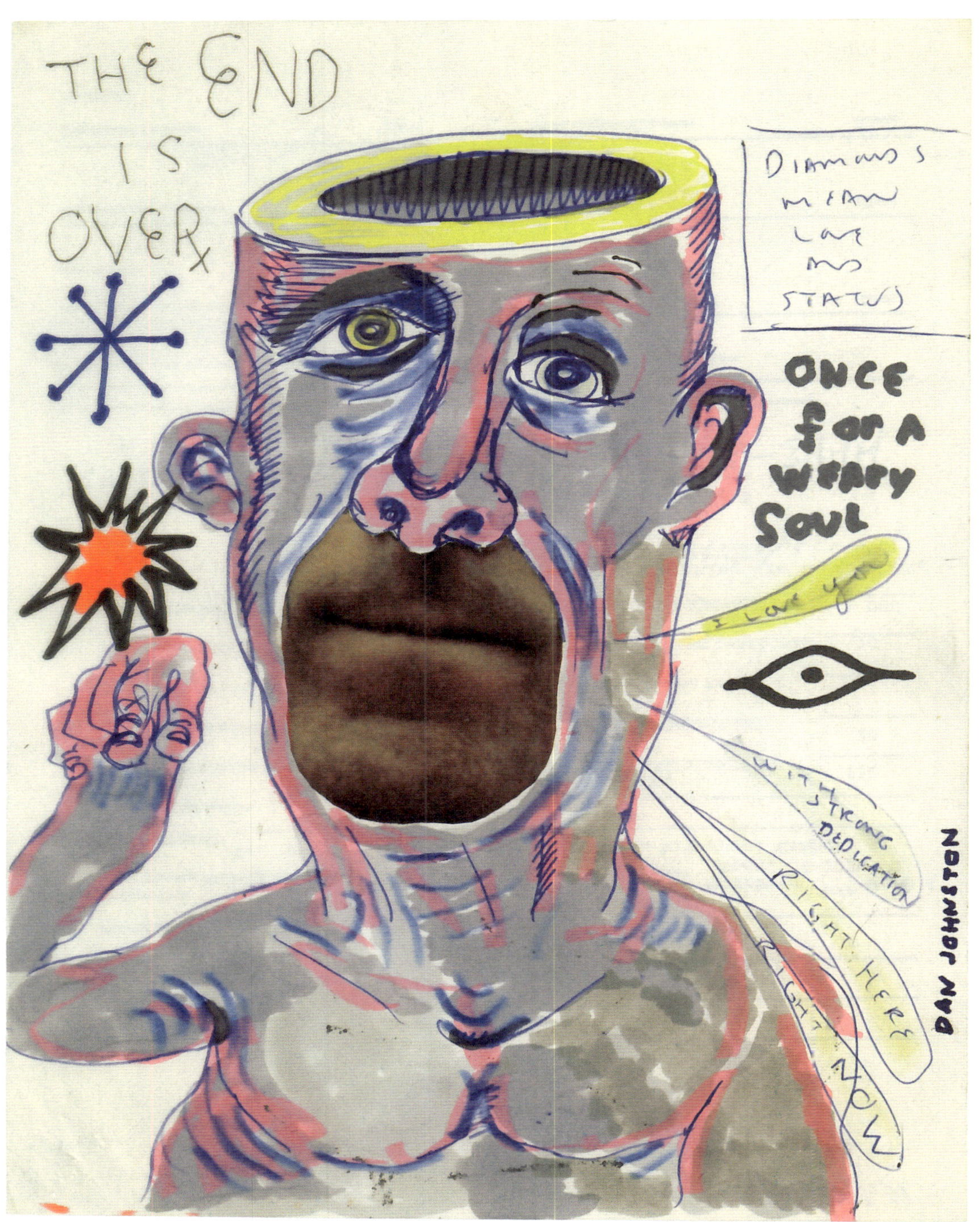

The End Is Over

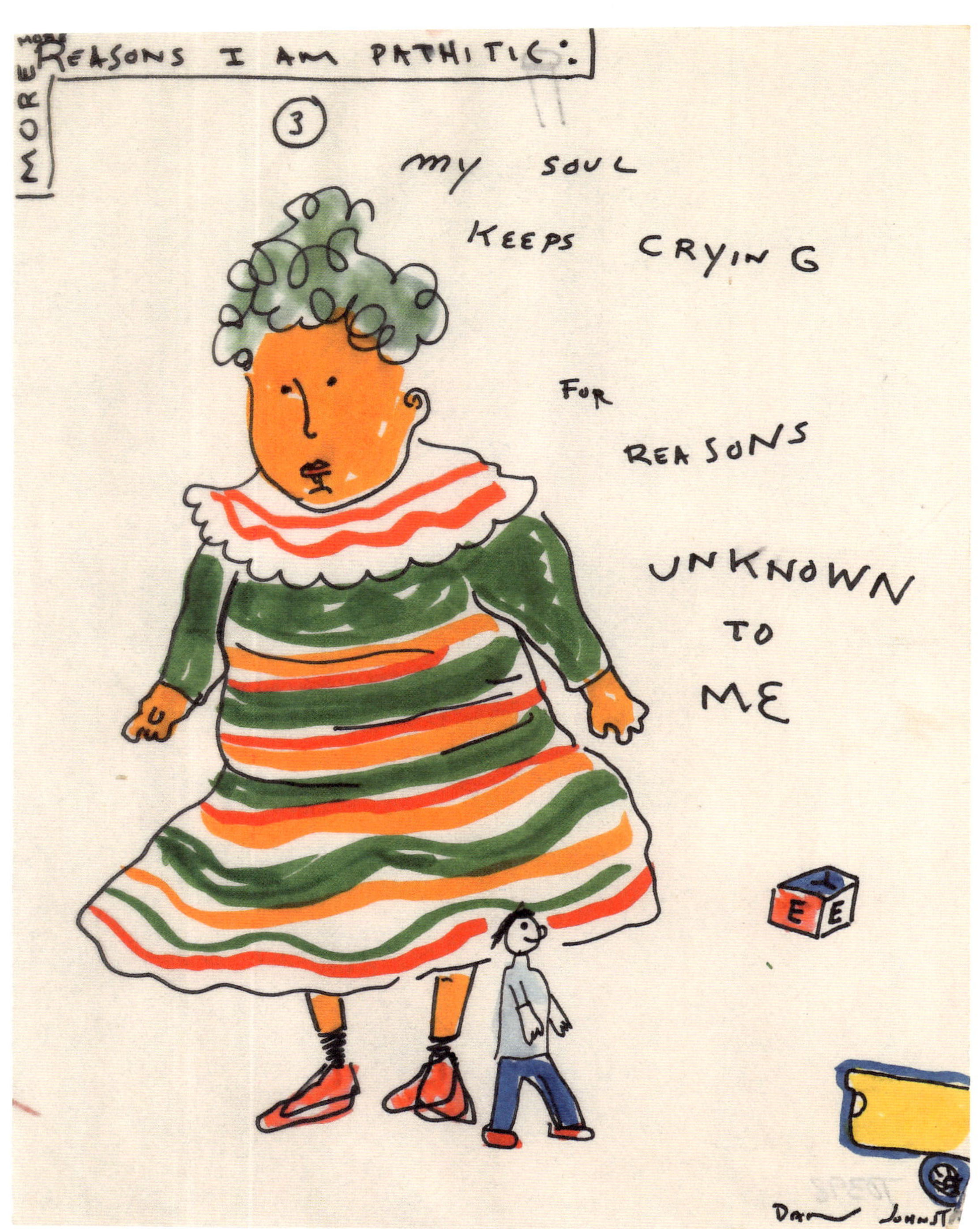

More Reasons I Am Pathitic

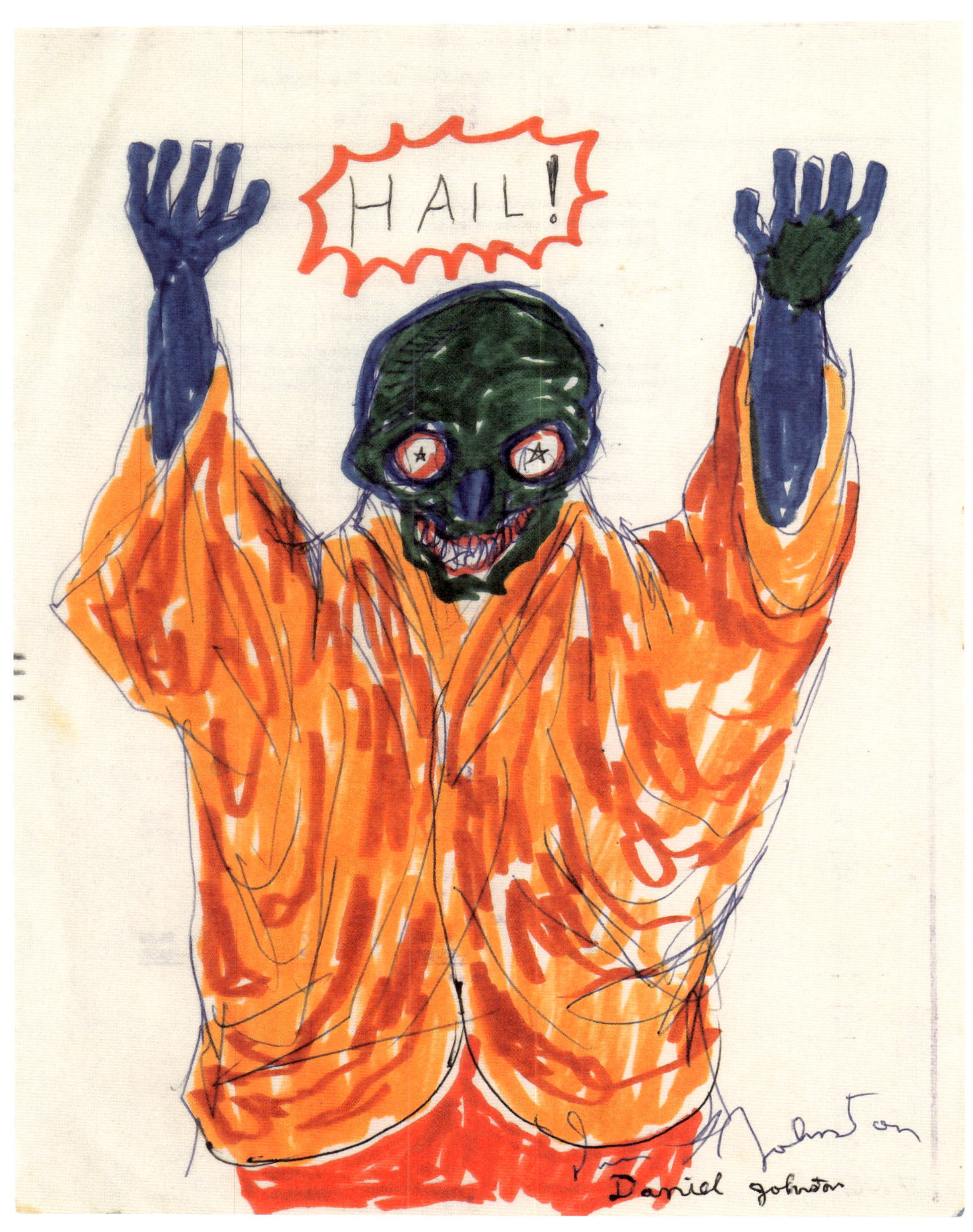

Hail!

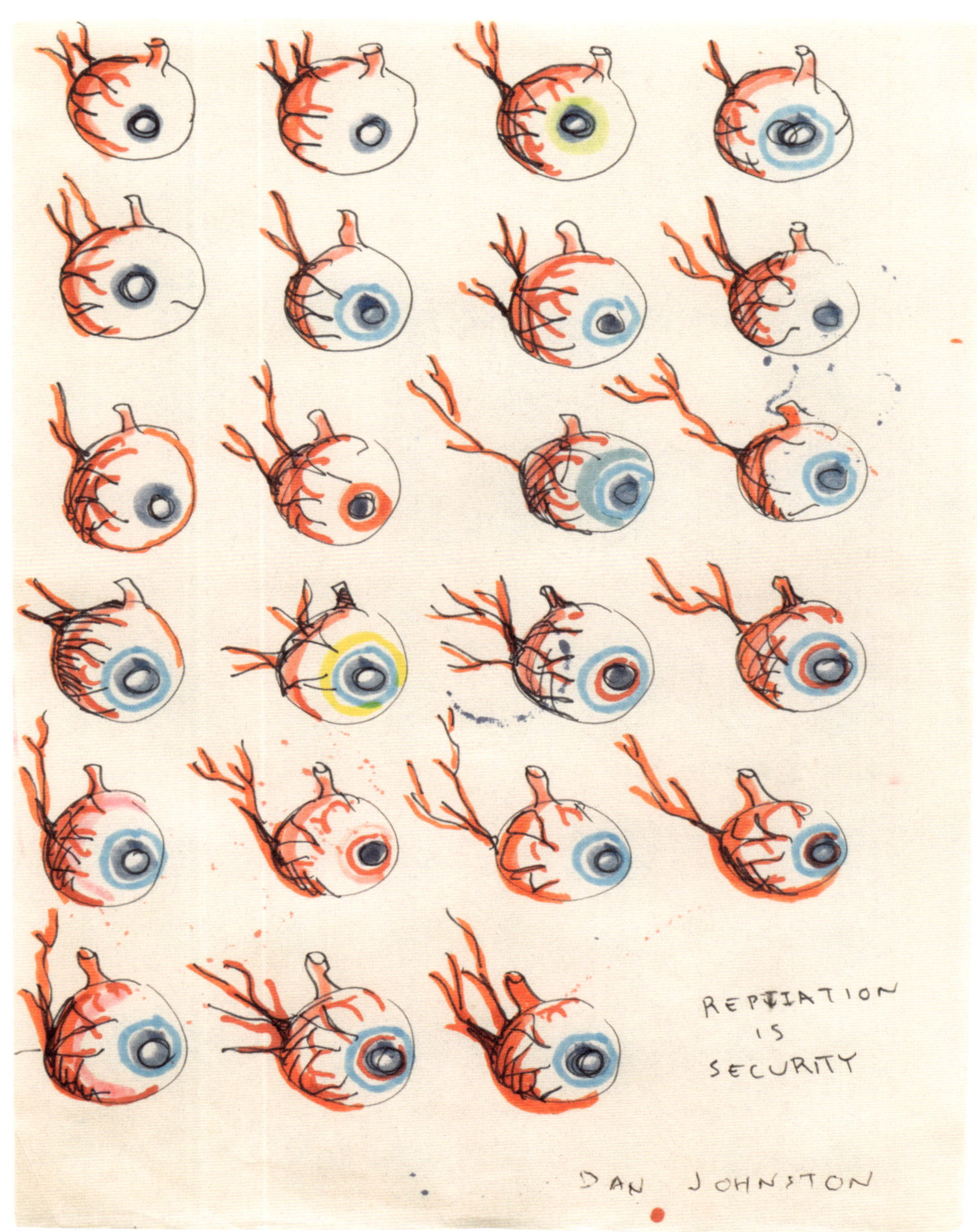

Reptiation Is Security

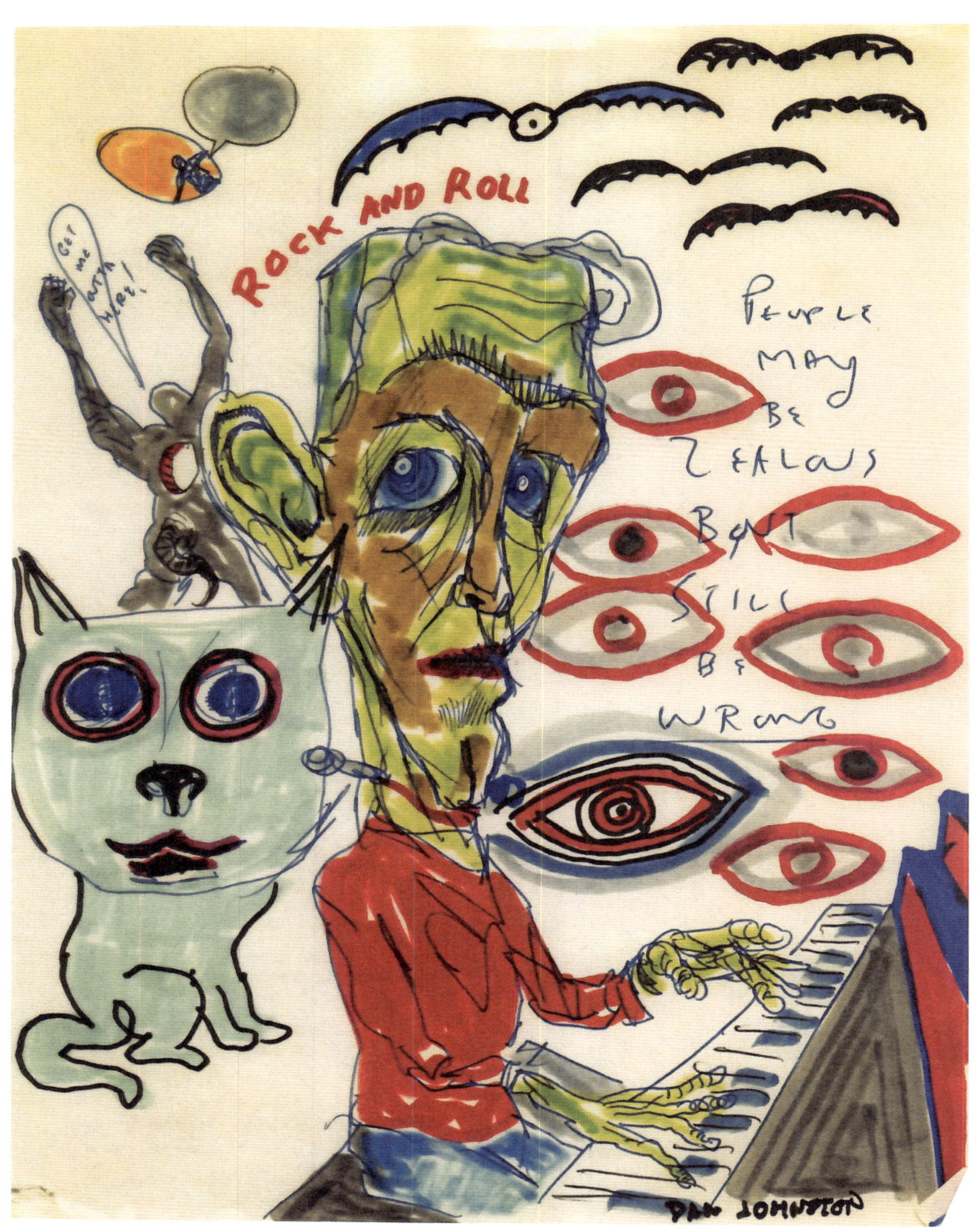

Rock and Roll

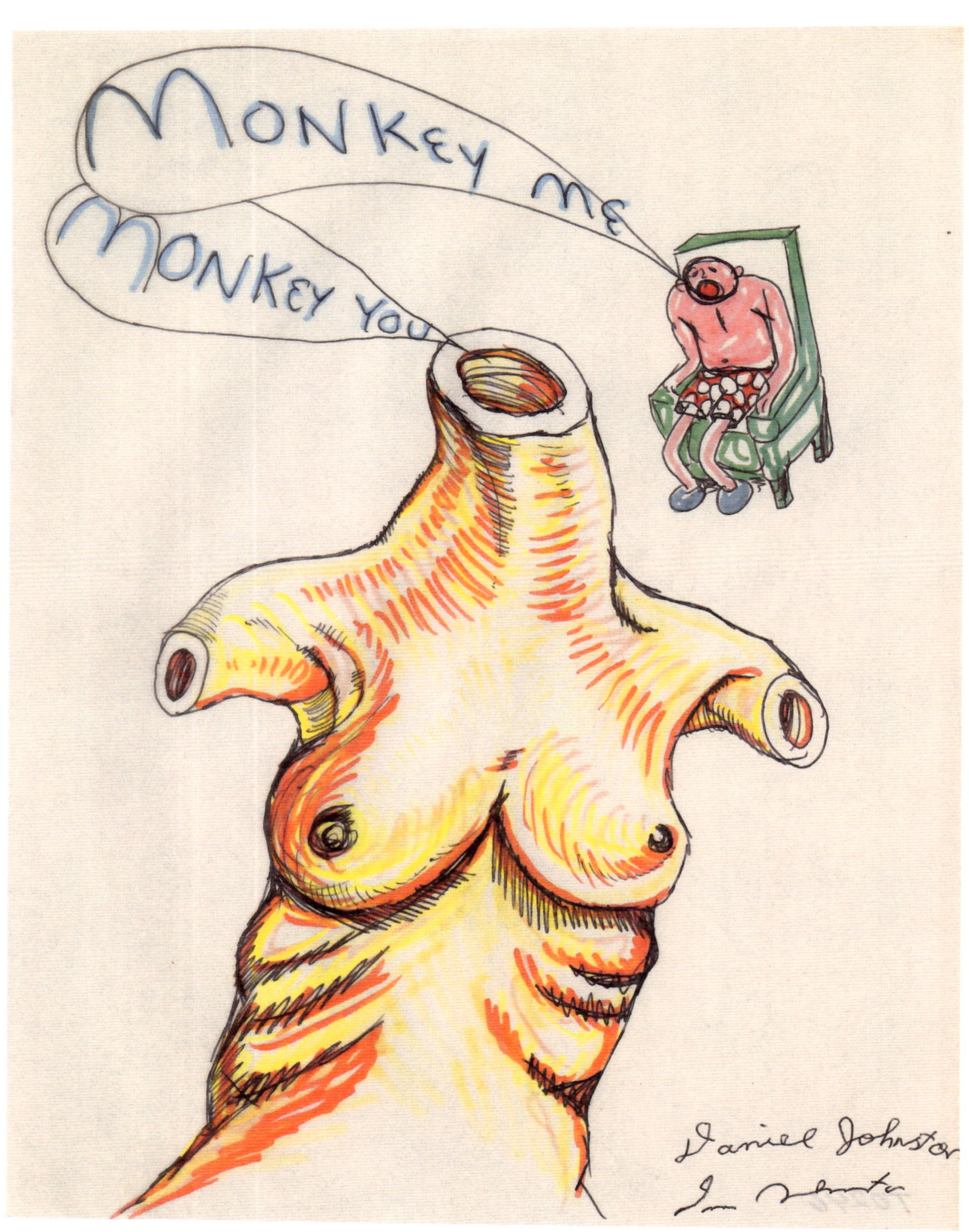

Monkey Me Monkey You

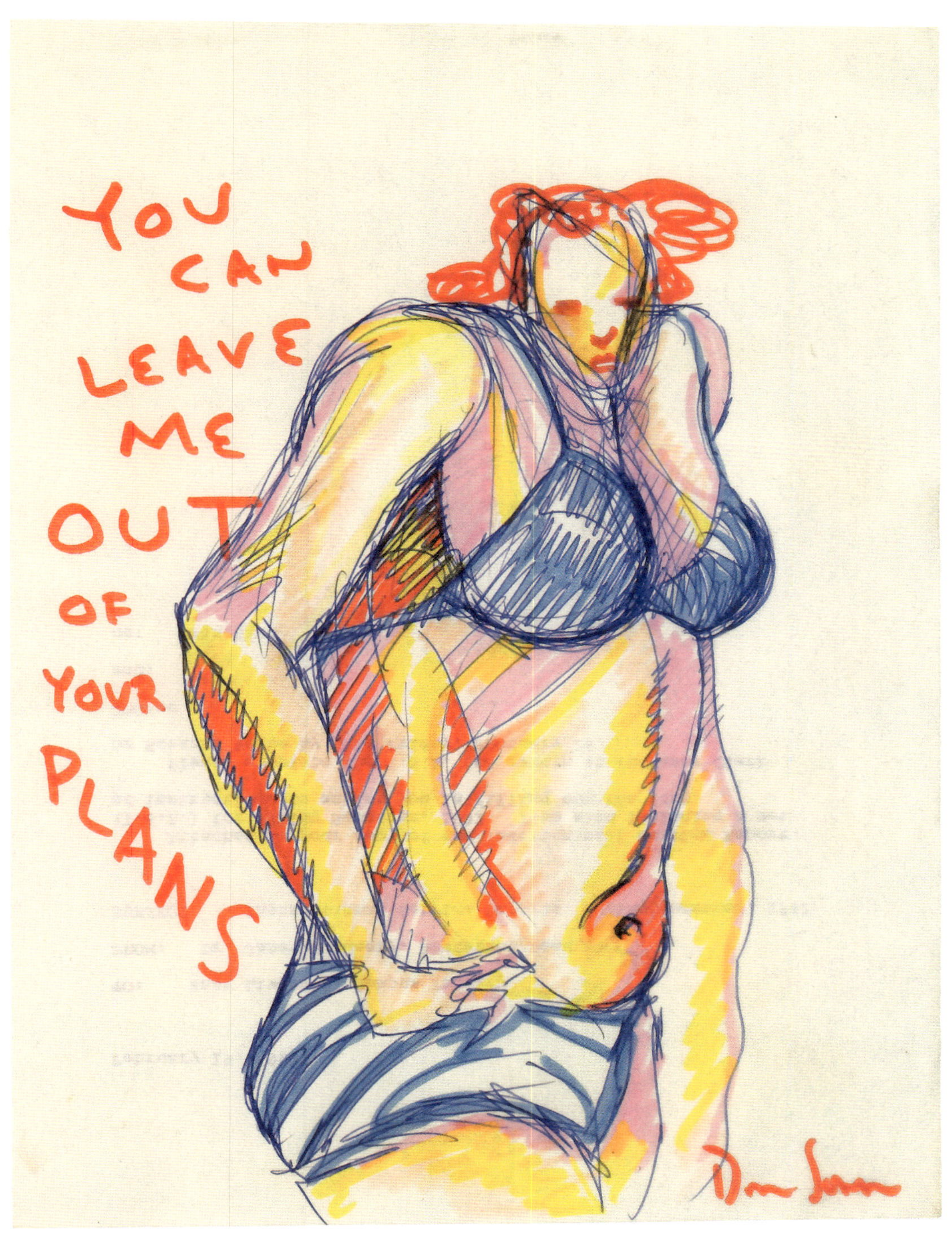

You Can Leave Me Out of Your Plans

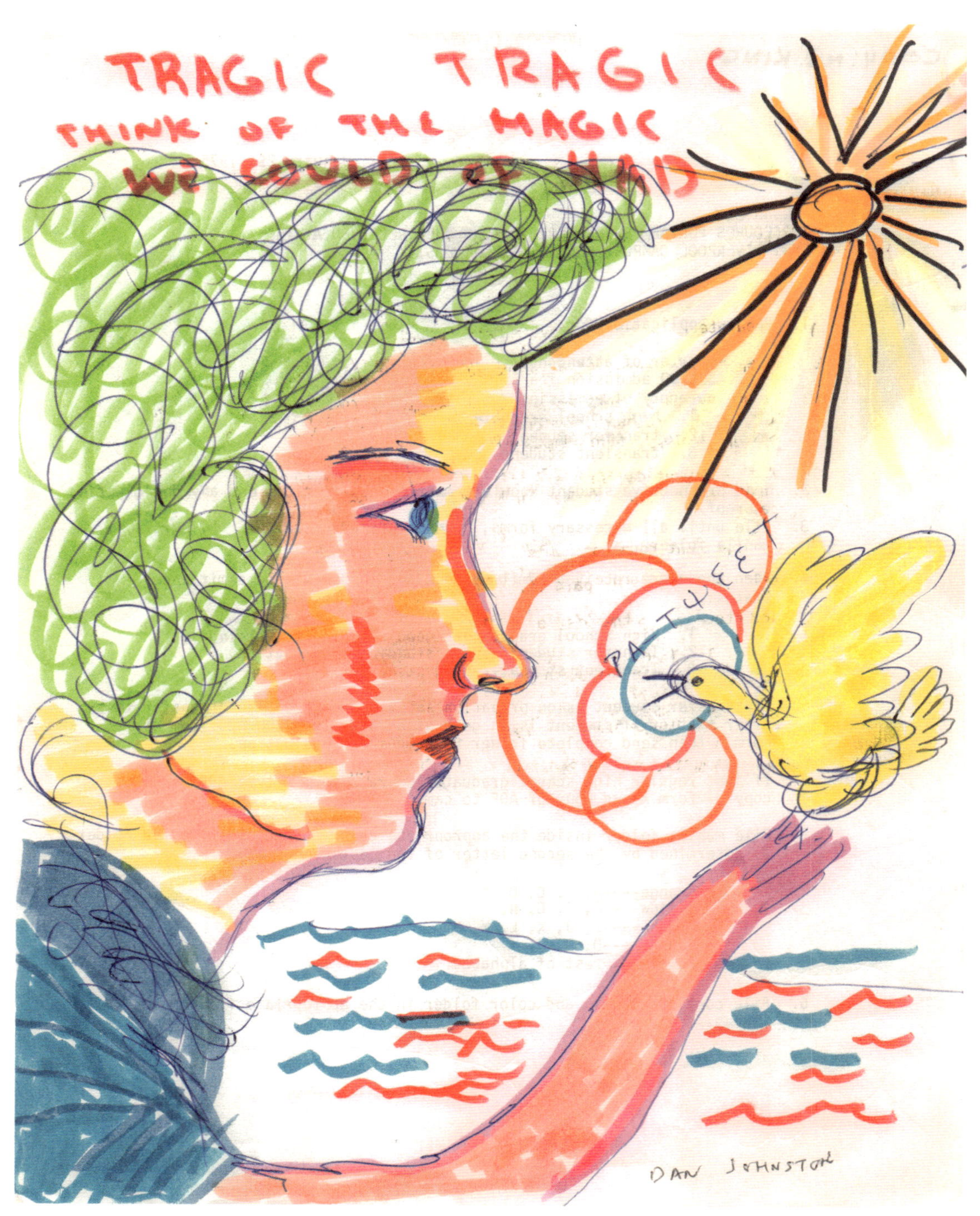

Tragic Tragic

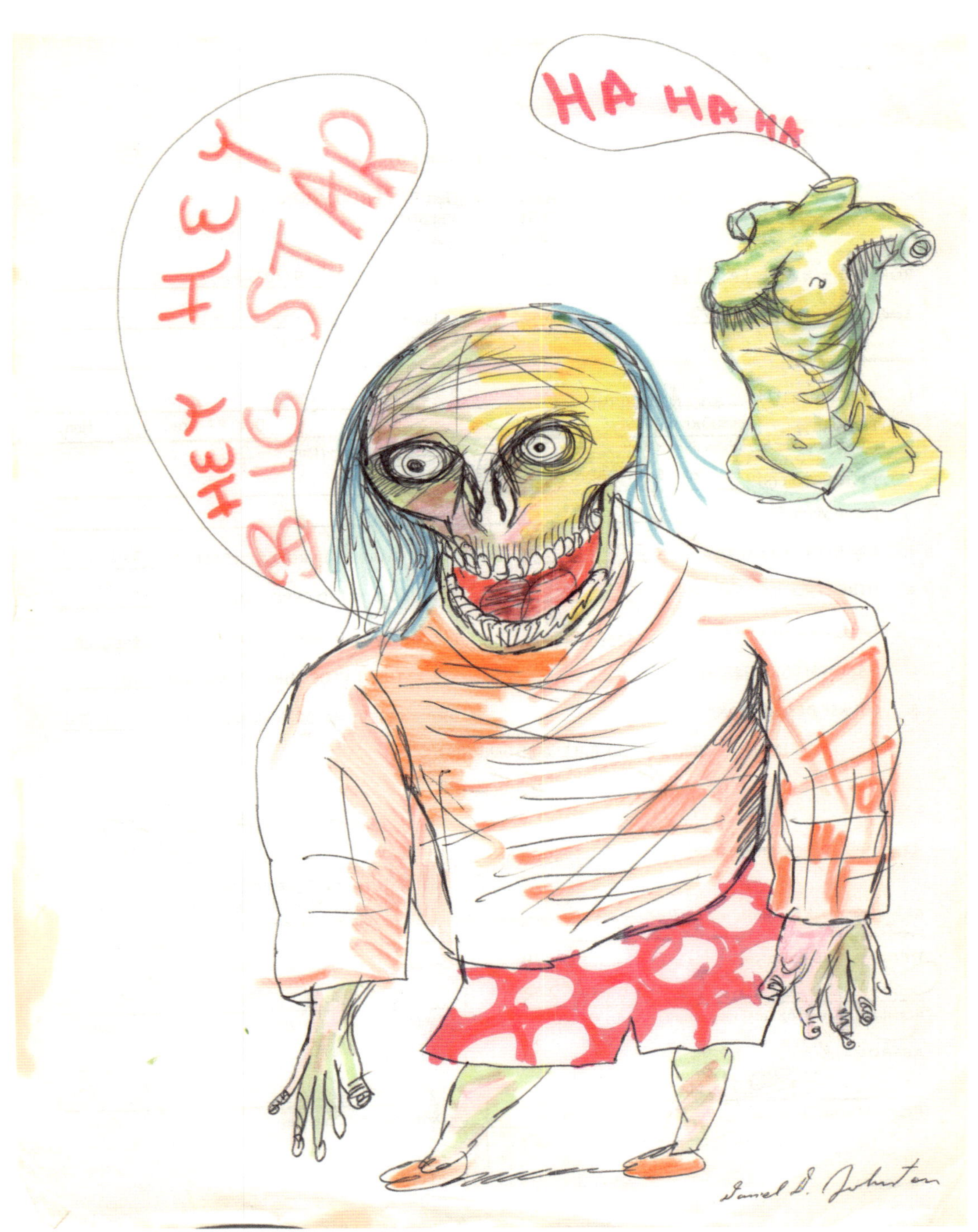

Hey Hey Big Star

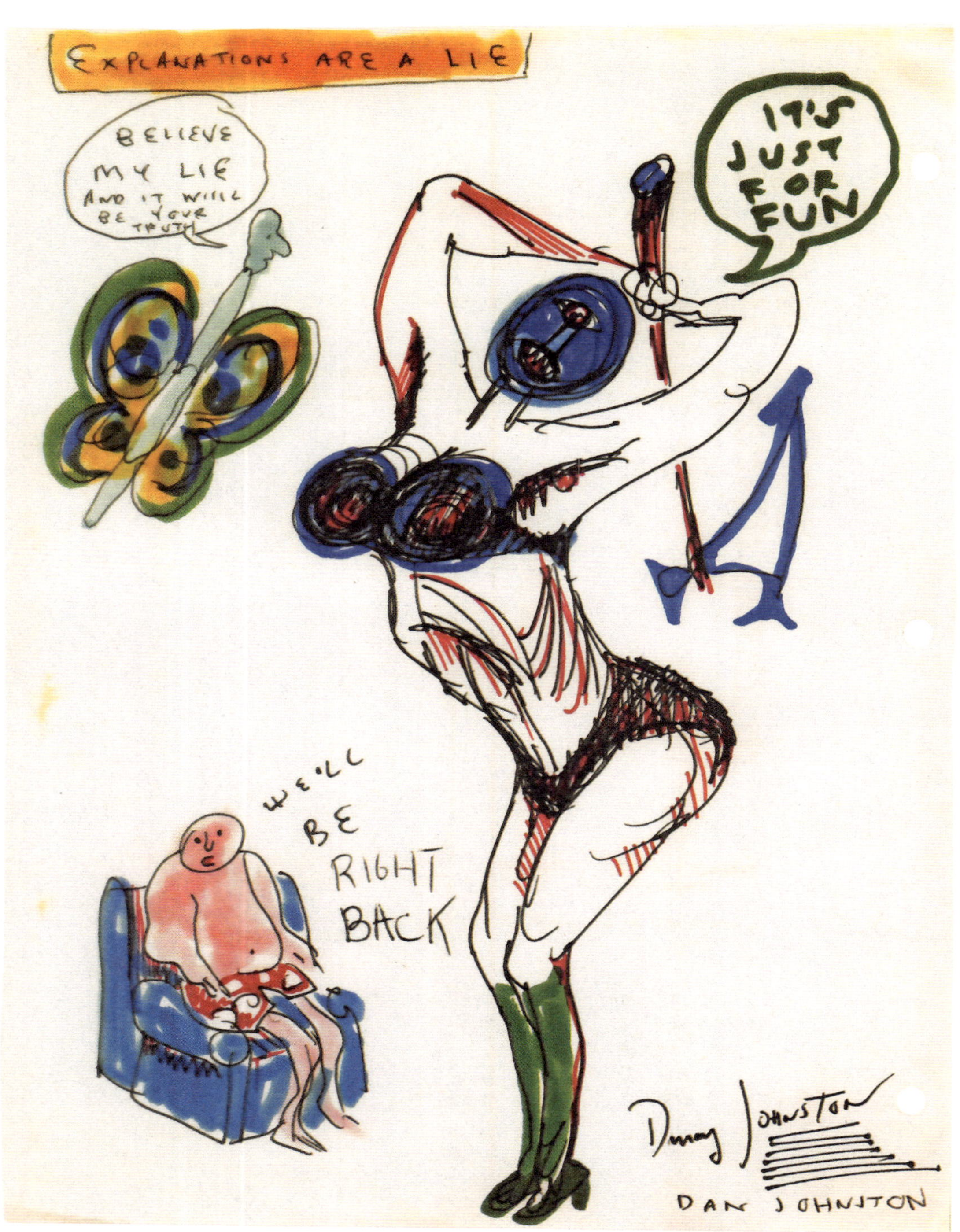

Explanations Are a Lie

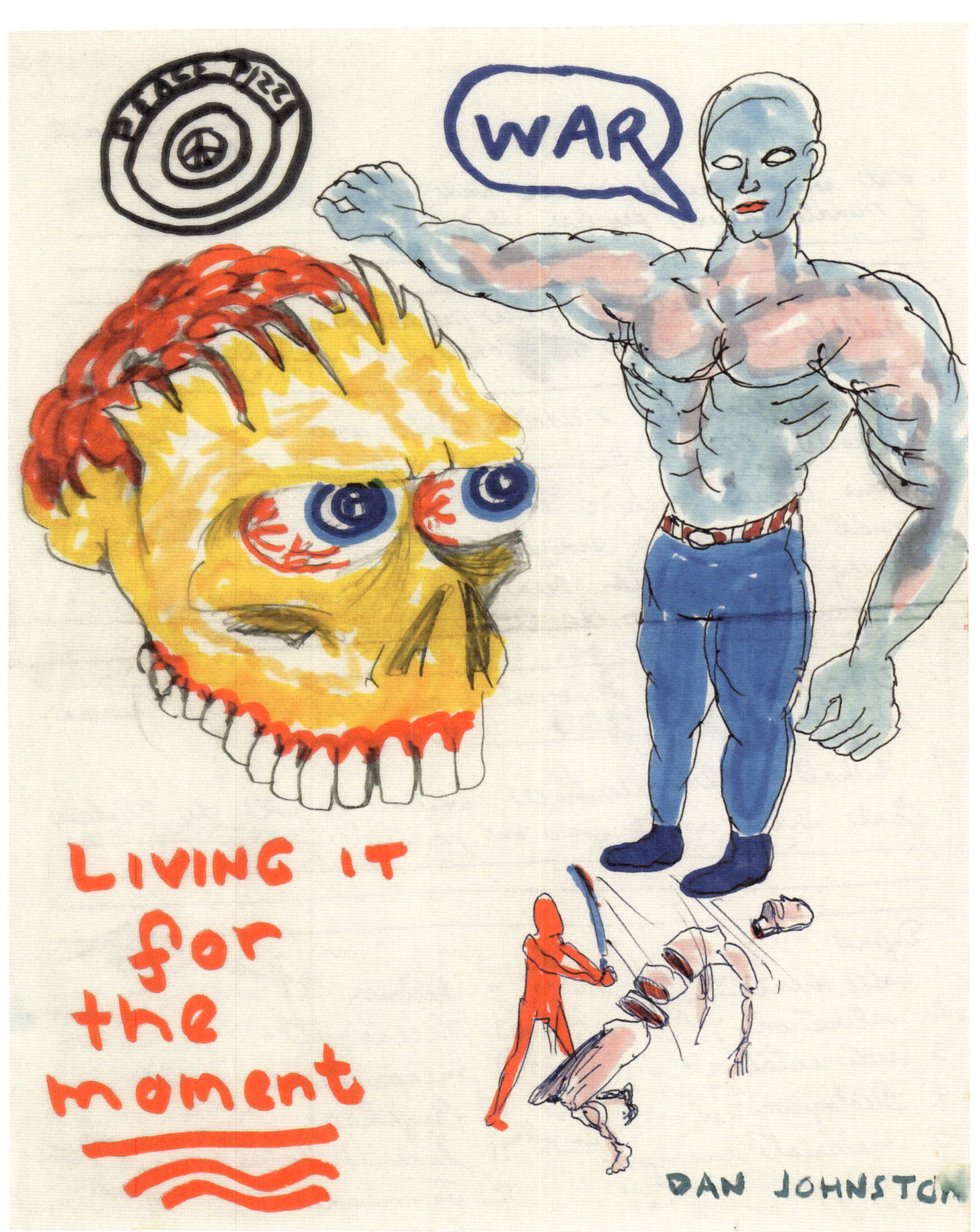

Living It for the Moment

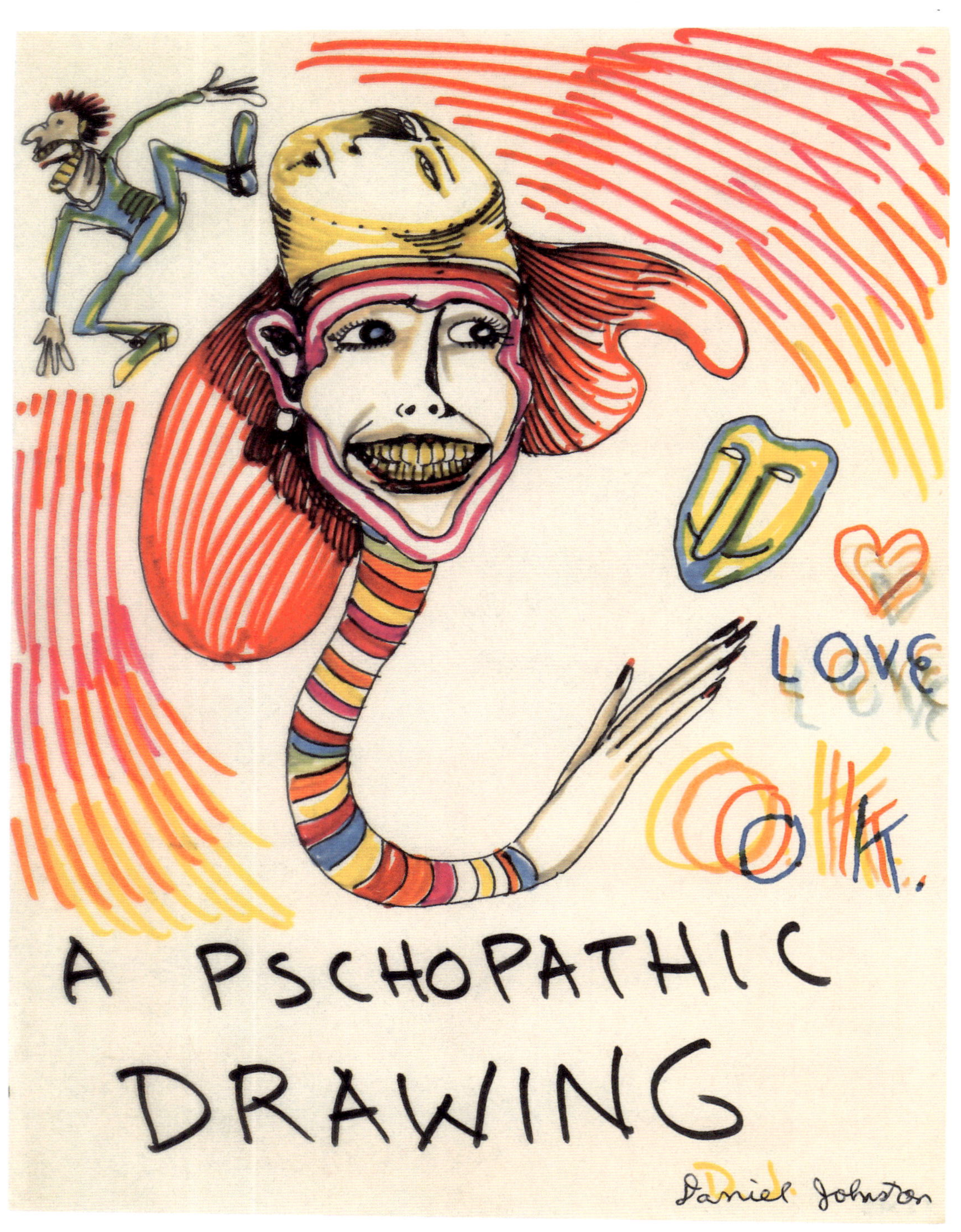

A Pschopathic Drawing

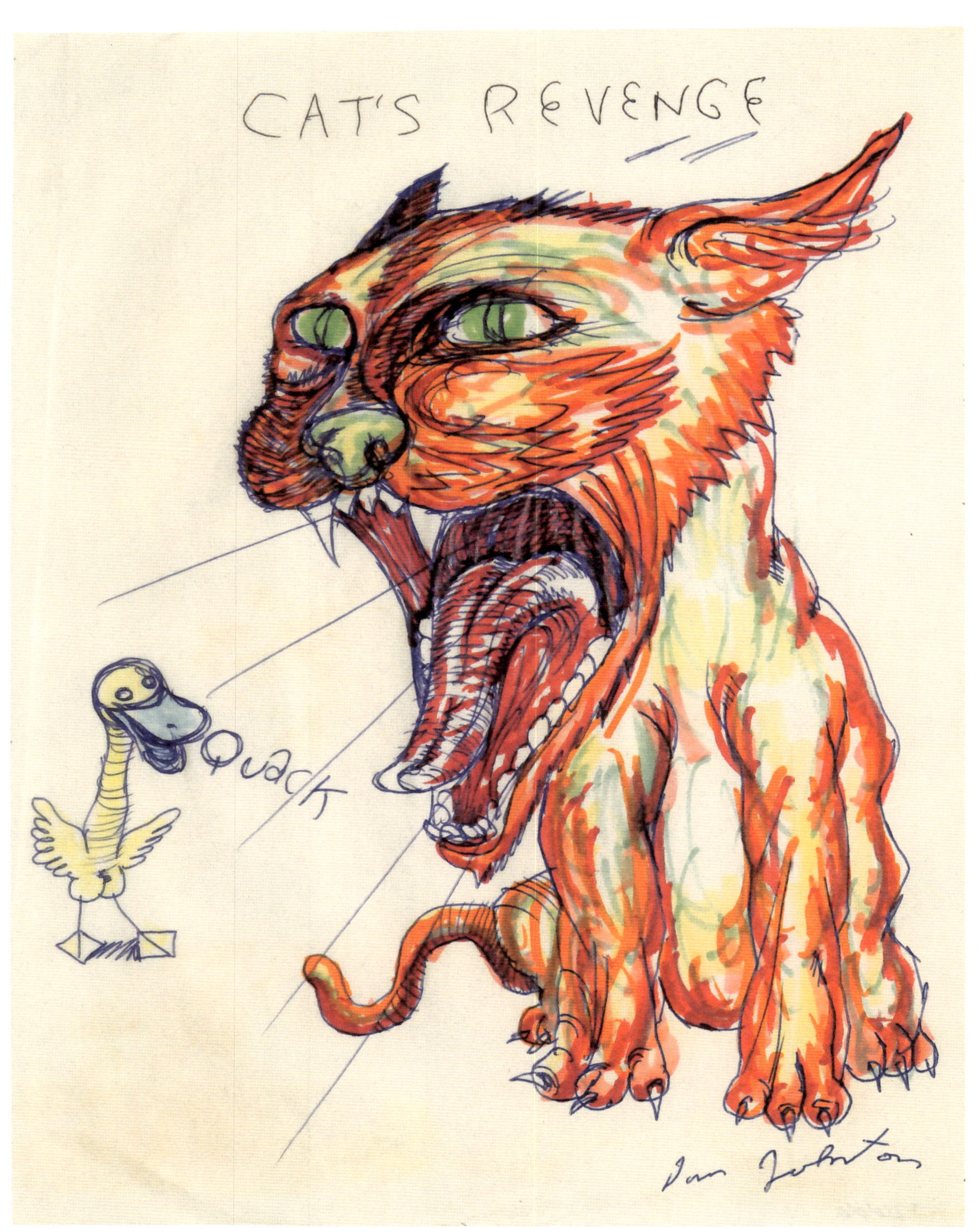

Cat's Revenge

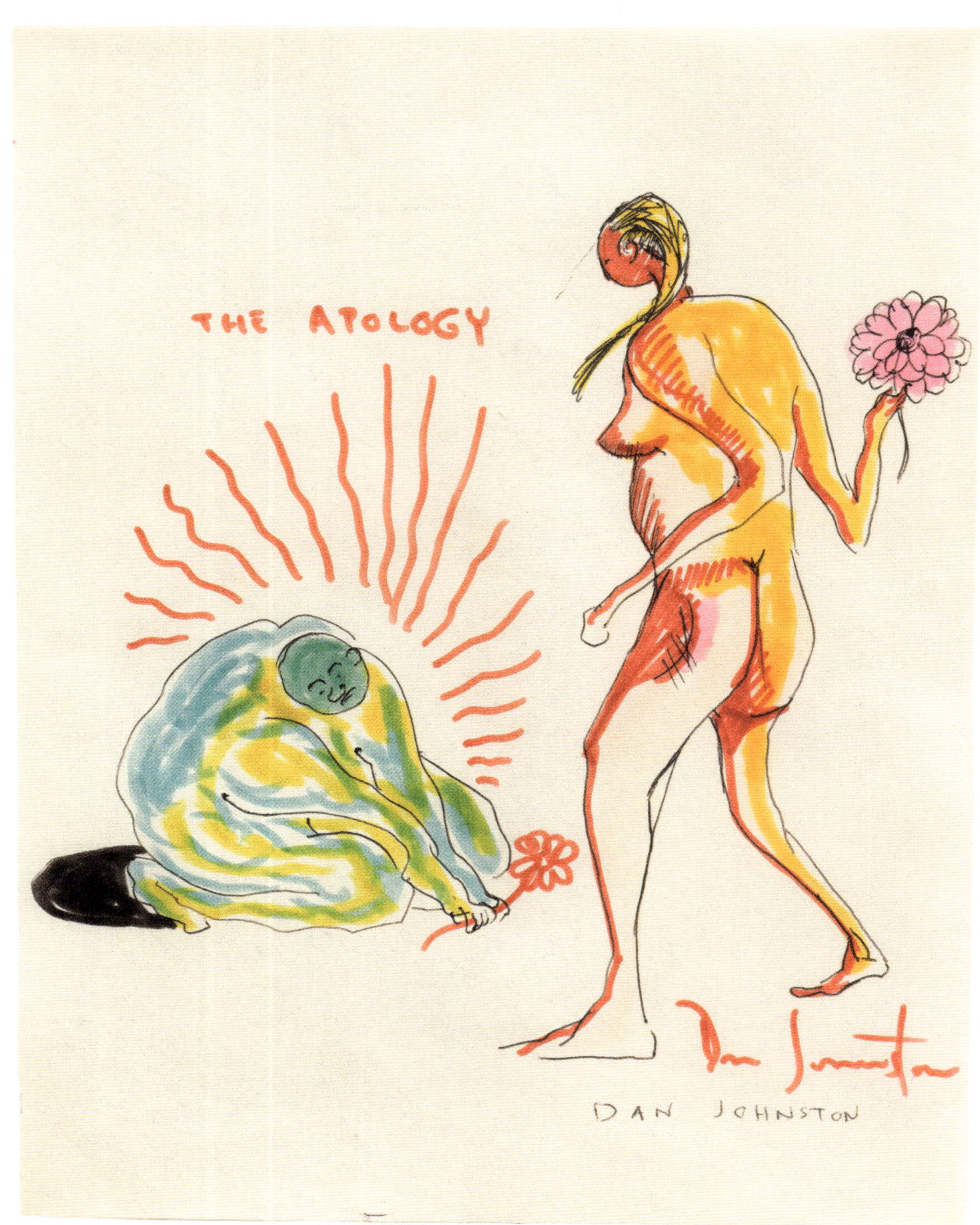

The Apology

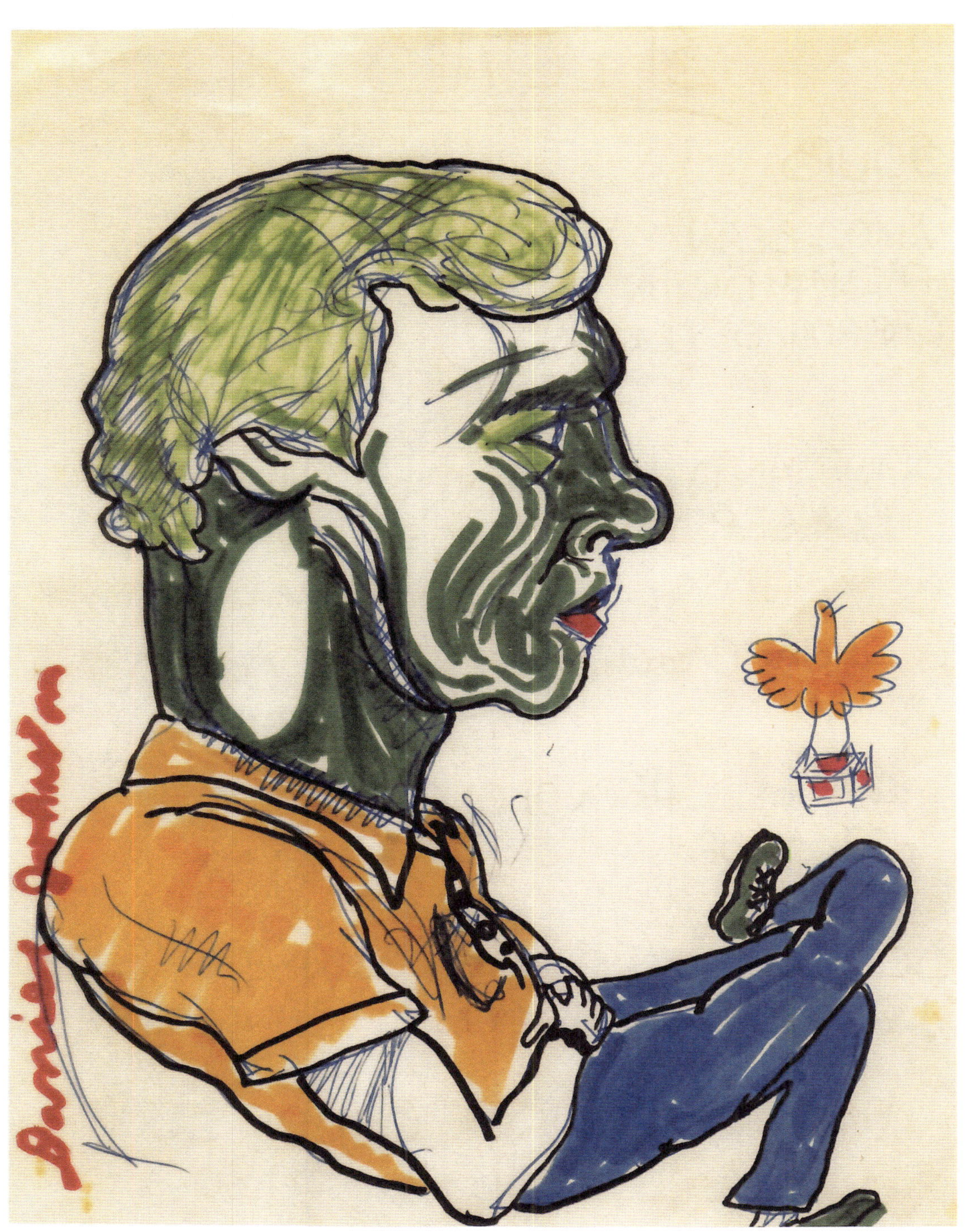

Untitled (Green Man)

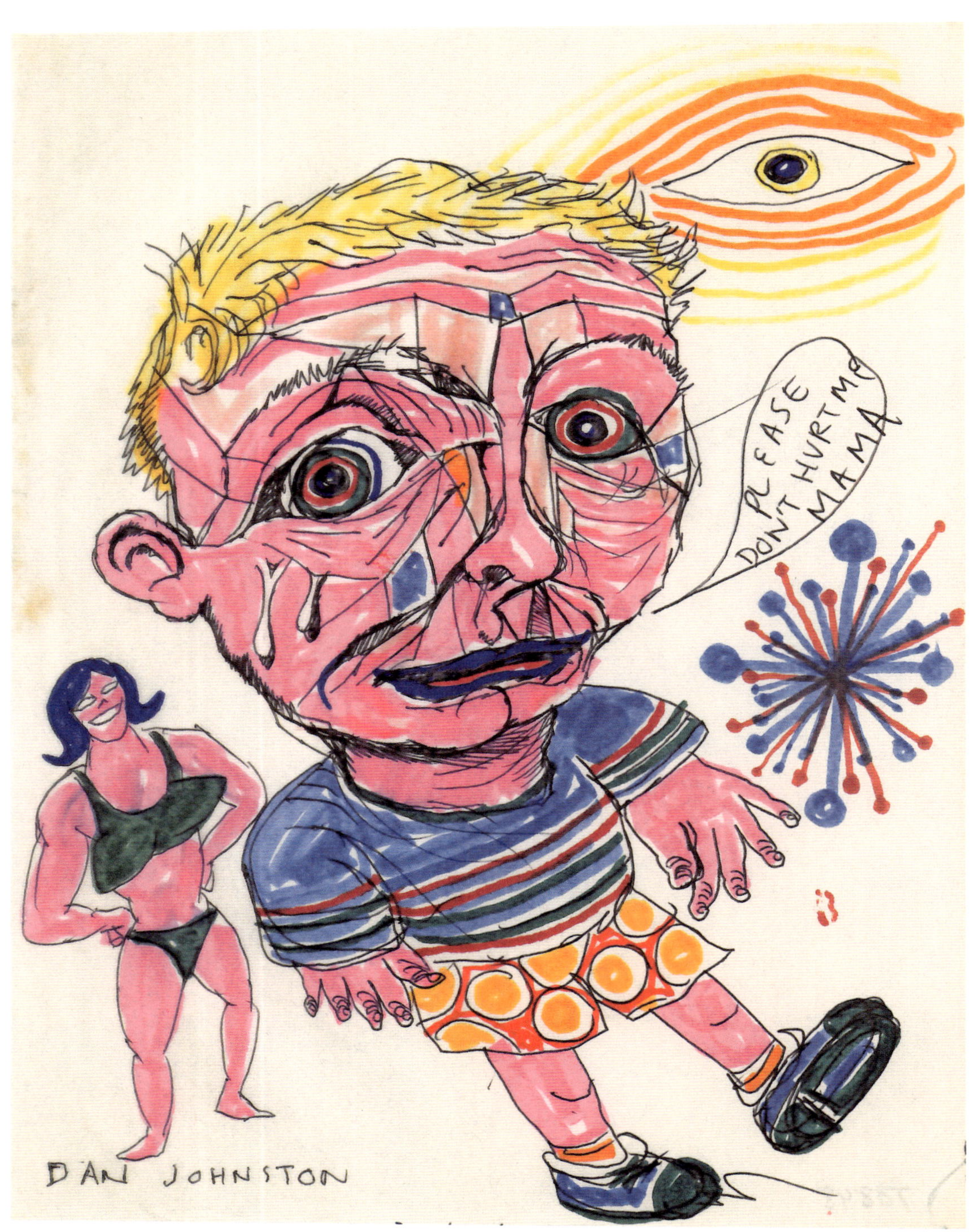

Please Don't Hurt Me Mama

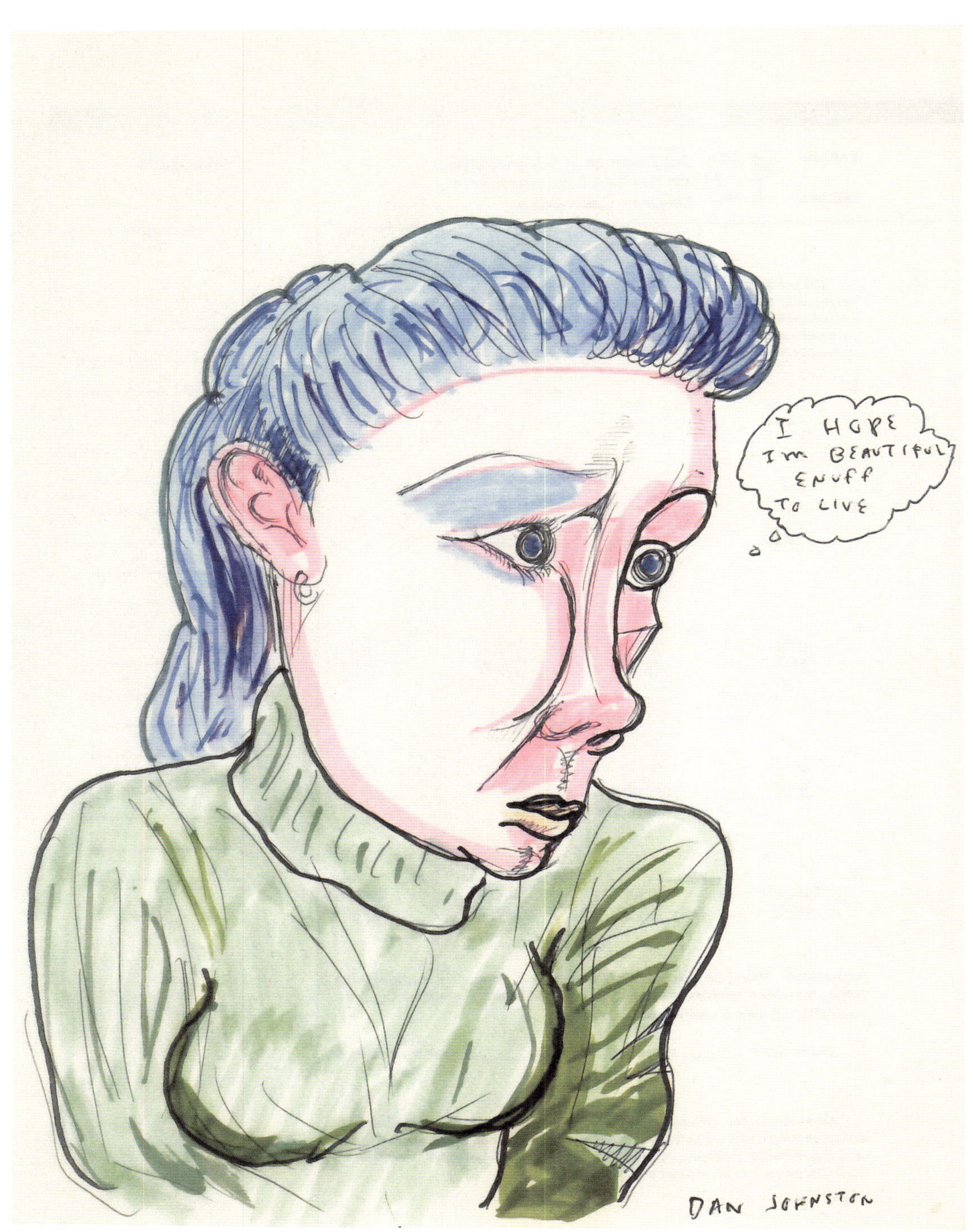

I Hope I'm Beautiful Enuff to Live

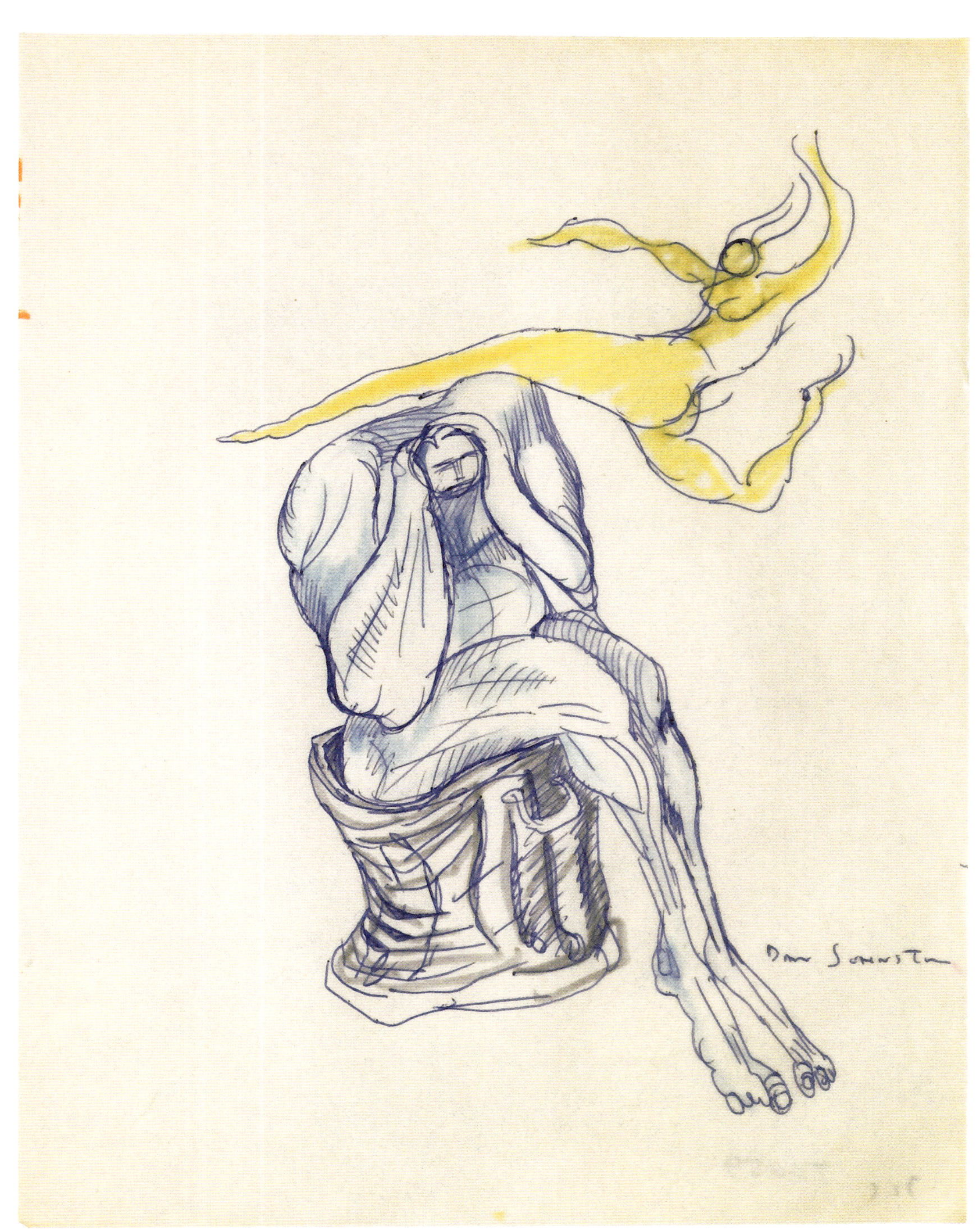

Untitled (Can't Think)

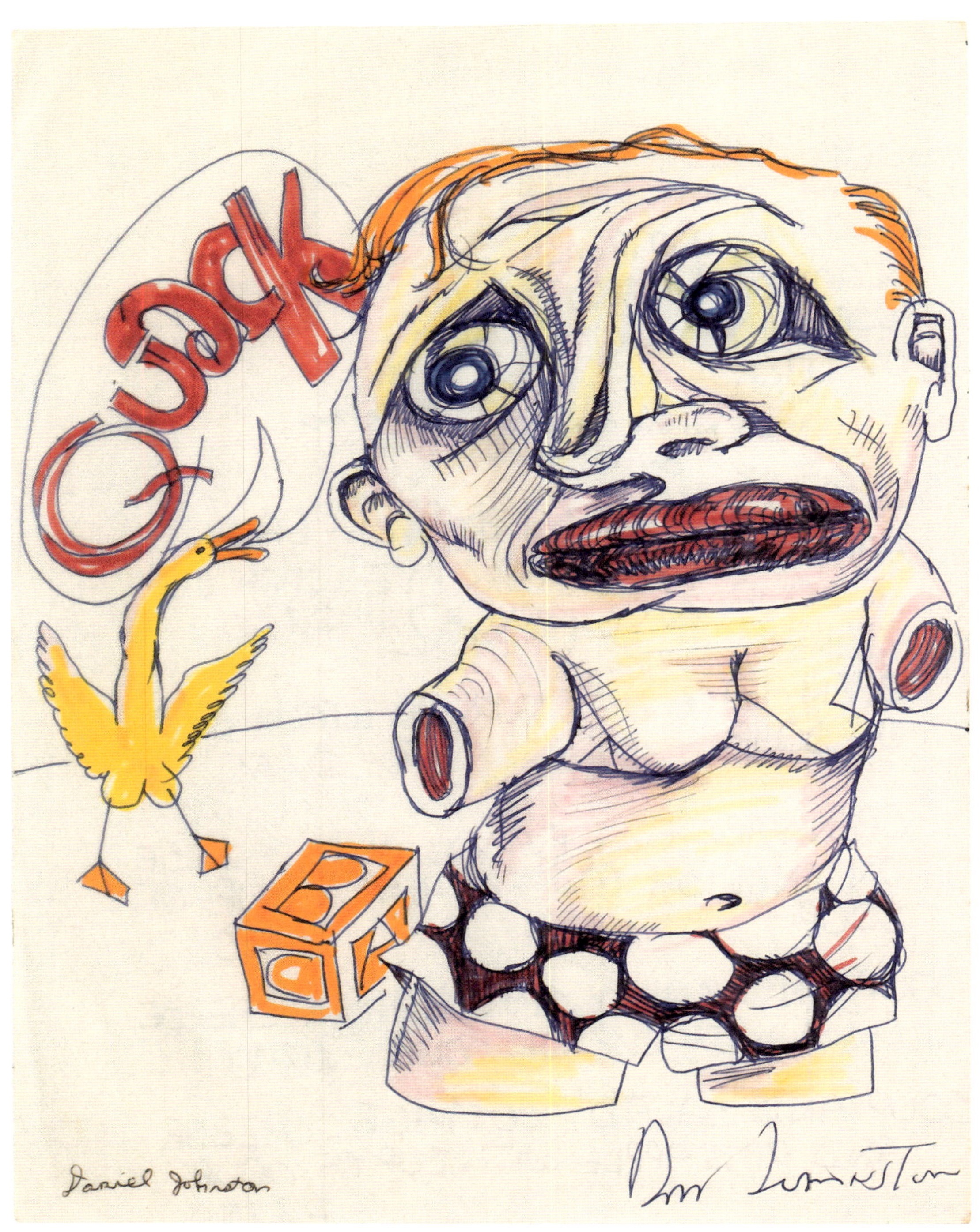

Quack

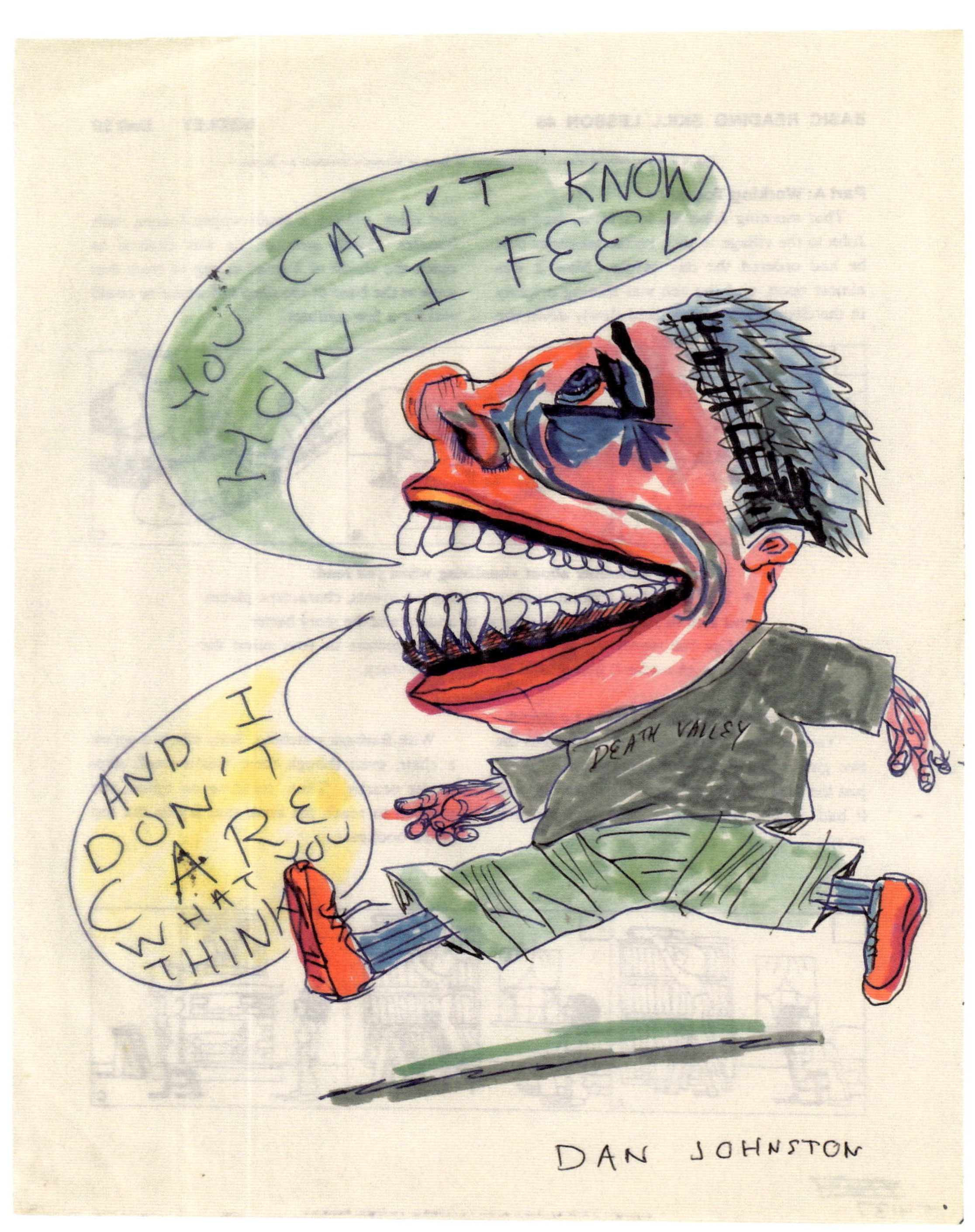

You Can't Know How I Feel

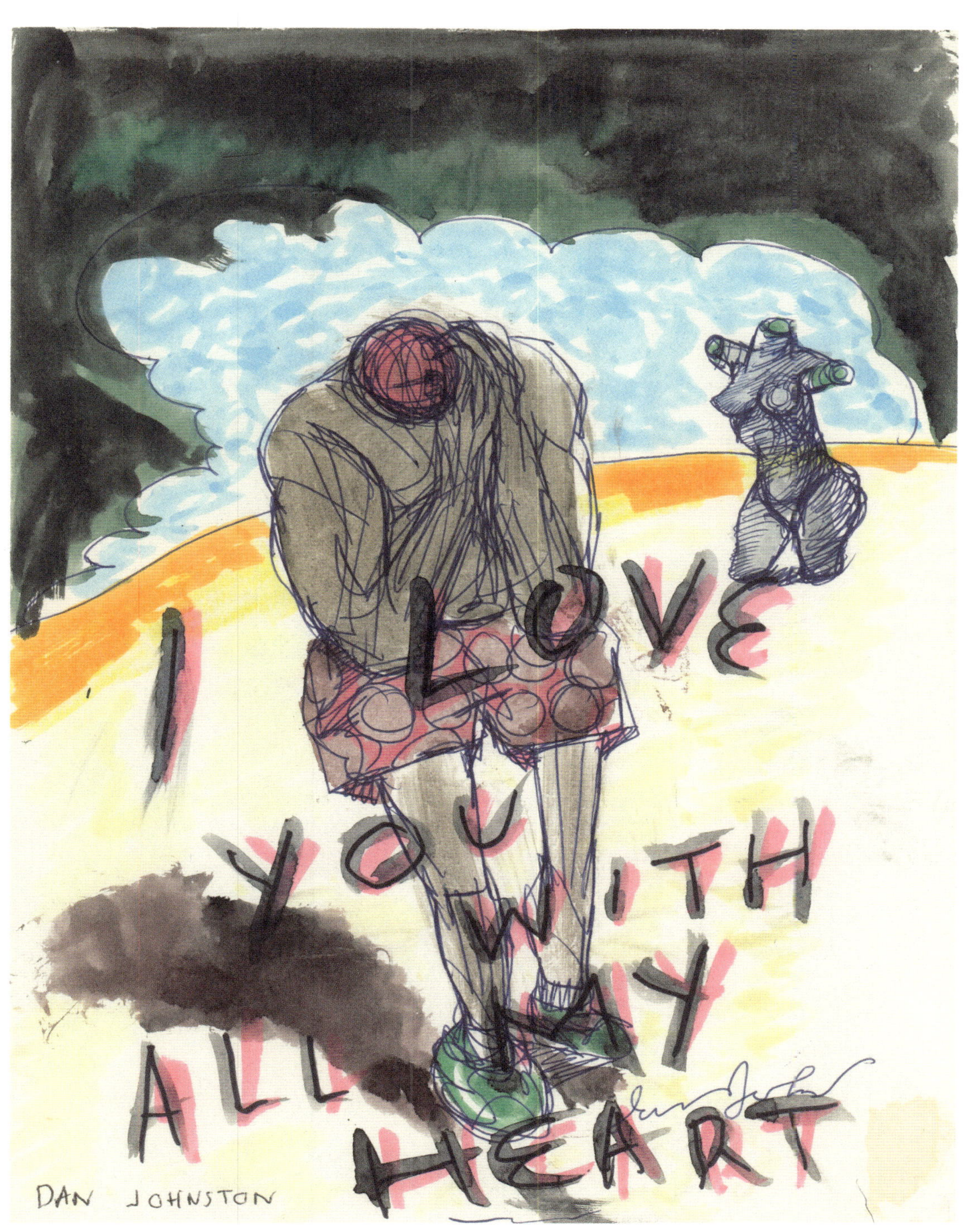

I Love You with All My Heart

People with unusual and "atypical" minds often contribute the most beautiful gifts of human expression. The best examples can be found among scientists, mathematicians, artists . . . and musicians. Ah, Daniel Johnston.

I never actually met Daniel, but I was lucky to see him play a show once in a small club in Austin. He remained seated alone on the dim stage, a nylon string acoustic guitar in hand—the whole set is still vibrant in my memory.

But it's the recordings that continue to haunt me. That mysterious and damaged sound quality, like it's coming from a sub-basement with the door closed. Then there's the heartbreaking, plaintive sonic register his voice occupies. And, of course, most striking of all—the painful, heartfelt, and often childlike lyrics that his voice and broken music carry so deliberately in their tentativeness.

In our house, we still have several of the original cassettes—precious artifacts. They include: *Yip/Jump Music*, *Retired Boxer*, and *The What of Whom*. Their "covers," with Daniel's alluring drawings, were xeroxed and glued onto the plastic boxes by his former manager Jeff Tartakov and Daniel's own hand, their edges now worn and curling, his molecules still magically present.

I remember talking with Tom Waits about our mutual love of his music many years ago. Tom was in the process of choosing one of Daniel's songs to cover for the compilation *The Late Great Daniel Johnston: Discovered Covered*. He eventually settled on "King Kong," but it was difficult—there were just so many "classics" to consider.

I also remember being quite distraught when hearing that Daniel Johnston had left us—now five years ago—and I immediately recalled him singing his song "Funeral Home" that one time I saw him in Austin: "Got me a coffin, shiny and black. I'm going to the funeral and I'm never coming back." Long live Daniel Johnston.

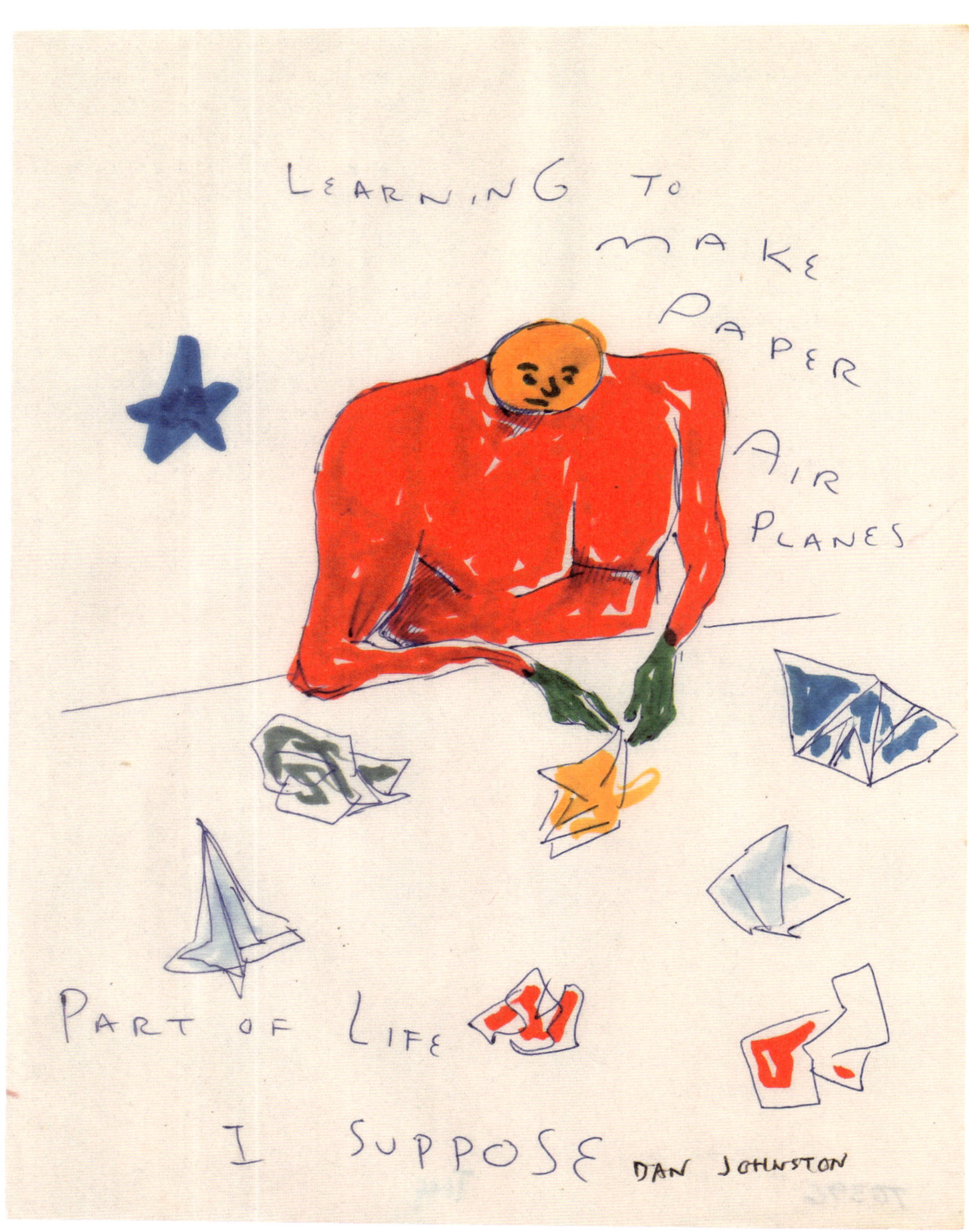

Paper Airplanes

VII.
Pleasure
1979–1985

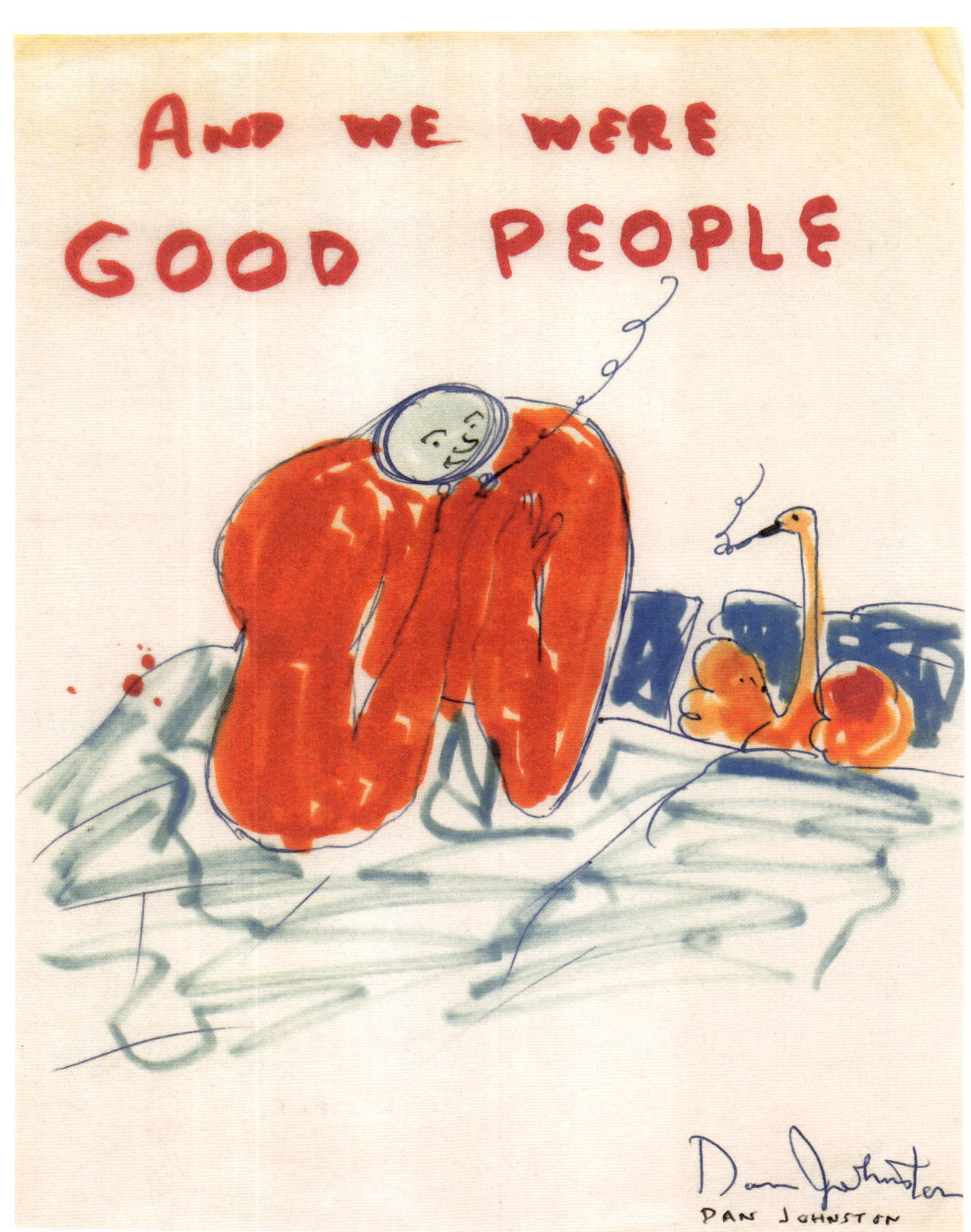

And We Were Good People

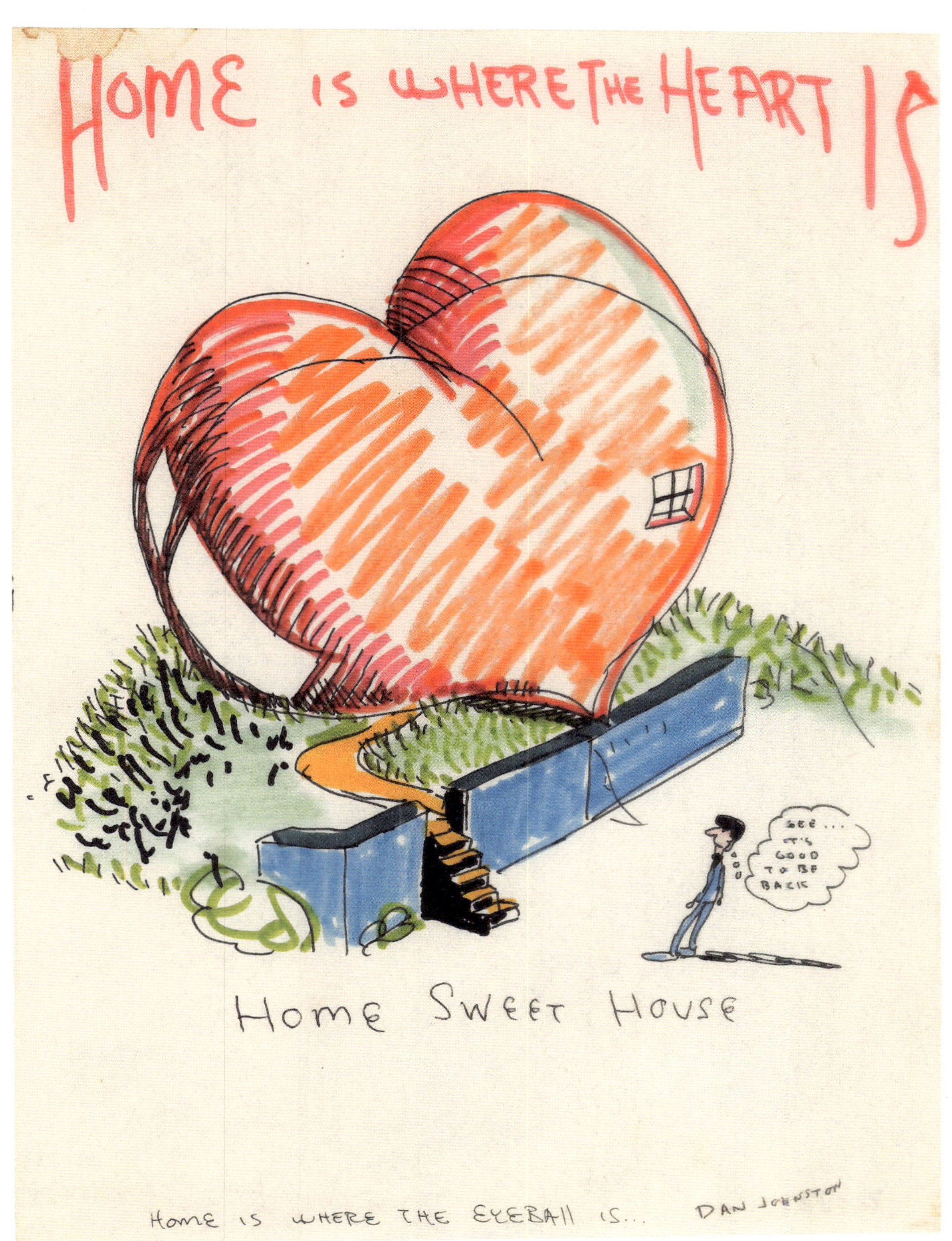

Home Sweet House

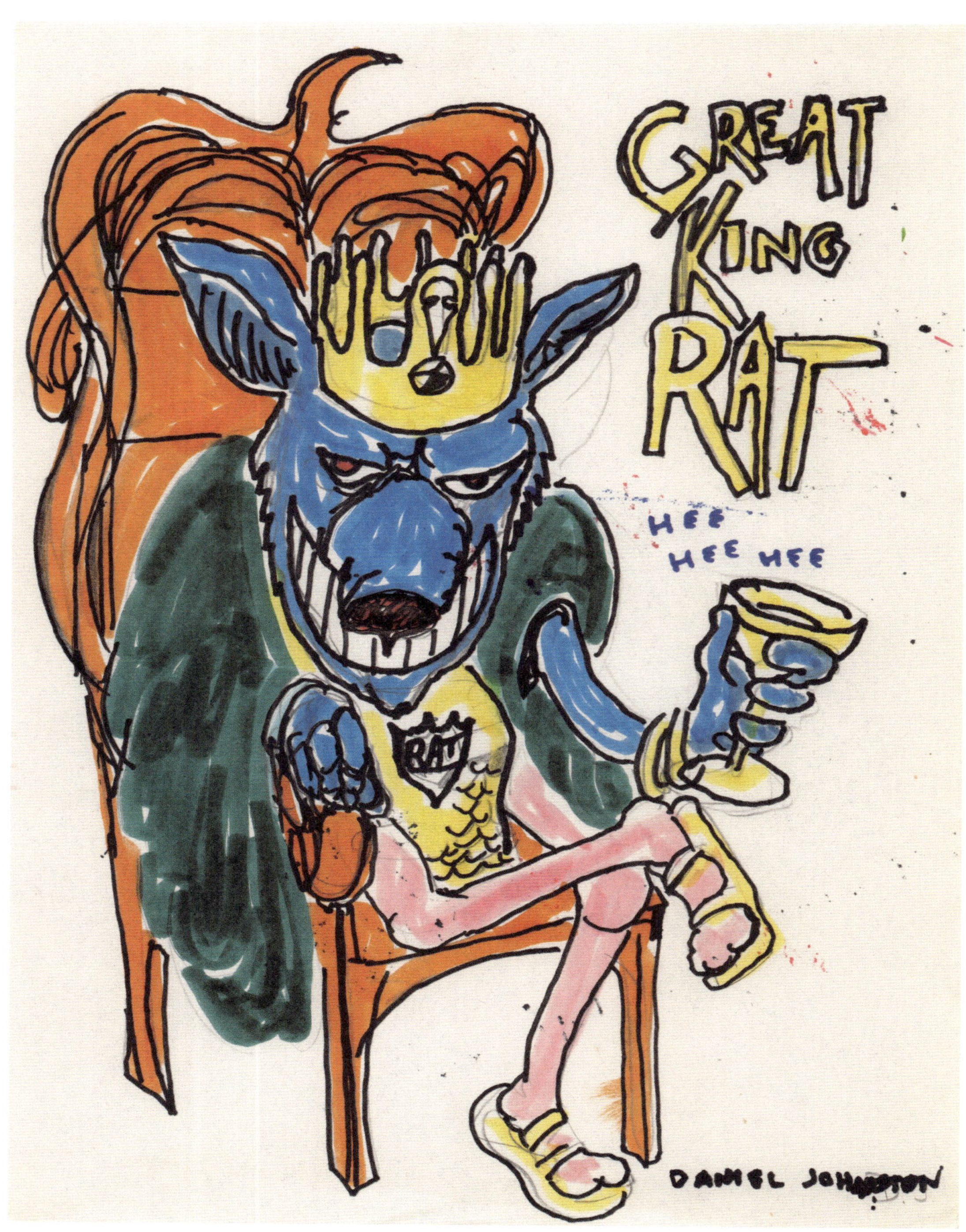

Great King Rat

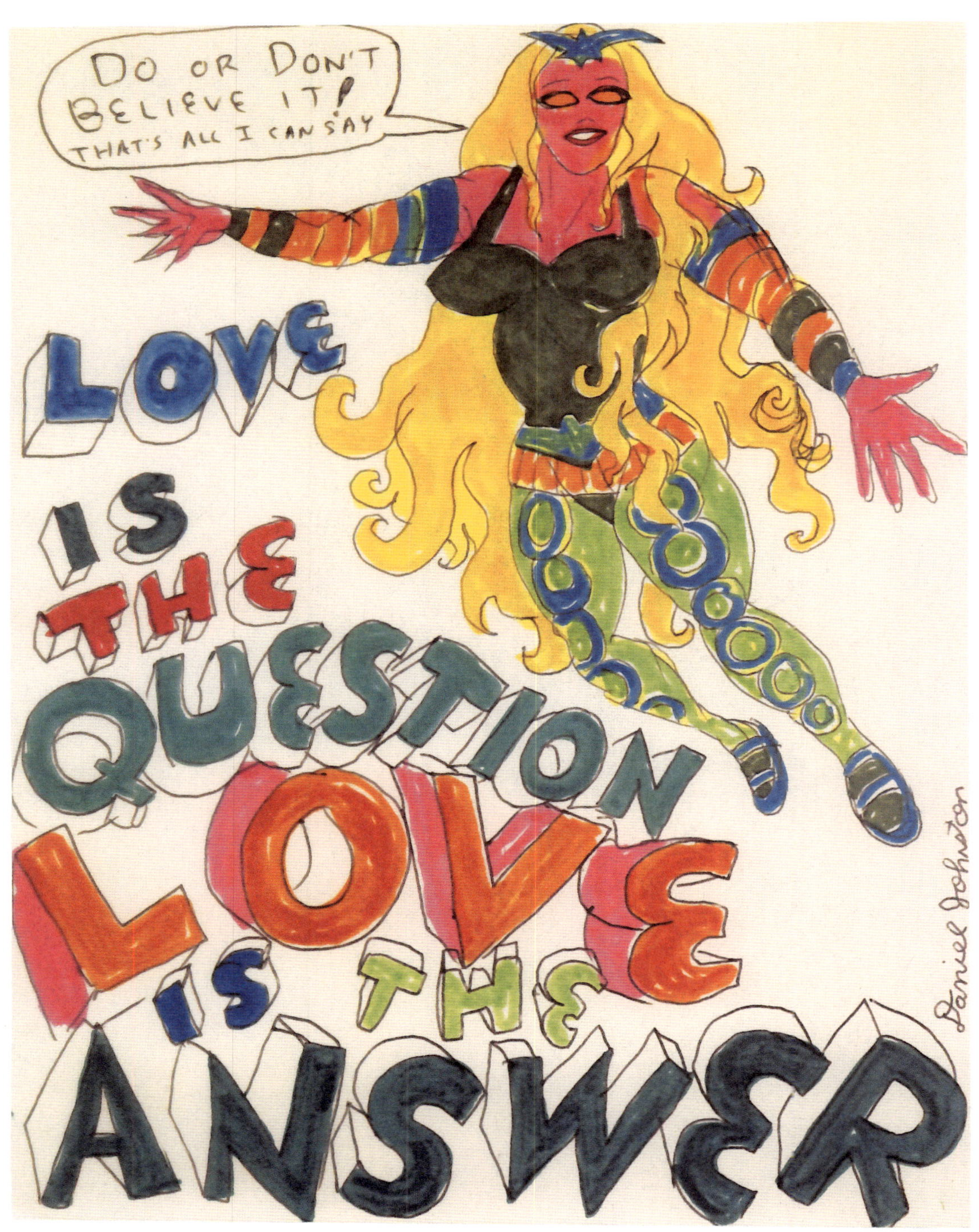

Love Is the Question Love Is the Answer

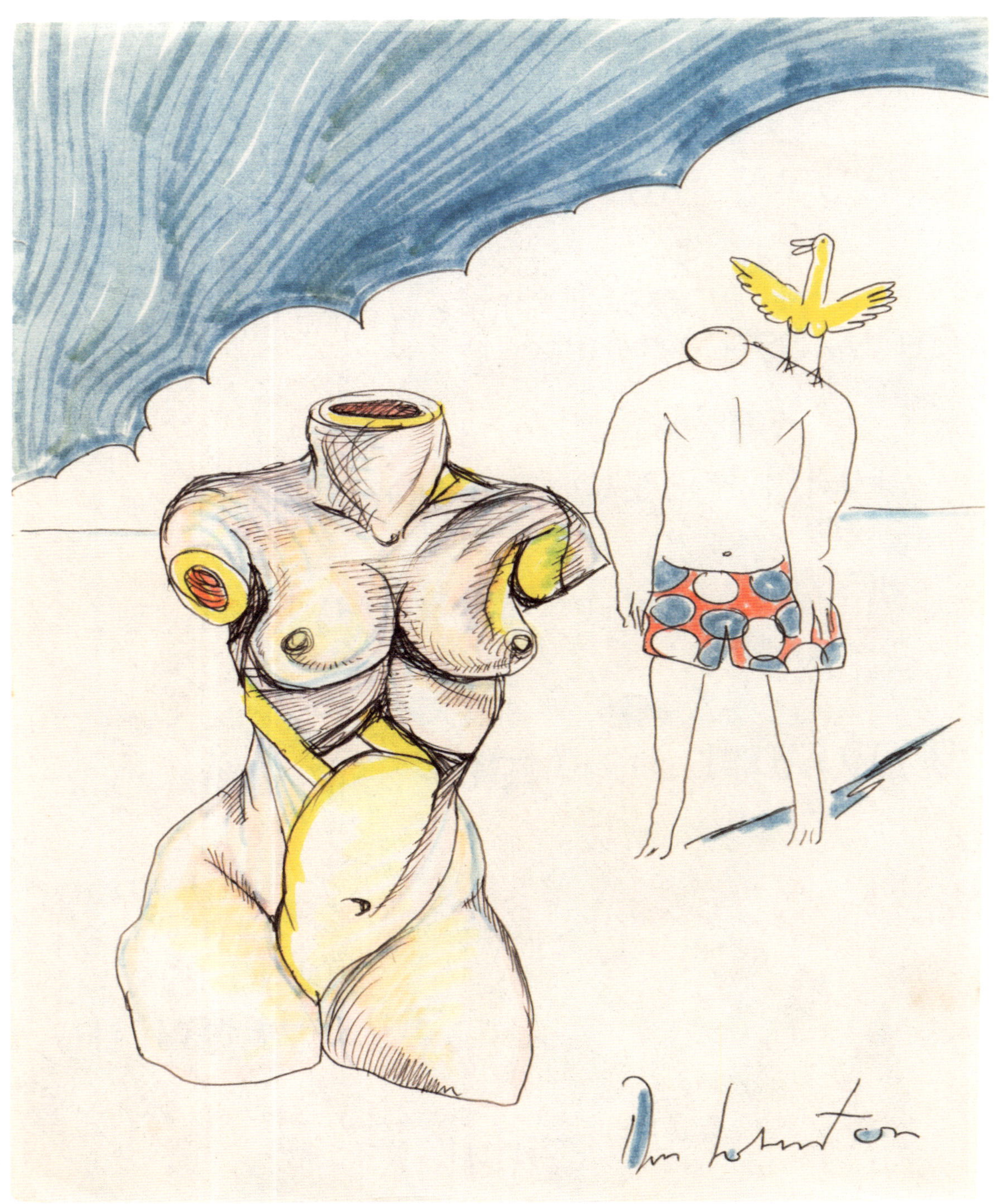

Untitled (Blue Sky Torso)

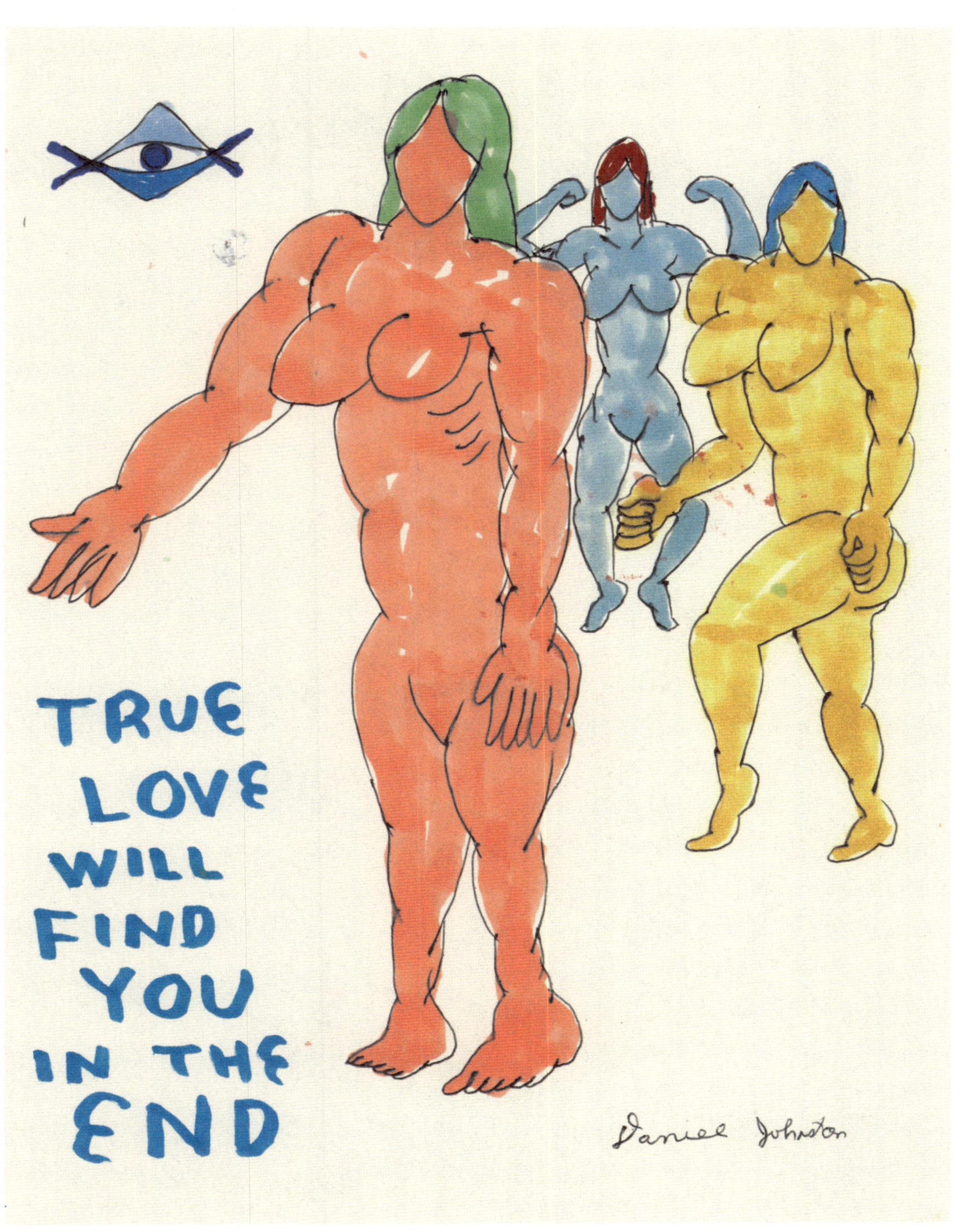

True Love Will Find You in the End

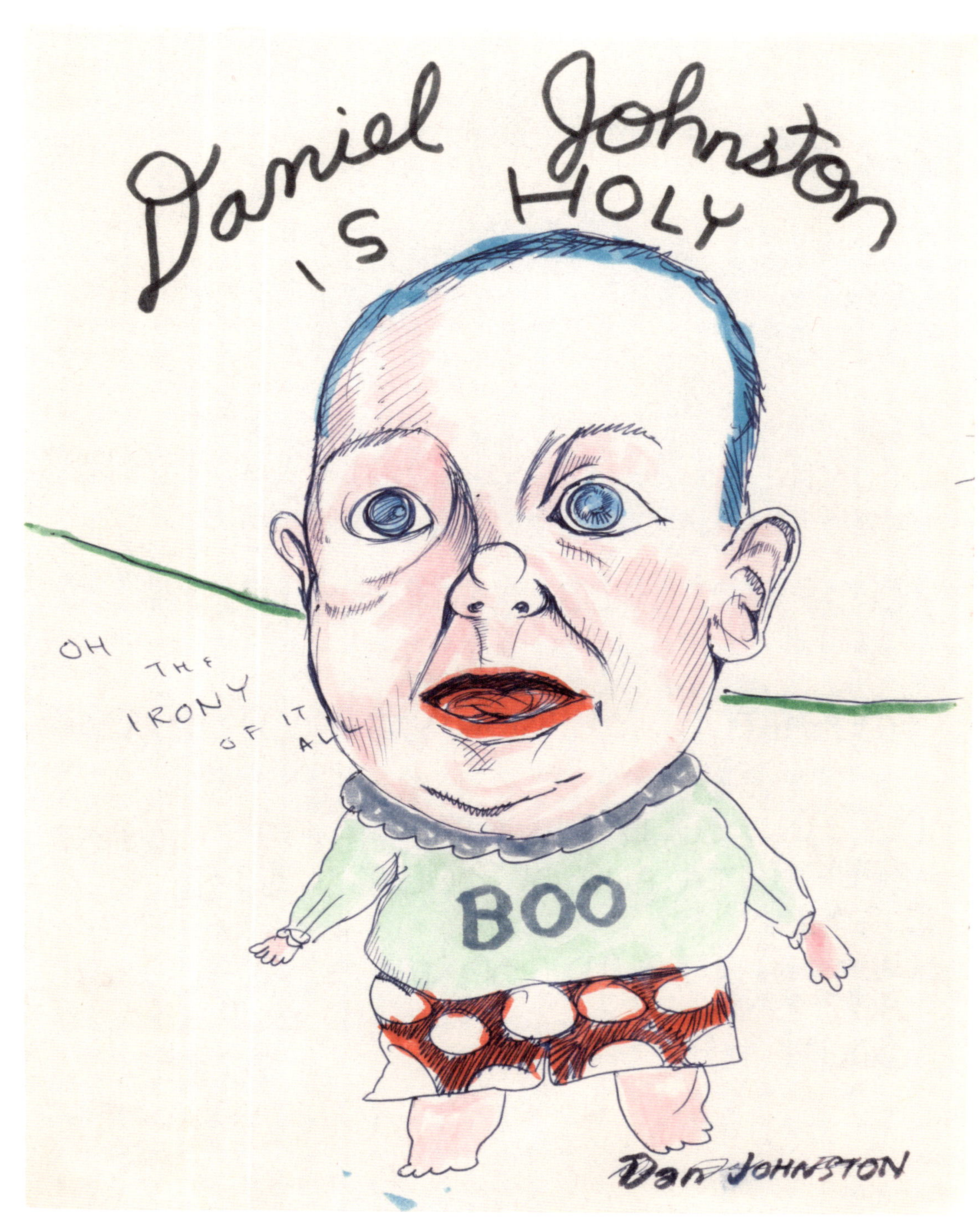

Daniel Johnston Is Holy

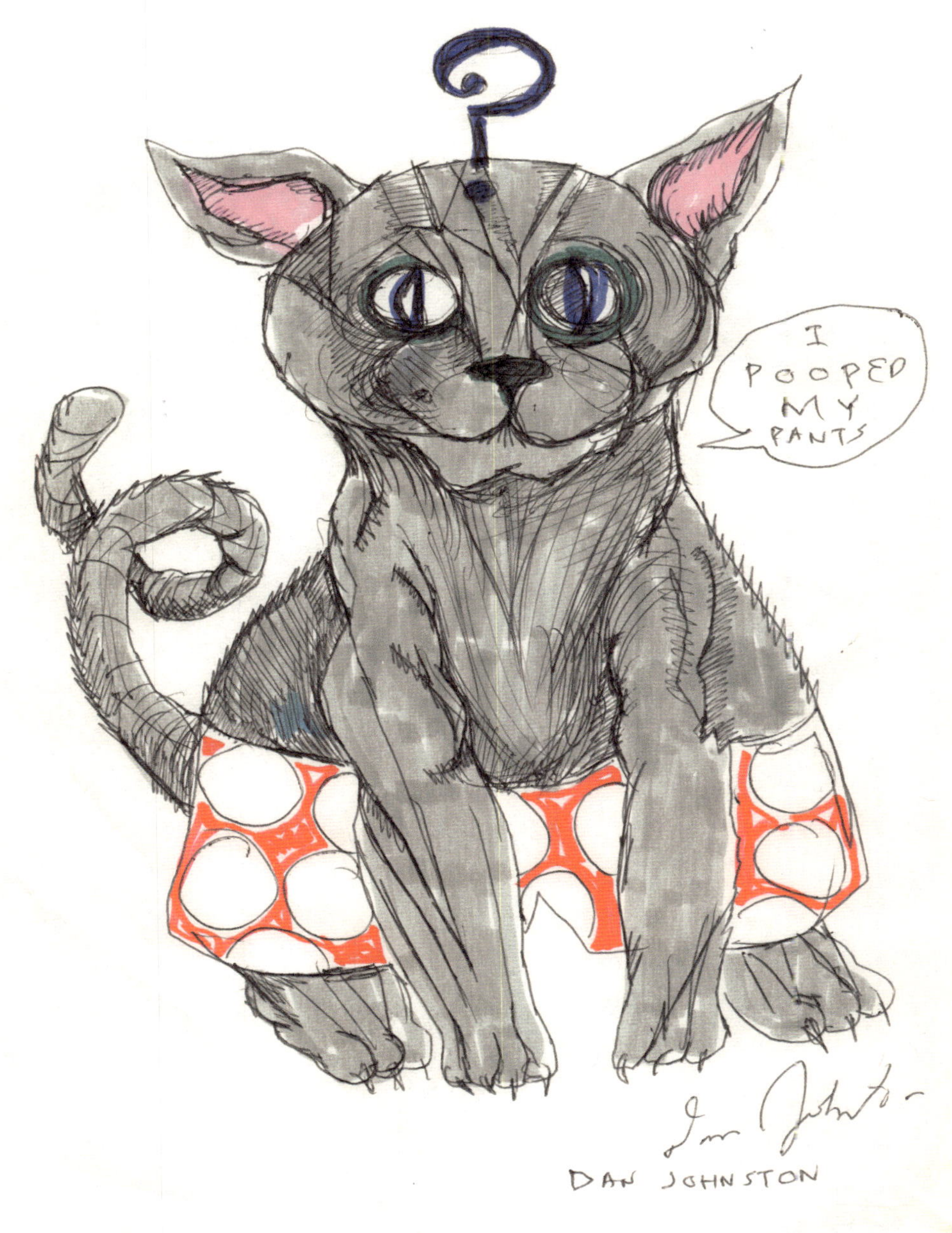

I Pooped My Pants

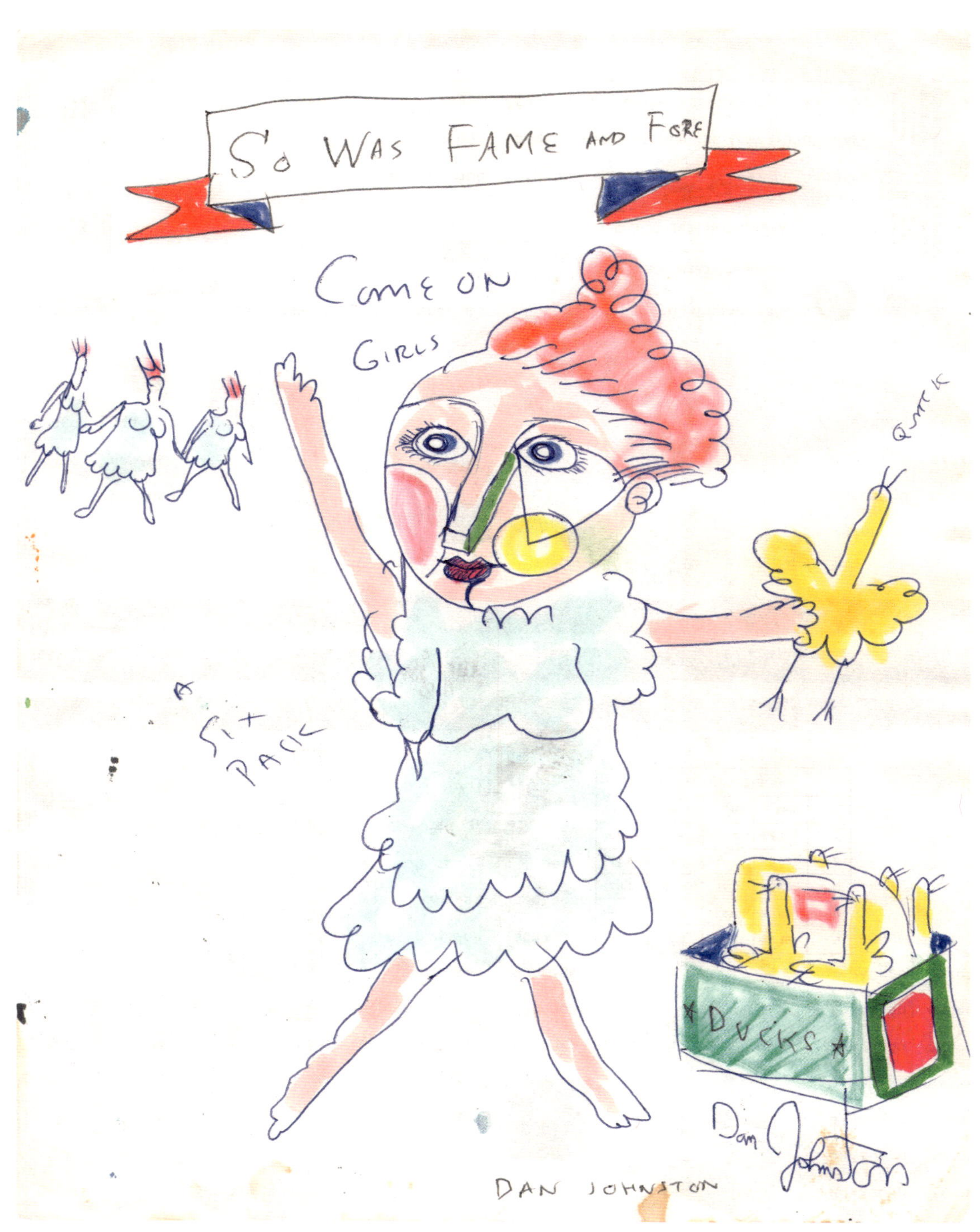

Come On Girls

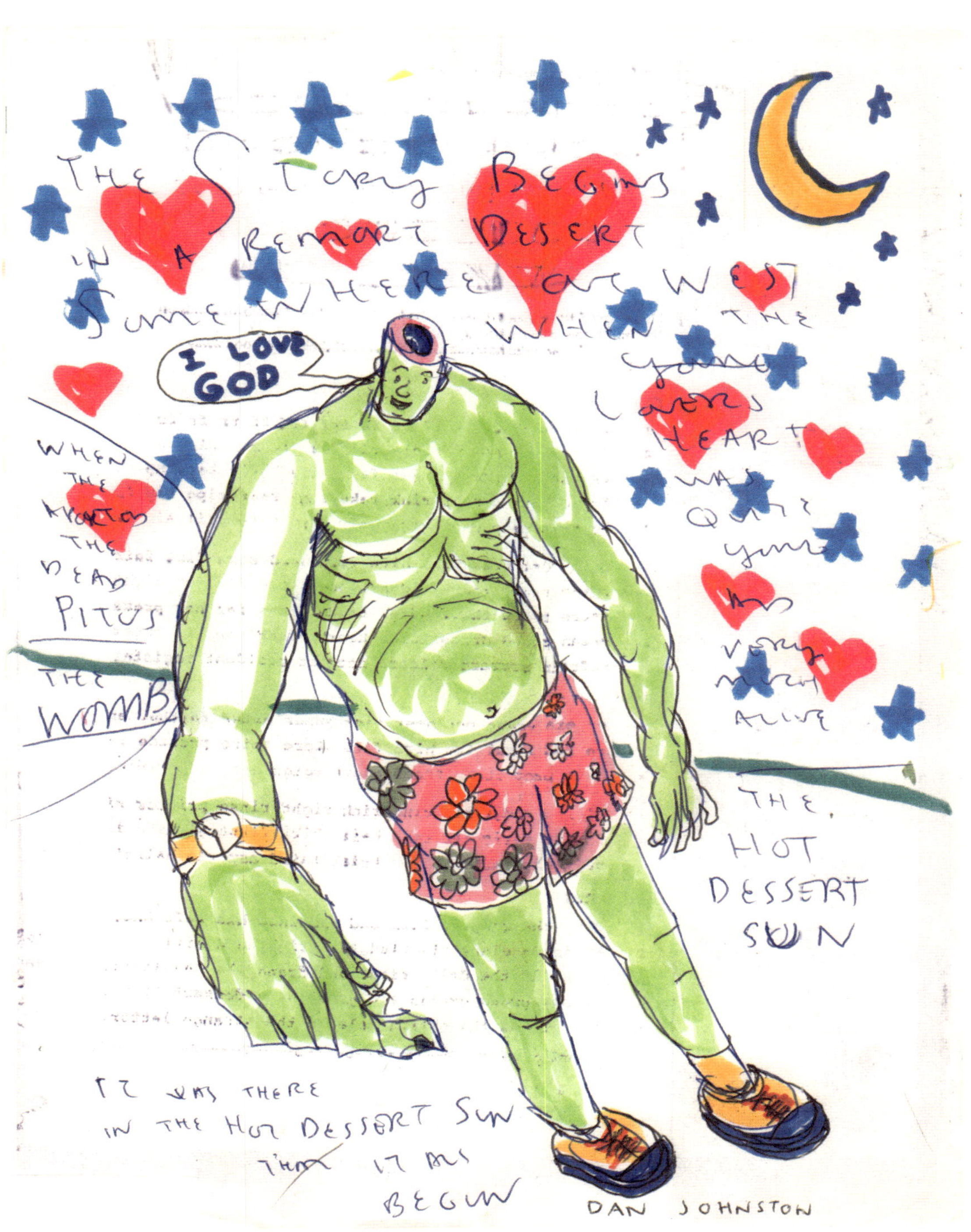
I LOVE GOD
THE WOMB
THE HOT DESSERT SUN
IT WAS THERE IN THE HOT DESSERT SUN
BEGUN
DAN JOHNSTON

I Love God

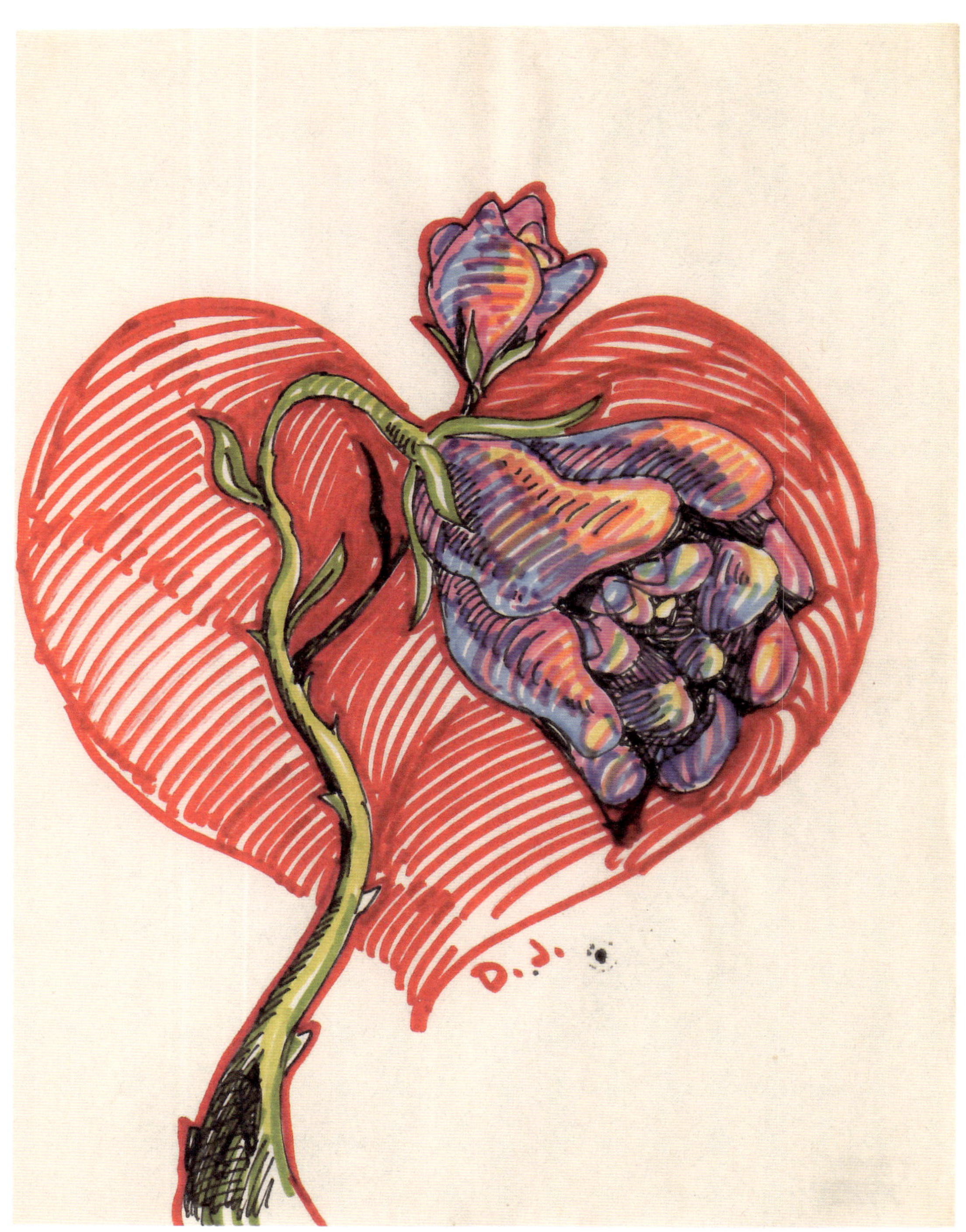

Untitled (Purple Rose)

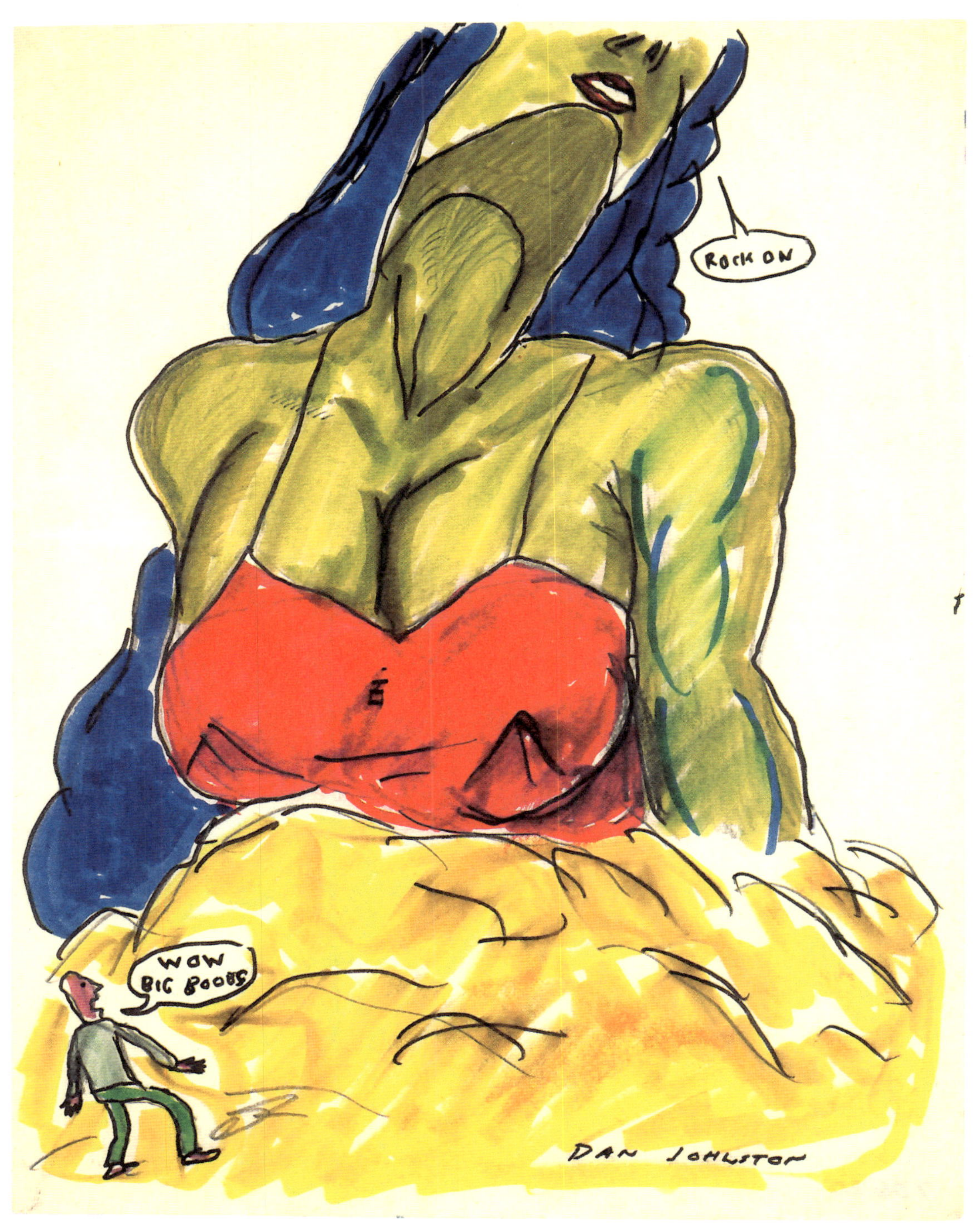

Wow Big Boobs

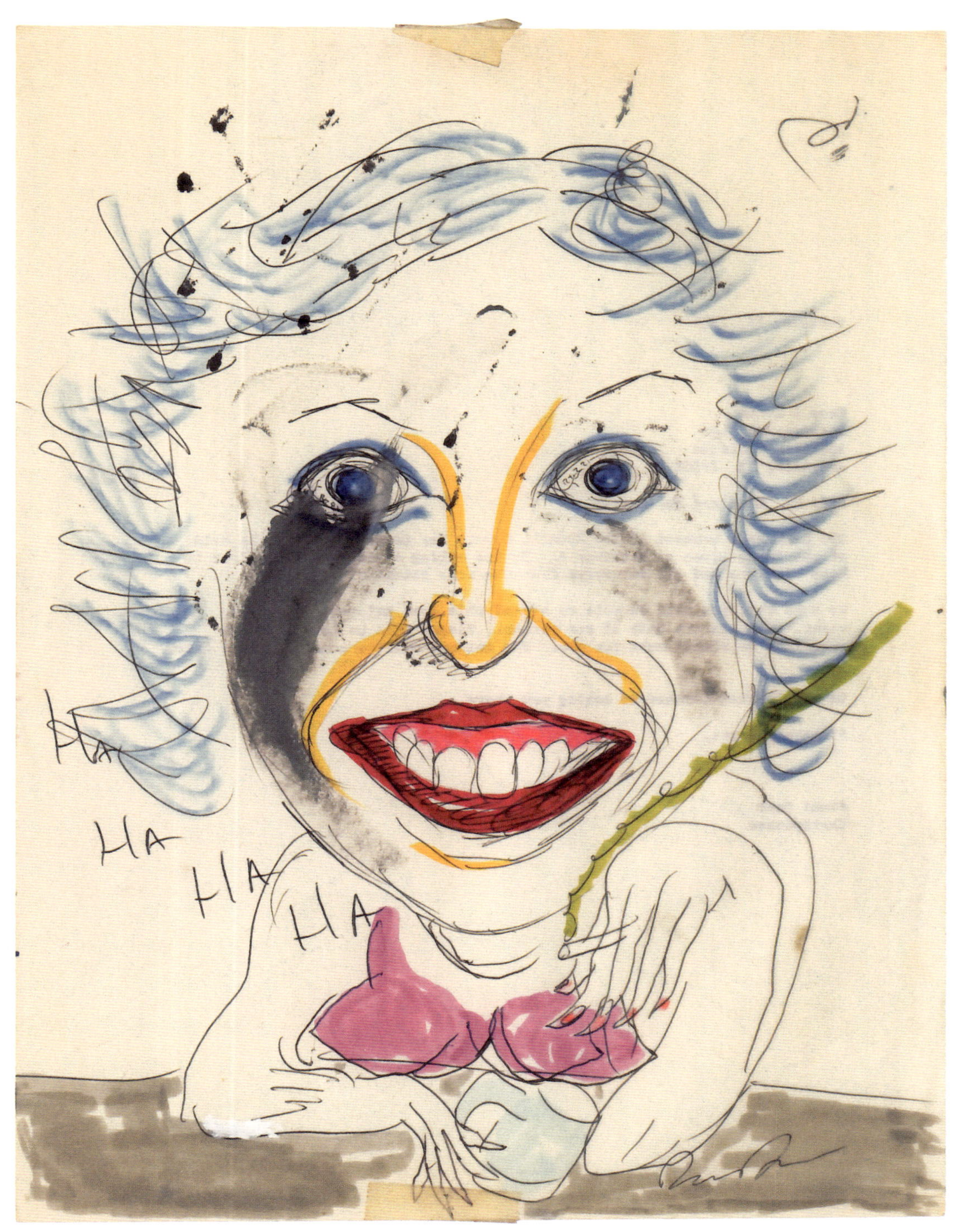

Ha Ha Ha Ha (Blue Hair)

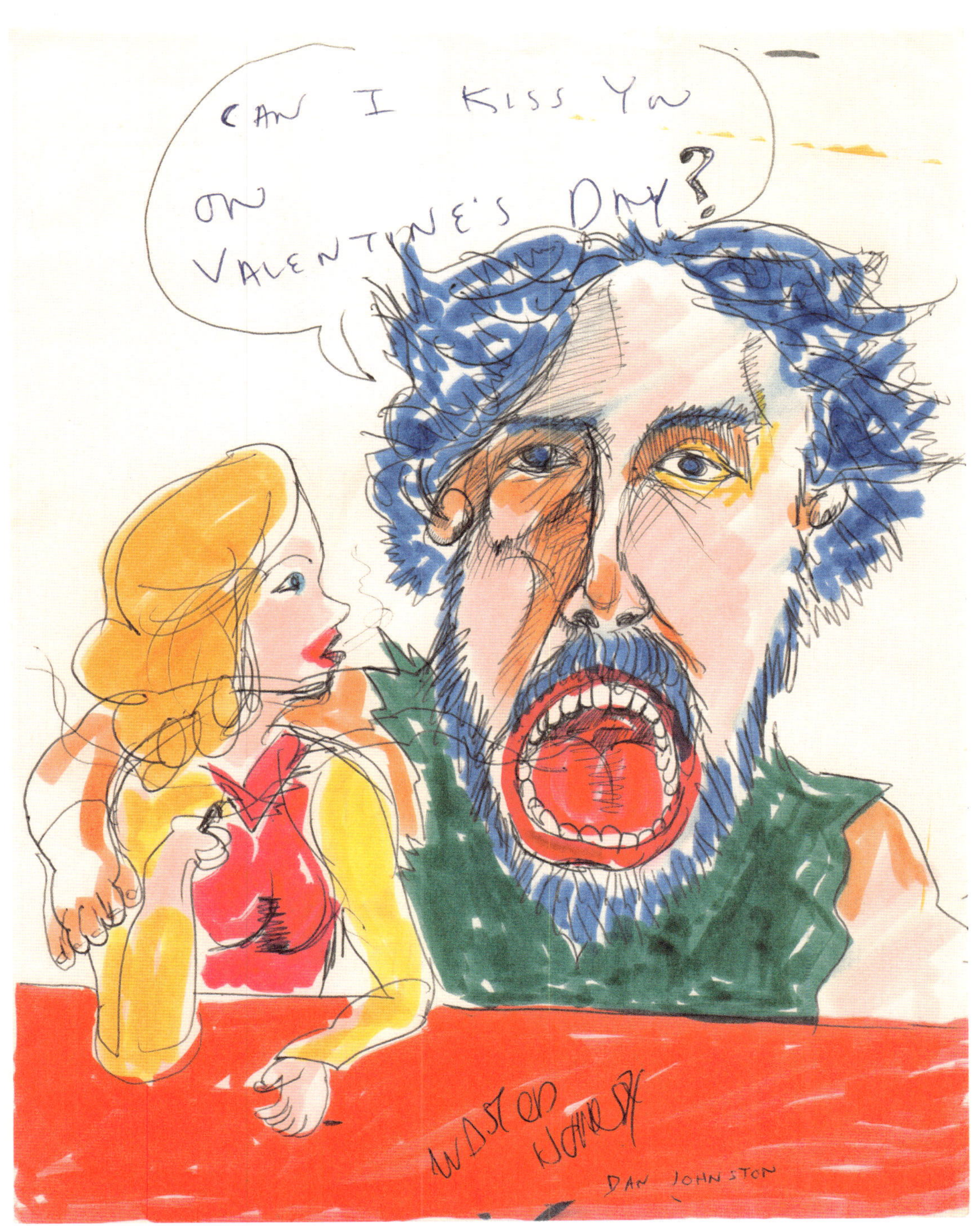

Can I Kiss You on Valentine's Day?

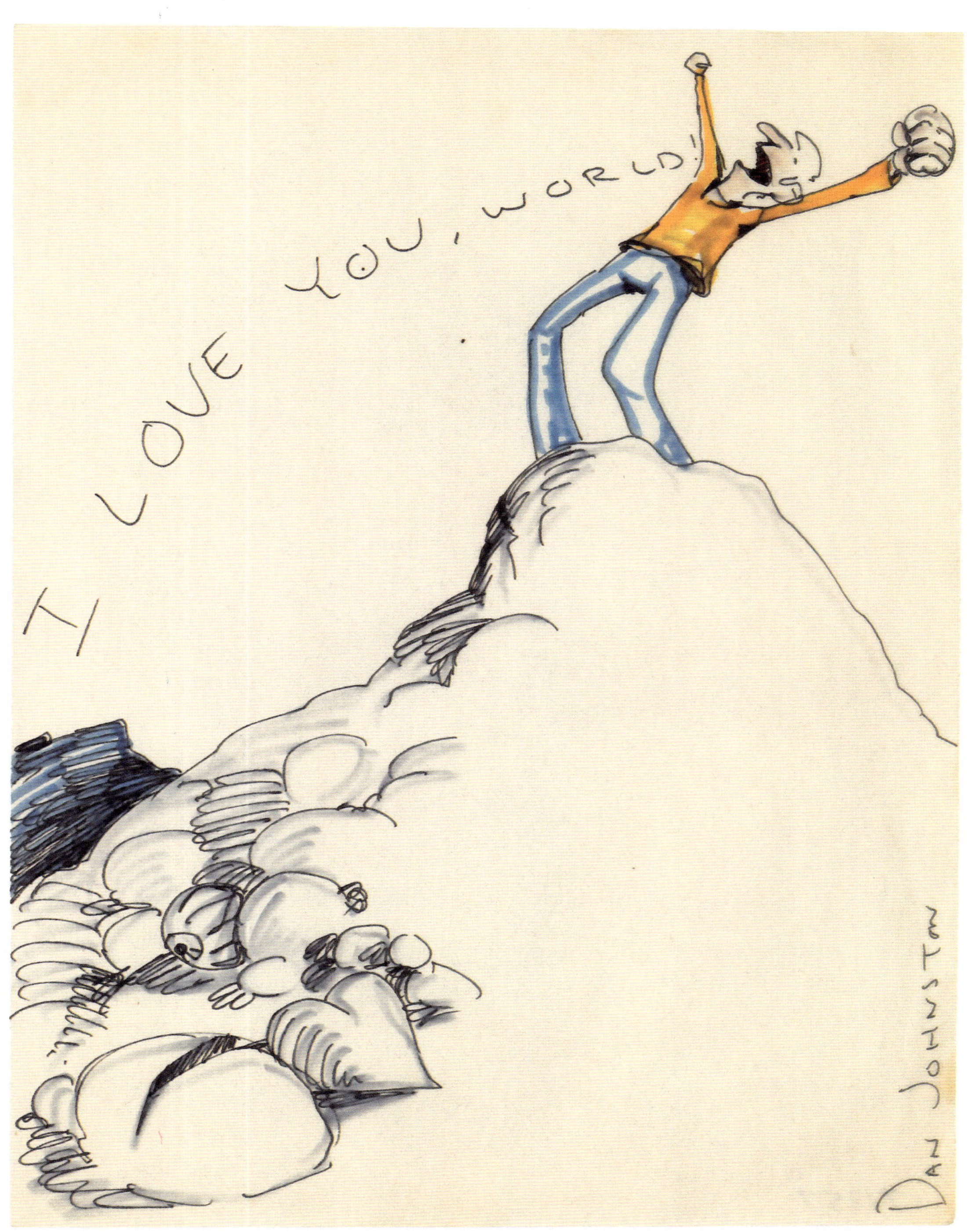

I Love You, World!

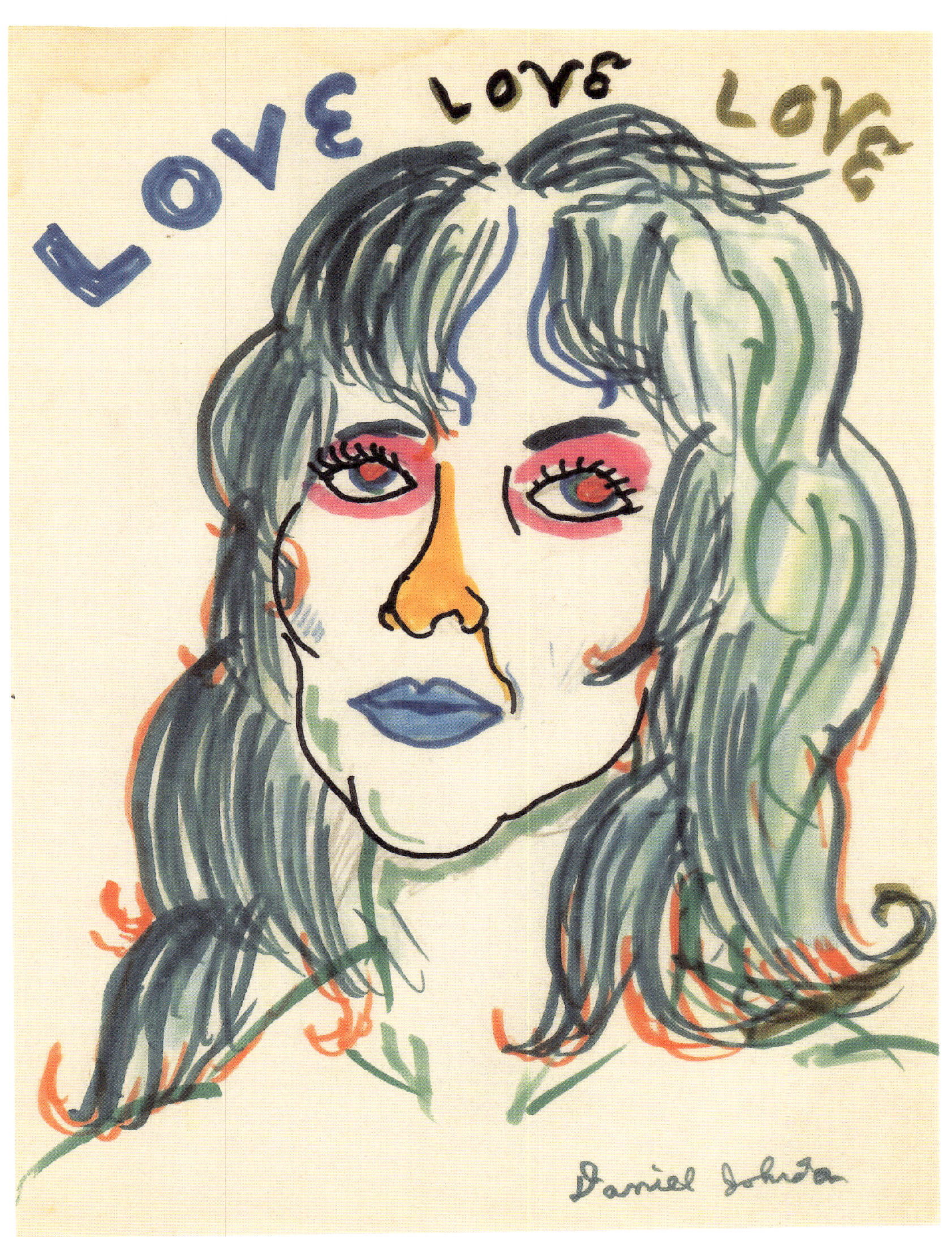

Love Love Love

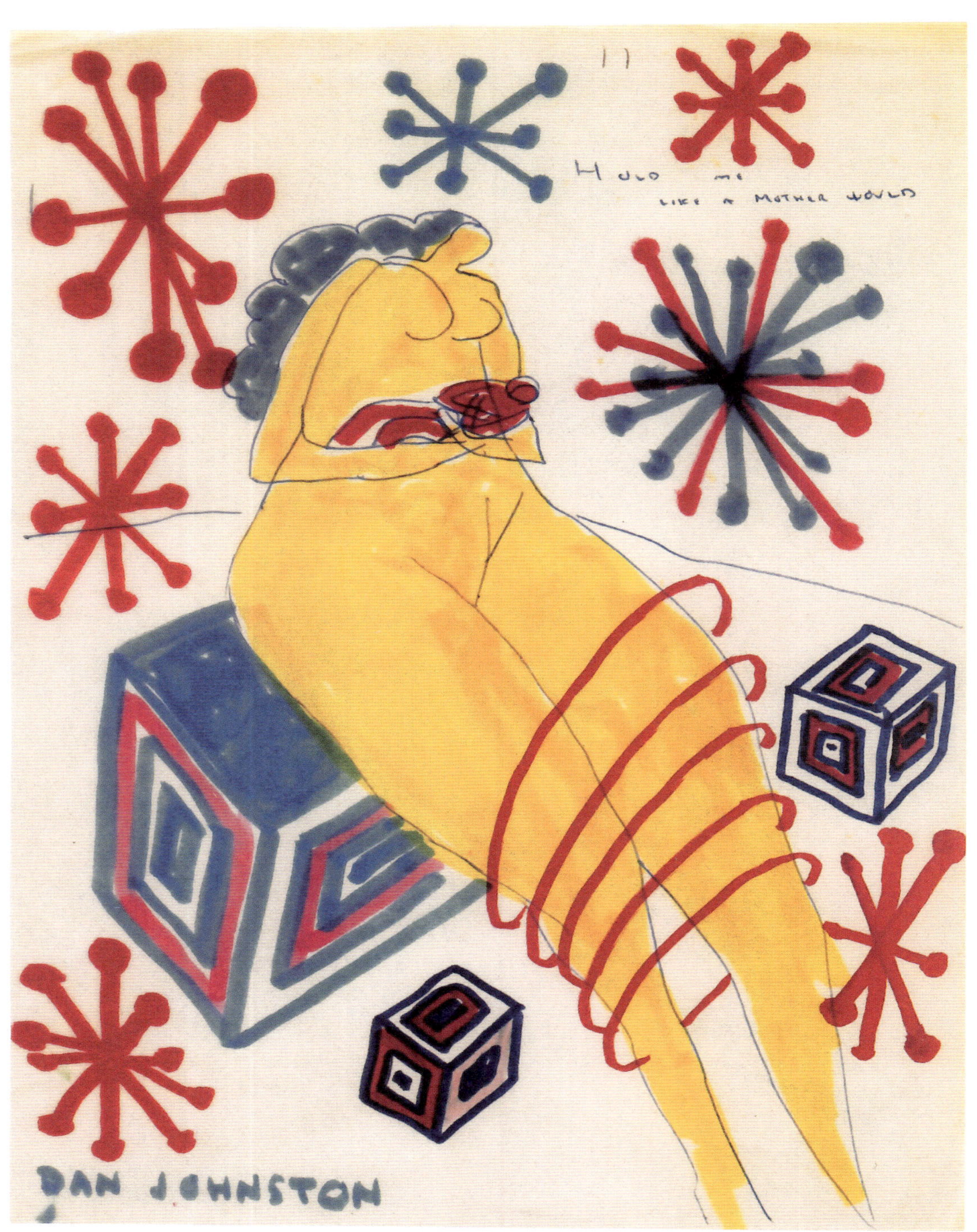

Hold Me Like a Mother Would

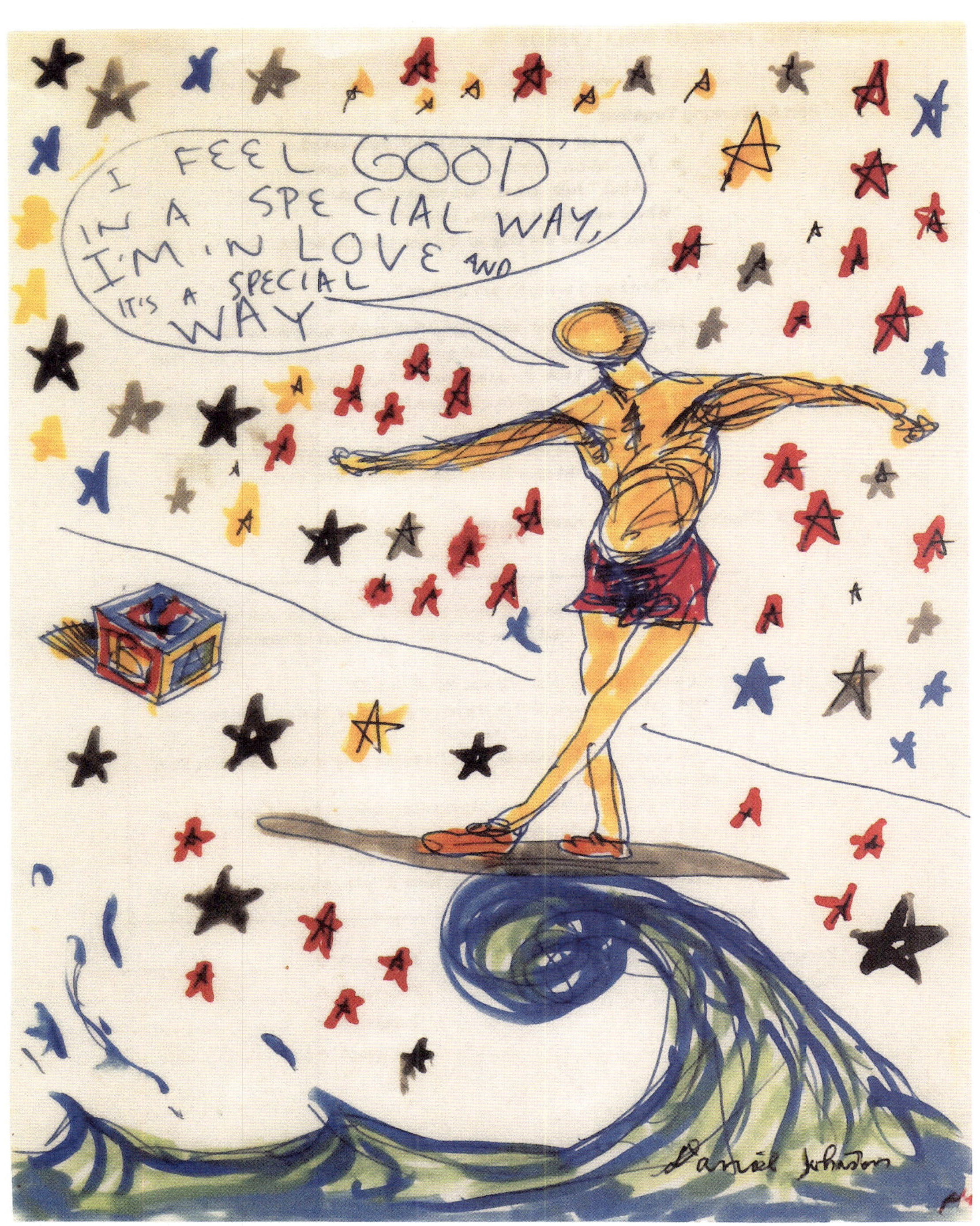

I Feel Good in a Special Way

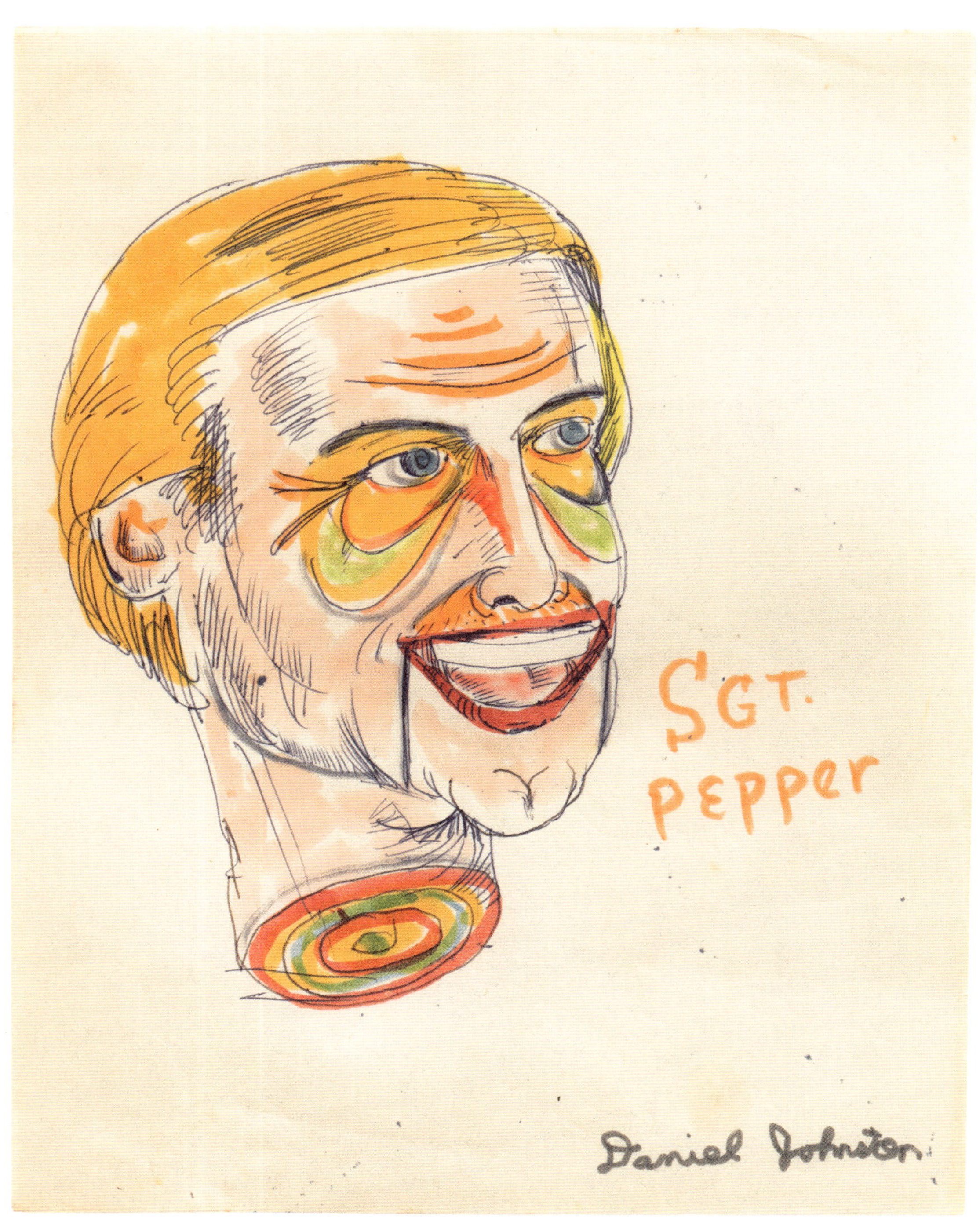

Sgt. Pepper

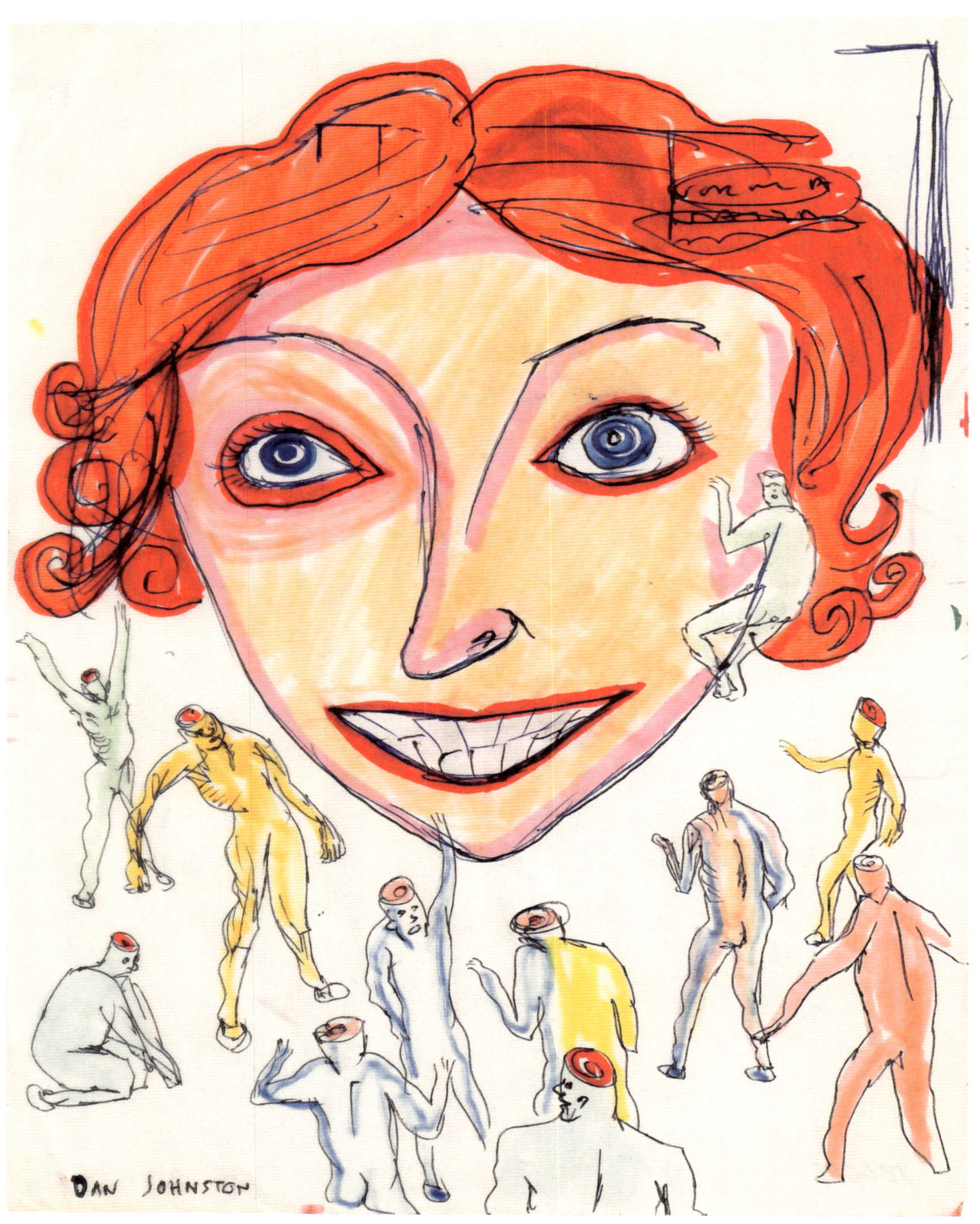

Untitled (Redhead)

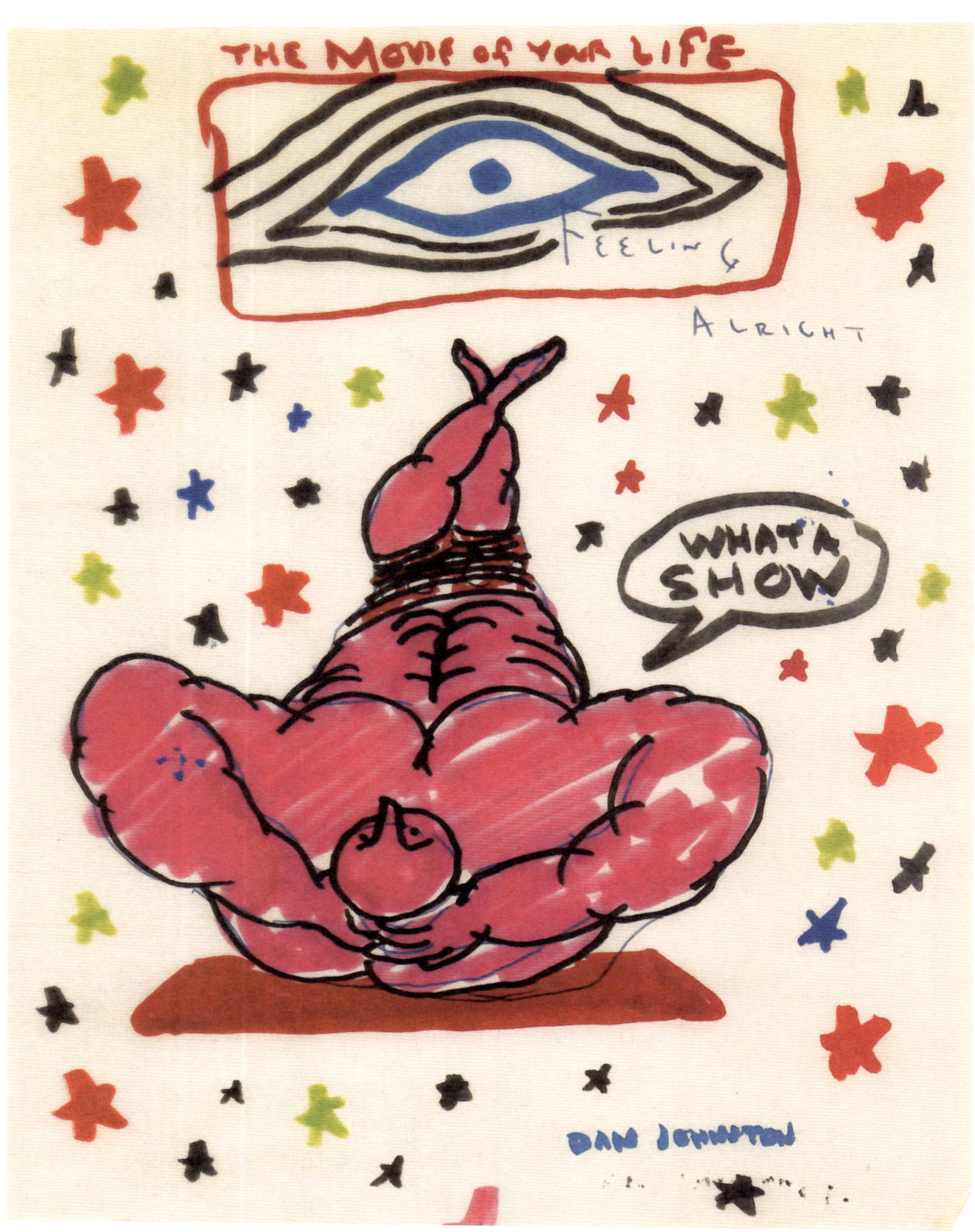

The Movie of Your Life (What a Show)

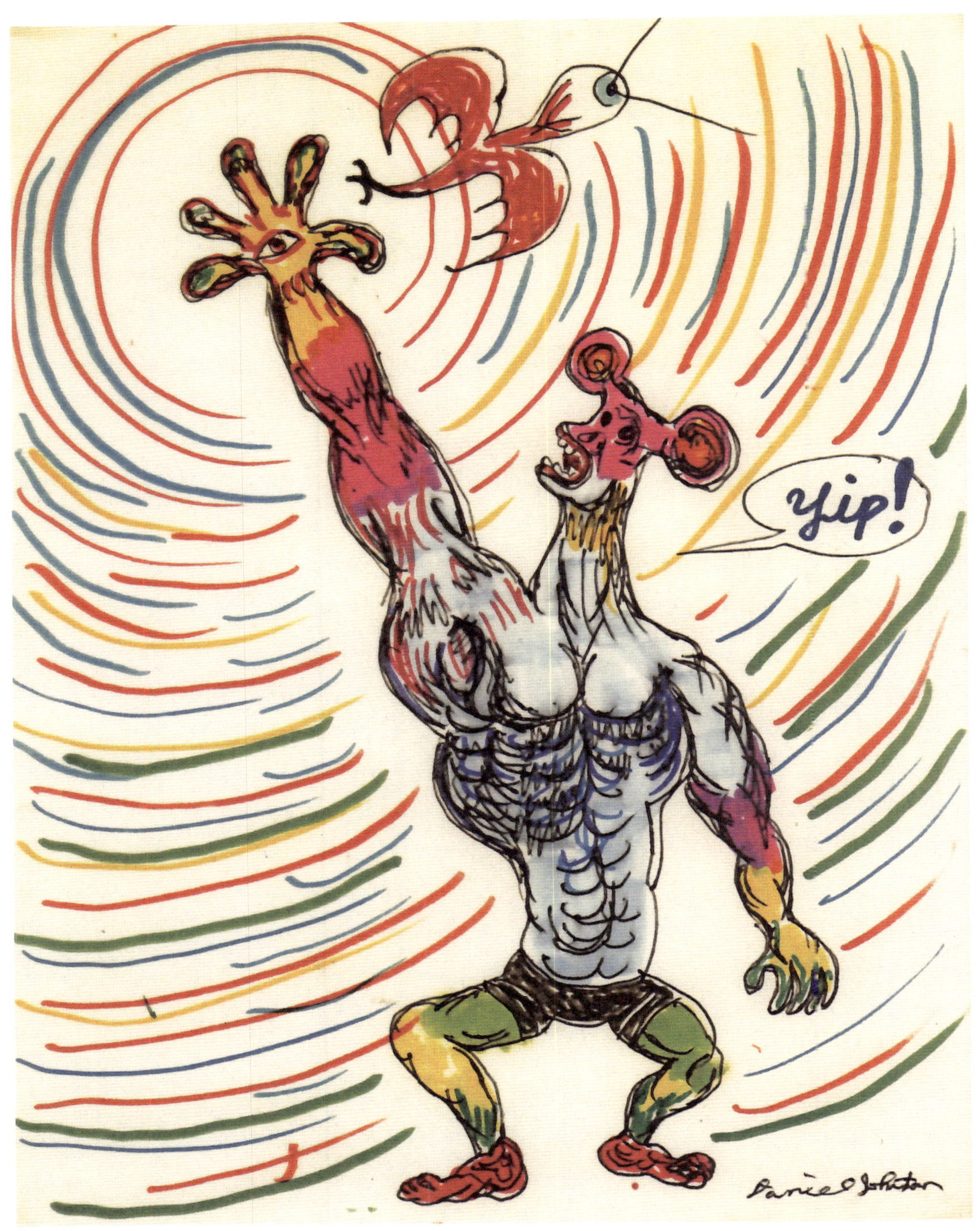

Yip!

In 2017, I had the opportunity to curate a set of songs and put together a band for two Daniel Johnston shows in Chicago. Those turned out to be among his very last shows anywhere, ever.

The experience was extremely bittersweet. I wish I could say that Daniel and I connected and had a feeling for each other. But that hope of mine was erased on the night of the second show, when Daniel introduced himself to me again and asked if I played music. Not only had we already played one show together, on the day off between the two shows, we invited Daniel to The Loft to have lunch and maybe make some music. At his request, we ordered spaghetti and drank Mexican Cokes.

The problem is, Daniel thought he was at a record store. So we let him take some records from the piles we had lying around. The conclusion that everybody had come to at this point in Daniel's life was gratitude that he had an interior life, an imaginary world that he was able to inhabit, free of the burdens that would be so obvious to most of us if we were in his condition.

The music, the comic books, the art, all of it stood to support a childlike world that was true to him. Remembering that lifted my spirits. It wasn't easy to be Daniel, but he seemed to find so much peace among so much mental anguish. The part of Daniel that made art—the best part of any of us—was intact. By the time I met him, there was hardly anything else there, besides his imaginary world.

We finally did get to sit down behind some instruments. Daniel was floating until a lyric sheet was in front of him. Then he knew exactly where he was. He might be playing a different song on the keyboard than the one he was singing, but imagine being able to do that. It's one of the most remarkable things I've ever seen.

His body of work—the incredible songs, the heartbroken songs, the funny songs, the terrifying songs, all of the vibrant, carefree art—could fill every gallery in the world or be celebrated on every refrigerator, depending on who you ask. He left all of it—he left all of himself—for us to embrace and be happy that it existed at all.

I know there are a lot of people who have struggled with whether or not it was voyeuristic or exploitative to shepherd someone with such mental health issues into the spotlight. I argue that we're celebrating the part of Daniel that kept him alive as long as he was able to stay alive. Learning that a part of Daniel was gone didn't make me love him less. It made me love what was there more. I'm grateful I had that experience, that I had the chance.

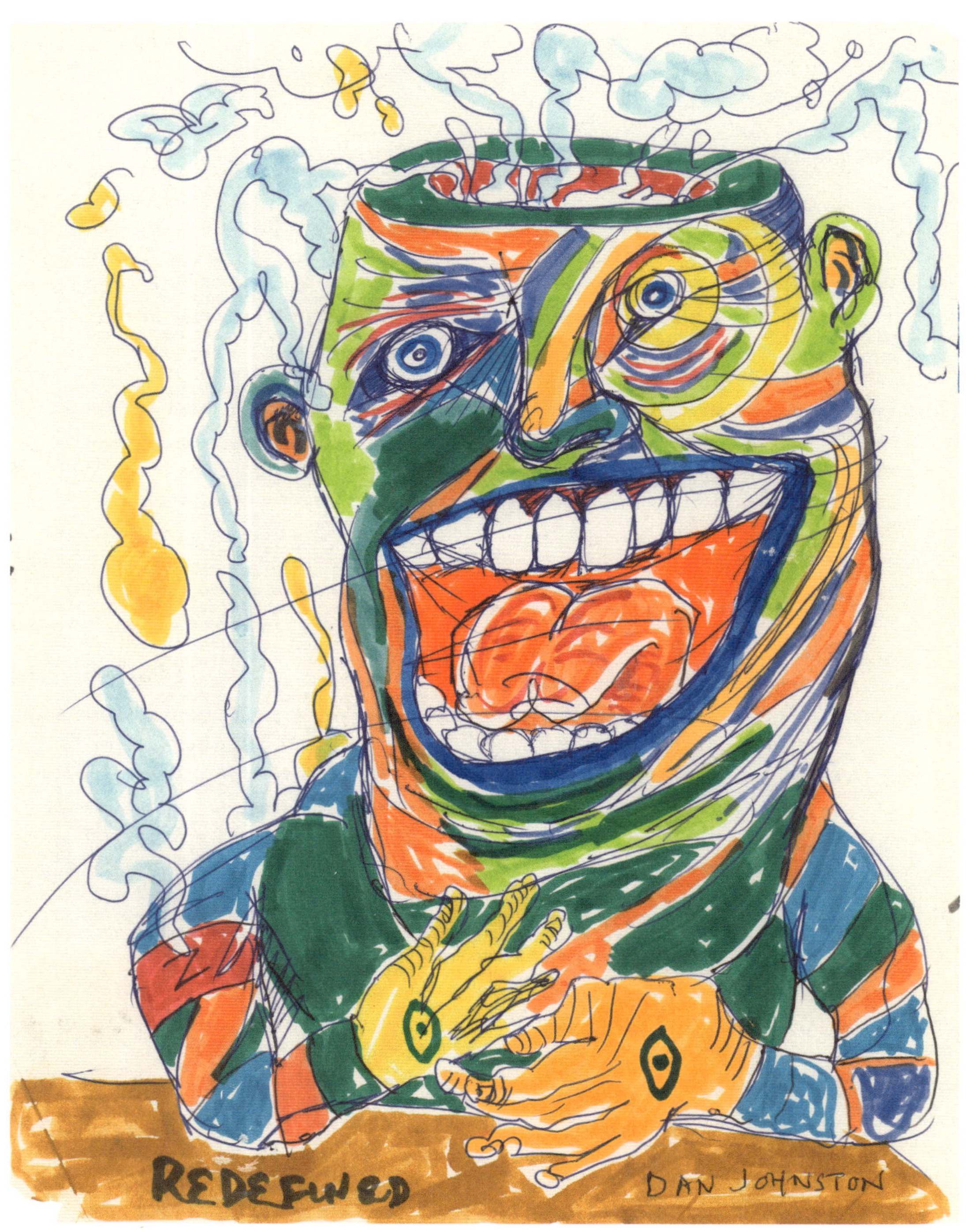

Redefined

VIII.
Psychomania
1970s–1980s

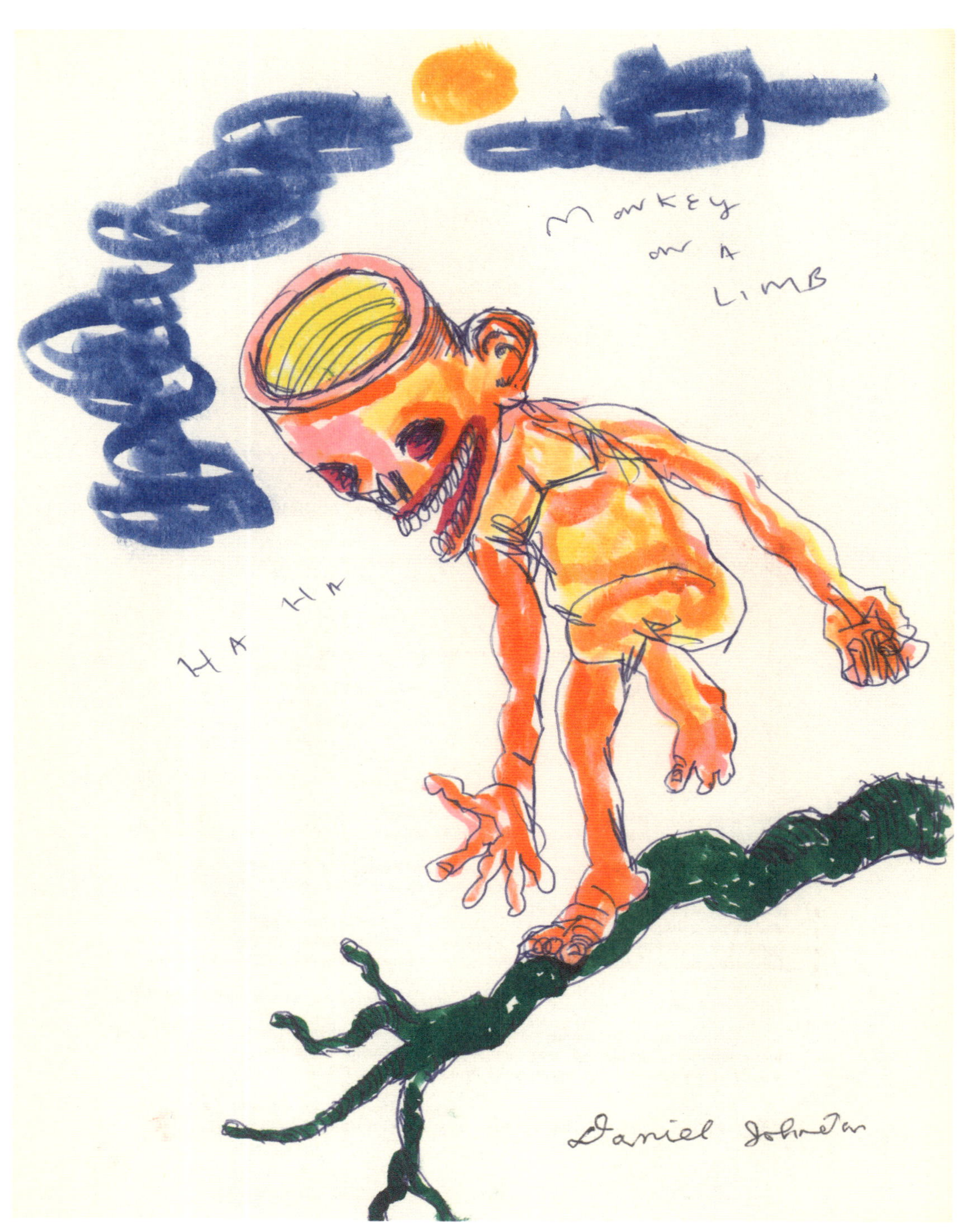

Monkey on a Limb

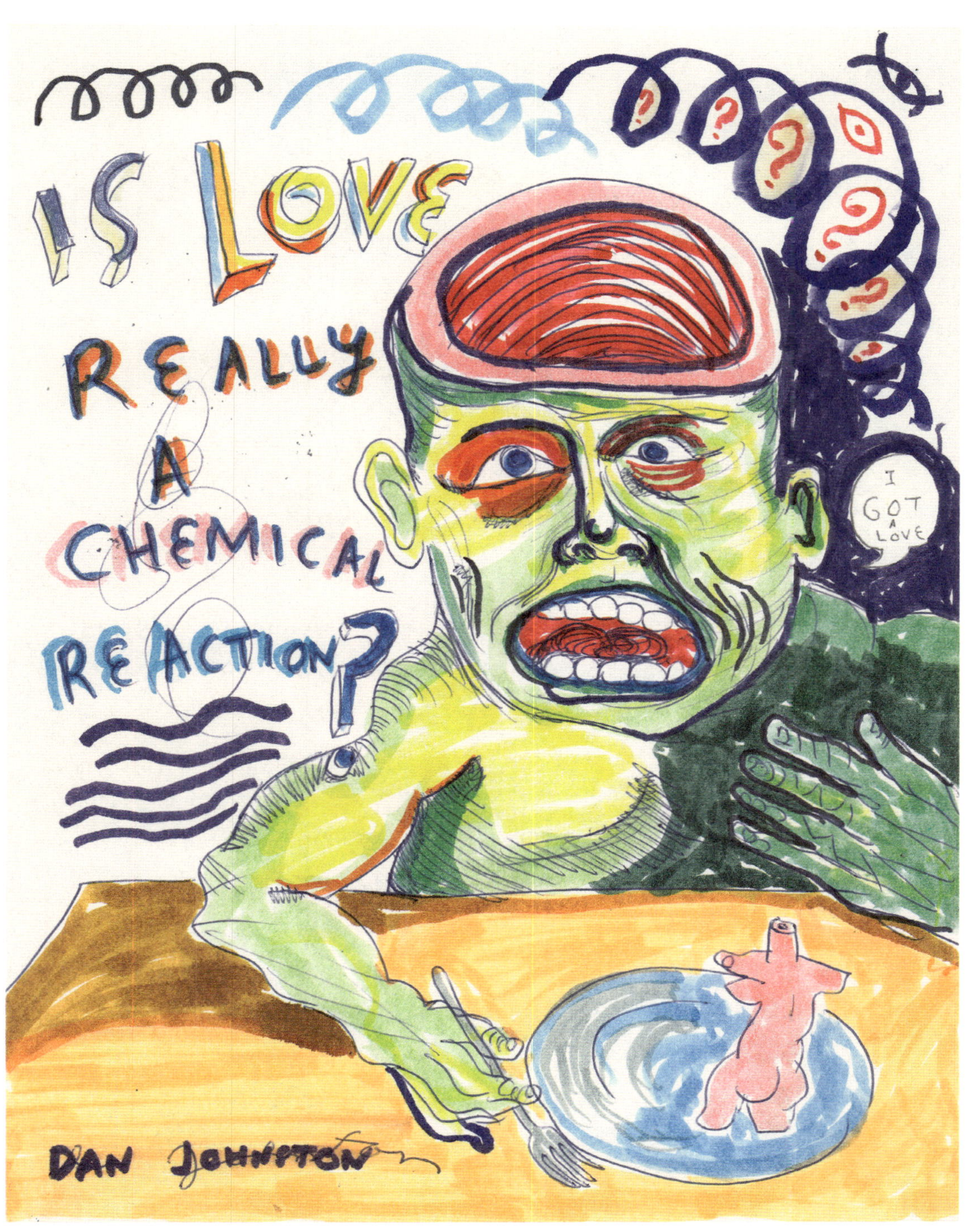

Is Love Really a Chemical Reaction?

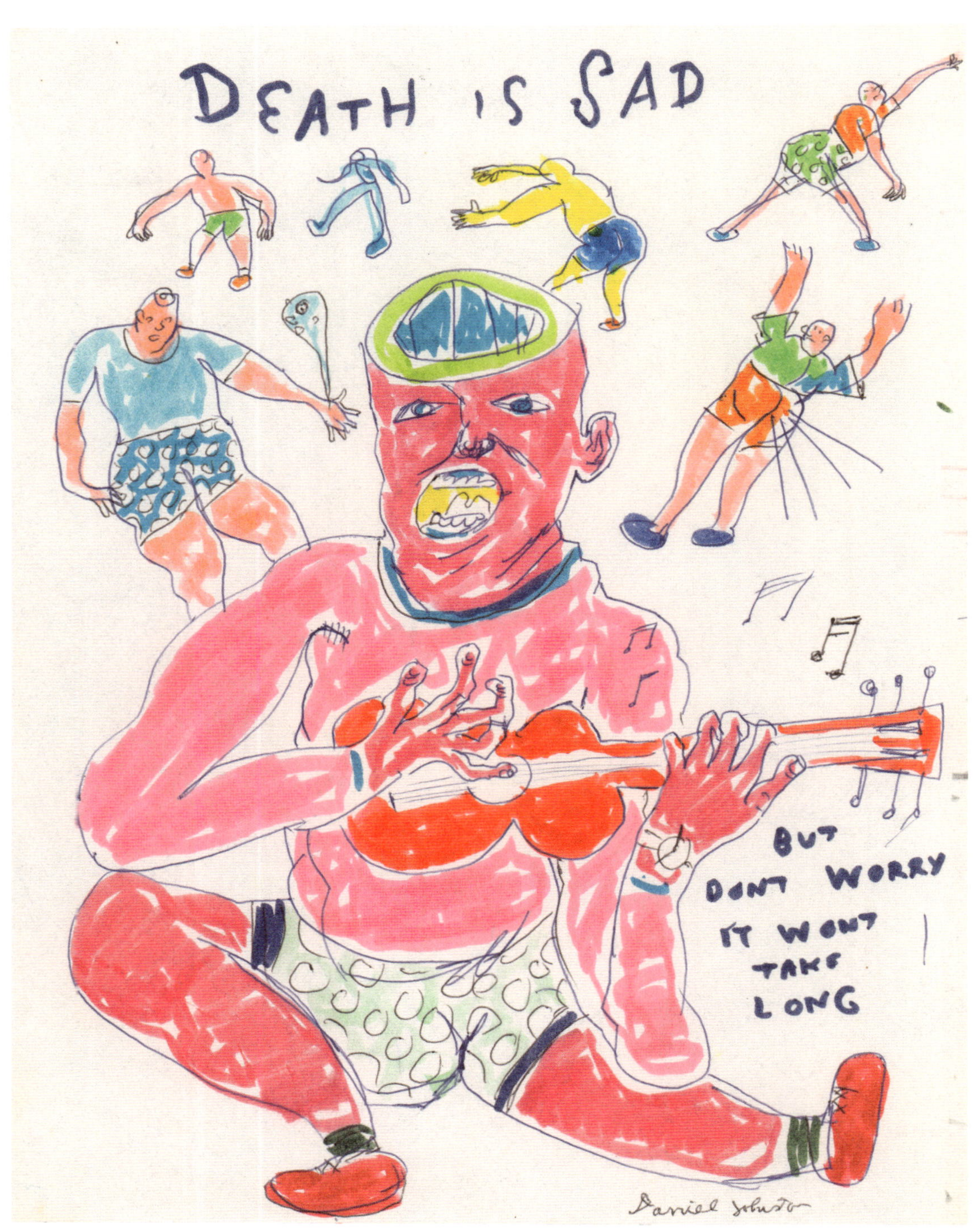
DEATH IS SAD
BUT
DONT WORRY
IT WONT
TAKE
LONG
Daniel Johnston

Death Is Sad

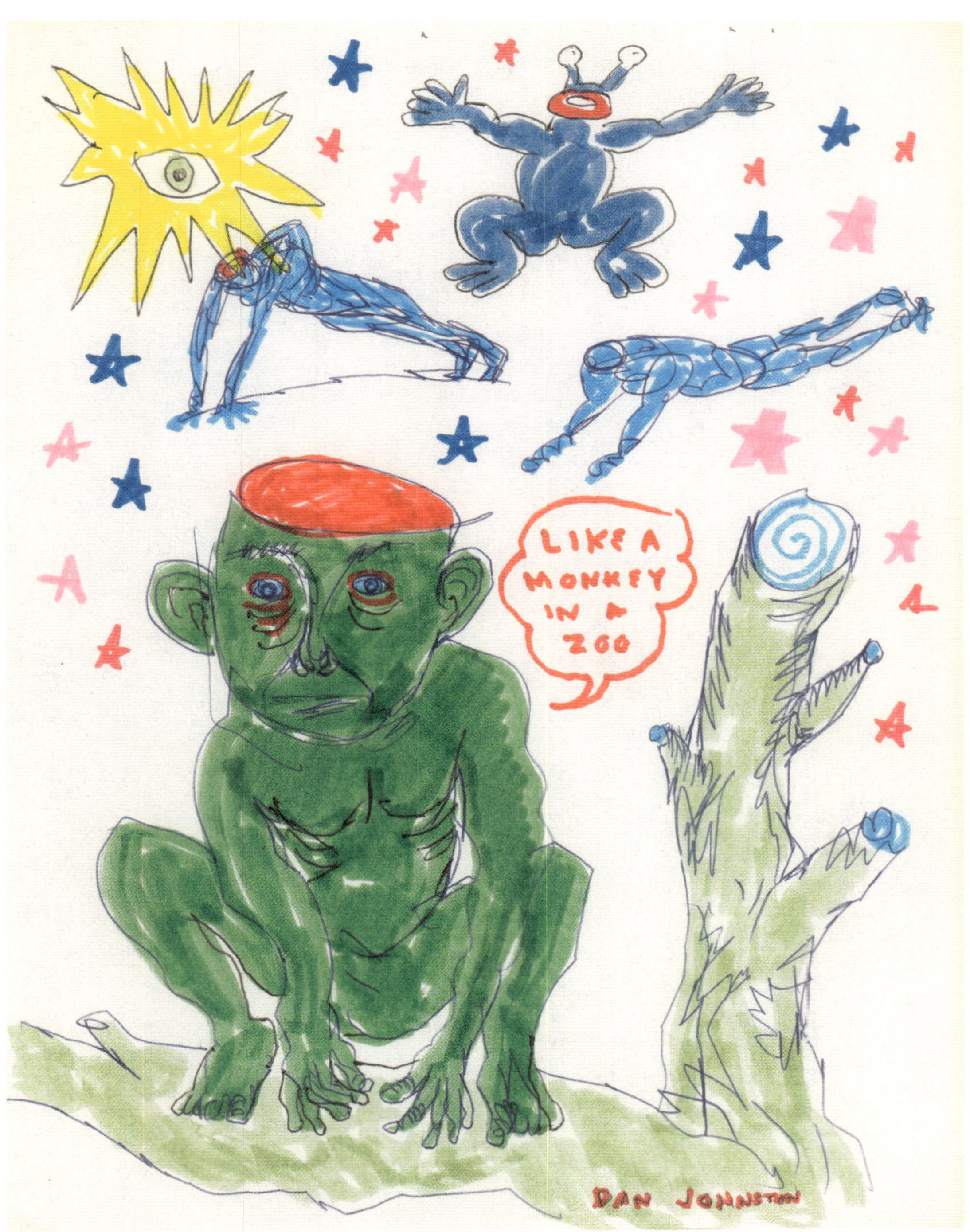

Like a Monkey in a Zoo

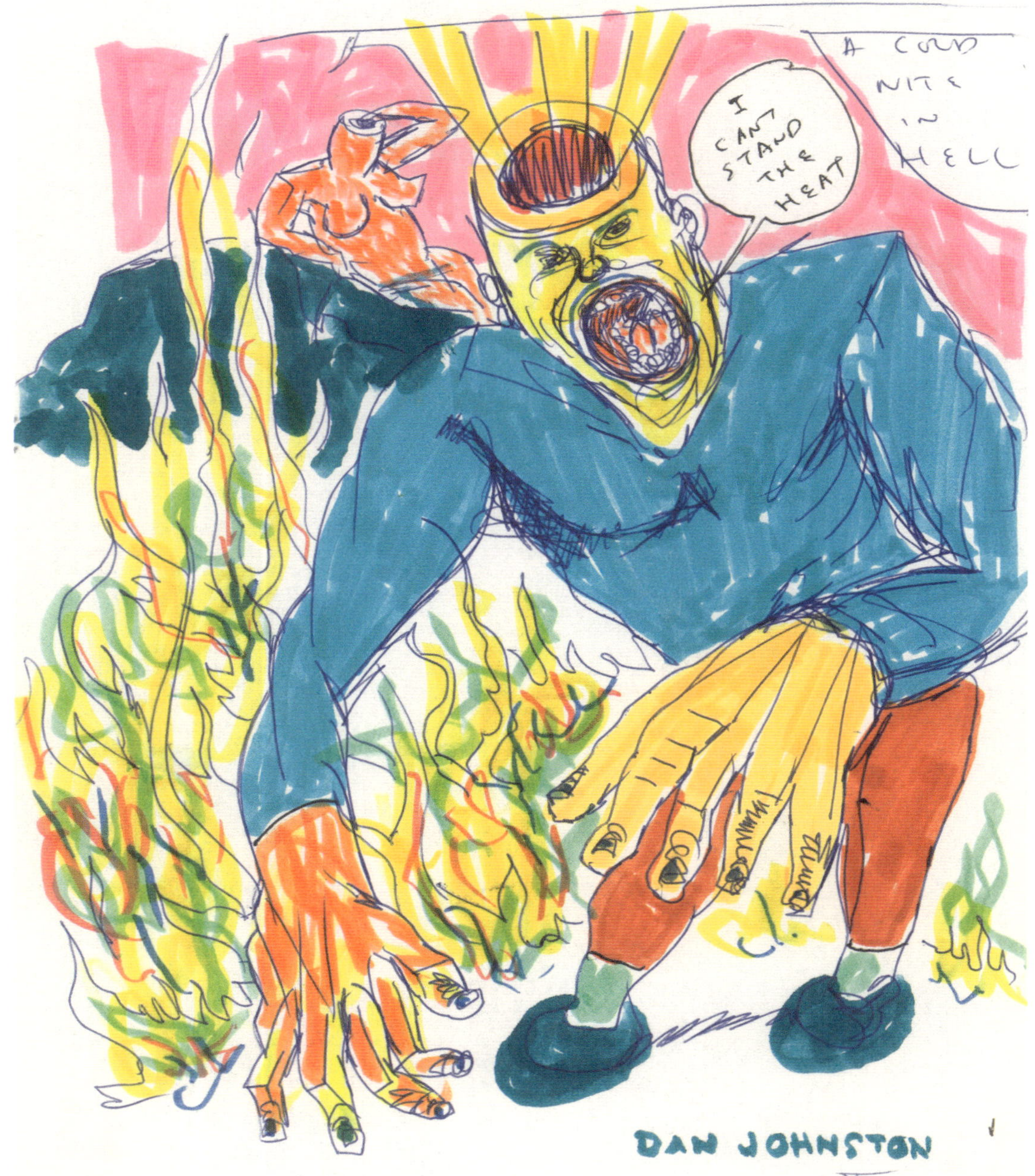

Give Up Mister Devil

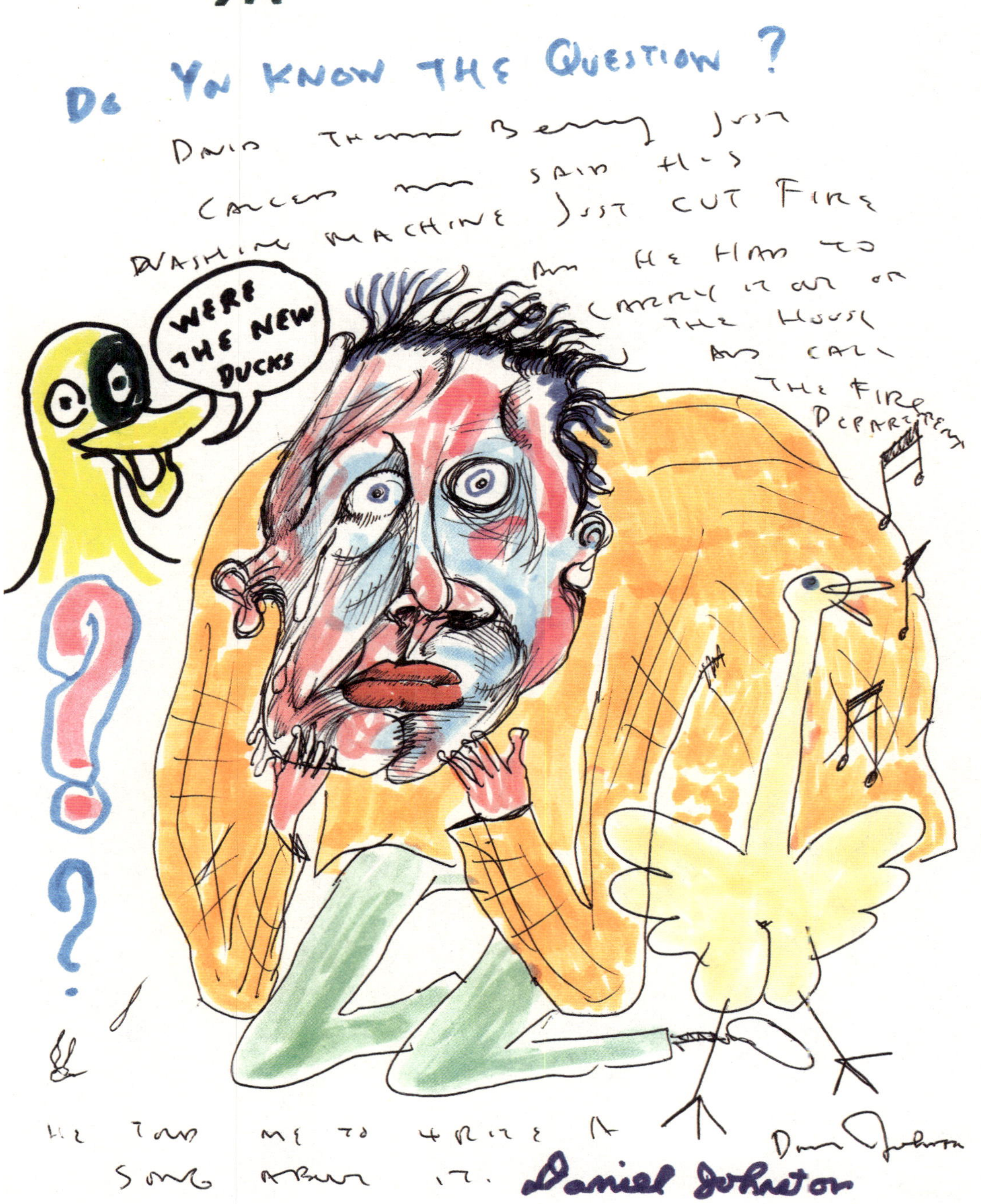

Do You Know the Question?

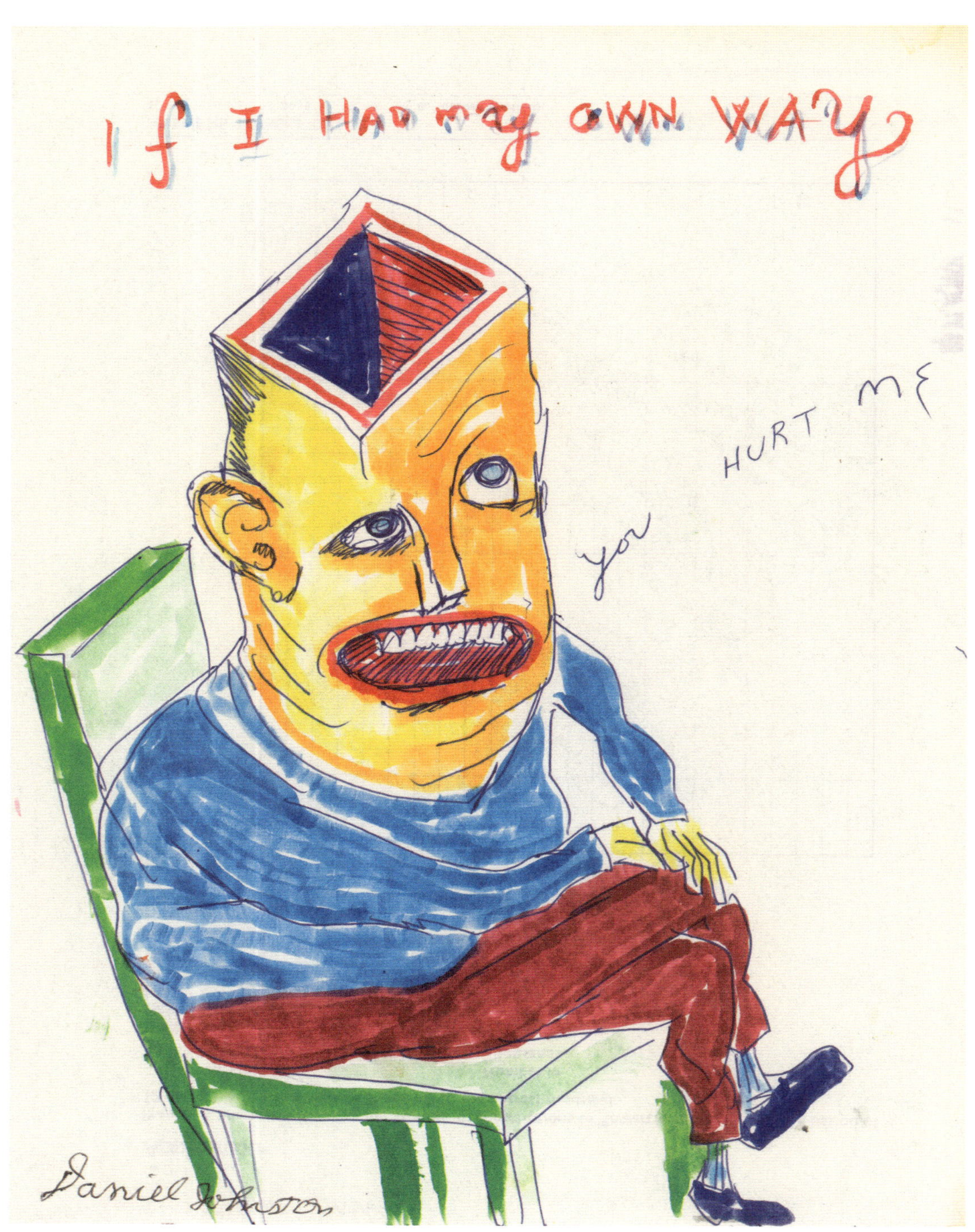

If I Had My Own Way (You Hurt Me)

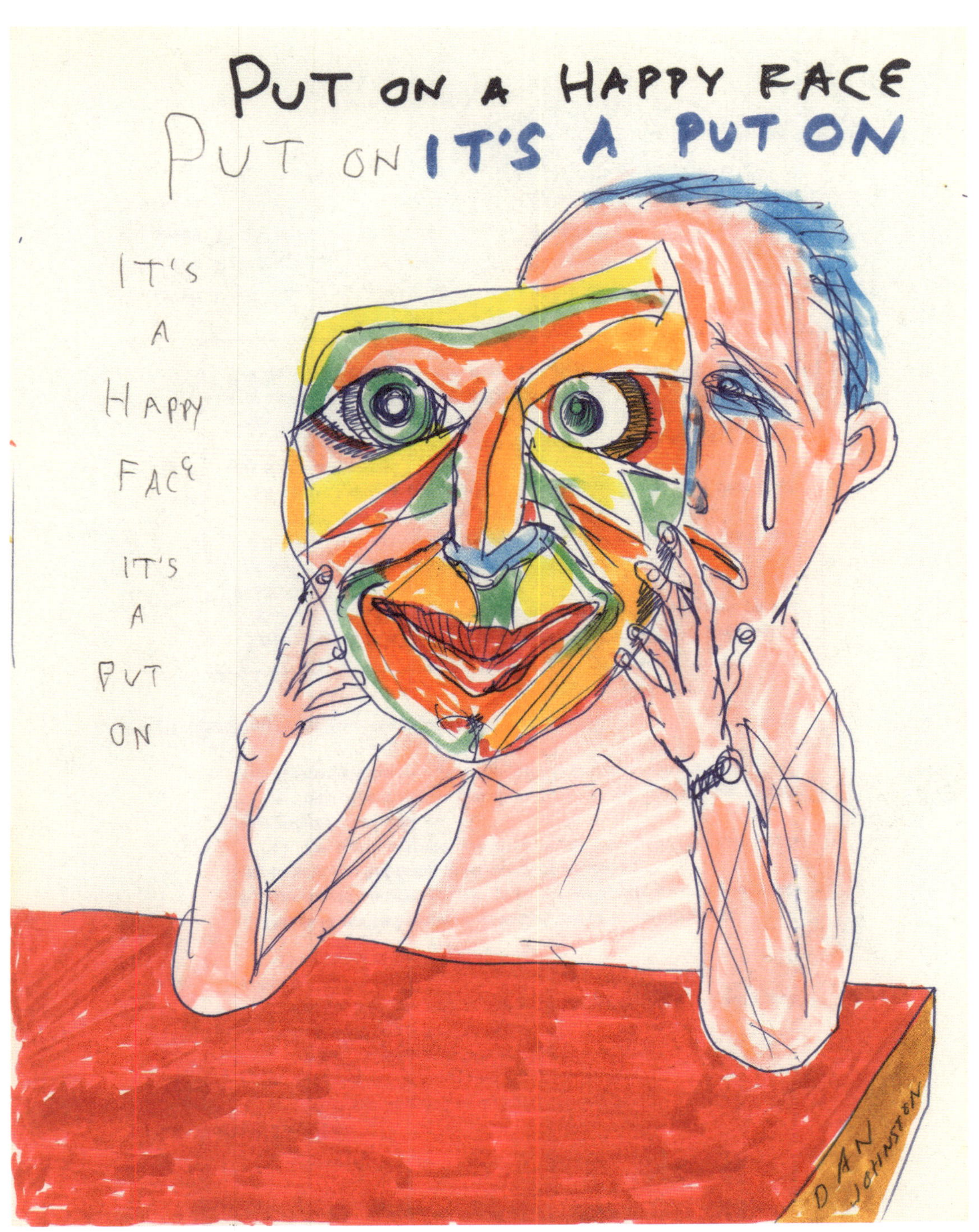

Put on a Happy Face (It's a Put On)

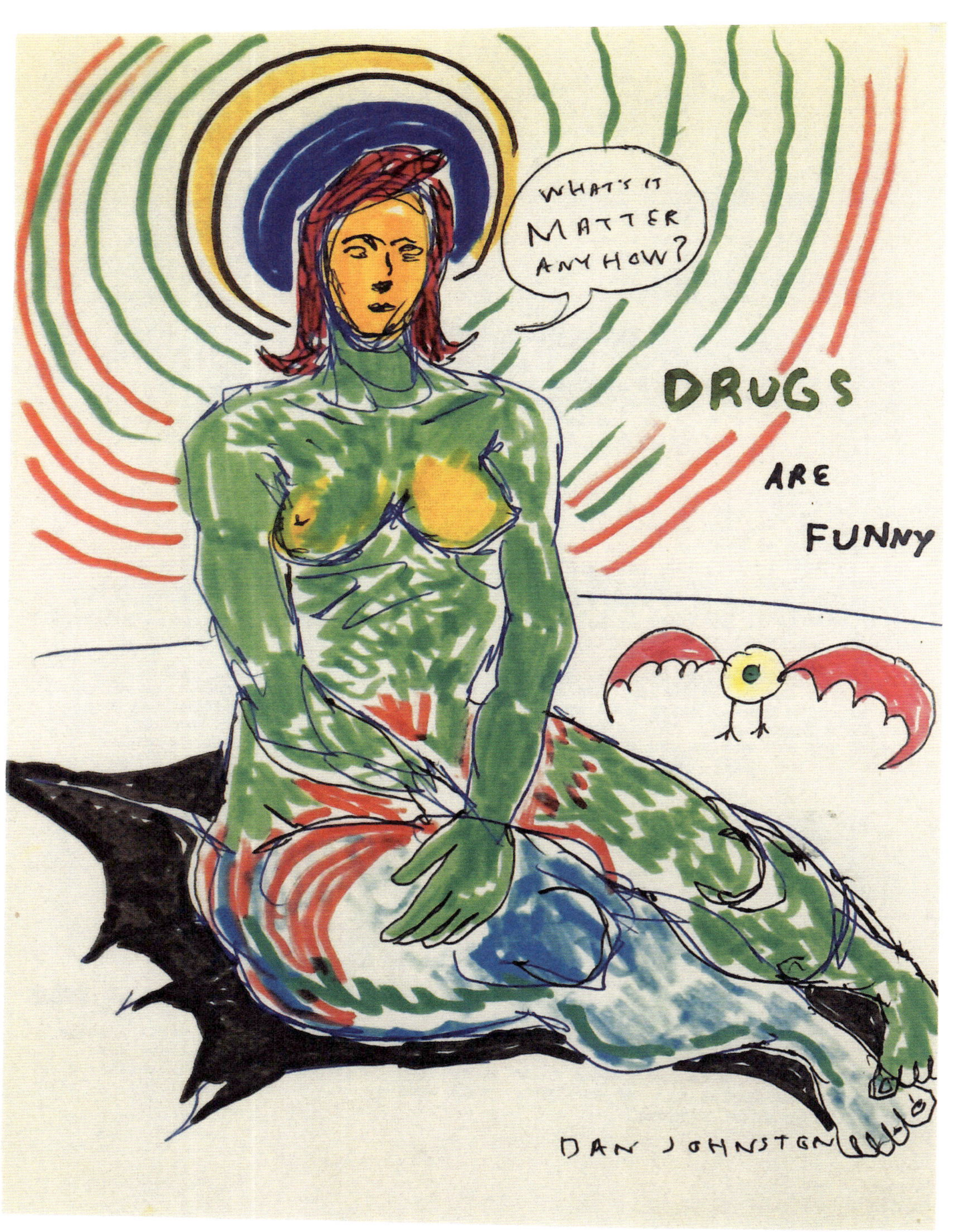

Drugs Are Funny

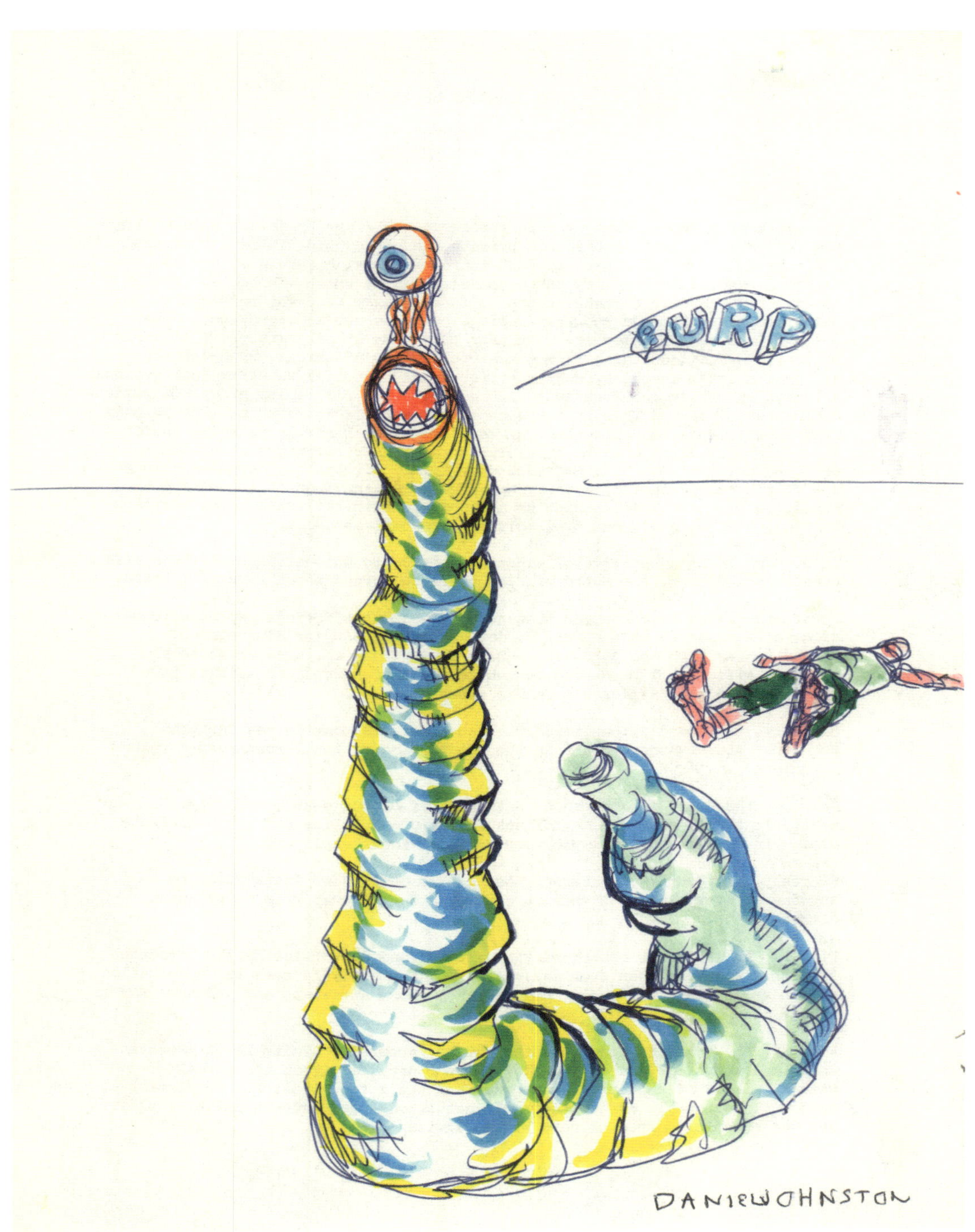

BURP

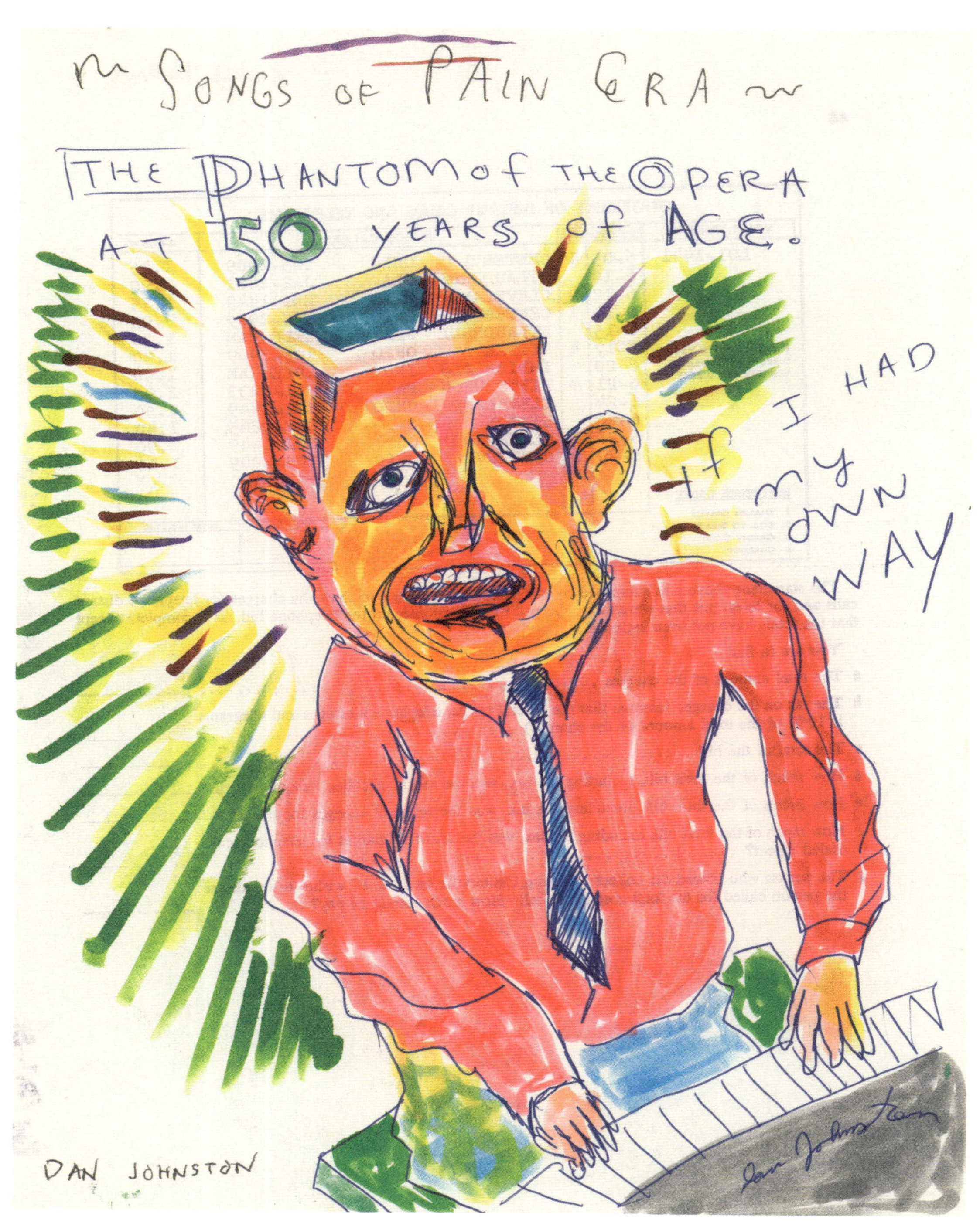

Songs of Pain Era (Phantom of the Opera)

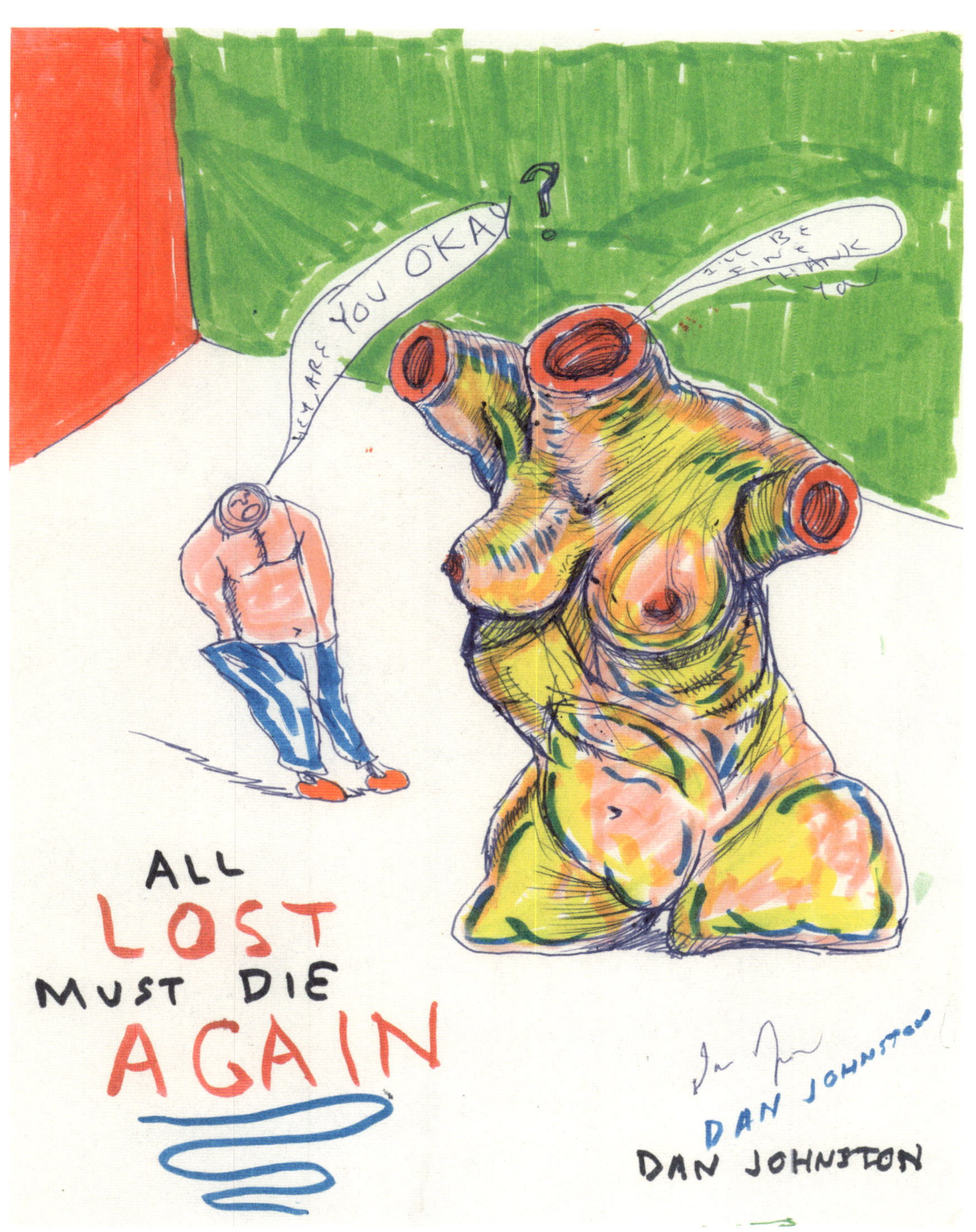

All Lost Must Die Again

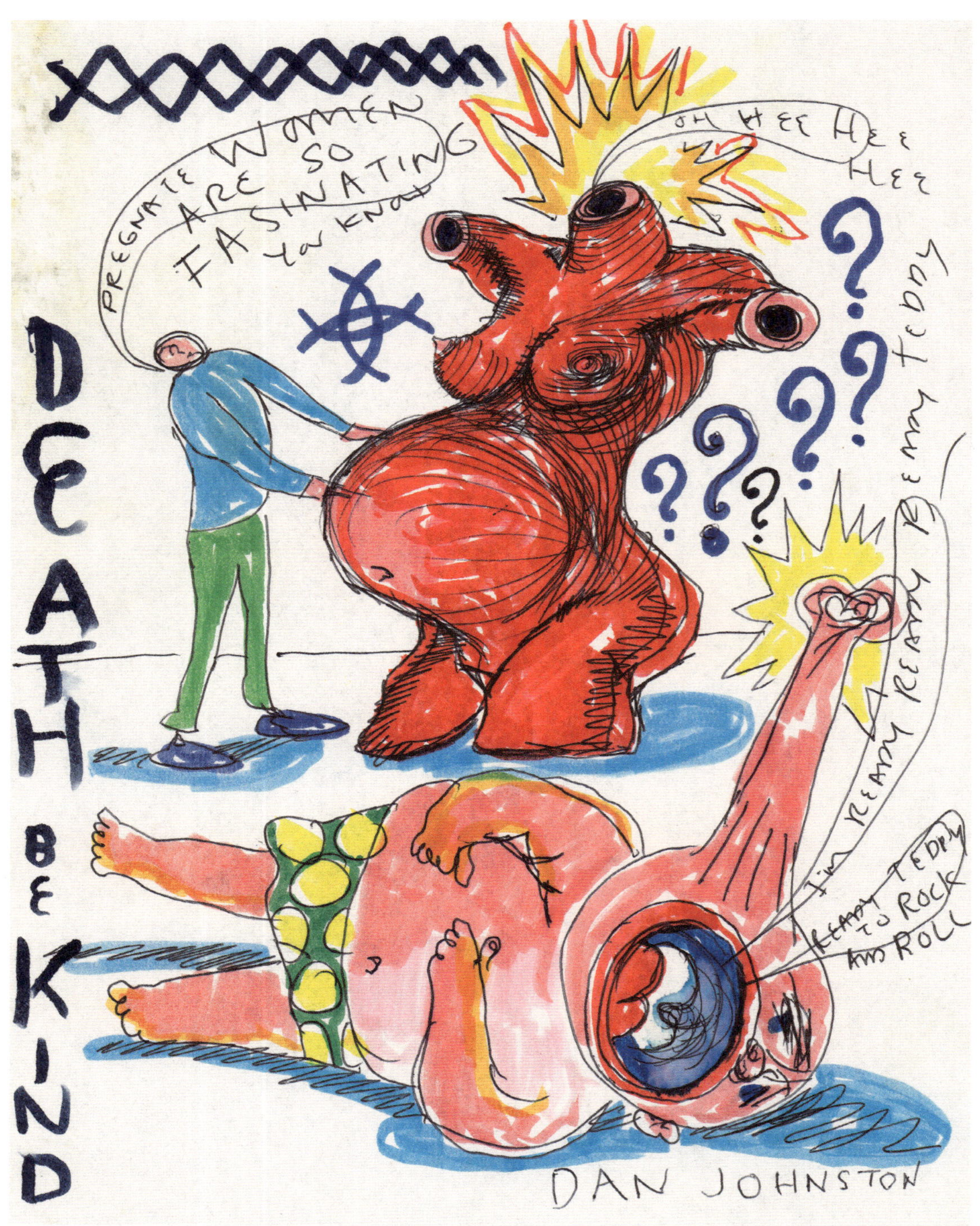

Death Be Kind

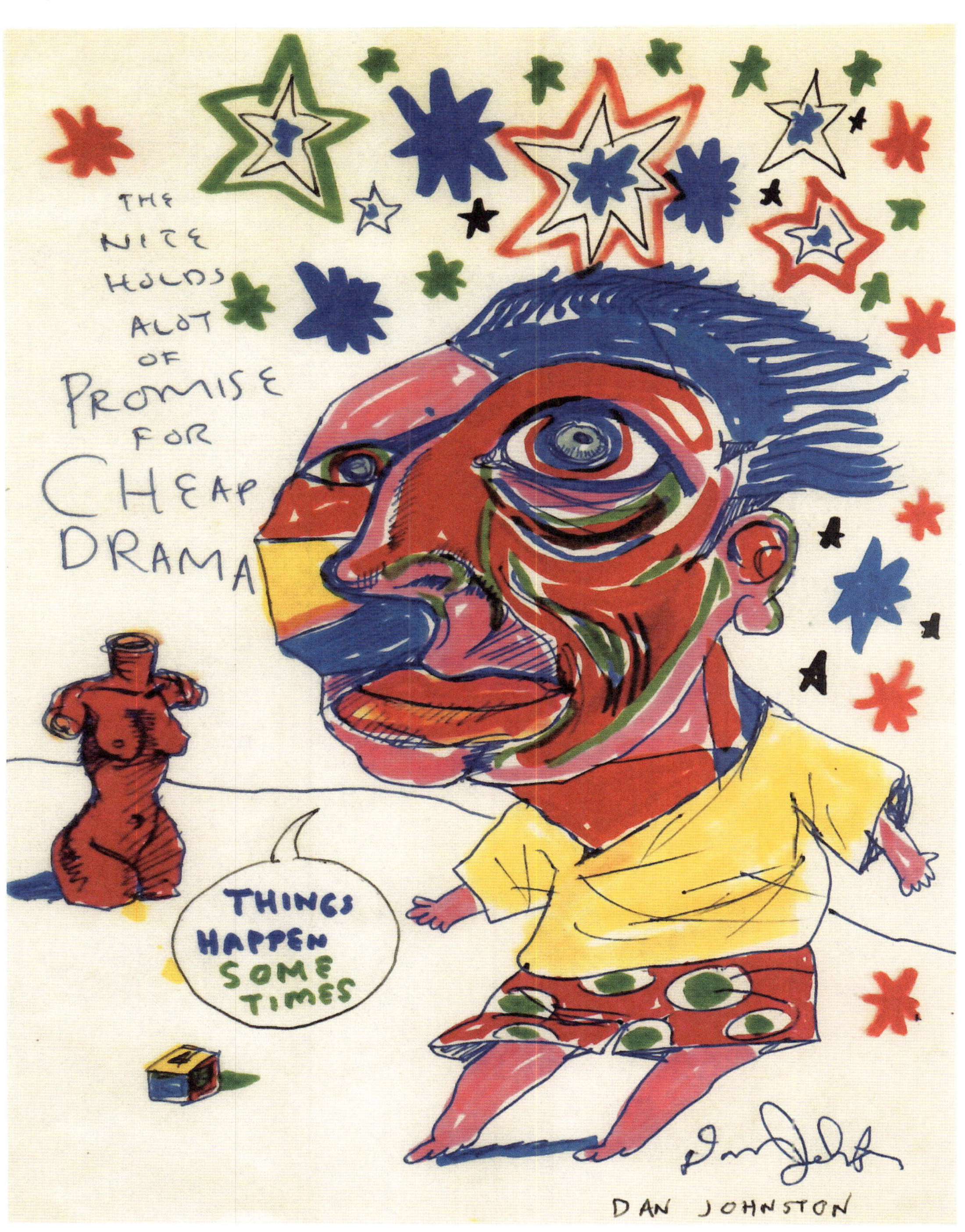

Promise for Cheap Drama

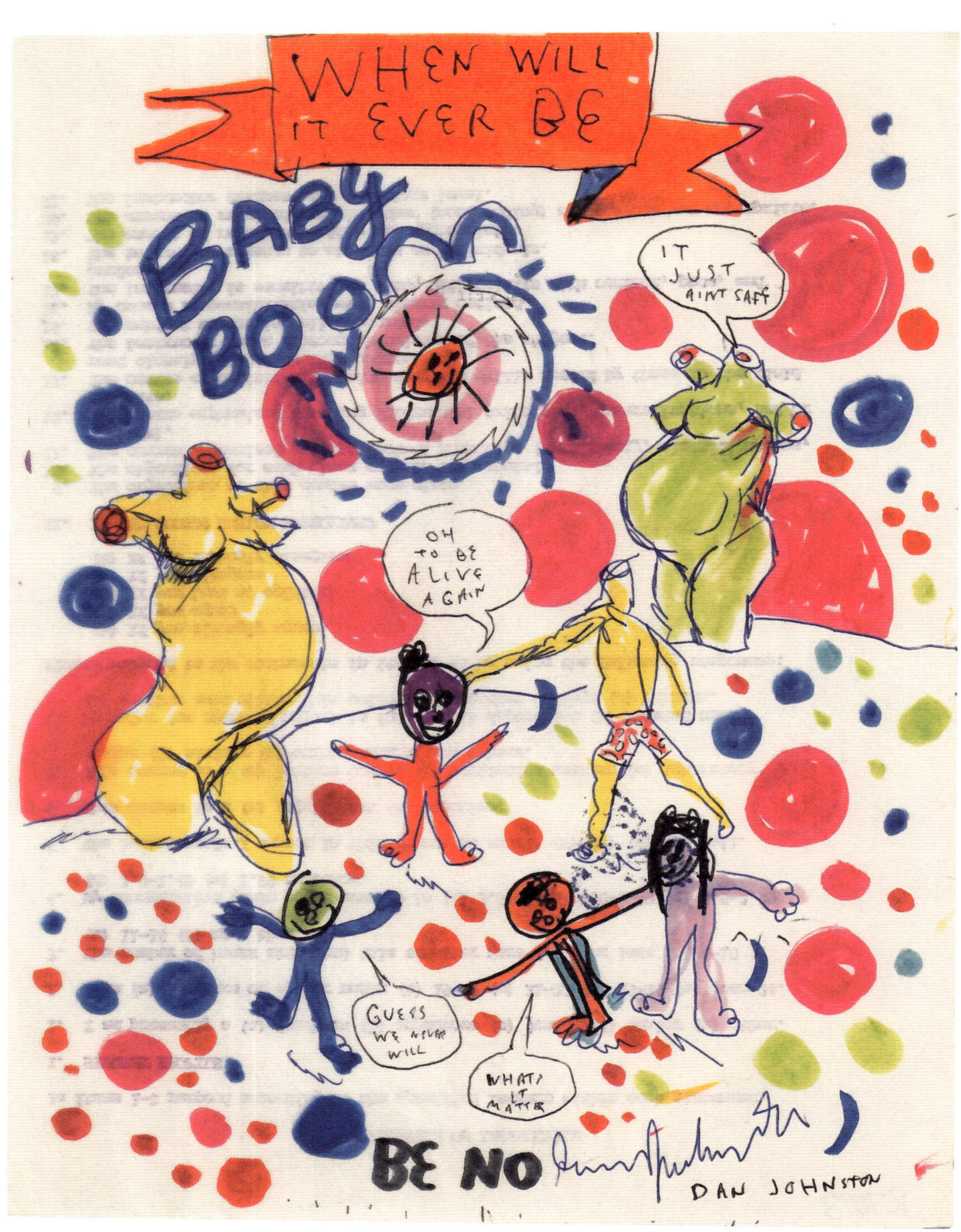

WHEN WILL
IT EVER BE
BABY BOO
IT JUST AINT SAFE
OH TO BE ALIVE AGAIN
GUESS WE NEVER WILL
WHAT'I IT MATTER
BE NO
DAN JOHNSTON

Baby Boom

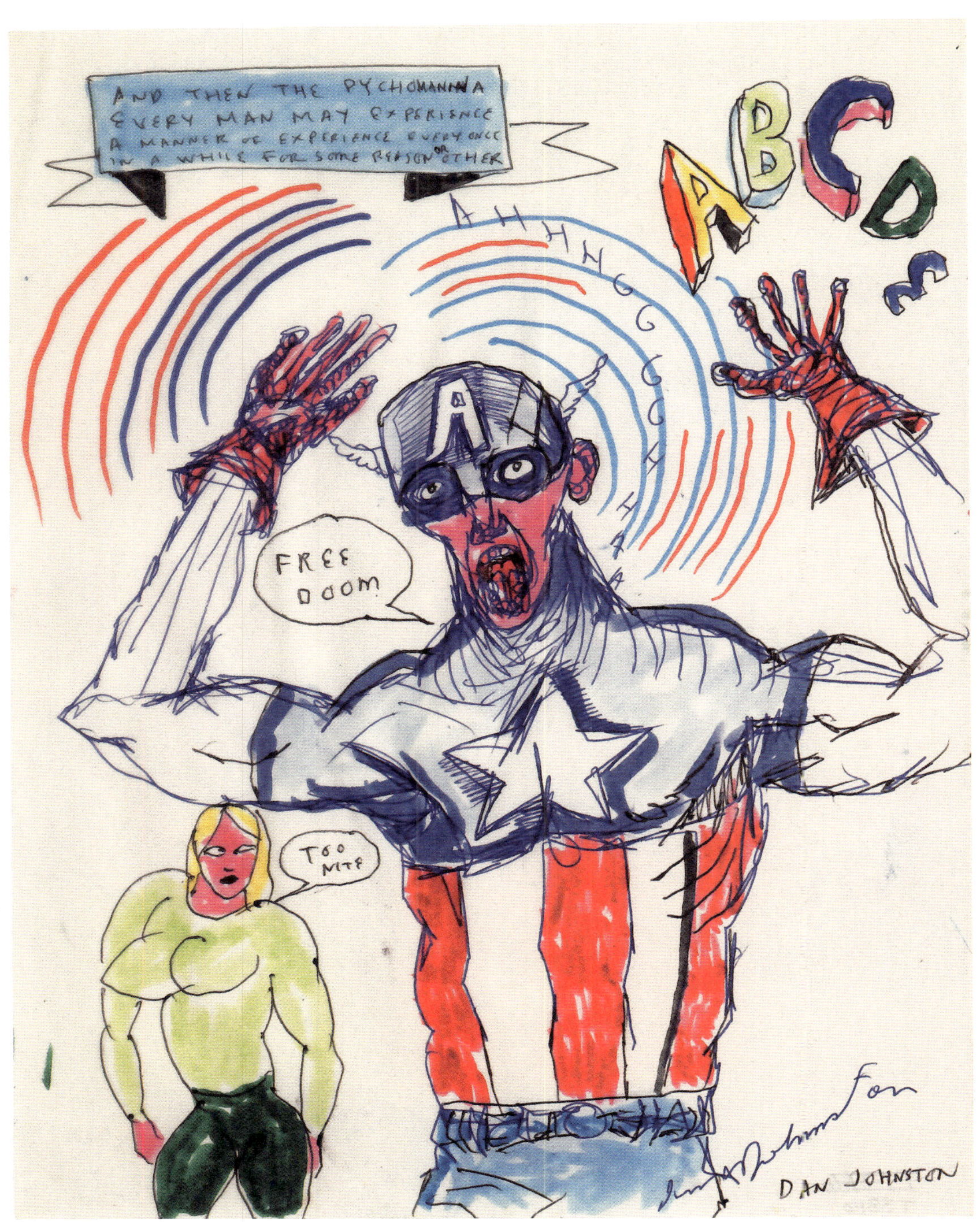

Free Doom (Captain America)

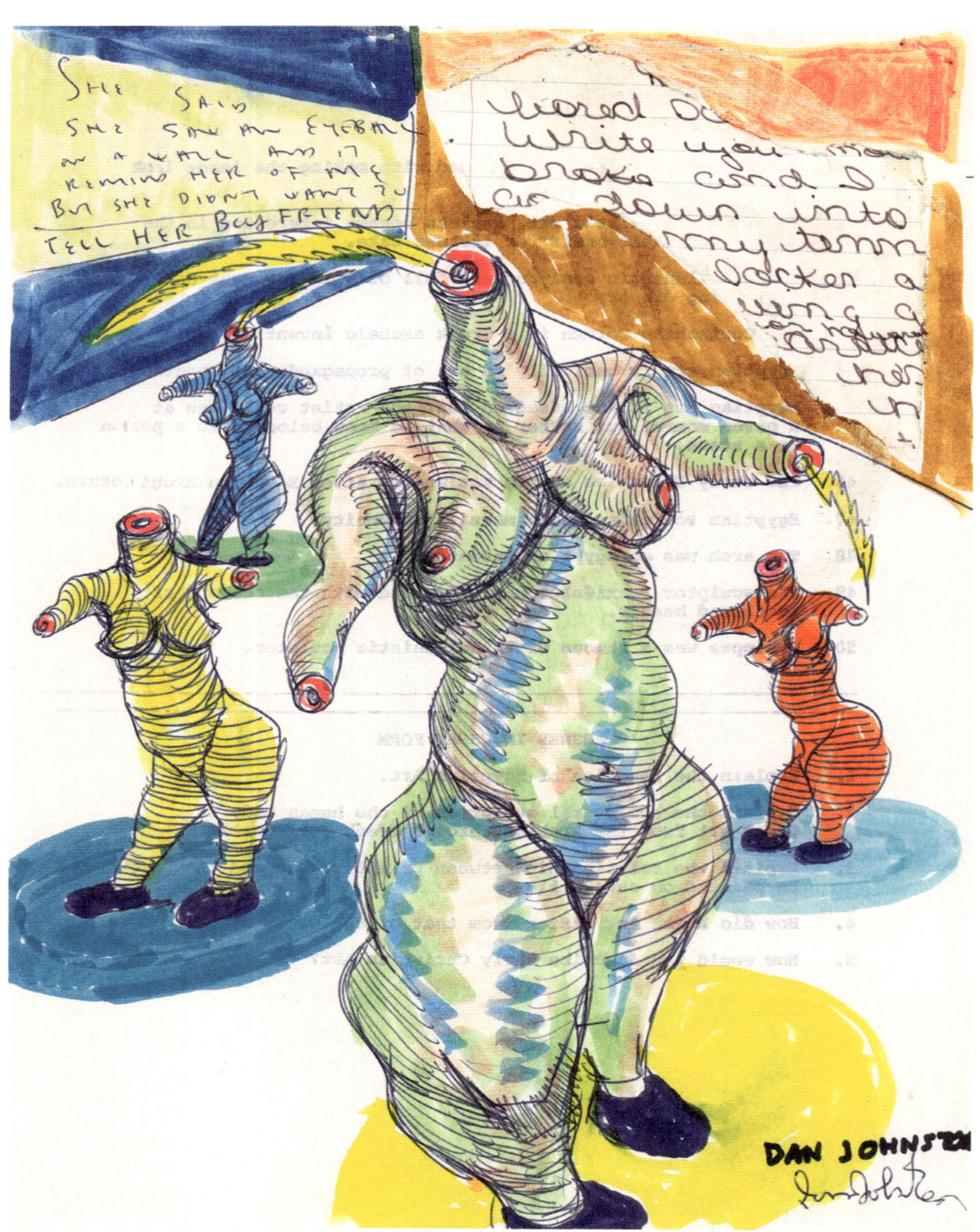

She Said She Saw an Eyeball

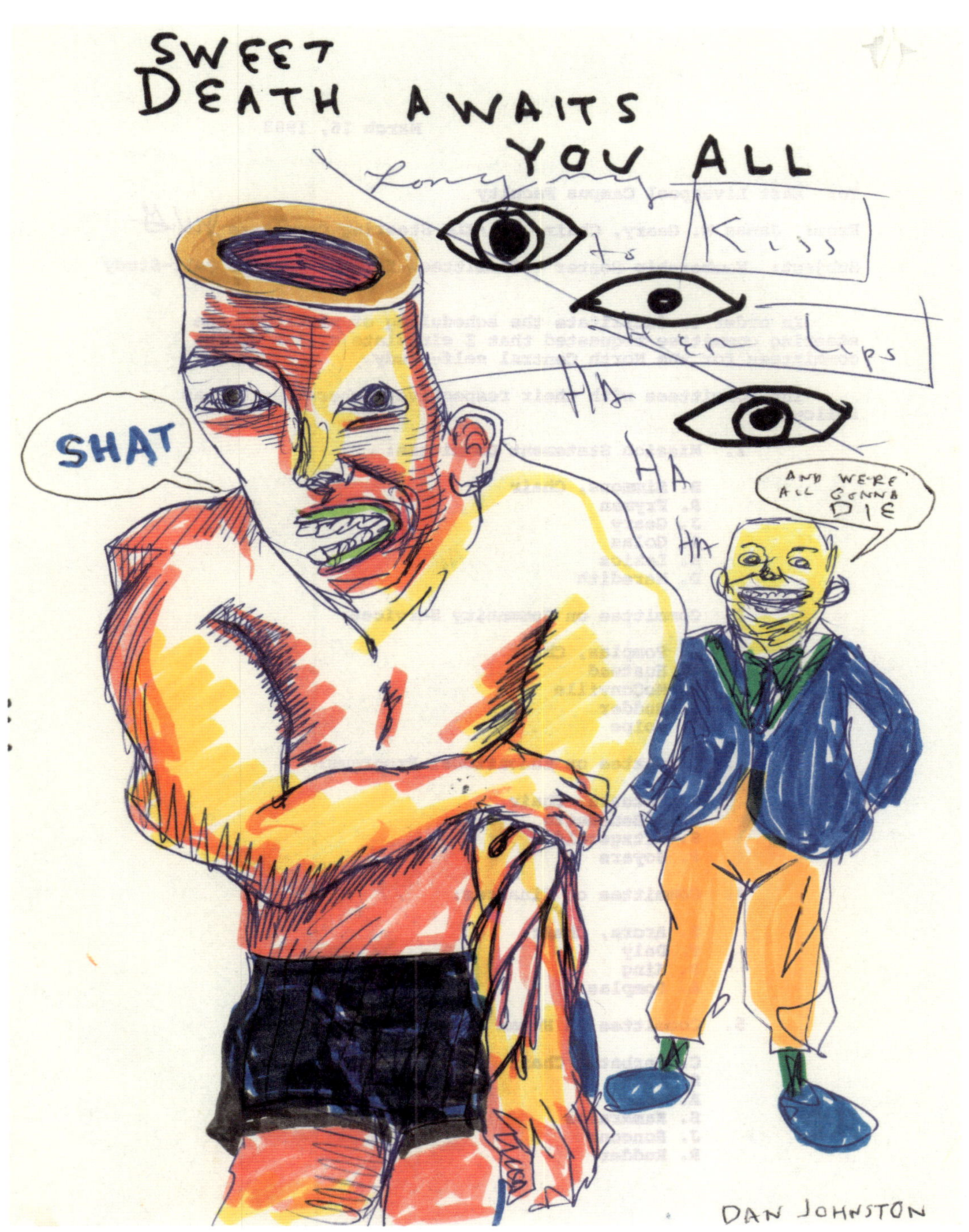

Sweet Death Awaits You All (Shat)

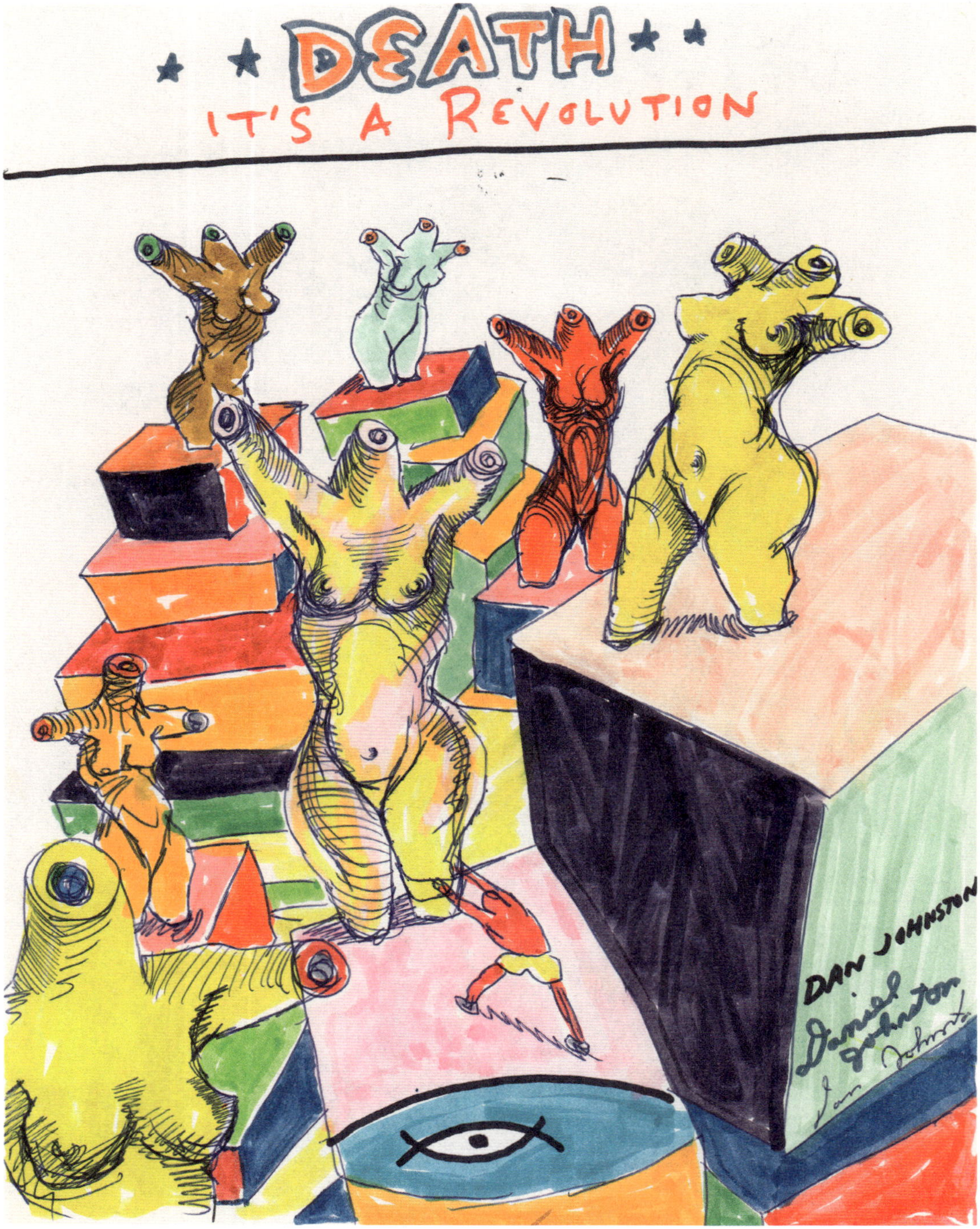

Death It's a Revolution

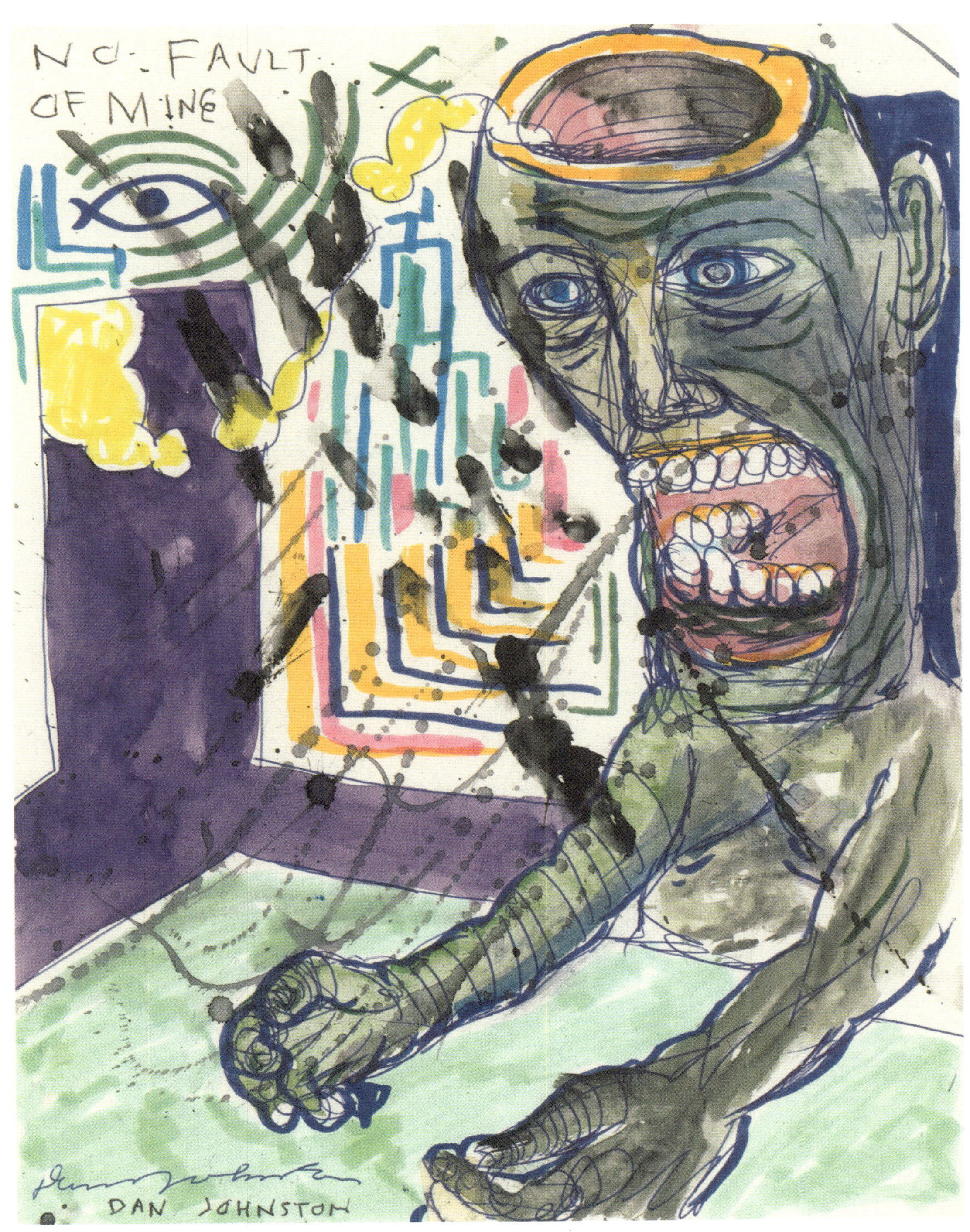

No Fault of Mine

It was the late 1990s—I was in film school—I heard Daniel Johnston was playing a show in Alphabet City, so I went to check it out.

When he came on, I was shocked—he's not a kid? WHAT?

He was this older guy, raw and trembling as he blew through some songs. I had to rearrange my brain. You hear that phrase "old soul" thrown around a lot, but what about the eternally young ones? That's Daniel. Maybe takes one to know one.

Cut to a few years later, and I'm listening to the Langley Schools Music Project sing their songs of innocence and despair to get in the zone for writing music for Spike Jonze's *Where the Wild Things Are*. I was thinking I'd try and get a kids' choir to sing weighty pop favorites; instead, Daniel's "Worried Shoes" popped into my head.

I sent it to Spike, and we were both pretty emotionally devastated by it. All that innocence and despair smooshed into a demo, with Daniel playing a pump organ, singing, "I took my lucky break and I broke it in two, / Put on my worried shoes." Pure pathos.

"Worried Shoes" was the theme at the heart of that film for me. I recall it was Maurice Sendak's favorite, too.

I don't know, it's hard to nail down what quality of Daniel's hooks me the most. I wonder if it's the yearning paired with the inexhaustible faith that things might just work out. He certainly makes heartbreak catchy.

Nope, I will never be the same after his music, and thank goodness for that. Thank you, Daniel.

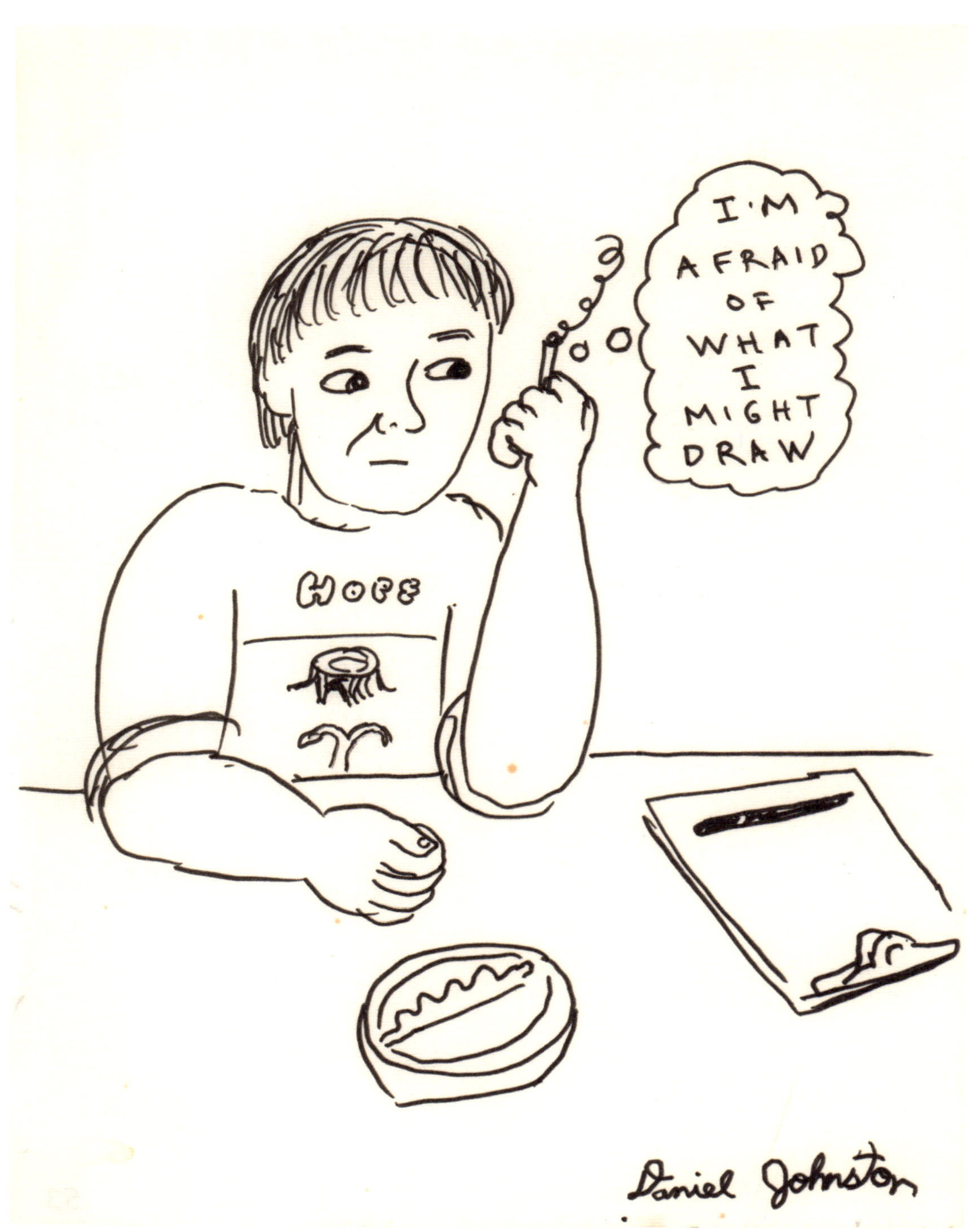

I'm Afraid of What I Might Draw

IX.
A Dreaming Man
1990s

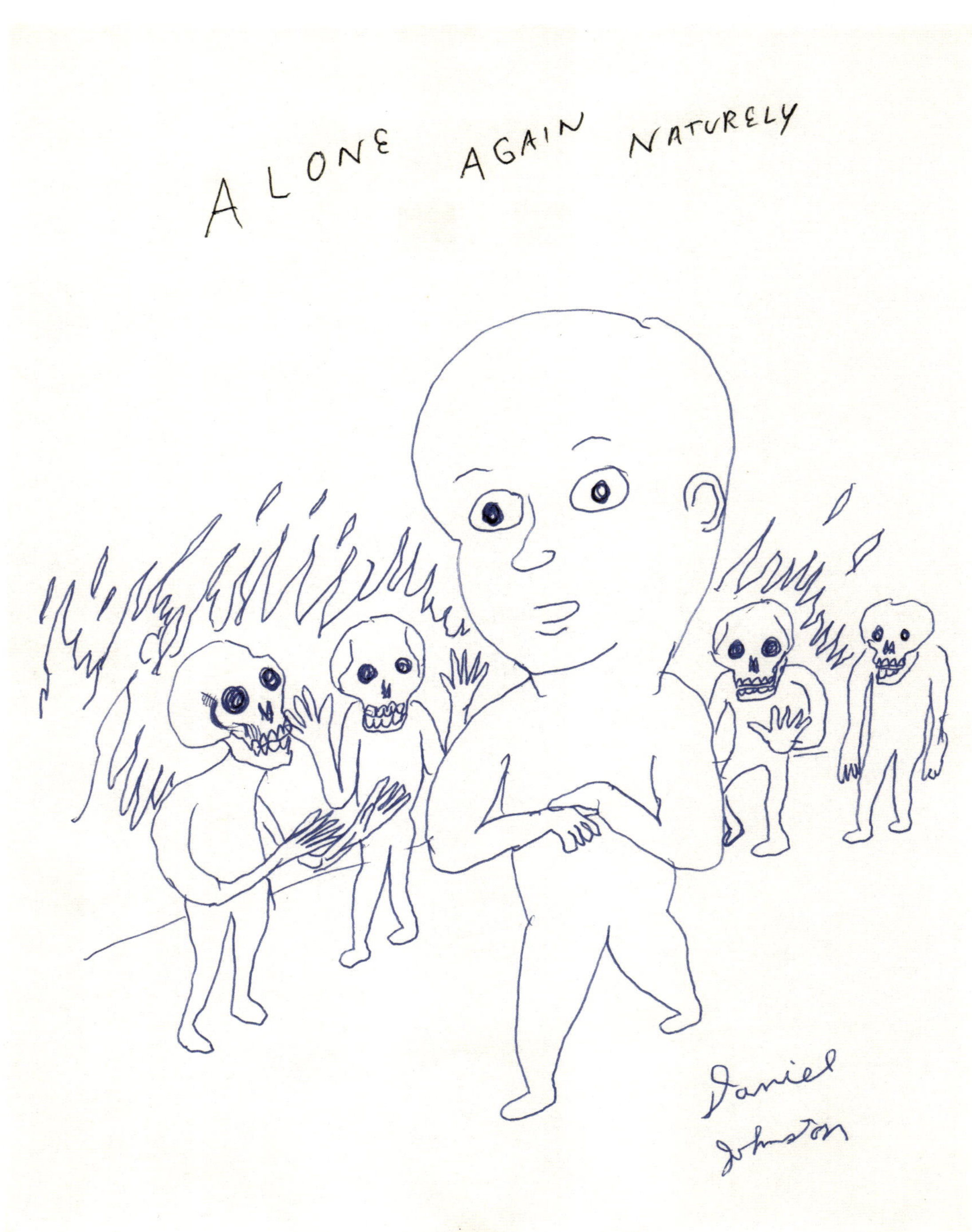

Alone Again Naturely

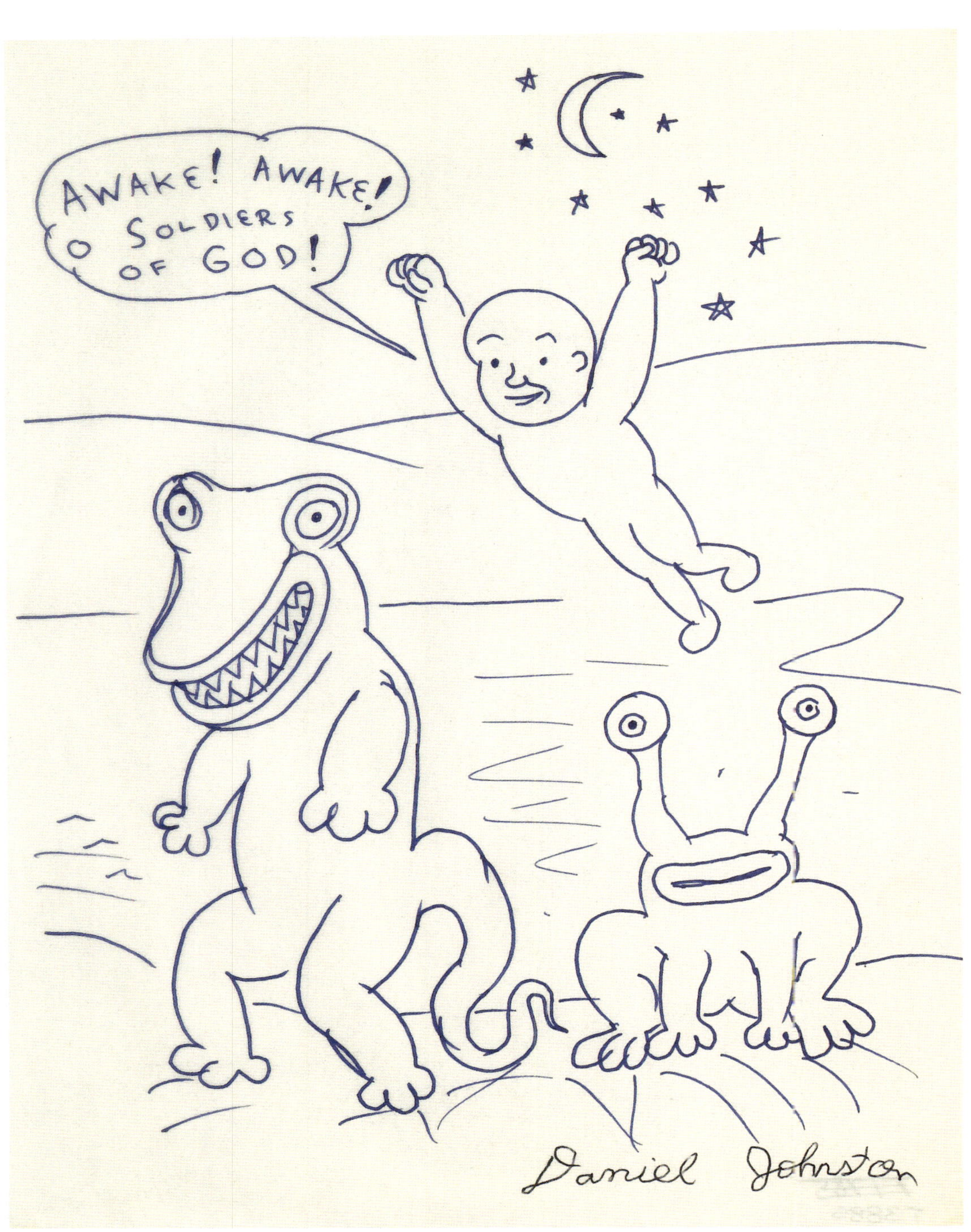

Awake! Awake! O Soldiers of God!

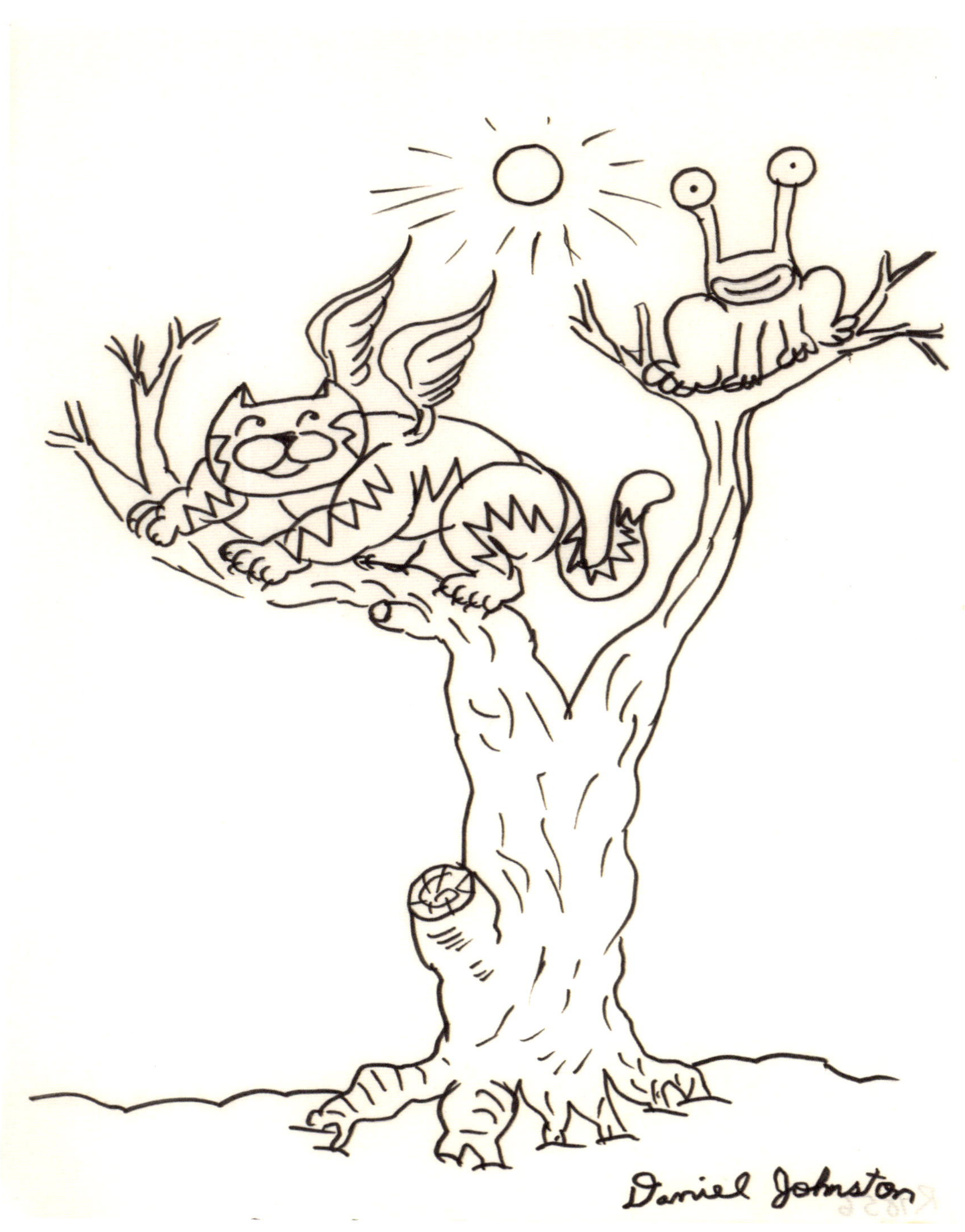

Untitled (Jeremiah & Sassy Frass)

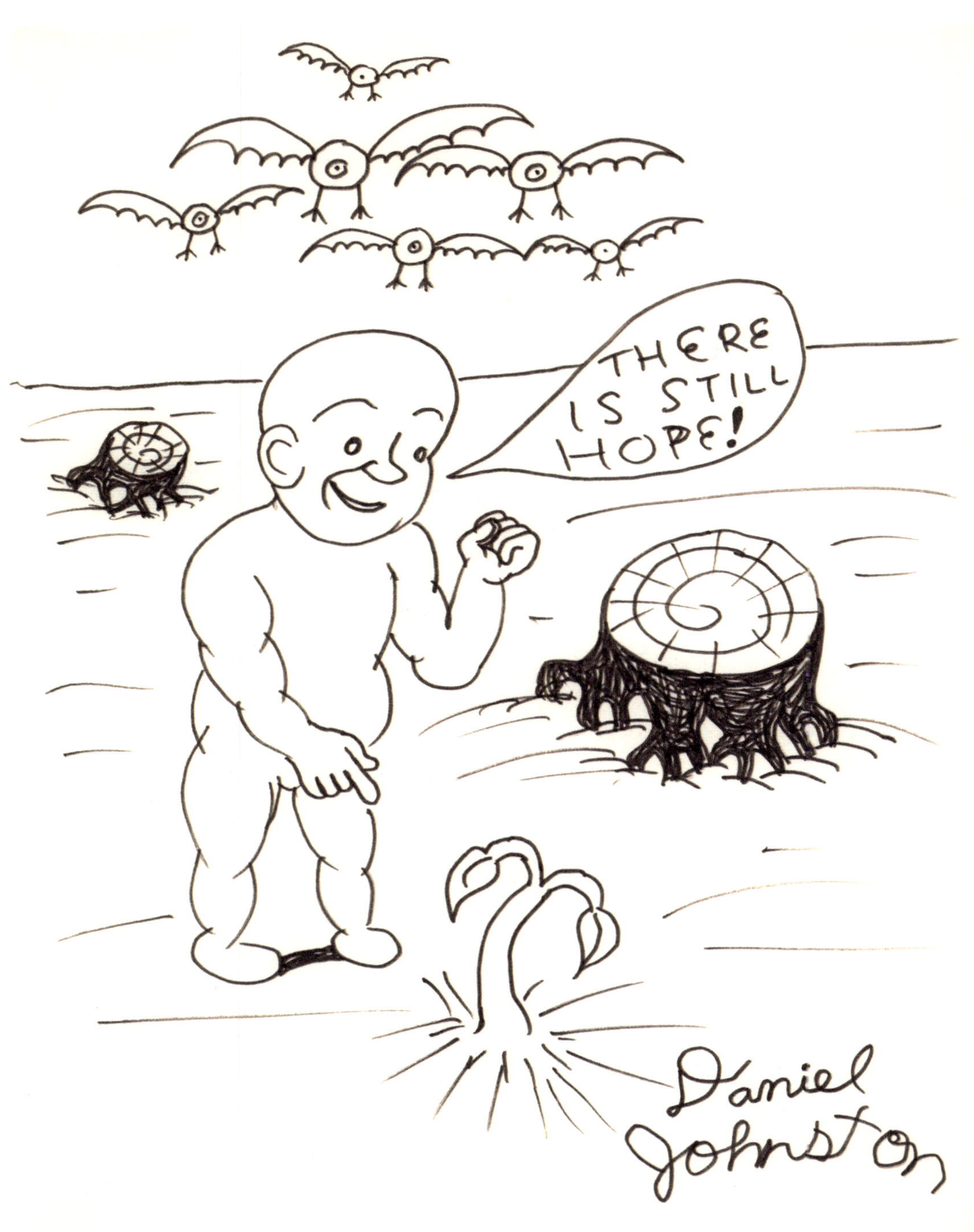

There Is Still Hope!

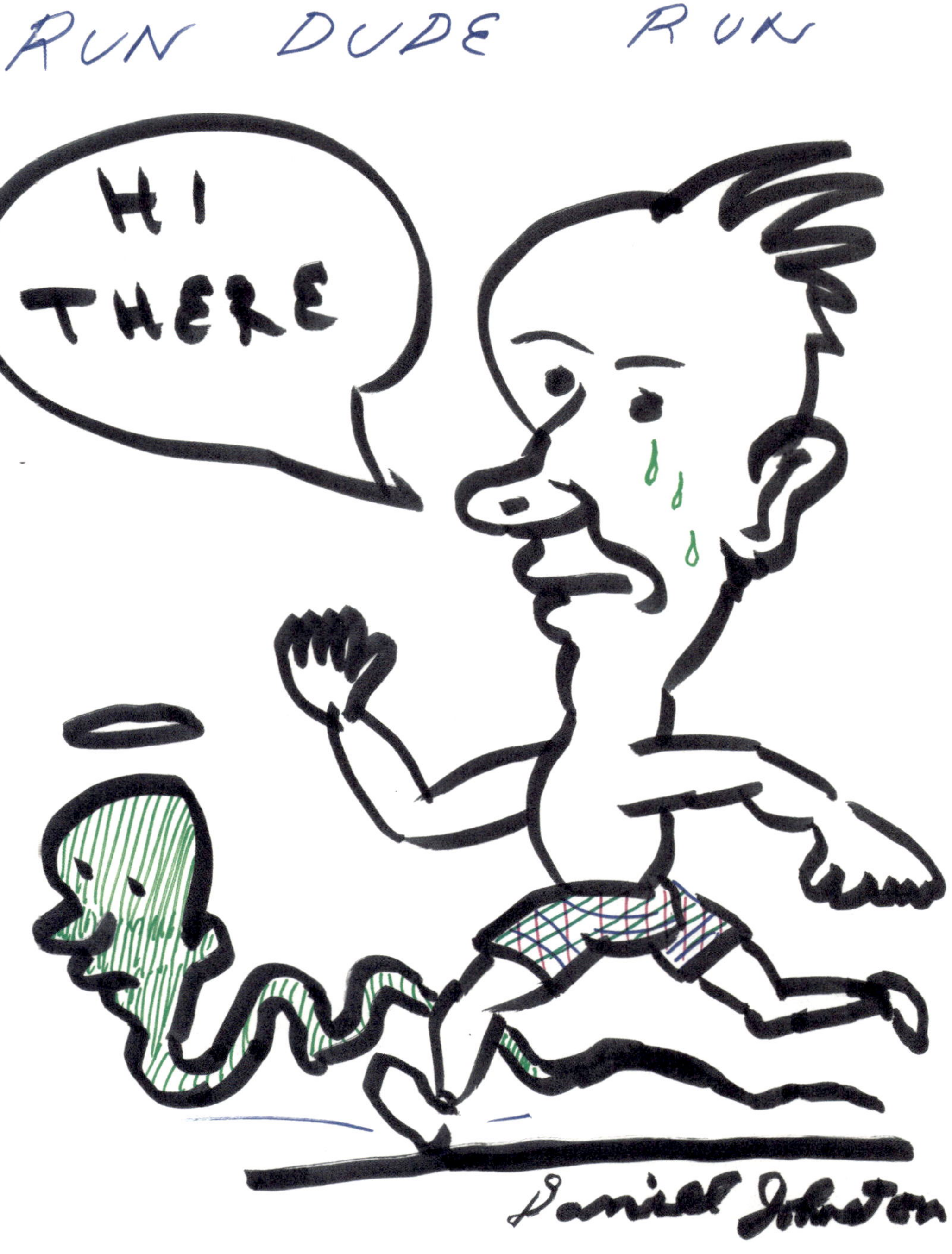

Run Dude Run

AND SO THE GHOST TORMENTED SATAN'S SEVERED HEAD FOR WHAT SEEMED A BRIEF INCIDENT BUT WAS ACTUALLY A PROLONGED MOMENT. THE POWER OF THE GHOST IS AMAZING!

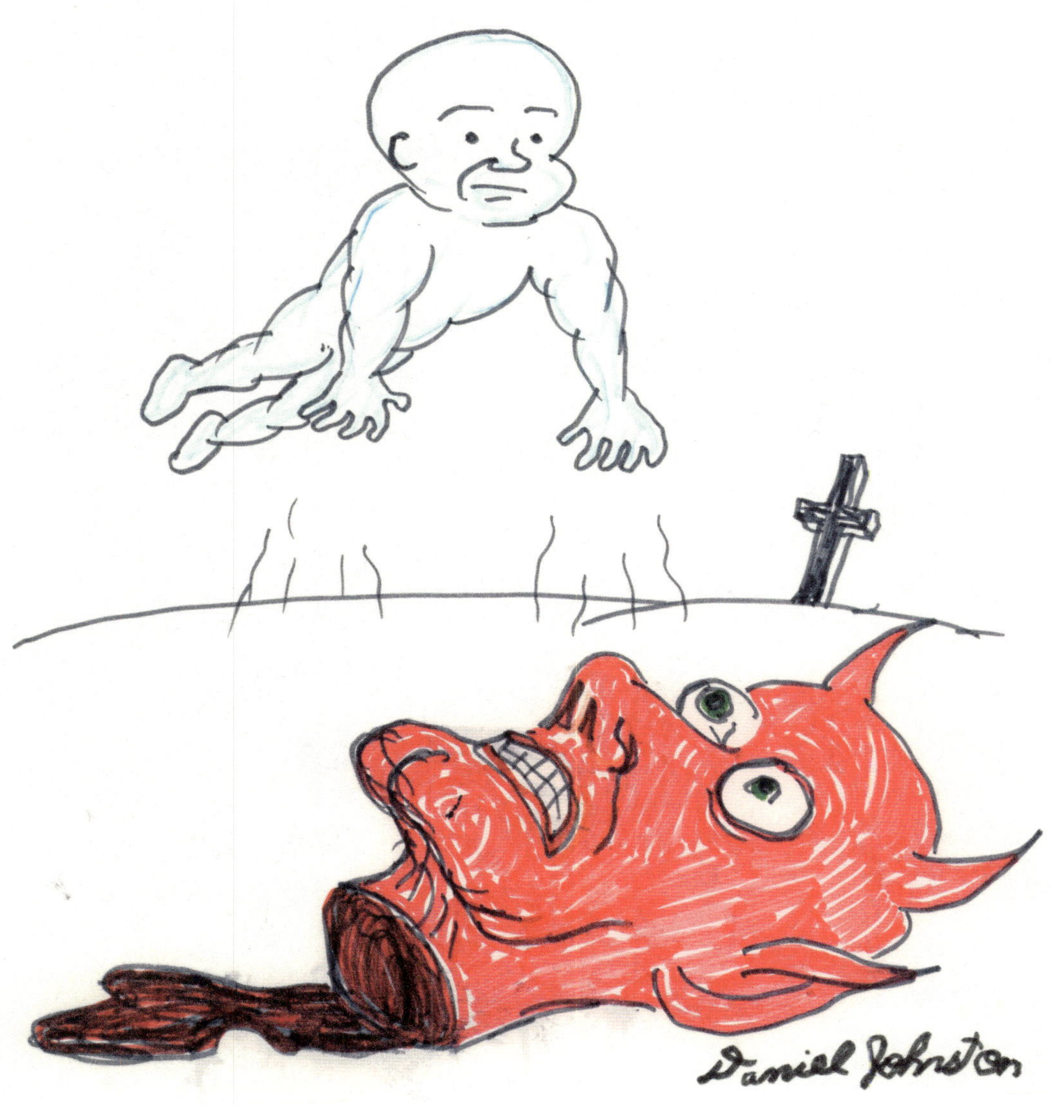

The Power of the Ghost Is Amazing! (Satan's Severed Head)

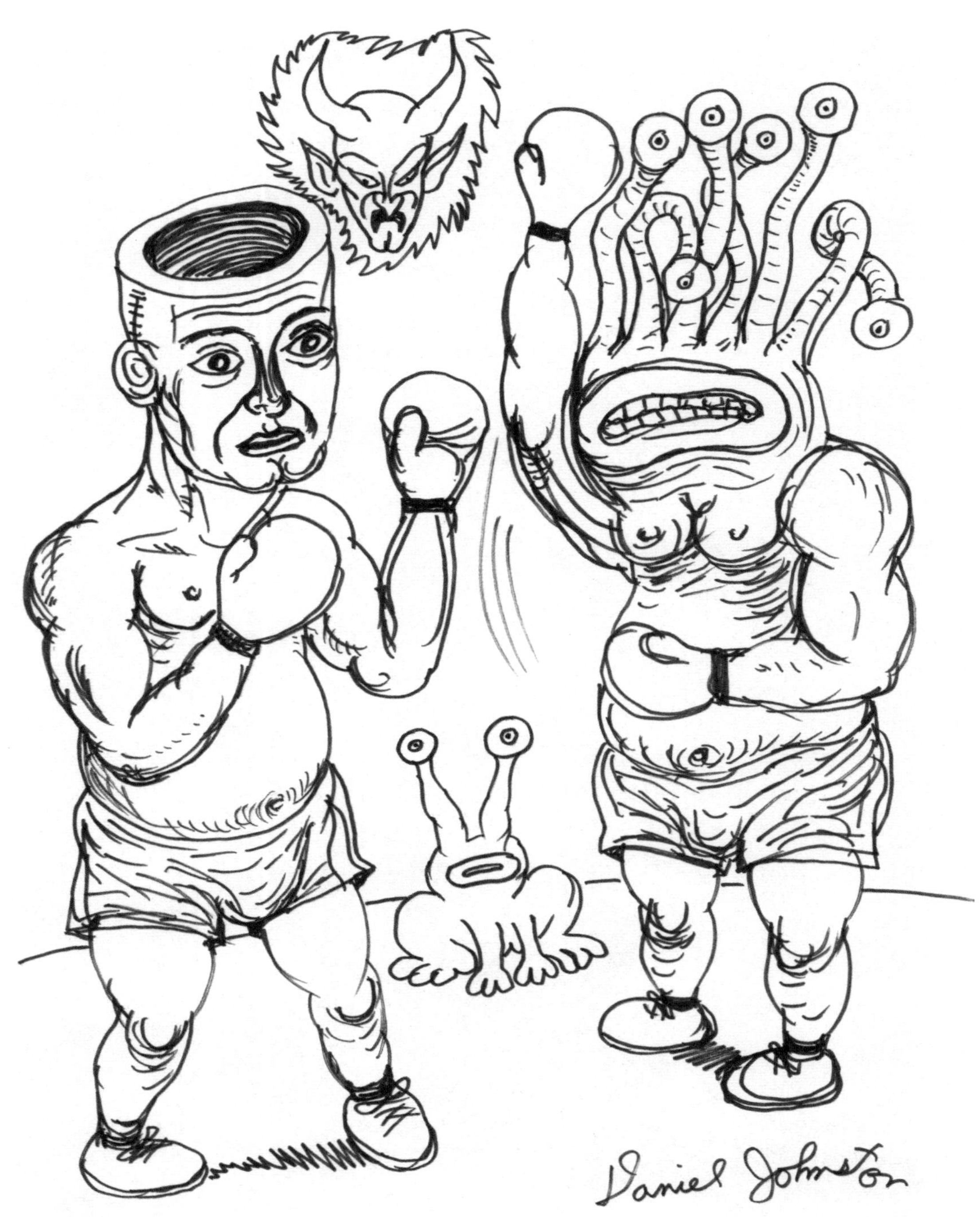

Untitled (The Eternal Battle, with Jeremiah)

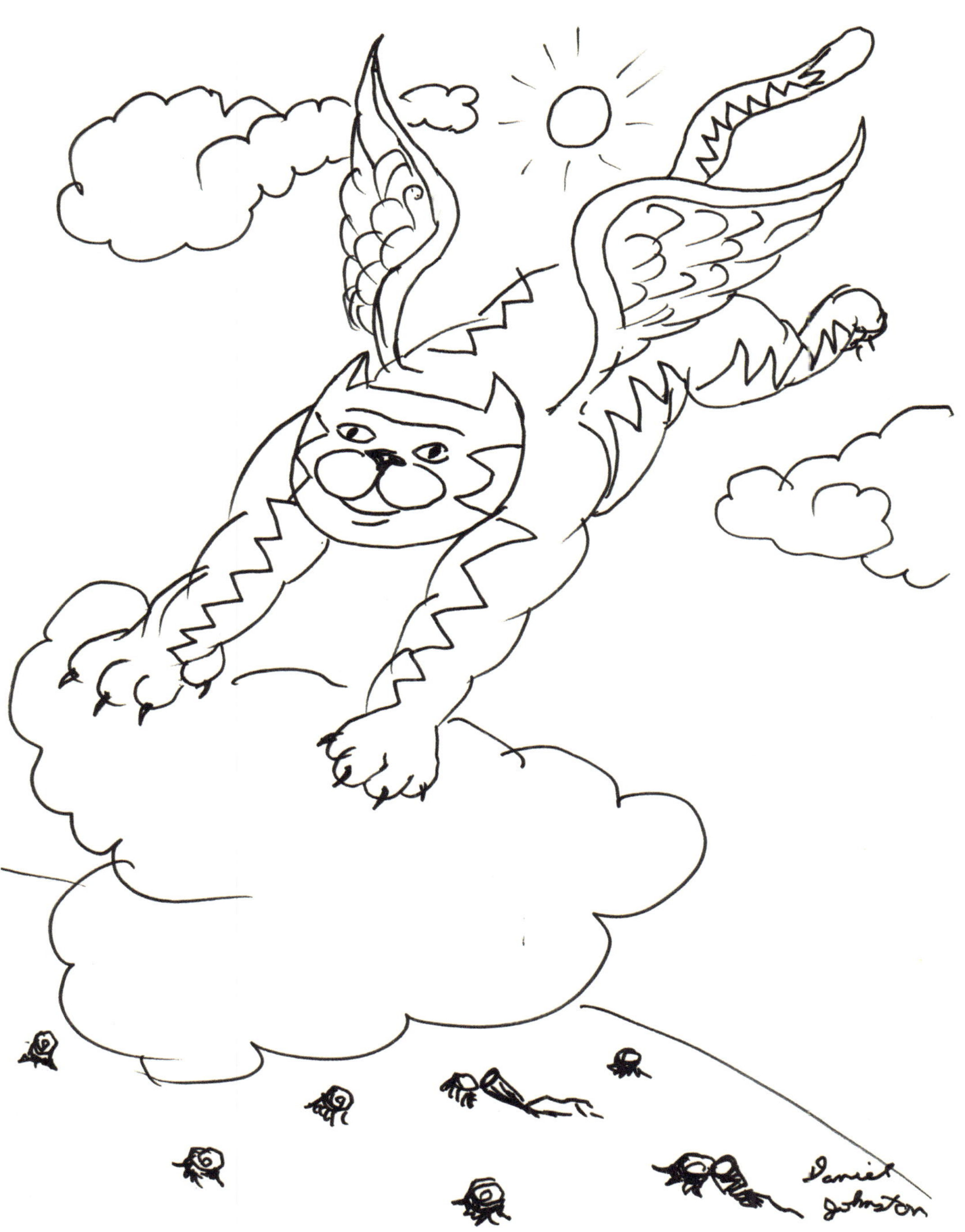

Untitled (Sassy Frass in Heaven)

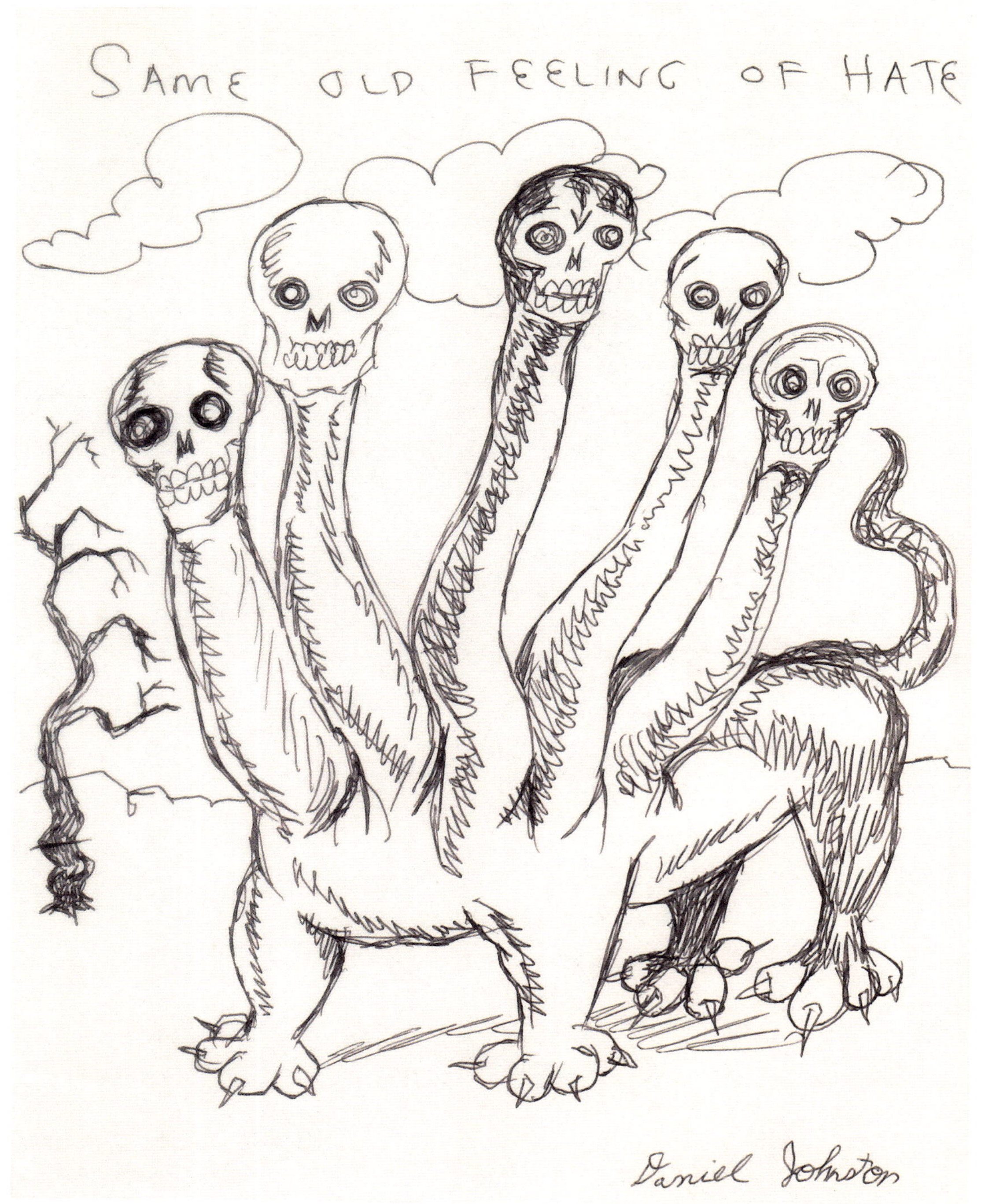

Same Old Feeling of Hate

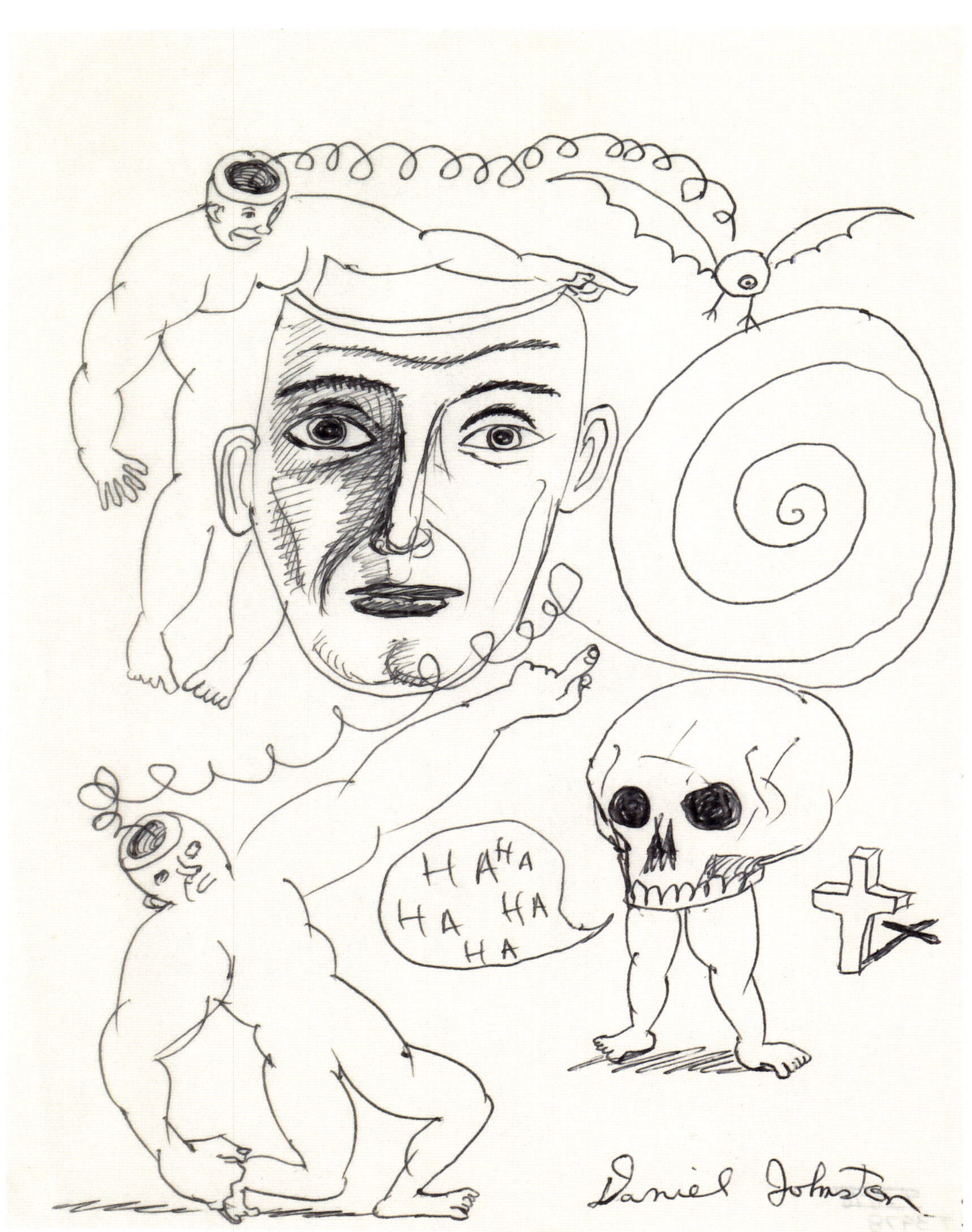

Ha Ha Ha Ha Ha (The Walking Skull)

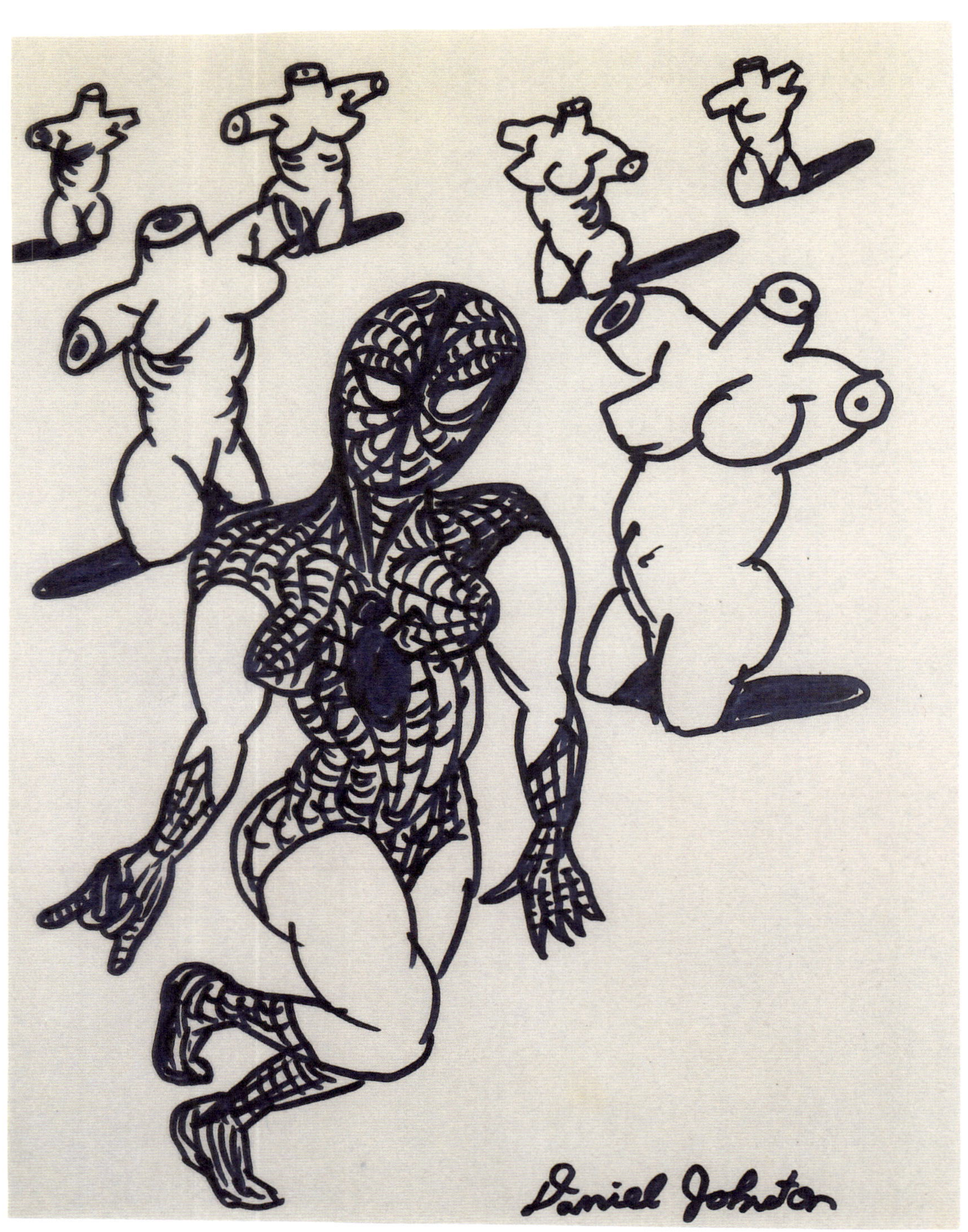

Untitled (Spiderwoman and Torsos)

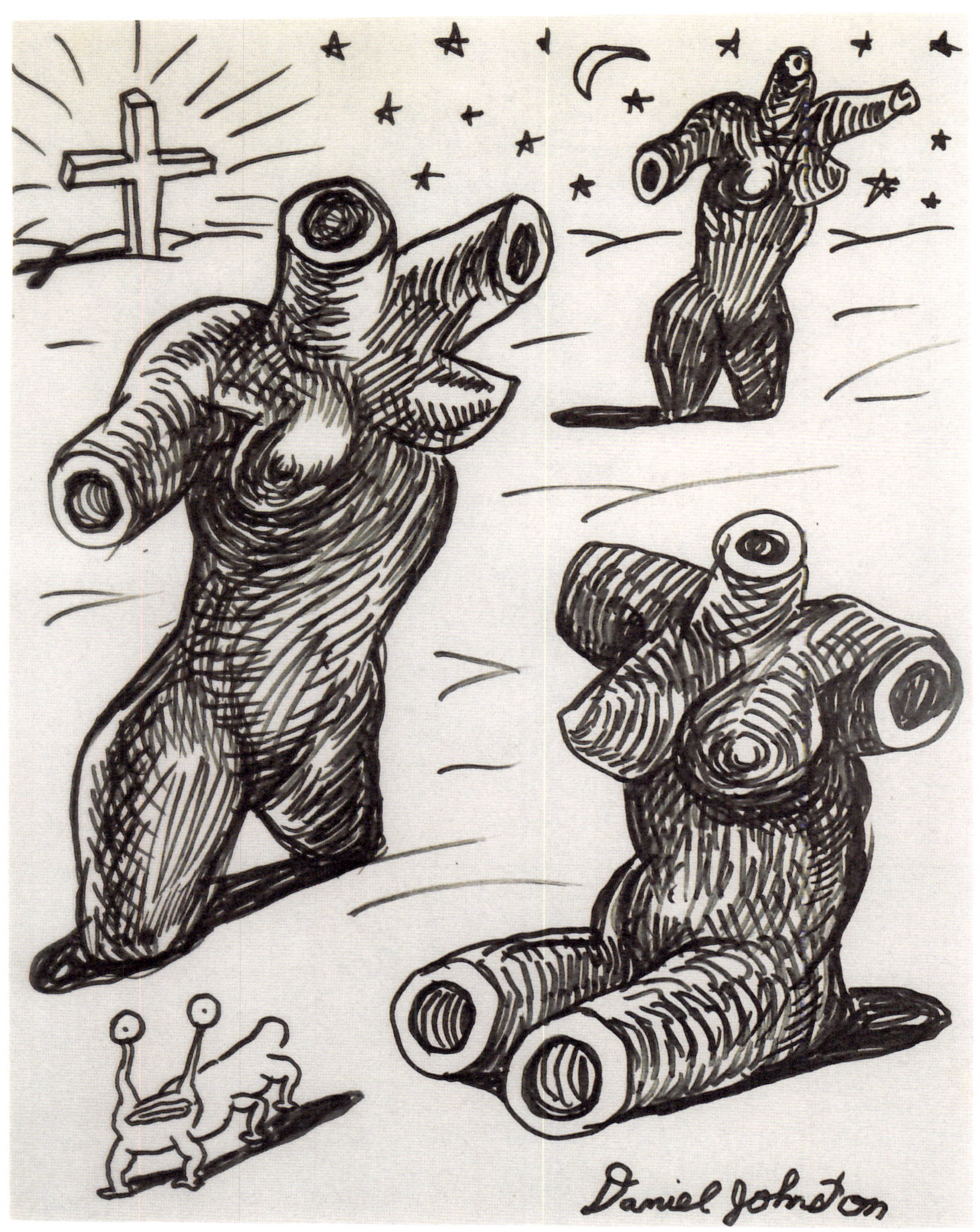

Untitled (Three Torsos)

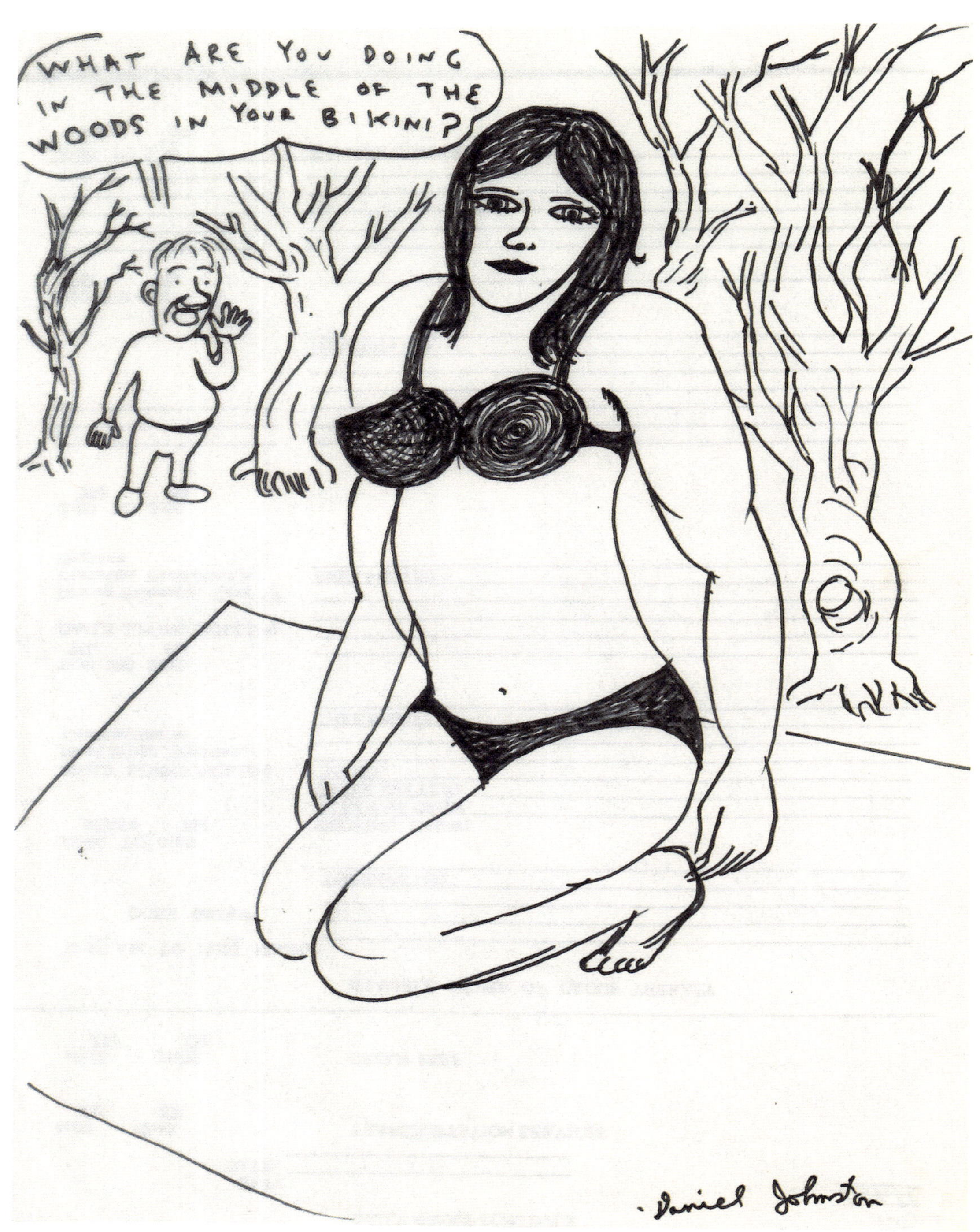

The Woods in Your Bikini?

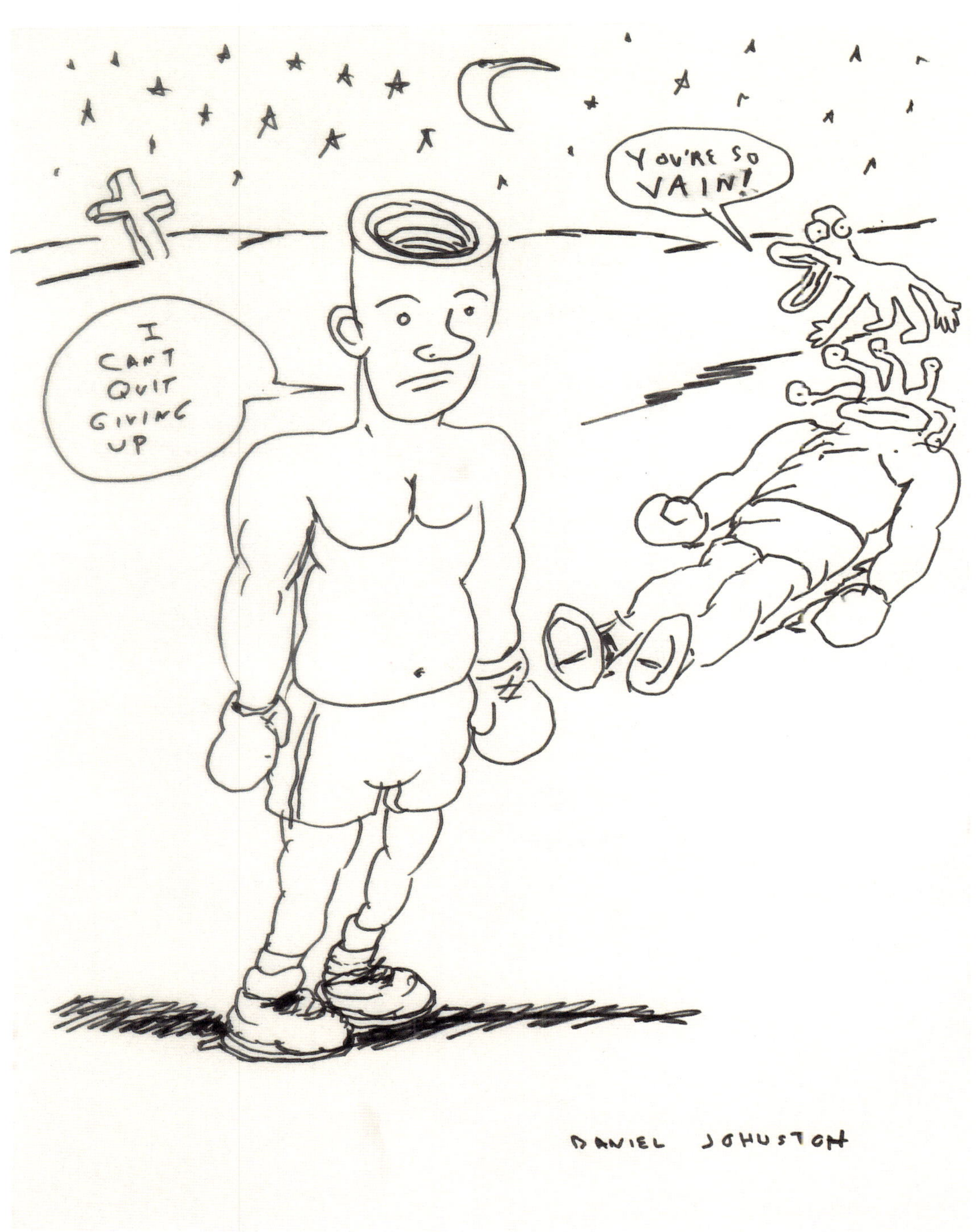

I Can't Quit Giving Up

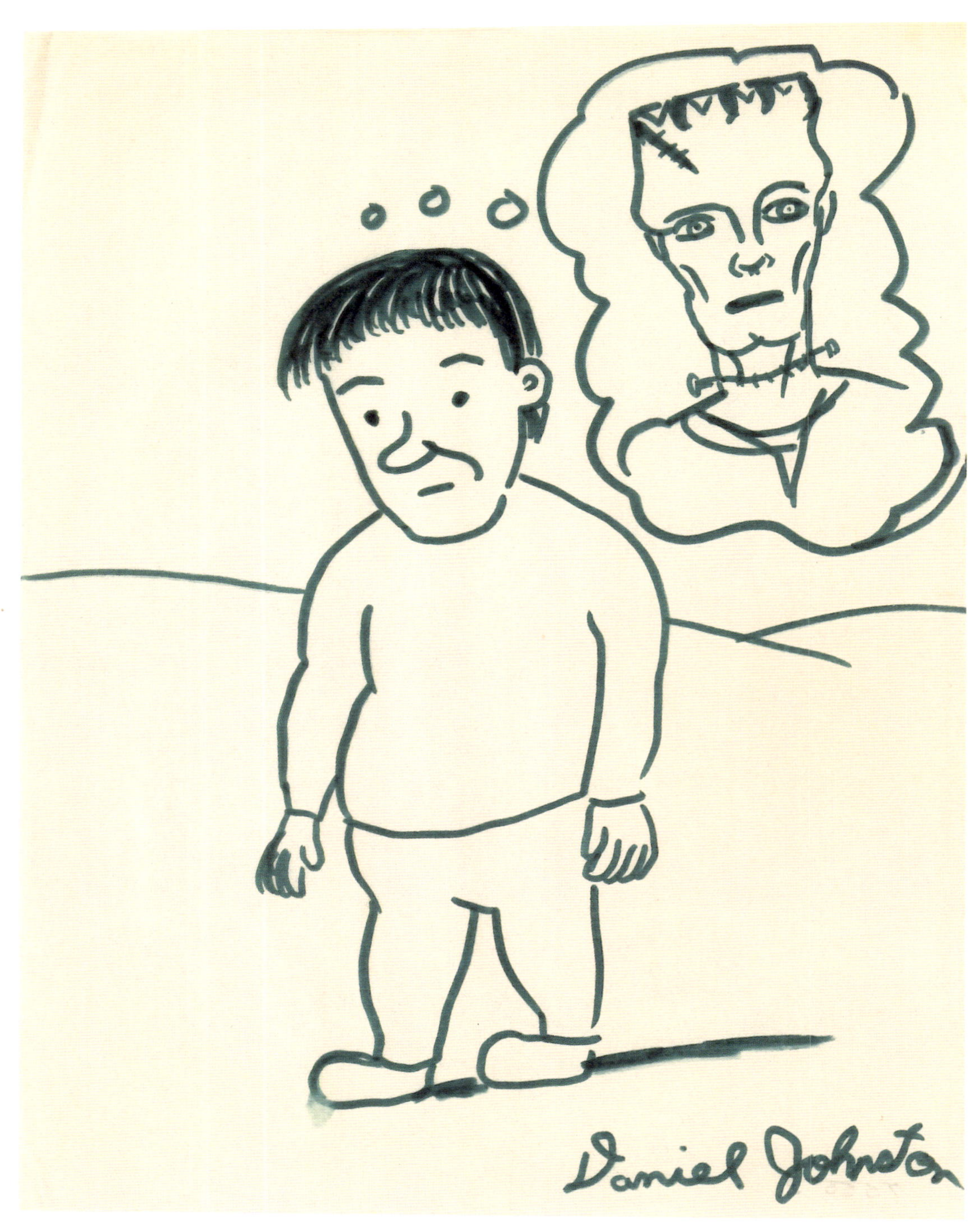

Untitled (Frankenstein)

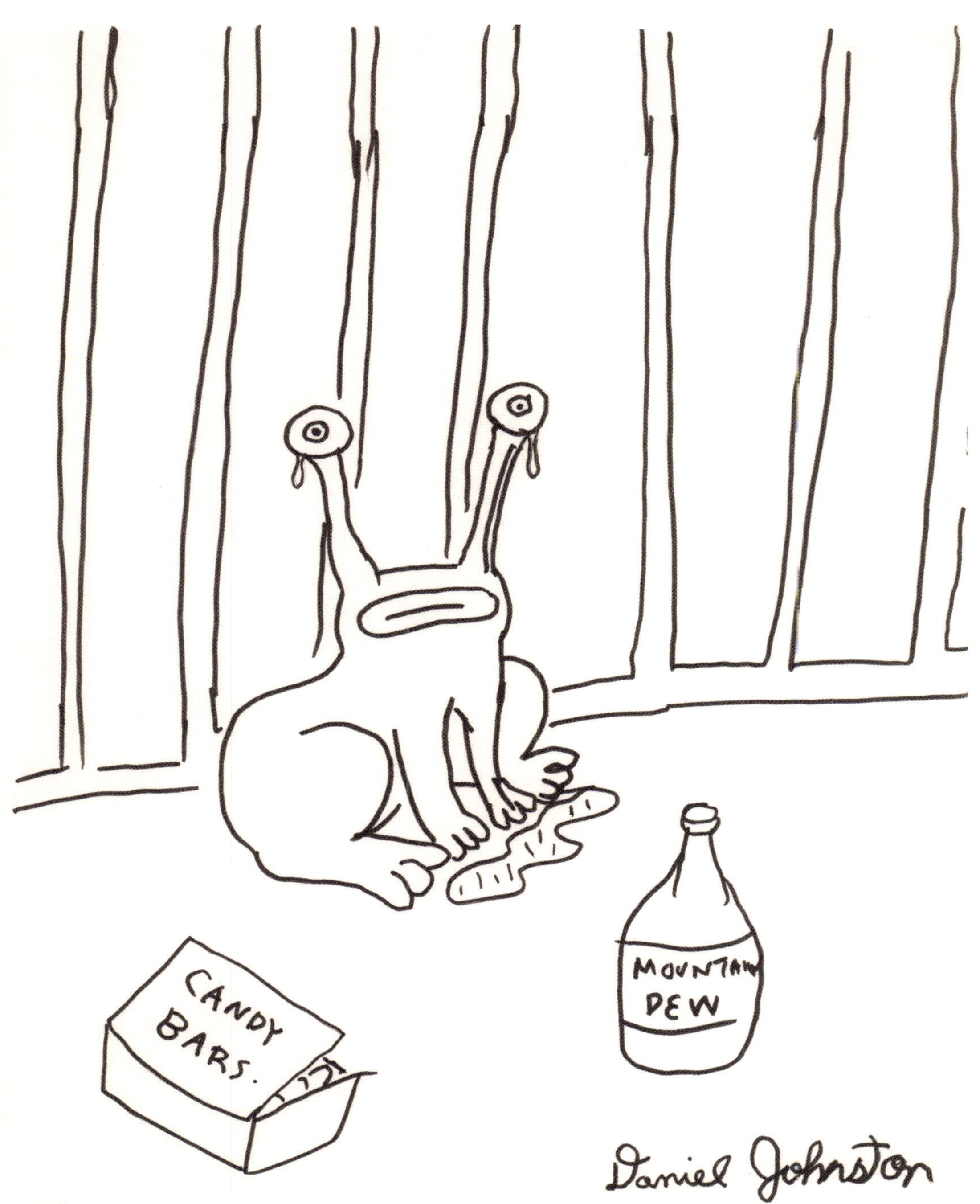

Untitled (Jeremiah in Jail)

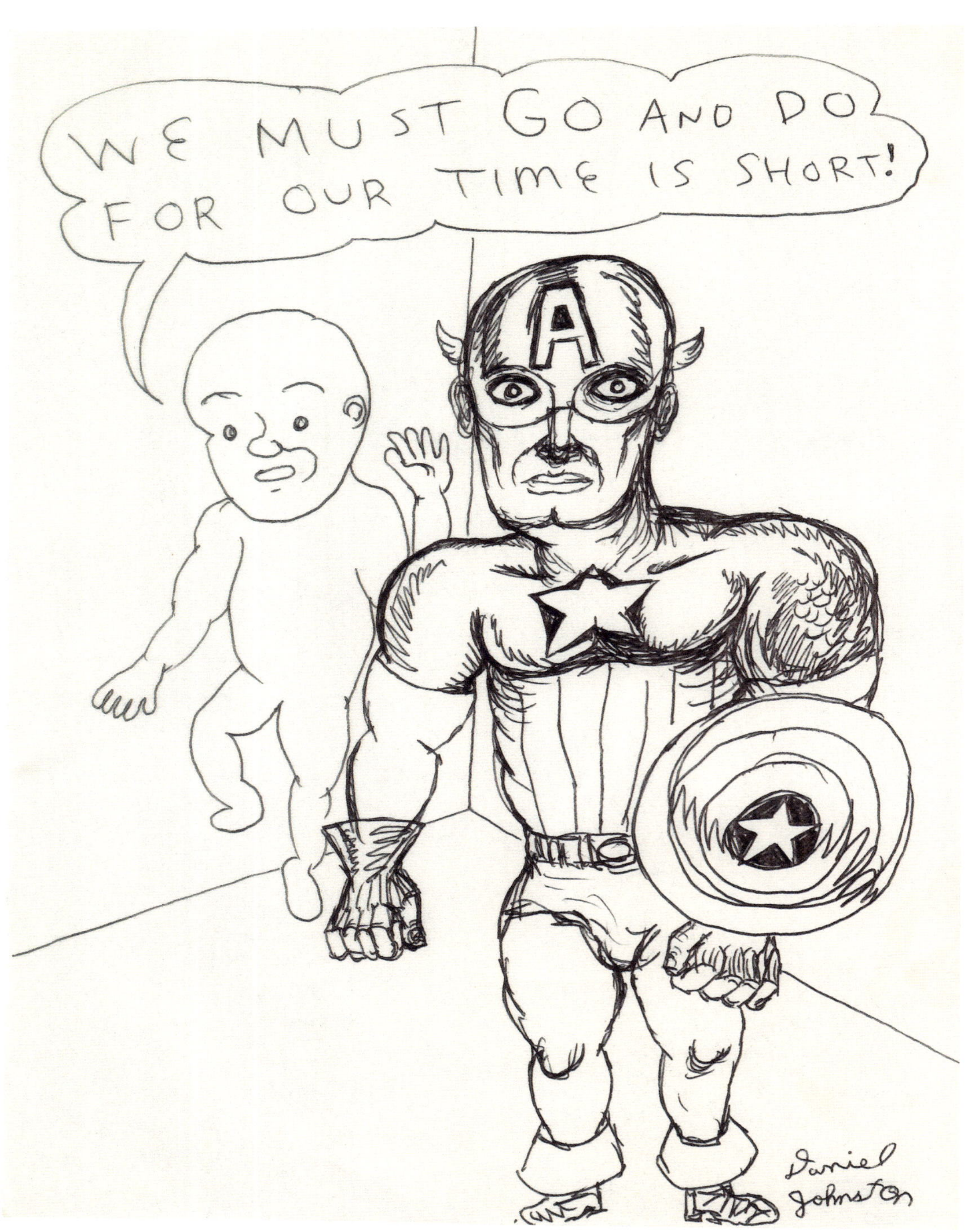

Our Time Is Short!

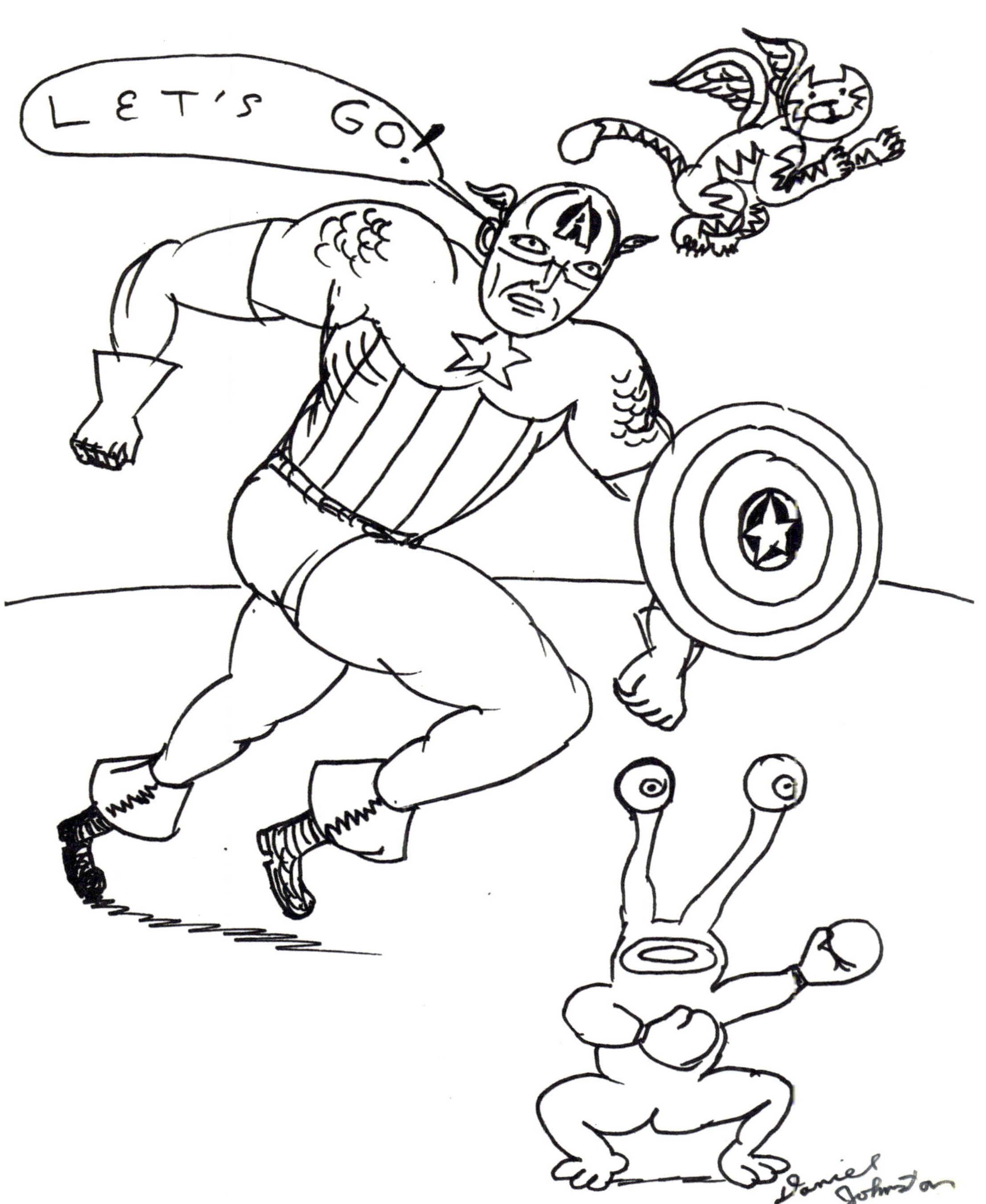

Let's Go!

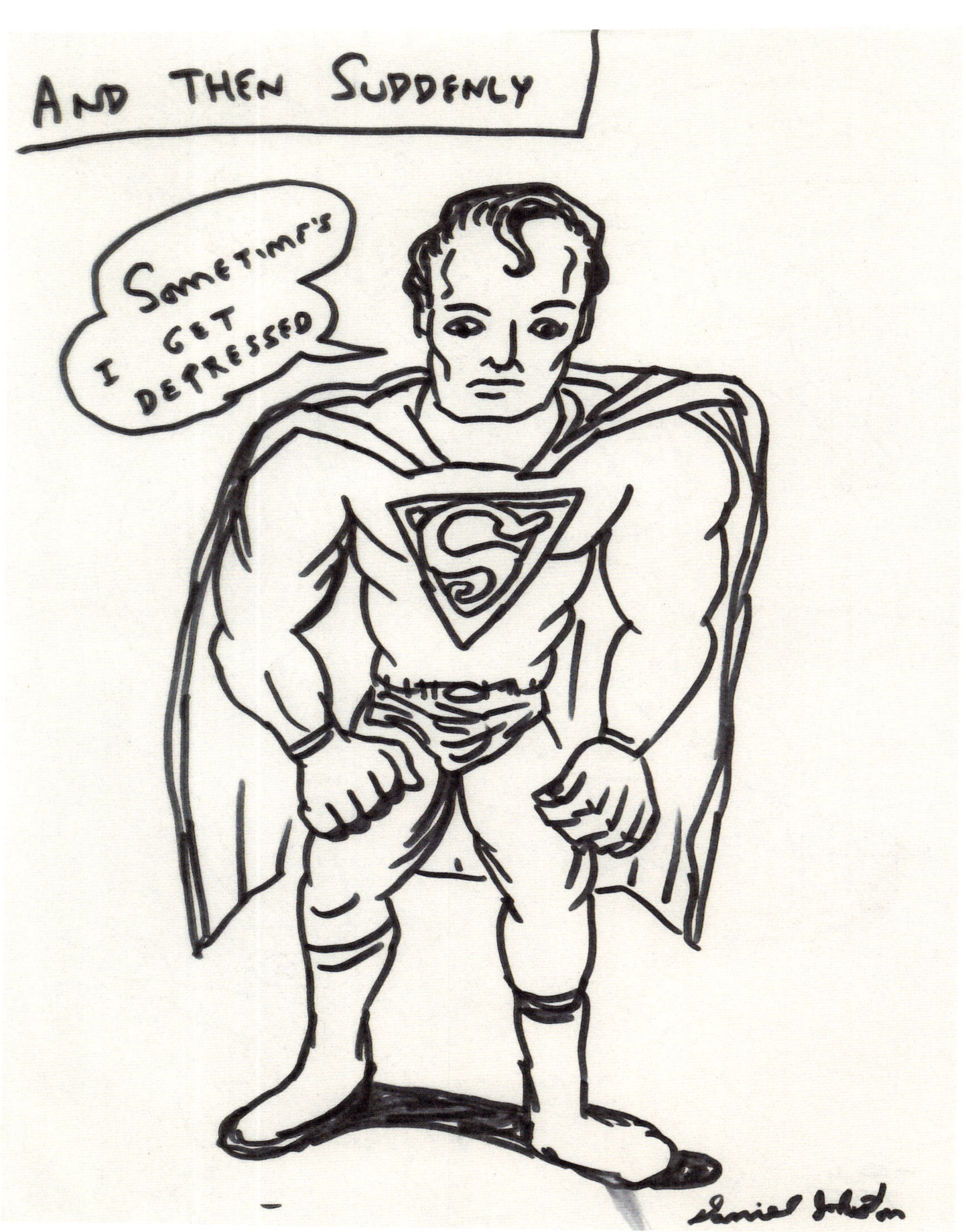

Sometimes I Get Depressed

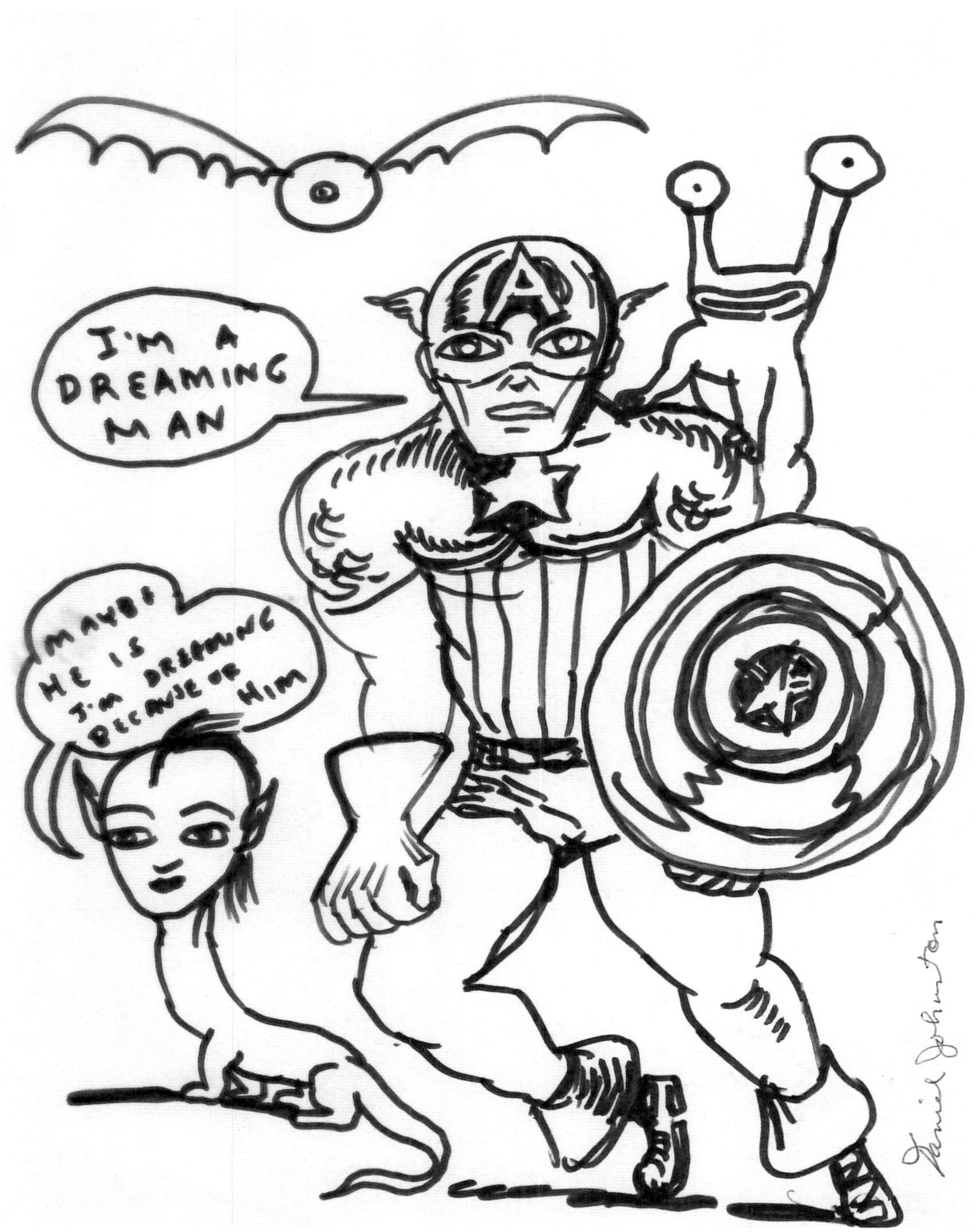

I'm a Dreaming Man

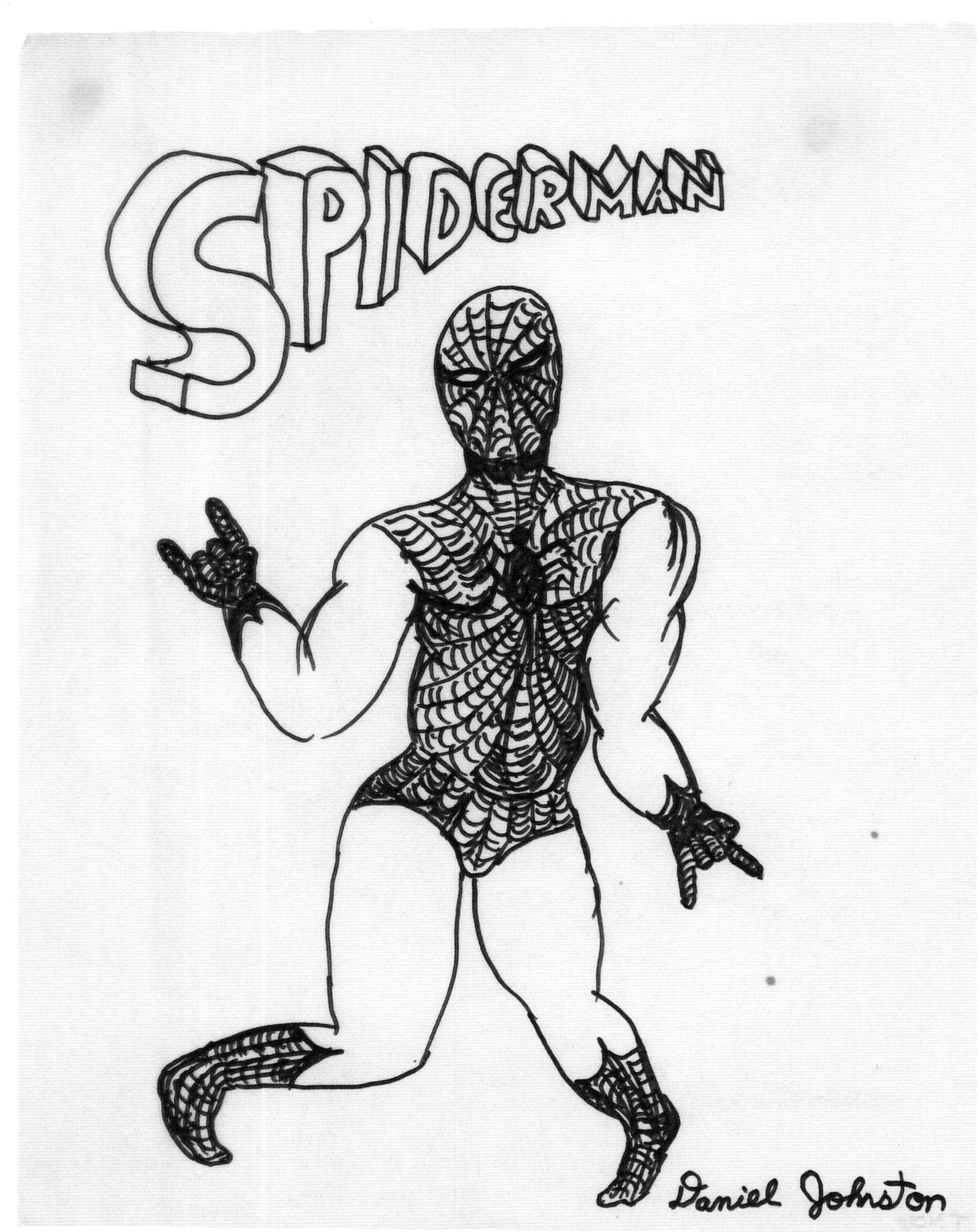

Spiderman

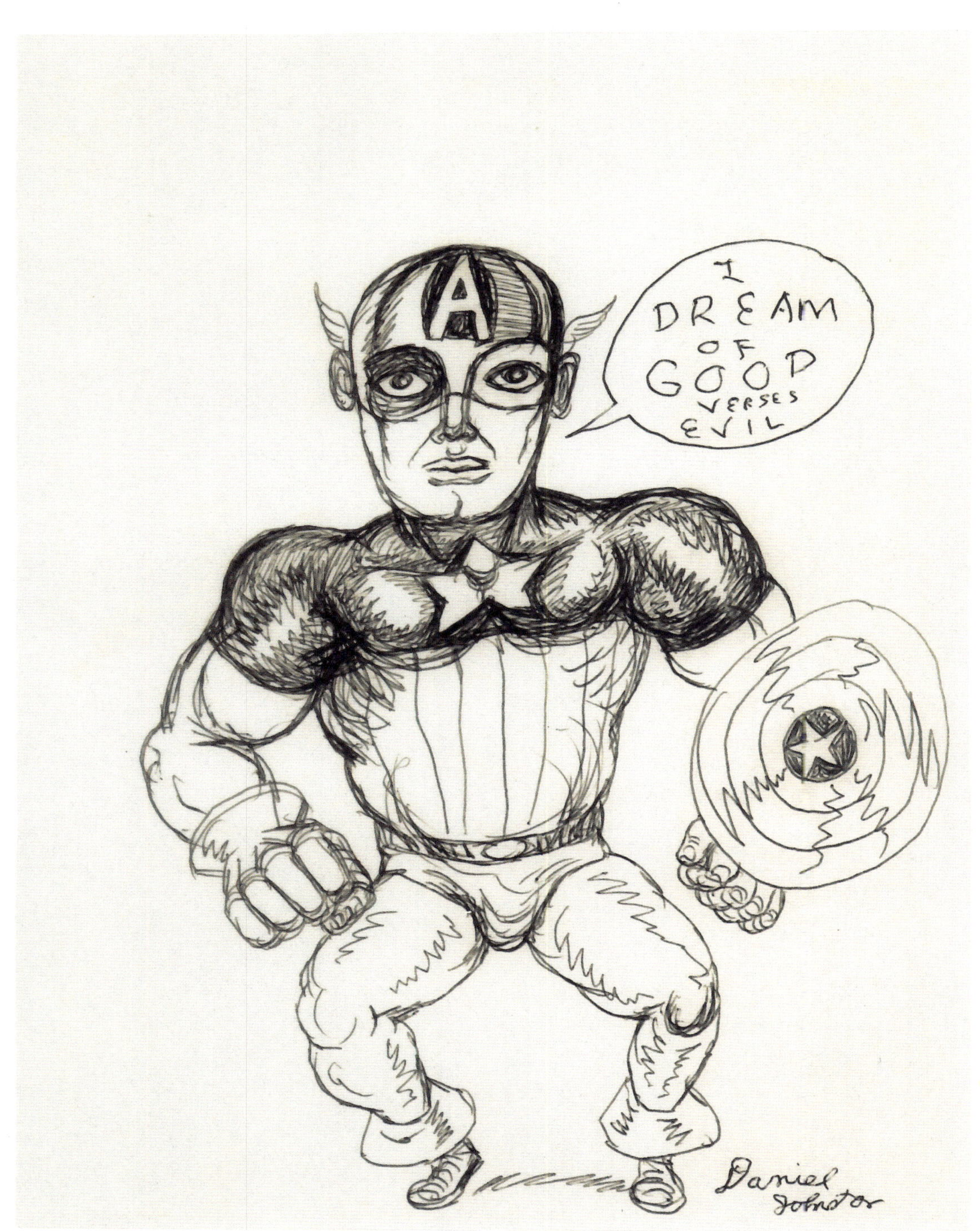

I Dream of Good Verses Evil

Fans loved to give Daniel Johnston hugs, but side-eyed, with a ready diagnosis, expert evaluation. As true pnkrckrs of indie mind, suspicious of success or sellout, of the insincere, the inauthentic.

Making it is not worth the effort; having arrived is where you do not want to be. MoMA or Carnegie Hall shows are sure signs of failure: the real ones WON'T ATTEND.

Historians of the Arts are wont to cite anything as founts of creation, usually determined at birth. From the infantile to infantilism. Were Richman, Picasso, Basquiat, Johnston true primitives? Or faux, feigned, affected, fey? Or cannily expressed by a measured hand and mind of design? Or all of the above?

Reducing it to a diagnosis of bipolar, while ignoring that polar opposites also attract, takes away too much, diminishes the artistry, which, to the real fans, is not to be denied.

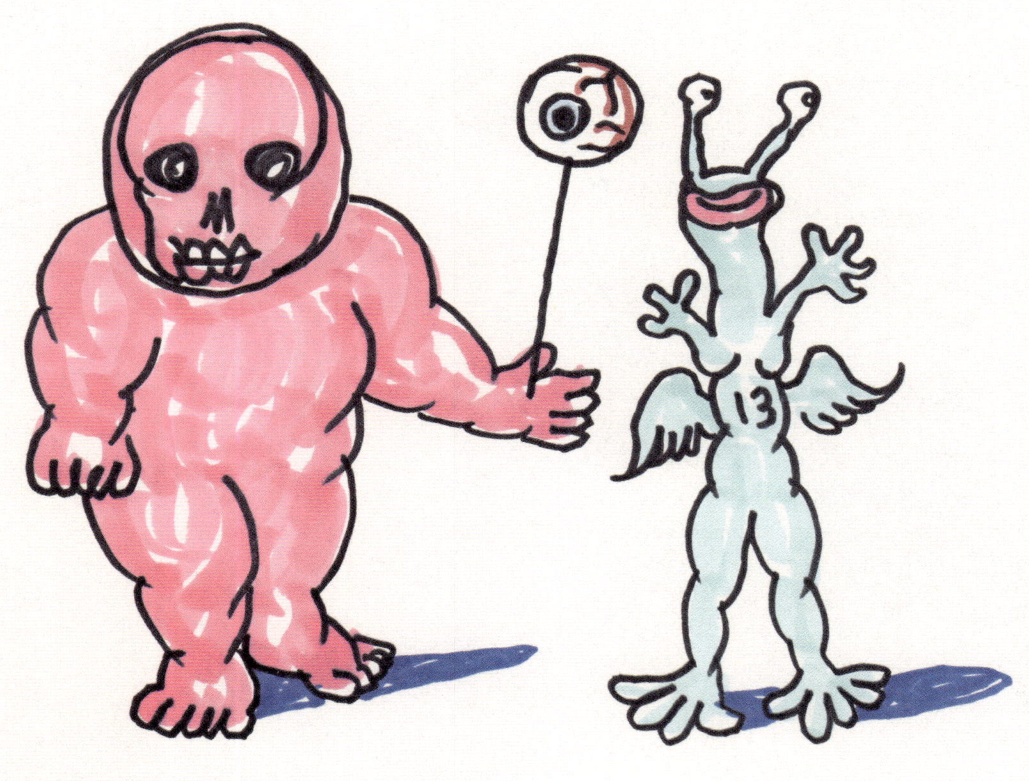

Love Is Always Drinking a Slurpe

X.
Eyeful of Adventure
1990s

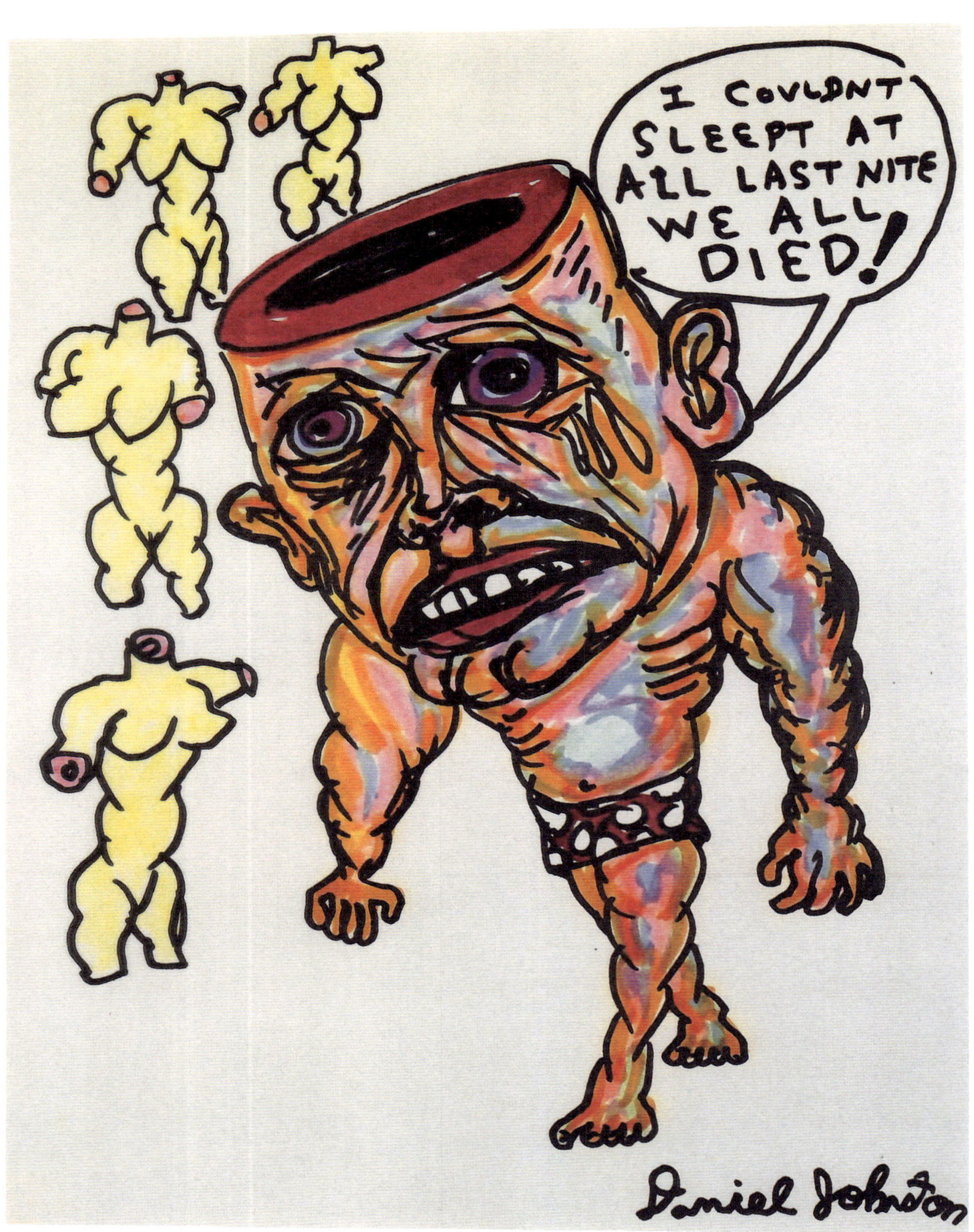
I COULDNT SLEEPT AT ALL LAST NITE WE ALL DIED!
Daniel Johnston

We All Died!

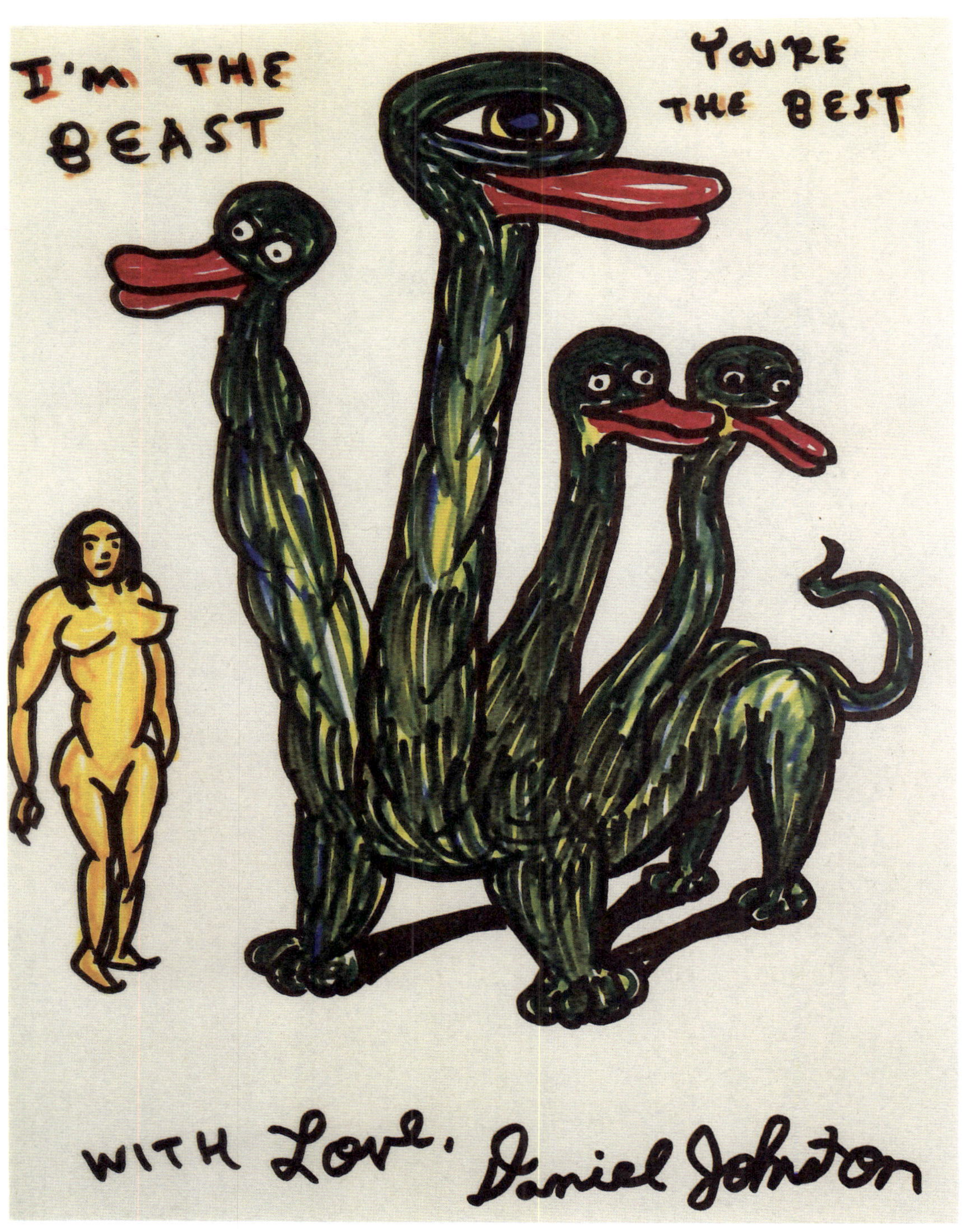

I'm the Beast You're the Best

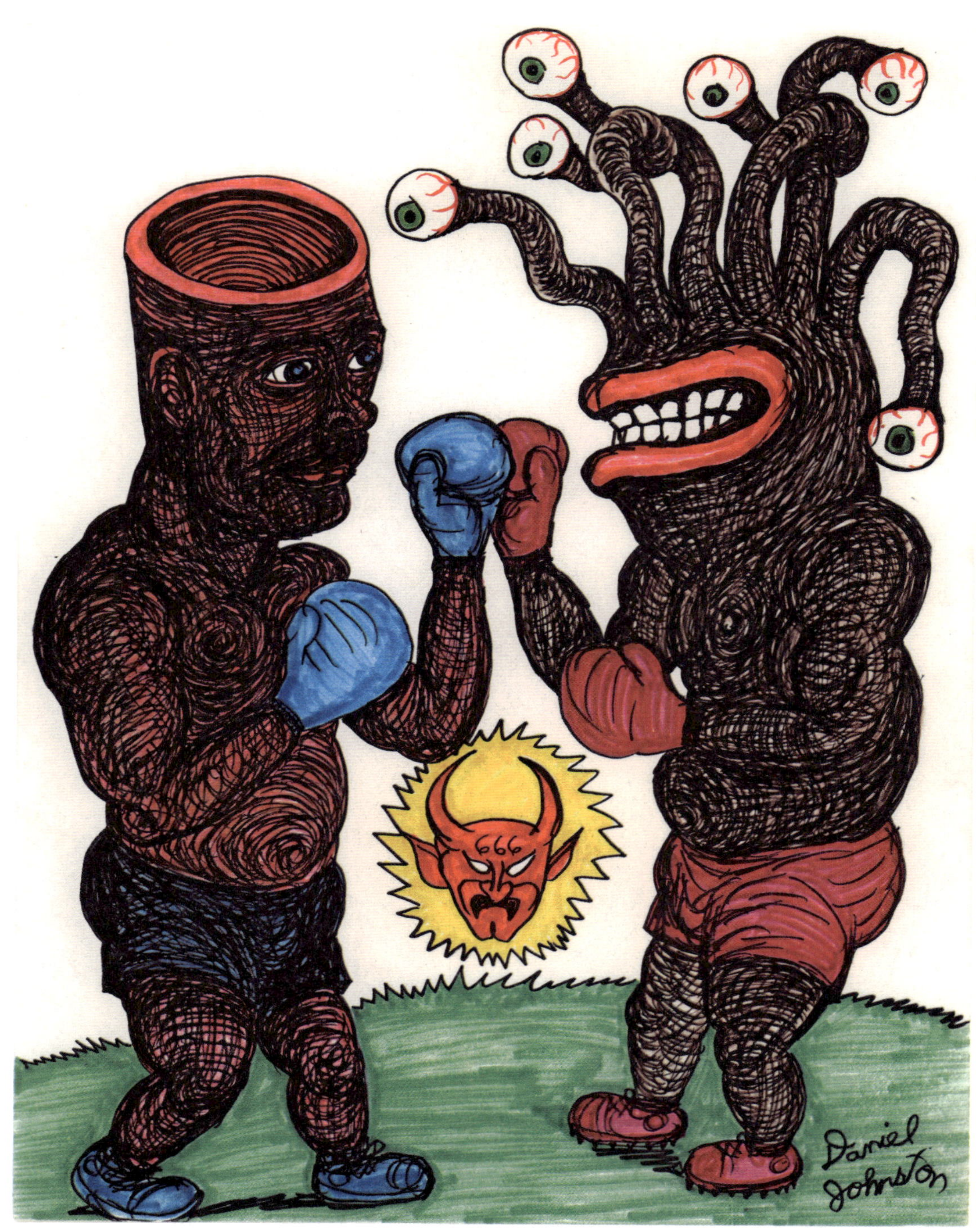

The Eternal Battle

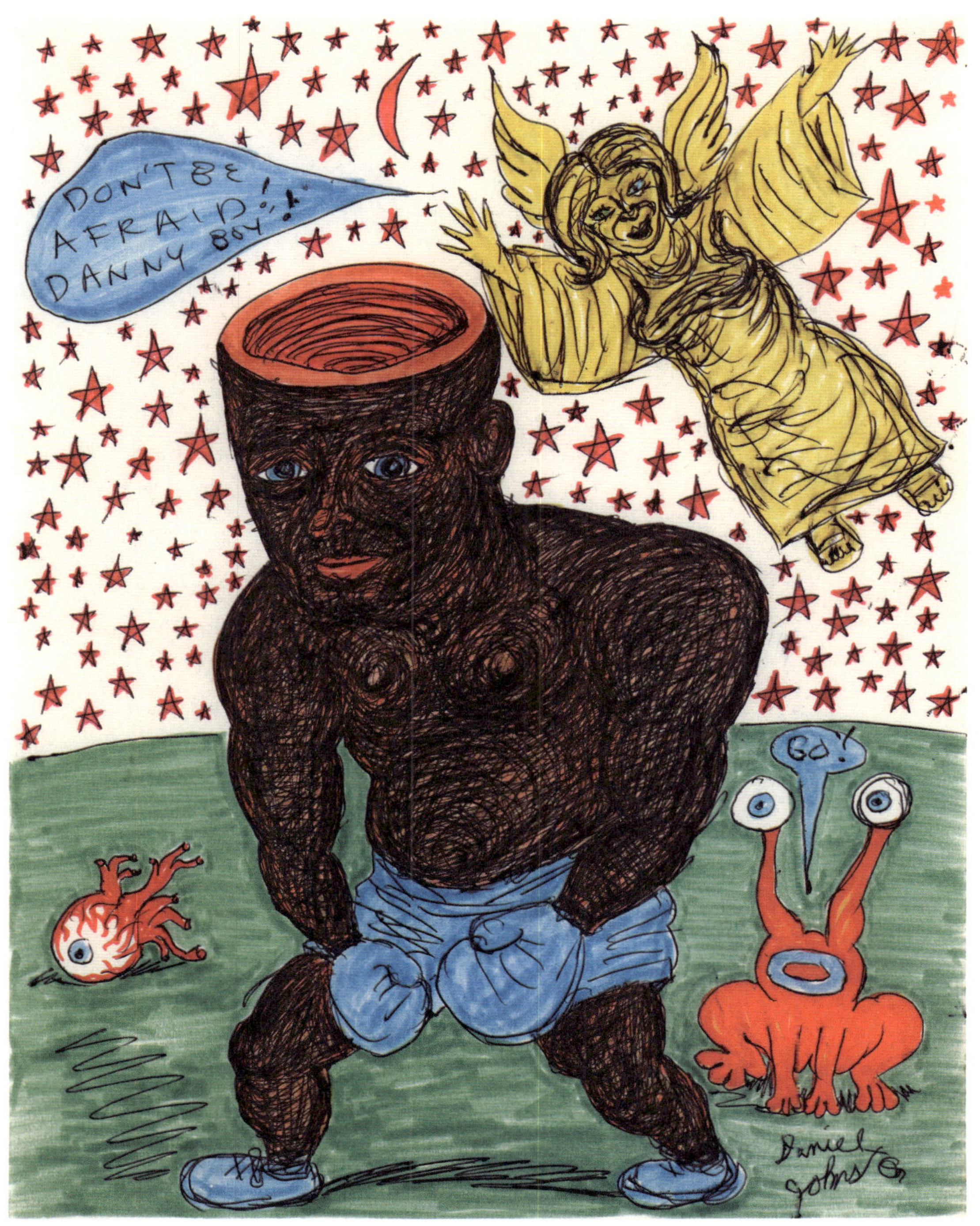

Don't Be Afraid Danny Boy!

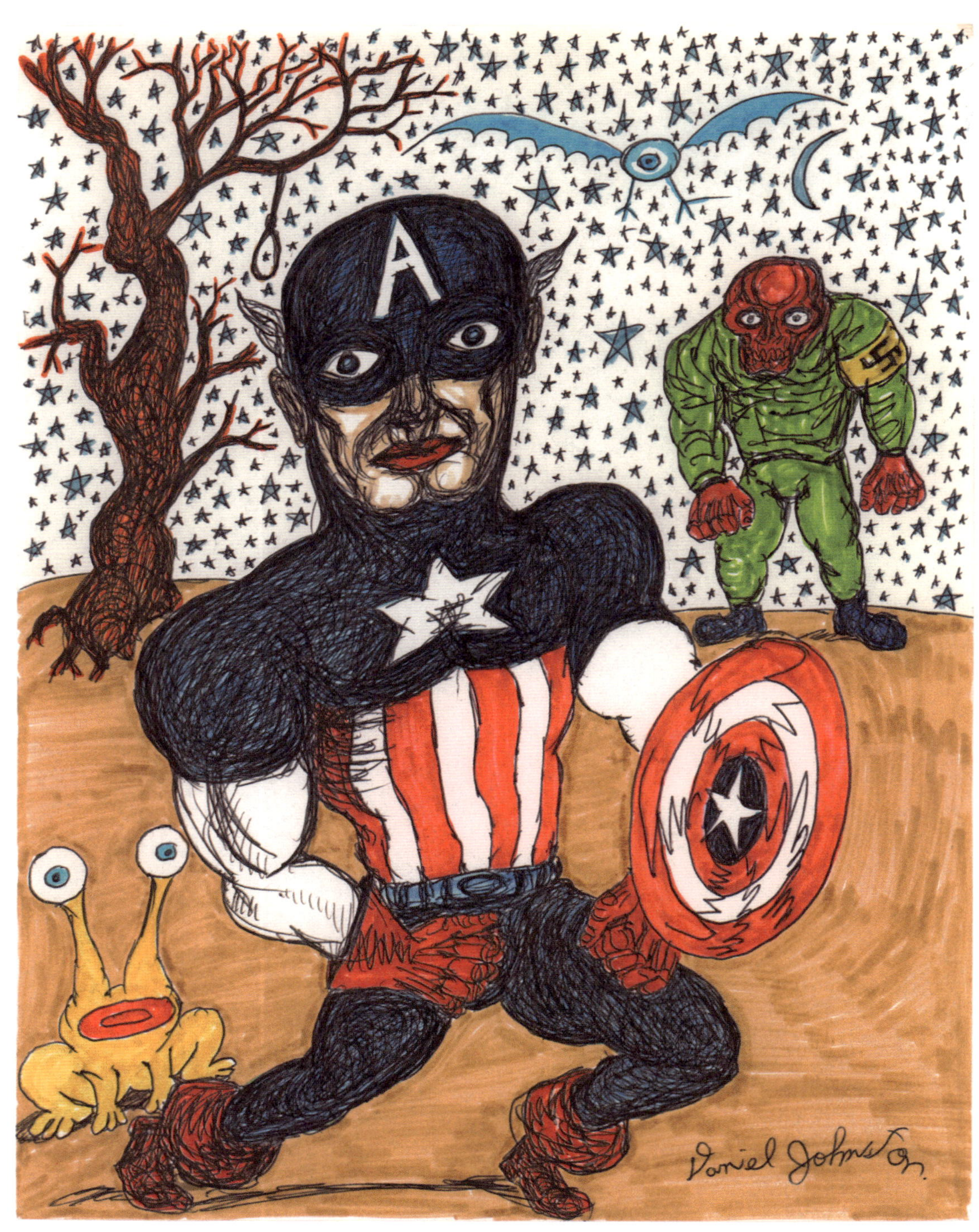

Untitled (Captain America, Red Skull)

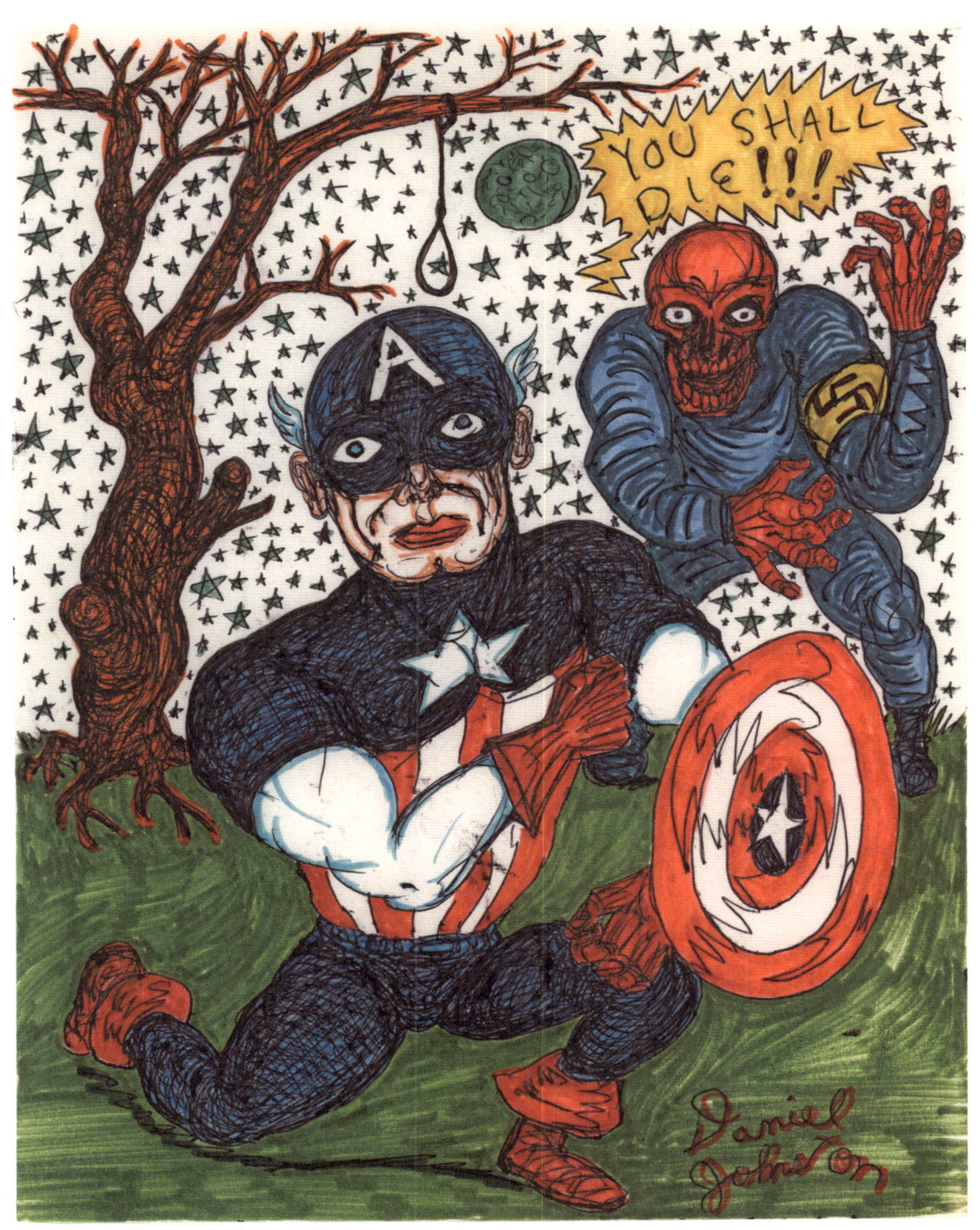

You Shall Die!

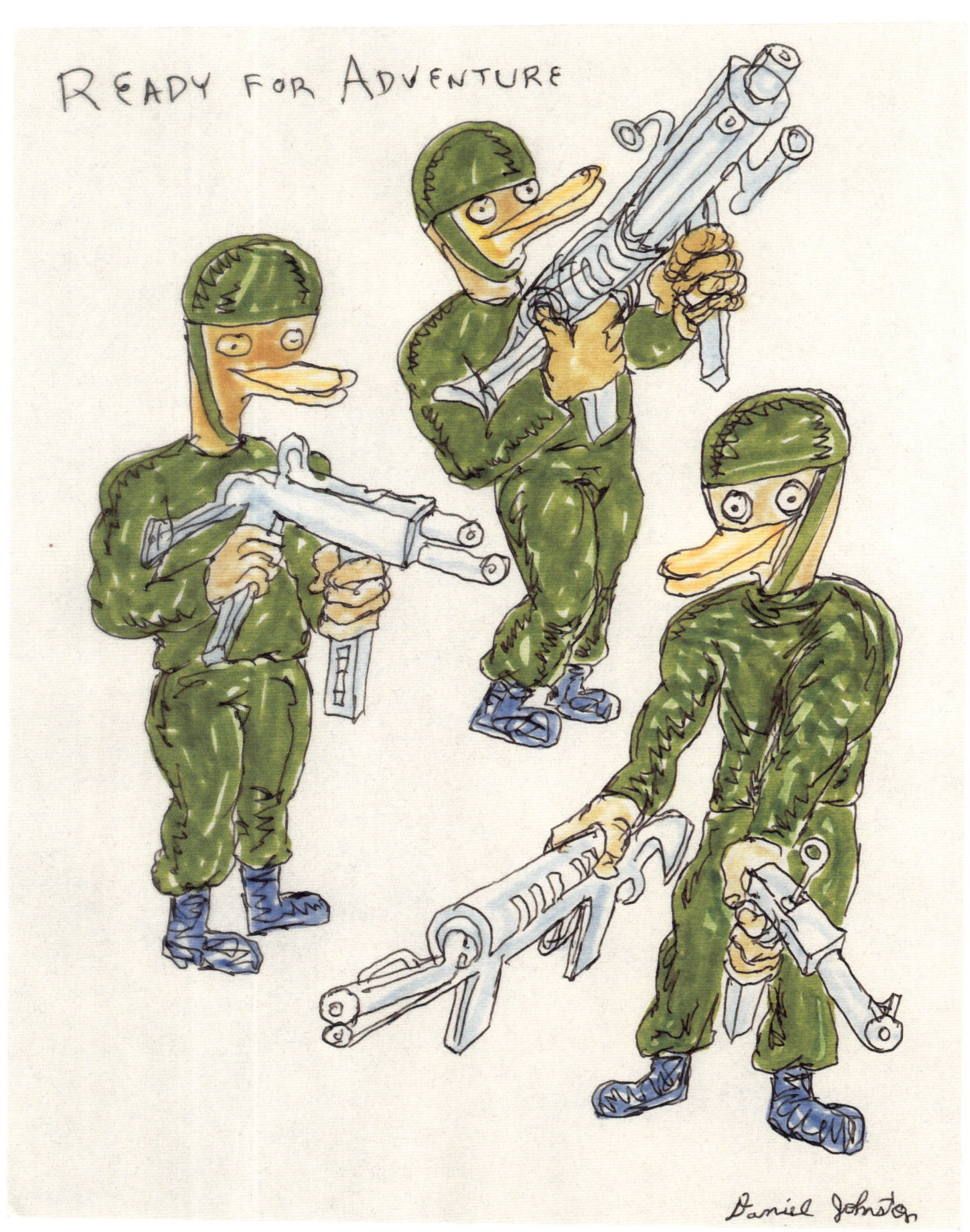

Ready for Adventure

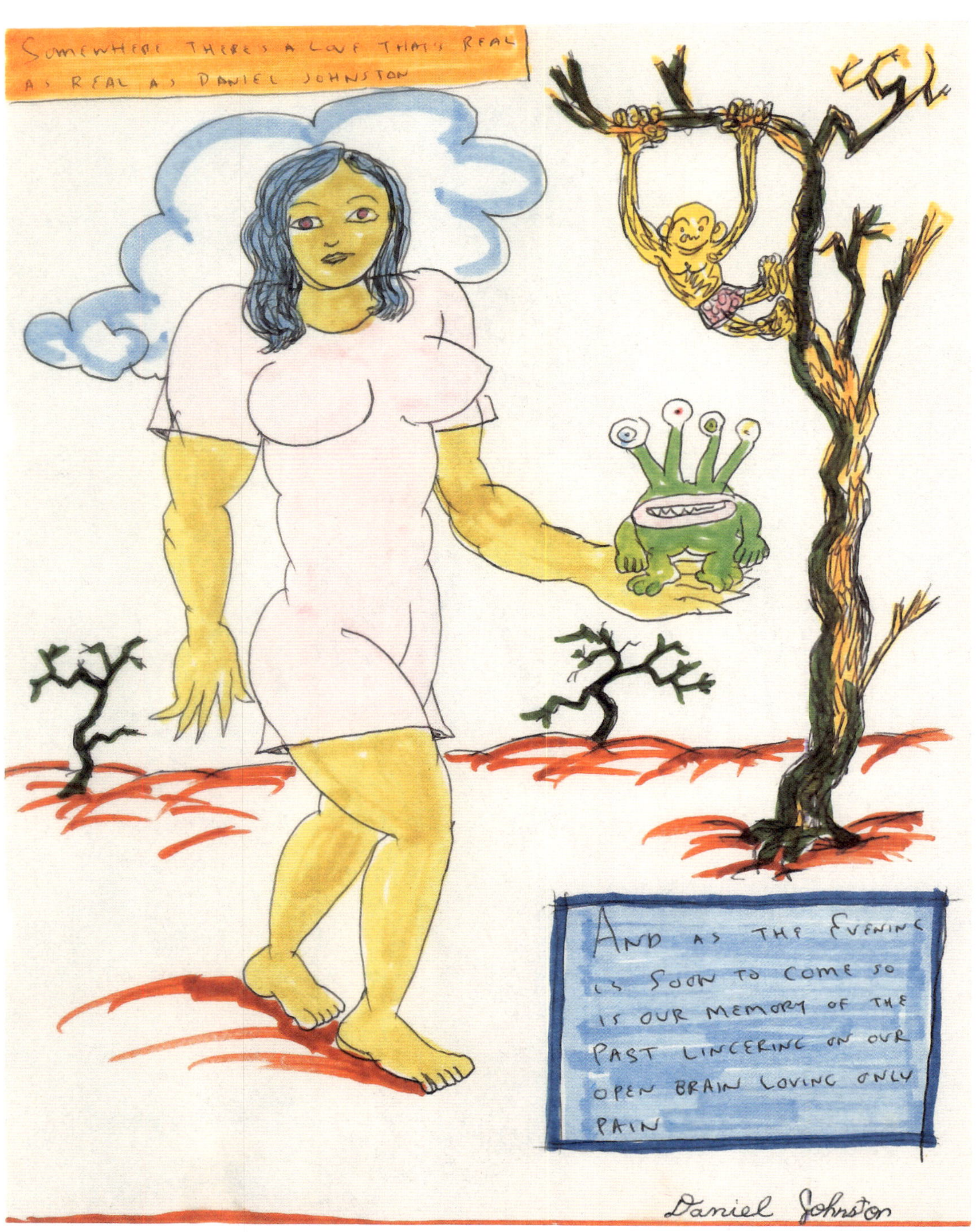

Somewhere There's a Love That's Real

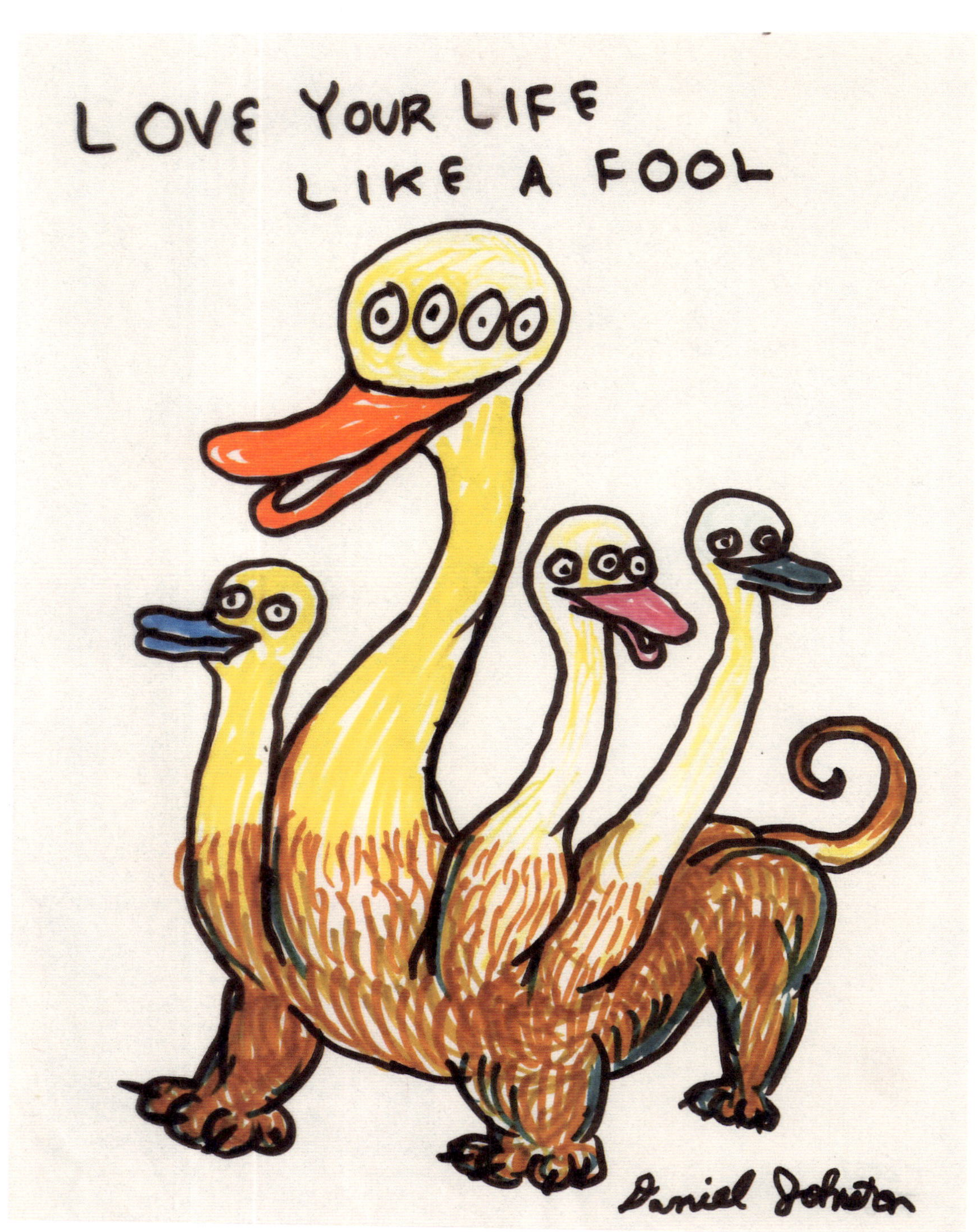

Love Your Life Like a Fool

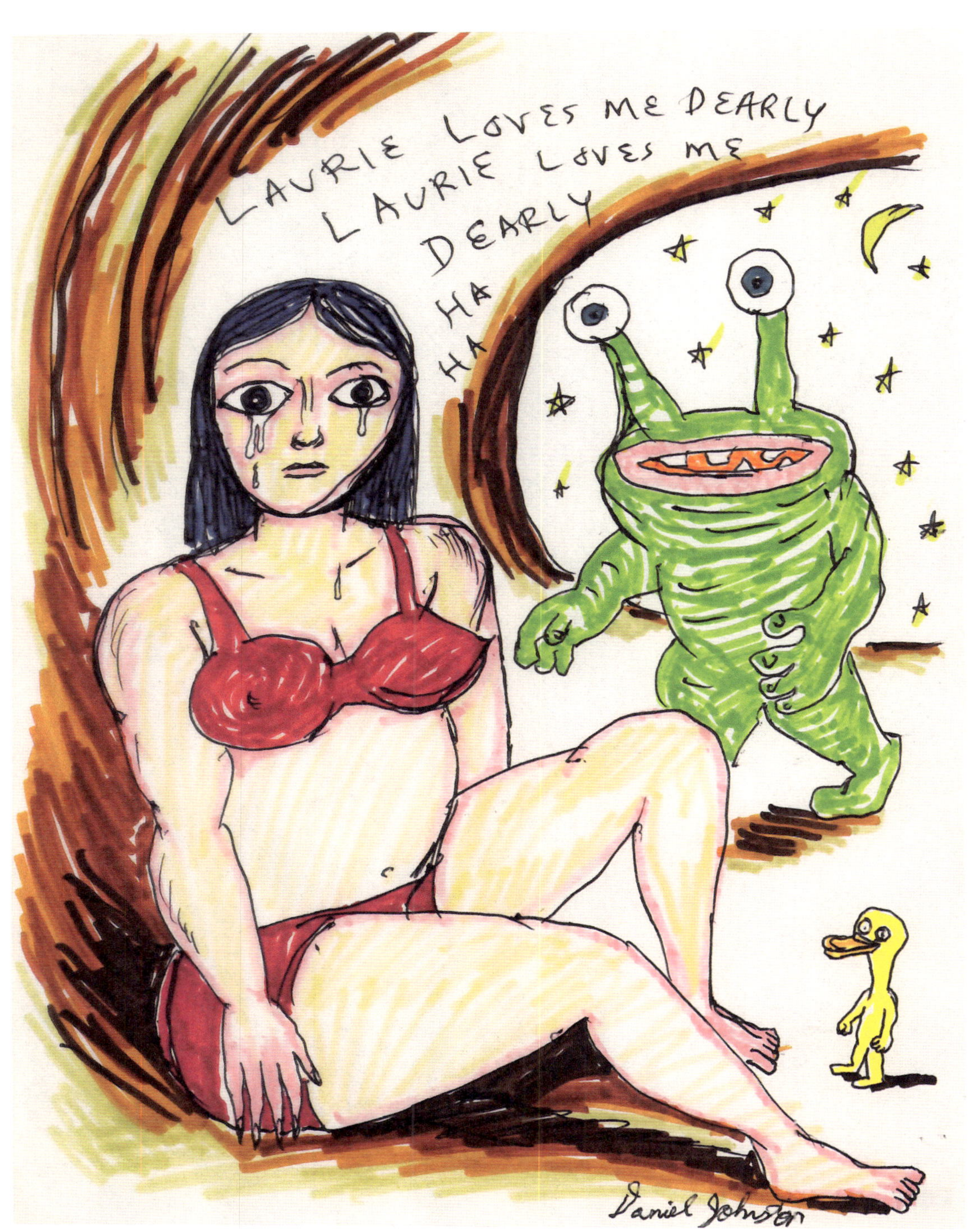

Laurie Loves Me Dearly

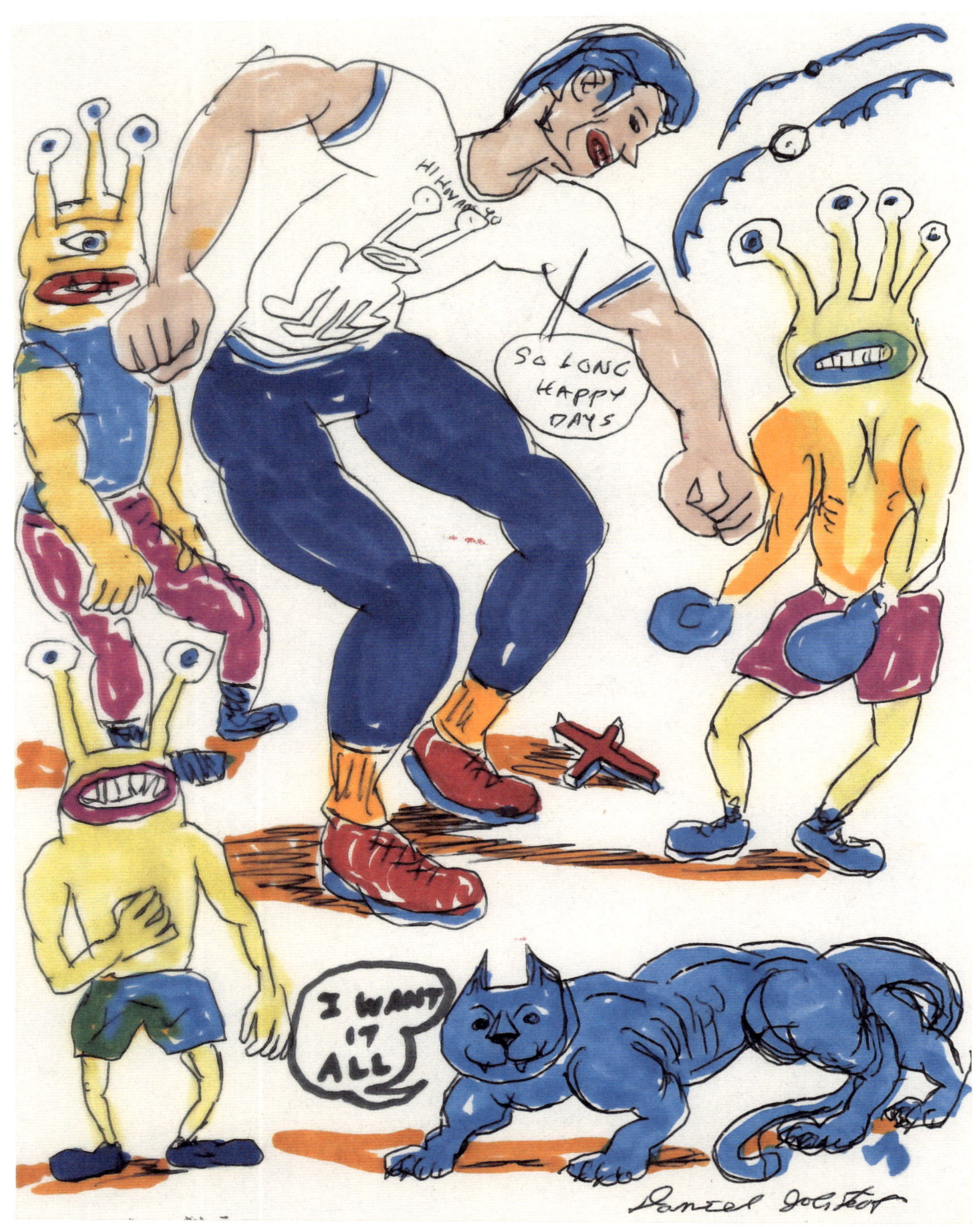

So Long Happy Days (I Want It All)

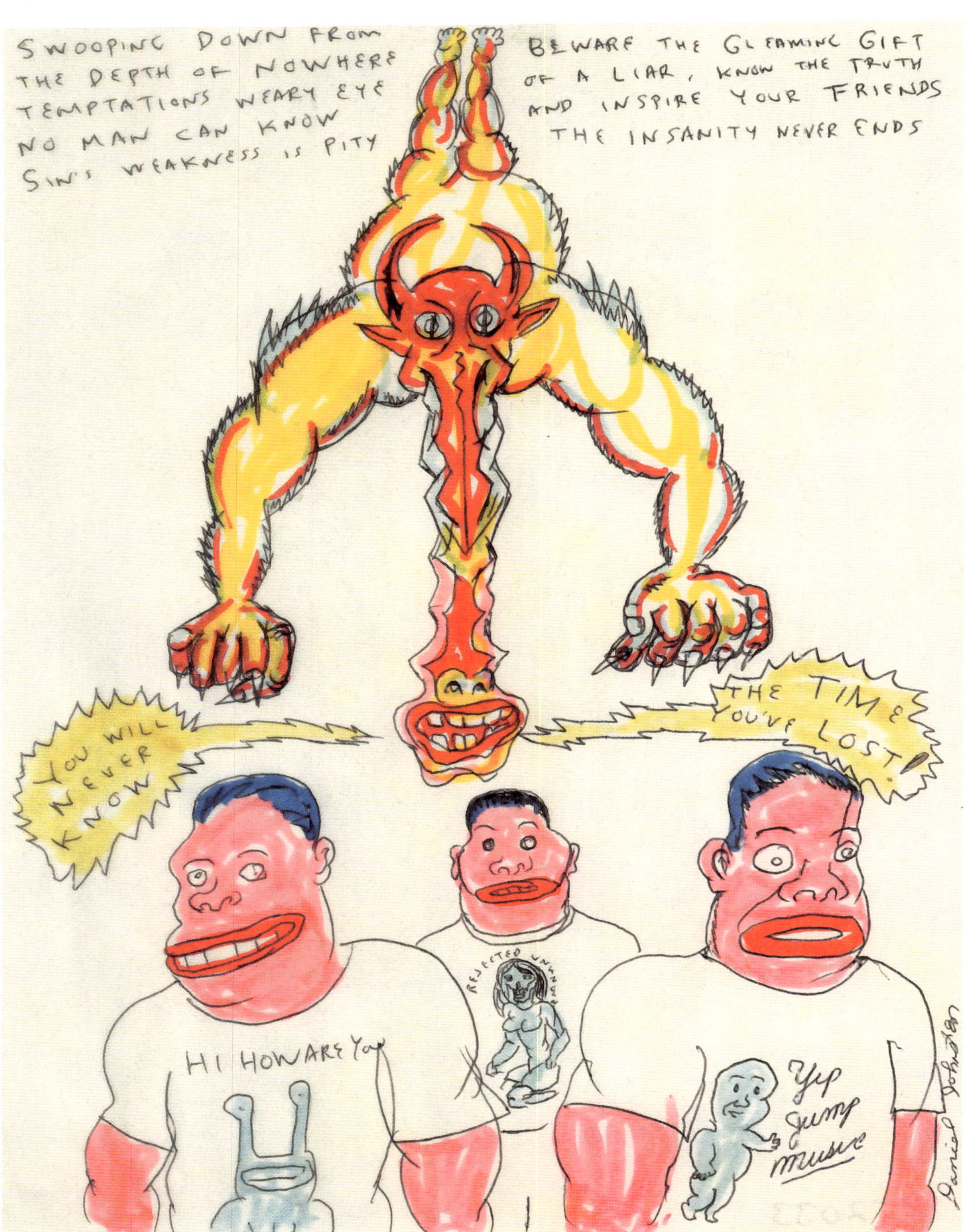

You Will Never Know the Time You've Lost

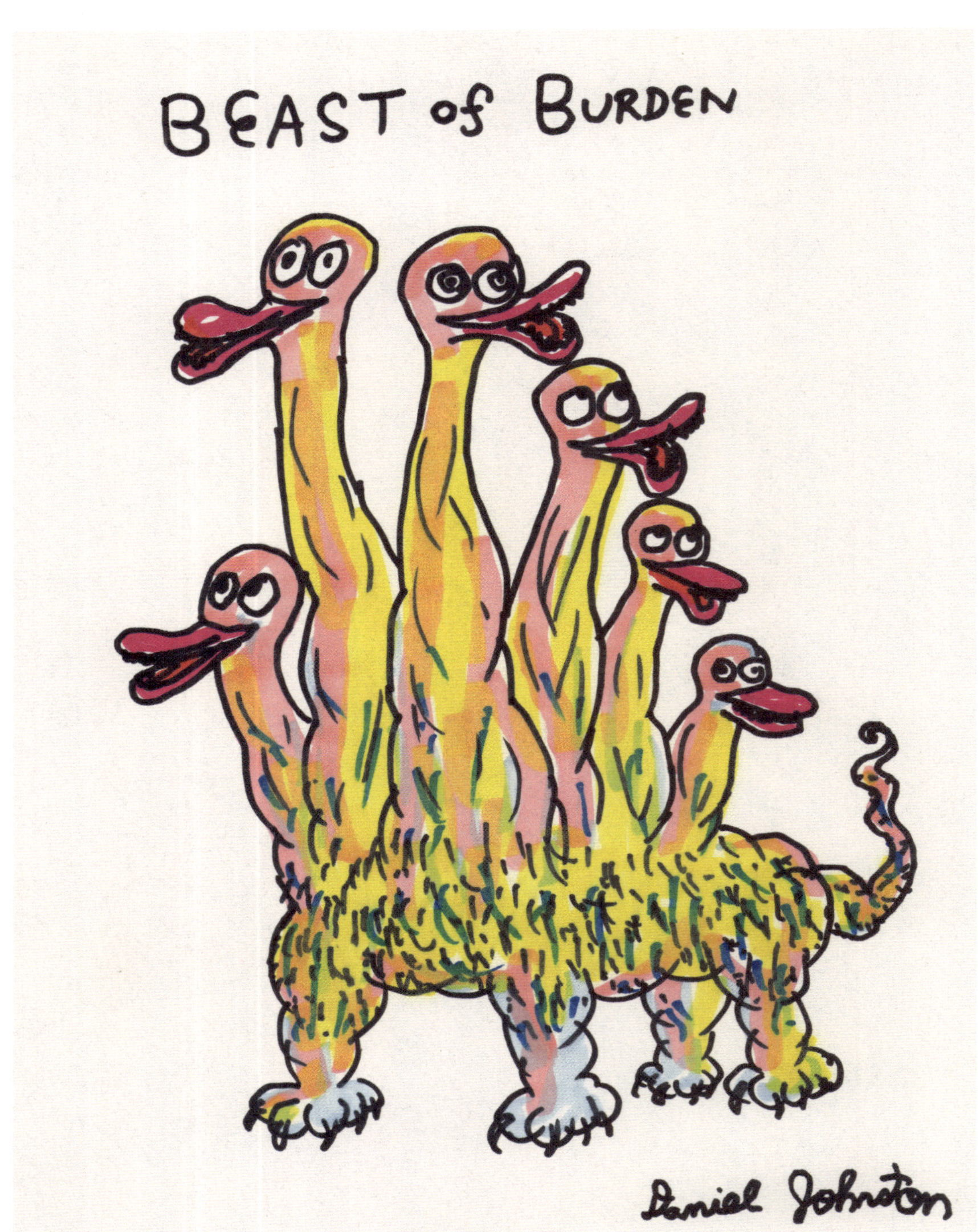

Beast of Burden

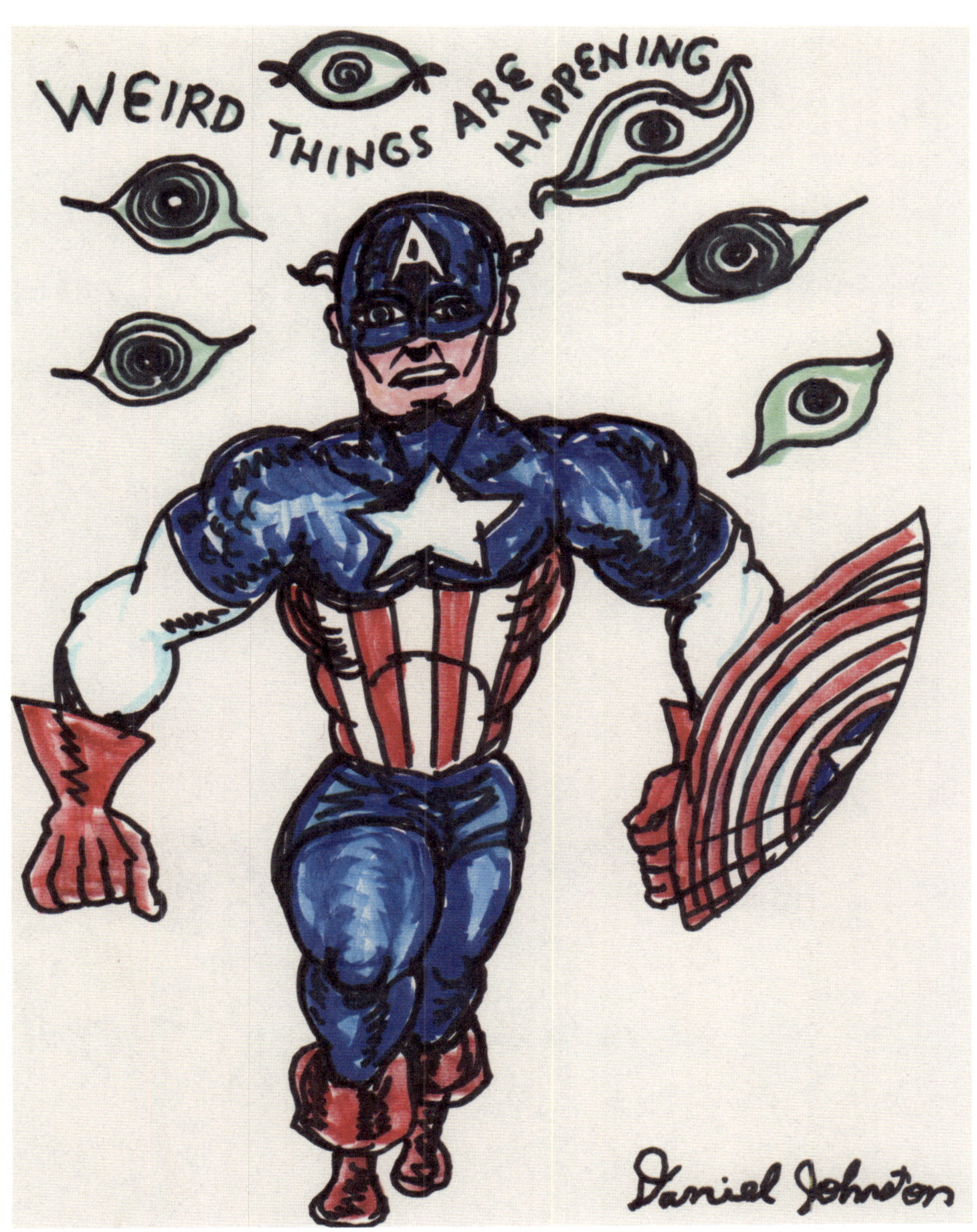

Weird Things Are Happening

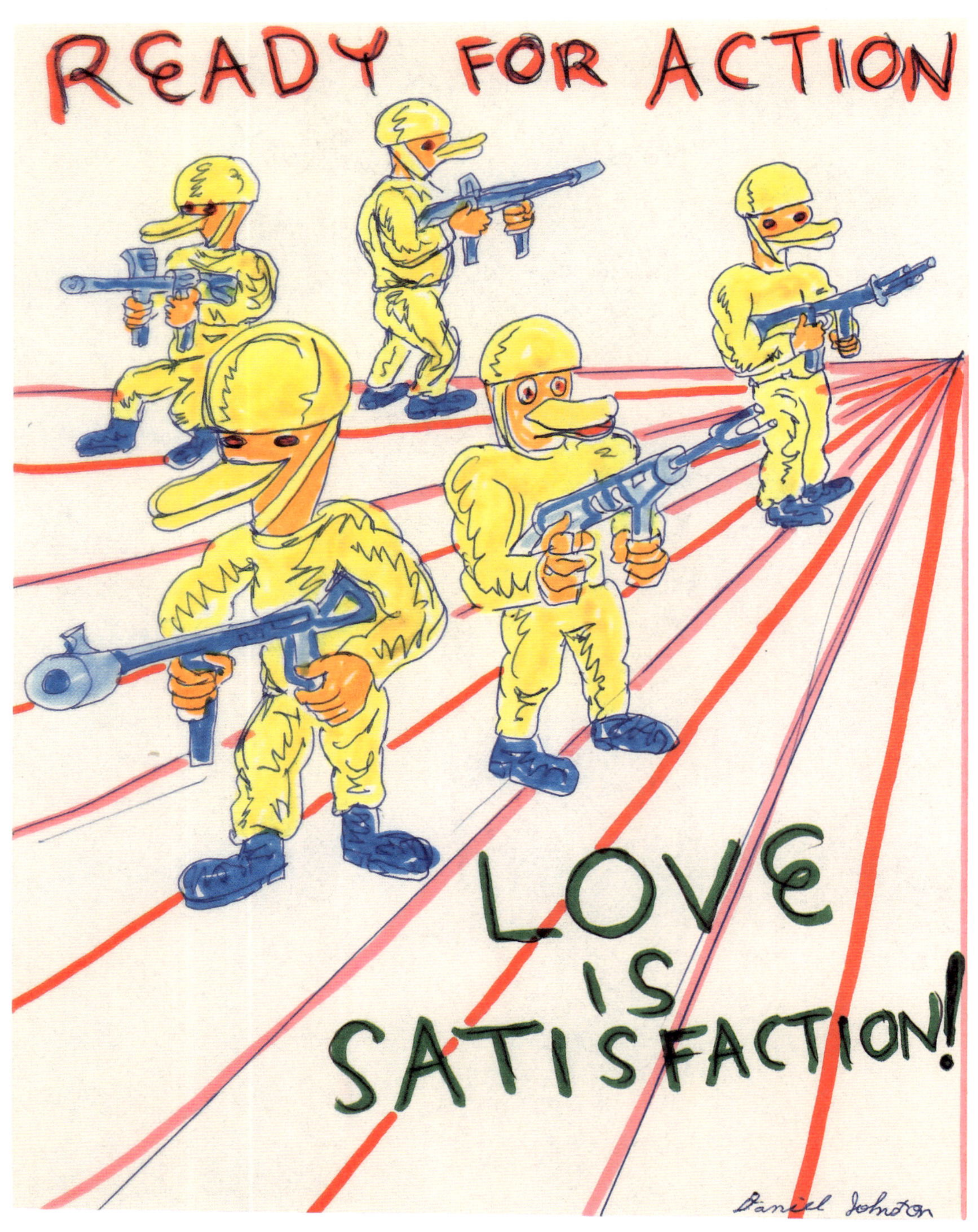

Ready for Action, Love Is Satisfaction!

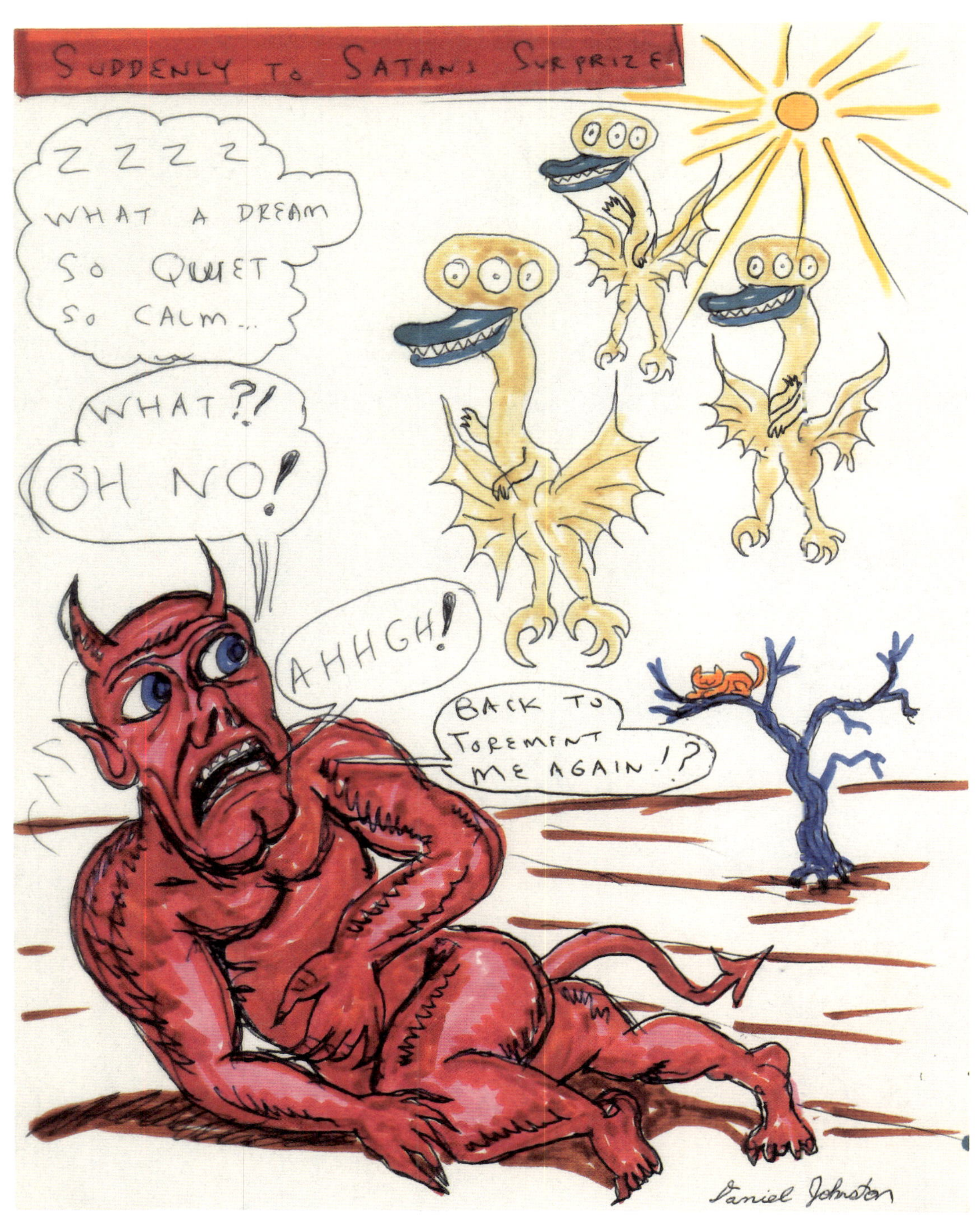

Suddenly to Satan's Surprize

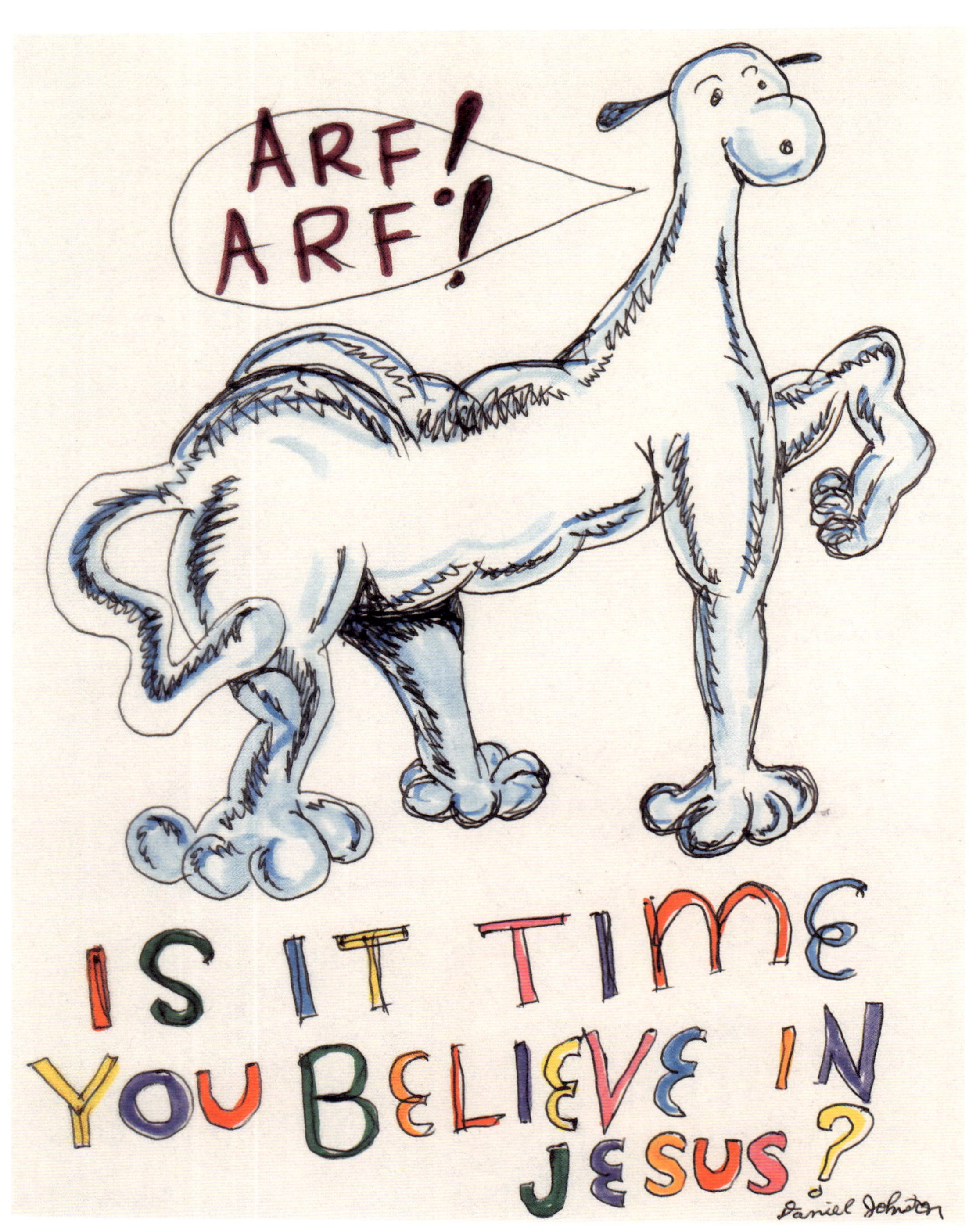

Is It Time You Believe in Jesus?

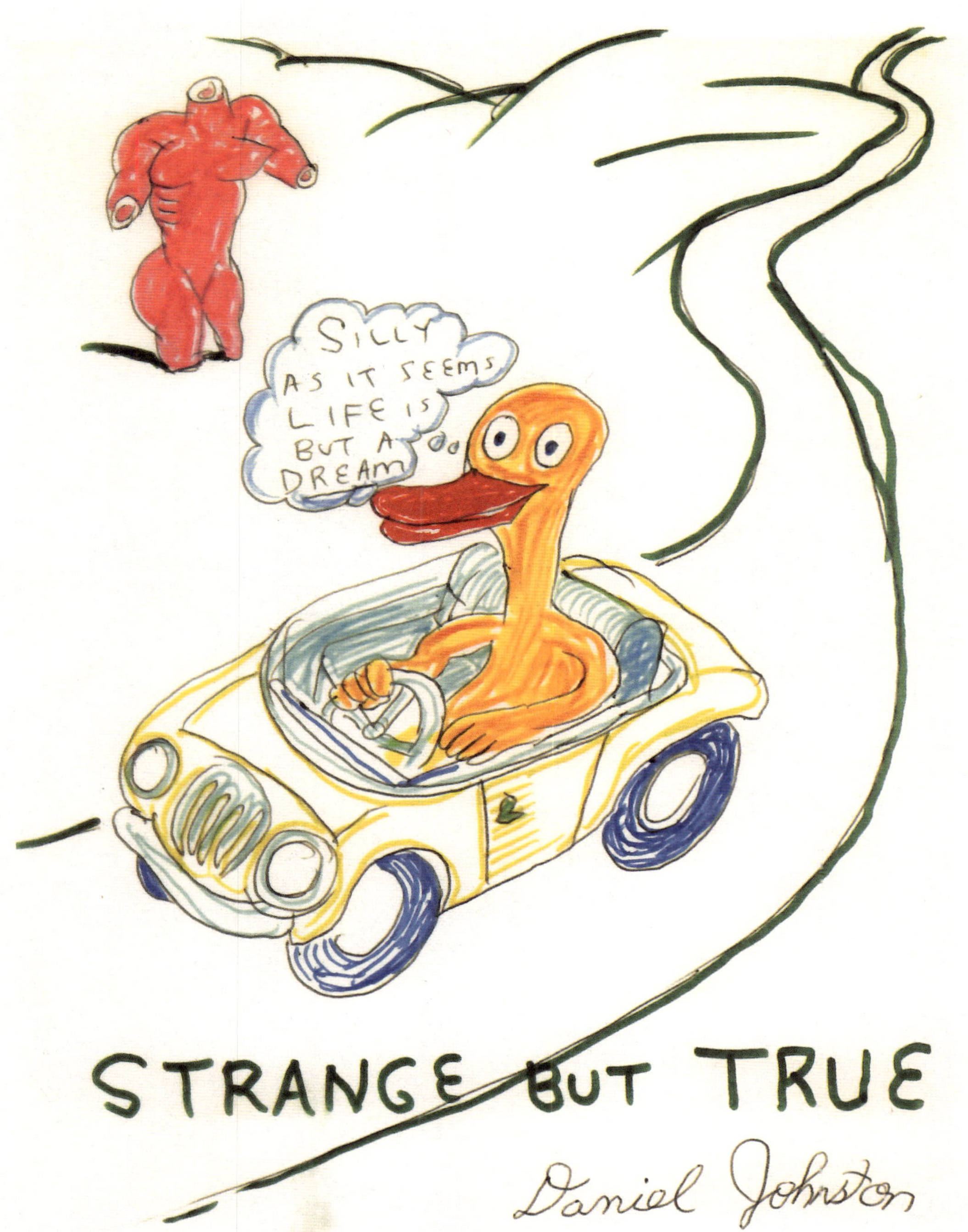

Strange but True

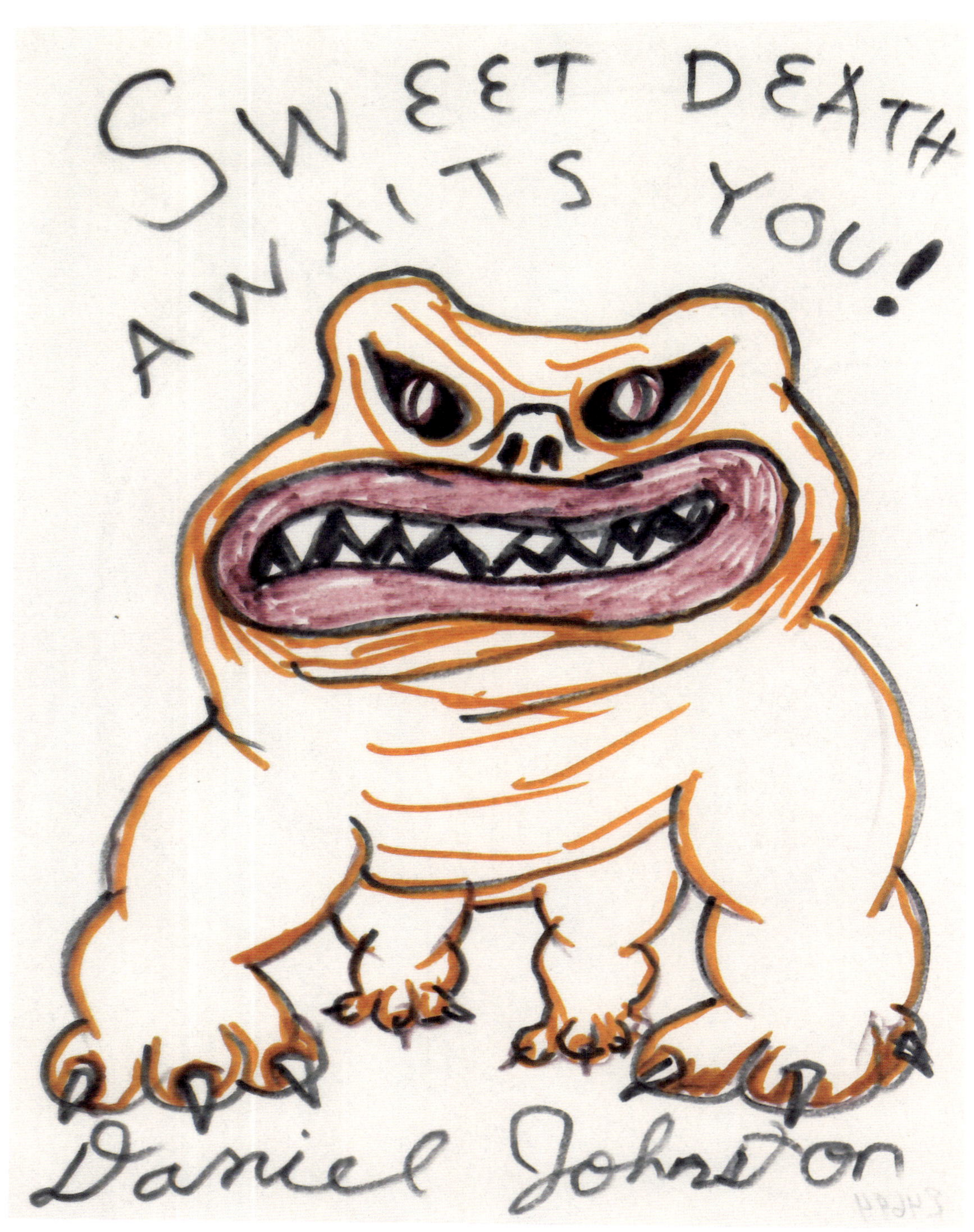

Sweet Death Awaits You!

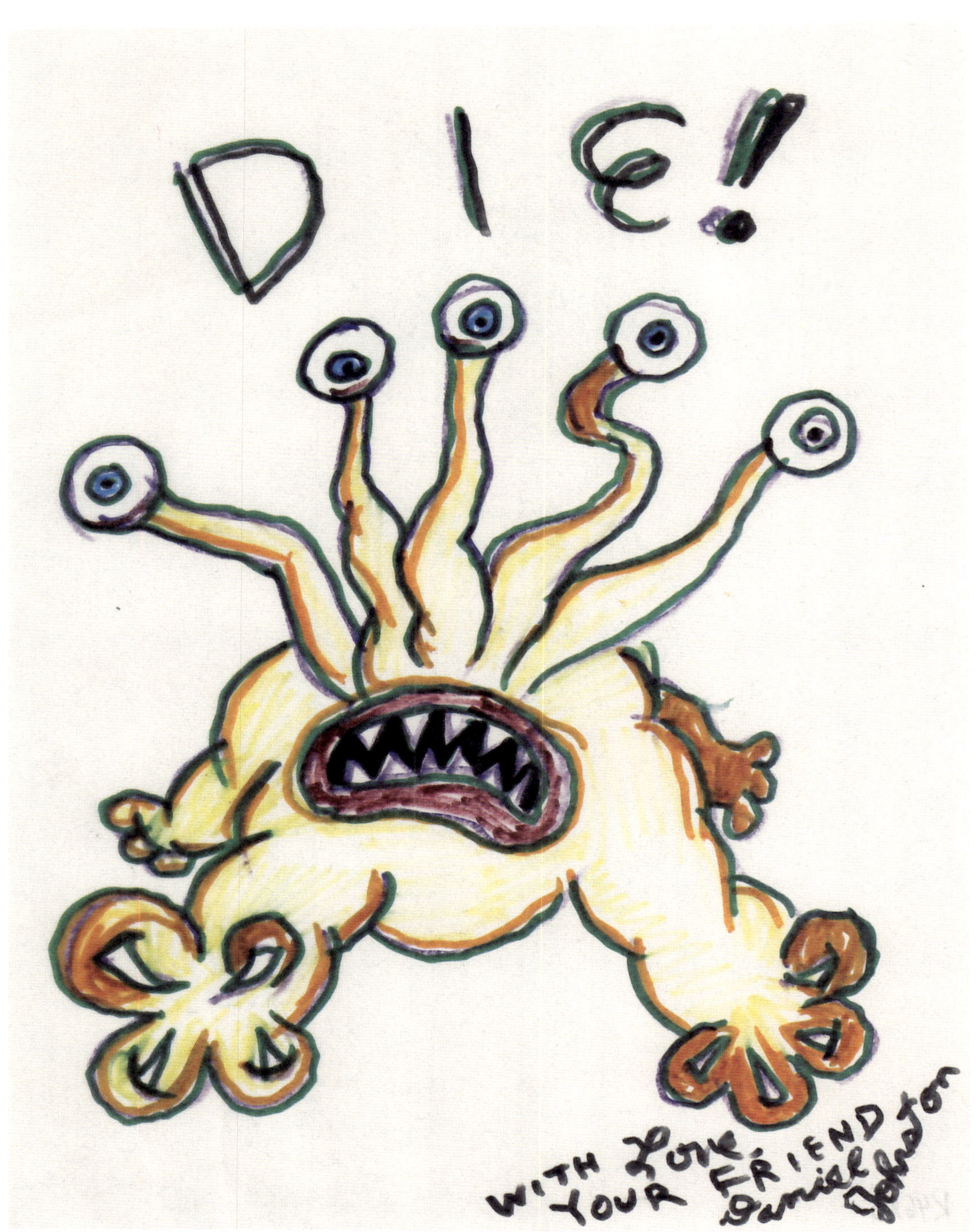

DIE!

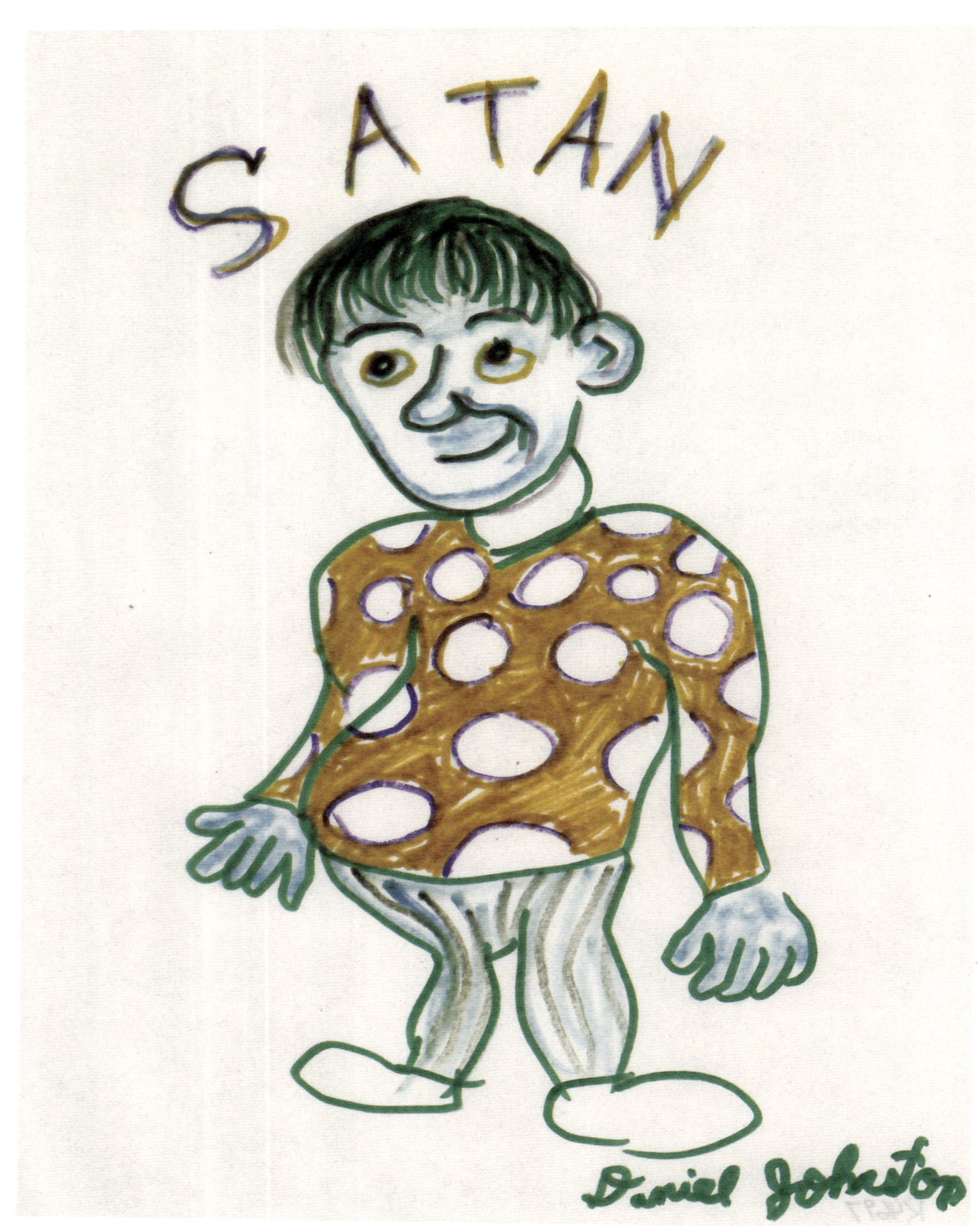

Satan

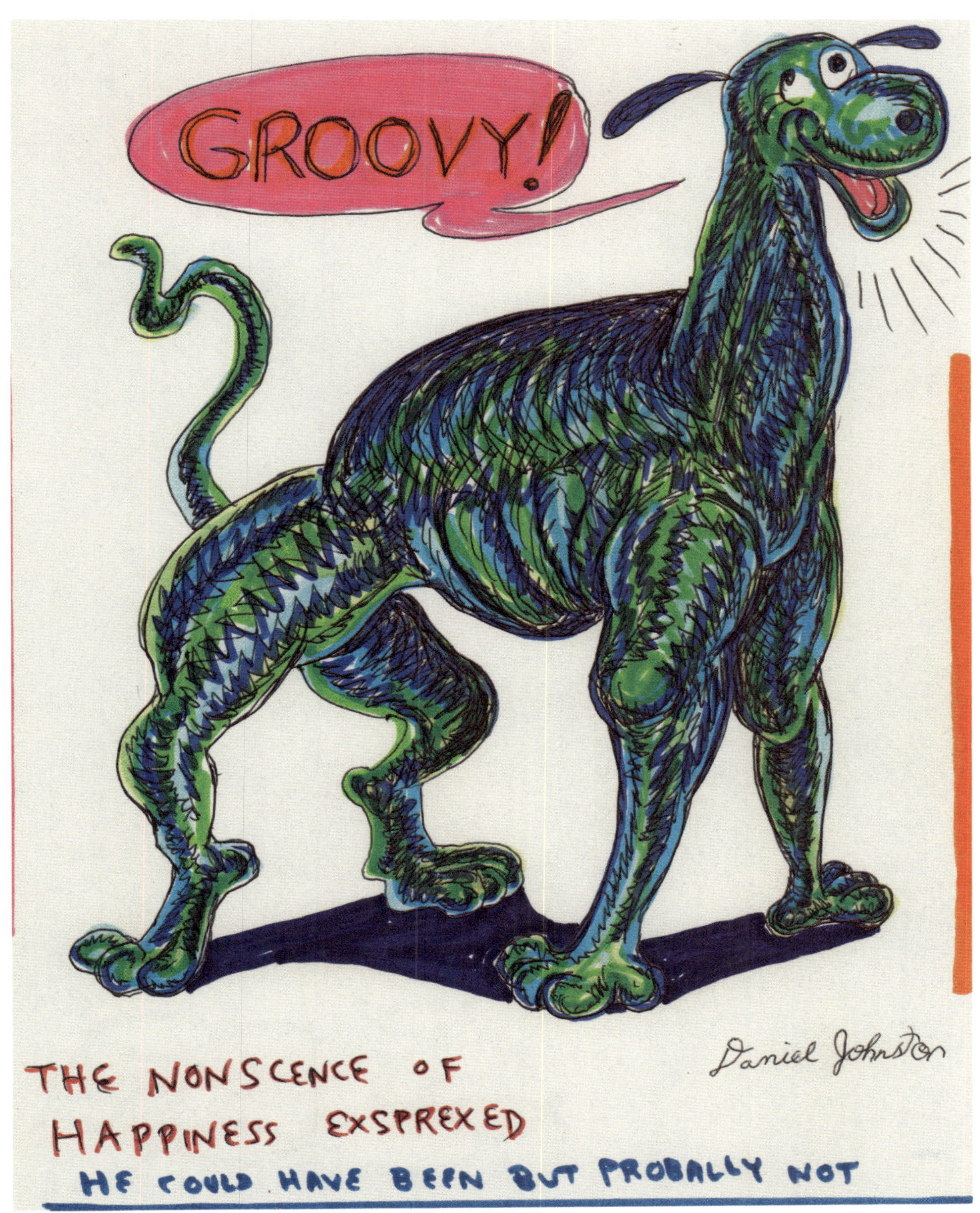
GROOVY!
Daniel Johnston
THE NONSCENCE OF
HAPPINESS EXSPREXED
HE COULD HAVE BEEN BUT PROBALLY NOT

Groovy!

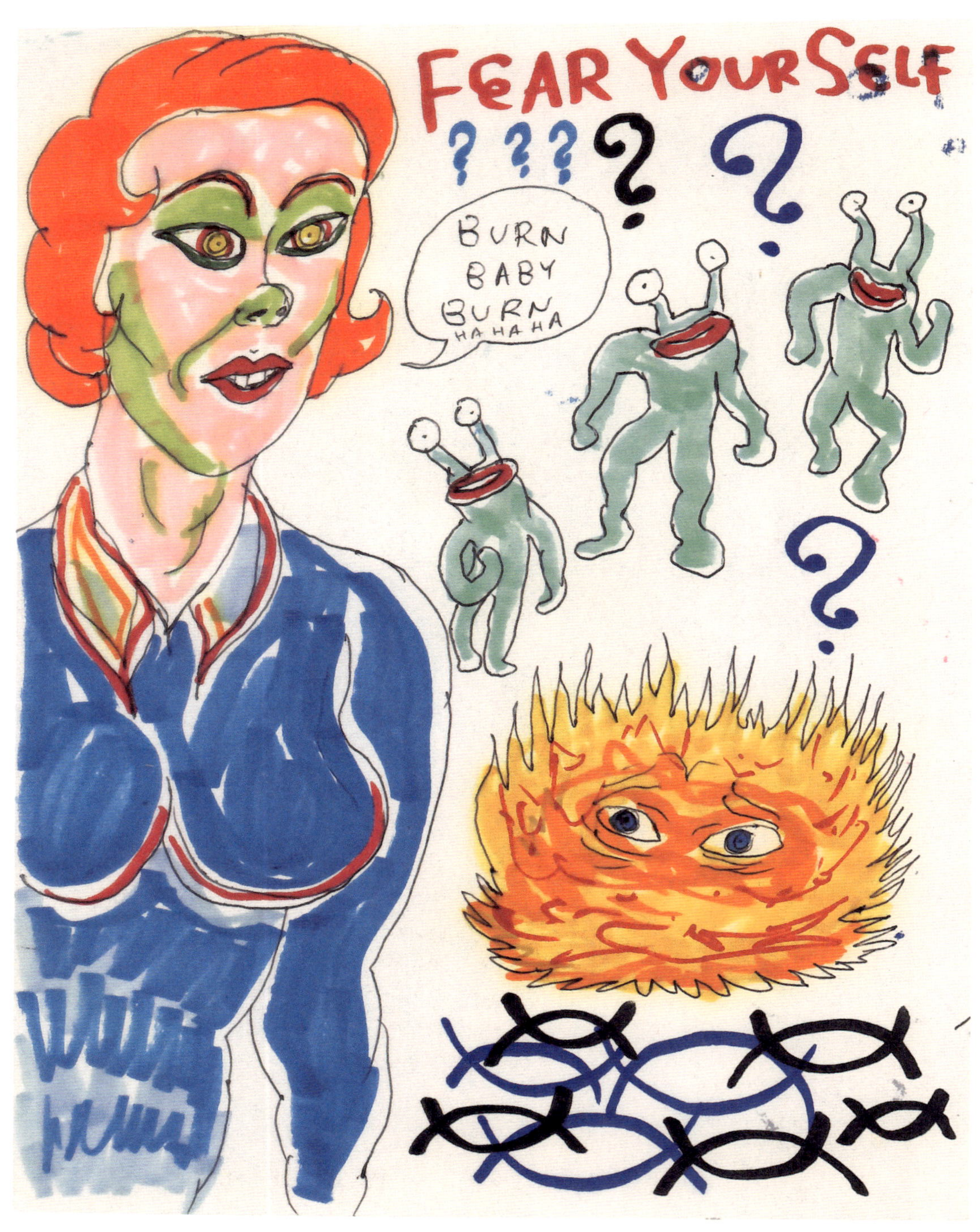

Fear YourSelf (Burn Baby Burn)

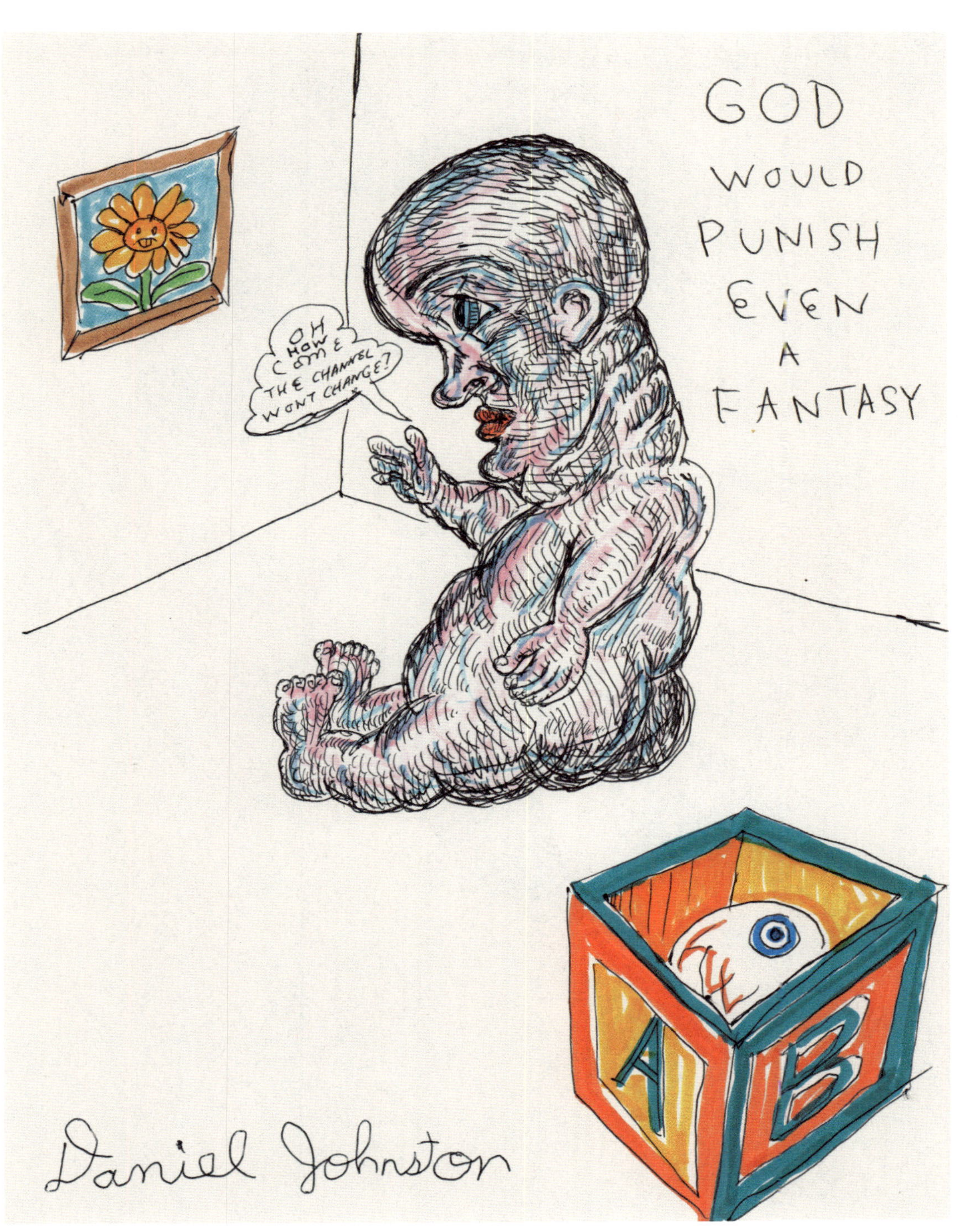

God Would Punish Even a Fantasy

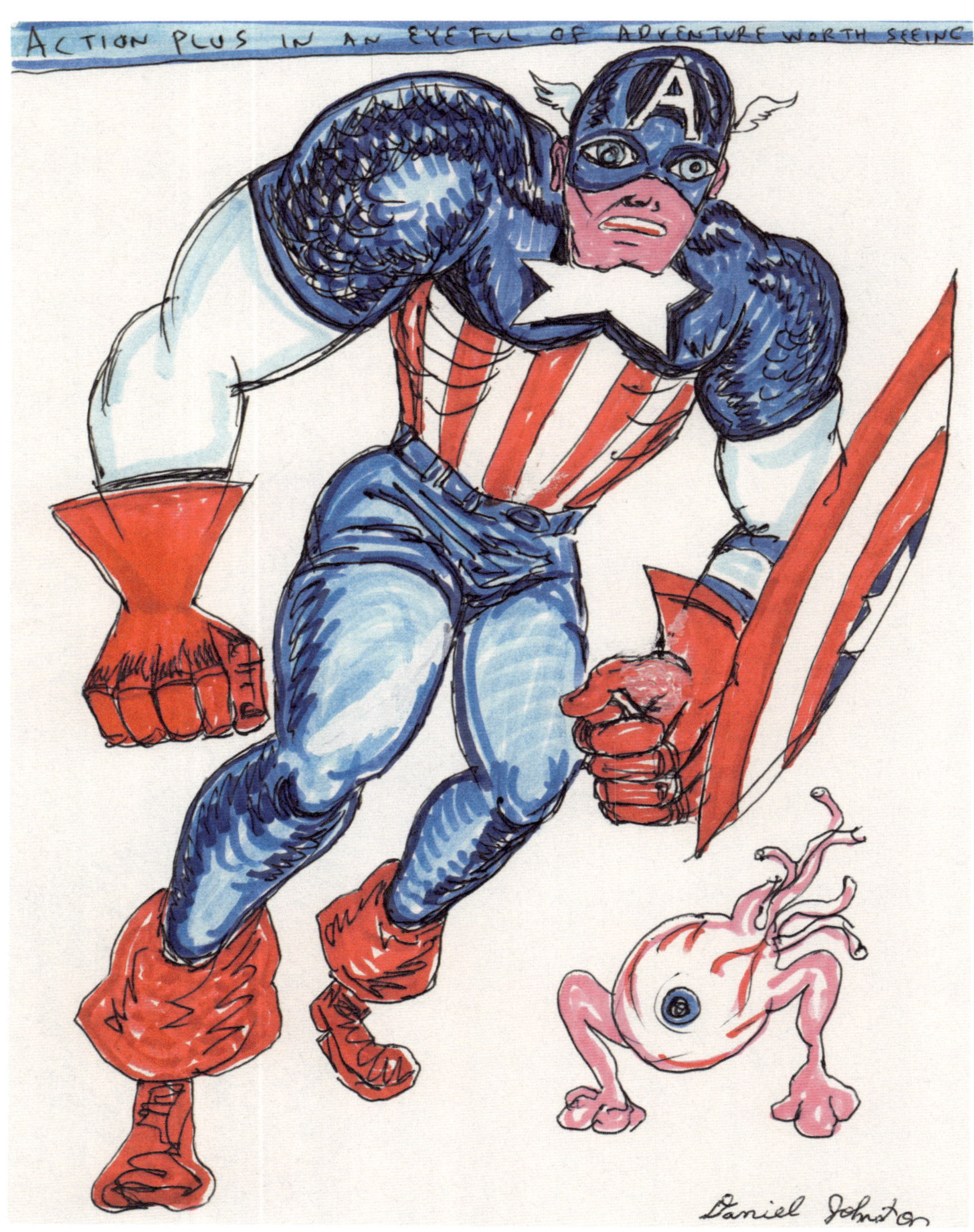

An Eyeful of Adventure

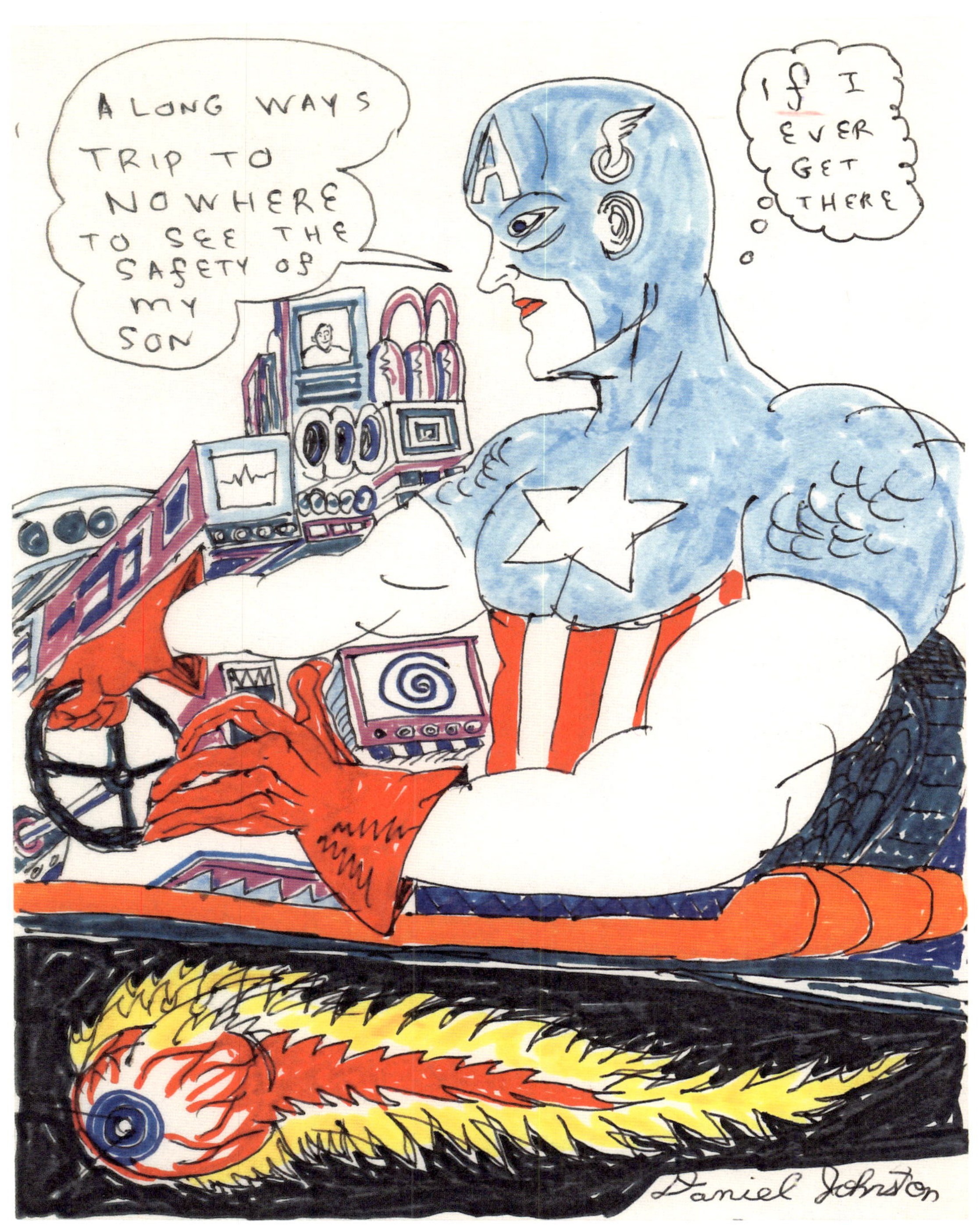

If I Ever Get There

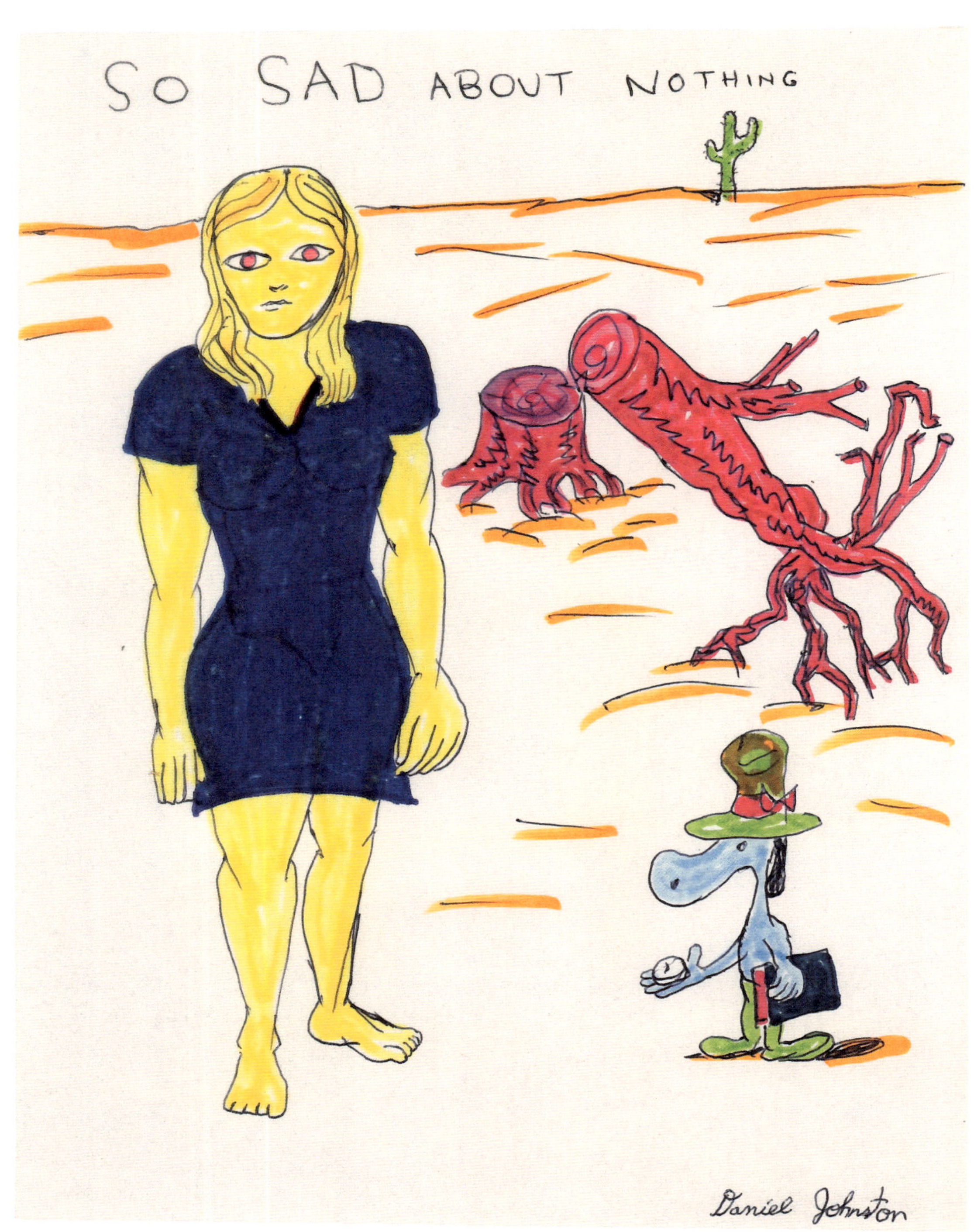

So Sad about Nothing

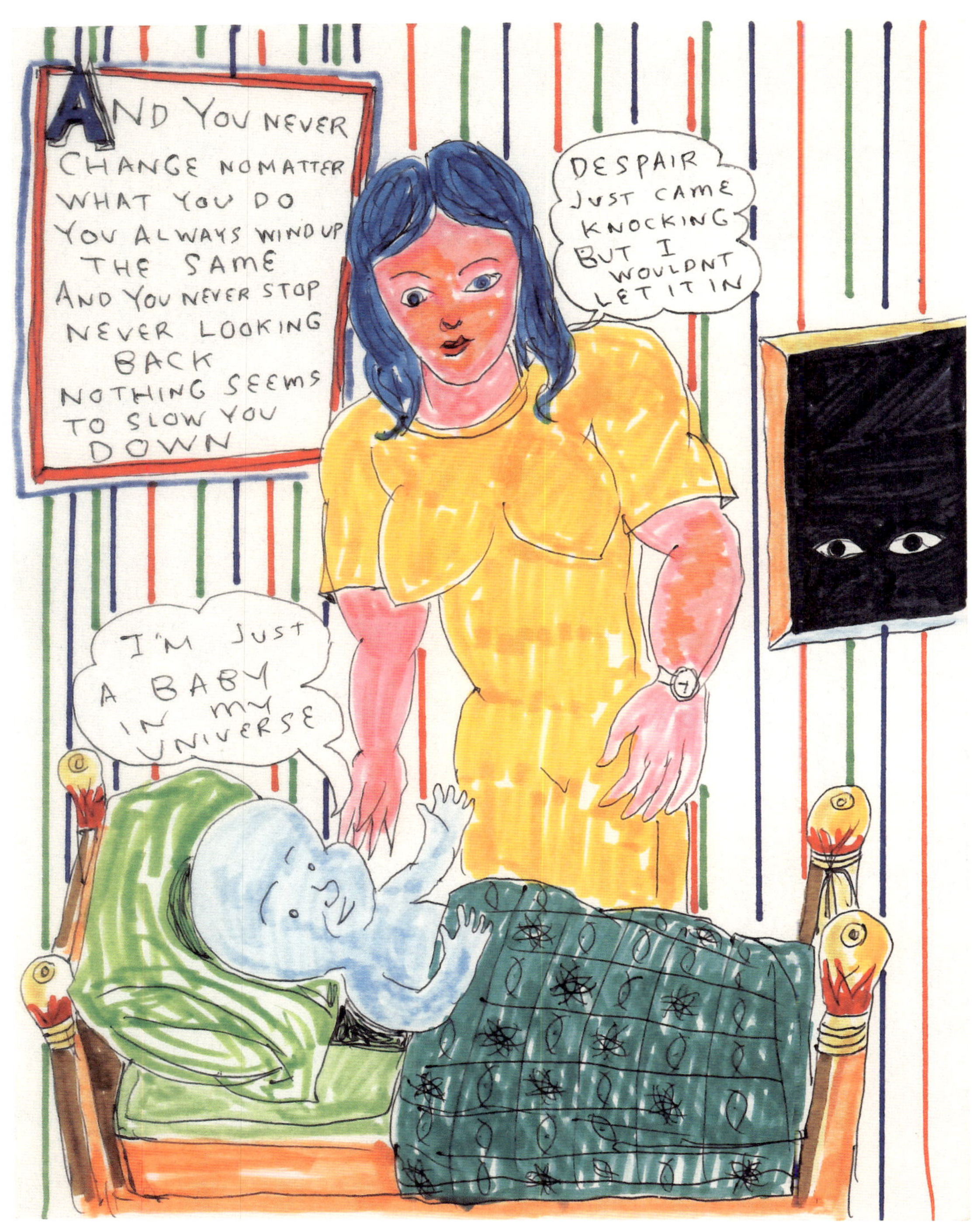

I'm Just a Baby in My Universe

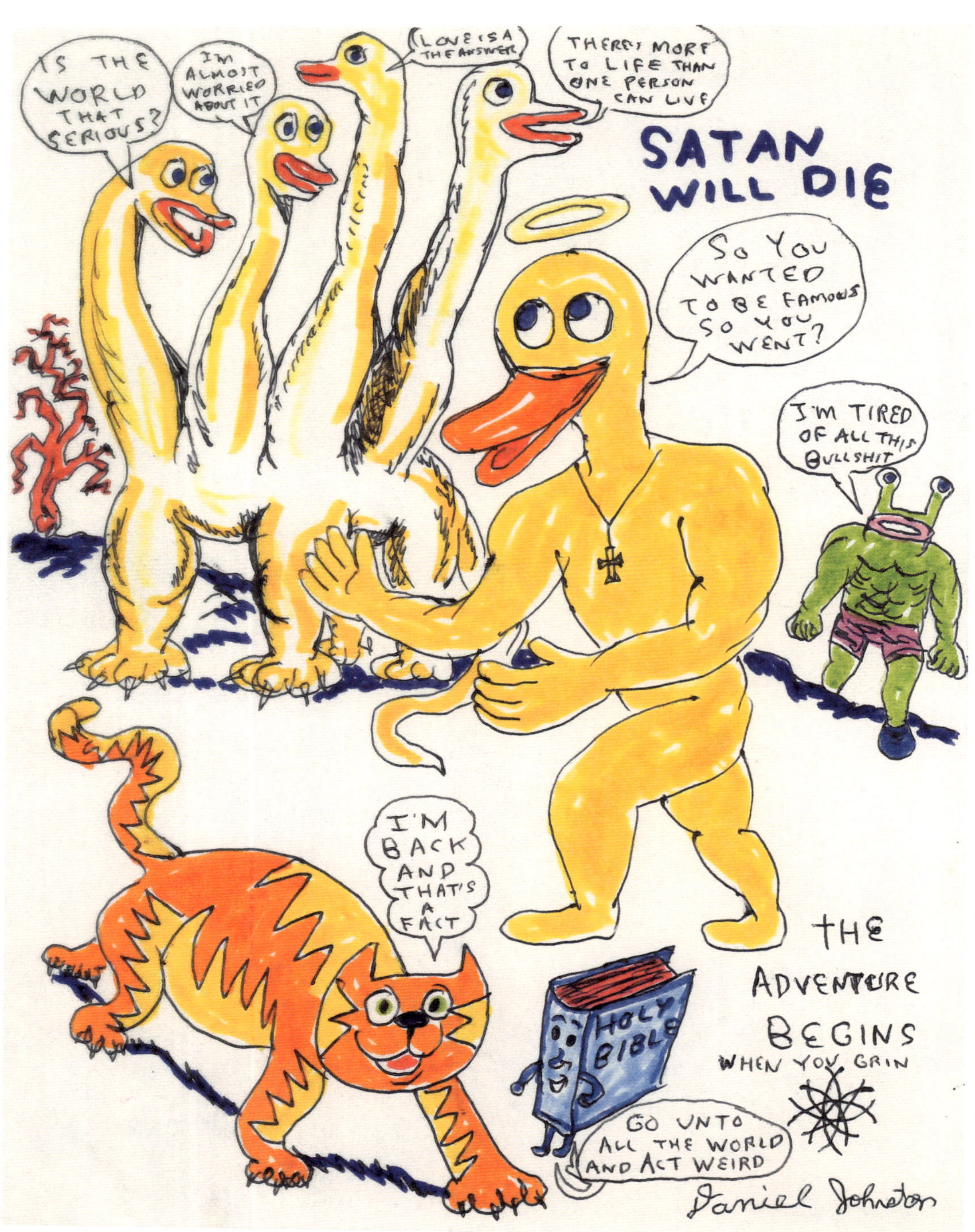

Satan Will Die

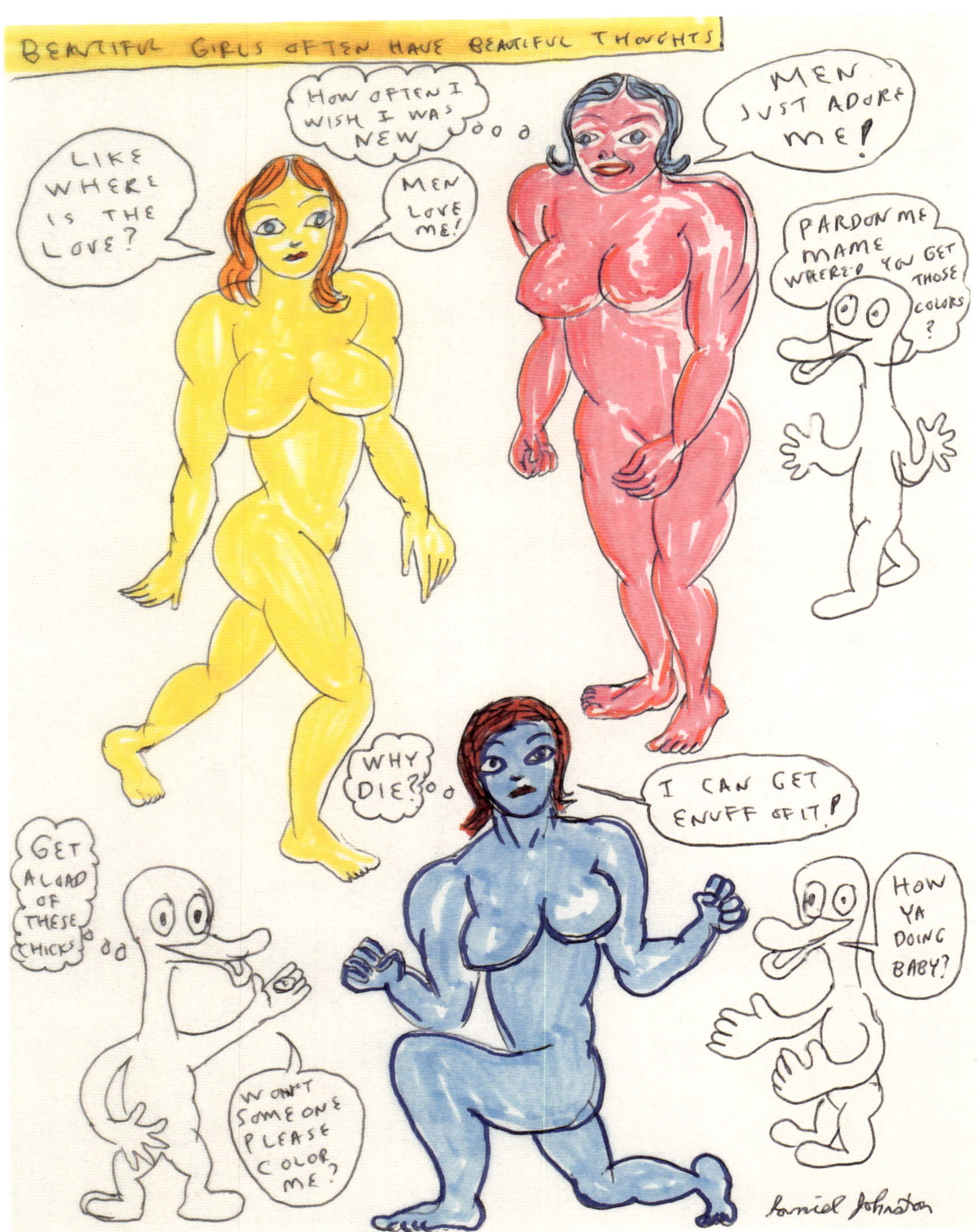

Beautiful Girls Often Have Beautiful Thoughts

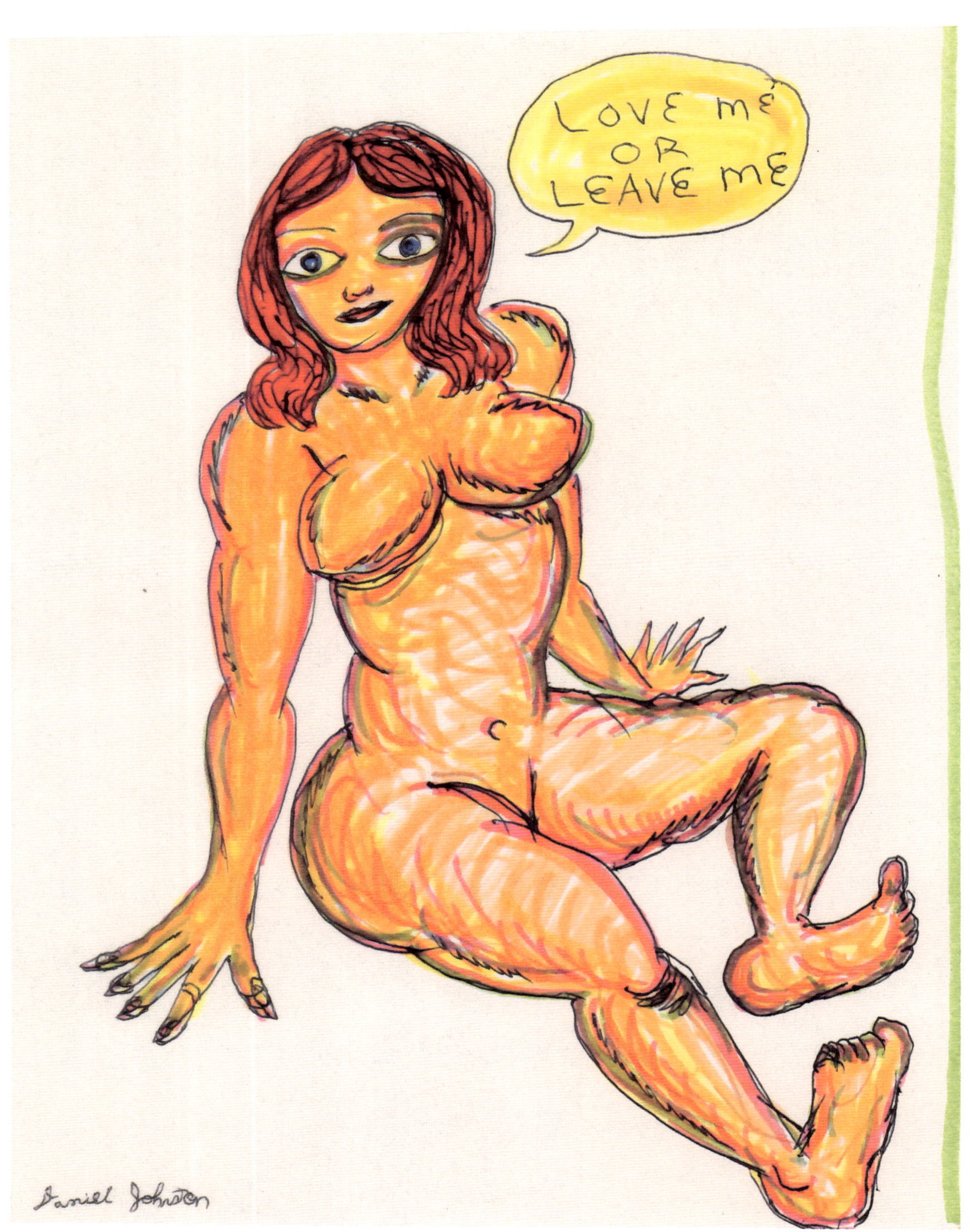

Love Me or Leave Me

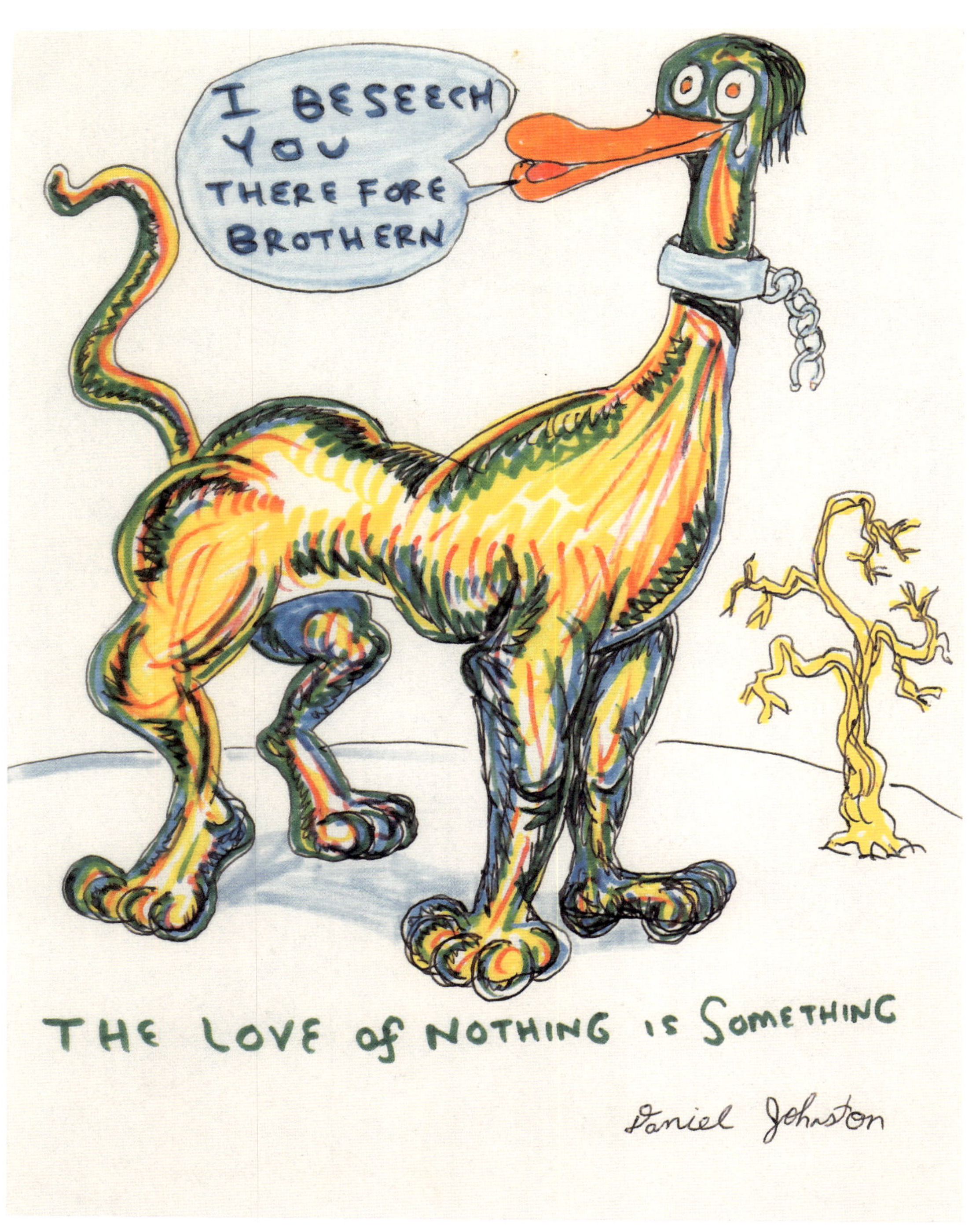

The Love of Nothing Is Something

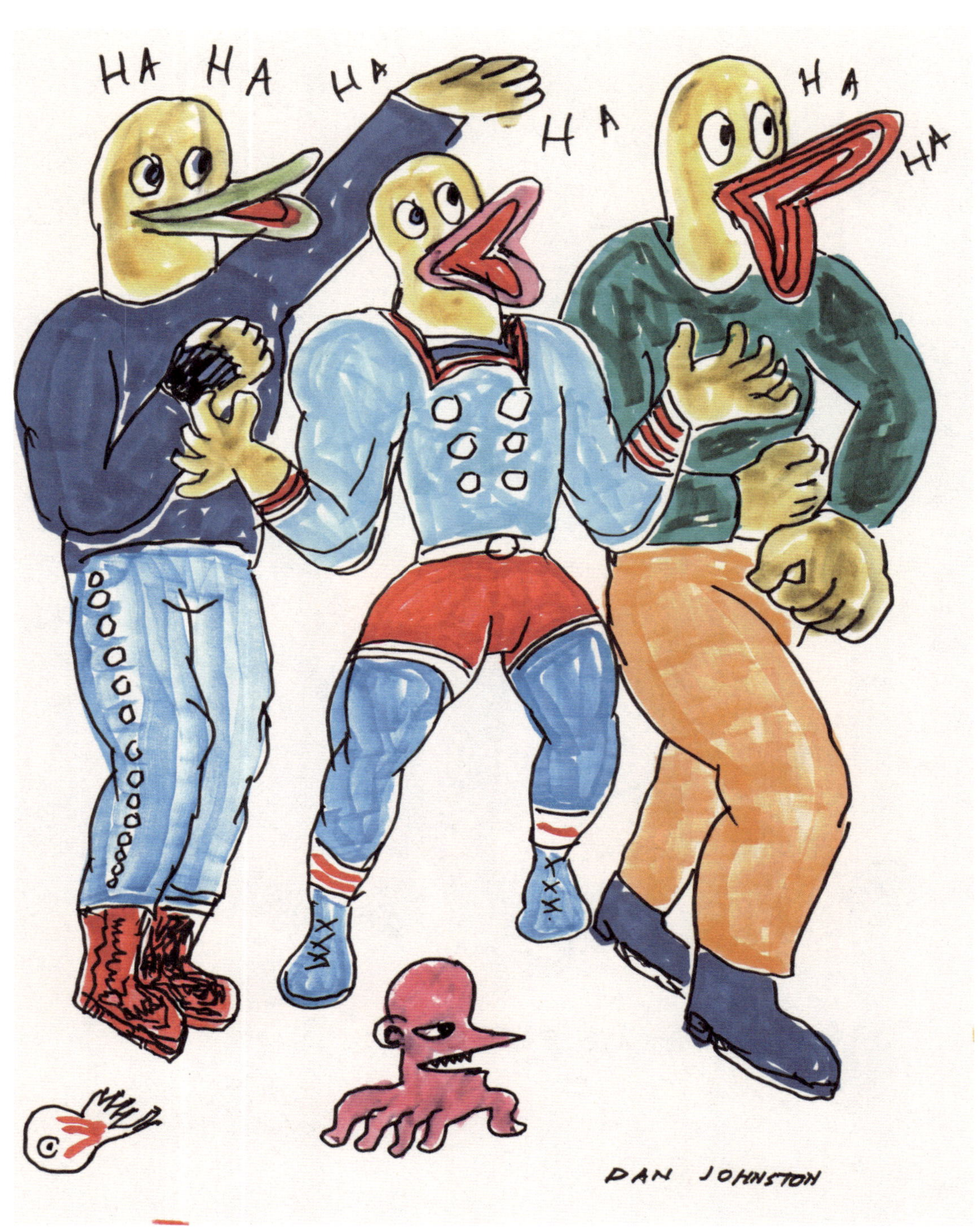

Ha Ha Ha Ha (Ducks Laughing)

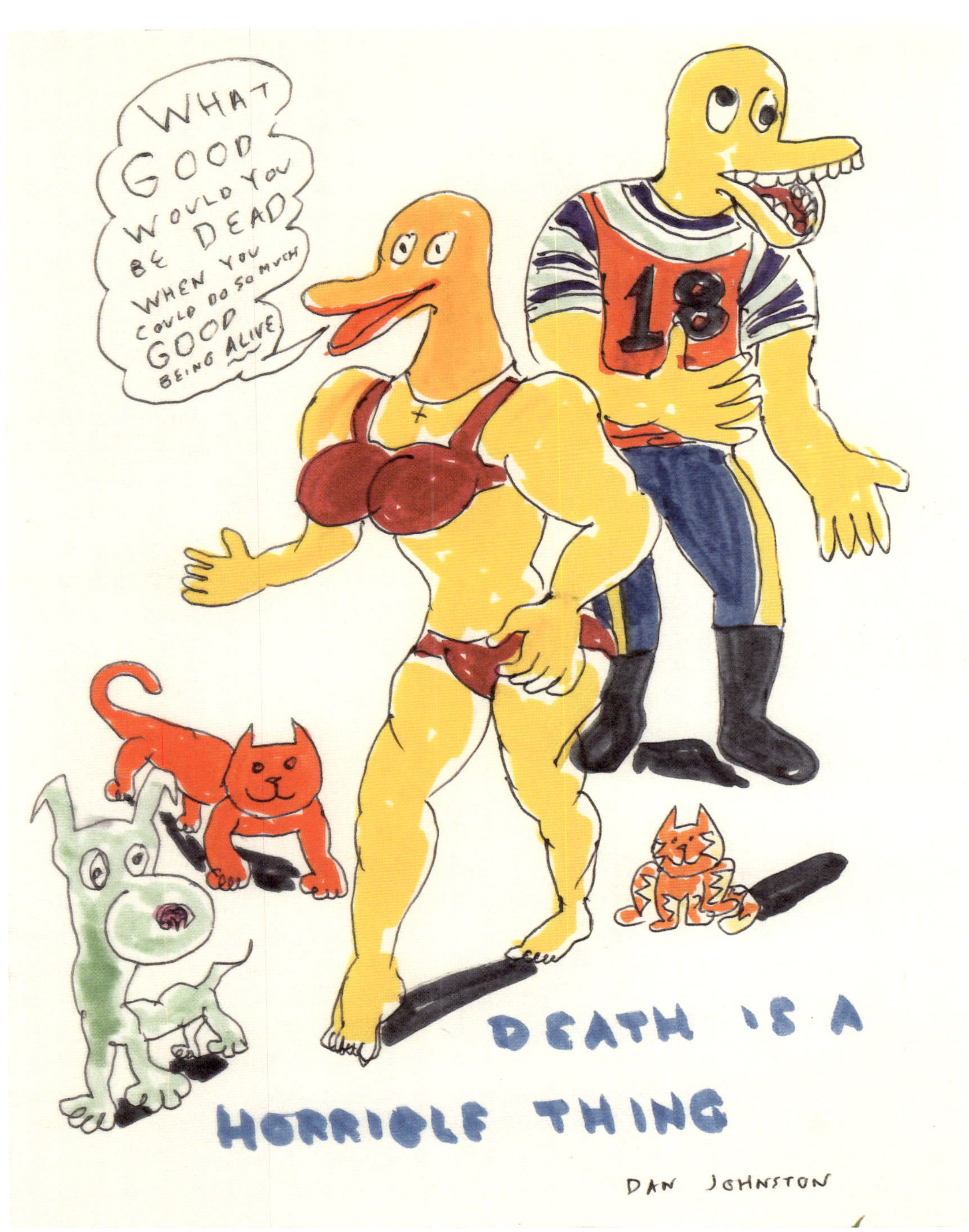

Death Is a Horrible Thing

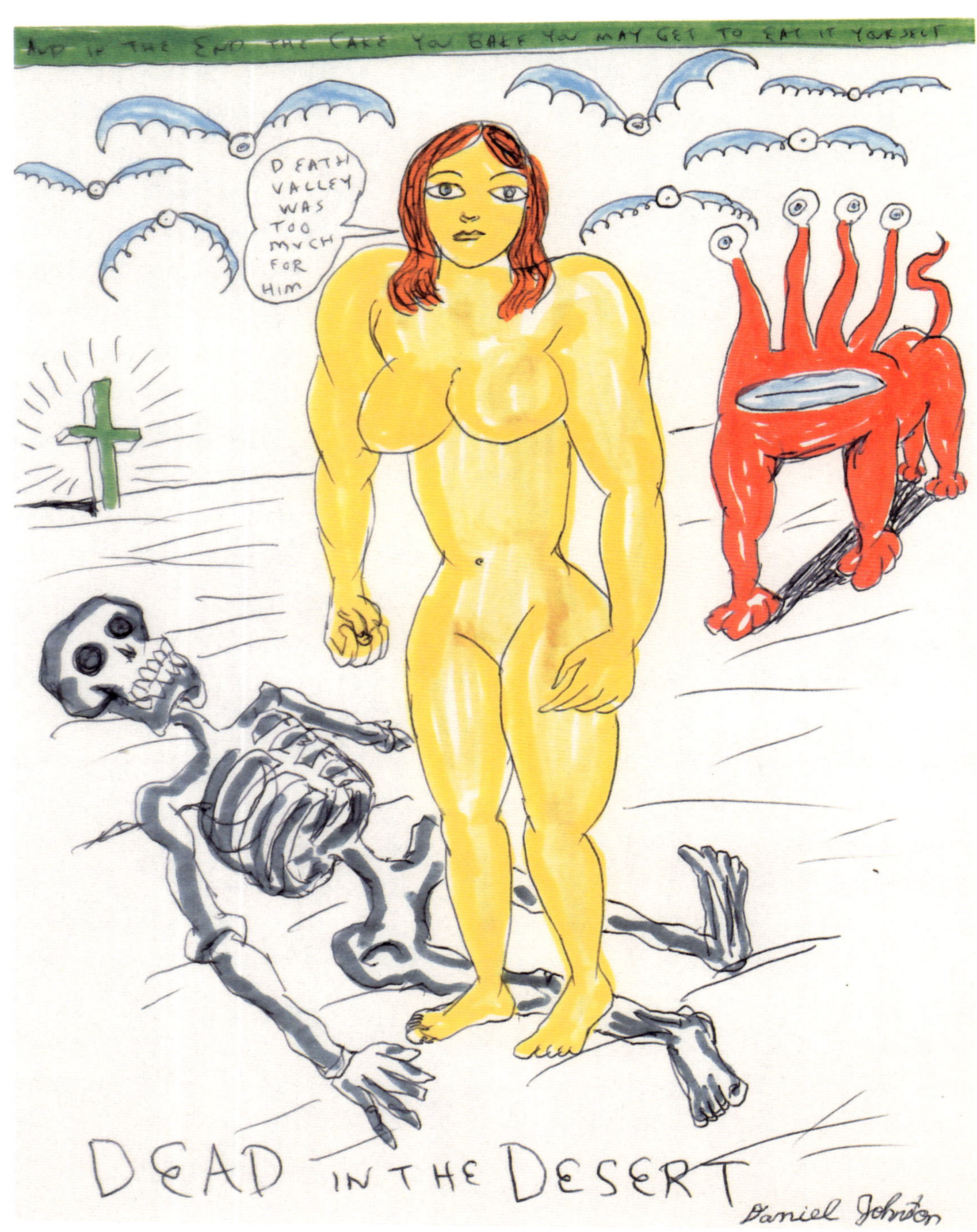

Dead in the Desert

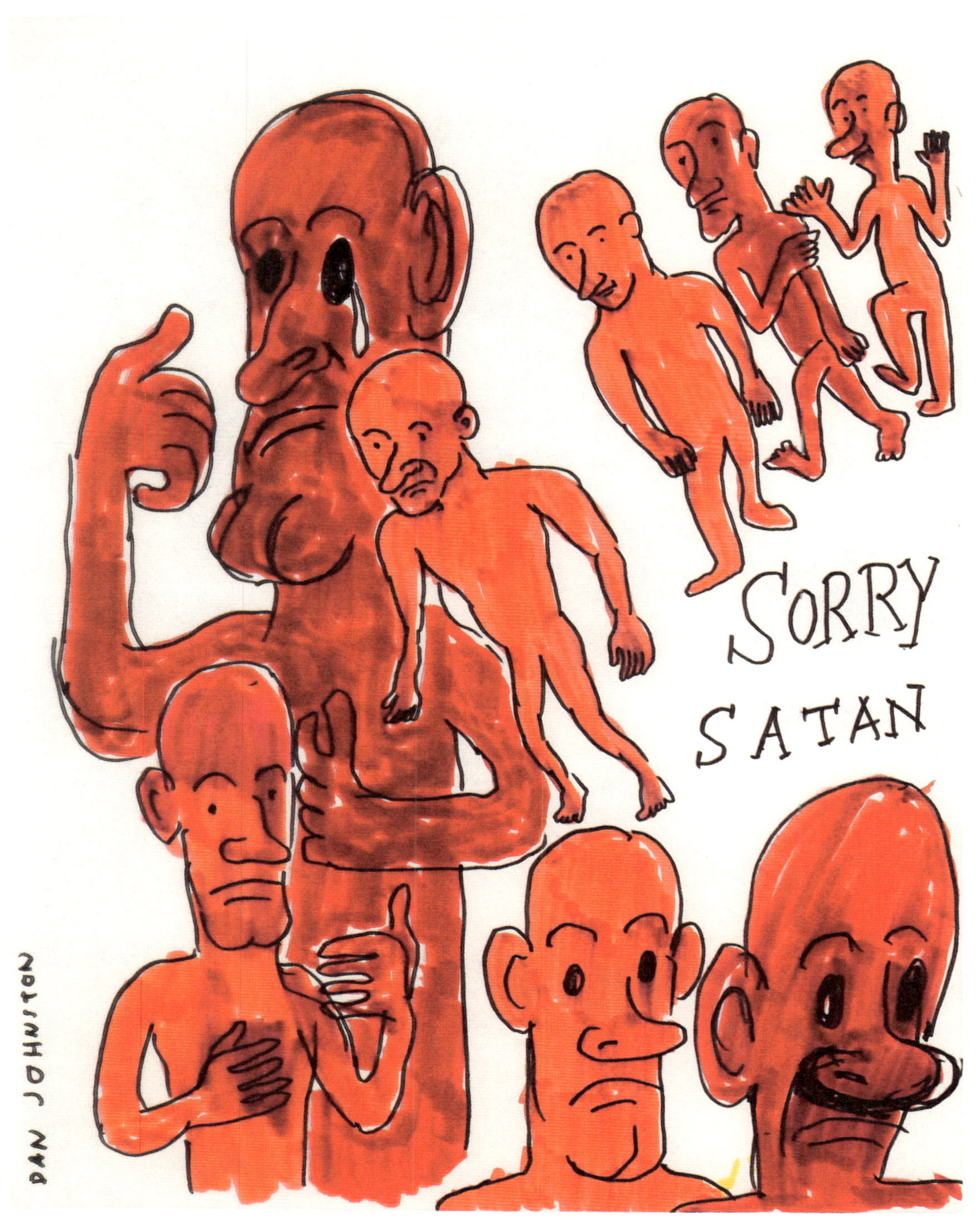

Sorry Satan

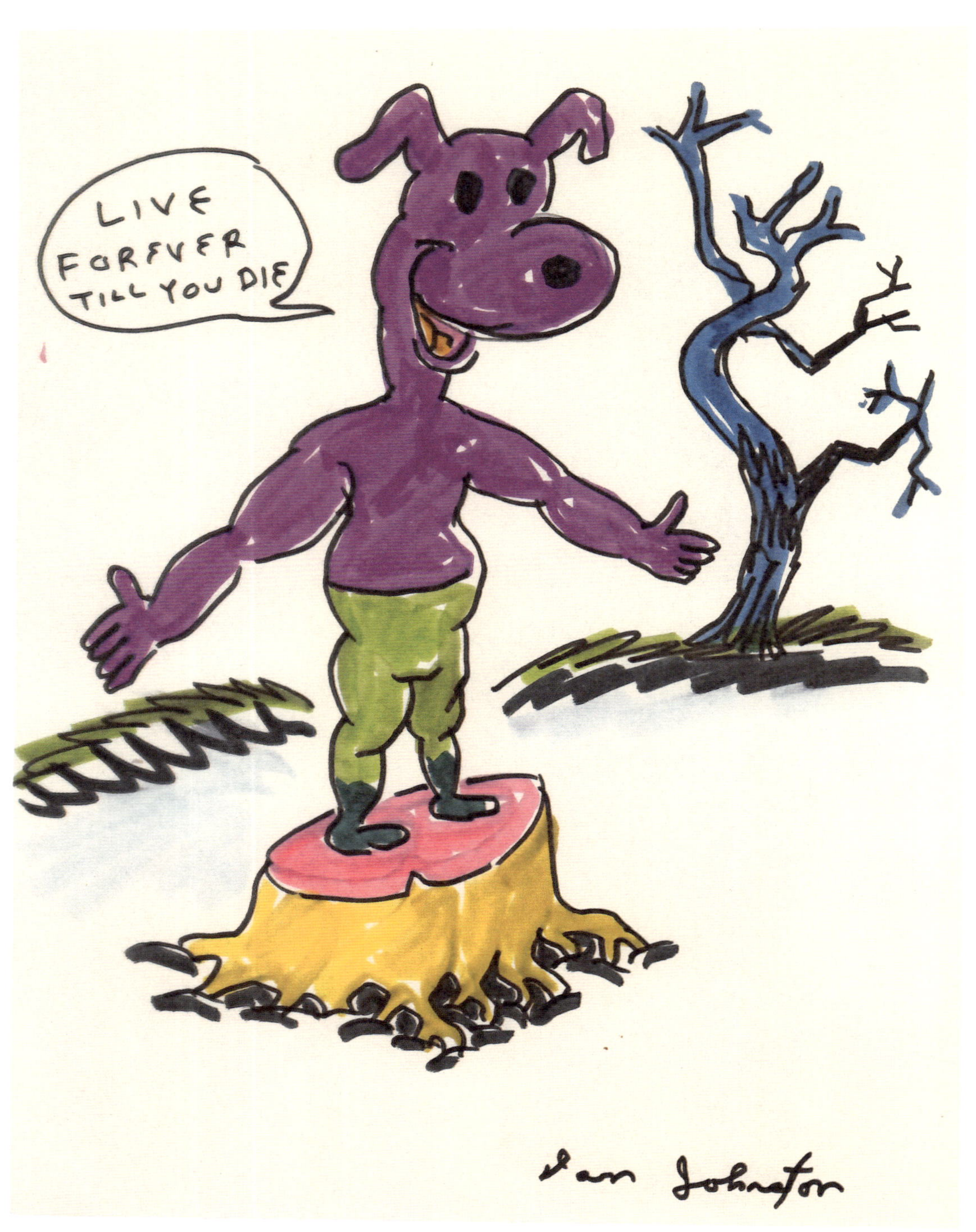

Live Forever Till You Die

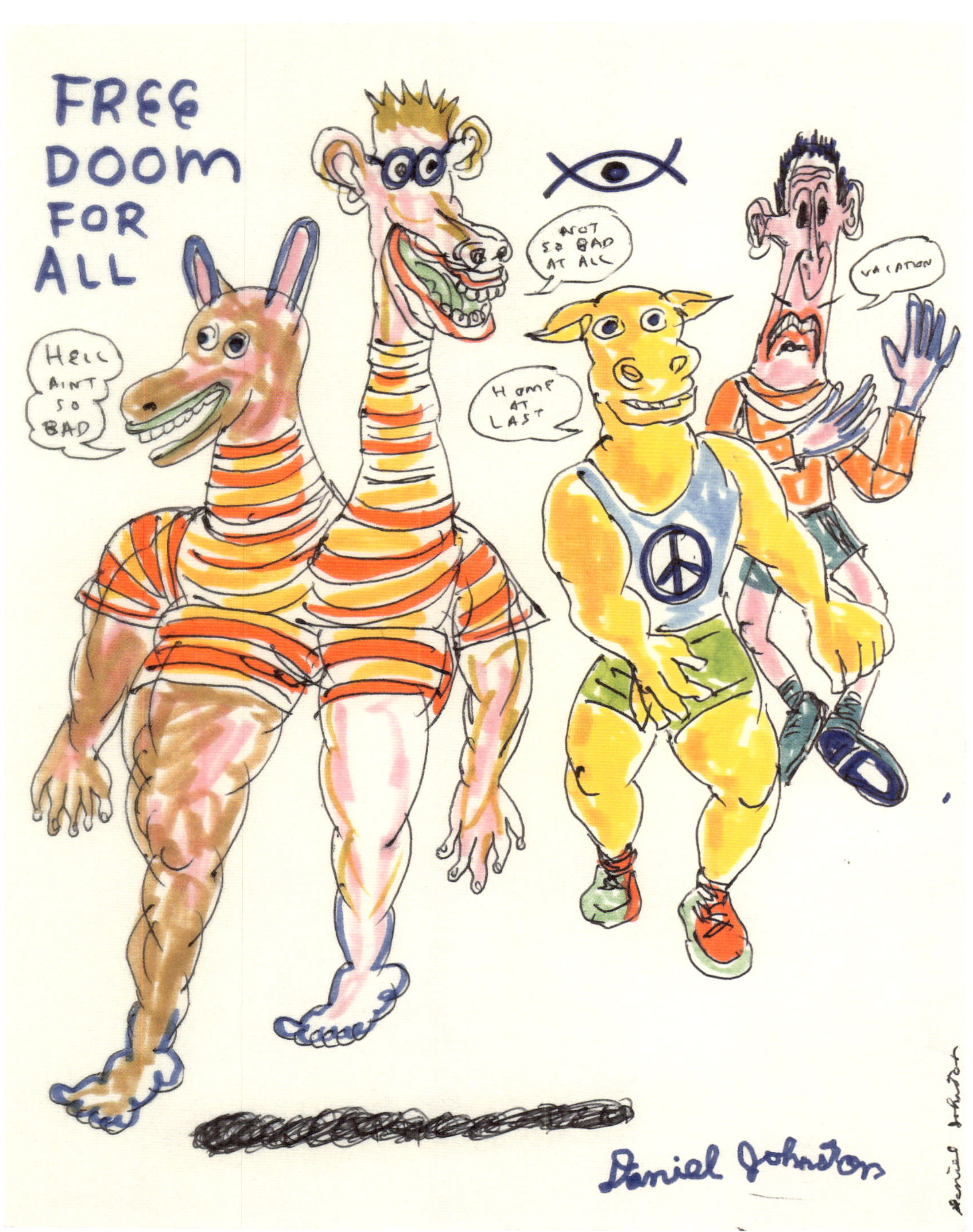

Free Doom for All

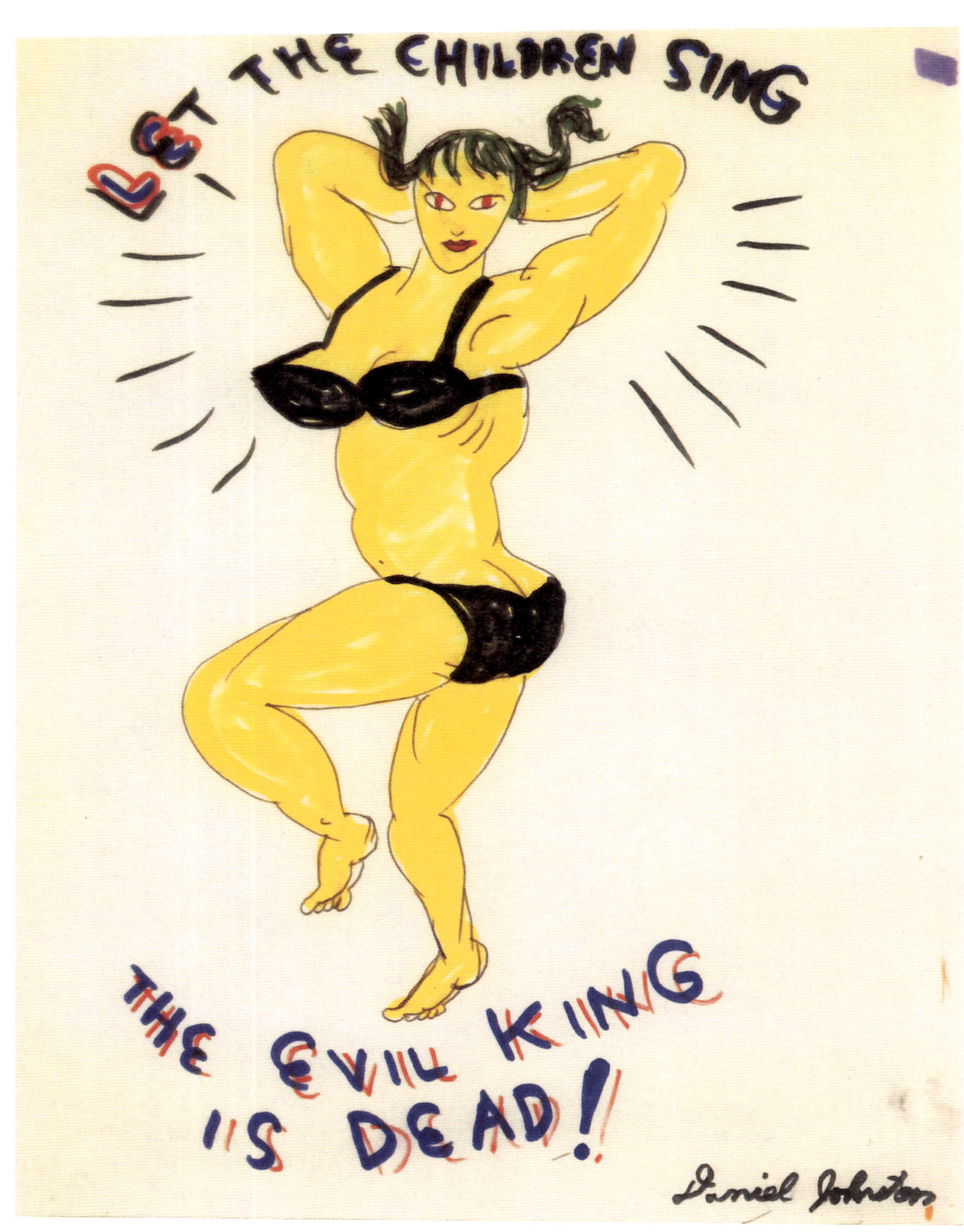

The Evil King Is Dead!

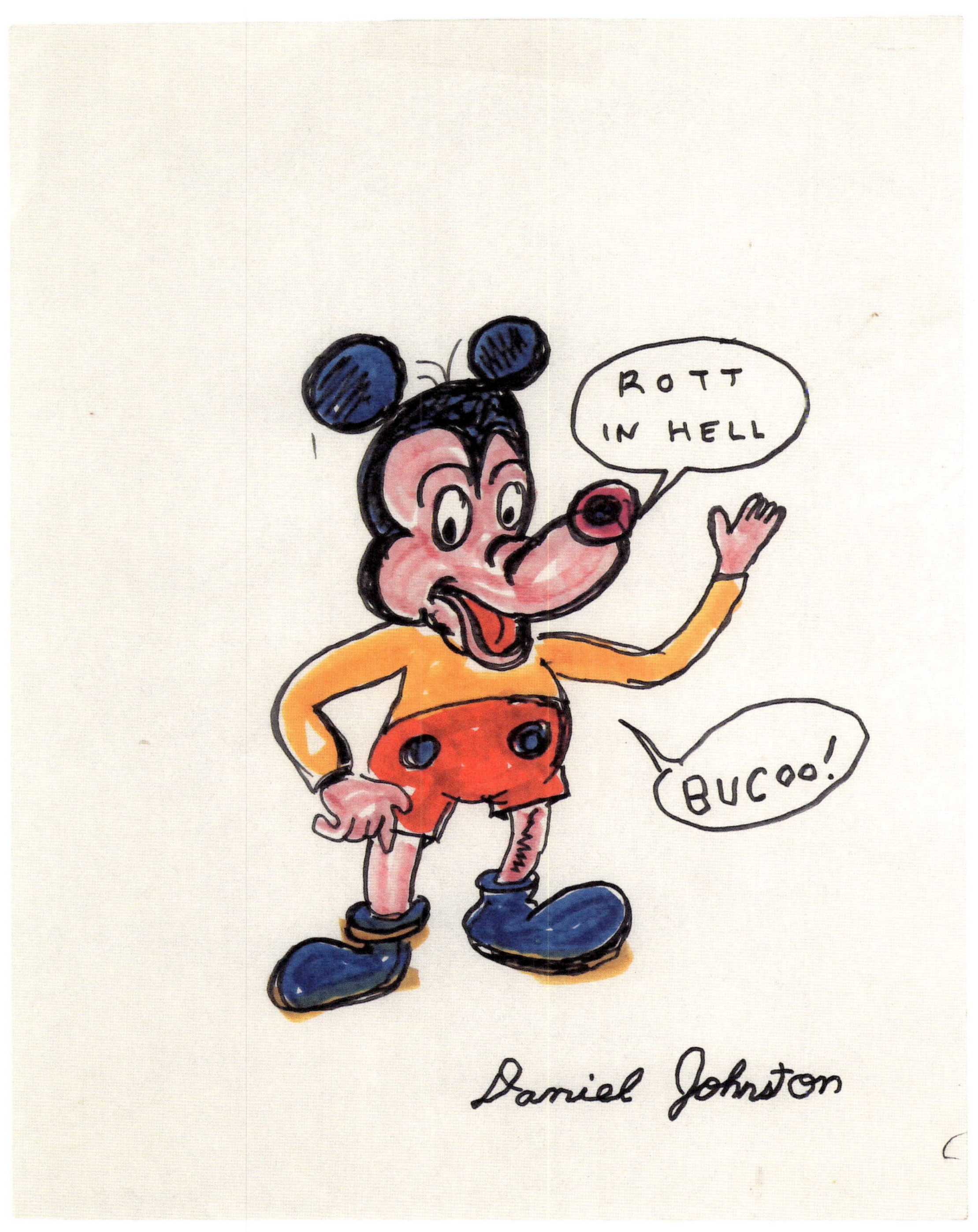

Rott In Hell (Bucoo!)

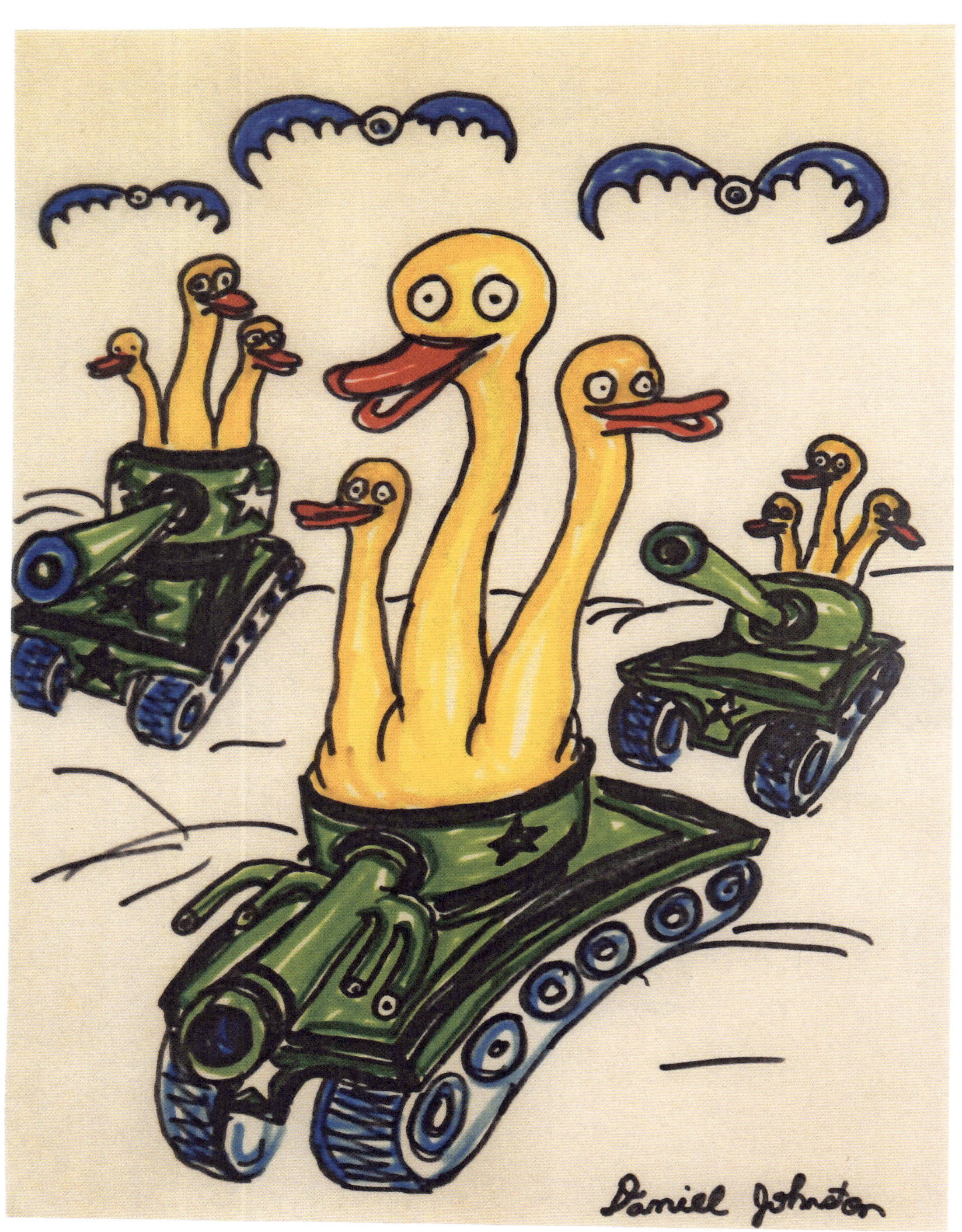

Untitled (Beast Tanks)

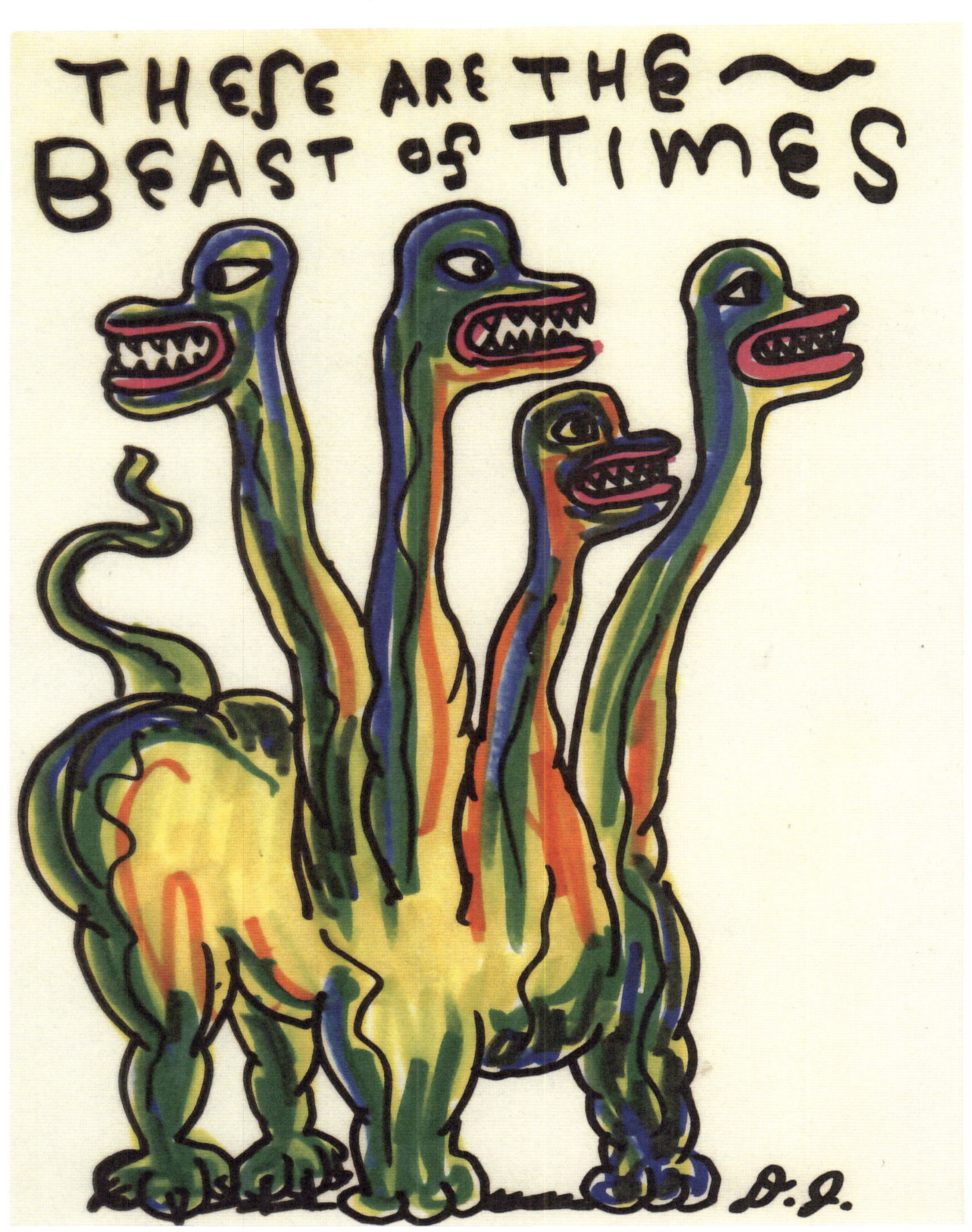

These Are the Beast of Times

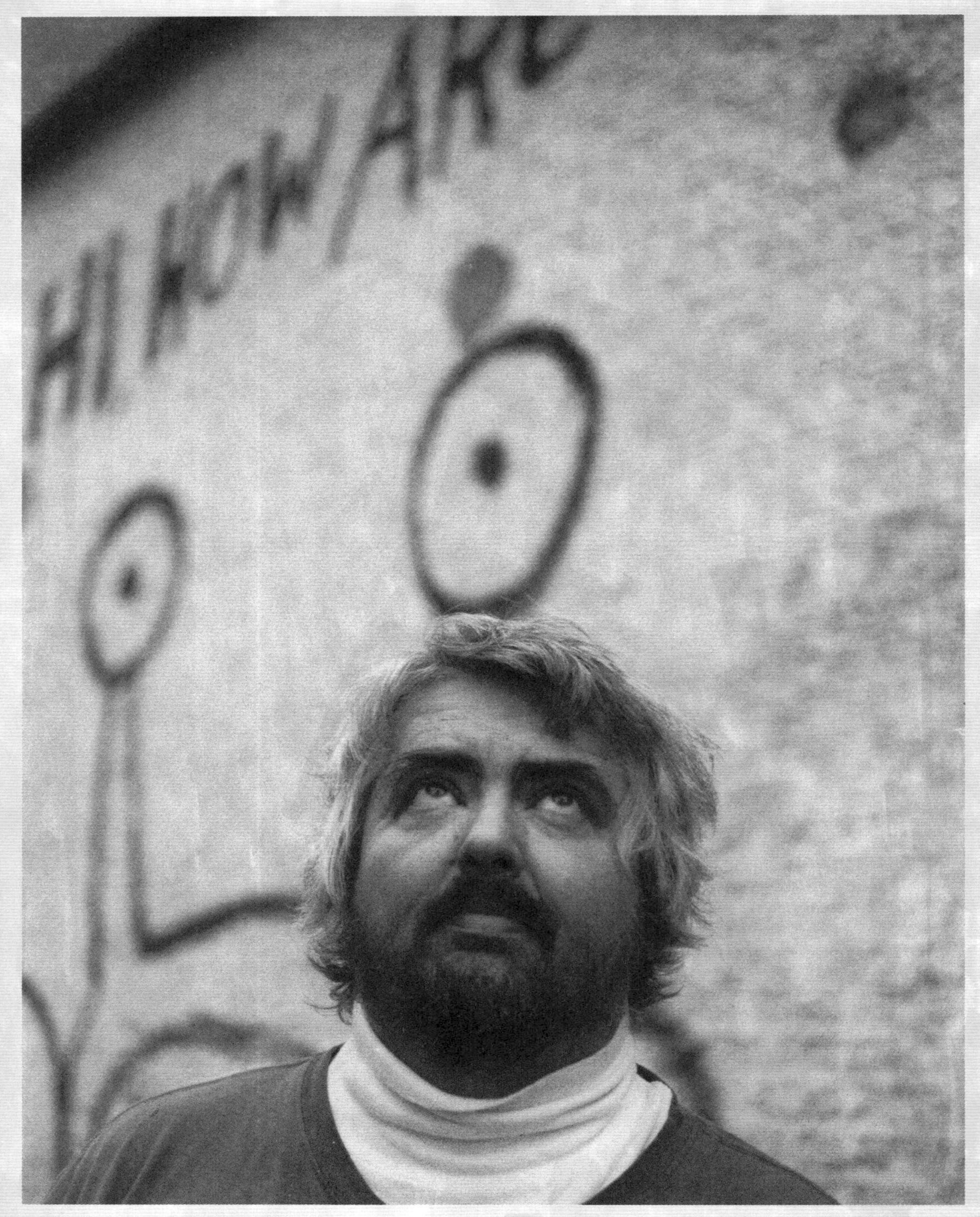
HI HOW

Robin K. Williams

Hi, How Are You: Myth and Daniel

In April 2023, I was driving down Guadalupe Street in Austin, along a commercial stretch beside the University of Texas (UT) known as "the Drag." After decades of traveling this road almost daily, I was shocked to see Daniel Johnston's beloved "Hi, How Are You" mural standing naked, surrounded by rubble, with the building that supported it in ruins. I parked in the nearby student neighborhood to document the scene. "RIP, 2100 Guadalupe," I thought with some sadness, even though I knew the mural would be preserved on-site with the new construction.

Johnston painted the mural in 1993 on the south facade of what was, at the time, a fixture of Austin's thriving music scene, the record store Sound Exchange. The store's employees had commissioned the mural from Daniel on somewhat of a whim. The building's eastern facade, facing Guadalupe, was already covered with colorful neon and artwork by other Austin artists, including the influential rock poster artist Frank Kozik, while the southern facade's large, white wall begged for an intervention. One day, as store employees stood around talking about who should do it, in walked Daniel Johnston; they invited him on the spot.

Daniel had been part of the Sound Exchange community since he first arrived in Austin in 1984–85. The store was the first one to sell his cassettes and supported his visual art by selling his drawings. As a music lover and collector, Daniel also shopped there frequently. Former store manager Craig Koon explained how he and other employees offered Daniel one hundred dollars and all the records he could carry with him.

Returning the next day, Daniel painted the iconic image of Jeremiah the Innocent with "Hi, How Are You" scrawled above it—the same image he used for his 1983 album by that name—along with a "fly eye" off to the left side. "The choice of image was Daniel's," Koon told me, "and the whole thing took him maybe an hour."

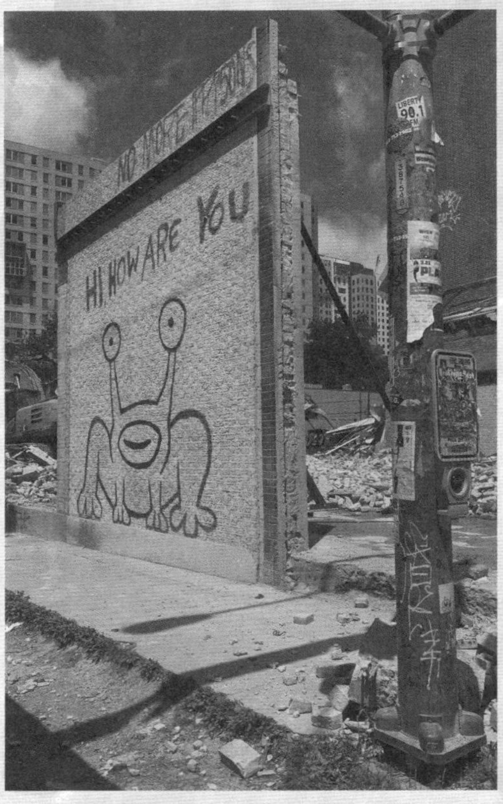

Daniel's fly eye didn't survive long. The Catholic church next door objected, falsely believing the bat-winged eyeball represented some kind of satanic symbolism, and the store painted over it. Conversely, the mural of Jeremiah with his friendly greeting has stood as a beacon of Austin's visual and cultural landscape for more than thirty years.

Sound Exchange closed in 2003, during my junior year at UT, after twenty-two years on the Drag. I began shopping there as a young teenager in the mid-1990s, shortly after Daniel painted his mural.

At that time, I was your average Kurt Cobain–crushing Nirvana fan, familiar with Daniel's "Hi, How Are You" image not only from the mural but also from the famous photographs of Kurt wearing the shirt—photographs many of my friends and I had taped, collage-style, to our bedroom walls. Thanks to an older friend, I was also a Yo La Tengo fan and knew of Daniel's music from their "Speeding Motorcycle" cover on *Fakebook*, though most likely I first heard Daniel's own voice in "Casper" in the 1995 film *Kids*. Without fully understanding it at the time, I already inhabited a cultural world deeply influenced by Daniel's artistic impact on others.

I remember seeing all of Daniel's cassettes arrayed on the Sound Exchange counter, right by the register, and sometime before starting college I bought two of them: *Hi, How Are You* and *Yip/Jump Music*. I still have these tapes, their covers browned from the aged glue and no longer adhered to the cases. It wasn't until years later that I learned Sound Exchange also kept some of Daniel's drawings for sale behind the register. They pulled them out for people they deemed worthy.

In 2004, the fast-food chain Baja Fresh moved into the space, igniting a controversy surrounding Johnston's mural. Locals noticed construction crews preparing to puncture large windows along the building's façades, prompting protests to save the mural from destruction. In response, recognizing the mural's significance among the community, the developer revised the architectural plans to preserve and incorporate it.

By 2013, the location had again changed hands, and the incoming Thai restaurant renamed itself "Thai, How Are You," honoring the mural with Johnston's blessing. The image had become firmly cemented as a local landmark.

Around the same time, as a graduate student from 2012 to 2017, I taught art history at UT and began each semester with a discussion of Daniel's mural. Projecting a current image on screen, I would ask the students if they recognized it. Almost everyone would; many lived nearby or passed it daily. Then, I would ask what they knew about it. "It's the 'Keep Austin Weird' frog," someone would invariably say, and they weren't entirely wrong. Although the image is known worldwide among Daniel Johnston fans, locally it had become tied to a campaign promoting small businesses, with the "weird" reflecting Austin's role as a regional creative hub and alternative to Texas's historically larger and more conservative cities. The "Hi, How Are You" image also appears on T-shirts and other merchandise representing Austin, often without context or mention of Daniel's name. I've even seen parody graffiti and T-shirts with stony-eyed imitation frogs and the phrase "How High Are You" replacing Daniel's Jeremiah's innocence.

To me, the recent shock of seeing the mural standing isolated amid the building's rubble underscored how drastically the image's layered significance could be stripped away. In my teaching, I had wanted to illustrate the importance of historical context in interpreting visual culture. Moving from Daniel's mural to a discussion about Pompeii dramatized how quickly cultural memory can fade and the meanings of images can change. If, by the 2010s—roughly ten years since the store closed and twenty since Daniel painted the mural—most students no longer knew the space was formerly a record store, much less the artist's name, where would the local memory be in another decade, where we are now, when the original building no longer even stands? What replaces historical specifics, I would suggest, is myth.

* * *

Myth thickly cloaks the figure of Daniel Johnston. He is an artist remembered for his innocence and sincerity—a tortured genius too rare for this world. The 2005 documentary *The Devil and Daniel*

Johnston, a brilliant film showcasing thoughtful research and compelling storytelling, introduced the artist to a much wider audience than his music alone had so far reached. But, with the tragic realities surrounding his lifelong struggles with mental illness, the attention often paid to Daniel's biography risks overshadowing his reception as an artist.

Recently, I had the honor of organizing the retrospective *Daniel Johnston: I Live My Broken Dreams*, which opened at The Contemporary Austin in September 2021. In developing the exhibition, I worked closely with Johnston's estate, particularly Lee Foster, who became a friend as we regularly discussed Daniel's art and shaped its presentation. Additionally, being a long-time Austinite, I tapped into a broad community of people who knew Daniel personally and generously shared their deep knowledge about his and Austin's music history, along with many objects and recordings loaned to the exhibition. As part of my research, I conducted dozens of interviews, trying to pierce the myth of "Daniel Johnston" in search of someone real.

David Thornberry, Daniel's best friend since high school, told me he believes there was no "real" Daniel Johnston. "He was always performing," Thornberry said. He had in mind Daniel's self-presentation, comparing him to Andy Kaufman and Pee-wee Herman for their ability to transform their entire physicality when embodying their characters. Dave's wife, Kathy McCarty—a songwriter and musician, frontwoman of the legendary Austin post-punk band Glass Eye, and, for a few weeks in 1985, Daniel's girlfriend—wholeheartedly agreed with Dave. They insisted it was not as if Daniel was intentionally acting or trying to deceive people; it's just how he was. "Dan was always trying to entertain, and he used his physical presence to become a character . . . by making himself appear smaller or larger [to seem] more innocent or heroic," Dave said, emphasizing the difficulty of conveying how Daniel did this with such completeness.

I understood Dave's point, in part, from having watched many videos and listened to hours of audiotapes Daniel recorded in his daily life, especially in the 1980s. One tape stood out to me because it narrated Daniel's inner life surrounding his eventual move to Austin. In 1983, Daniel was living with his brother, Dick, in Houston. He wanted to be in Austin because of its creative community, for music as well as underground comics, but was afraid to make the move.

On the tape, he plays two sides of himself against each other. There's the afraid Daniel, who says things like, "I don't want to go . . . I'm *scared* [*whiny voice*]," and the strong Daniel, who counters with, "*I'm* taking over now, *I'm* running the show—we're *doing* this [*tough-guy voice*]." These characters struck me as both stock figures from popular culture and sincere representations of Daniel's

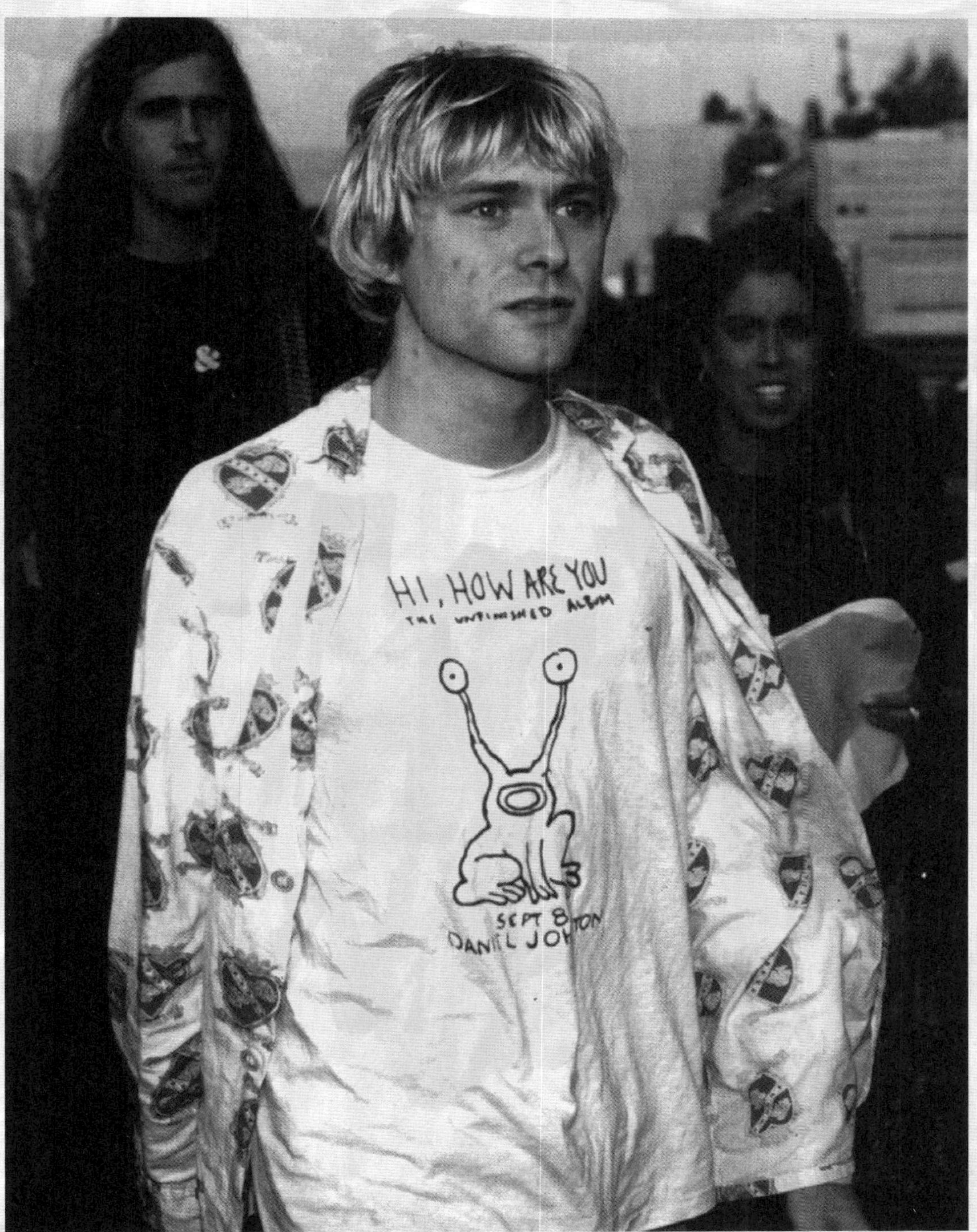
HI, HOW ARE YOU
THE UNFINISHED ALBUM
SEPT 8

inner dialogue, as he spontaneously played them back and forth, never pausing or breaking the bit. By experiencing many similar examples, while also studying so much of his artwork, I began to perceive Daniel as something like a medium through which a rich trove of cultural influences, dialogues, images, and references flowed.

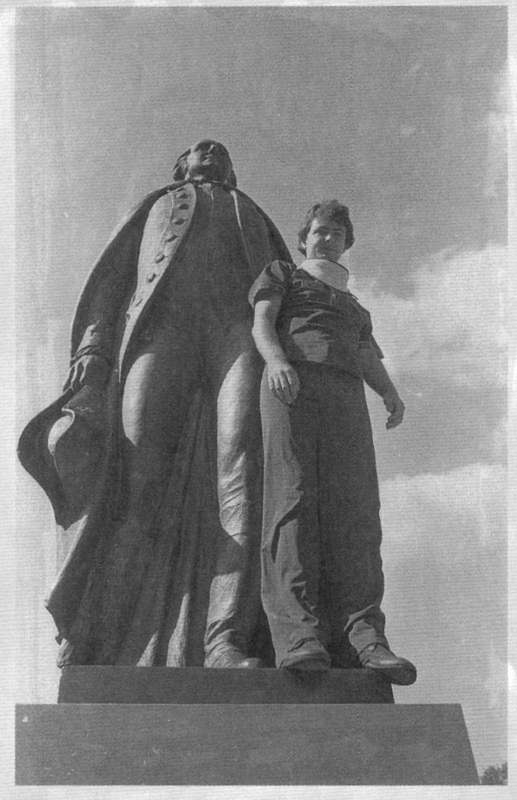

Daniel's unique genius, I believe, is partly his unparalleled ability to ingest the vast cultural products of the twentieth century, interpreting and recontextualizing them within the framework of his own imagination and the holistic mythology of his inner world. In some ways, we all do something like this when we love a song or an artwork; in consuming it, we make it part of ourselves, experiencing it through our own interiorities. The line between what is objective and subjective in this appreciation is, thankfully, not worth parsing. With Daniel, this process would be impossible to fully parse anyway; his consumption was so thorough and his synthesis so extraordinary that he could intake a galaxy of stars and create an entirely new universe.

Consider the meta-structure of Daniel's mythology, which combines the oppositions of good and evil, light and dark, found in the Bible with these same forces enacted through a cast of superheroes and other characters, both known and invented. Daniel's favorite superhero, Captain America, features in his artwork more than any other single figure; a tight selection of eighty Captain America drawings appeared in the Austin exhibition. Across these drawings, Daniel's Captain adheres both more and less faithfully to how his art hero, Jack Kirby, originally depicted him. Sometimes he's fighting Nazis or other villains, and other times he's flirting with girls or hanging out with Daniel's charmed characters like Casper, Jeremiah, or Laurie. For Daniel, the patriotic Captain served as an avatar at times for his own father, a WWII veteran, and at other times for Jesus or as a symbol of ultimate Good.

Sometimes, the Captain was also just a dude. Daniel's art abounds with these tendencies toward abstracting, analogizing, and compounding.

Daniel was a mythmaker. In his constant compulsion to create, through any and every means available, he shaped a universe with himself at its center. By peering into this universe, we can witness his relentless quest to make sense of the world and how to live in it. He approached the world with insatiable curiosity, absorbing everything as source material. The multiplicity of his characters keenly reflects the inherent multiplicity of meaning in everything. Daniel perhaps recognized the chaos of reality better than most, allowing it to exist instead of attempting to limit and control it. At the same time, the playfulness with which he shaped this chaos in his own likeness manifested a dense fabric of allusions integrating elements of himself, his art and music, and the external world.

Daniel's mythmaking extended to shaping his artistic image. No doubt, compared to so many people who move through life chasing cool, Daniel projected an air of authenticity or aloofness, but he wasn't naive about it. Around 1990, he made a comic about how he met journalist Louis Black in 1985 at the *Austin Chronicle* office. In the comic, Daniel hands Louis a tape, and Louis tells him they'll consider it for a review. This exchange is depicted in dialogue, but in thought bubbles, we see Louis thinking, "He has a certain innocence," while Daniel thinks, "I have a certain innocence, but I know how to use my innocence!"

* * *

In 1985, filmmaker Richard Linklater created a short documentary about Woodshock, a music festival held on a sprawling property near Austin. In it, he briefly interviews Daniel, who was among the crowd. "Ask me a question," Daniel suggests, so Linklater does, asking, "Where do you work?" Holding his tape up to the camera, Daniel replies, "I work at McDonald's, and this is my album *Hi, How Are You*. It's an old album, but if you get a chance, please listen to it." He smiles warmly, and after a short pause, asks, "Are you gonna listen to it?" Linklater says he will, and Daniel sweetly urges, "All right, please do."

It's a treasure of a documentary moment that captures how Daniel introduced himself in those early Austin days, when he was a newcomer eagerly wanting to connect. In witnessing the exchange, I feel endeared to him and can vividly sense how he quickly made such a strong impression on the community through both his personality and his music.

The same summer, in 1985, Daniel made it onto MTV for the first time, in an episode of *The Cutting Edge* spotlighting Austin's music scene. As his friends from the scene recall, although the producers had not originally intended to include Daniel, by the time they arrived he was the talk of the town, and they wisely slotted him in. He first appears in a segment filmed at a backyard barbecue. Speaking to the camera, Daniel introduces himself and his album *Hi, How Are You*, mentioning that he made it during "a nervous breakdown." In a different segment filmed at the music venue, he addresses the camera with an earnest grin: "This is to David Thornberry from Daniel Johnston. Dave, here I am on MTV holding up my tape *Hi, How Are You* . . . Remember when we used to watch MTV back home? Look, I'm on MTV, David."

The episode features many amazing Austin bands of the time—including Dharma Bums, Glass Eye, Poison 13, Timbuk3, True Believers, and Zeitgeist—but Daniel stole the show performing his song "I Live My Broken Dreams." Flashing a quick smile to the camera, he steps onstage with his guitar and sings, with his slight quiver, about the journey that brought him to Austin:

When I was out in San Marcos / a year ago today / they probably would have put me in a home / But I threw all my belongings / into a garbage bag / and out into the worldness I did roam

I love this song because it speaks to Daniel's courage and self-possession, which I believe helps us begin to see through the myths surrounding him. Daniel didn't end up in Austin by chance; he moved intentionally, in the way he could, seeking out community and audiences, and he found them. In a town with many great songwriters and musicians, people in Austin recognized the magnitude of Daniel's talent and supported him. He emerged from this scene as "Daniel Johnston."

Famously, upon arriving in Austin, Daniel handed out copies of his cassettes as a way of introducing himself and his music. Although he occasionally gave them to cool-looking girls, he primarily gave them to people in bands he wanted to hear his music. This was how he got his first gig, opening for Glass Eye, after giving tapes to Kathy McCarty. "His cassettes were his business cards," said Daniel's former manager Jeff Tartakov. He used them strategically.

A common misconception is that each of these tapes was a unique recording. While multiple versions of his earliest albums made in West Virginia exist, by the time he arrived in Austin, Daniel was duplicating his cassette albums using a cheap boombox and the cheapest tapes he could find, though he assembled them all by hand. He even sold these early copies at Sound Exchange.

In 1986, Tartakov took over the duplication, assembly, and distribution of Daniel's cassettes through his label, Stress Records, with the goals of helping Daniel break even and sharing his music as widely as possible. Interestingly, the

Stress tapes closely resemble the versions Daniel himself earlier duplicated. Jeff told me that when he began this work, Daniel sat him down for a two-hour training session to teach him how to do everything, including hand-cutting and gluing the labels. Daniel used rubber cement glue, and Jeff recalls how Daniel half-joked with him, "You'd better open the window—you're not used to the hard drugs like me."

Daniel's reputation quickly grew nationally as his Stress cassettes were distributed through Systematic in San Francisco, K Records in Olympia, and Dutch East in New York. Bands like Sonic Youth and Yo La Tengo paid attention. Kurt Cobain got the shirt when Tartakov gave it to the UK-based music journalist Everett True, who then passed it on to him. The rest is history.

Much of Daniel's early success relied on physical exchanges of material culture. Whether it was Daniel introducing himself by holding up *Hi, How Are You* or handing out his cassettes, music industry staffers listening to and circulating his music, or kids like me discovering his songs through mixtapes, covers, or magazine spreads about Nirvana, it would be compelling to trace a material history of how Daniel's music circulated early on. In many ways, Sound Exchange and places like it would be central to this story.

Soon enough, a new college dormitory will rise at 2100 Guadalupe, and Daniel's mural will proudly stand as a local icon. Through the Hi, How Are You Project, it will also raise awareness about mental health—a crucial message for the young people who will frequently see it. As this transformation takes place, I hope we can also remember how the mural got there in the first place. It is vital to acknowledge the essential role spaces like record stores and music venues play in enabling creative communities to thrive. As Daniel has shown us, these spaces have fostered some of the most surprising artists who have gone on to alter the course of popular culture. The ripple effects and the inspiration for future young creatives cannot be overestimated.

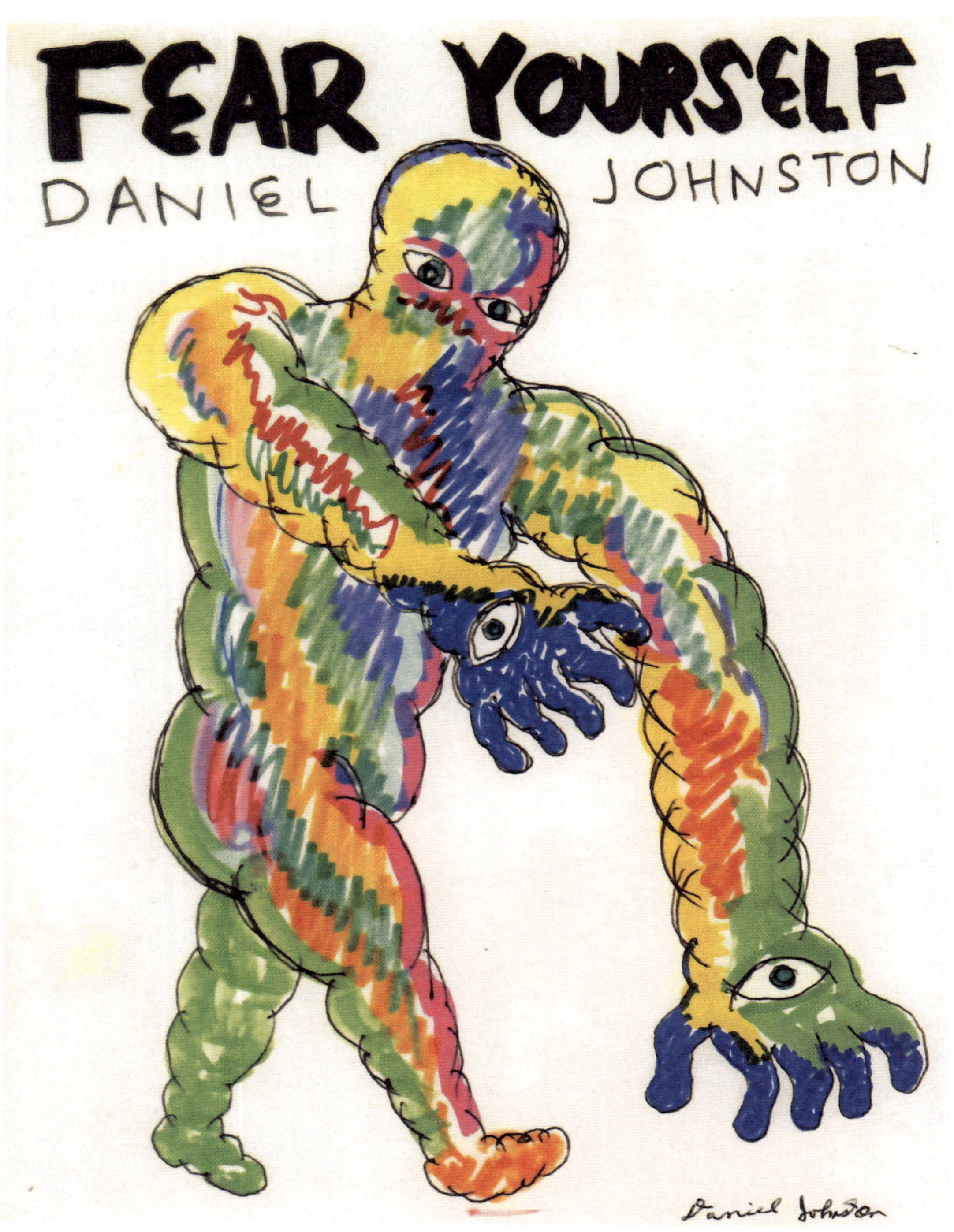

Fear Yourself

XI.
Fear Yourself
2000s

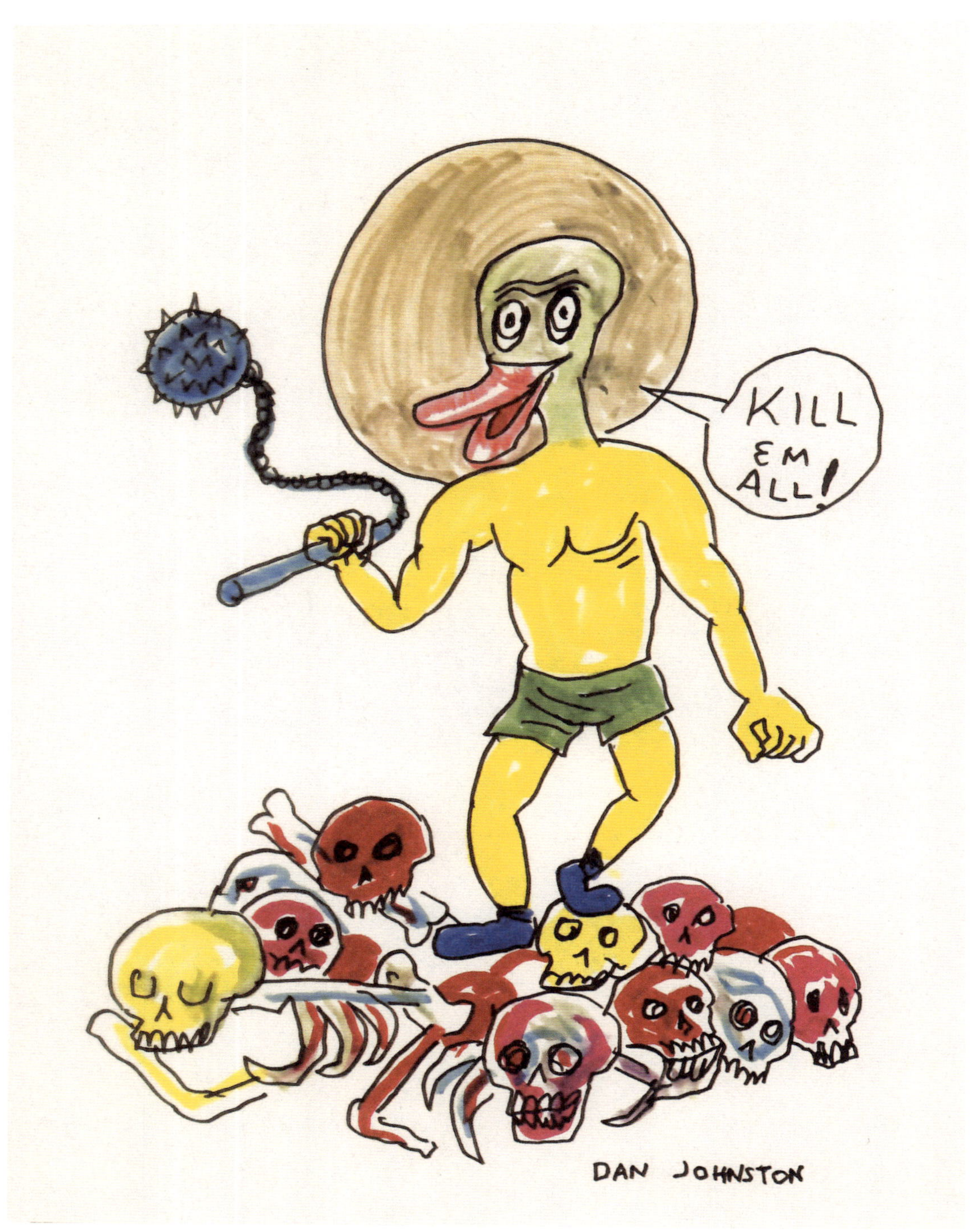

Kill Em All!

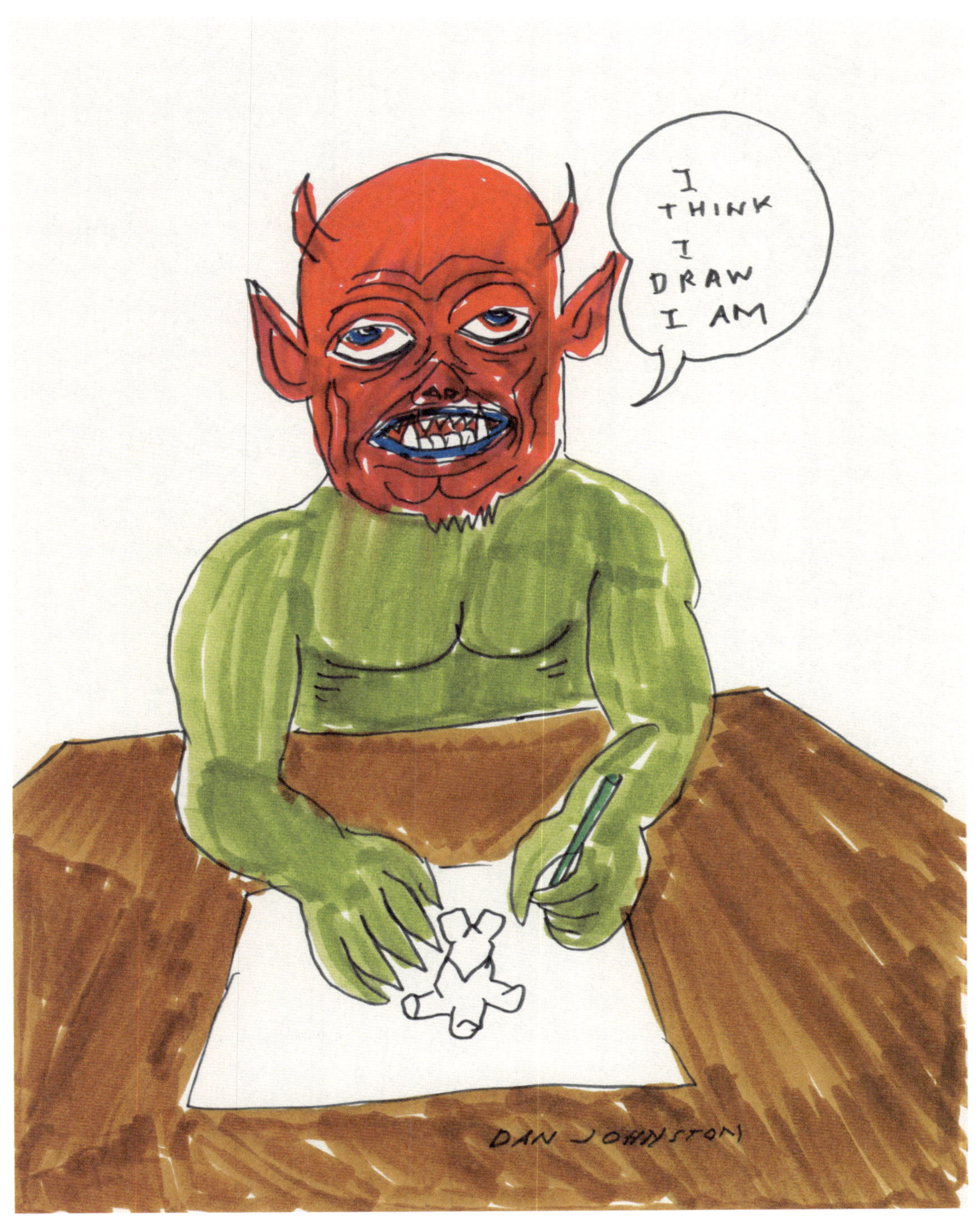

I Think I Draw I Am

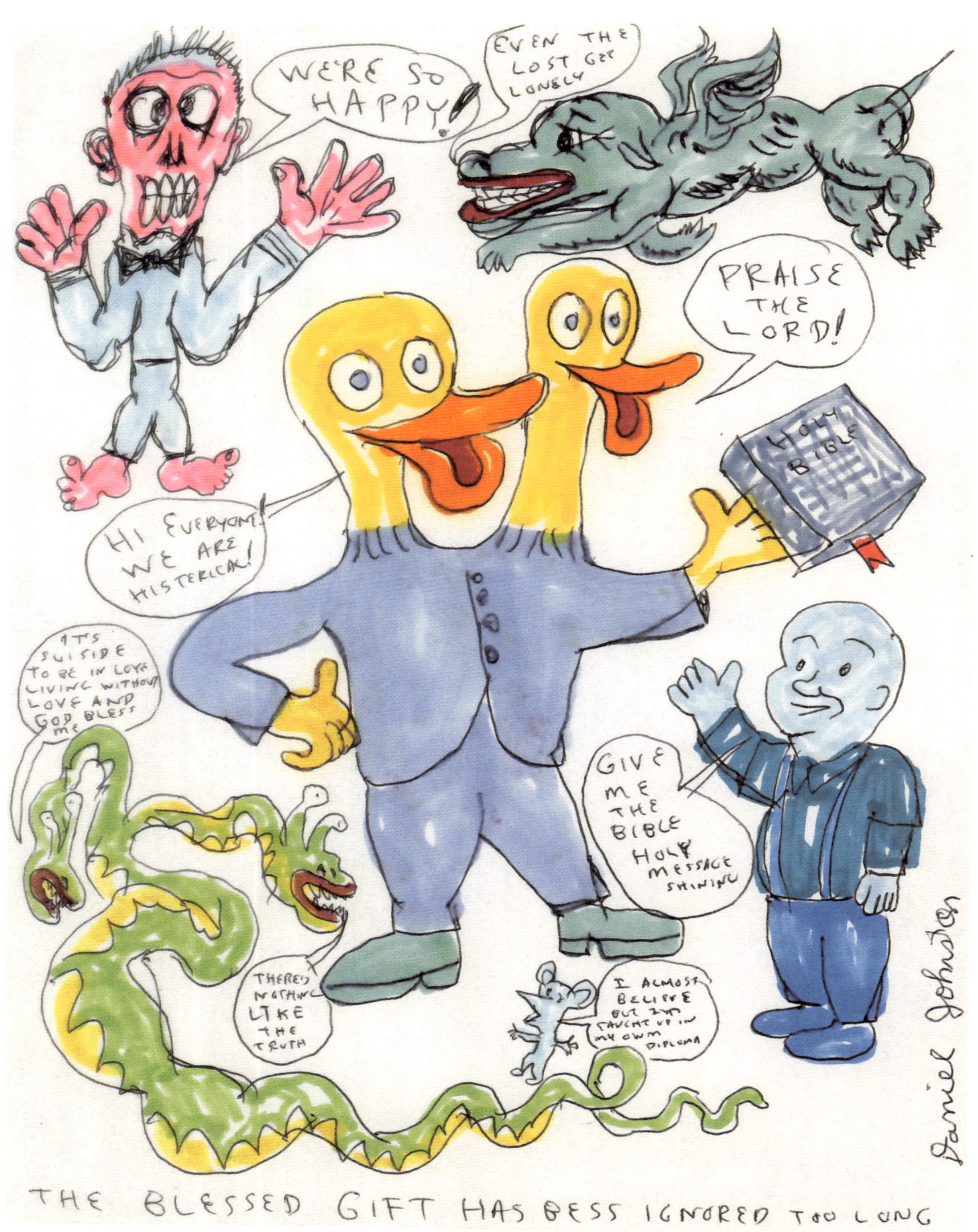

Even the Lost Get Lonely

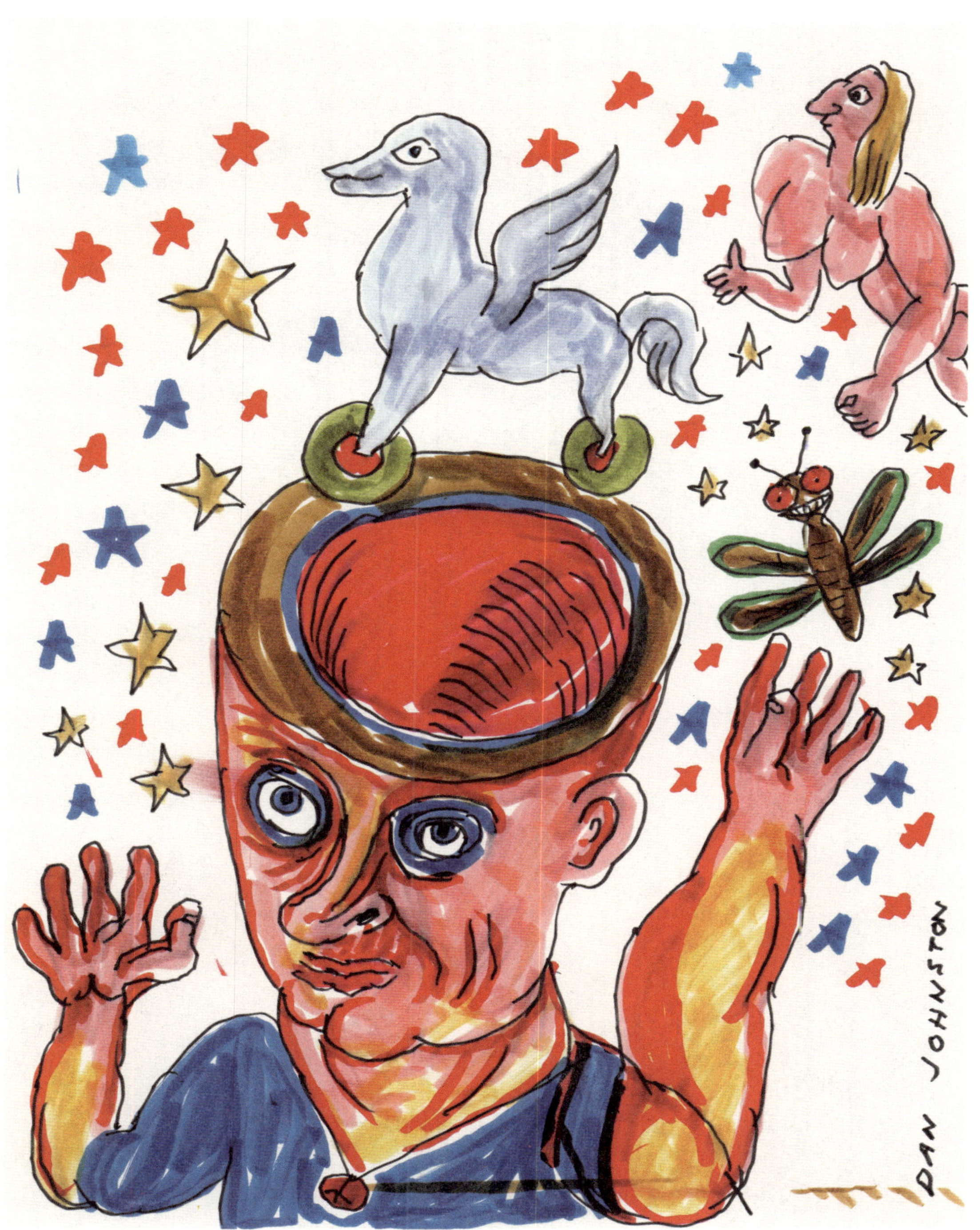

Untitled (Imagine)

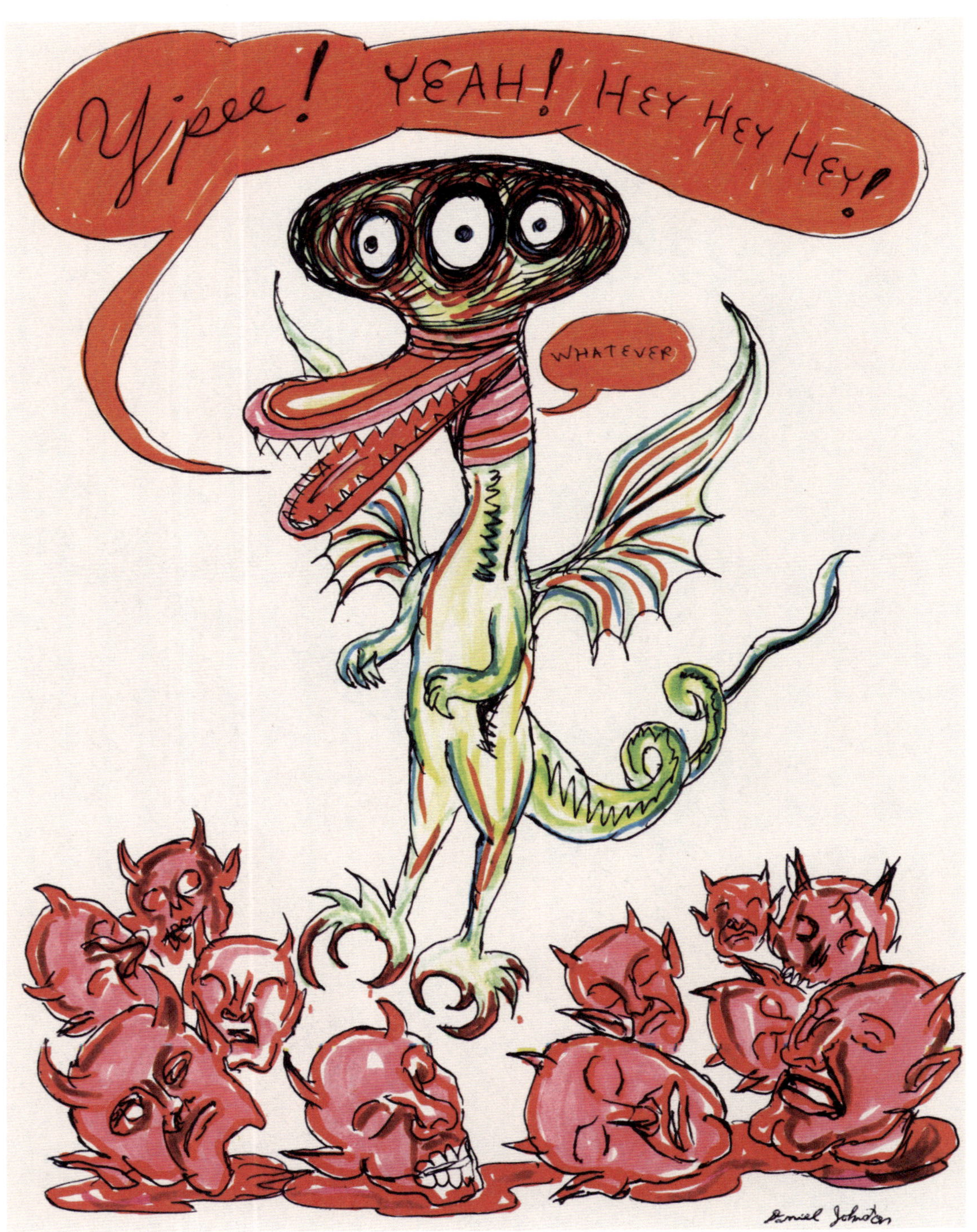

Whatever

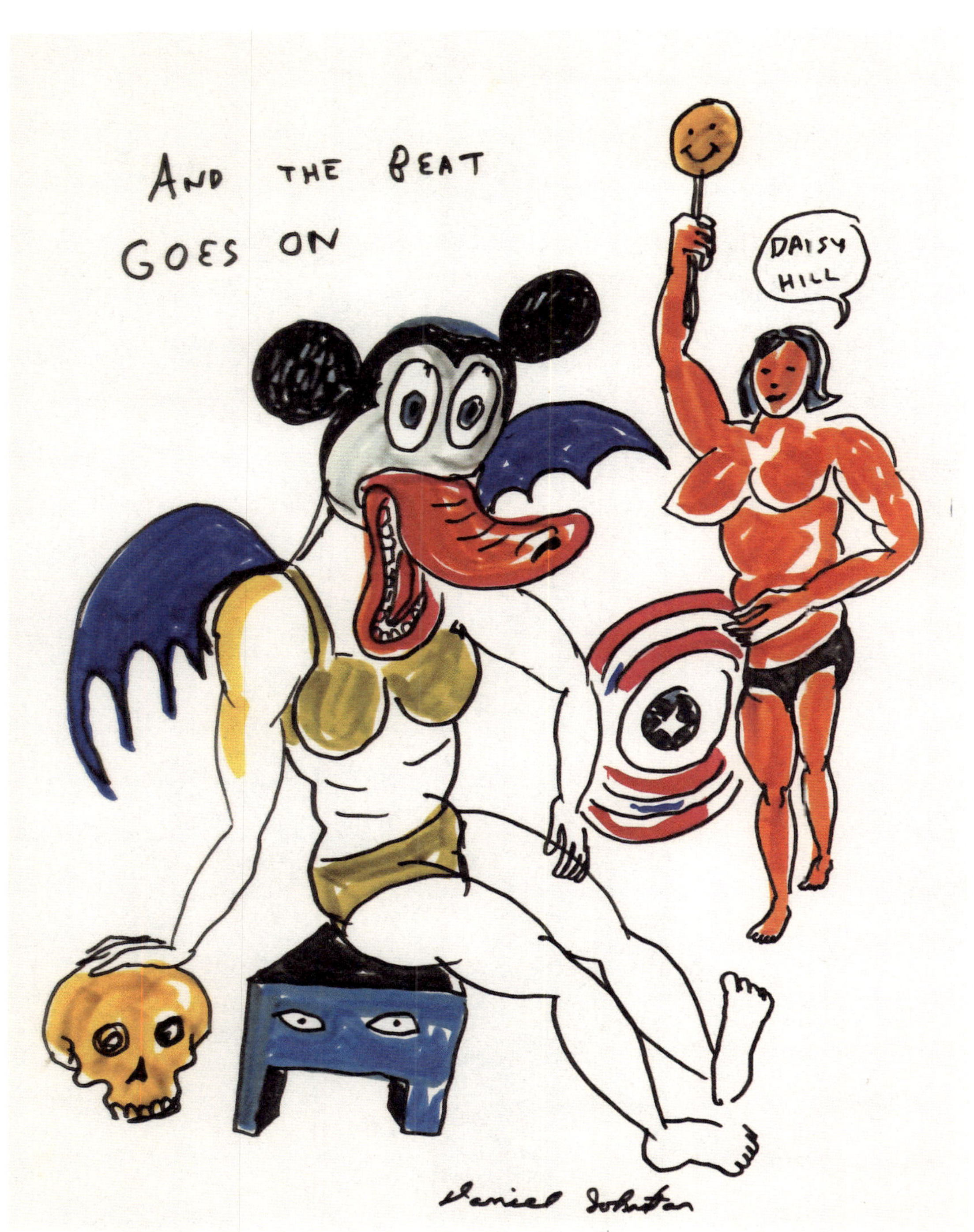

And the Beat Goes On

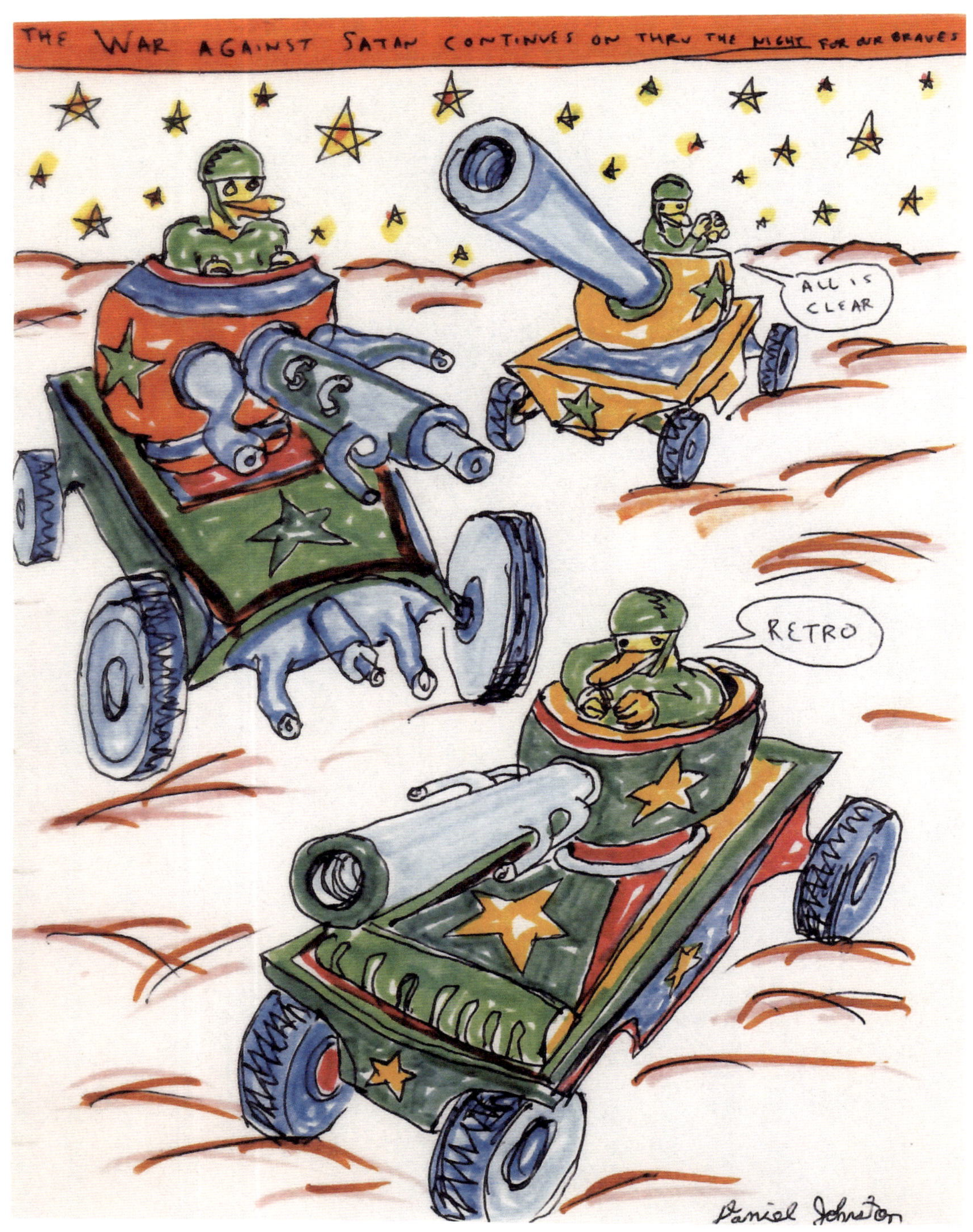

The War against Satan

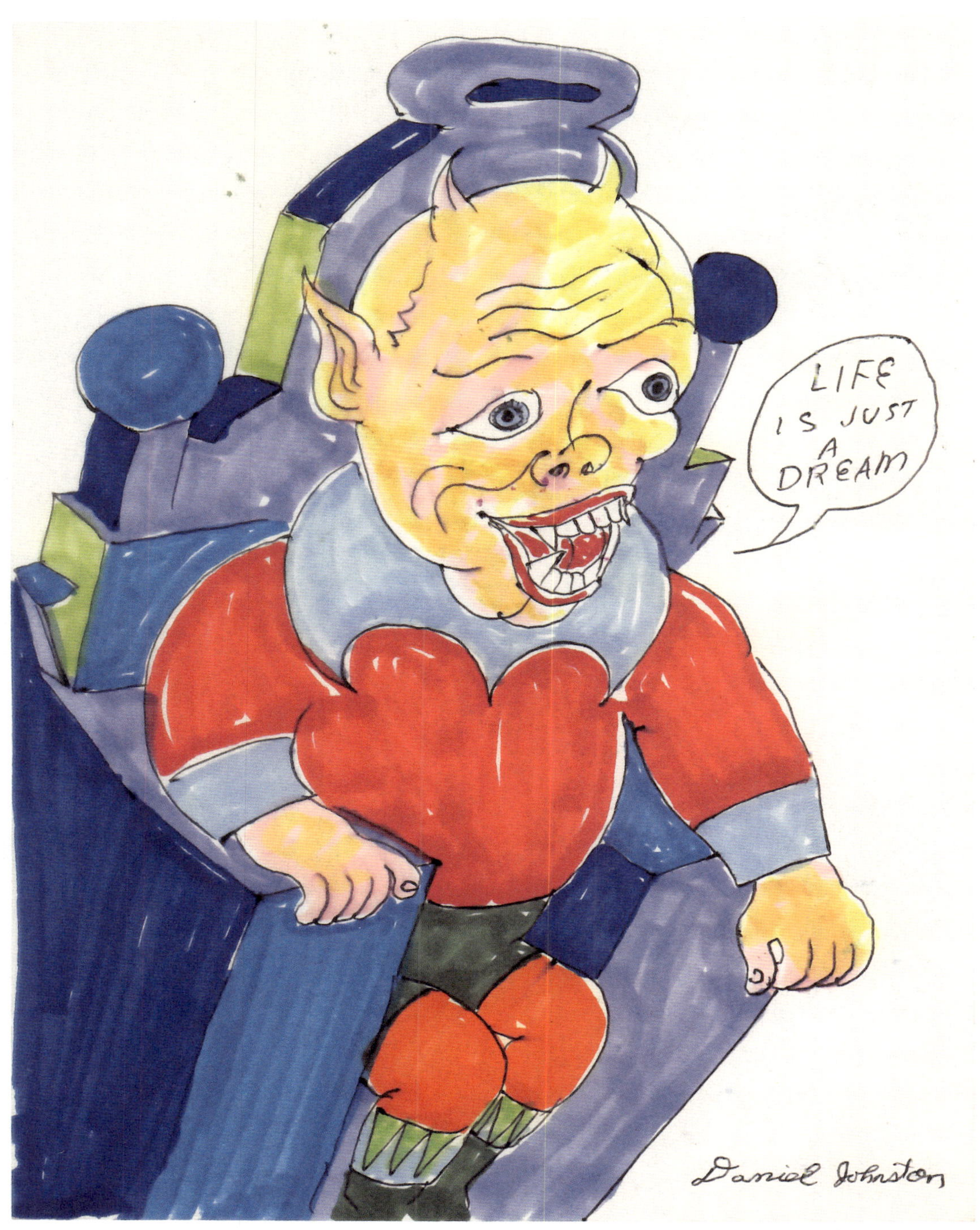

Life Is Just a Dream

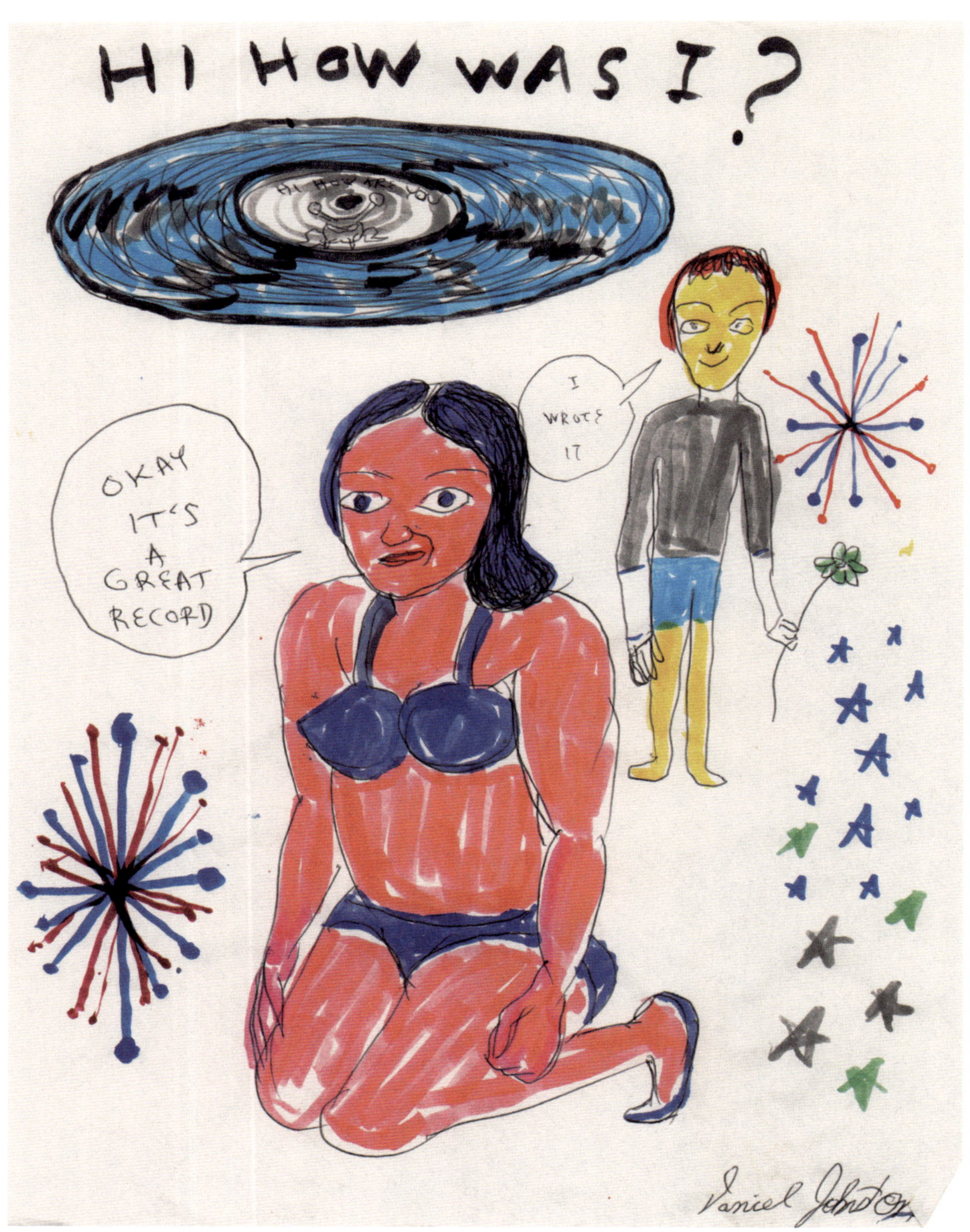
HI HOW WAS I?
HI HOW ARE YOU
I WROTE IT
OKAY IT'S A GREAT RECORD
Daniel Johnston

Hi How Was I?

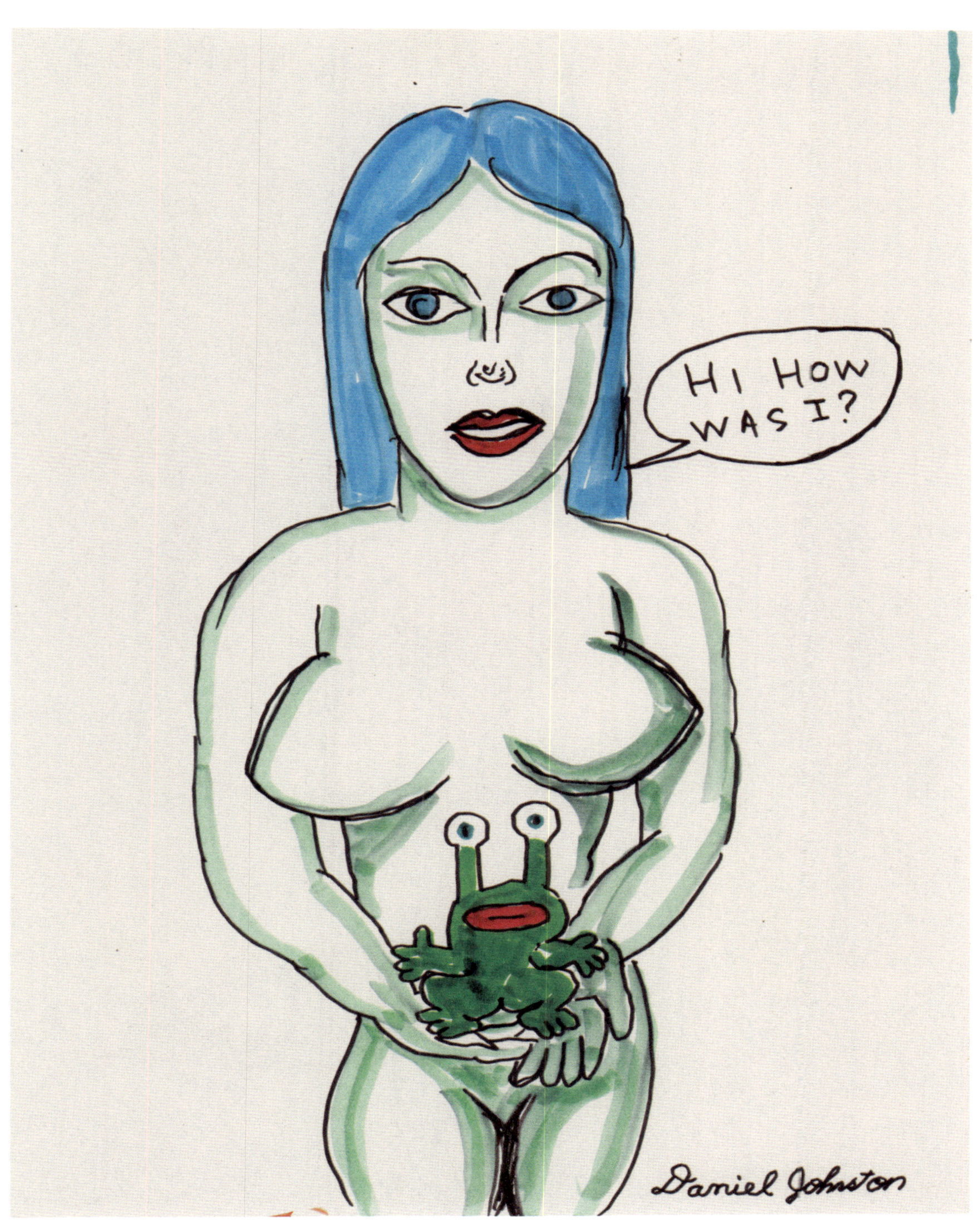

Hi How Was I? (with Jeremiah)

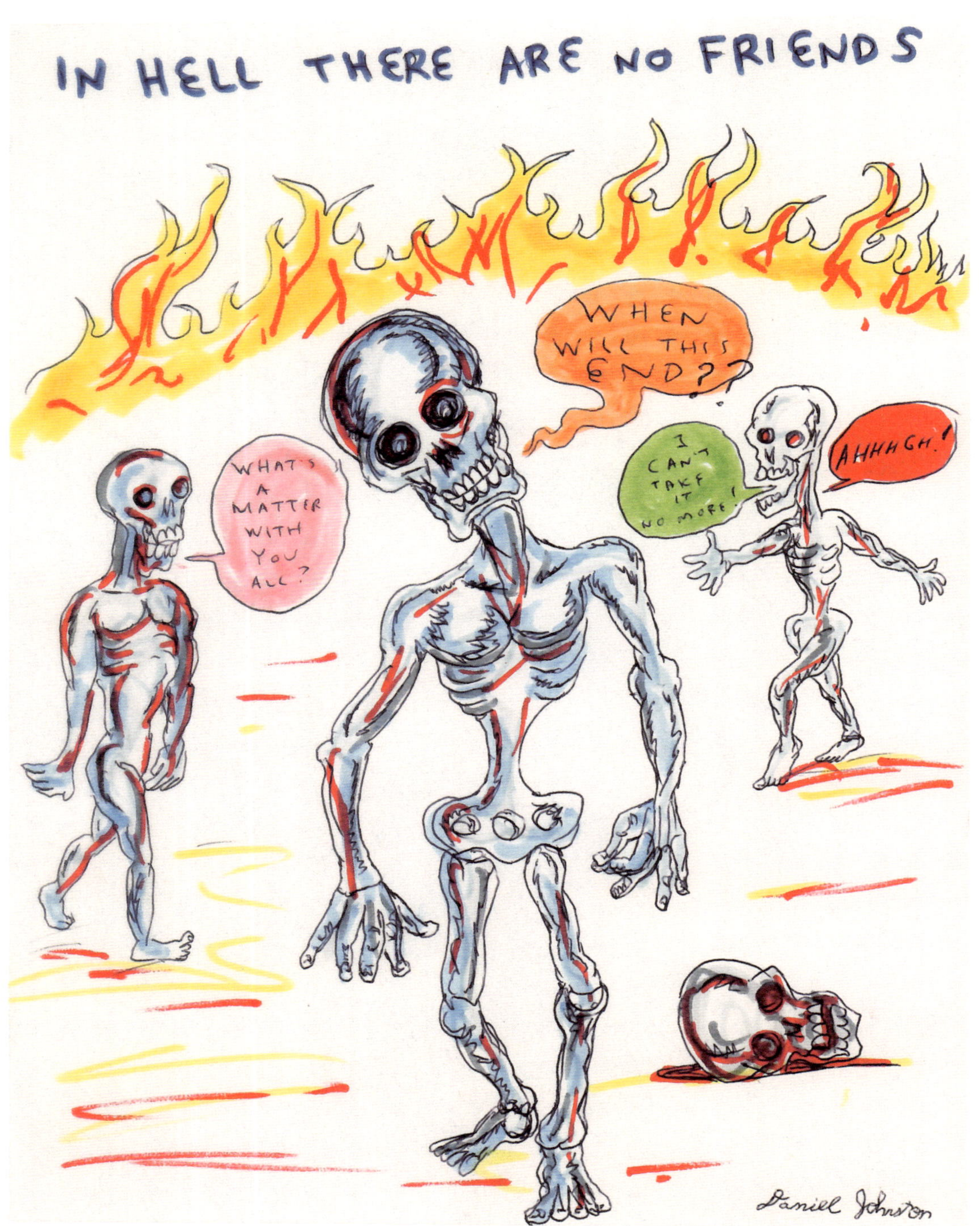

In Hell There Are No Friends

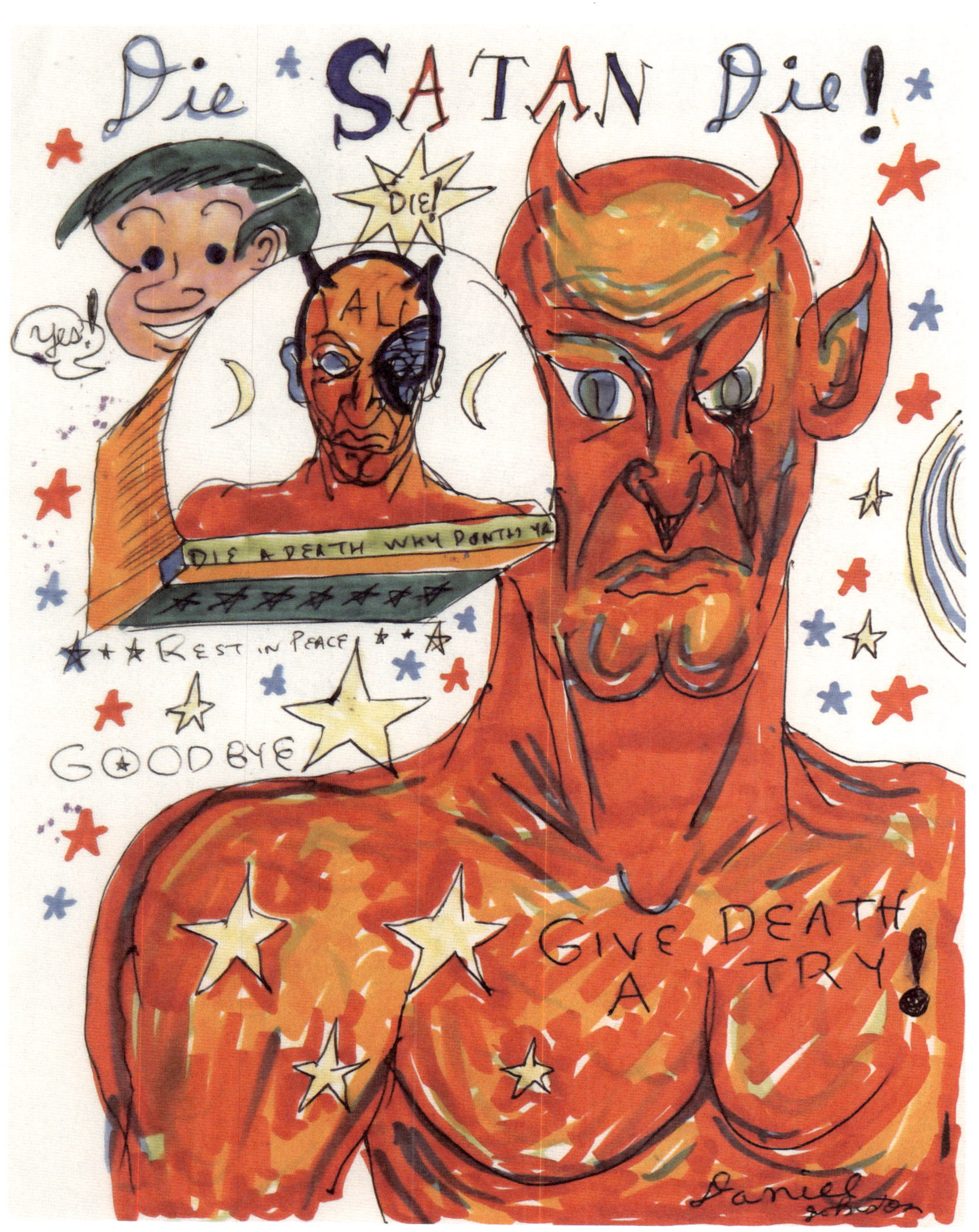

Die Satan Die!

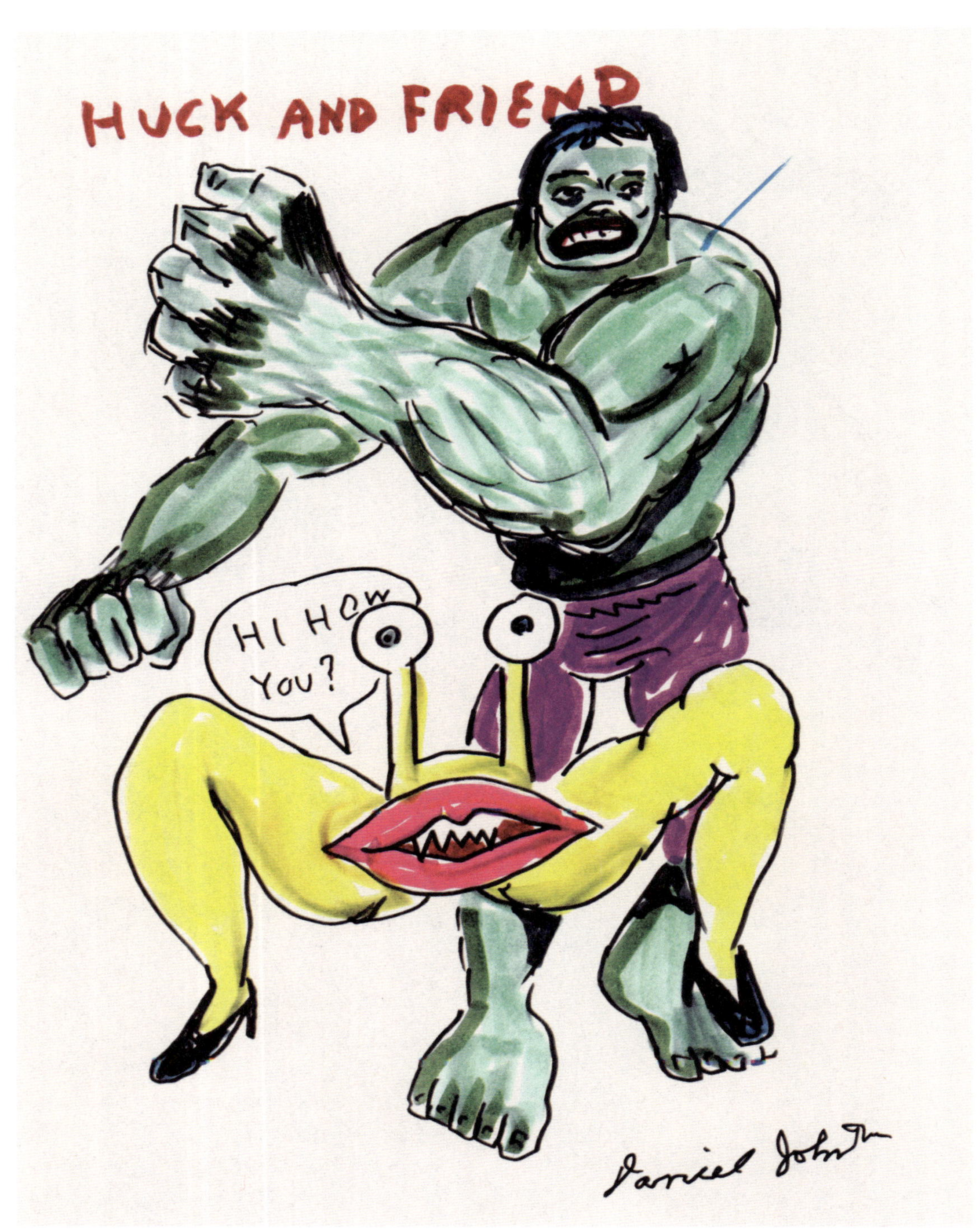

Hulk and Friend

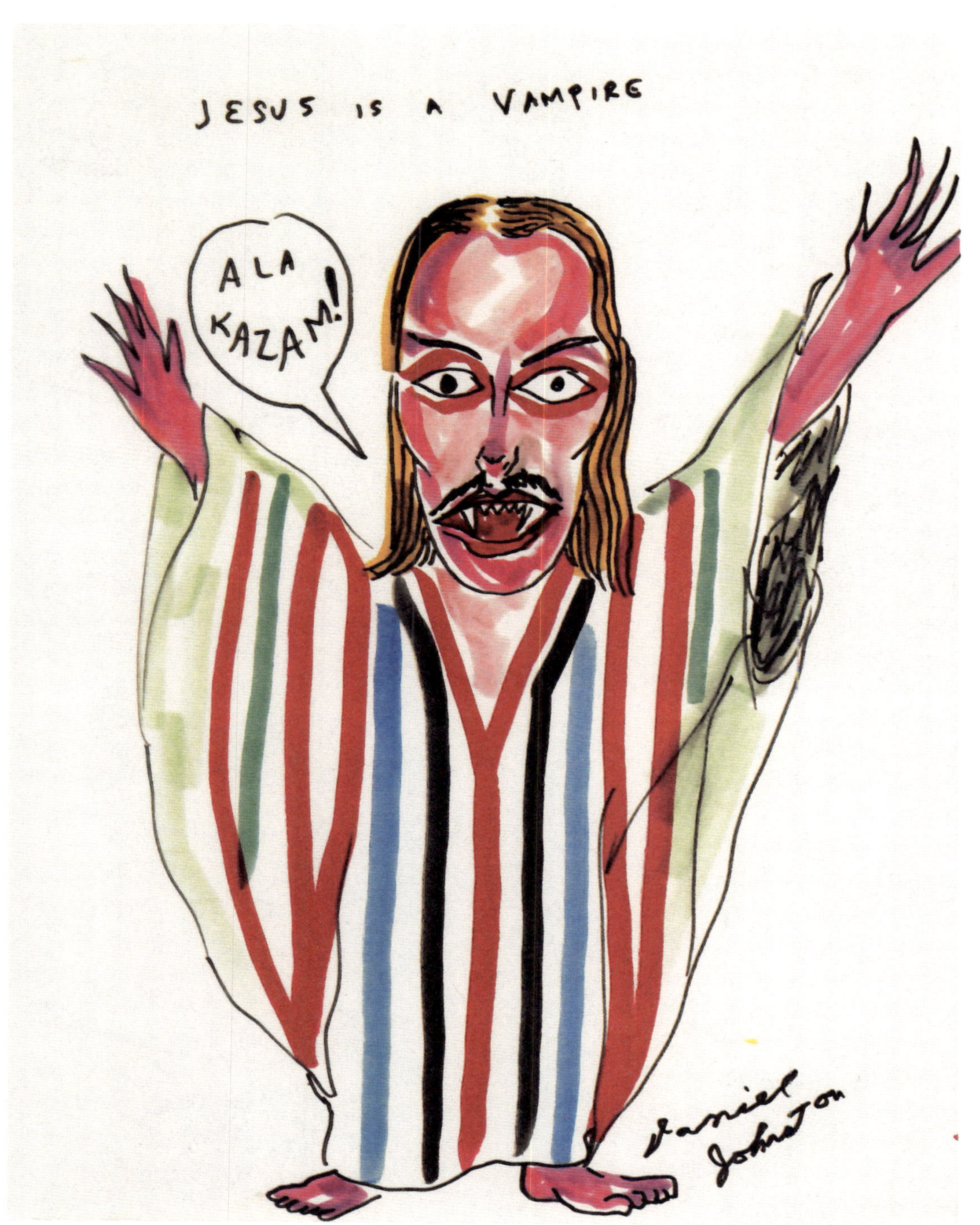

Jesus Is a Vampire

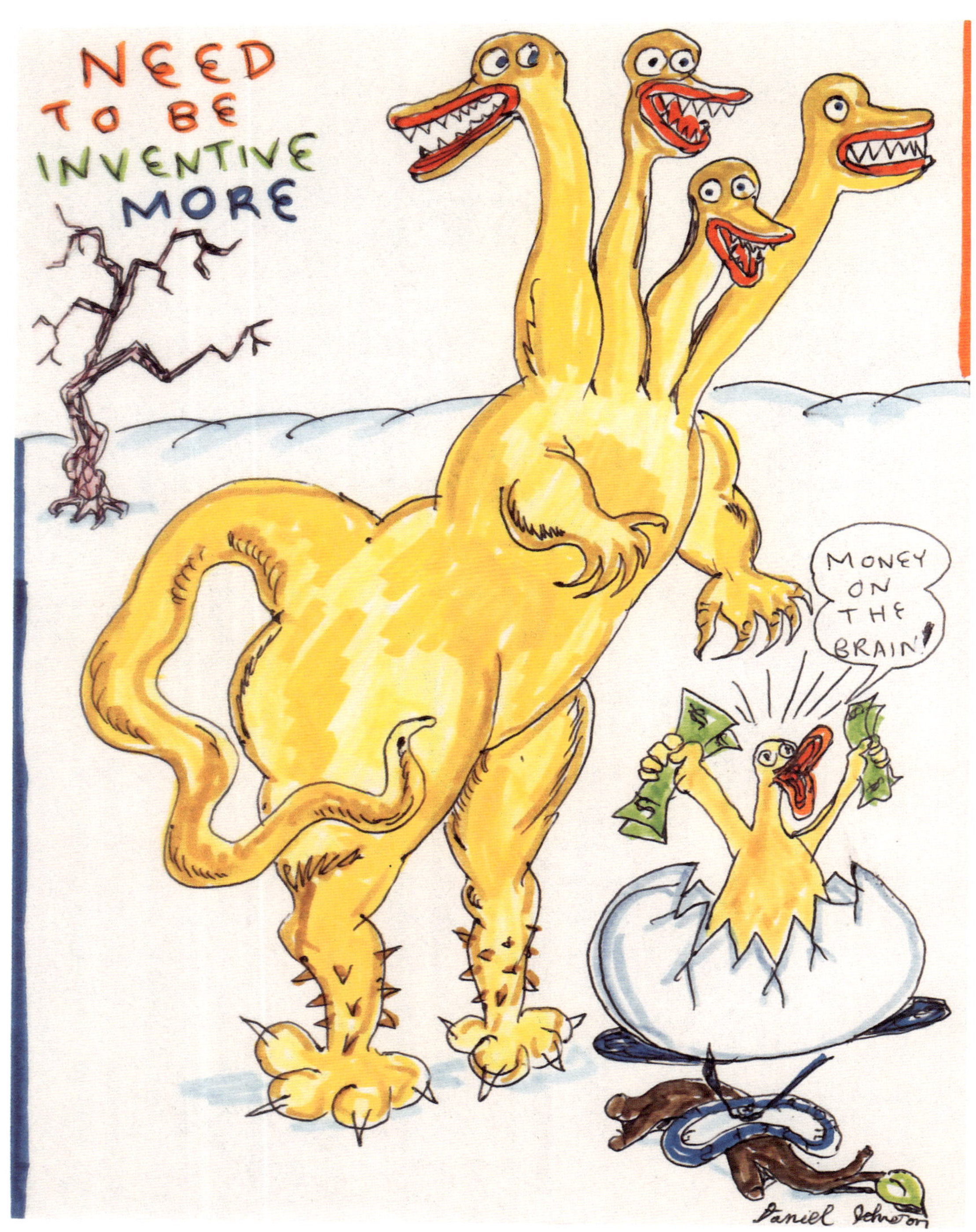

Need to Be Inventive More

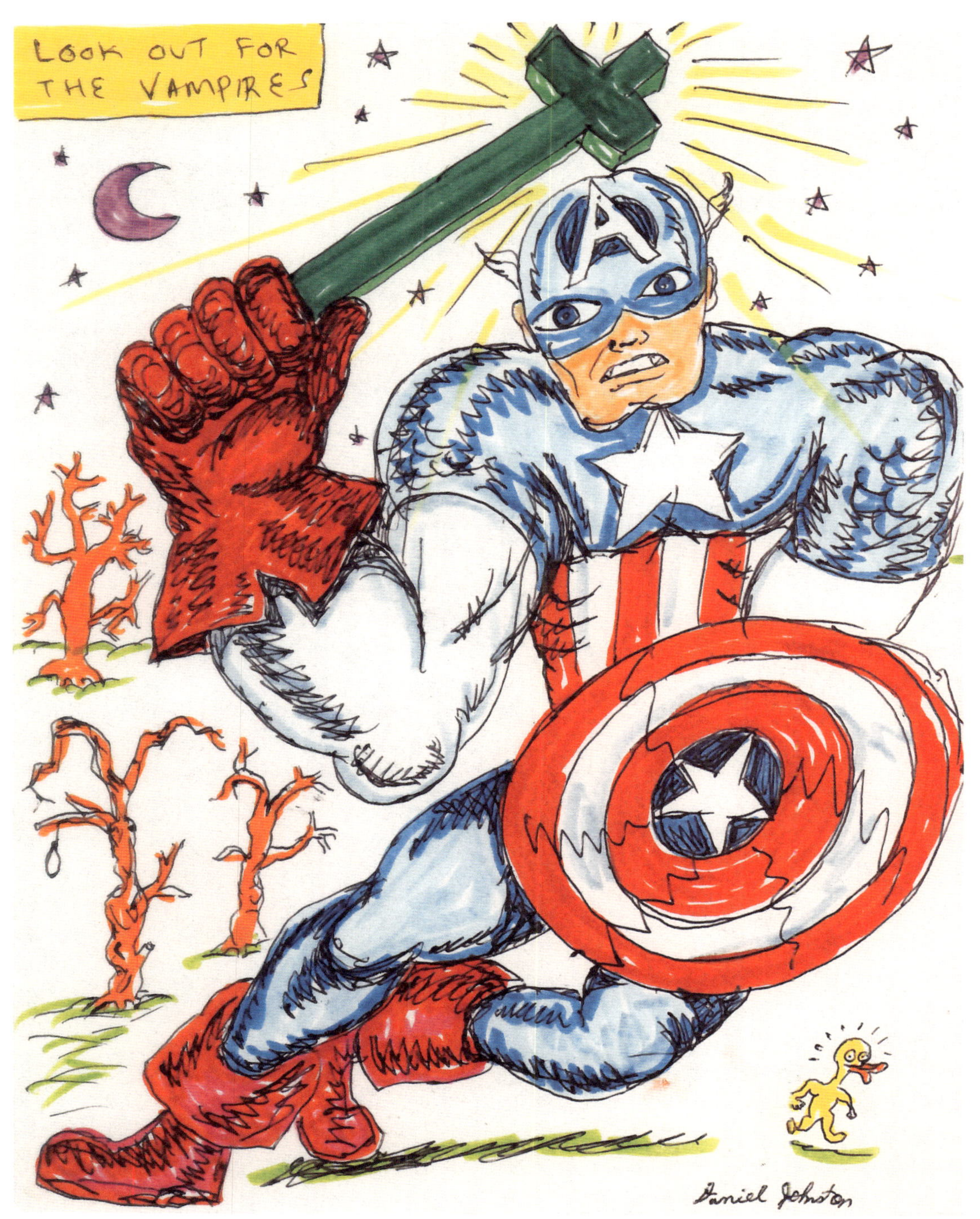

Look Out for the Vampires

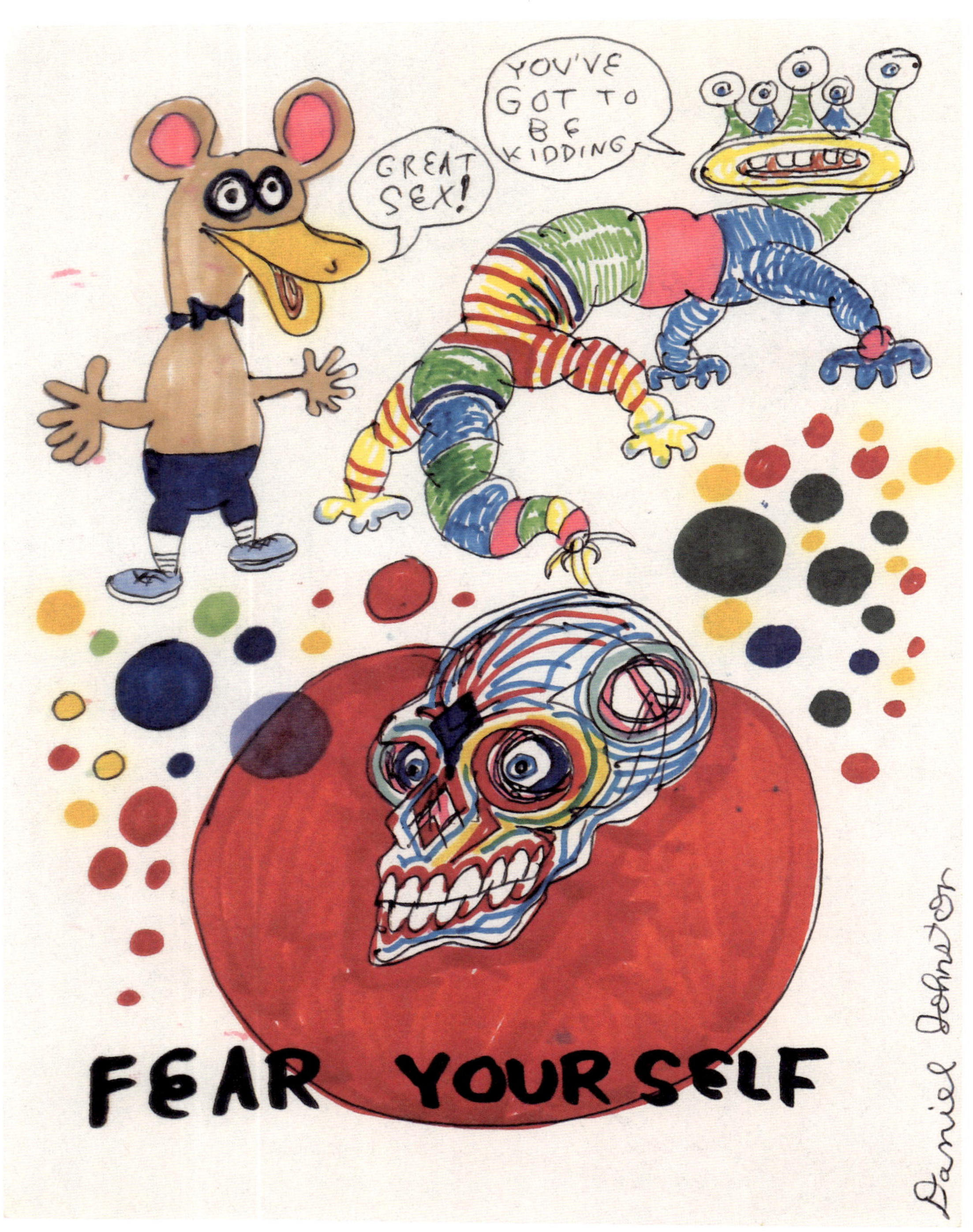

Fear Yourself (You've Got to Be Kidding)

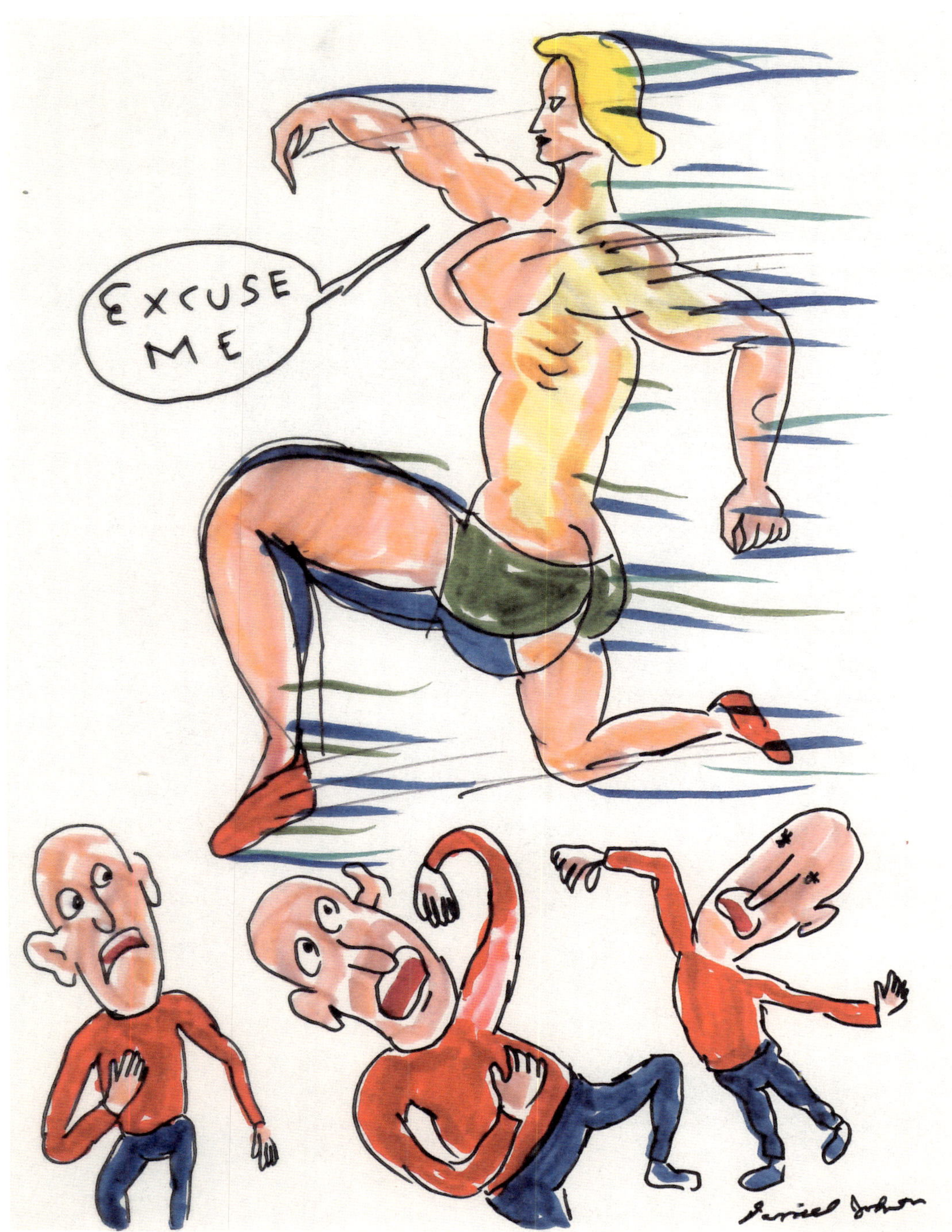

Excuse Me

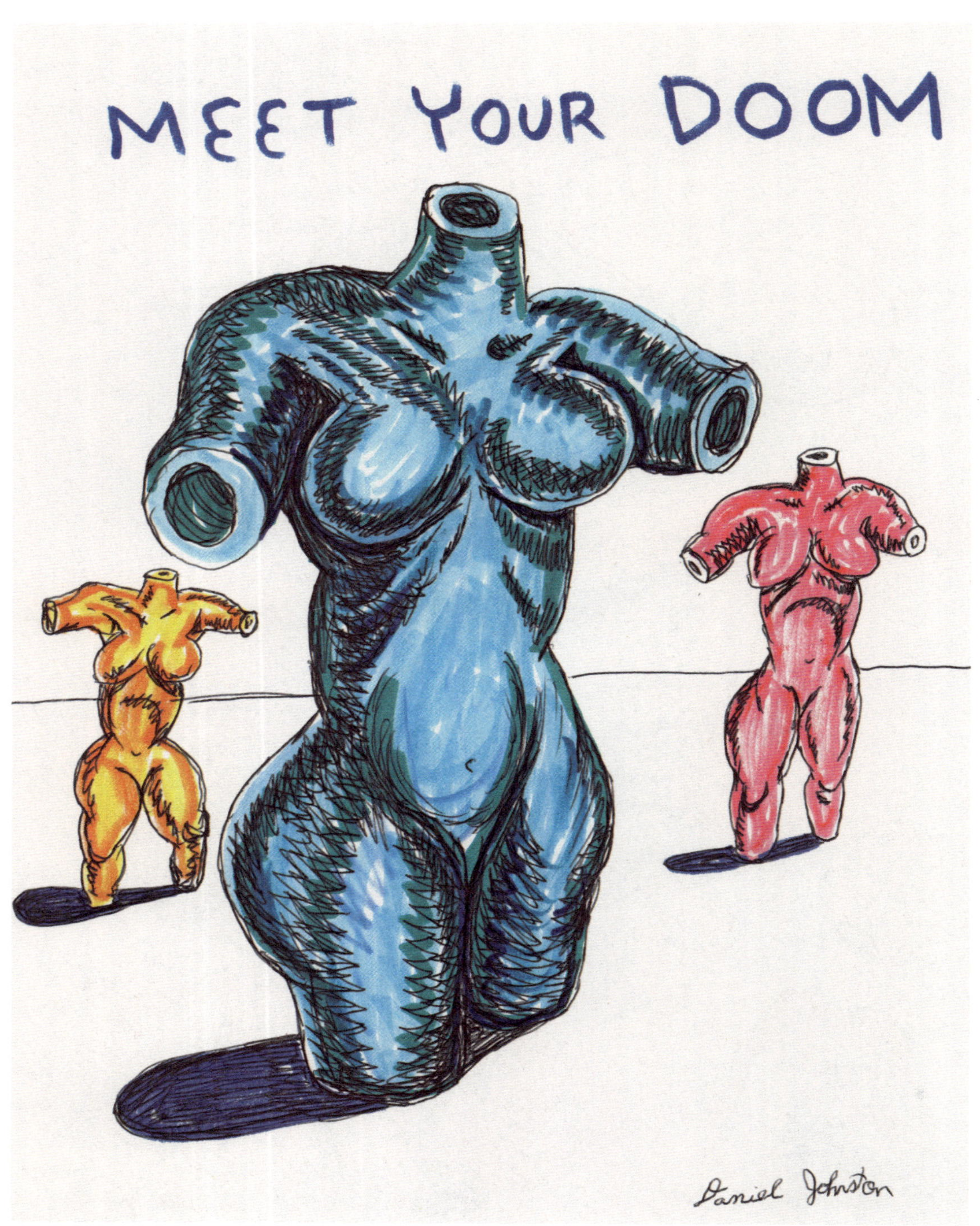

Meet Your Doom

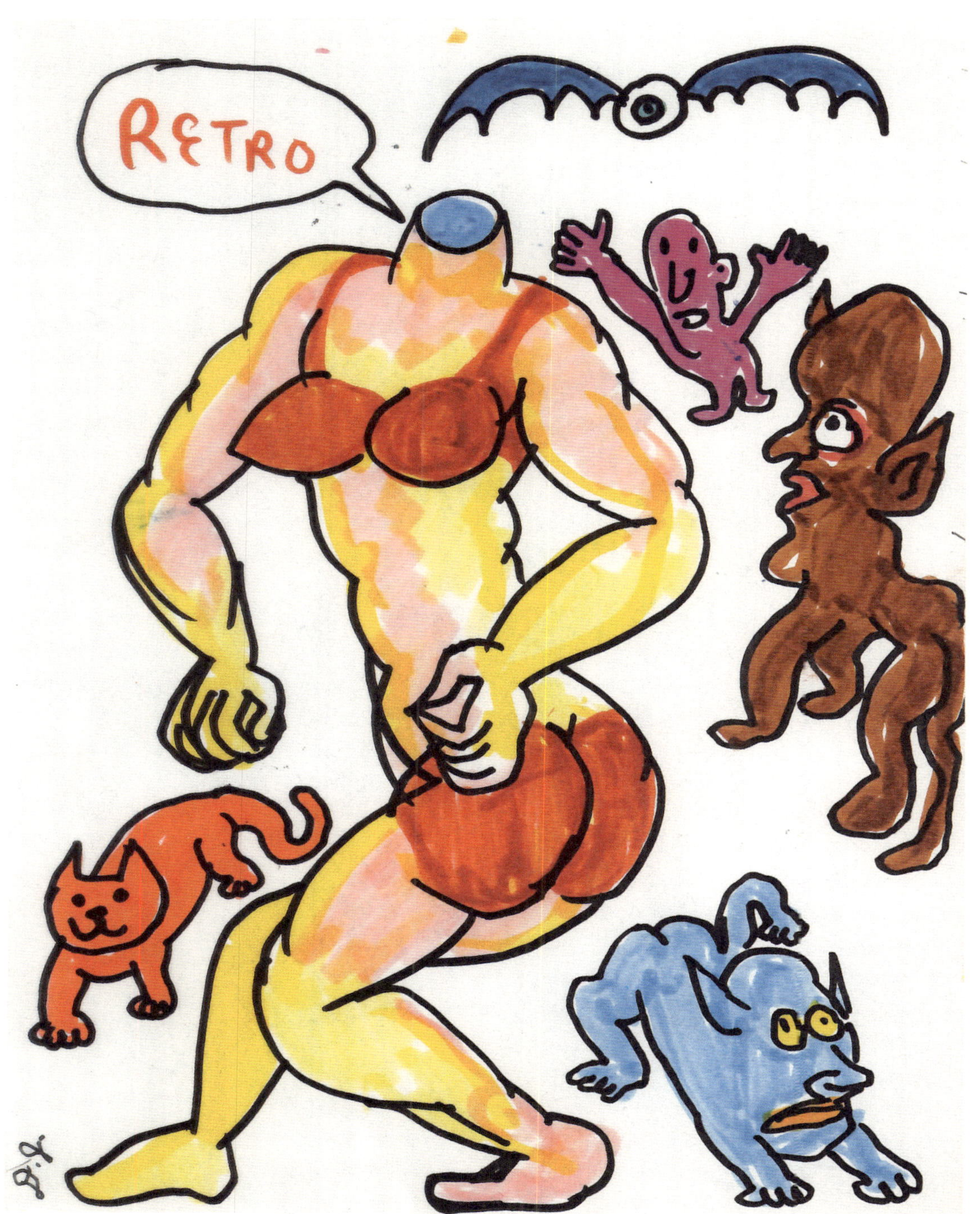

Retro

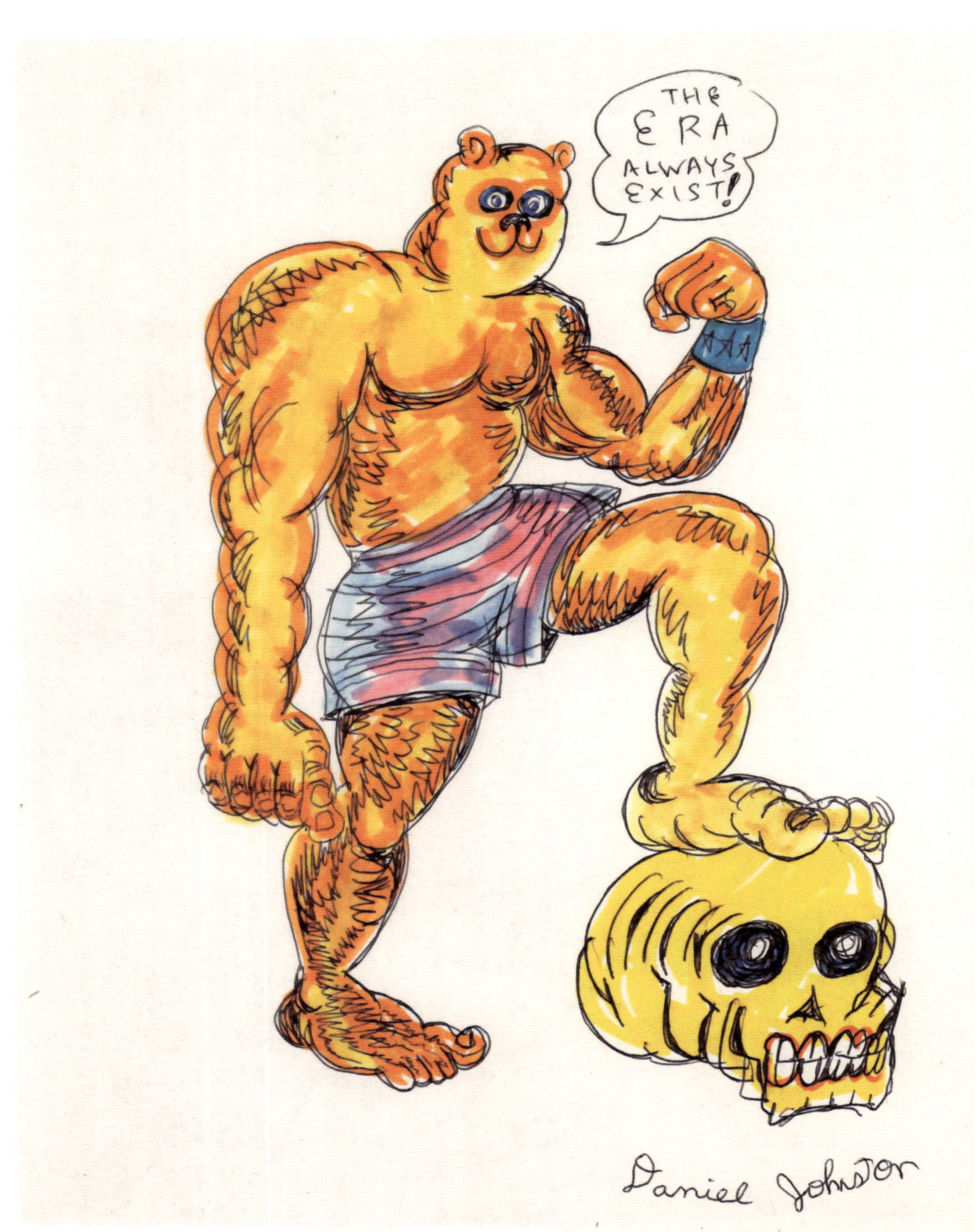

The Era Always Exist!

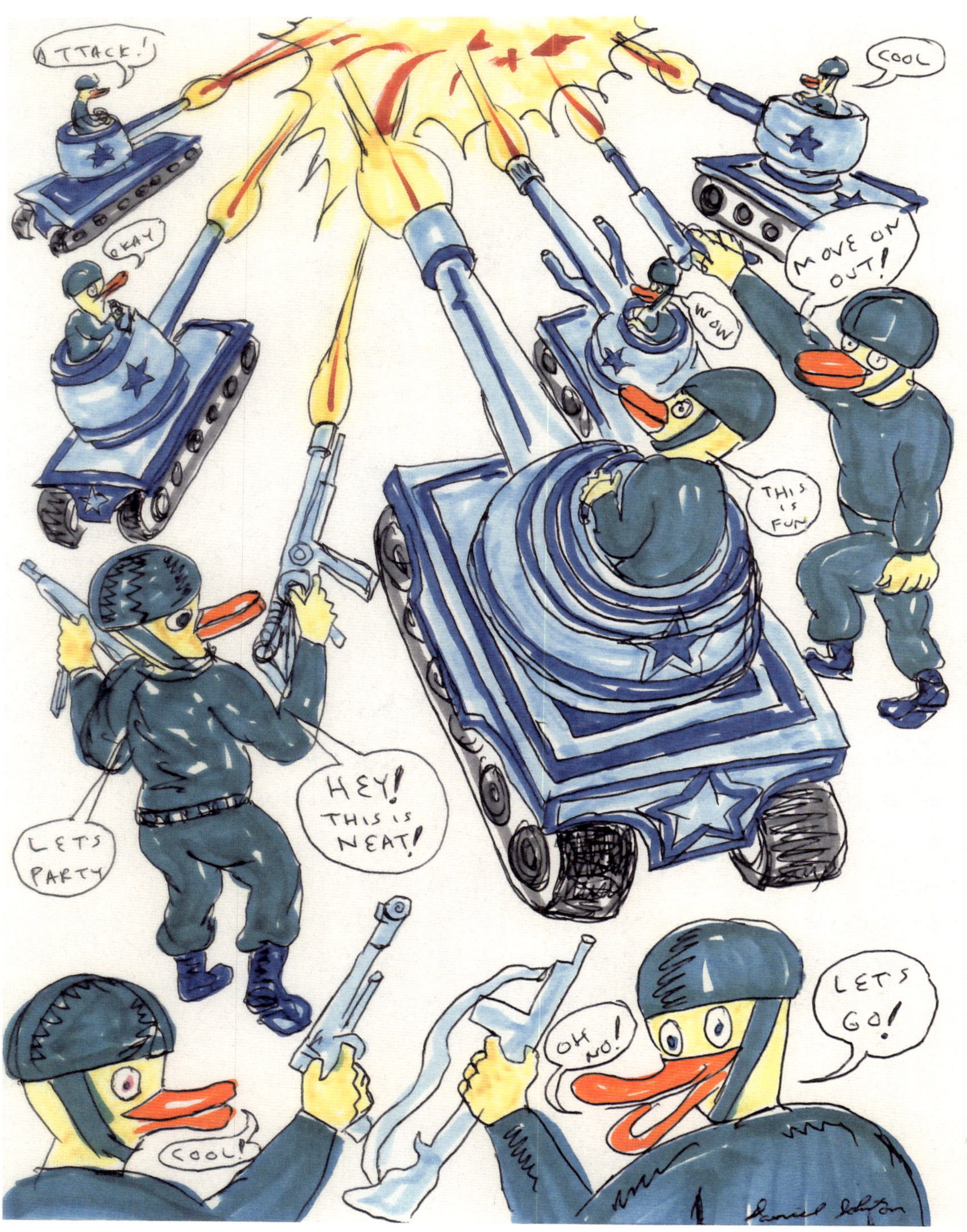
ATTACK!
COOL
OKAY
MOVE ON OUT!
WOW
THIS IS FUN
HEY! THIS IS NEAT!
LET'S PARTY
OH NO!
LET'S GO!
COOL!

Let's Party

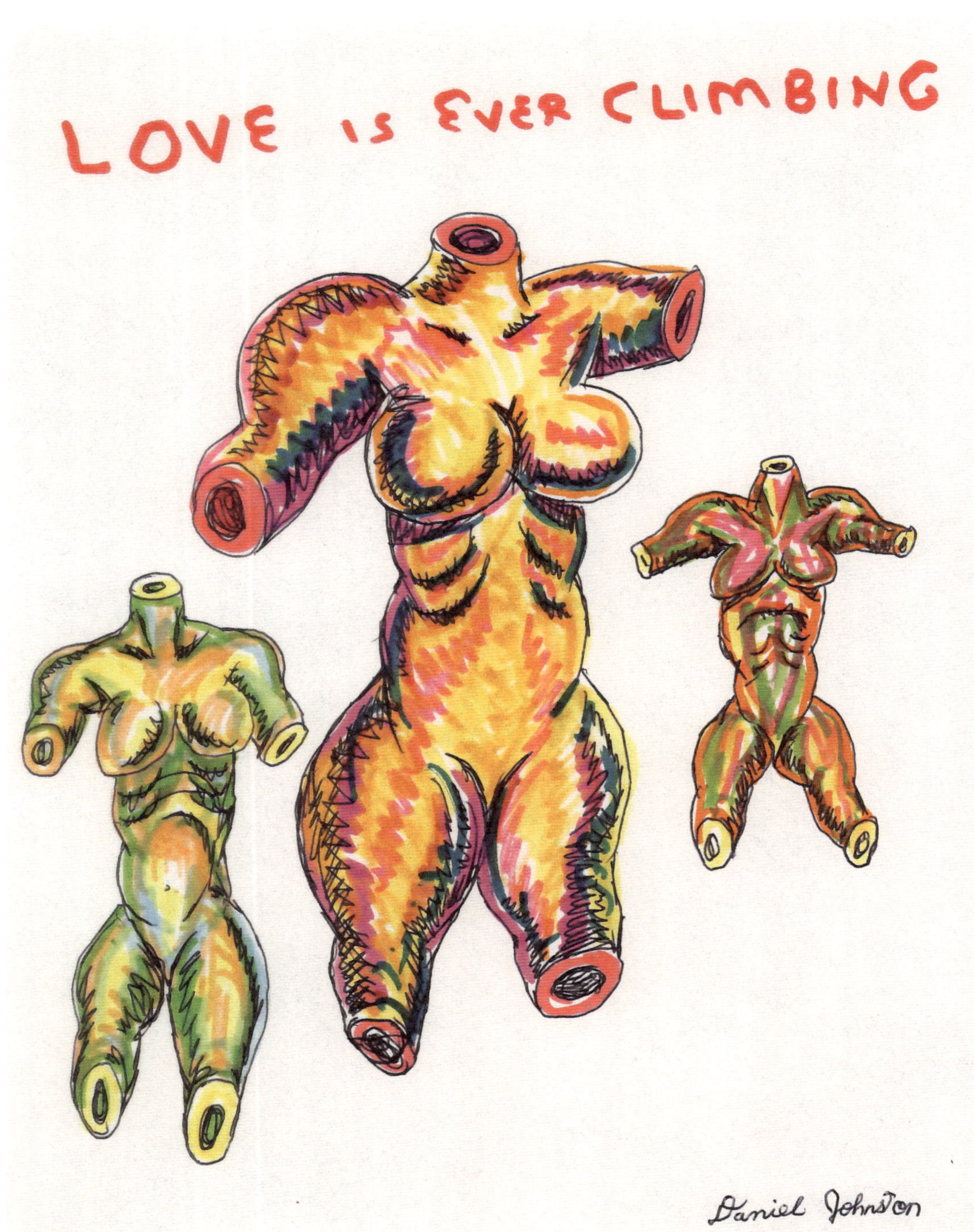

Love Is Ever Climbing

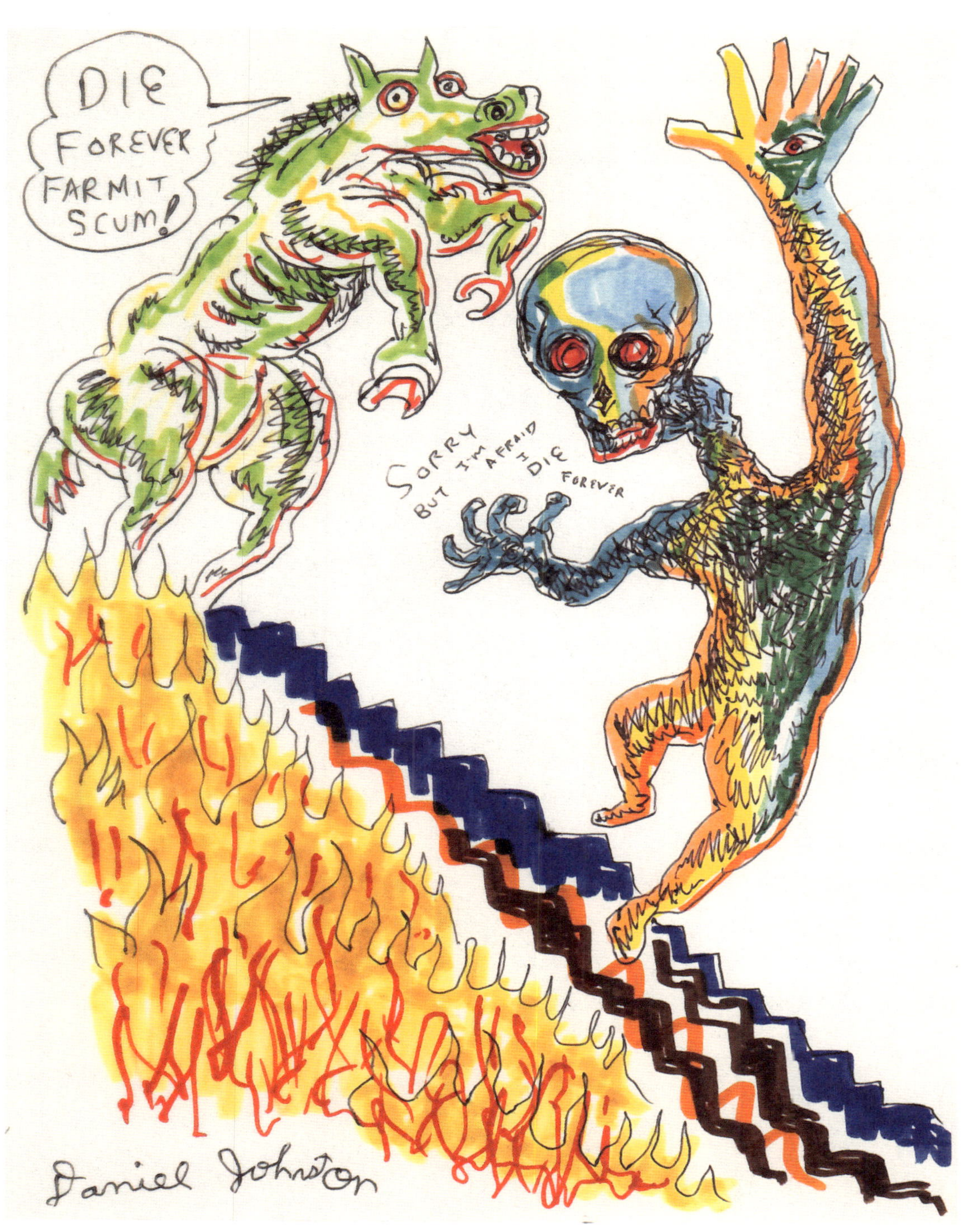
DIE FOREVER FARMIT SCUM!
SORRY BUT I'M AFRAID I DIE FOREVER
Daniel Johnston

Die Forever

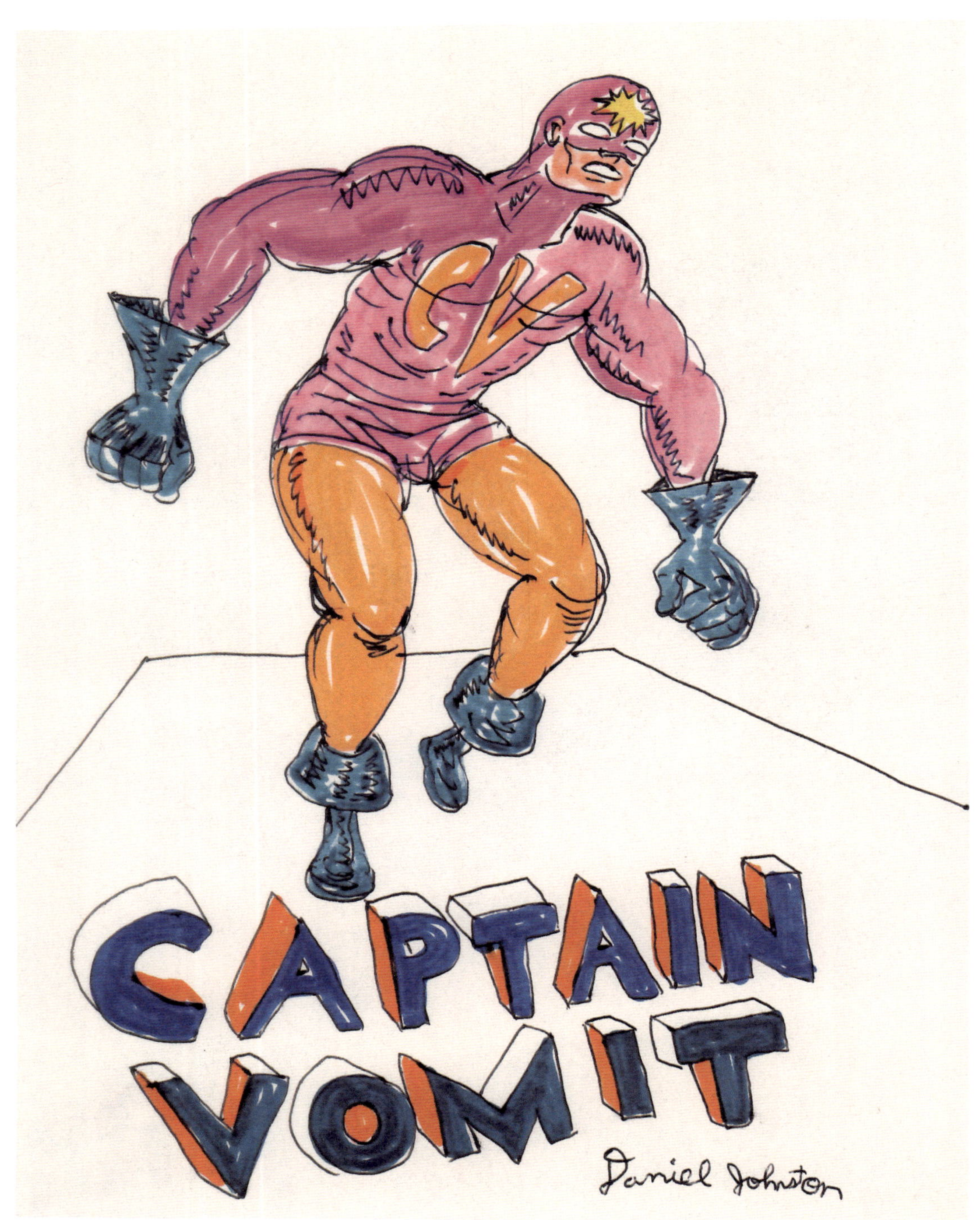

Captain Vomit

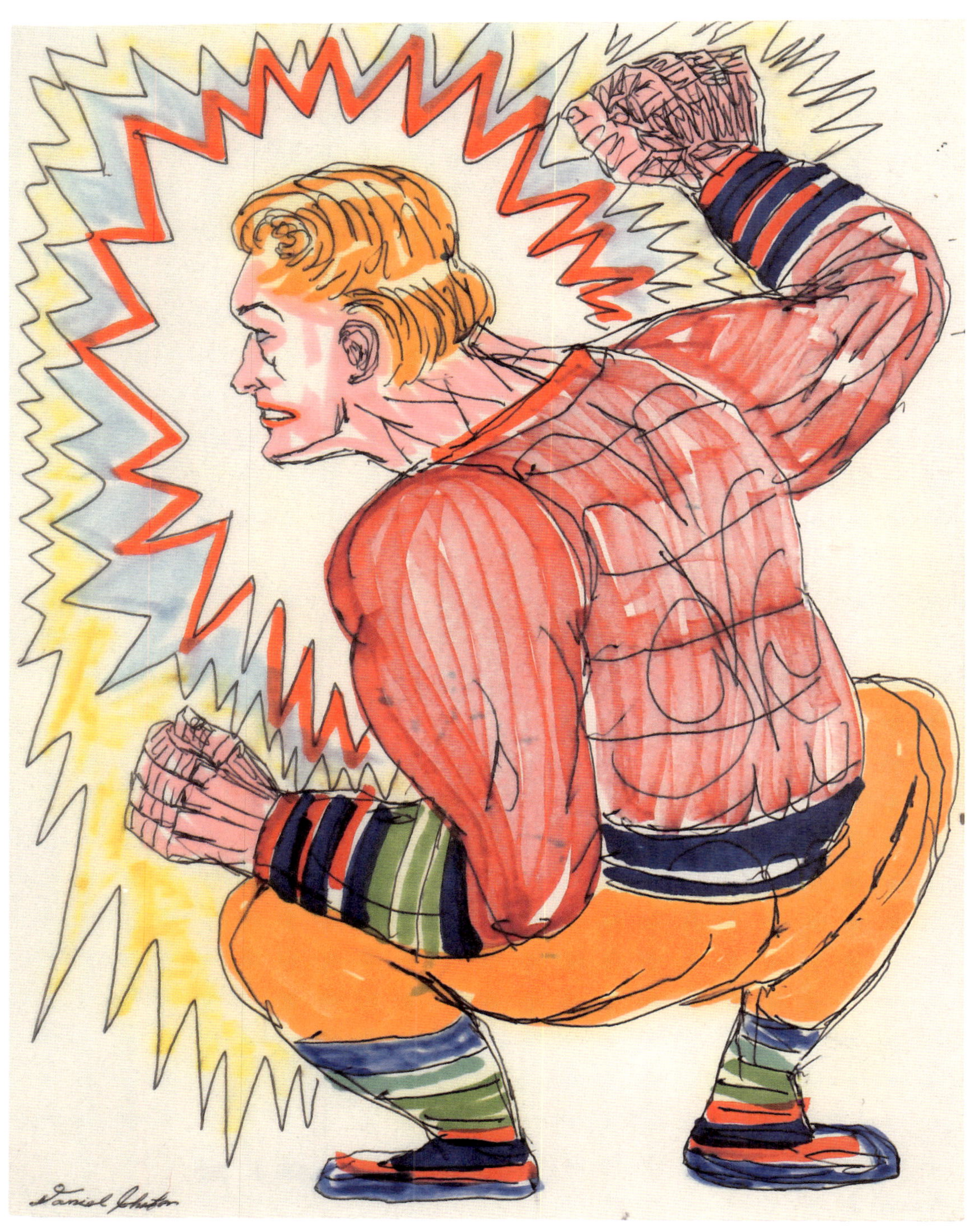

Untitled (Surprised Red Sweater)

Coming from a puritanical background, I was always drawn toward mischievous, rebellious stories like the one from *The Devil and Daniel Johnston*. "You're an unprofitable servant!" Mrs. Johnston's words rang in my ears and bounced around my skull, as if they had come from the mouth of my own mother, a sentiment she had expressed to me many times throughout my childhood.

Daniel was the kind of special that we wrongfully assign to any person that finds themselves on a stage. As artists, I believe, we all have that thought, when too often we are only in a war for acknowledgment and attention. Only a few of us have a light that's not angled in our direction; only a few of us defy it as it falls on us.

Daniel simply was and is: he did it because if he didn't, he would atrophy. His obsession with the beyond was sincere.

There was no symmetry in his relationship with praise, and no symmetry in his relationship with the world, and as a result he found himself suspended in the kind of air we search for our whole lives.

I was introduced to the album *Hi, How Are You* some years ago and was hyper-fixated on it for months. I bought drawings, watched interviews, anything to bring me closer to his freedom. At one point, I found "True Love Will Find You in the End." I will never forget how I felt then, awe and jealousy. It was a song that had to exist, and he was the rightful custodian. The clear Beatles influence without compromising his identity—it just transported me to high school when I first heard the Beatles, like seeing in color for the first time.

The comic-book energy of the visual art was so undeniably him but also so strongly nostalgic. But you got the feeling while looking at it that nostalgia wasn't his intention when making it—an unintentional by-product. Strong feelings emerged when you saw it. It all felt very impulsive: the characters were interacting with each other, but there didn't appear to be a grand narrative uniting them all. Instead, it appeared to be a moment in many separate, complex lives: all these different characters, unrelated, crossing paths in this exact moment on this piece of paper. It made you curious as to what his thoughts looked like. As I went through his work, it became clear that there was so much beauty and pleasantness, along with great darkness and existential dread. One can only imagine.

Artists like Daniel come once in all lifetimes. He won't return, and that's the beauty: the music encourages us to continue. Lyrics so bare, pictures so childlike but assertive in any room. Art that is unconcerned with commerce. If we listen closely, Daniel will help us return there.

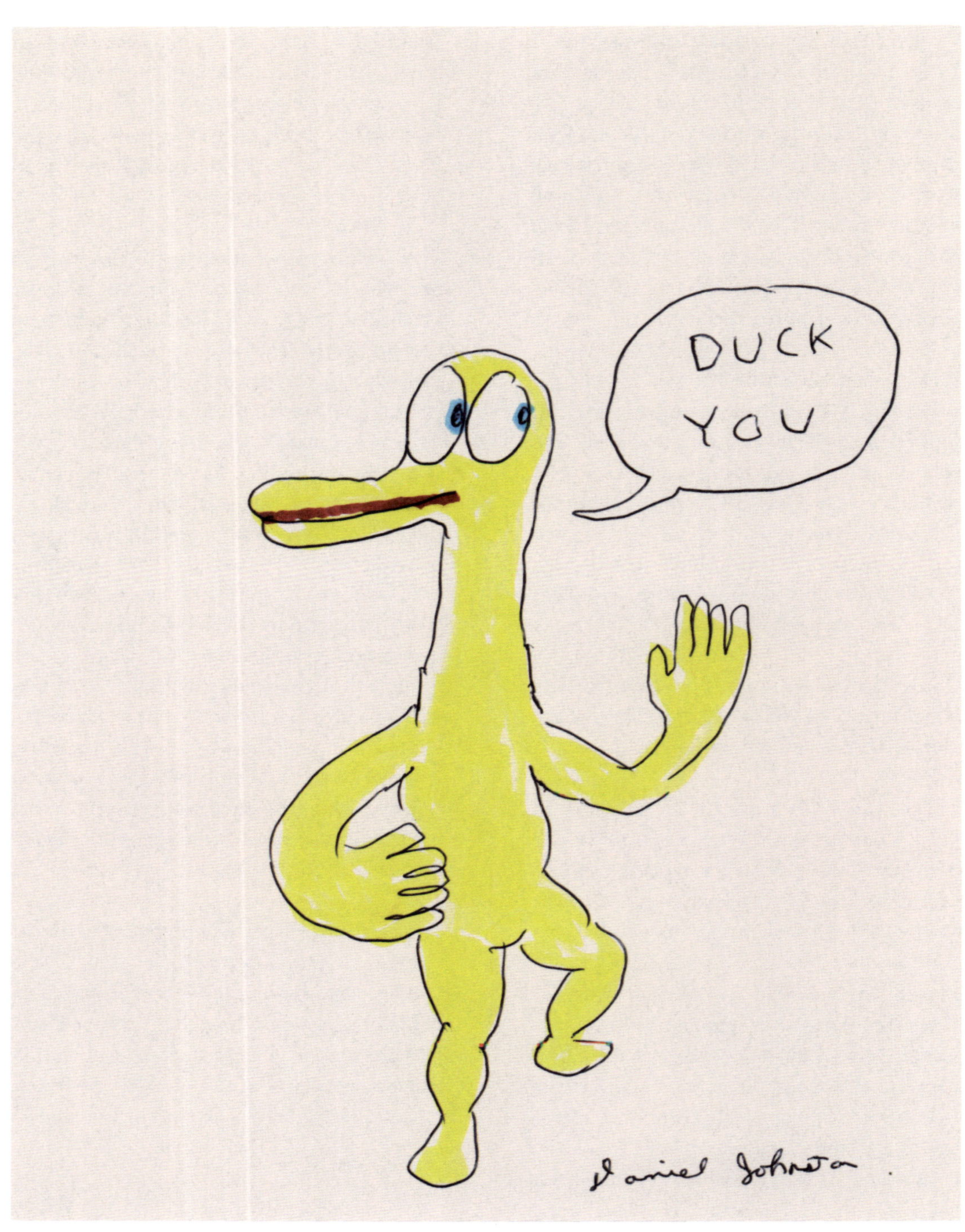

Duck You

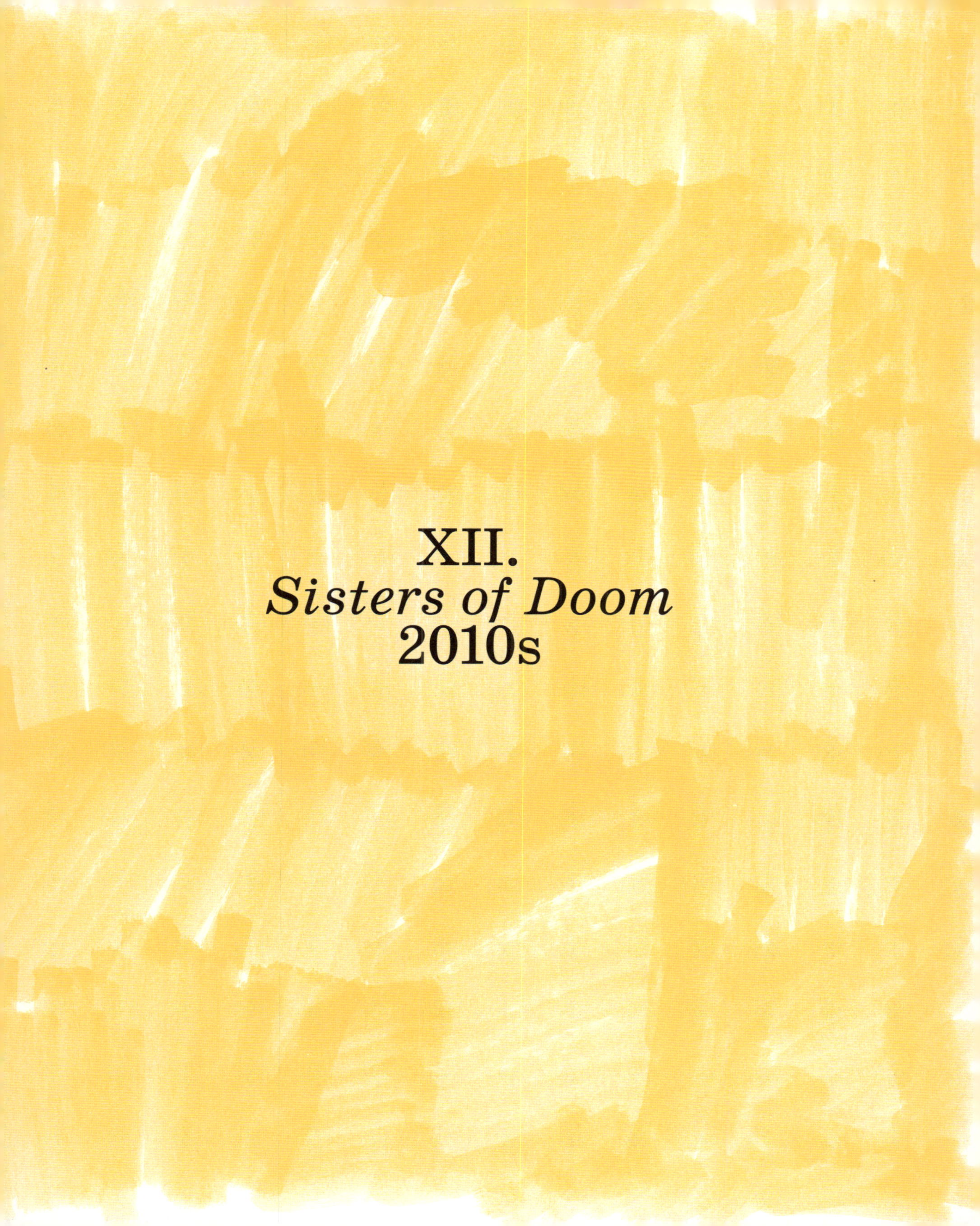

XII.
Sisters of Doom
2010s

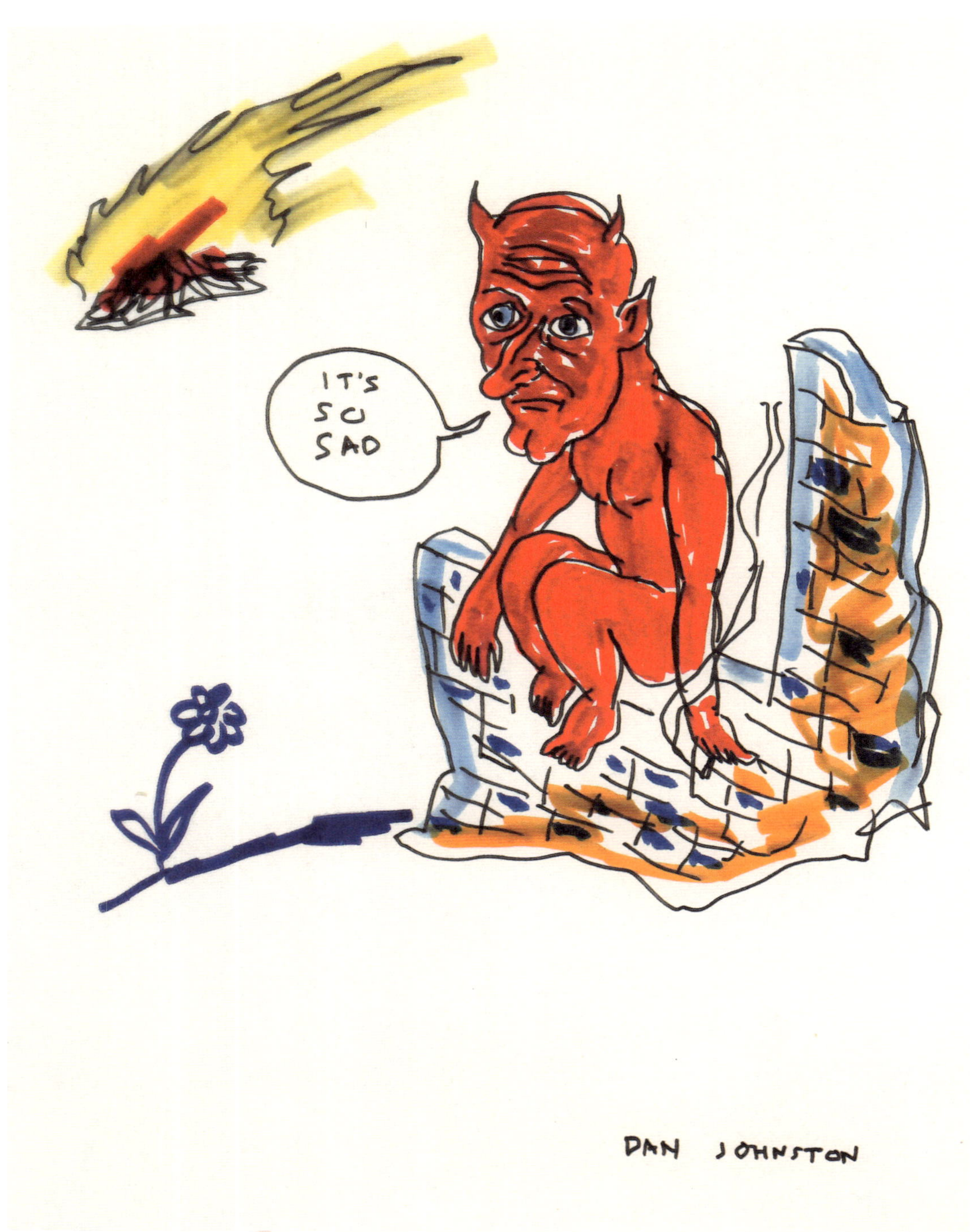

It's So Sad

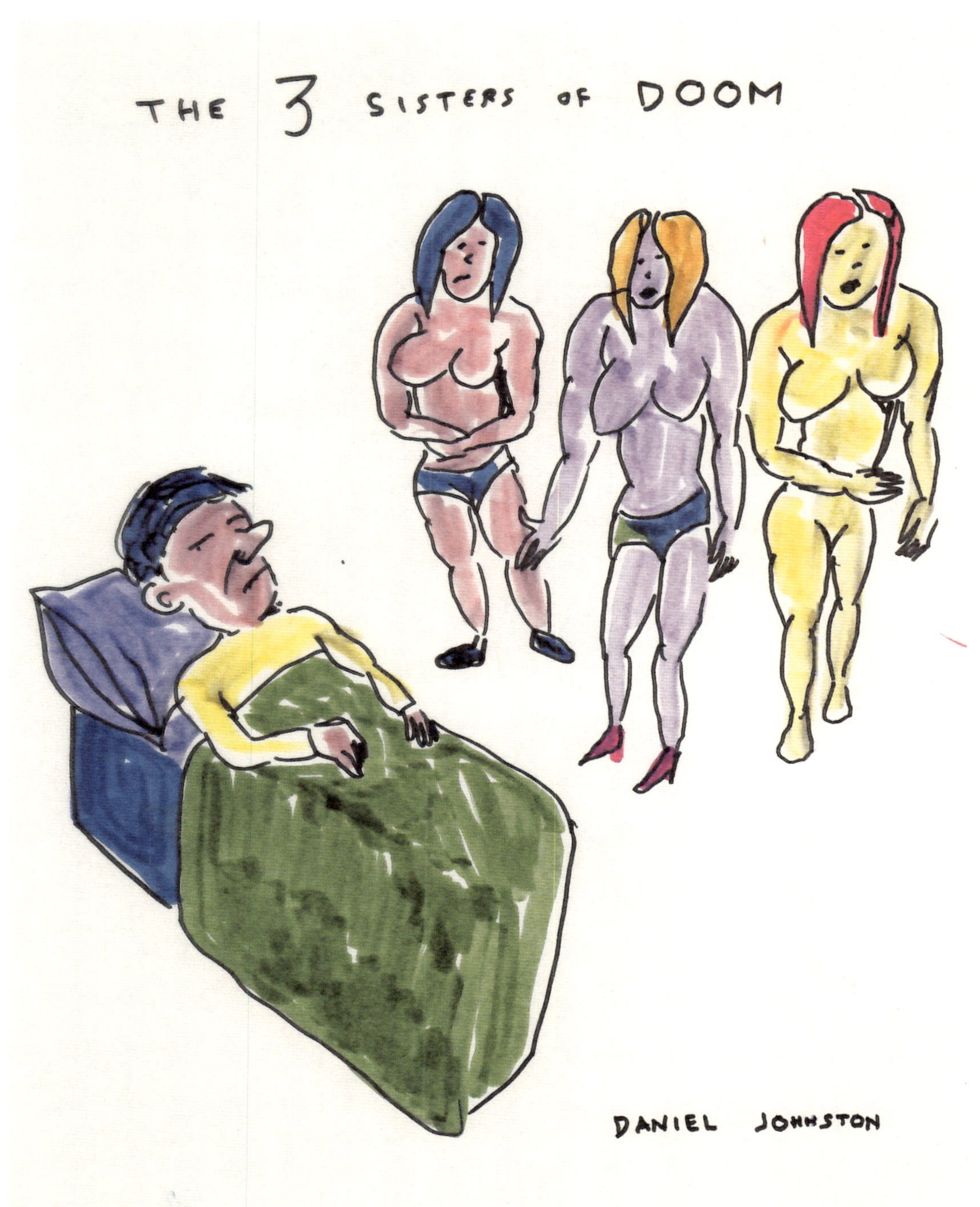

The 3 Sisters of Doom

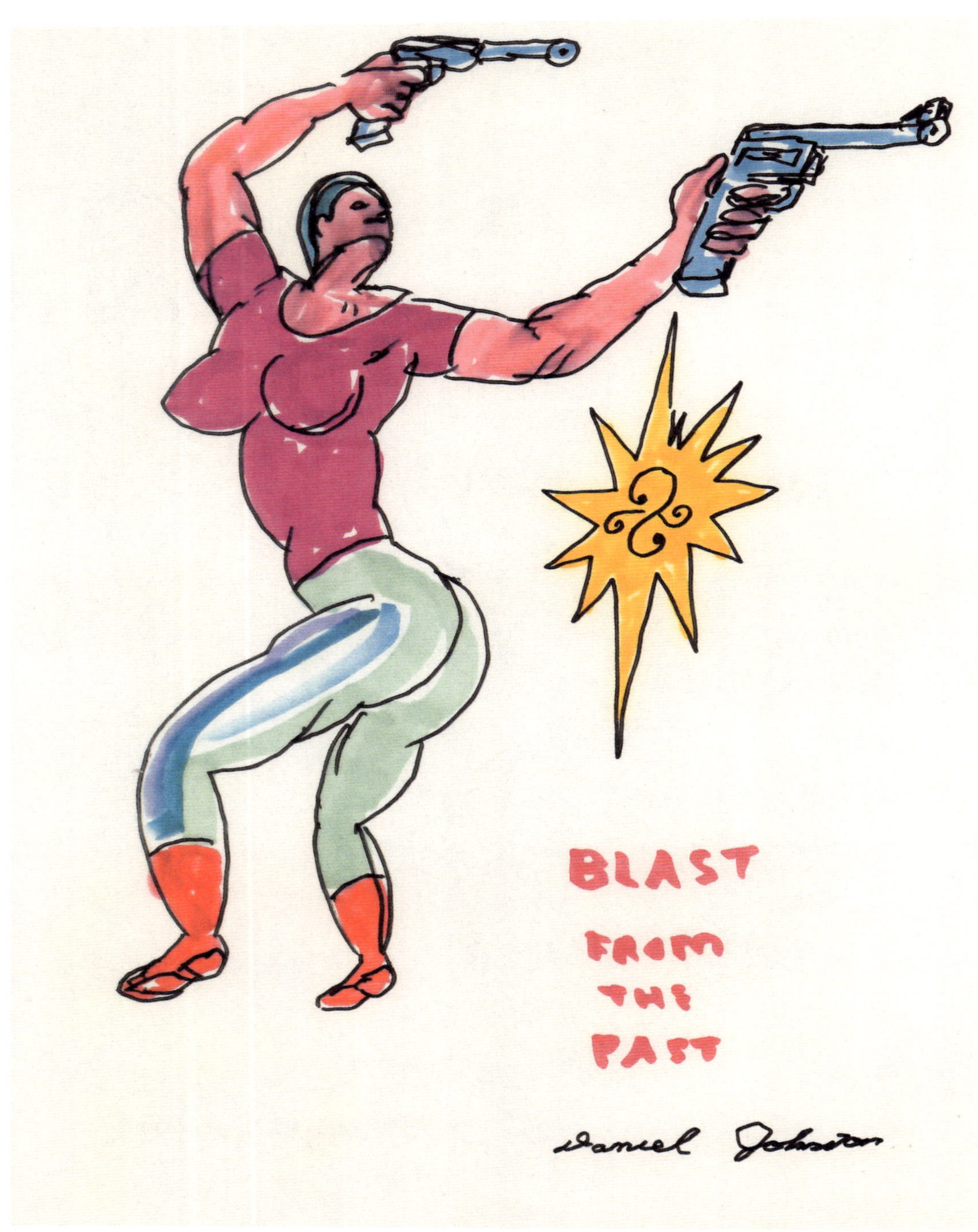

Blast from the Past

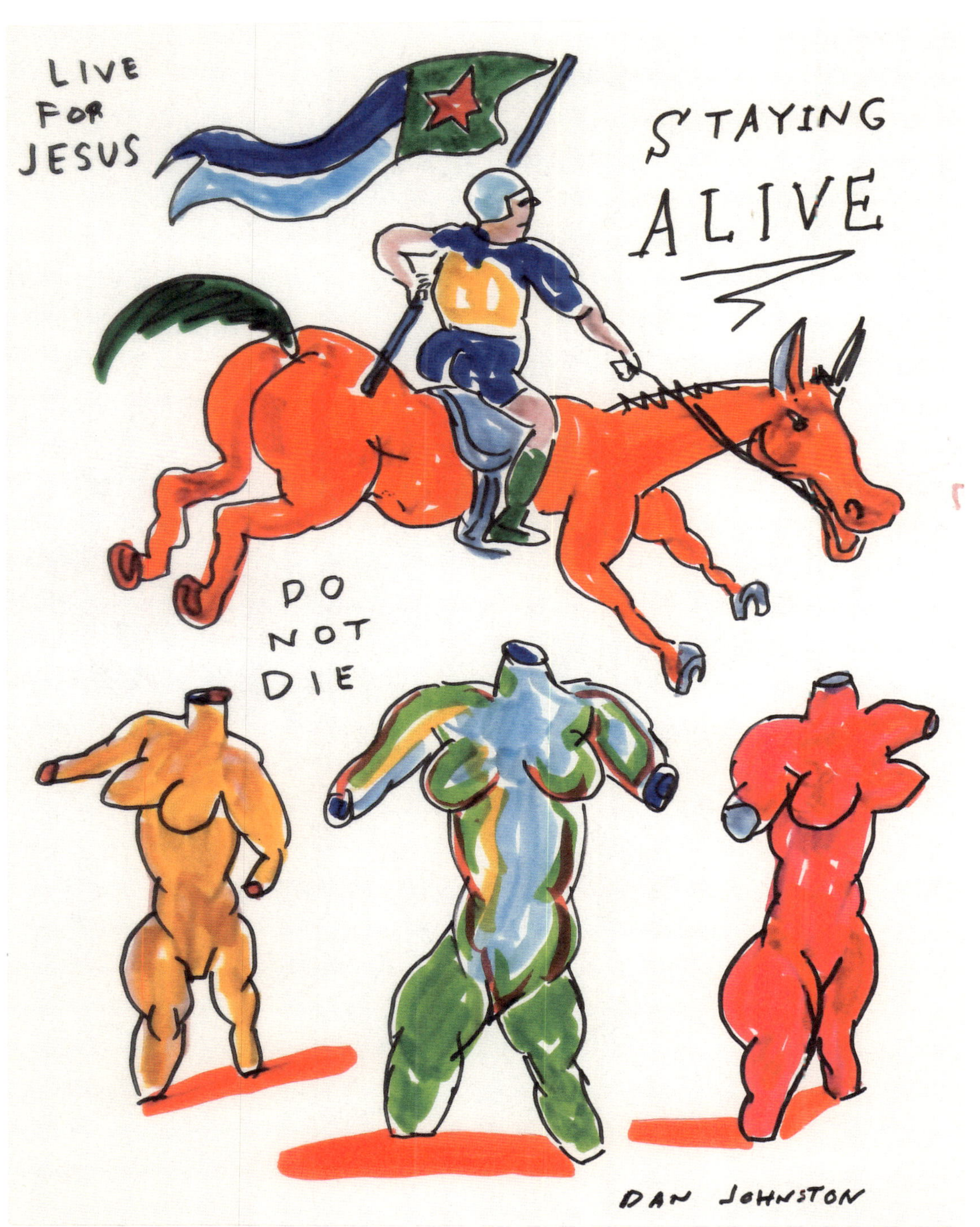

Staying Alive (Do Not Die)

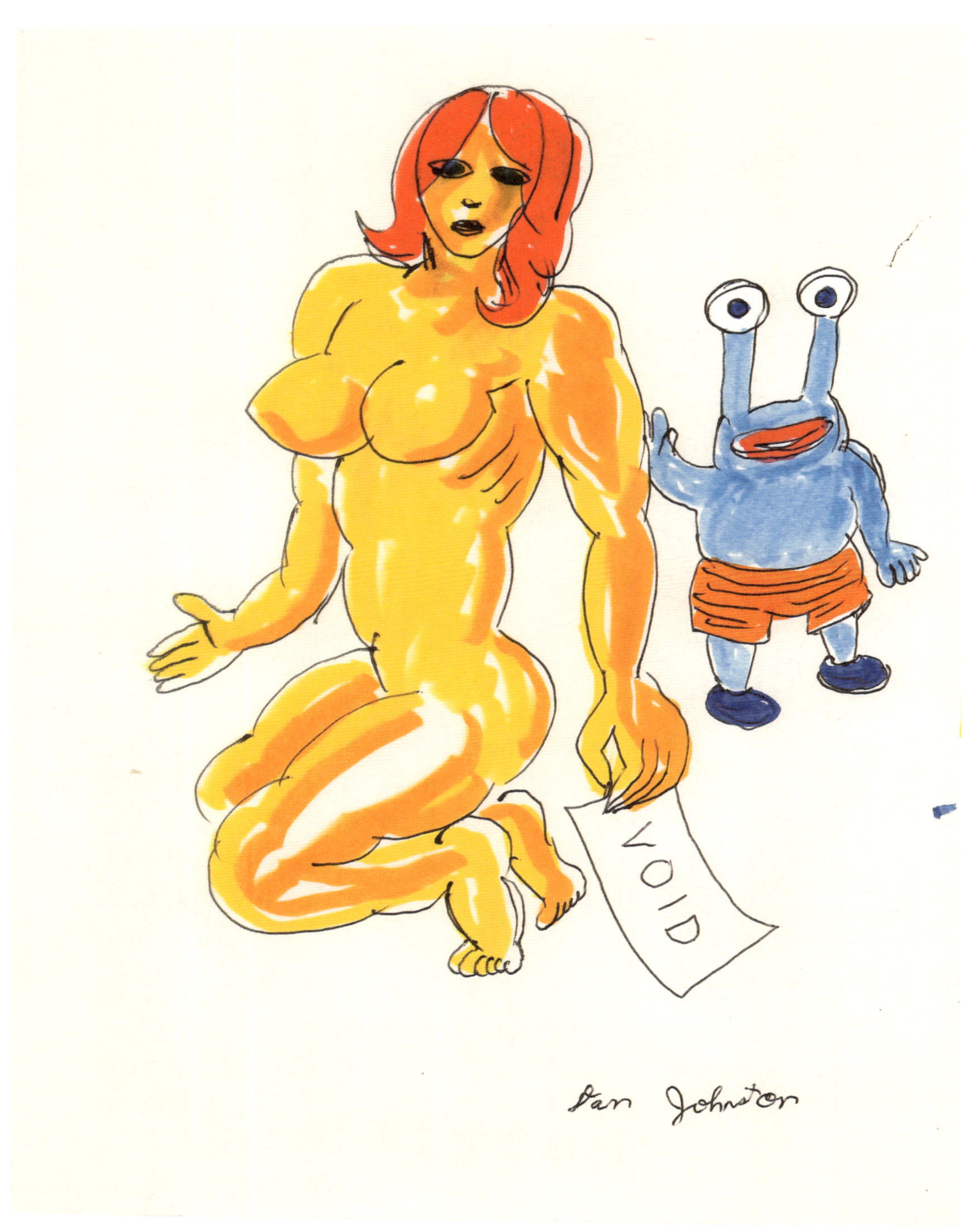

VOID

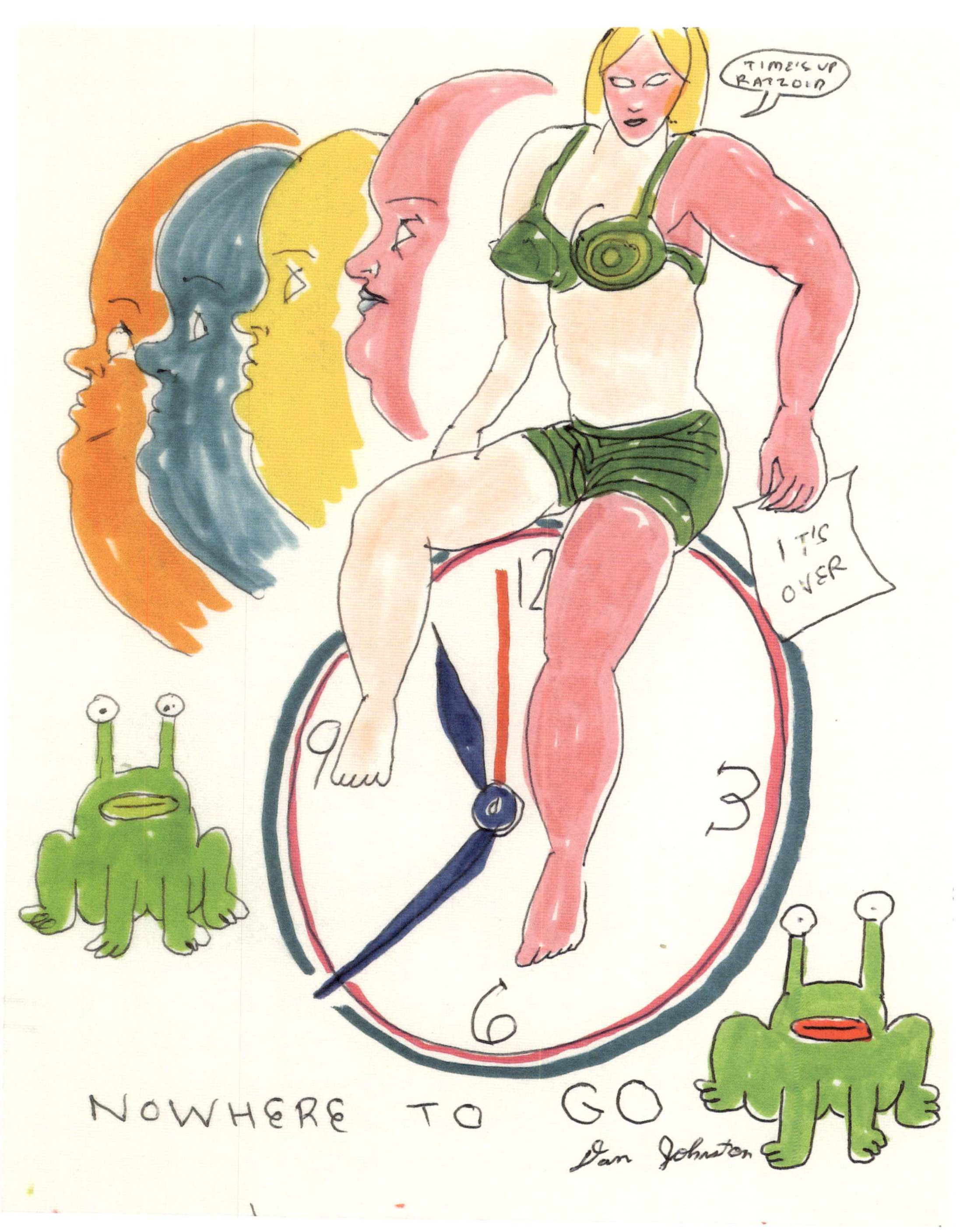

Nowhere to Go (It's Over)

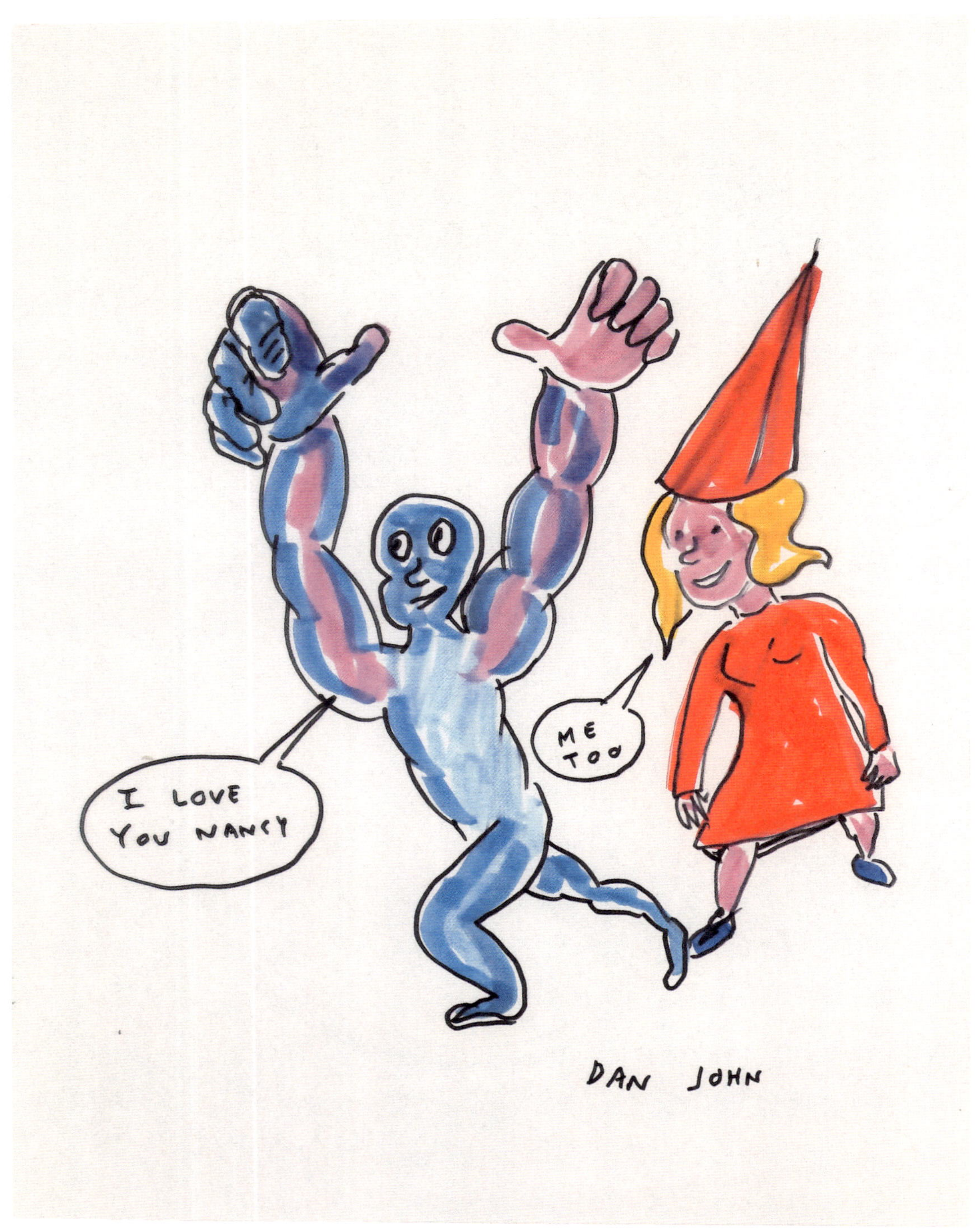

I Love You Nancy

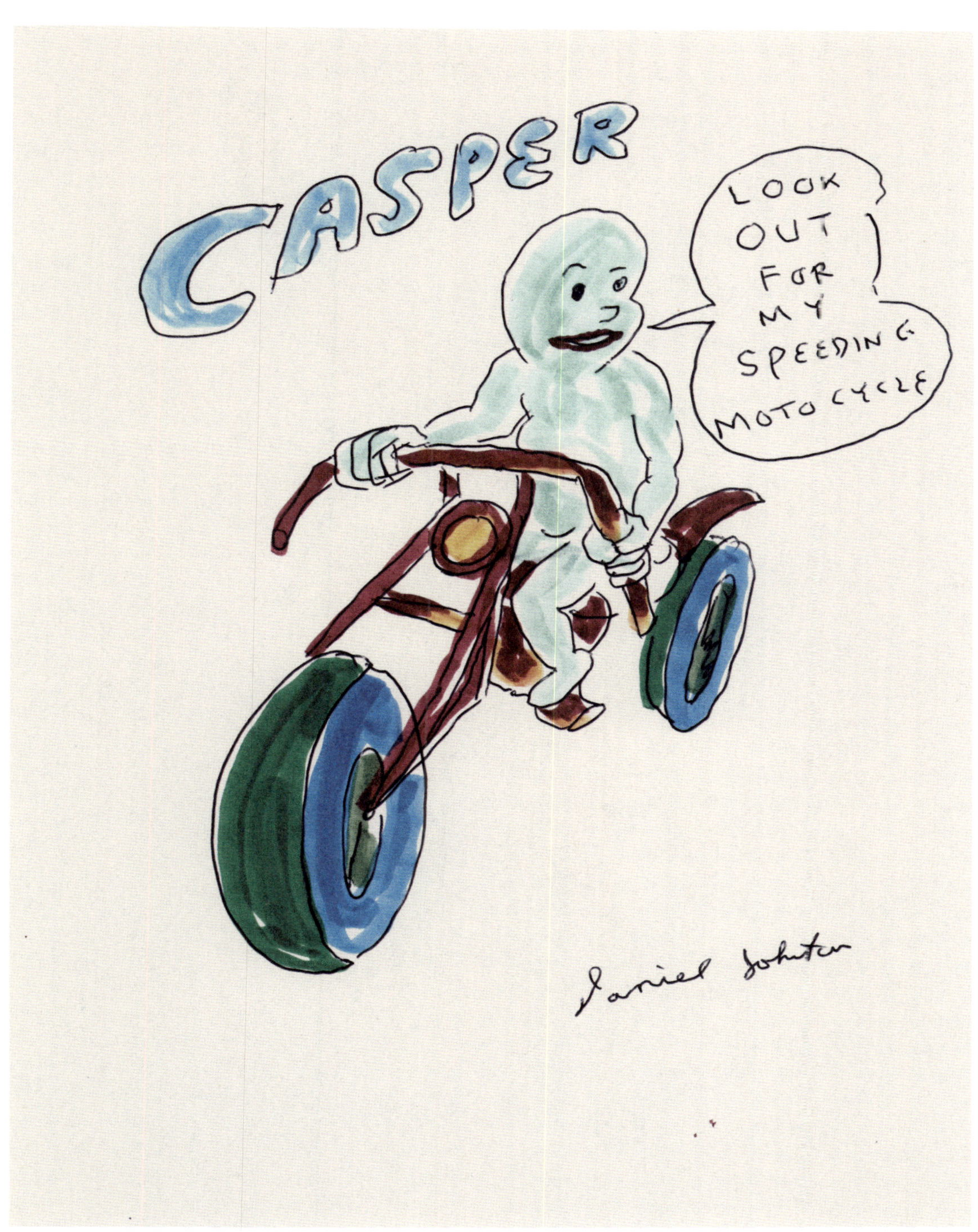

Look Out for My Speeding Motocycle (Casper)

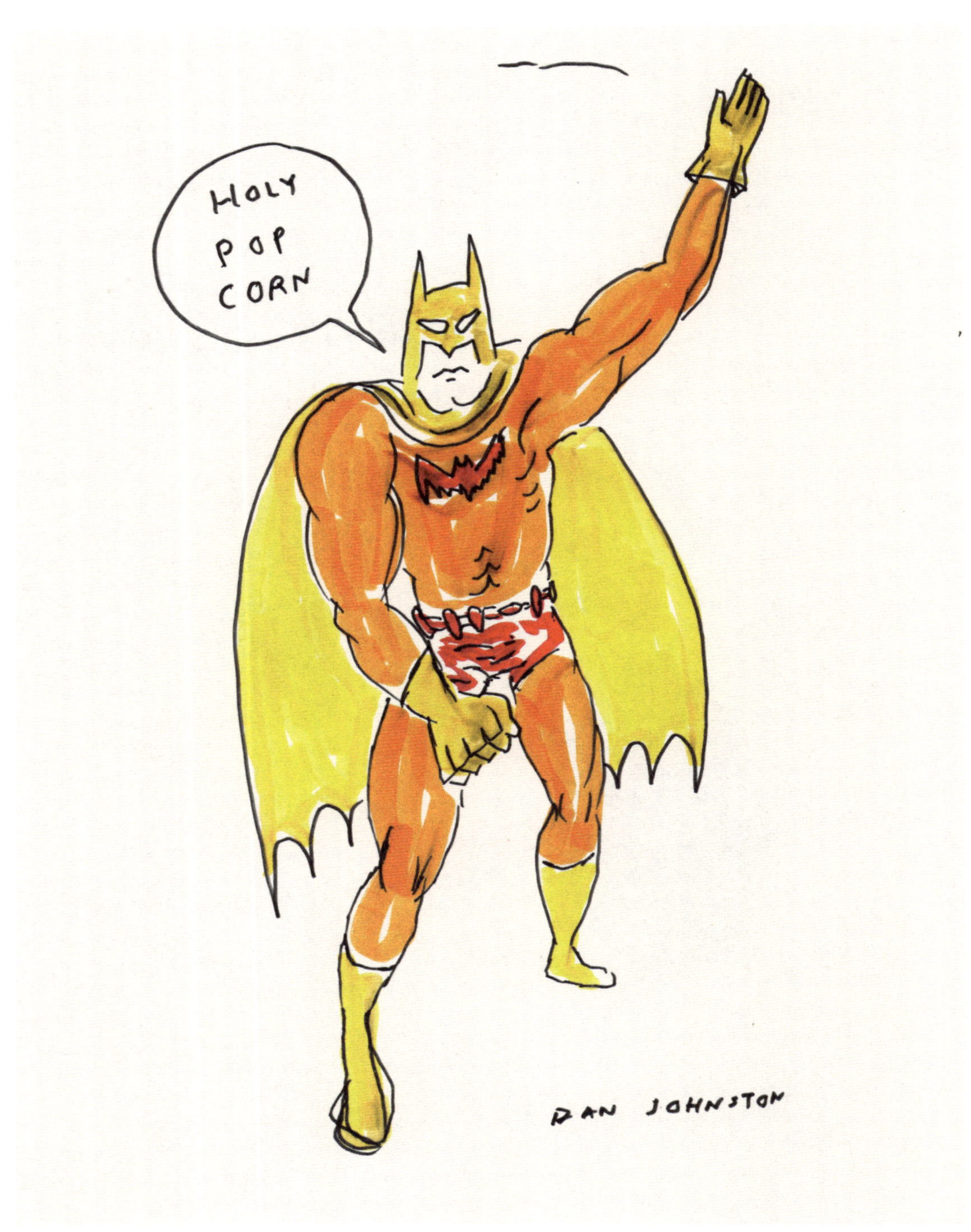

Holy Pop Corn

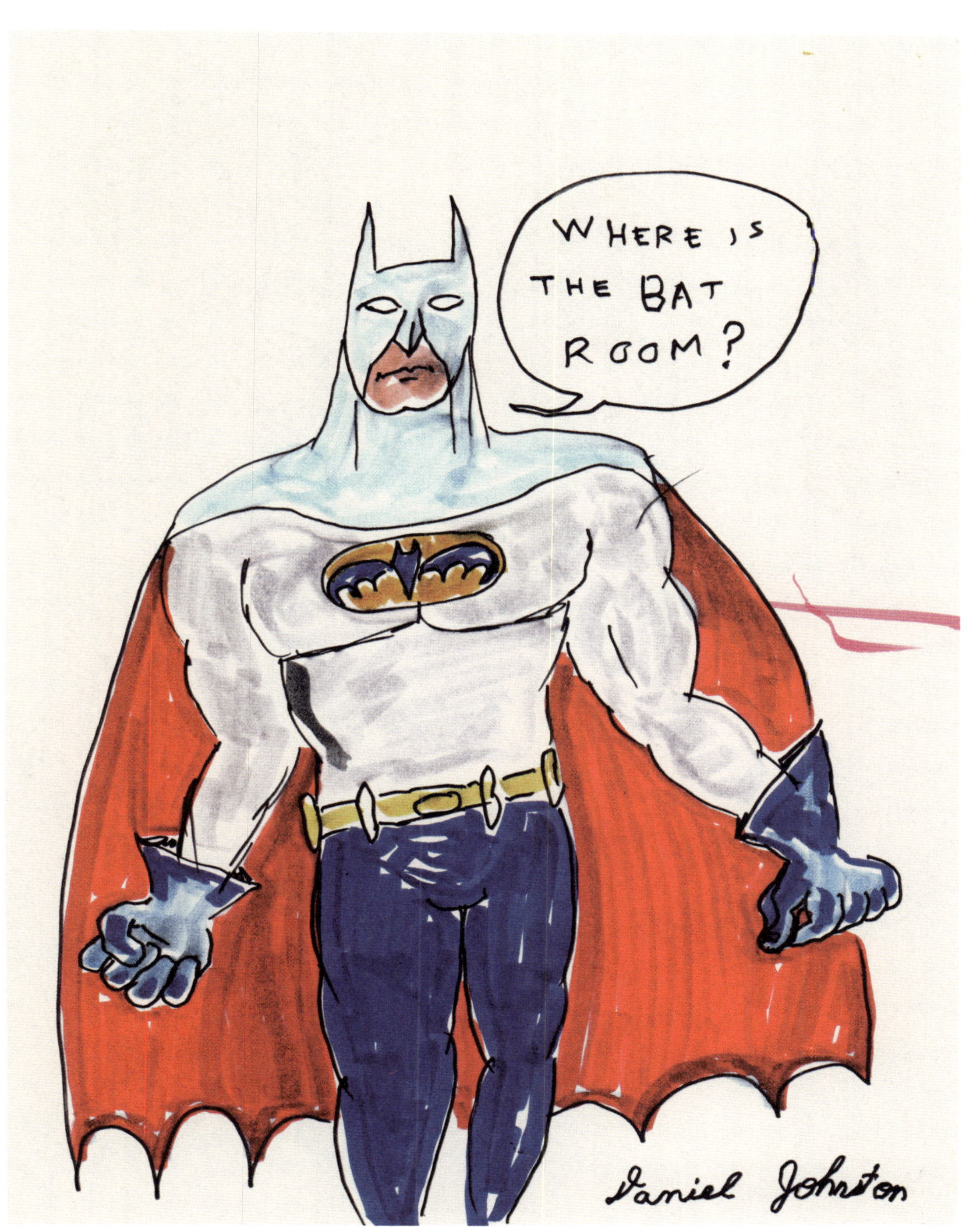

Where Is the Bat Room?

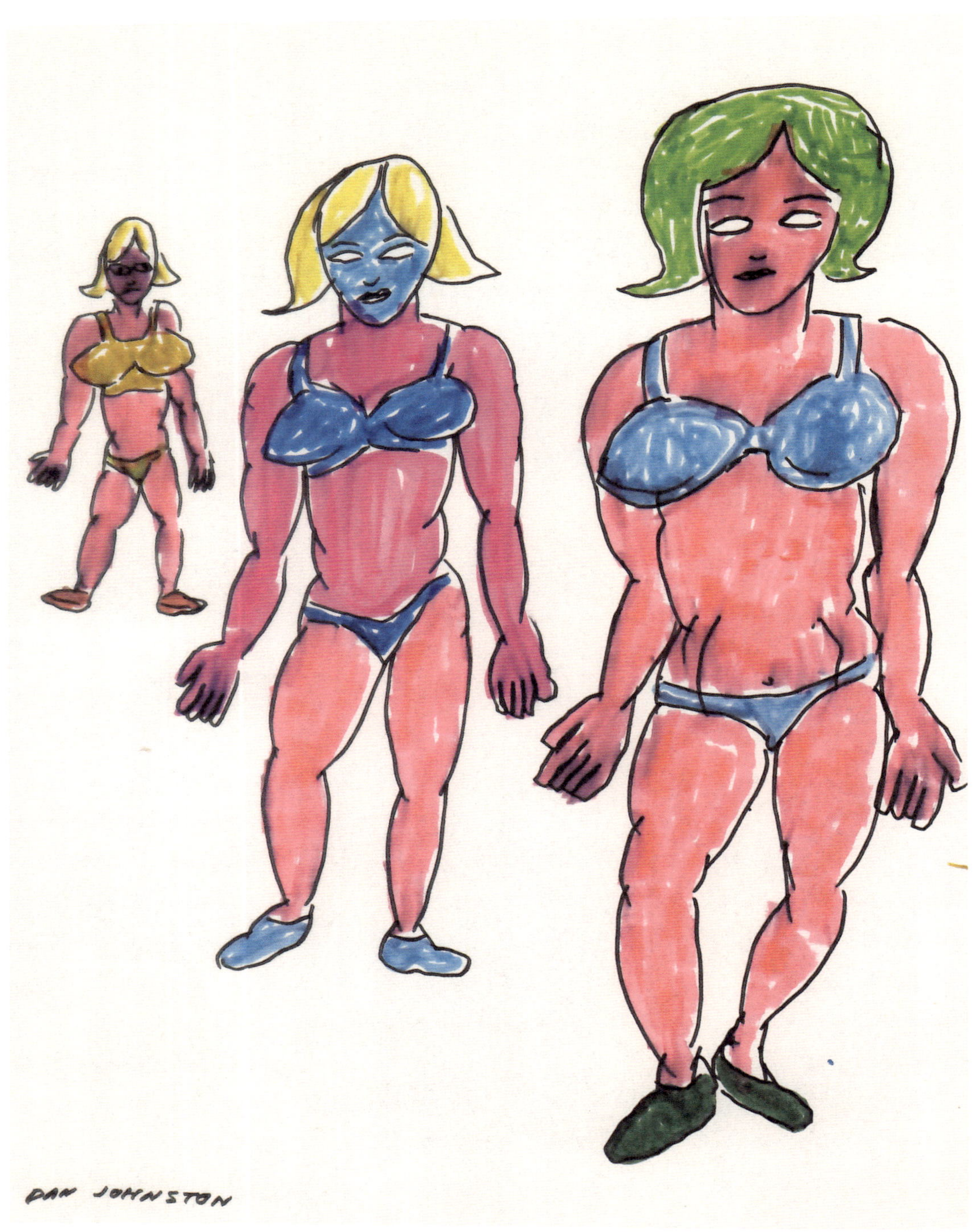

Untitled (Pink Ladies)

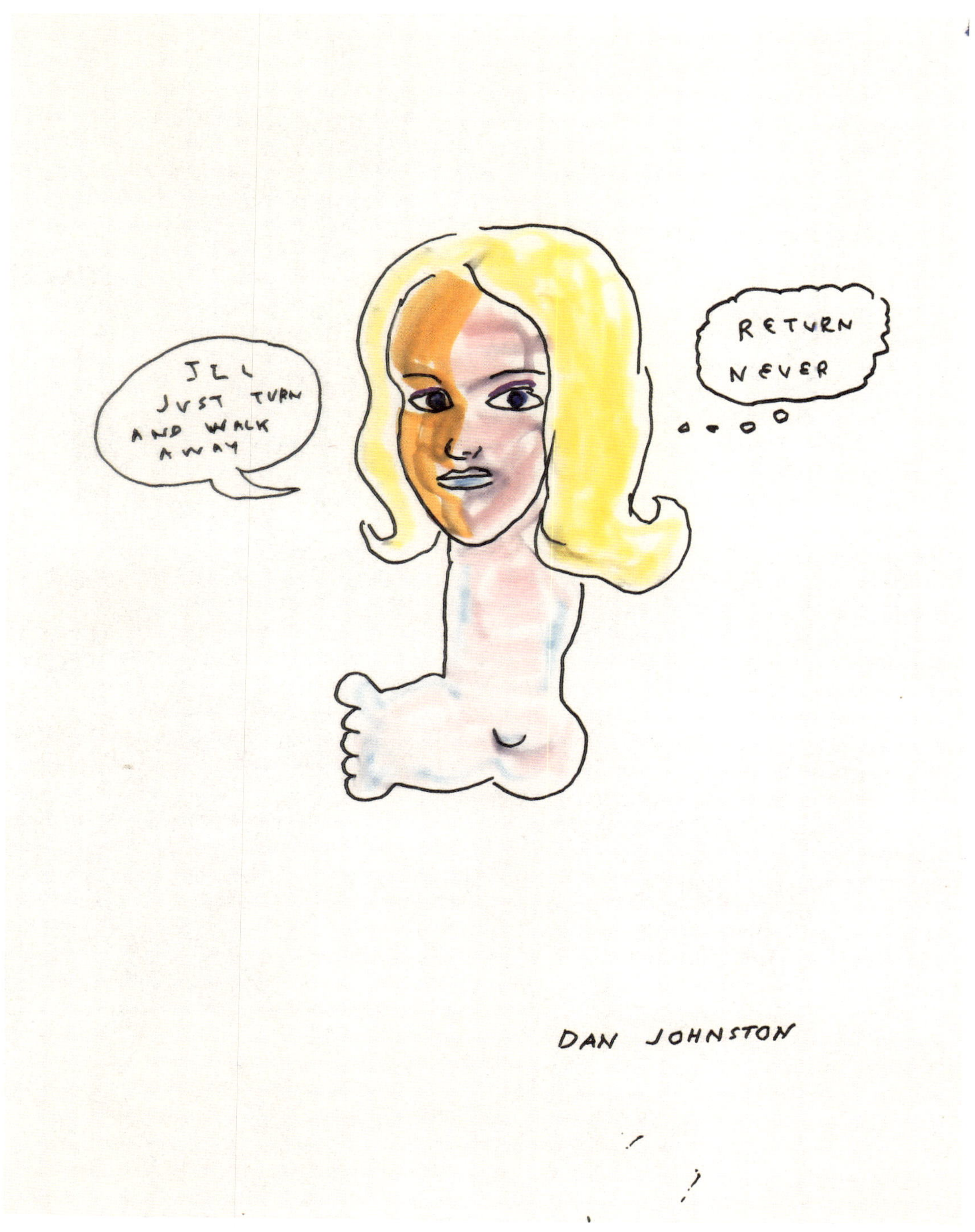

Return Never

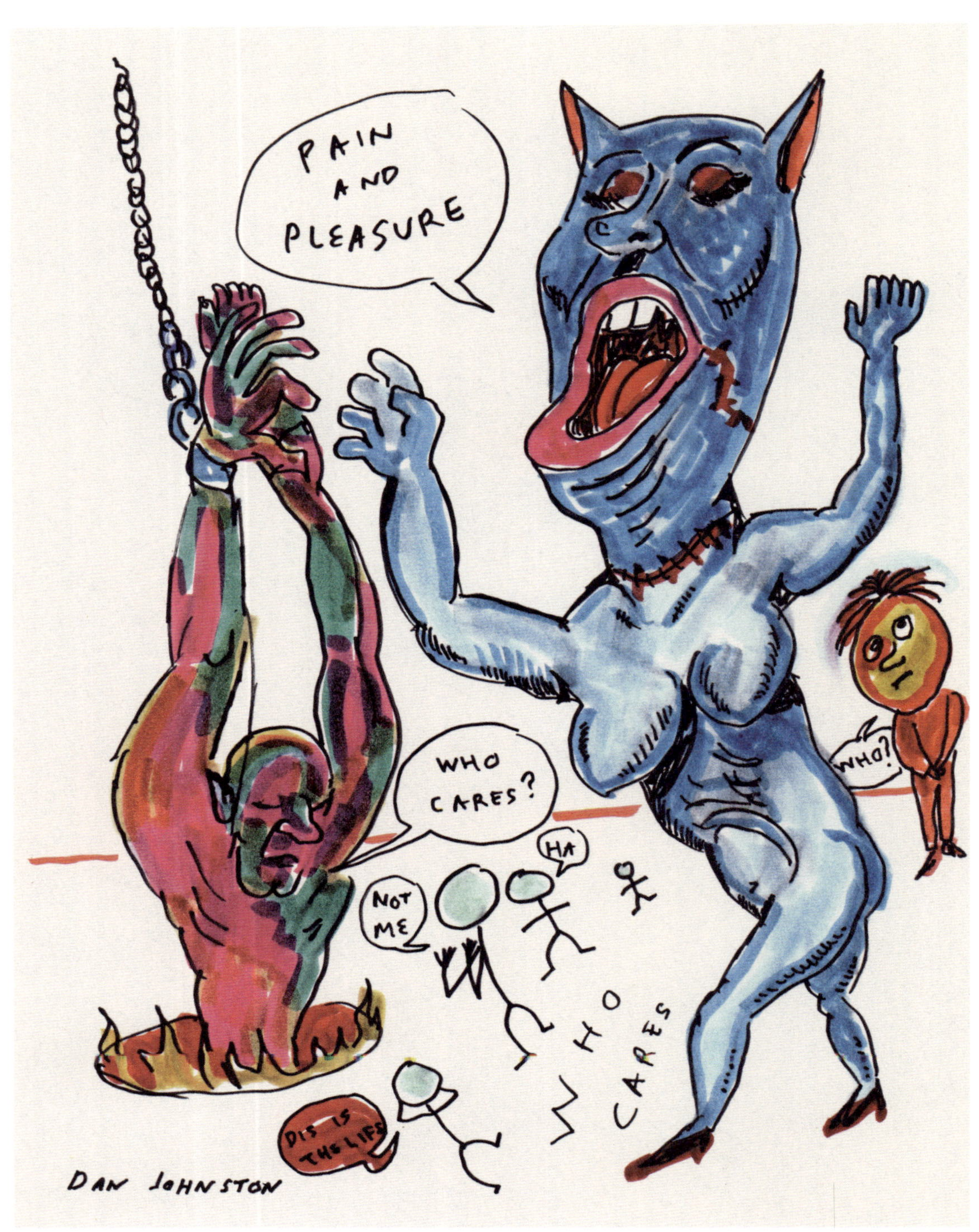

Pain and Pleasure

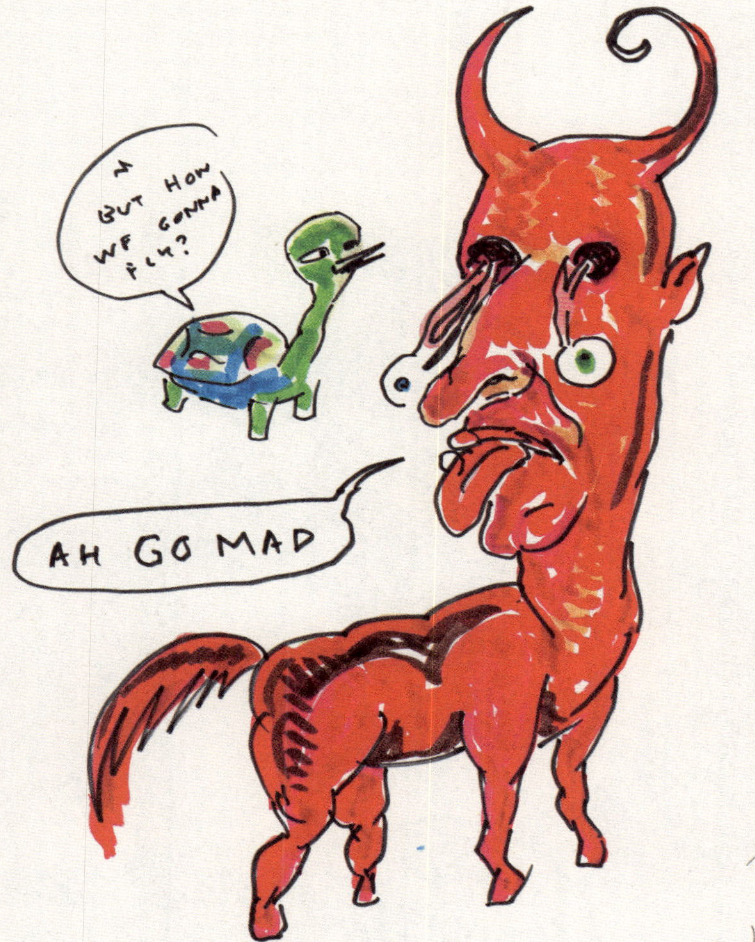

Vomet Was Once a Cheese Sandwich

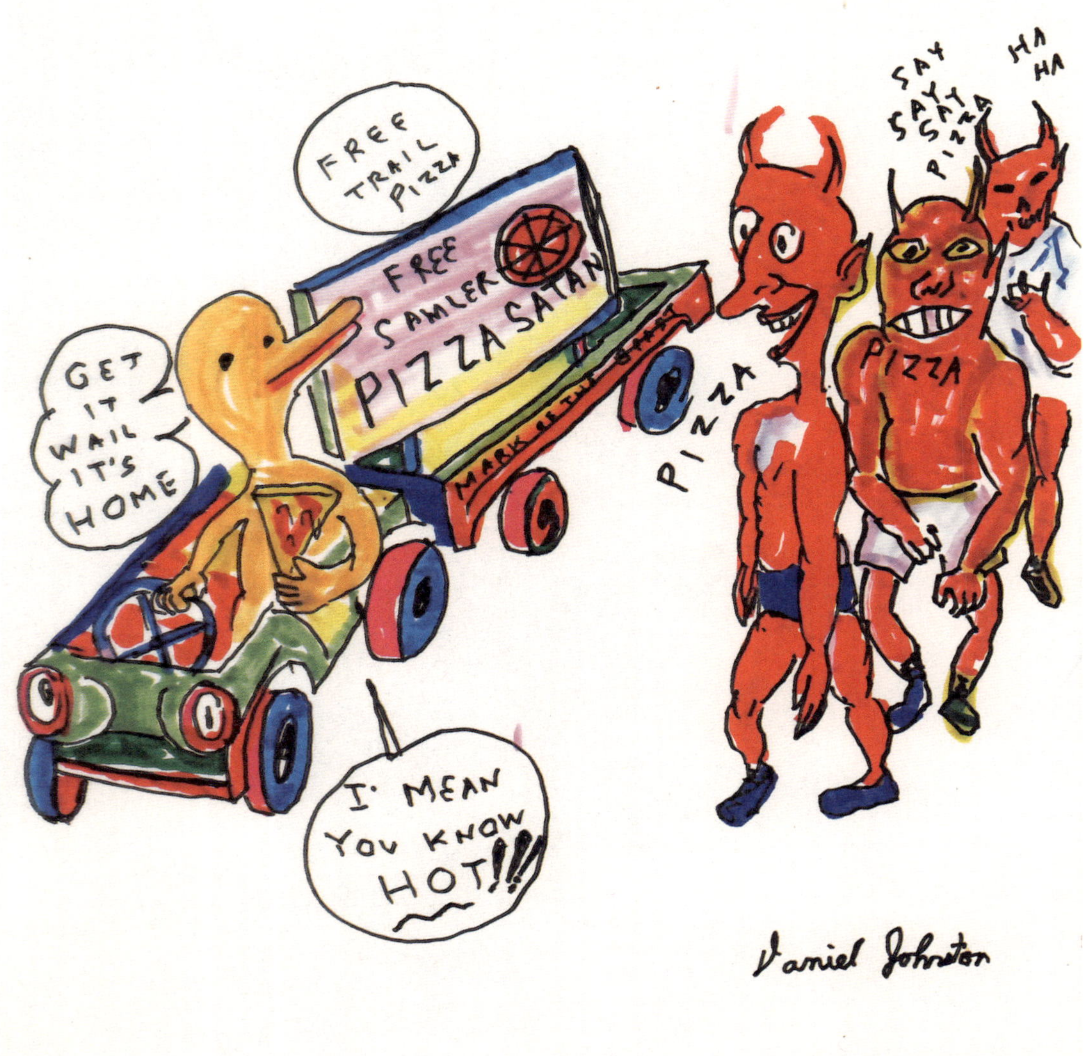

Temptags8onHard to Find

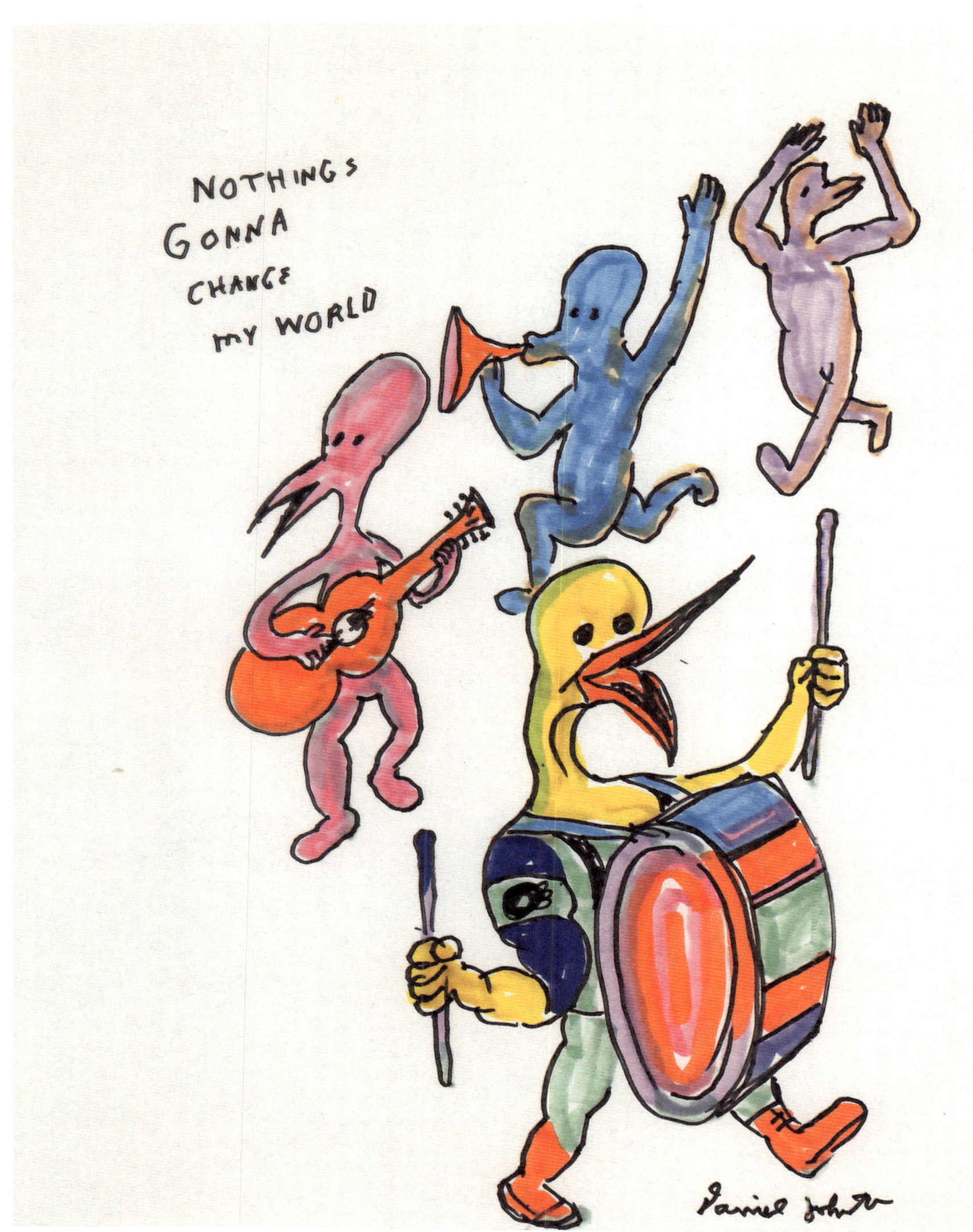

Nothings Gonna Change My World

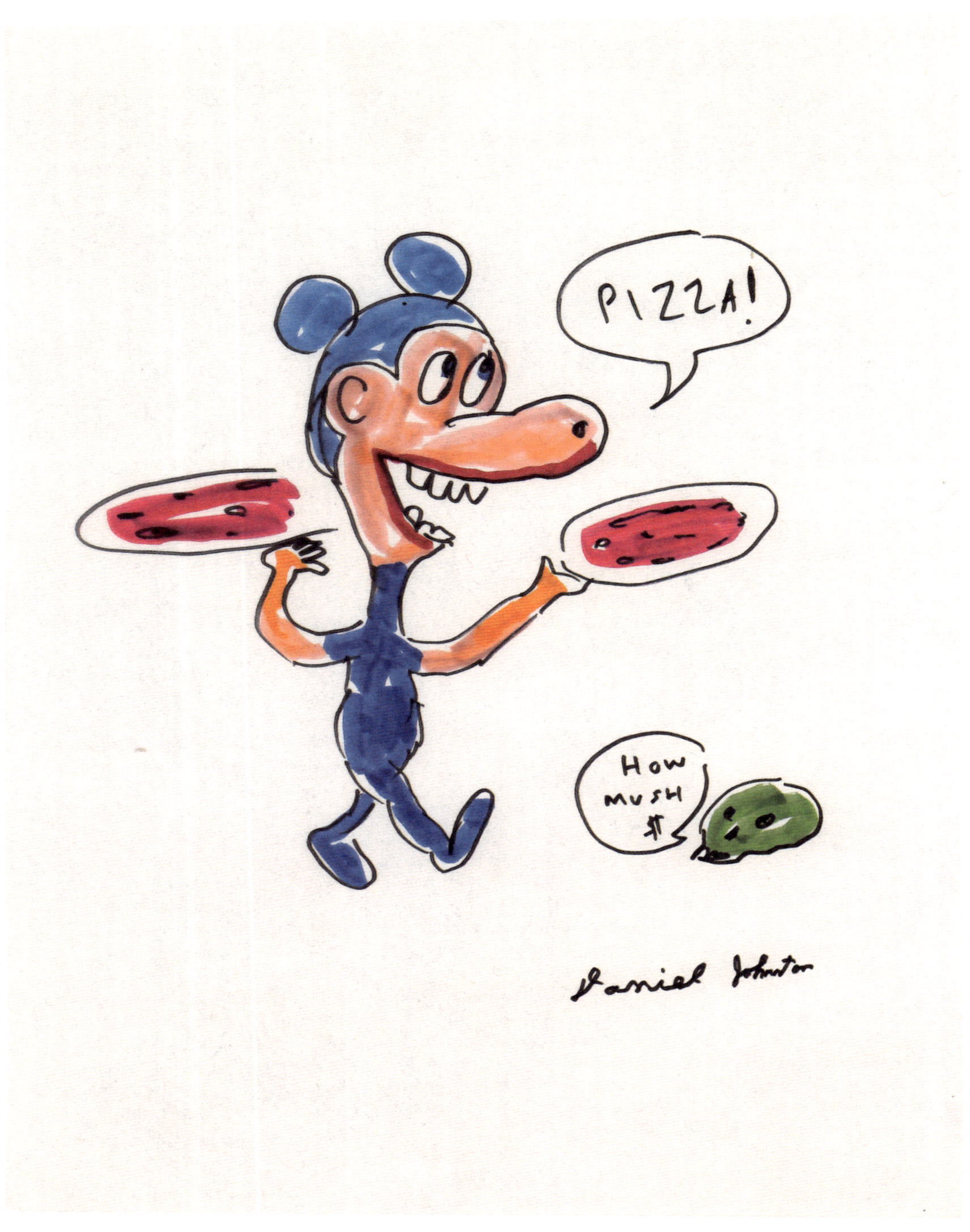

Pizza! (How Mush)

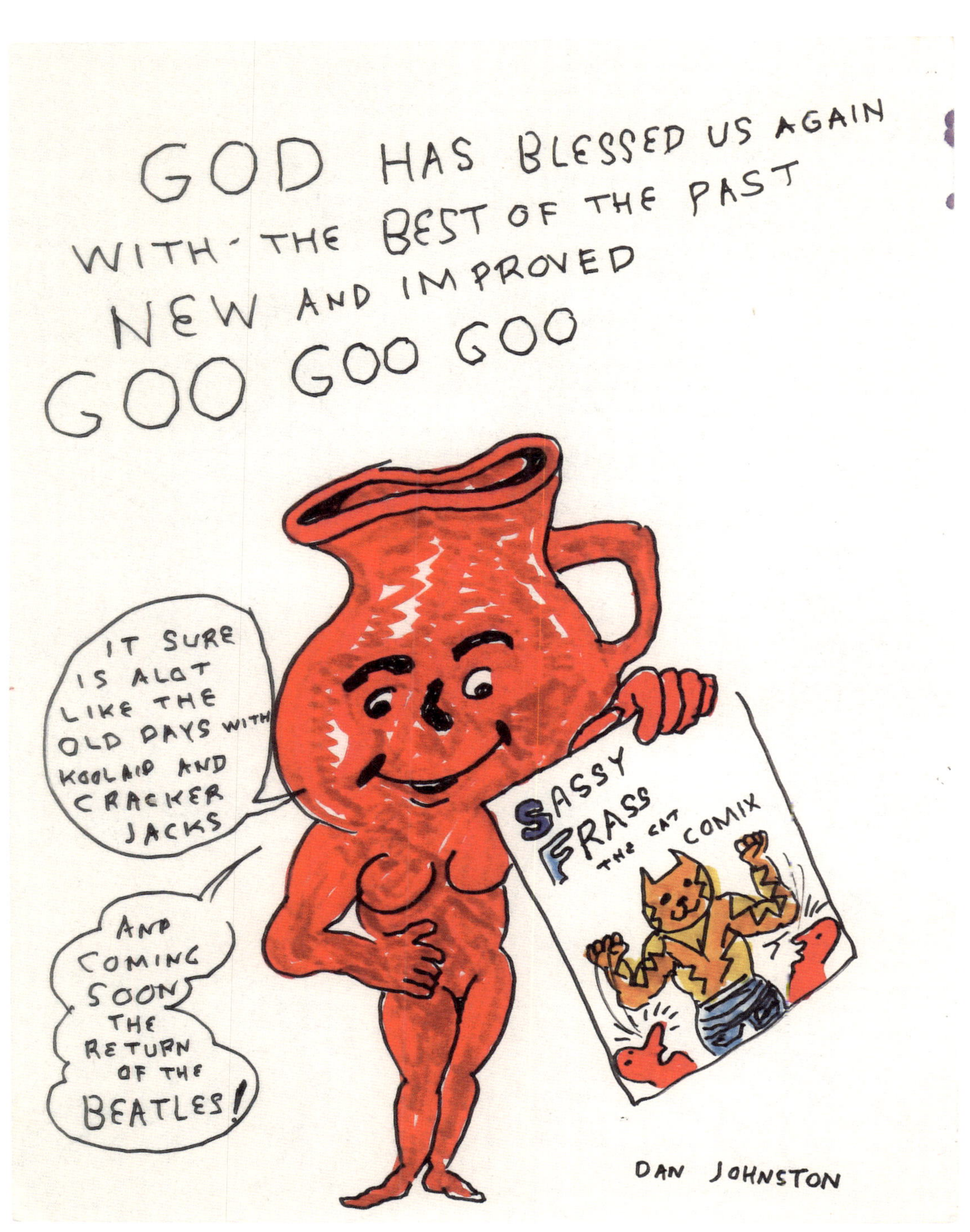

The Return of the Beatles

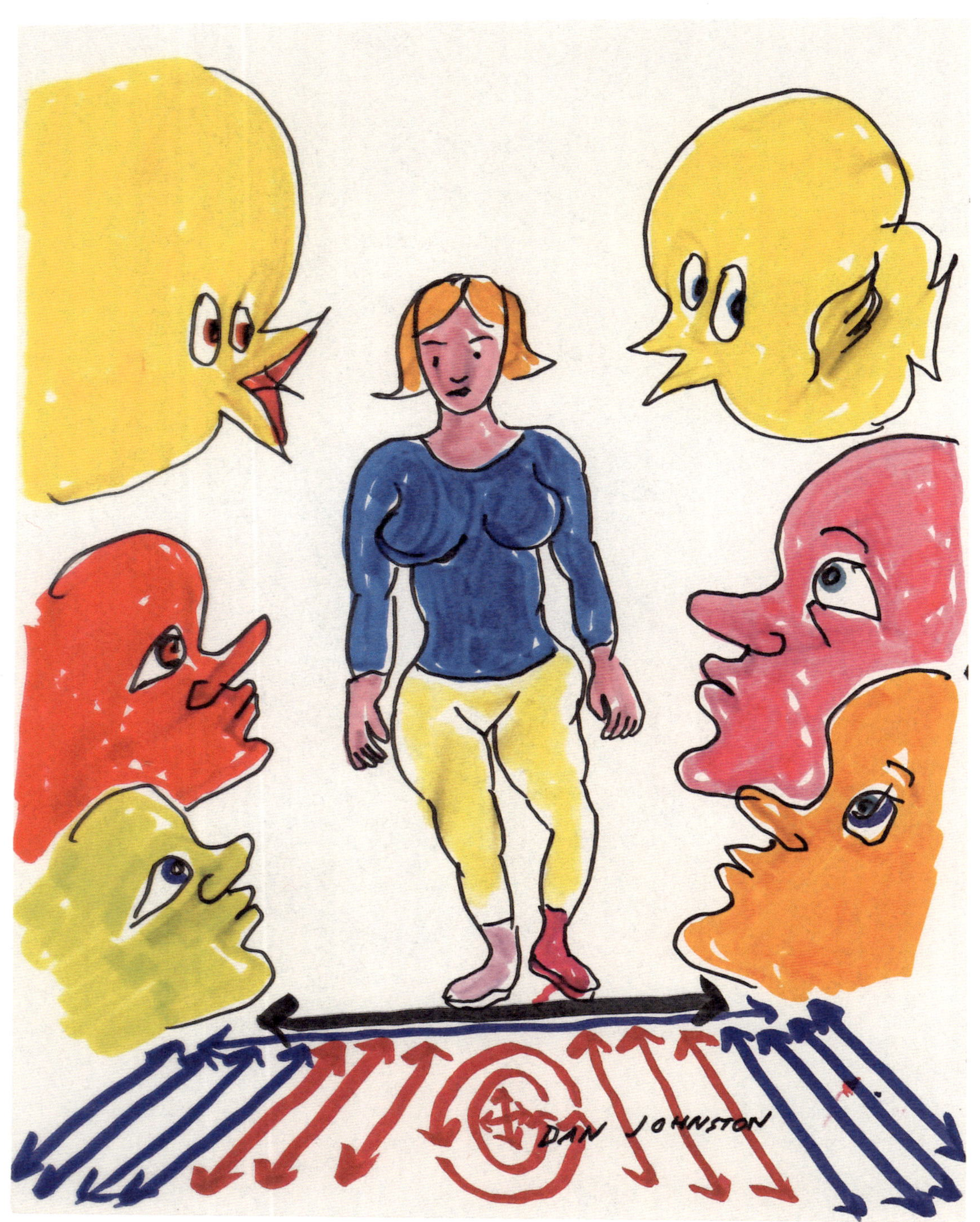

Untitled (All Eyes on Her?)

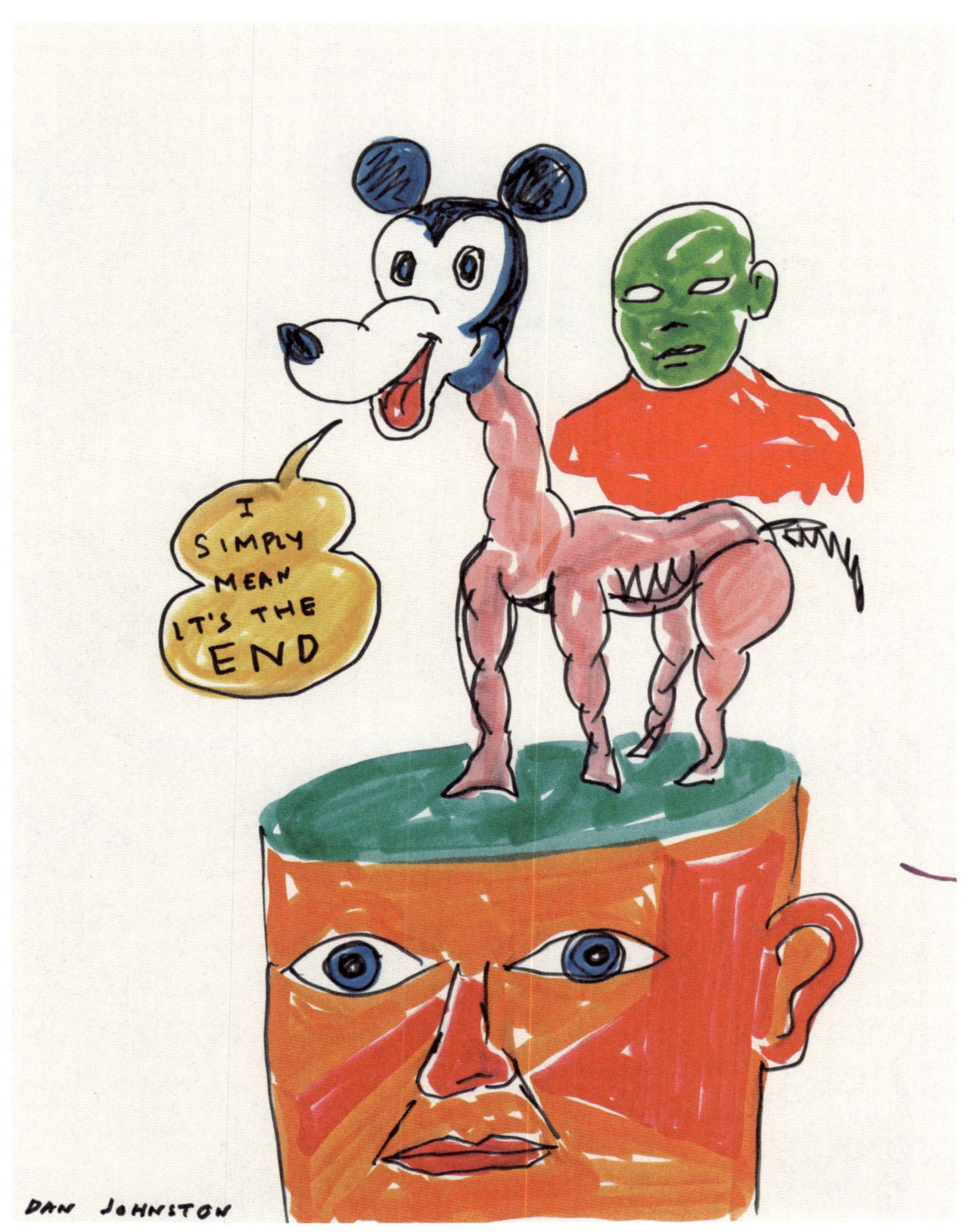

I Simply Mean It's the End

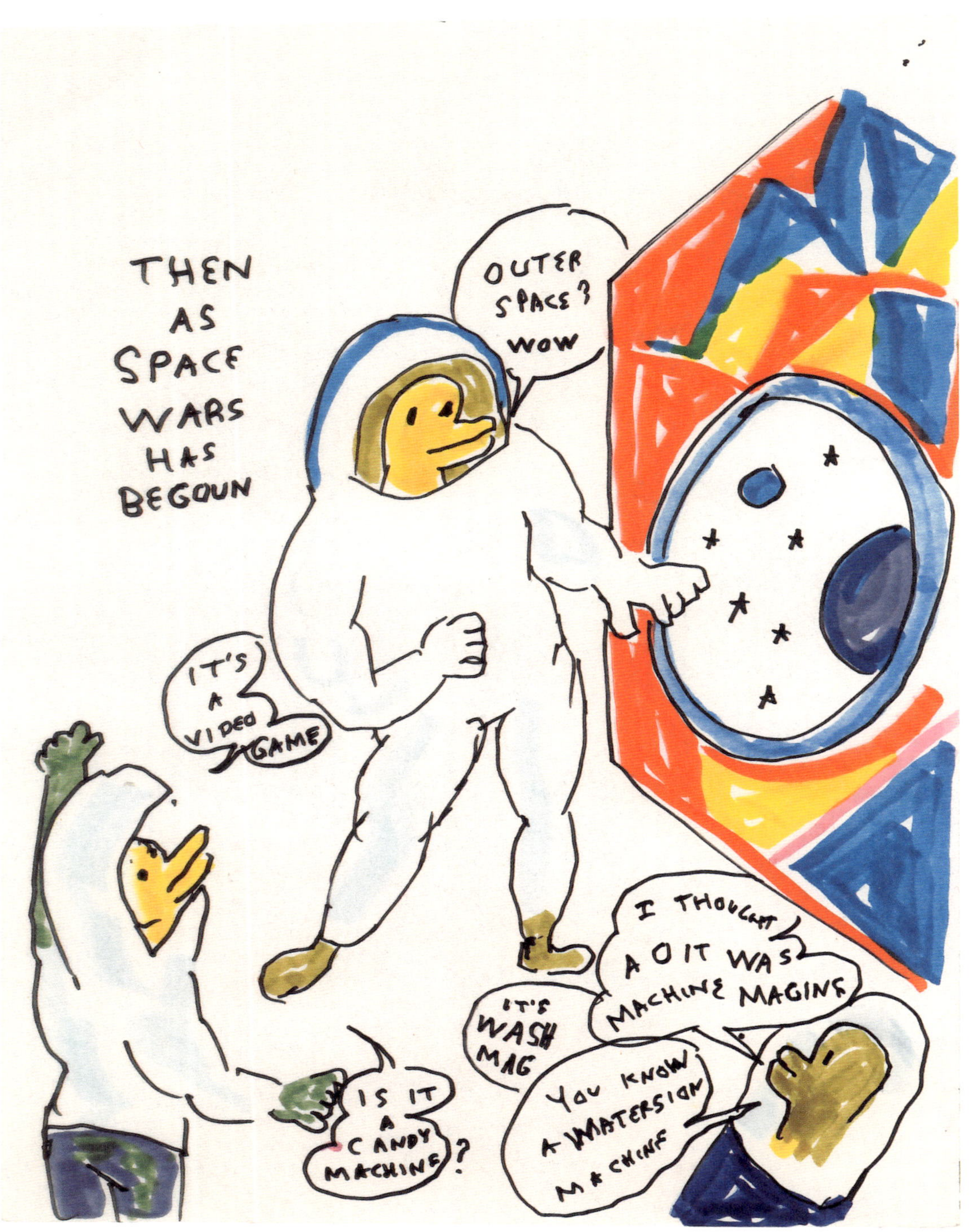
THEN AS SPACE WARS HAS BEGOUN
OUTER SPACE? WOW
IT'S A VIDEO GAME
IS IT A CANDY MACHINE?
IT'S WASH MAG
I THOUGHT A O IT WAS MACHINE MAGINE
YOU KNOW A WATERSION MACHINE

Space Wars

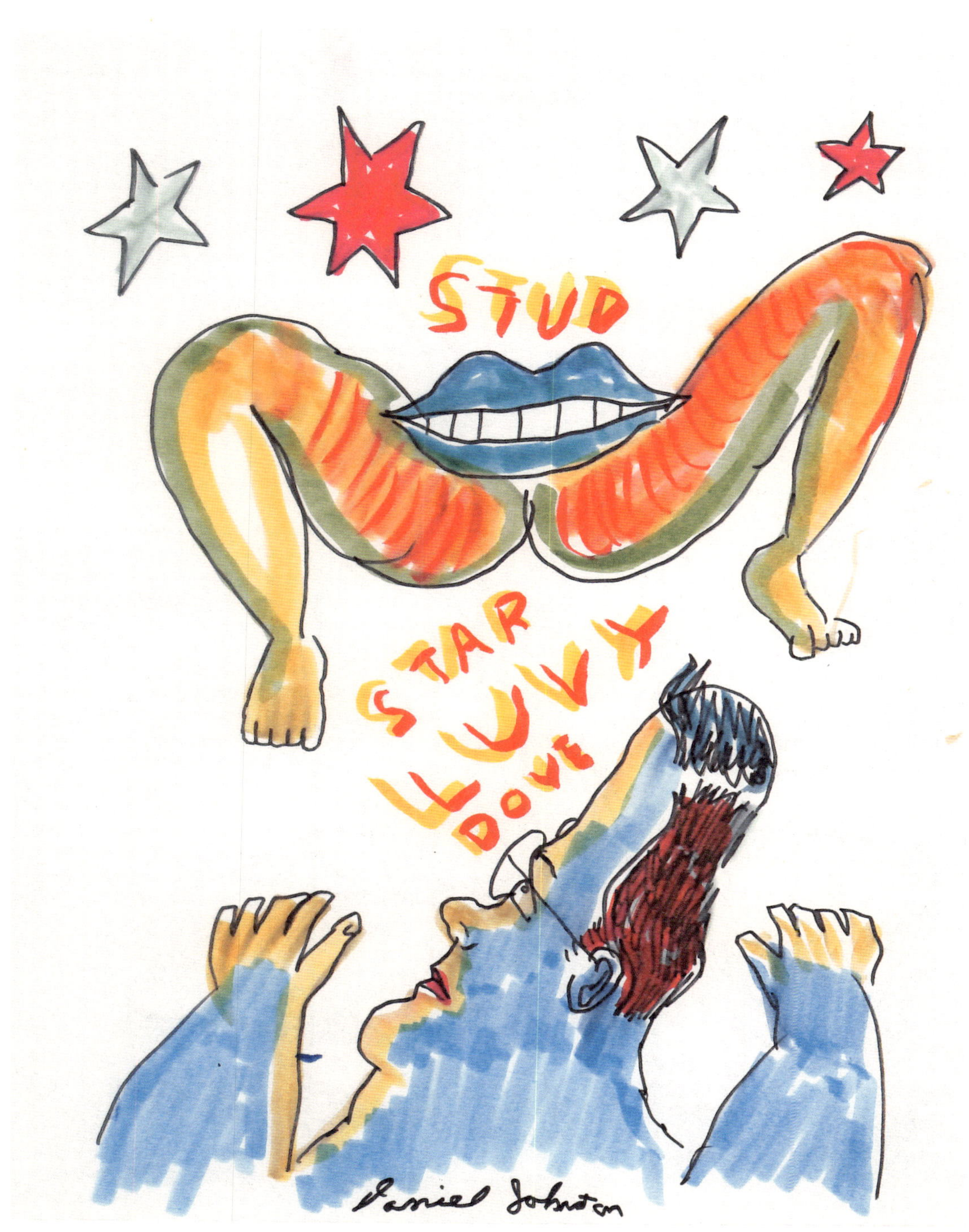

Stud (Star Luvy Dove)

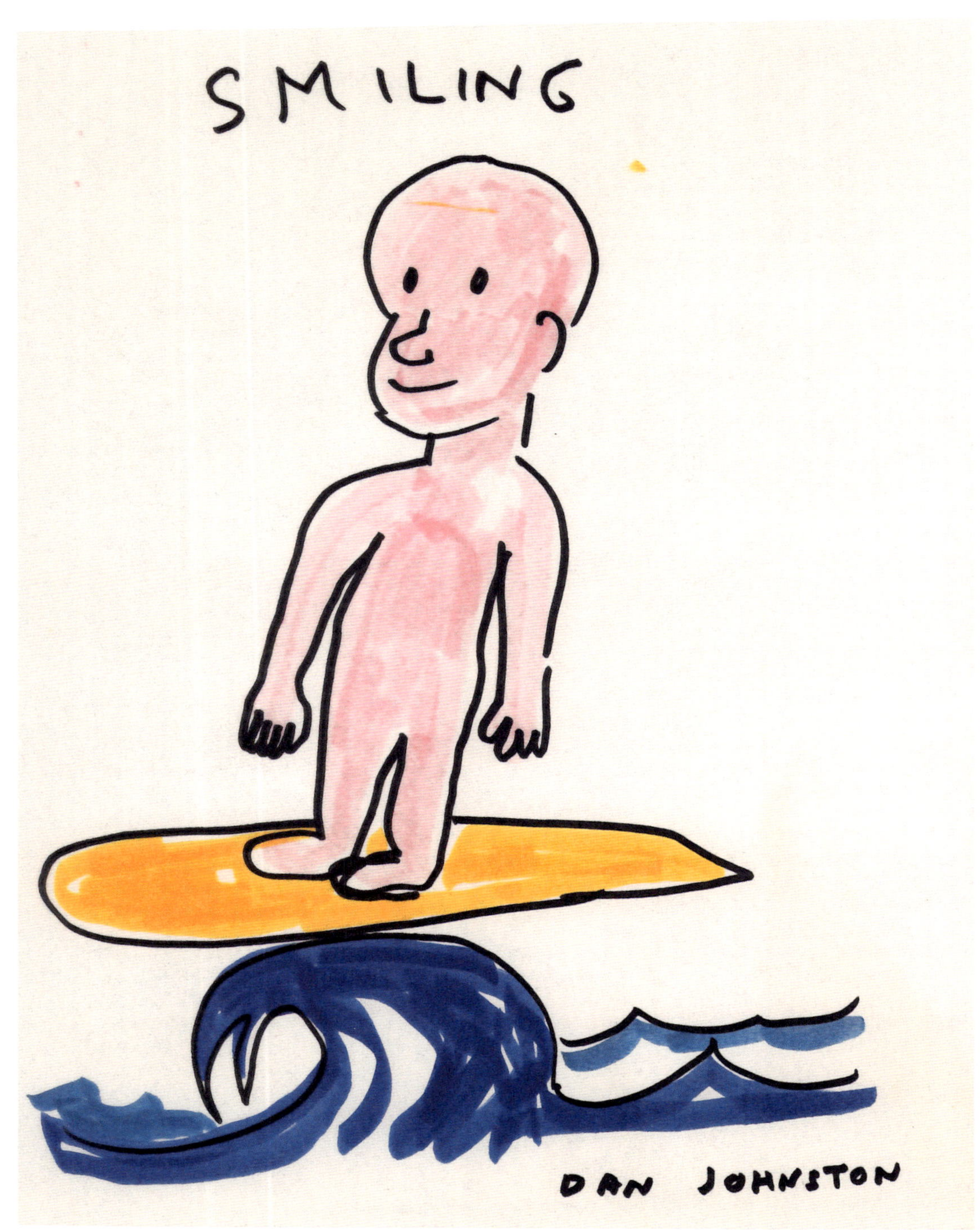

Smiling

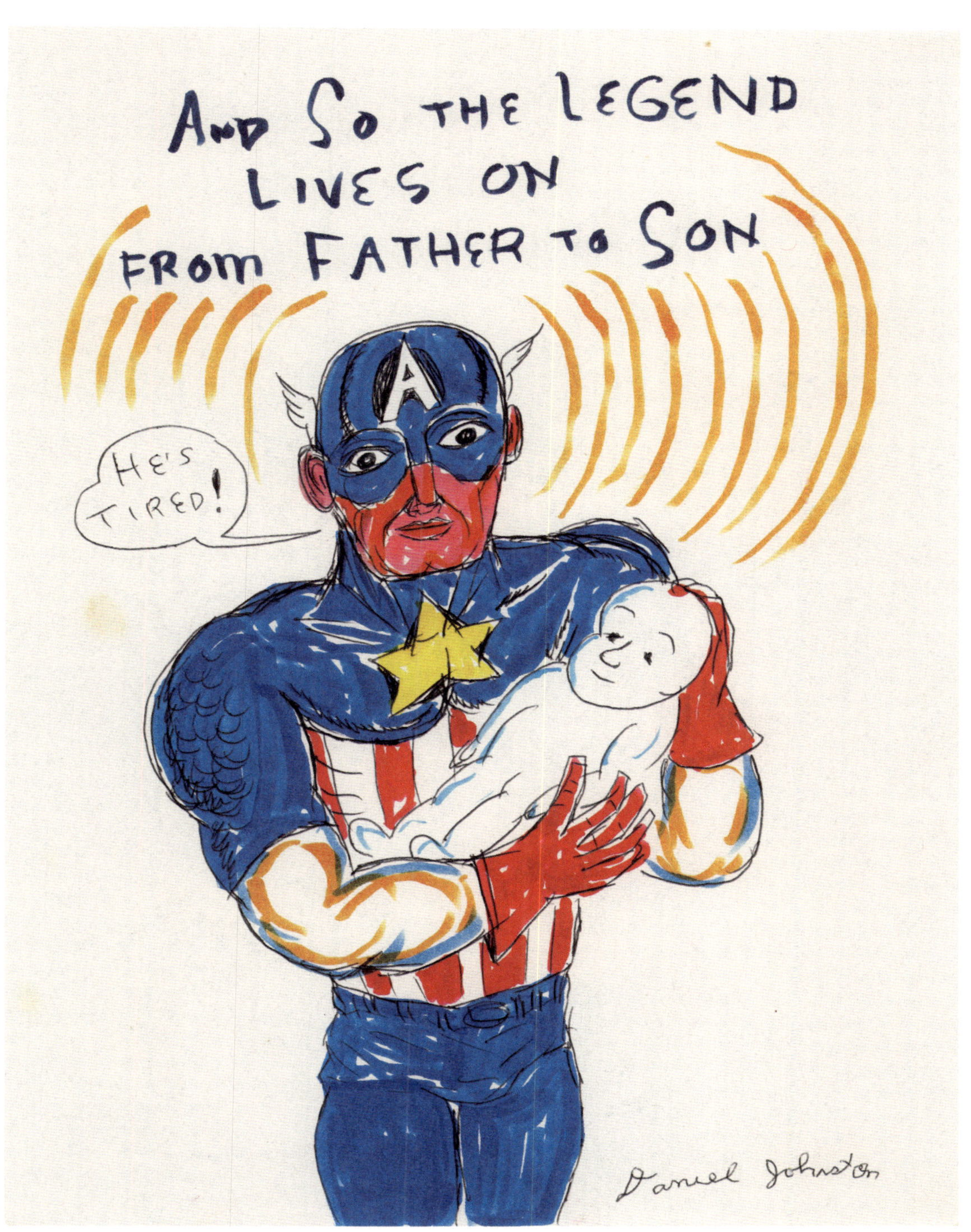

And So the Legend Lives On (Cap & Casper)

BLESS FOR THE DAY

LOOK
I'M SORRY
SO SORRY

WE'VE
ONLY JUST
BEGUN

Daniel Johnston

Bless for the Day

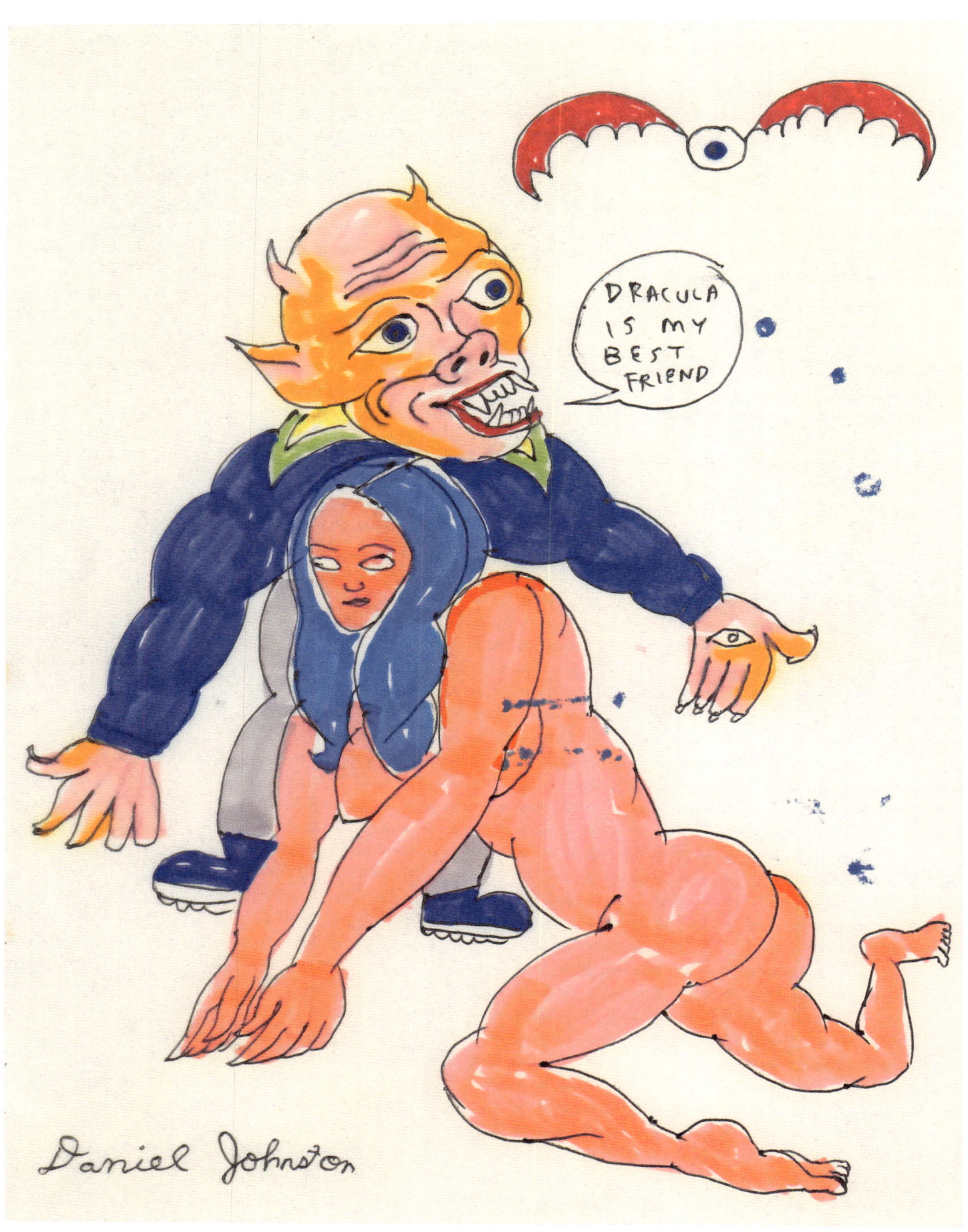

Dracula Is My Best Friend

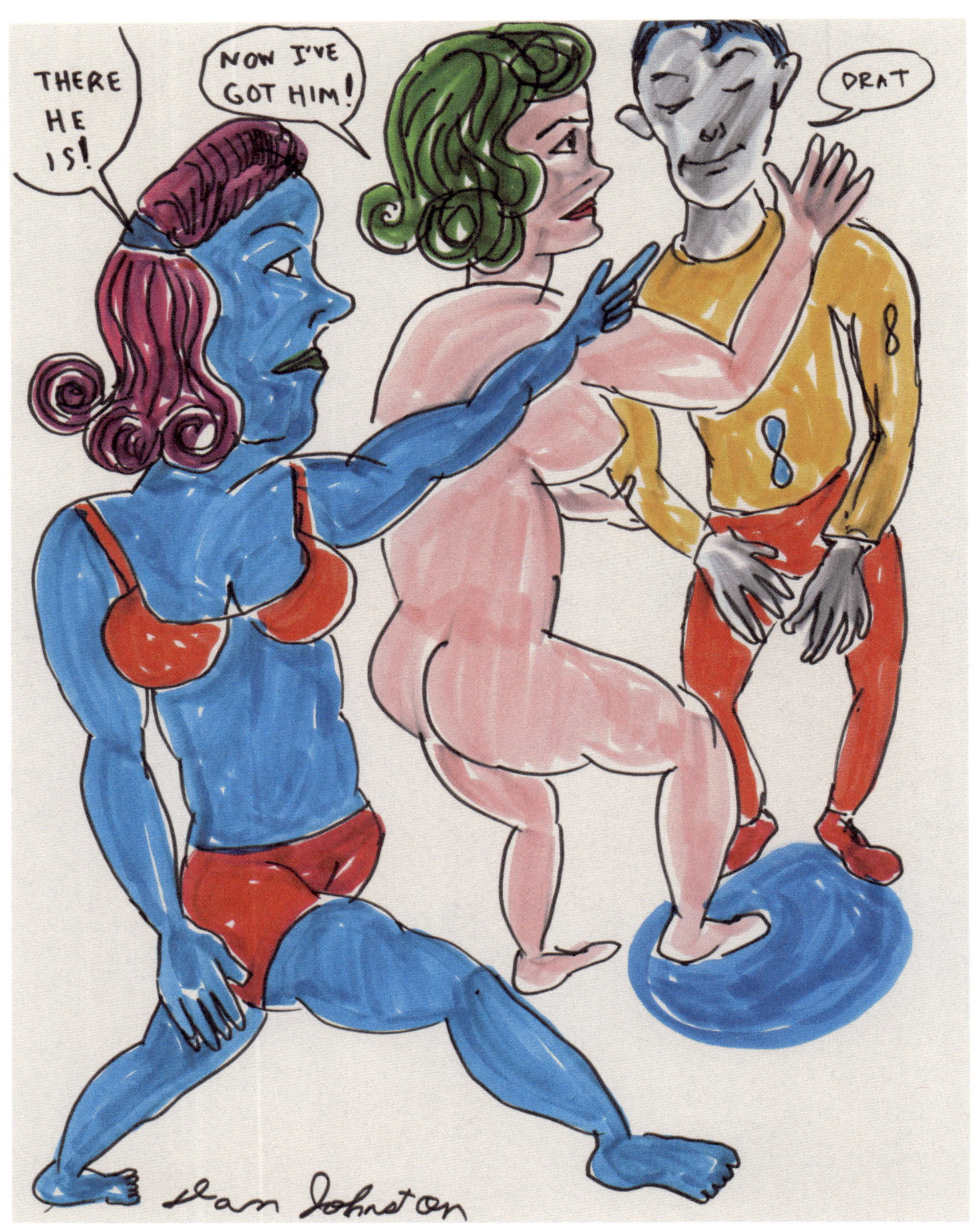

There He Is!

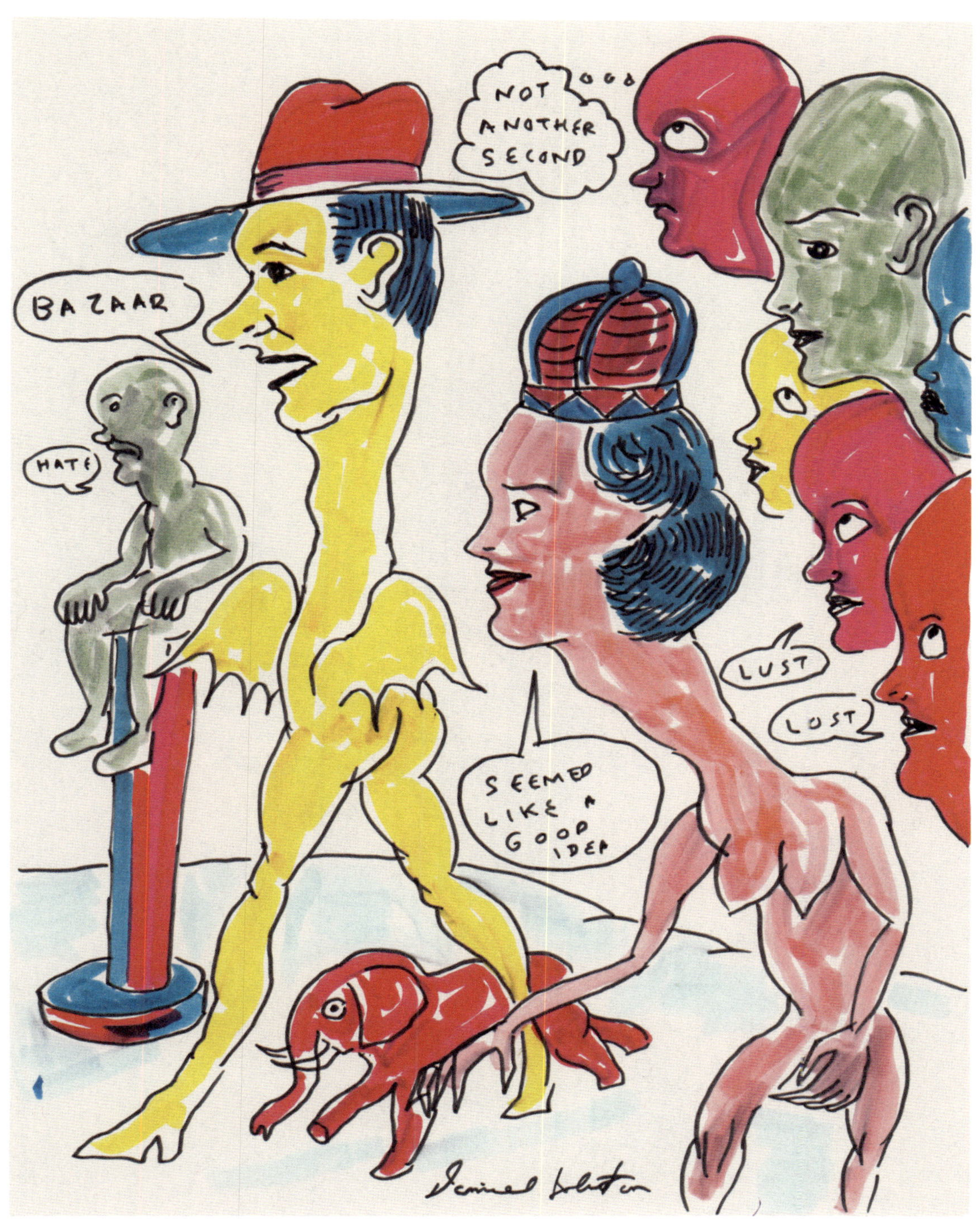
NOT ANOTHER SECOND
BAZAAR
HATE
LUST
LOST
SEEMED LIKE A GOOD IDEA

Bazaar

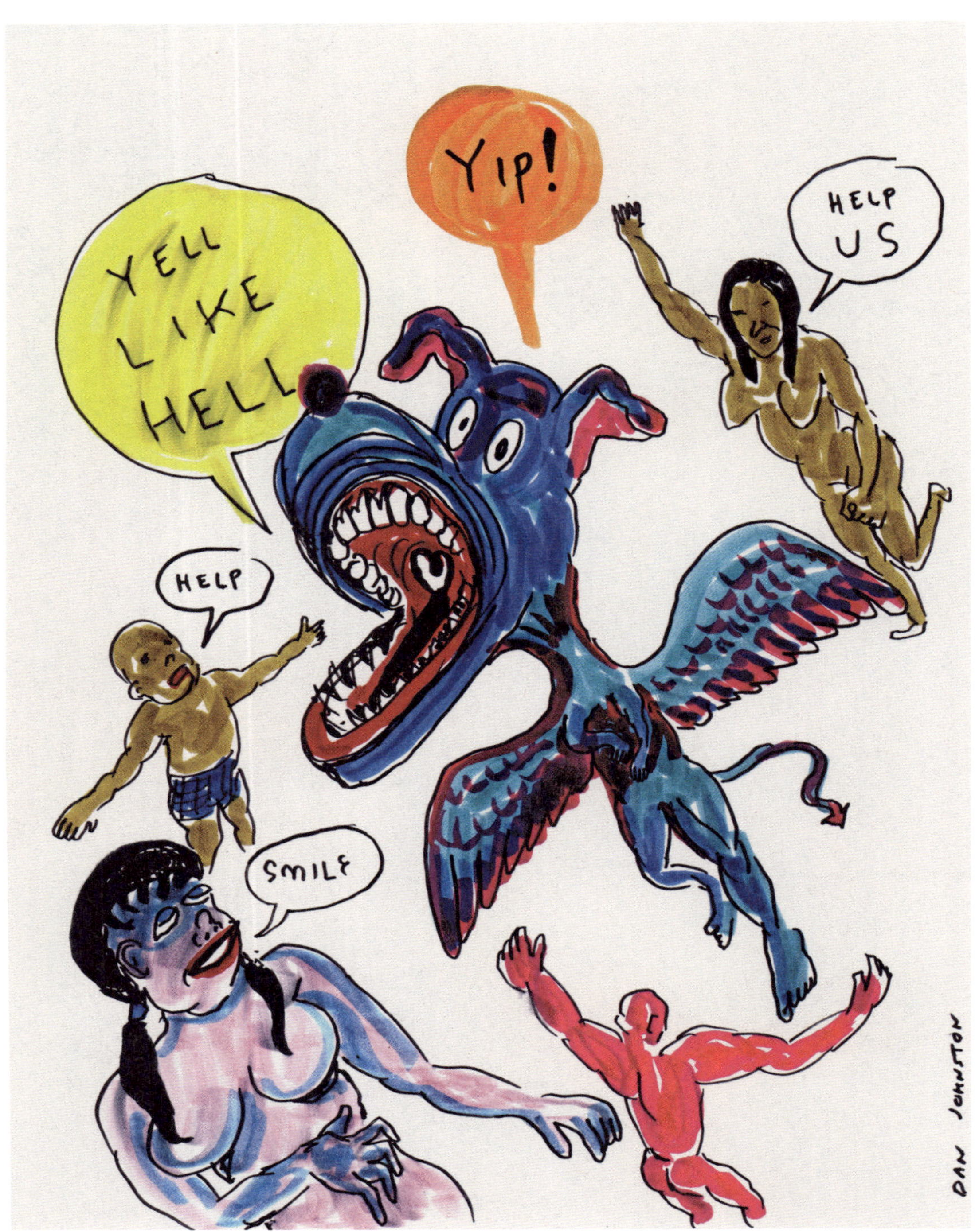

Yell Like Hell

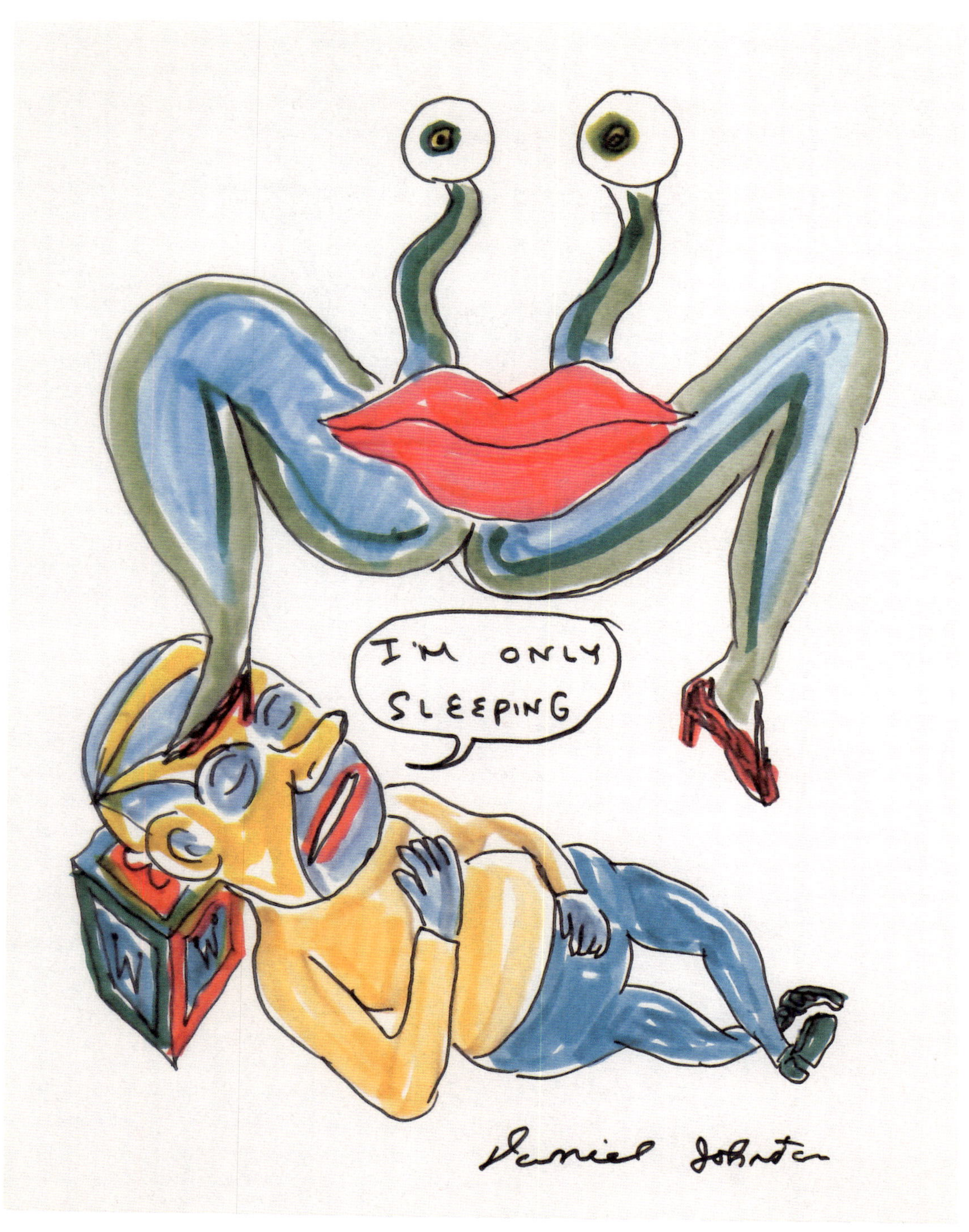

I'm Only Sleeping

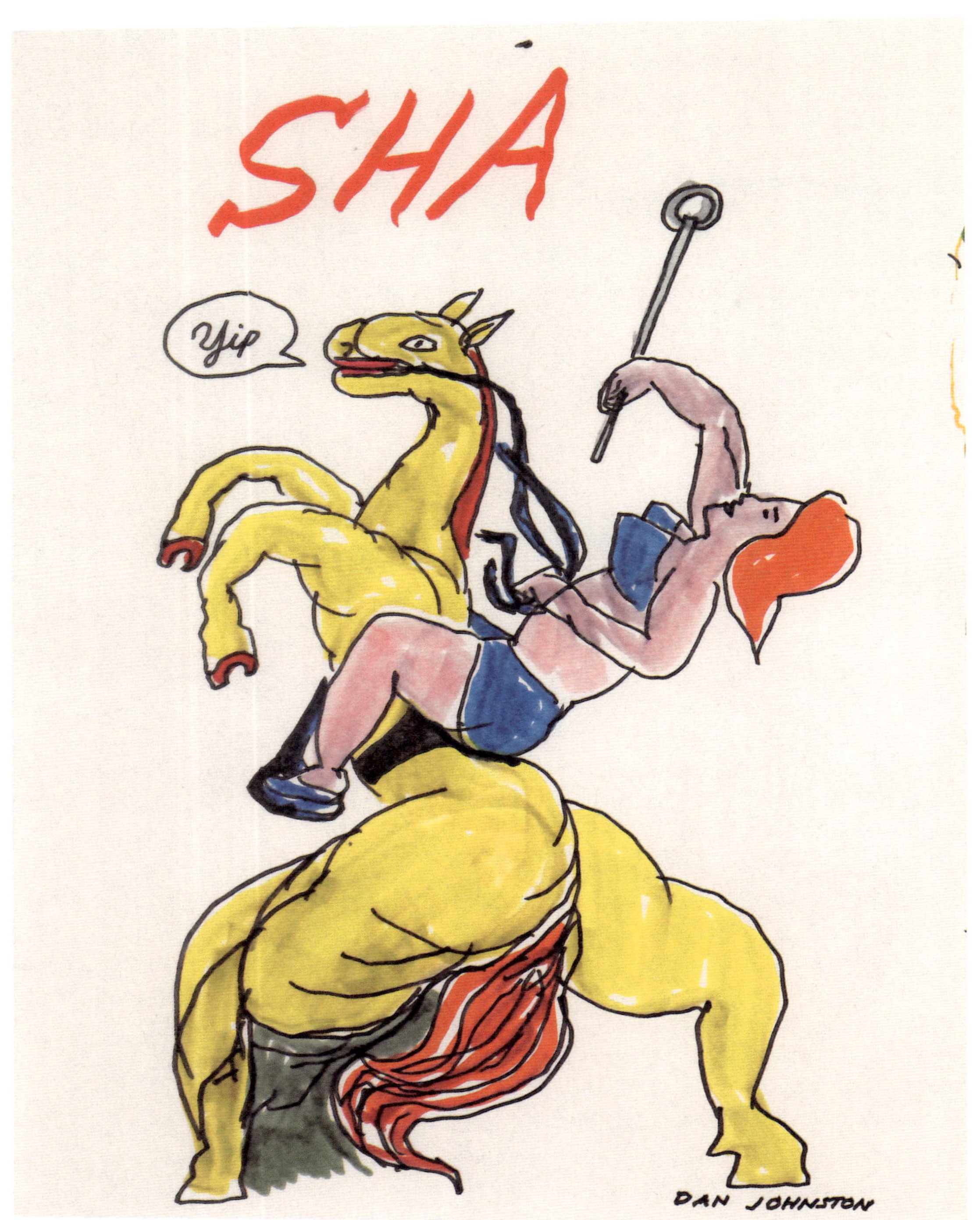

SHA

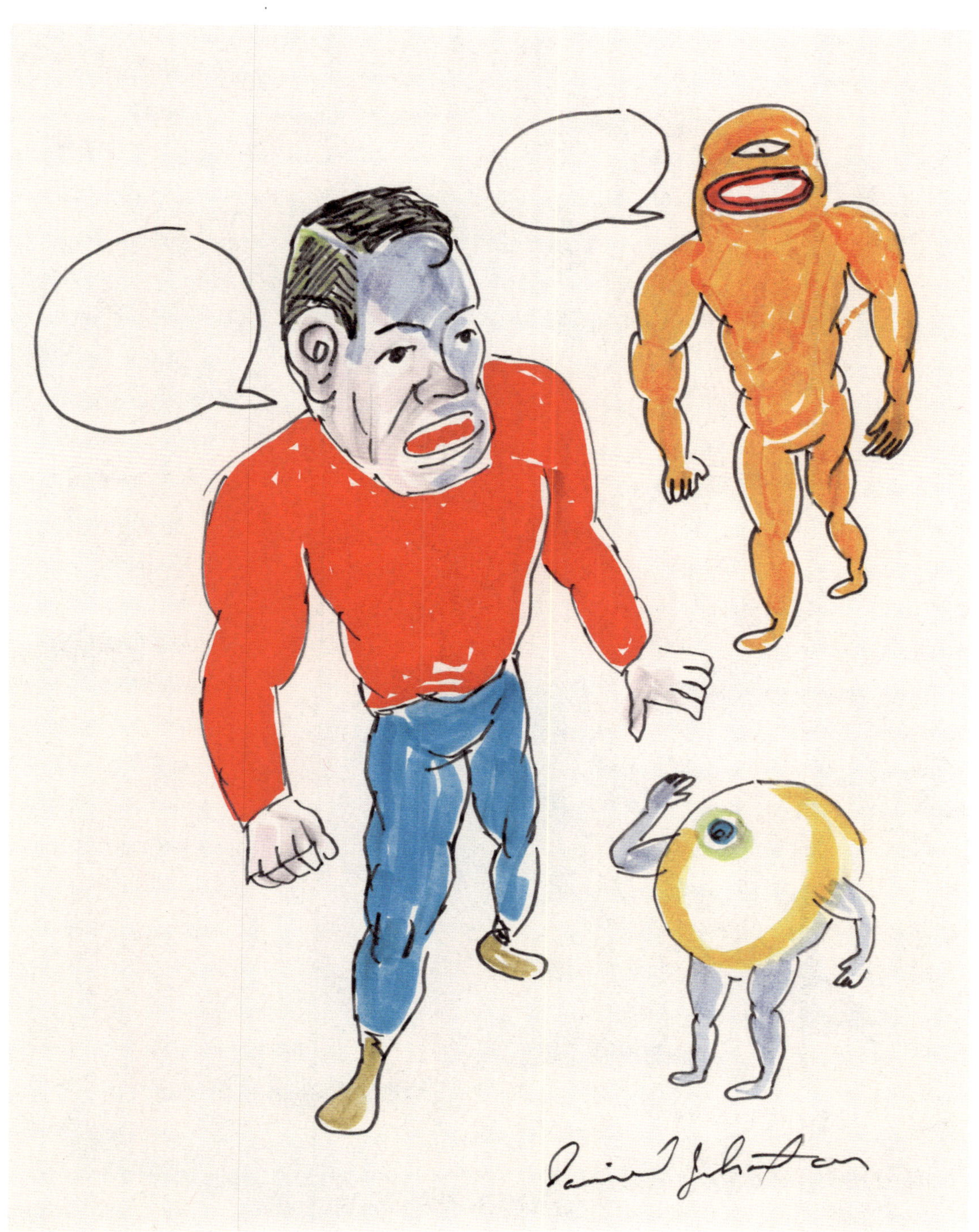

Untitled (No Words)

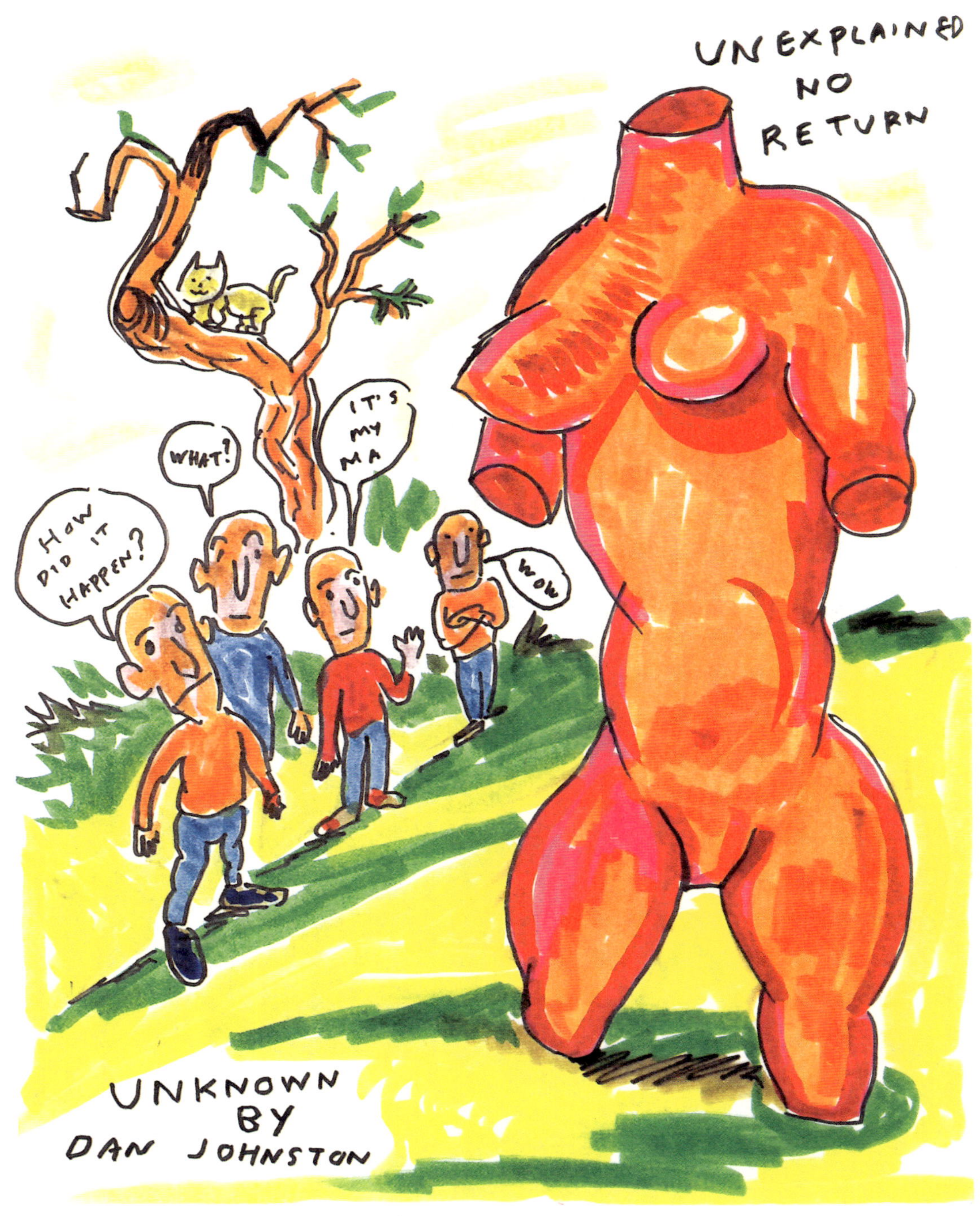

Unexplained No Return

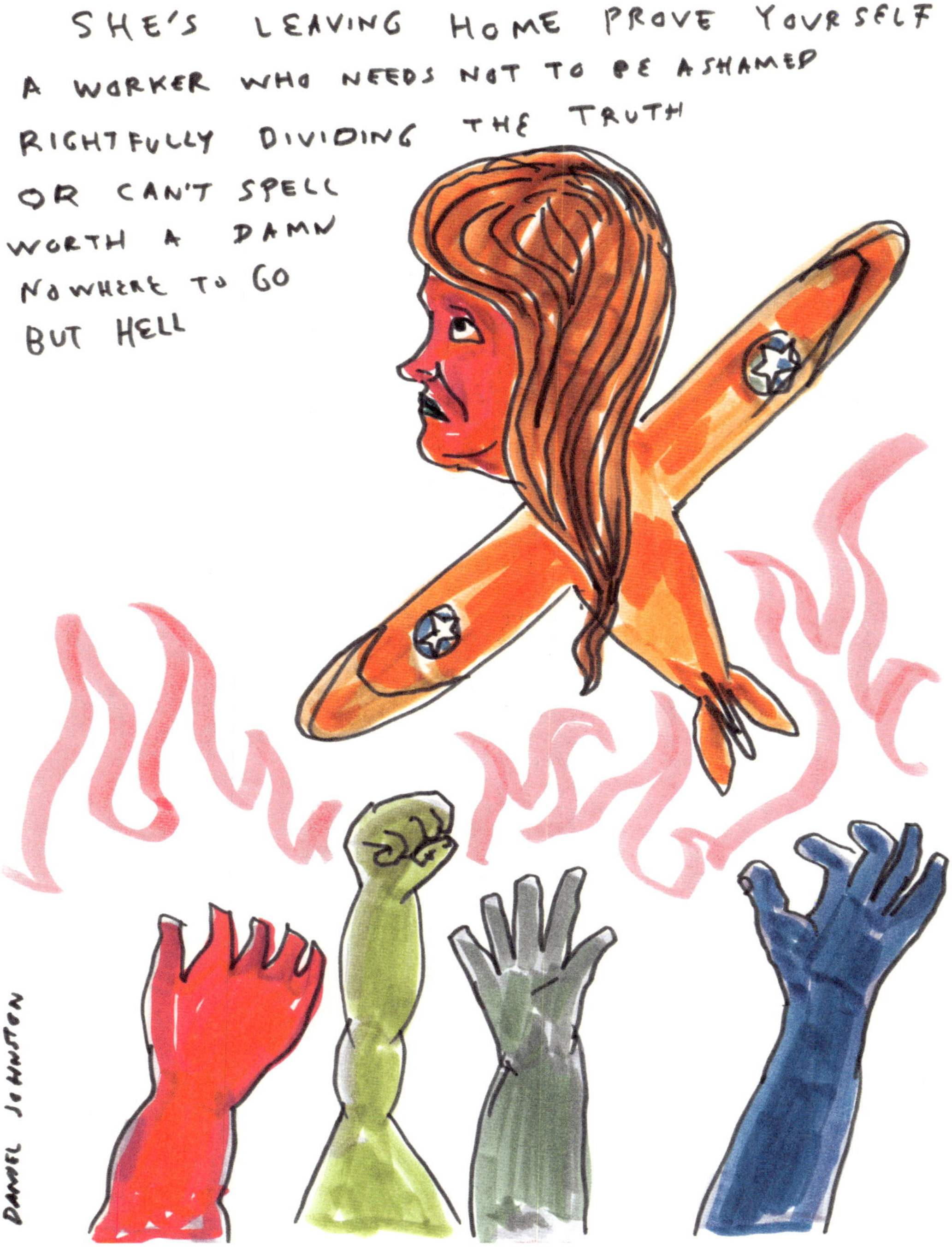

SHE'S LEAVING HOME PROVE YOURSELF
A WORKER WHO NEEDS NOT TO BE ASHAMED
RIGHTFULLY DIVIDING THE TRUTH
OR CAN'T SPELL
WORTH A DAMN
NOWHERE TO GO
BUT HELL

DANIEL JOHNSTON

Nowhere to Go but Hell

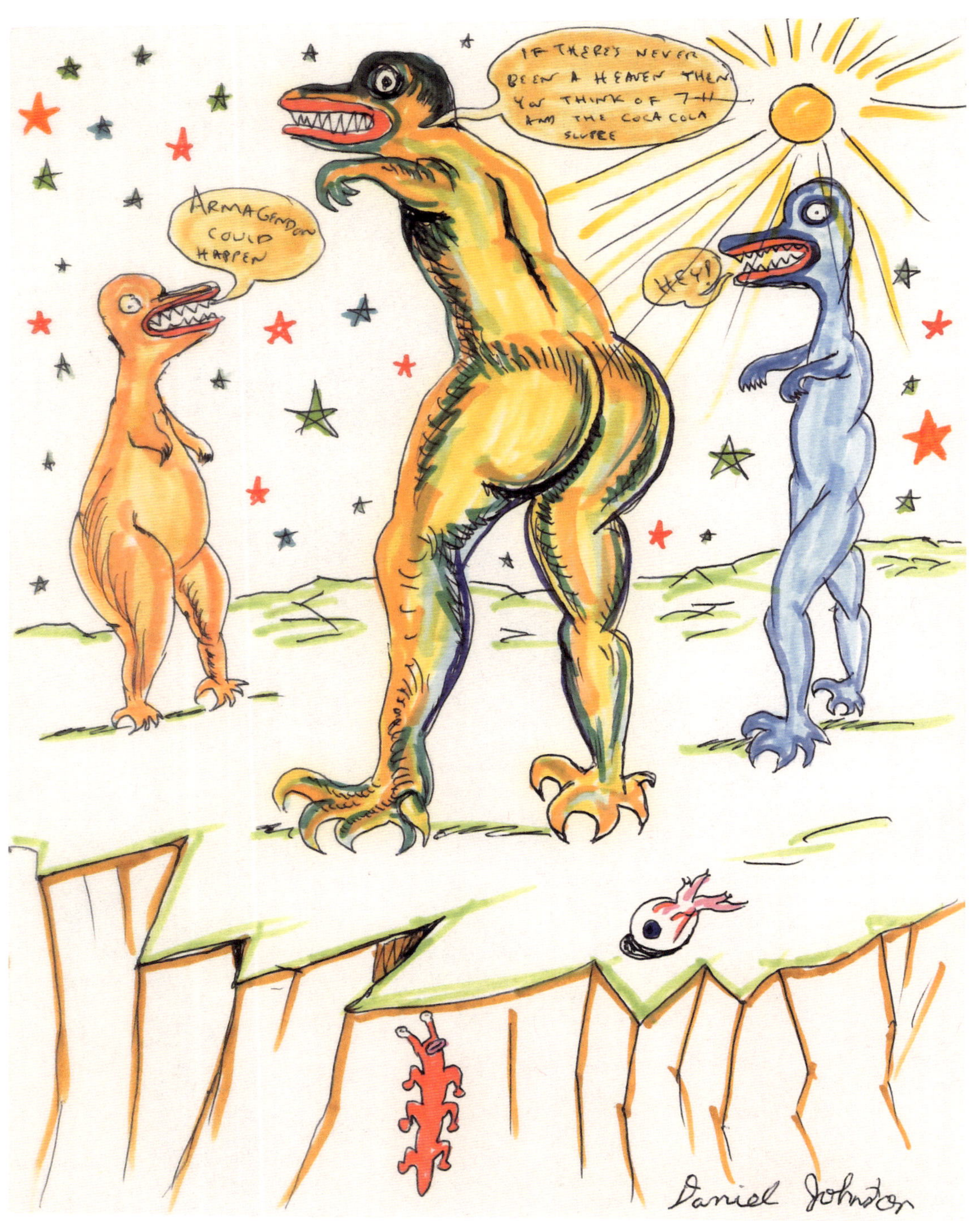

Armagendon Could Happen

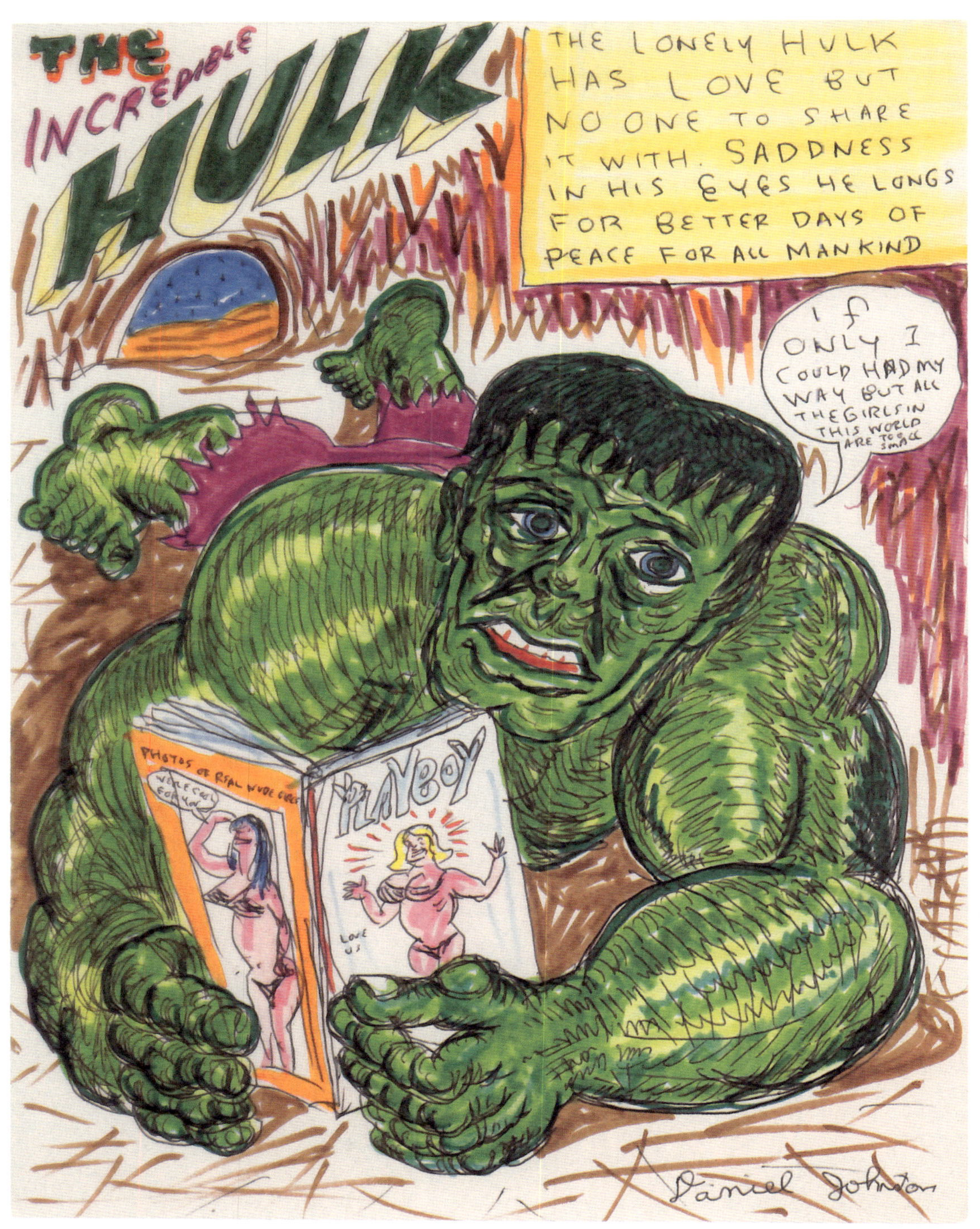

The Lonely Hulk

I first heard Daniel Johnston's music when I was seventeen, then immediately watched *The Devil and Daniel Johnston*. That film hit me so hard. It was made during Daniel's most successful moments and also his most vulnerable ones. I watched the film and felt I could totally relate to him—he was just this kid who didn't fit in and made things in his bedroom and didn't expect anything. He was peculiar. He was motivated. I wanted to be just like him.

That was around the time I started my musical career. I was completely obsessed with Elliott Smith and Daniel Johnston. I was so inspired by them both. I even got tattoos inspired by them. The Daniel tattoo is the bat from *Continued Story* (1985, self-released)—an early tag he did in school notebooks and on the school walls (a bit like the one on p. 146).

I spent so much time with his music. His lyrics are just so completely genuine and honest. Now everything I write has no filter. I say it straight, just like Daniel. Even the production has nothing to hide—like all of Daniel's broken keyboard sounds, simple song structures, and shitty-sounding recordings.

He didn't purposefully set out to make music in a lo-fi way, or want to create a trend. But he inadvertently started the DIY sound that people search for. He was the one who did it, because he just *did* it.

I guess that's why I was so drawn to him.

His words weren't complicated, but they were brave and in your face, unapologetic. Music was his way to communicate the feelings he struggled to understand at times—and the seventeen-year-old me found a lot of comfort in that. He expressed it in his songs and in his art.

Everything he created has left a mark on me: his tapes, his lyrics—the drawings and interviews. Daniel made me realize that music and art don't have to be intricate to be impressive or make sense. As long as it's heartfelt and genuine, it will be special to someone.

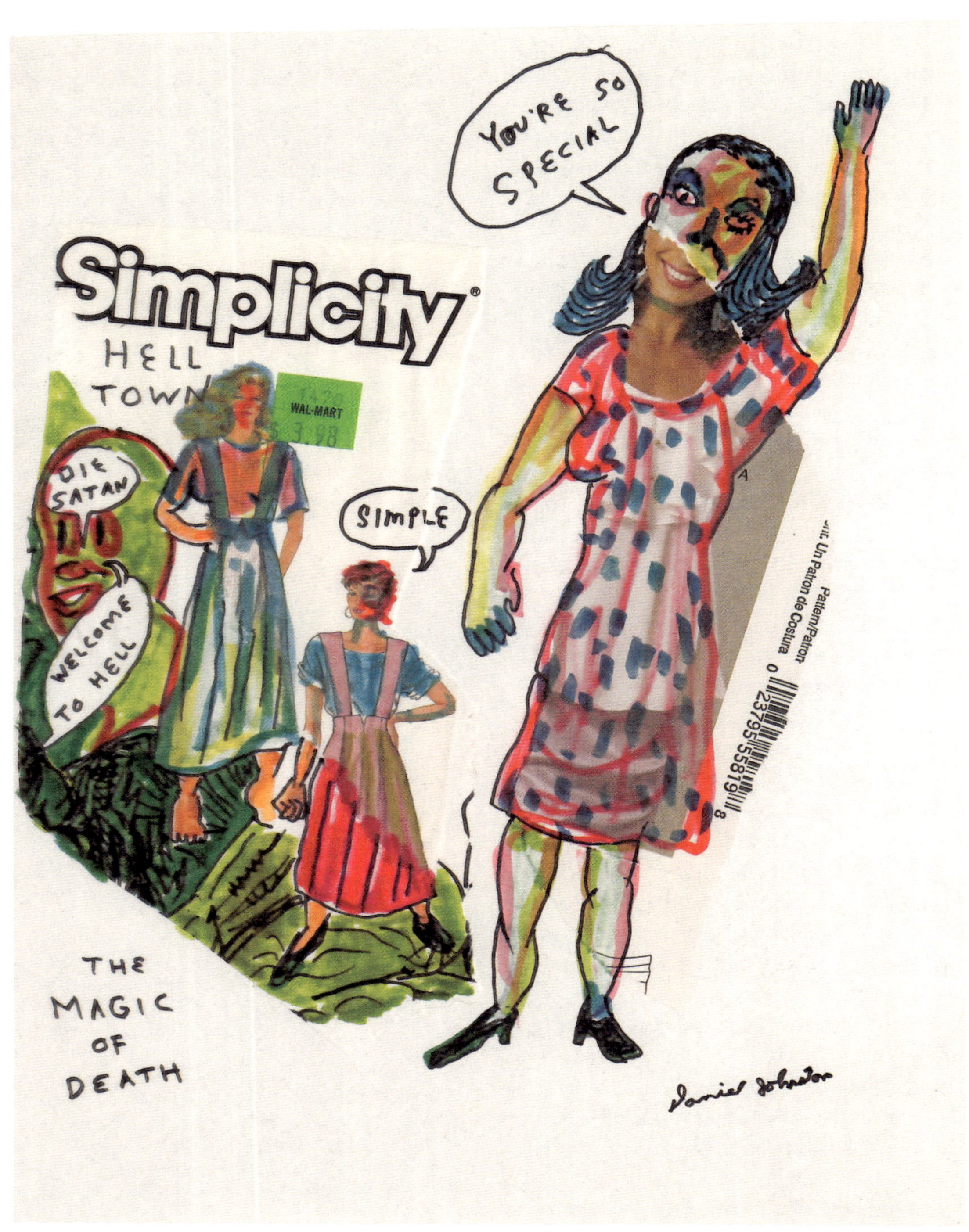

Simplicity (The Magic of Death)

XIII.
Collages
2015–2019

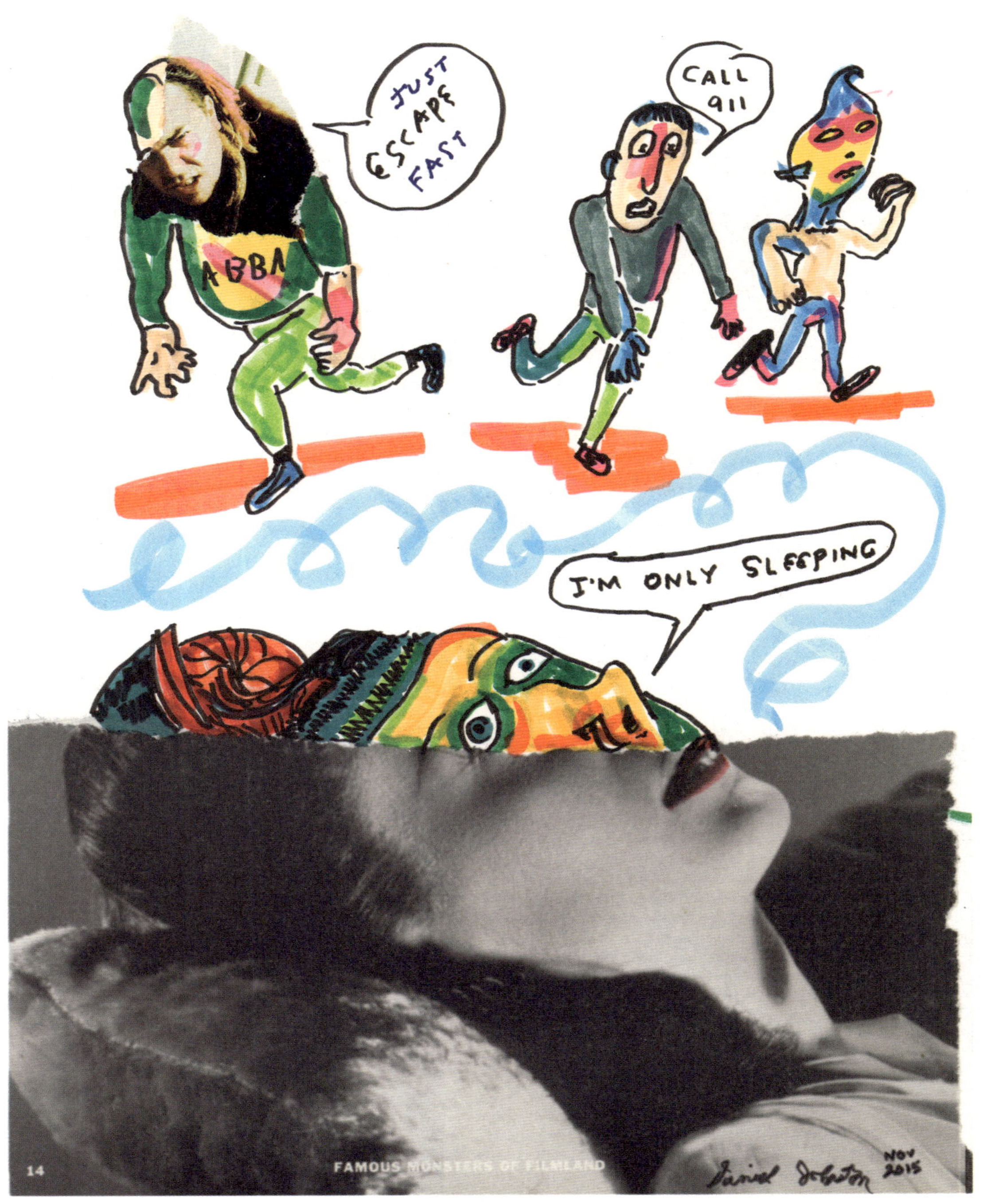

Just Escape Fast (Famous Monsters of Filmland)

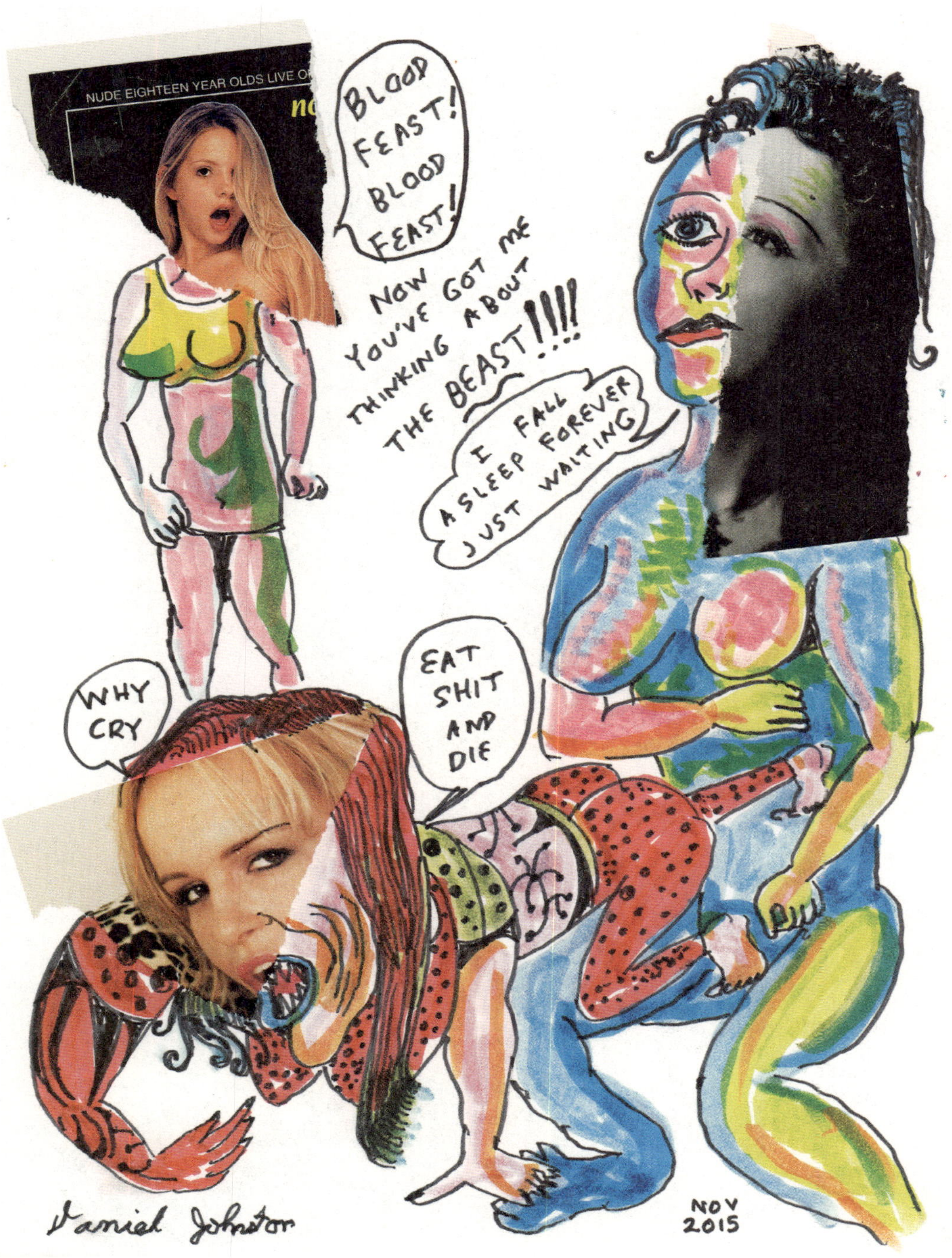
NUDE EIGHTEEN YEAR OLDS LIVE O
BLOOD FEAST! BLOOD FEAST!
NOW YOU'VE GOT ME THINKING ABOUT THE BEAST!!!!
I FALL ASLEEP FOREVER JUST WAITING
WHY CRY
EAT SHIT AND DIE
Daniel Johnston
NOV 2015

Blood Feast!

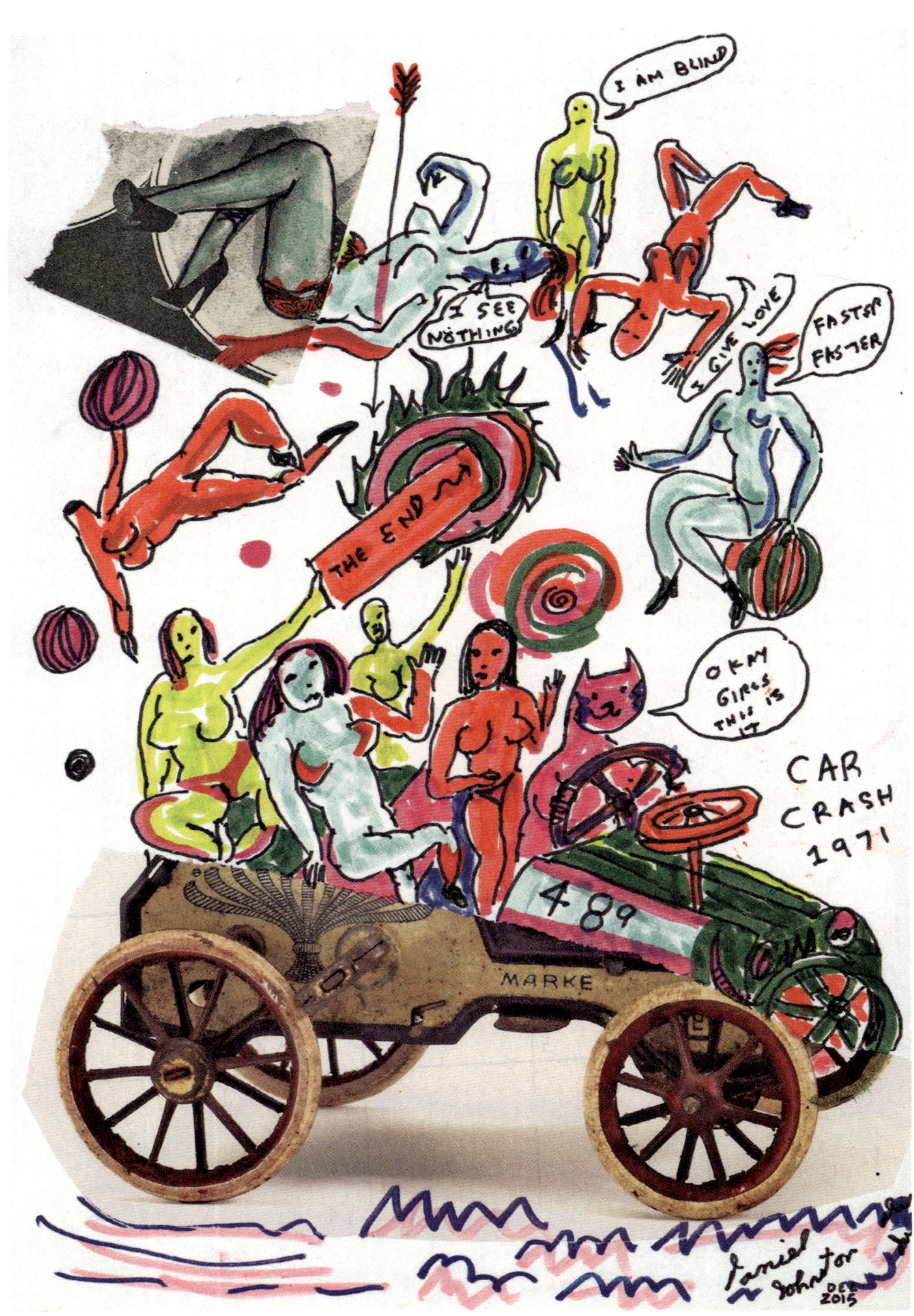

Car Crash 1971

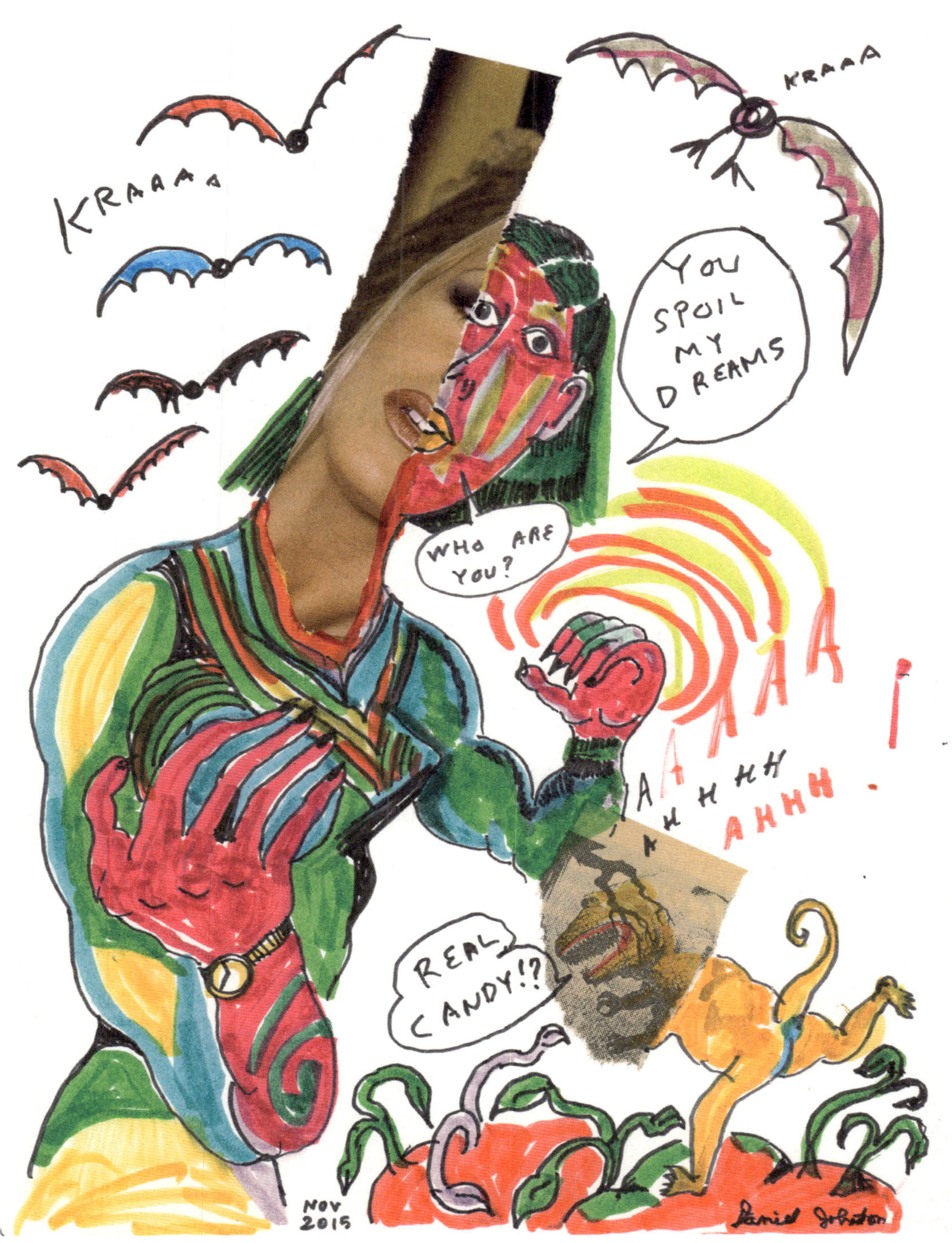
KRAAAA
KRAAA
YOU SPOIL MY DREAMS
WHO ARE YOU?
AAAAA!
AHHHH
AHHH.
REAL CANDY!?
NOV 2015
Daniel Johnston

Real Candy!?

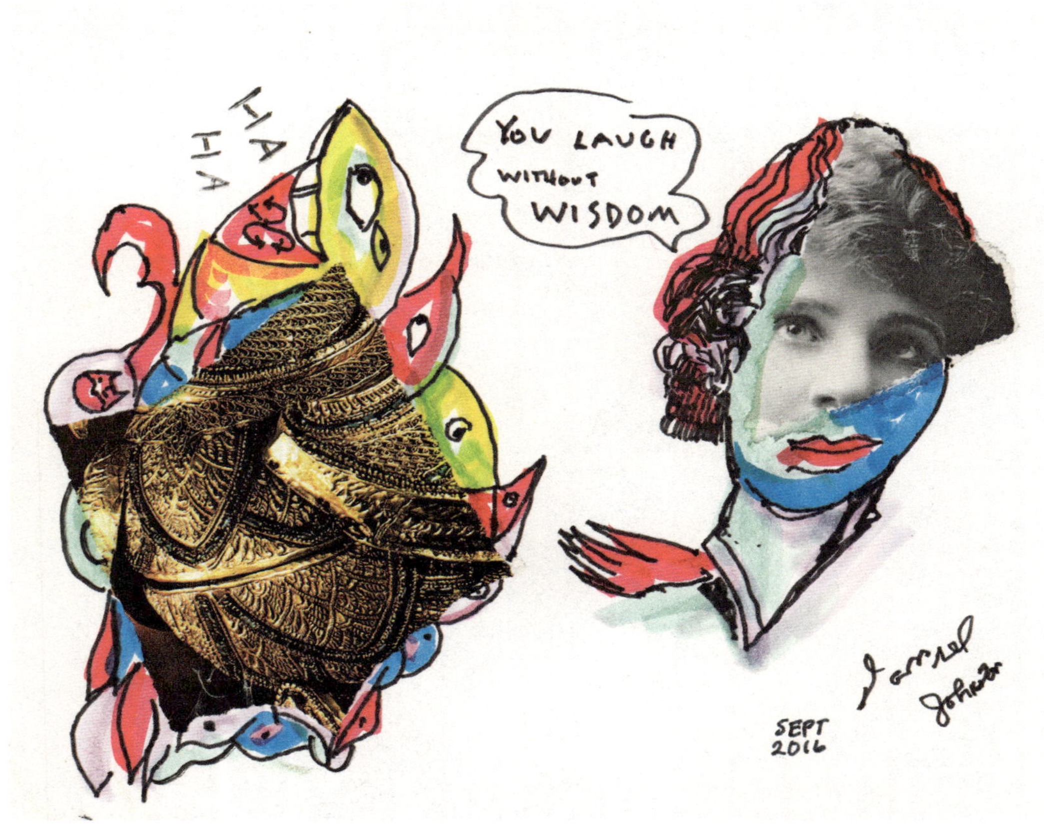

You Laugh without Wisdom

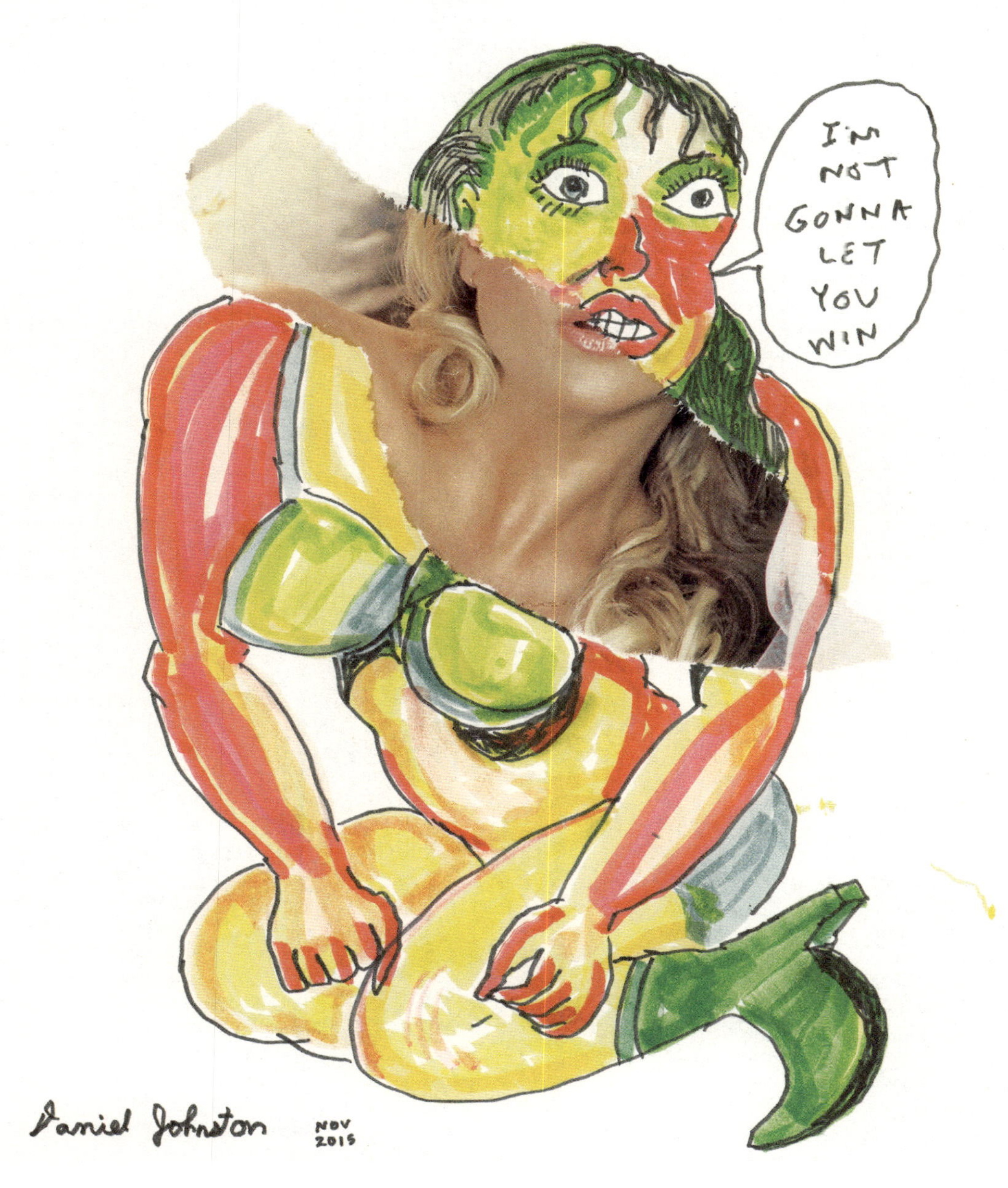

I'm Not Gonna Let You Win

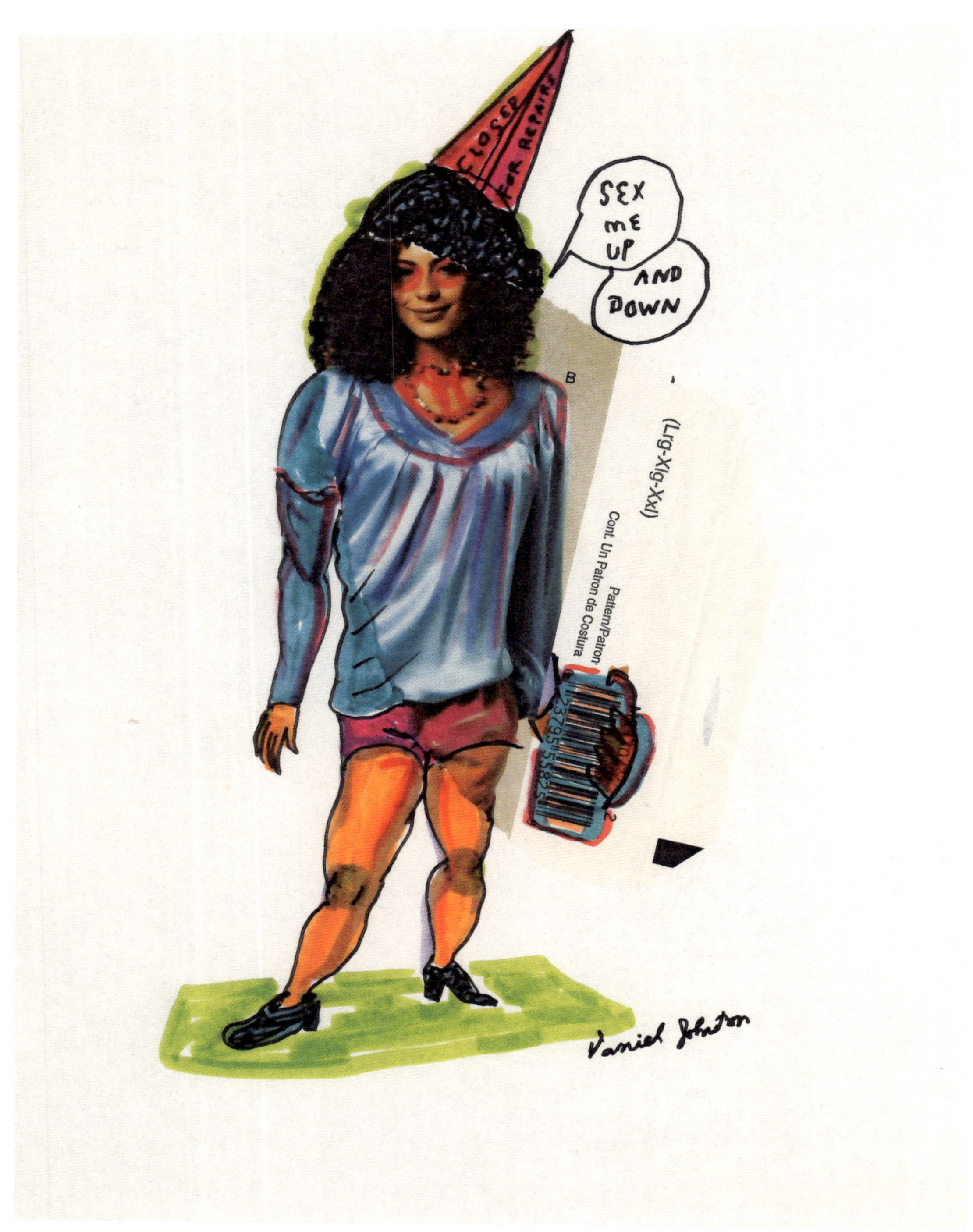

Sex Me Up (and Down)

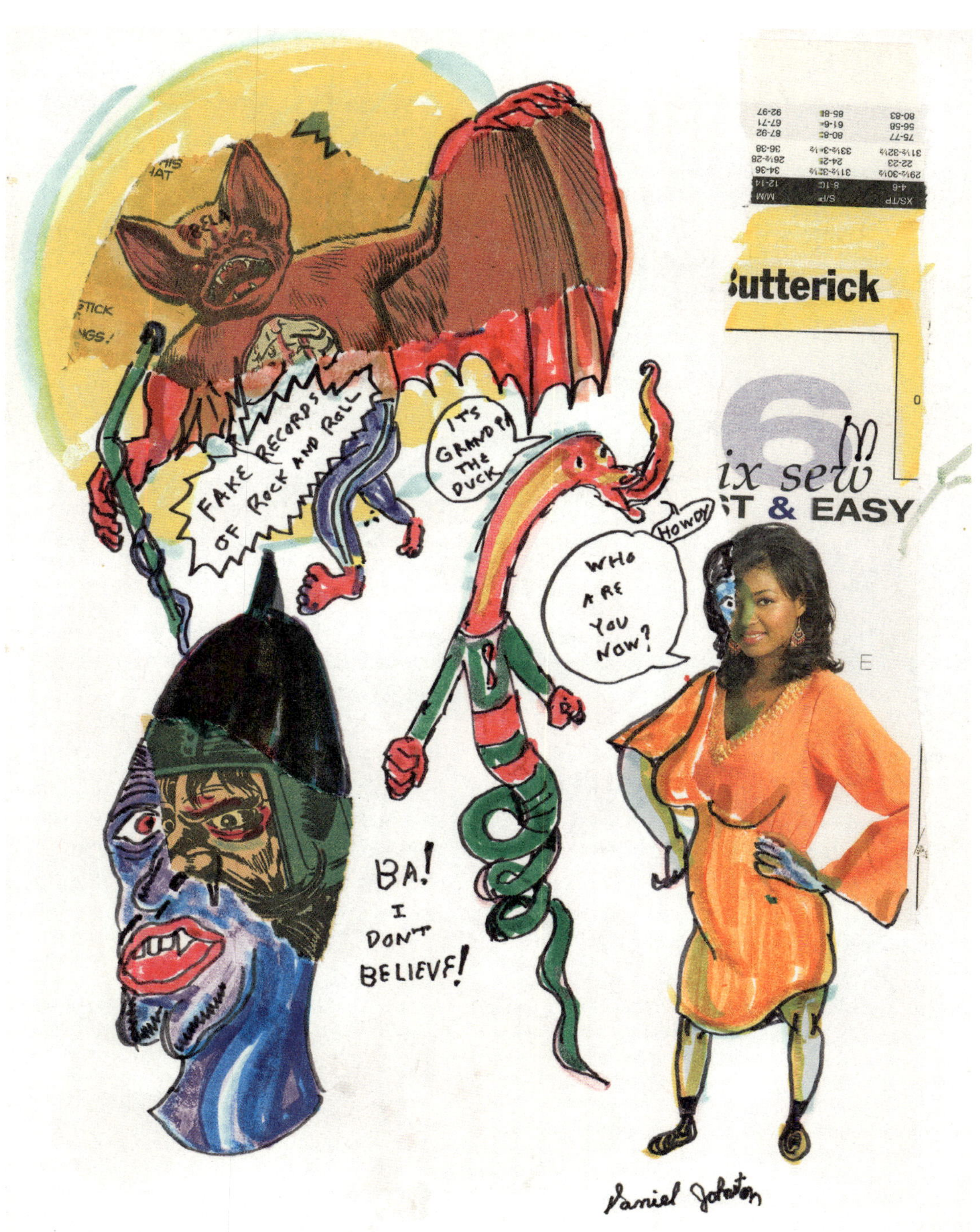

Fake Records of Rock and Roll

January 22, 1961
Birth: Daniel Johnston is born in Sacramento, California.

1965
Move to West Virginia: Johnston's family moves to New Cumberland, West Virginia, where Daniel spends his formative years.

1980–1982
Enrollment at Kent State University: Daniel briefly enrolls at Kent State University to study art, though he later drops out due to personal challenges and his focus on music.

1981–1982
First Homemade Cassettes: Johnston records *Songs of Pain* (1981), *Don't Be Scared* (1982), and *The What of Whom* (1982) and gains a local following.

1983
Move to Houston: Johnston stays with his brother, Dick Johnston, and starts recording *Yip/Jump Music* (1983).

1983
Album Release, *Hi, How Are You*: One of Johnston's most iconic albums, featuring his famous frog character from the album's cover.

1984–1985
Move to Austin: Johnston releases *Respect* and *Continued Story* (Stress Records), and finds a larger audience in Austin's underground music scene.

1985
National Broadcast: Johnston featured on MTV's *The Cutting Edge*, a show dedicated to alternative music.

1985–1986
Austin Music Awards: Johnston wins Songwriter of the Year and Best Folk Act in a live ceremony.

1990
Nervous Breakdown: After experiencing severe mental health issues, Johnston is hospitalized following an incident in which he caused a small plane to crash by wrestling the controls from his father. Despite this, he continues creating music and art.

1990–1991
First Studio Albums: Releases *1990* and *Artistic Vice* (1991).

1992
MTV Music Awards: Kurt Cobain first wears *Hi, How Are You* shirt during Nirvana's performance at the MTV Video Music Awards, bringing widespread attention to Johnston.

1994
Album Release, *Fun*: Johnston signs with Atlantic Records and releases his first major label project.

2001
Album Release, *Rejected Unknown*: Johnston returns from a seven-year recording hiatus.

2003

Album Release, *Fear Yourself*: Johnston releases a studio album with Gammon that includes an eight-page booklet of drawings.

2005

Documentary, *The Devil and Daniel Johnston*: A critically acclaimed documentary about Johnston's life and struggles with mental illness premieres at the Sundance Film Festival, and wins Documentary Directing Award.

2006

Album Release, *Lost and Found*: Sketchbook Records releases Johnston's sixteenth album.

2006

Whitney Biennial, *Day for Night*: Fourteen of Johnston's drawings are included in *Day for Night*, curated by Chrissie Iles and Philippe Vergne at the Whitney Museum of American Art, New York.

2009

Album Release, *Is and Always Was*: Johnston releases another well-received album, produced by Jason Falkner; *Is and Always Was* showcases a more polished recording style.

2010

Album Release, *Beam Me Up!*: Johnston releases a live tour album with a jazz ensemble in Europe.

2012

Album Release, *Space Ducks*: Johnston releases his second album with Eternal Yip Eye Music, his last studio album.

2017

Final Tour: Johnston embarks on his final tour, with guest musicians from prominent bands including Wilco performing with him at each stop.

2018

First "Hi, How Are You Day" Concert: The "Hi, How Are You Day" concert in Austin opens with an official proclamation by Mayor Steve Adler. This would be Johnston's final live music performance.

September 11, 2019

Death: Daniel Johnston passes away from natural causes at the age of fifty-eight in Waller, Texas, leaving behind a legacy of music and art.

Daniel's early managers, Ron Harris, Randy Kemper, Jeff Tartakov, and Tom Gimbel, all stepped up with little reward and a lot of grief, because they believed Daniel needed to be heard. Brian Beattie, Don Goede, Jordy Trachtenberg, Jeff Feuerzeig, and so many others spread the Daniel Johnston message as a personal passion. Art in this book has been graciously offered from the collections of Lee Foster, Electric Lady Studios, Margy Johnston, and others. Lee Foster came to Texas on a mission to explore Daniel's art legacy, and we became dear friends. Lee's professional acumen and personal passion for Daniel have yielded greater results than I could have imagined. Lee has tirelessly and selflessly contributed so much, including working with Robin K. Williams to organize the exhibition that opened at The Contemporary Austin in 2021. I have called Lee Daniel's art evangelist, but he is also Daniel's art ambassador. I cannot adequately thank him for the labor of love of the past five years and especially the untold months of effort he has put into making this book the best it can be.

—Dick Johnston

My deepest gratitude to Daniel Johnston for his art and music. Thank you, Dick Johnston, for your trust, generosity, and friendship—and for the latitude you have given me to create this book. To the team, Tom Gimbel, Donny Veloz, Dexter Tesch, and Don Goede, for your hard work and steadfast dedication to Daniel's memory. Thank you, Marjory Johnston, for your tremendous insight into Daniel's imaginativeness, for your collaboration and contributions to the book. Thank you, Jeff Tartakov, for your time, expertise, and willingness to share your knowledge of Daniel's creative life and work.

Endless thanks to my friends and fellow Daniel lovers, Robin, Lana, Jack, Phoebe, Claire, Daniel, Bea, Karen, Jeff, Dev, and Jim—it is such a joy and honor to have you all be part of this. Thank you, Rizzoli publishing. Thank you, Loren Olson, for your unwavering leadership of this book, for your endless patience and readiness to solve every puzzle with me. To Keith Stoltz, for your partnership and belief in me always. And to Karen Elson, for your love, support, inspiration, and optimism. I love you.

To my friends, coworkers, and colleagues without whom this book would not be possible: Sarah Grant, Clover Singsen, Brenna Kennedy, Justin Gressley, Darin Harmon, Jamie Oborne, Michele Fleischli, Crystal Myers, Alexis Rosenzweig, Mike Ahern, Lysee Webb, Sarah Patellos, Deanna Miesch, Marie Javins, Jung Kim, Arielle de Saint Phalle, Luc Swift, Conner Deck, Lauren Marquez, Margeaux McCaughey, Nick Gambini, and Magali van Caloen.

Thank you, Eric Kaplan.

—Lee Foster

The Hi, How Are You Project (HHAY) is a nonprofit organization dedicated to promoting mental wellness and raising awareness about mental health challenges, with a particular focus on young people between the ages of fourteen and twenty-four. Founded in 2018, the organization was inspired by the iconic artist and musician Daniel Johnston, whose struggles with mental illness were openly expressed throughout his life and work. HHAY continues his legacy by fostering open conversations about mental health, breaking down stigmas, and encouraging people to check in with one another.

The mission of the Hi, How Are You Project is to create environments where mental health issues can be openly discussed without fear or judgment. The organization recognizes the unique mental health challenges faced by young people, who often experience significant transitions during adolescence and early adulthood. These challenges can include anxiety, depression, and stress related to school, relationships, and social pressures. By focusing on this critical age group, HHAY aims to equip young people with the tools they need to navigate these challenges and seek help when needed.

Through various programs, initiatives, and events, HHAY fosters mental health education, advocacy, and community engagement. The annual Hi, How Are You Day (celebrated on January 22, Daniel Johnston's birthday) is a key event that encourages people to start conversations about mental health. The project also collaborates with schools, universities, and community organizations to provide educational resources and workshops that raise awareness about the importance of mental health and self-care.

A core belief of the Hi, How Are You Project is the idea that the simple question "Hi, how are you?" can open the door to important conversations and connections. This message is woven into all of the organization's outreach efforts, as they aim to destigmatize discussions around mental health and encourage empathy and support within communities.

HHAY is committed to providing young people with the resources they need to prioritize their mental health and seek help when necessary. By promoting mental wellness education and fostering a culture of compassion and openness, the Hi, How Are You Project is helping to create a world where mental health is understood, supported, and nurtured. Learn more at www.hihowareyou.org.

First published in the United States of America in 2025 by

Rizzoli International Publications, Inc.
49 West 27th Street
New York, NY 10001
www.rizzoliusa.com

Publisher: Charles Miers
Editor: Loren Olson
Design: Sarco
Production Manager: Barbara Sadick
Copy Editor: Natalie Danford
Proofreader: Richard Slovak

ISBN-13: 978-0-8478-2800-5
Library of Congress Control Number: 2024946657

The authorized representative in the EU for product safety and compliance is Mondadori Libri S.p.A., via Gian Battista Vico 42, Milan, Italy, 20123
www.mondadori.it

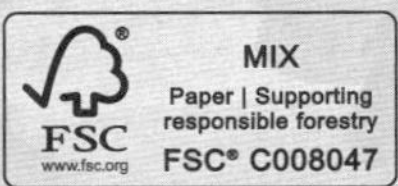

Printed in China
2026 2027 2028 / 10 9 8 7 6 5 4 3

p. 2: Young Daniel with guitar, c. 1985.
Photo: Jeffrey Niles Fuller
p. 6: Daniel composing in Austin, 1992.
Photo: J. McConnico
p. 30: Daniel playing the guitar, c. 1990s.
Photo: Deb Pastor
p. 33: Daniel with drawings, c. 1985.
Photo: Estate of Daniel Johnston
p. 36: Daniel drawing in his father's garage, Waller, Texas, c. 1993.
Photo: Yves Beauvais
p. 39: Daniel in Waller, Texas, 2010.
Photo: Jung Kim
p. 84: Daniel, West Virginia, c. 1970.
p. 87: Daniel, West Virginia, c. 1968.
p. 88: Daniel, West Virginia, c. 1976.
Photos: Estate of Daniel Johnston
p. 91: Daniel Johnston cleans tables at an Austin McDonald's, 1985.
p. 92: Daniel in Austin, 1985.
p. 95: Daniel in Waller, Texas, c. 1997.
Photos: Deb Pastor
p. 298: Daniel, Austin, 2004.
Photo: Todd V. Wolfson
p. 300: Daniel Johnston's Jeremiah mural at 2100 Guadalupe Street, Austin, 2023
Photo: Robin K. Williams
p. 303: Kurt Cobain at the MTV Video Music Awards, 1992.
Photo: Paul Harris, Getty Images
p. 304: Daniel in Austin, 1985.
Photo: Deb Pastor
p. 377: Adapted from a tribute quoted by Thomas Smith that first appeared in *NME Blogs*, September 12, 2019

Instagram.com/RizzoliBooks
Facebook.com/RizzoliNewYork
Youtube.com/user/RizzoliNY